Mathematics for A and AS level

Pure mathematics

The School Mathematics Project

CAMBRIDGE
UNIVERSITY PRESS

PUBLISHED BY THE PRESS SYNDICATE OF THE UNIVERSITY OF CAMBRIDGE
The Pitt Building, Trumpington Street, Cambridge CB2 1RP, United Kingdom

CAMBRIDGE UNIVERSITY PRESS
The Edinburgh Building, Cambridge CB2 2RU, United Kingdom
40 West 20th Street, New York, NY 10011-4211, USA
10 Stamford Road, Oakleigh, Melbourne 3166, Australia

First published 1997

Printed in the United Kingdom at the University Press, Cambridge

Typeset in Sabon 10/12 $\frac{1}{2}$ pt

A catalogue record for this book is available from the British Library

Adapted from the original 16–19 Mathematics material by Chris Belsom

Main authors

Simon Baxter	Barrie Hunt	Paul Roder
Stan Dolan	Mike Leach	Jeff Searle
Tim Everton	Tim Lewis	David Tall
Doug French	Lorna Lyons	Brian Wardle
Andy Hall	Tom Patton	Thelma Wilson
Ron Haydock	Richard Peacock	Phil Wood

Team leaders   Stan Dolan   Barrie Hunt
                     Ron Haydock

16–19 project director   Stan Dolan

ISBN 0 521 56617 7

Acknowledgements
The publishers would like to thank the following for supplying photographs:

page 78 (l)	John and Irene Palmer/Oxford Scientific Films;
(r)	David Thompson/Oxford Scientific Films;
page 81	The Ancient Art and Architecture Collection (Ronald Sheridan's Photo Library);
page 117 (l)	ESA/PLI/Science Photo Library;
(r)	Simon Fraser/Science Photo Library;
page 310	George East/Science Photo Library

Contents

Introduction for the student

The material in this book provides a suitable preparation for the pure mathematics content of most A level and AS level courses in mathematics, and includes the core content of all new syllabuses, as implemented beginning in 1998. It is based on six units from the SMP *16–19 Mathematics* course – *Foundations, Introductory calculus, Functions, Problem solving, Mathematical methods* and *Calculus methods.*

The book is a self-contained resource, consisting of explanatory text and exercises. All exercises are provided with solutions at the end of the book. The textual material is written in such a way that you yourself become involved in the development of the ideas; *it is a text to be worked through, rather than read passively.* You learn mathematics by actually doing it yourself, and this is constantly encouraged through the text.

Throughout the body of the text, as material is being developed, you will meet blocks of questions indicated as follows:

 2 .3A

1 (a) Explain how the details of the graph . . .

The questions in these **development sections** are designed in such a way that ideas are opened up, explored and developed before results or observations are formalised. They are a crucial part of the learning process, making you more familiar with the ideas that you will eventually apply in more straightforward and conventional exercises. Answers, or more detailed solutions, are provided at the back of the book both for these sections and the exercises. You should check your work as you go along, correcting as necessary. Do not be tempted to look at the solutions too readily when you encounter a problem – wrestling with a difficulty is a better way of coming to terms with it than giving up too early.

At various points in the text you will also be directed towards a number of **tasksheets,** located just after the body of the text. These contain either **extension material** (and are labelled E tasksheets, for example 2.3 TS E1) or **supplementary support material** (labelled 2.3 TS S1, for example). These are important in that they provide extra material for you to study. However, they are additional to the main flow of the text, and may be omitted if appropriate. Extension tasksheets provide further enrichment material or ideas, and if you are able to cope with the mainstream material confidently enough, then you should certainly attempt them. Supplementary tasksheets provide extra help at certain points if needed, for instance in solving inequalities or in extra differentiation practice. You need not do these if you are confident with the ideas that they take you through.

There is also a complete revision guide for the *16–19 Mathematics* course, SMP *16–19 Revision*, which you will find very helpful as you prepare for examinations. The revision book summarises all of the material and important results, chapter by chapter, and provides further revision examples (with solutions).

Presentation and precision

Before you start your work in mathematics, a timely word about presentation is in order! Mathematics is often described as a language, and it has its own grammar which should be practised and rigorously applied. Mathematics is a means of expressing and communicating ideas. You should develop good habits of presentation and use of appropriate notation, so that your work can be easily followed by others, with each statement correctly and logically following from previous work. It is particularly important not to be careless with notation. For example, sloppy use of the equals sign must be avoided: **equals** in mathematics means precisely that! What is on one side of the equals sign exactly and precisely equals what is on the other – no more, no less. Again, in using the **implies** symbol $\Rightarrow$, you know for example that $x = 2$ implies that $x^2 = 4$, but it is *not* true that $x^2 = 4$ implies $x = 2$ (x might be -2). So

$$x = 2 \;\Rightarrow\; x^2 = 4 \quad \text{is correct, but} \quad x^2 = 4 \;\Rightarrow\; x = 2 \quad \text{is wrong.}$$

Look at your presentation: can it be followed easily by someone else? Is it mathematically precise, with the correct mathematical language? The ability to communicate effectively is an important and valuable skill, in mathematics itself and more generally.

Mathematics has been described as one of the greatest of all human intellectual achievements; its study is a challenging but rewarding activity which requires much hard work and practice. We hope that you will enjoy the challenge and become confident with the skills developed, so that you may use mathematical ideas in your further studies or in employment, either within mathematics itself, or in the countless areas to which it can be applied.

1 Foundations

.1 Graphs

1.1.1 Introduction

Drawing and sketching graphs is an important and useful skill in mathematics, often helping to illustrate an idea more effectively, or as an aid to solving problems generally.

It is important, therefore, to be fully conversant with graphs of important and common functions, and we concentrate initially on the graph of the straight line, followed by the graphs of quadratic functions.

The following example considers a problem where the solution is greatly simplified by drawing appropriate graphs.

 .1A

A market trader finds that she can sell 60 transistor radios each week if she reduces her profit margin to zero, but sales drop when she increases her price. In fact, at £6.00 profit per radio she sells none at all. What profit margin should she choose to achieve the greatest possible total profit?

To help decide what profit margin to choose, the trader models her sales figures with the straight-line graph shown.

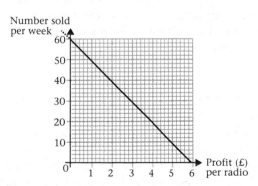

1 (a) Use the graph to copy and complete this table.

Profit (£) per radio	0	1	2	3	4	5	6
Number of radios sold	60						0
Total profit (£) from sales						50	

(b) Draw a graph from the table, plotting total profit against profit per radio. (The solution to the trader's problem should now be quite easy to see.)

(c) What profit per radio should she choose?

2 Suppose the profit is £x per radio.

(a) Find the number of radios that the trader sells per week in terms of x.

(b) What is her total profit from sales in terms of x?

(c) What are the equations of the straight-line graph shown on page 1 and the graph that you have drawn?

When considering the graphs of functions it is very useful to recognise certain properties of the graphs, which not only provide an aid to sketching graphs in general ('curve sketching'), but also give an insight into the properties of the function and to relationships between functions. These ideas are explored more fully throughout the course.

In the following work you should use a graph plotting calculator (or computer package) to explore properties of the graphs of a variety of functions. Many of the functions will be new to you but you will soon become more familiar with them.

 .1B

1 Use a graph plotter to draw each of the following basic functions and their graphs. Sketch them and note any features which you think are interesting. Look out for and note any features such as reflection or rotational symmetry.

(a) $y = x$ (b) $y = x^2$ (c) $y = x^3$ (d) $y = x^4$

(e) $y = \sqrt{x}$ (f) $y = \sqrt[3]{x}$ (g) $y = \dfrac{1}{x}$ (h) $y = \dfrac{1}{x^2}$

(i) $y = \sin x$ (j) $y = \cos x$ (k) $y = \tan x$ (l) $y = \log x$

(m) $y = 3^x$ (n) $y = (\tfrac{1}{2})^x$ (o) $y = |x|$ (p) $y = \text{int}\,(x)$

2 Plot the graphs of $y = -x$, $y = -x^2$, $y = -x^3$ and $y = -x^4$. How are they related to the graphs of question 1?

(Note: $-x^2$ means square first, then change sign. This can cause confusion sometimes with a graph plotter, and it may be necessary to include brackets, $-(x^2)$, to ensure the correct meaning.)

3 Compare and comment on the graphs of $y = x^2$ and $y = \sqrt{x}$, and $y = x^3$ and $y = \sqrt[3]{x}$.

1.1.2 Linear graphs

When a function has a straight-line graph, it is said to be **linear**.

Examples of straight-line graphs may be found in a wide range of subjects.

(a) The distance against time graph of a body moving with constant speed is a straight line.

(b) Economists often assume that the demand for a commodity decreases linearly with price.

(c) The amount by which a metal rod expands when it is heated is proportional to its temperature and so the graph of length against temperature is linear.

Linear graphs are simple to deal with. Sometimes you can approximate more complex graphs by linear graphs, as in the example which follows.

 .1c

A long-distance walker aims to cover the 800 miles from John O'Groats to Land's End at the rate of 30 miles per day.

The graphs below illustrate his progress after t days.

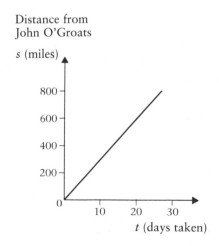 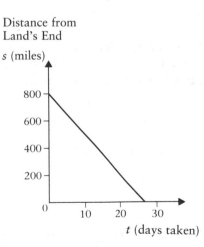

(a) What distance has the walker covered after one day and how far is he from Land's End?

(b) How far has he walked after two days and how far is he from Land's End?

(c) How far has he walked after t days and how far is he from Land's End?

(d) What are the equations of the two graphs of distance against time?

Both graphs have the following features.

- They are both straight-line or linear graphs. For this reason, $30t$ and $800 - 30t$ are called **linear functions** of t.
- The graph of $s = 30t$ passes through the origin and has a **gradient** of 30.
- The graph of $s = 800 - 30t$ crosses the s-axis at 800. The number 800 is called the **intercept** on the s-axis. This function is decreasing, the graph having a **negative gradient** of -30.

An introduction to straight-line graphs is provided in supplementary tasksheet S1.

▶ 1.1 Tasksheet S1 – The equation of a straight line (page 523)

> y is a **linear function** of x if it can be expressed in the form $mx + c$.
>
> The graph of y against x is then a straight line.
>
> m is the **gradient** of the line.
>
> c is the value of y when x is zero and is the **intercept** on the y-axis.

There are a number of ways of finding the equation of a line if you know a couple of points on the line. A method which is quick and easy to use is illustrated in example 1.

Example 1
Find the equation of the straight line through $(1, 2)$ and $(3, 8)$.

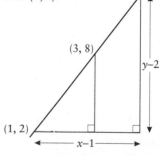

Solution

$$\text{Gradient} = \frac{y - 2}{x - 1} \quad \text{or} \quad \frac{6}{2} = 3$$

So $\dfrac{y - 2}{x - 1} = \dfrac{6}{2}$

$\Rightarrow \quad y - 2 = 3(x - 1) \quad (\Rightarrow \text{ means 'implies'})$

$\Rightarrow \quad y = 3x - 1$

> A straight line of slope m passing through the point (x_1, y_1) has
> equation $\dfrac{y - y_1}{x - x_1} = m \quad \text{or} \quad y - y_1 = m(x - x_1)$

1.1 Exercise 1

1 Draw the straight lines whose equations are:

(a) $y = 2x + 4$ (b) $s + 2t = 7$ (c) $2y - 4x + 3 = 0$

(d) $x + y = 4$ (e) $y = 5$ (f) $x = 3$

2 Write down the equation for each of the following straight lines.

(a)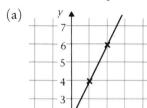

(b)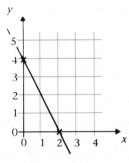

(c)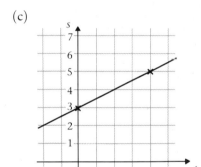

(d)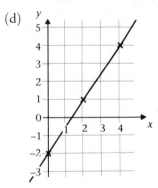

3 Find the equations of the straight lines passing through the points:

(a) $(0, 3)$ and $(2, 7)$ (b) $(1, 4)$ and $(2, 6)$

(c) $(1, -5)$ and $(-4, 0)$ (d) $(1, 2)$ and $(-2, 1)$

4 Which of the following equations have straight-line graphs?

(a) $y = x^2 - 2$ (b) $2y + x = 4$ (c) $x^2 + y^2 = 9$

(d) $xy = 5$ (e) $x = 5 - 2y$ (f) $x - y = 2x - y + 6$

(g) $y - 3 = 4(x + 1)$ (h) $\dfrac{x}{2} + \dfrac{y}{3} = 1$ (i) $\sqrt{y} = 1 + \sqrt{x}$

5 Find the equation of the straight line:

(a) of slope 4 which passes through the point $(2, 1)$

(b) which passes through $(2, 5)$ and is parallel to $y = 3x + 1$

(c) which passes through $(2, 3)$ and is parallel to $2x + 3y + 4 = 0$

1.1.3 Quadratic functions

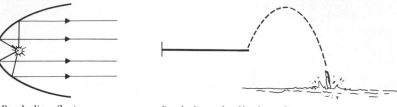

Parabolic reflector   Parabolic path of body under gravity

You can see the curve known as a **parabola** in various everyday situations and it arises in mathematics most simply as the graph $y = x^2$.

The graph of $y = x^2$ has line symmetry in the y-axis, and a **vertex** at the origin. In this case the vertex is the minimum point. For inverted parabolas it would be the maximum point.

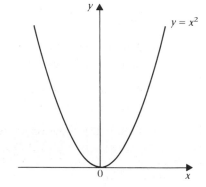

Polynomial functions of x are functions formed by adding together powers of x. Examples are:

$$3x + 1$$

$$x^2 + 5x - 2$$

$$5x^4 - 3x^3 + 2x^2 + 7x - 5$$

(Note: the powers of x *must be non-negative whole numbers*.)

You have already looked at linear functions where the highest power of x present is the first power, x^1 (or just x). In this section we will concentrate on **quadratic functions** of the form

$$y = ax^2 + bx + c \qquad (a \neq 0)$$

where the highest power is x^2. If $a = 0$, then this is a linear function.

You should use a graph plotter to confirm that the graph of $ax^2 + bx + c$ is always a parabola, whatever the values of a, b and c ($a \neq 0$). Note, for example, the effect of making a negative.

We will now look at some of the simplest transformations of $y = x^2$ and find that $y = ax^2 + bx + c$ is not always the most helpful form of the equation of a quadratic function.

 .1D

1 Plot the graph of $y = x^2$ and superimpose the graph of $y = x^2 + 3$.

2 Superimpose various graphs of the form $y = x^2 + q$, for both positive and negative values of q. Write down your conclusions.

3 Plot the graph of $y = x^2$ and superimpose the graph of $y = (x + 4)^2$.
   Describe carefully the relationship between the graphs.

4 Repeat question 2 for the family of curves with equations $y = (x + p)^2$.

5 (a) Describe carefully how any curve of the form $y = (x + p)^2 + q$ is related to the curve $y = x^2$.

   (b) What are the coordinates of the vertex of the parabola
       $y = (x + p)^2 + q$?

   (c) What is the equation of its line of symmetry?

6 Suggest *possible* equations for the following curves. The curve $y = x^2$ is shown dotted in each case and the coordinates of the vertex are given. Use a graph plotter to check your equations.

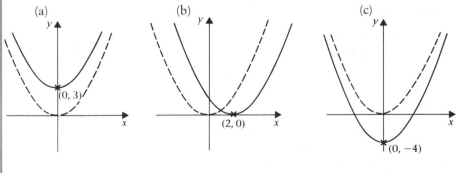

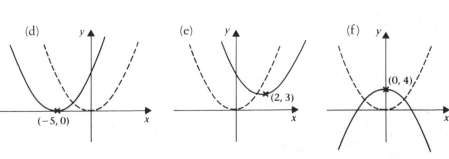

(g)

(h)

(2, 4)

(i)

(3, 0)

(−2, 5)

7   Sketch the curves $y = x^2 - 4$ and $y = 4 - x^2$. What are the coordinates of the points where they meet?

8   Sketch the curves $y = (x - 3)^2 + 2$ and $y = 11$ and find the coordinates of the points where they meet.

9E   The curve $y = ax^2$ passes through the vertex of $y = (x + 2)^2 + 3$. What is the value of a?

10E   The curves $y = (x - a)^2 + b$ and $y = (x - c)^2 + d$ never intersect. By comparing their graphs, find what relationships exist between any or all of a, b, c and d.

The graph of $y = (x + p)^2 + q$ is a **translation** of the graph of $y = x^2$.

Using **vector notation**, this translation can be described as $\begin{bmatrix} -p \\ q \end{bmatrix}$

i.e. the curve is moved by $-p$ units in the x direction and by q units in the y direction.

This is an important result which will be used later.

Example 2

Sketch the graph of $y = (x + 3)^2 - 7$.

Solution

The graph of $y = (x + 3)^2 - 7$ is

obtained by translating the graph of

$y = x^2$ through $\begin{bmatrix} -3 \\ -7 \end{bmatrix}$.

As the vertex of $y = x^2$ is at $(0, 0)$, you can see that the vertex of $y = (x + 3)^2 - 7$ is at $(-3, -7)$.

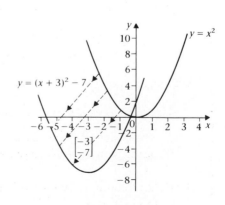

1.1.4 Completing the square

We shall now investigate the relationship between the two forms $y = x^2 + bx + c$ and $y = (x + p)^2 + q$.

You may find it helpful to revise how to multiply brackets quickly and easily, and in particular how to calculate squares. Practice is provided on tasksheet S2 if needed.

 1.1 **Tasksheet S2 – Multiplying brackets (page 526)**

Example 3

Multiply out: (a) $(x + 5)(x - 3)$ (b) $(x - 3)^2 + 1$

Solution

(a) $(x + 5)(x - 3) = x(x - 3) + 5(x - 3)$

$$= x^2 - 3x + 5x - 15$$

$$= x^2 + 2x - 15$$

(b) $(x - 3)^2 + 1 = (x - 3)(x - 3) + 1$

$$= x^2 - 6x + 9 + 1$$

$$= x^2 - 6x + 10$$

You have seen that the graphs of $(x + p)^2 + q$ and $x^2 + bx + c$ are always parabolas. When written in the form $(x + p)^2 + q$, it is easy to locate the vertex and sketch the quadratic. In the following questions you will see how the two forms are related and how to express $x^2 + bx + c$ in the form $(x + p)^2 + q$. This is known as **completing the square**.

1 .1E

1 (a) Plot the graph of $y = x^2$ and superimpose the graph of $y = x^2 + 2x$.

   (b) Consider the vertices to decide what translation maps $y = x^2$ onto $y = x^2 + 2x$. Hence write $x^2 + 2x$ in the form $(x + p)^2 + q$.

2 Taking values of b as: (a) 10   (b) -6 (c) 7

   (i) plot the graph of $y = x^2$ and superimpose the graph of $y = x^2 + bx$;

   (ii) write down the translation which maps $y = x^2$ onto $y = x^2 + bx$, and hence write $x^2 + bx$ in the form $(x + p)^2 + q$.

3 (a) On the basis of your work in question 2 write $x^2 + 4x$ in the form $(x + p)^2 + q$.

(b) Hence write $x^2 + 4x + 9$ in the form $(x + p)^2 + q$.

(c) Check your answer to part (b) by plotting the graphs of $x^2 + 4x + 9$ and $(x + p)^2 + q$.

4 Write the following in the form $(x + p)^2 + q$.

(a) $x^2 + 14x + 2$ (b) $x^2 - 8x + 5$ (c) $x^2 - 3x + 1$

5 (a) If $x^2 + bx = (x + p)^2 + q$, express p and q in terms of b.

(b) Describe how you would express $x^2 + bx + c$ by completing the square.

6 (a) Express $x^2 - 2x + 1$ in completed square form.

(b) Explain why $x^2 - 2x + 1$ can never be negative.

7 Write in completed square form and hence sketch (*without* the aid of a graph plotter) the graph of:

(a) $x^2 + 4x - 2$ (b) $x^2 - 5x + 3$ (c) $x^2 + 12x - 5$

8E Complete the square and hence solve the quadratic equation

$$2x^2 + 6x - 9 = 0$$

Sketch a graph to illustrate your solution.

$y = (x + p)^2 + q$ and $y = x^2 + bx + c$ are equivalent forms for the quadratic function, and both give useful information – about the graph of the function, for example. The relationship between the two forms can be shown algebraically.

$$(x + p)^2 + q = x^2 + 2px + p^2 + q$$

Comparison with $x^2 + bx + c \Rightarrow b = 2p$ or $p = \frac{1}{2}b$

$$\text{and } c = p^2 + q \quad \text{or } q = c - p^2.$$

In order to complete the square on $x^2 + bx + c$:

(a) write $x^2 + bx$ in the form $(x + p)^2 + q$
where $p = \frac{1}{2}b$ and $q = -p^2$;

(b) adjust the constant term by adding on c.

Although not all quadratics are perfect squares it is always possible to express them in the form $(x + p)^2 + q$ using the method developed above.

Example 4

Complete the square on $x^2 + 6x + 2$.

Solution

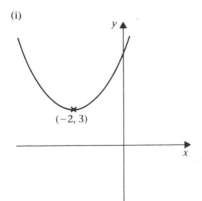

$$x^2 + 6x = (x + 3)^2 - 9$$

$$x^2 + 6x + 2 = (x + 3)^2 - 9 + 2$$

$$x^2 + 6x + 2 = (x + 3)^2 - 7$$

1.1 Exercise 2

1 For each of the following equations:

(a) $y = x^2 + 8x + 5$ (b) $y = x^2 - 4x - 3$

(c) $y = x^2 - 5x + 6$ (d) $y = x^2 - 7x - 3$

   (i) complete the square;

   (ii) check your answer by multiplying out;

   (iii) without using a graph plotter, sketch the corresponding graph.

2 (a) Write down a possible completed square form for the quadratic functions whose graphs are shown below.

  (b) Hence write down the equations of the quadratic functions in the form $y = x^2 + bx + c$.

(i)

(ii)

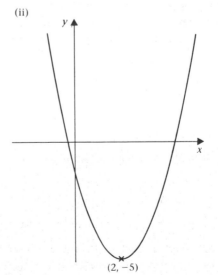

1.1.5 Zeros of quadratics

The axis of symmetry and the vertex of the parabola are important features of the graph, but they are by no means the only ones. Also useful are the points at which the graph crosses the axes, if it does! The graphs of all quadratic functions of x must cross the y-axis, but some graphs, such as those below, do not cross the x-axis.

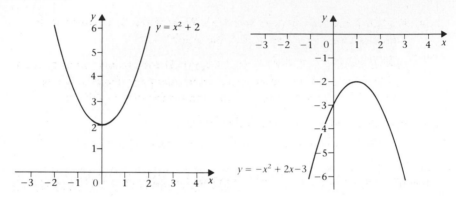

For the graph of any function, the point of intersection with the y-axis is easily found by putting $x = 0$ in the function. The values of x at the points of intersection with the x-axis are called the **roots** of the equation $y = 0$, and are also known as the **zeros** of the function because they make the function equal to zero. The zeros of $x^2 - x - 6$ are -2 and 3.

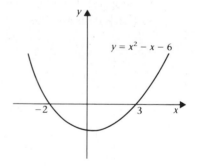

If the product of two numbers a and b equals zero, then either a or b (or both) are zero. This means that it is possible to solve easily equations written in **factorised form** (i.e. written as a product of factors).

Example 5

Solve the equations: (a) $x(x + 1) = 0$
    (b) $(x - 3)(2x + 7) = 0$
    (c) $x^2 + 6x = 0$

Solution

(a) $x(x + 1) = 0 \Rightarrow x = 0$ or $x = -1$

  i.e. $x = 0$ and $x = -1$ are *both* solutions to the equation $x(x + 1) = 0$ (or $x^2 + x = 0$).

(b) $(x - 3)(2x + 7) = 0 \Rightarrow x = 3$ or $x = -\frac{7}{2}$

(c) $x^2 + 6x = 0 \Rightarrow x(x + 6) = 0 \Rightarrow x = 0$ or $x = -6$

The ease with which equations may be solved when written in factorised form is a major reason why finding the factors of algebraic expressions is important. Equally, factorised form gives important information about the graph of a function.

 .1F

1 (a) Plot the graph of $y = (x + 1)(x + 5)$. What is the significance of the numbers 1 and 5 with respect to the graph?

   (b) Investigate the graph of $y = (x + \alpha)(x + \beta)$ for various values of α and β, including positive and negative values, zero and the case where $\alpha = \beta$. What is the significance of α and β for the graph?

2 What is the relationship between the graphs of
$$y = (x + \alpha)(x + \beta) \qquad \text{and} \qquad y = -(x + \alpha)(x + \beta)?$$

The quadratic expressions above are in **factorised form**.

3 Suggest possible equations for the following curves and use a graph plotter to check your answers.

(a)

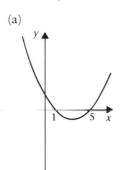

(b)

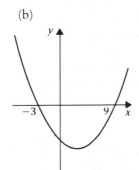

(c)

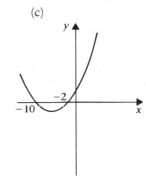

(d)

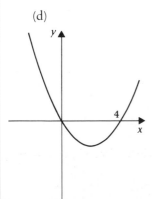

(e)

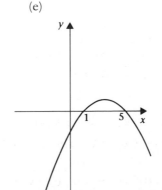

(f)

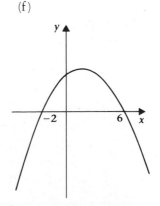

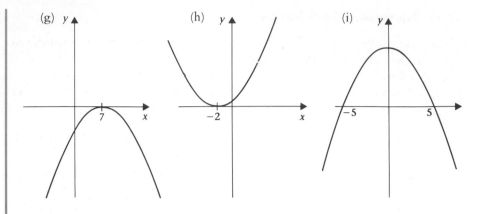

4 *Without the aid of a graph plotter*, make neat sketches of the graphs of:

(a) $y = (x + 2)(x - 1)$ (b) $y = (x - 2)^2$ (c) $y = x^2 + 5x + 6$

(d) $y = -(x + 1)^2$ (e) $y = x^2 - 4$

Sketching a quadratic

You have seen that a quadratic function in expanded form such as

$$x^2 + 6x + 5$$

may also be expressed in completed square form

$$(x + 3)^2 - 4$$

or in factorised form

$$(x + 1)(x + 5)$$

The zeros of $(x + 1)(x + 5)$ are the roots of $(x + 1)(x + 5) = 0$ and are found by putting $x + 1 = 0$ and $x + 5 = 0$ to give $x = -1$ and $x = -5$.

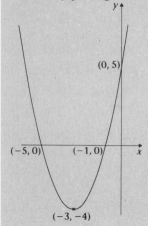

The point $(0, 5)$ is most easily obtained from the form $y = x^2 + 6x + 5$.

The points $(-1, 0)$ and $(-5, 0)$ are obtained most easily from the factorised form $y = (x + 1)(x + 5)$.

The vertex $(-3, -4)$ is obtained most easily from the completed square form $y = (x + 3)^2 - 4$.

1.1.6 Factorising quadratics

To find where the graph of a quadratic function crosses the x-axis it is helpful to have the quadratic expression in a factorised form such as $(x+1)(x+5)$. You must therefore be able to factorise the form $ax^2 + bx + c$ whenever this is possible. Initially we shall only consider examples with $a = 1$. Tasksheet S3 gives you practice at factorising quadratic expression if needed.

The relationships illustrated here for the quadratic $x^2 - 9x + 18$ enable you to factorise quadratic expressions which have integer roots.

$$+18 = (-3) \times (-6)$$

$$x^2 - 9x + 18 = (x-3)(x-6)$$

$$-9 = (-3) + (-6)$$

$$\Rightarrow x^2 - 9x + 18 = (x-3)(x-6)$$

▶ 1.1 **Tasksheet S3 – Further factorisation (page 528)**

1.1 **Exercise 3**

1 Factorise the following. You may check your answers by using a graph plotter to plot the graphs of each of the two forms.

(a) $x^2 + 7x + 12$ (b) $x^2 - 2x - 3$ (c) $x^2 - 7x + 10$

(d) $x^2 - 4$ (e) $x^2 - 7x$ (f) $x^2 - 6x + 9$

(g) $x^2 + 3x + 2$ (h) $x^2 + 4x + 4$ (i) $x^2 - 49$

2 Use a graph plotter to plot the graphs of:

(a) $y = x^2 + 3x + 2$ (b) $y = x^2 + x - 1$ (c) $y = x^2 - x + 1$

In each case determine whether

(i) the quadratic function has any zeros;

(ii) the quadratic expression can be factorised.

3 Solve the following equations by factorisation.

(a) $2x - 3x^2 = 0$ (b) $x^2 + x = 90$

(c) $x^3 = 9x$ (d) $x^3 + 3x^2 + 2x = 0$

4 Simplify $(x-1)(x-5) + (x-1)(x+2)$. Hence solve the equation

$$(x-1)(x-5) + (x-1)(x+2) = 0$$

5 Find the two times when a projectile is at a height of 140 m, if the height h metres, after time t seconds, is given by the expression $h = 40t - 5t^2 + 80$.

6E A rectangular garden 12 m long and 10 m wide consists of a rectangular lawn bordered with flower beds of the same width round the two longer sides and one of the shorter sides. If the area of the flower beds is half the area of the garden, what is the width of the flower beds?

7E 100 m of fencing form three sides of a rectangular enclosure of area 1200 m². Find the dimensions of the enclosure.

8E A rectangle has a perimeter of 46 cm and an area of 120 cm². Using a quadratic equation, find the dimensions of the rectangle.

After working through section 1.1 you should:

1 be able to find the gradient and the equation of a line joining two points;

2 be familiar with linear functions and the equations of straight lines;

3 be able to translate the graph of $y = x^2$ and find the equation of its image;

4 know how to complete the square to find the position of the vertex and the equation of the line of symmetry for the graph of a quadratic function;

5 be able to find, when possible, the zeros of a quadratic function from the factorised form;

6 know how to rewrite one form of the quadratic into any other using the scheme outlined below.

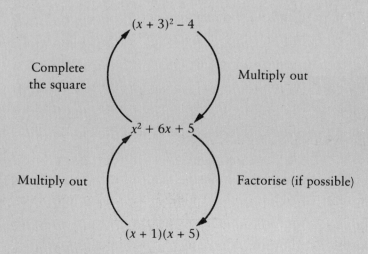

1 Foundations

.2 Sequences

1.2.1 Introduction – notation

Sequences, or lists of numbers, occur in many contexts. From an early age we learn simple sequences such as the 5-times table

$$5, \quad 10, \quad 15, \quad 20, \quad 25, \quad 30, \quad \ldots$$

or we look for patterns in puzzles such as

$$2, \quad 1, \quad 4, \quad 2, \quad 6, \quad 3, \quad 8, \quad 4, \quad \ldots$$

To aid the description of a sequence, certain notations are used. If U is the sequence $\quad 3, \quad 7, \quad 11, \quad 15, \quad 19, \quad \ldots \quad$ then

$u_1 = 3$ is the first term,

$u_2 = 7$ is the second term,

$u_5 = 19$ is the fifth term, and so on.

 .2A

1 U is the sequence $\quad 2, \quad 8, \quad 14, \quad 20, \quad \ldots$

(a) What are the values of u_1 and u_4?

(b) What value would you expect for u_5?
Give an equation connecting u_5 and u_4.

(c) Give an equation connecting u_{i+1} and u_i.

2 T is the sequence defined by $t_1 = 4$ and $t_{i+1} = t_i + 9$.

(a) What are the values of $\quad t_2, \quad t_3, \quad t_4, \quad t_5$?

(b) What is the value of t_{20}?

A sequence U may be given by an **inductive definition**. Such a definition requires:

(i) a starting value or values, for example u_1, the first term;

(ii) a **recurrence relation**, i.e. a formula which will generate any term from the previous term or terms, for example $u_{i+1} = u_i + 6$.

Example 1

Find an inductive definition for the series   1,   2,   6,   24,   120,   ...

Solution

$u_1 = 1$ and the pattern is then

$$u_2 = 2 \times u_1, \quad u_3 = 3 \times u_2, \quad u_4 = 4 \times u_3, \quad \text{and so on.}$$

So $u_1 = 1$, $u_{i+1} = (i+1)u_i$.

Some properties of sequences are investigated below.

 .2B

1 For each sequence write out the first five terms and the value of the 20th term.

(a) $u_1 = -5$ and $u_{i+1} = u_i + 2$ (b) $u_1 = 15$ and $u_{i+1} = u_i - 4$

(c) $u_1 = 2$ and $u_{i+1} = 3u_i$ (d) $u_1 = 3$ and $u_{i+1} = \dfrac{1}{u_i}$

We can use diagrams to illustrate the behaviour of sequences.

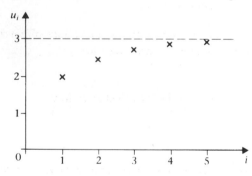

$2, \quad 2\frac{1}{2}, \quad 2\frac{3}{4}, \quad 2\frac{7}{8}, \quad 2\frac{15}{16}, \quad \ldots \quad$ converges.

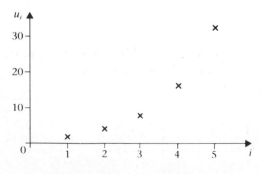

$2, \quad 4, \quad 8, \quad 16, \quad 32, \quad \ldots \quad$ diverges.

2 For each of the sequences below, sketch a diagram to illustrate its behaviour (obtain sufficient terms to be able to describe the behaviour or pattern of the sequence). You may find it interesting to use a variety of starting values.

(a) $u_{i+1} = -2u_i$ (b) $u_{i+1} = 2u_i + 4$ (c) $u_{i+1} = (i+1)u_i$

(d) $u_{i+1} = \dfrac{1}{i+1}u_i$ (e) $u_{i+1} = \dfrac{2}{u_i}$ (f) $u_{i+1} = u_i + 2i + 1$

3E For different starting values, obtain a sufficient number of terms to enable you to describe the behaviour or patterns of each sequence.

(a) $u_{i+2} = u_i + u_{i+1}$ (You will need starting values for both u_1 and u_2.)

(b) $u_{i+1} = \dfrac{20 - 3u_i}{2u_i}$ (You will need to generate a considerable number of terms to be sure of the pattern.)

4E Investigate the following sequence, using various whole-number starting values.

$$s_{i+1} = \begin{cases} 3s_i + 1, & \text{when } s_i \text{ is odd} \\ \dfrac{s_i}{2}, & \text{when } s_i \text{ is even} \end{cases}$$

You are recommended to begin with starting values of between 1 and 10. What happens with numbers greater than 10?

The various types of sequence can be classified as follows.

Convergent

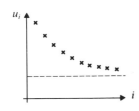

The values get closer and closer to a fixed value.

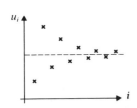

The values of this convergent sequence **oscillate** back and forth about one value.

Divergent

Any sequence which does not converge to a fixed value is called divergent.

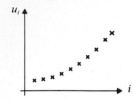

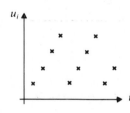

This sequence diverges to $+\infty$. The values grow in size, eventually becoming infinitely large.

This sequence is **periodic**. A set of values is repeated at regular intervals.

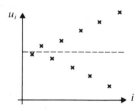

This sequence is both oscillatory and divergent.

1.2 Exercise 1

1 Write down the first five terms of the sequence U where $u_{i+1} = 2u_i$ and $u_1 = 4$ and describe the properties of the sequence.

2 Which of the following sequences converge?

(a) $u_{i+1} = \dfrac{2}{3}u_i, \ u_1 = 9$ (b) $u_{i+1} = \dfrac{1}{u_i^2}, \ u_1 = 2$ (c) $u_{i+1} = \dfrac{5}{u_i}, \ u_1 = 1$

3

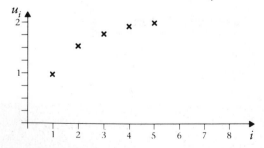

The diagram above illustrates the first five terms of the sequence U where

$$u_{i+1} = u_i + \left(\tfrac{1}{2}\right)^i \text{ and } u_1 = 1$$

Describe fully the properties of the sequence.

4 Investigate and describe the sequence T where $t_{i+2} = t_i + t_{i+1}$ and $t_1 = 1, \quad t_2 = 2$.

5 Investigate and describe the sequence T where

$$t_{i+1} = \frac{27}{(t_i)^2} \text{ and } t_1 = 2$$

6 Find inductive definitions for the sequences:

(a) $1, \quad \frac{1}{2}, \quad \frac{1}{4}, \quad \frac{1}{8}, \quad \frac{1}{16}, \quad \ldots$ (b) $1, \quad -\frac{1}{2}, \quad \frac{1}{4}, \quad -\frac{1}{8}, \quad \frac{1}{16}, \quad \ldots$

1.2.2 The general term

During a training run, a coach makes an athlete run at $6\,\mathrm{m\,s}^{-1}$. Let s_t metres be the distance covered in t seconds, so that $s_1 = 6$.

 .2c

1 (a) What is s_{50}?

(b) What is s_t?

(c) Why is it inappropriate to use an inductive method to calculate s_{50}?

Clearly, there are drawbacks if only inductive definitions are used to generate the terms of a sequence. It can be very useful to have a formula for the general term.

2 (a) Why is $2 \times 3^{n-1}$ the general term of the sequence T where

$$t_{i+1} = 3t_i \text{ and } t_1 = 2?$$

(b) What are the terms of the sequence U where

$$u_i = (-1)^i \frac{1}{i^2}?$$

A sequence of alternating signs can be achieved by using a factor of $(-1)^i$ or $(-1)^{i+1}$ in the general term.

Example 2

Find an expression for the ith term of the sequence $-1, \quad 3, \quad -5, \quad 7, \quad \ldots$

Solution

It is helpful to think of the terms as

$$-1 \times 1, \quad +1 \times 3, \quad -1 \times 5, \quad +1 \times 7, \quad \dots$$

The $-1, \quad +1, \quad -1, \quad +1, \quad \dots$ sequence is generated by $(-1)^i$.

The $1, \quad 3, \quad 5, \quad 7, \quad \dots$ sequence is generated by $2i - 1$.

So $u_i = (-1)^i(2i - 1)$.

1.2 Exercise 2

1

 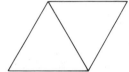 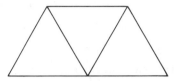

The set of patterns above can be made using matchsticks. How many matchsticks would be required for the next pattern in the sequence? Copy and complete the table.

No. of triangles	1	2	3	4	5	10	20	100	i
No. of matchsticks									

2 Copy and complete the table below for each of the following patterns of dots.

Position in pattern	1	2	3	4	5	10	20	100	i
No. of dots									

(a) • , •••• , •••••• , •••••••• , ---

(b) •• , ••• , •••• , ---

(c) • , • • , • • , • • , ---

(d) • , •••• , •••••• , ---

(e) •• , •••• , •••••• , ---

(f) ••• , •••• , •••••• , ---

3 Write out the first five terms of the sequence whose ith term is:

(a) $u_i = 3i + 2$ (b) $u_i = 5 \times 2^i$ (c) $u_i = 3i^2$

4 (a) Write out the first five terms of the sequence whose ith term is:

(i) $u_i = (-1)^i$

(ii) $u_i = (-1)^{i+1}$

(iii) $u_i = (-1)^{i+2}$

(iv) $u_i = (-1)^i 2^{i-1}$

(b) Write down the general term of the sequence:

(i) 3, −3, 3, −3, 3, ...

(ii) −3, 3, −3, 3, −3, ...

5 For each of the following sequences complete the table.

	Term								
	1	2	3	4	5	6	9	100	i
A	2	4	6	8					
B	2	5	8	11					
C	2	4	8	16					
D	6	12	24	48					
E	1	−1	1	−1					
F	−1	2	−3	4					
G	1	−2	3	−4					
H	2	−4	6	−8					
I	$\frac{1}{2}$	$\frac{1}{3}$	$\frac{1}{4}$	$\frac{1}{5}$					
J	1	−4	9	−16					

1.2.3 Arithmetic series

A car is accelerating from rest.

In the first second it moves 3 m.

In the second second it moves 5 m.

In the third second it moves 7 m.

In the fourth second it moves 9 m.

If this pattern continues, then the total distance travelled in the first ten seconds will be

$$S = 3 + 5 + 7 + 9 + 11 + 13 + 15 + 17 + 19 + 21$$

A sequence of numbers added together is called a **series**. In this case S will be the sum of the series. To calculate S for the first ten seconds is straightforward, if a little tedious, but had the sum been for the first thirty seconds, an algebraic technique would have been useful.

 .2D

> As a schoolboy, the German mathematician Carl Friedrich Gauss (1777–1855) spotted a simple fact which helped him to calculate the sum of the series
>
> $$1 + 2 + 3 + 4 + \cdots + 99 + 100$$
>
> Can you find a simple way to sum this series?

Where consecutive terms of a sequence *differ by a constant value*, such a sequence is known as an **arithmetic sequence**, or **arithmetic progression** (**A.P.**).

Gauss's observation makes it straightforward to sum any such series.

 .2E

> $$1 + 2 + 3 + 4 + 5 + 6 + 7 + 8 + 9 + 10$$
>
> This series may be summed by noting how each pair of values linked below has the same sum.
>
> $$1 + 2 + 3 + 4 + 5 + 6 + 7 + 8 + 9 + 10 = 10 \times \tfrac{11}{2} = 55$$
>
> You can use this method to find the sum of any arithmetic series.

1 (a) Find the sum of:

(i) $1 + 2 + 3 + 4 + \cdots + 20$

(ii) $1 + 2 + 3 + 4 + \cdots + 9$ (careful!)

(iii) $1 + 2 + 3 + 4 + \cdots + 29$

(b) Describe in your own words how to sum an arithmetic series.

2 Show that the series

$$5 + 6 + 7 + \cdots + 105$$

has 101 terms.

3 For the series below, state the number of terms and sum the series.

(a) $1 + 2 + 3 + 4 + \cdots + 50$

(b) $10 + 11 + 12 + \cdots + 90$

(c) $200 + 199 + 198 + \cdots + 100$

For an arithmetic series of n terms, whose first term is a and last term l, the sum of all n terms, S_n, is given by:

$$S_n = n\left(\frac{a+l}{2}\right)$$

4 For the series below, state the number of terms and use the result above to sum the series.

  (a) $1 + 3 + 5 + 7 + 9 + 11 + 13 + 15$

  (b) $4 + 7 + 10 + 13 + \cdots + 100$

  (c) $196 + 191 + 186 + \cdots + 71$

For some series, instead of being given the last term, you are given the number of terms. If this is the case you need to find the last term.

5 For each of the series below, find a formula in terms of i for the ith term.

  (a) $3 + 5 + 7 + 9 + \cdots$

  (b) $6 + 10 + 14 + 18 + \cdots$

  (c) $12 + 7 + 2 - 3 - \cdots$

6 For the series $5 + 9 + 13 + 17 + \cdots$

  (a) (i) calculate the 15th term;

     (ii) calculate the sum of the first 15 terms.

  (b) (i) Write down an expression for the ith term.

     (ii) Find a formula for the sum of the first i terms.

You can generalise the method of question 6 to a series having first term a and where each succeeding term is found by adding on d.

d is called the **common difference** for the sequence.

The first few terms are:

$$a, \quad a + d, \quad a + 2d, \quad \ldots$$

7 For the sequence $a, \quad a + d, \quad a + 2d, \quad \ldots$, write down:

  (a) the fifth term,   (b) the 50th term,

  (c) the nth term,   (d) the sum of the first 50 terms.

To obtain a general formula for the sum of n terms of the series, you need:

- the first term $= a$ • the last term $= a + (n - 1)d$

8 Show (by substitution into the earlier form for S_n) that the sum of n terms of the series is

$$S_n = n\frac{[2a + (n - 1)d]}{2} = \frac{n}{2}[2a + (n - 1)d]$$

You should now know and understand the following results.

- The average term of an arithmetic progression can be found by averaging the first and last terms. The sum of an A.P. is found by multiplying

    number of terms $\times$ average term

  For a series of n terms with first term a and last term l, this can be written as

  $$S_n = n\left(\frac{a + l}{2}\right)$$

- For an arithmetic series, whose first term is a and whose common difference is d, a useful formula for the sum of the first n terms is

  $$S_n = \frac{n}{2}[2a + (n - 1)d]$$

Example 3
Sum the series:

(a) $3 + 5 + 7 + \cdots + 99$ (b) $4 + 11 + 18 + \cdots$ as far as the 50th term.

Solution

(a) The first term is 3, the last 99, so the average is $\dfrac{3 + 99}{2} = 51$.

   The difference between the first and last terms is $99 - 3 = 96$.

   With a common difference of 2, 99 is $\frac{96}{2} = 48$ terms on from 3.

   Thus the total number of terms is $48 + 1 = 49$ and the sum is $49 \times 51 = 2499$.

(b) The first term $a = 4$, and the common difference $d = 7$, so from the formula, $S_{50} = 25(8 + 49 \times 7) = 8775$.

1.2 Exercise 3

1 Find the sum of the arithmetic series:

(a) $4 + 9 + 14 + 19 + \cdots + 199$

(b) $3 + 9 + 15 + \cdots$ as far as the 50th term

(c) $1 + 1\frac{1}{2} + 2 + 2\frac{1}{2} + \cdots + 100$

(d) $99 + 97 + 95 + \cdots + 25$

2 Complete the following table.

	First term	Common difference	Number of terms	Last term	Sum
(a)	8	2	18		
(b)	6	9		303	
(c)	3		25	195	

3 A small terrace at a football ground comprises a series of 15 steps, which are 50 m long and built of solid concrete. Each step has a rise of $\frac{1}{4}$ m and a tread of $\frac{3}{4}$ m.

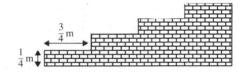

By calculating the area under each step and forming a series, calculate the total volume of concrete required to build the terrace.

4 A child builds a pattern with square building bricks using the sequence of steps as shown.

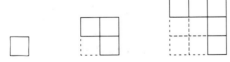

The total number of bricks used is $1 + 3 + 5 + \cdots$

(a) How many bricks does the child use on the nth step?

(b) If the child has 60 bricks, how many steps can be completed?

(c) Use the formula for summing an arithmetic series to show that the total number of bricks used will be n^2.

5E Another child builds a square pattern using bricks that are twice as long as they are wide.

(a) How many bricks does the child use on the nth step?

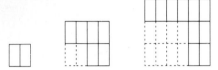

(b) Use the formula for summing an arithmetic series to find the total number of bricks used.

6E Each year Mrs Smith gives her nephew a birthday present of money (in £) equal to five times his age in years. The money is put into a bank account, but unfortunately does not attract any interest and he is not allowed to withdraw any money until he is 18. She makes the first payment on his first birthday and continues until he is 18.

(a) How much does he have in the account on his 18th birthday?

(b) How old is he when the sum of money in the account first exceeds £500?

7E 220 m of video tape are wound onto a reel of circumference 8.2 cm. Because of the thickness of the tape, each turn is 0.1 cm longer than the previous one. How many turns are required?

1.2.4 Finance – APR

When borrowing money or deciding where to put savings, the interest rate is not the only factor to be taken into account. When obtaining a house mortgage, for example, it can be very important that the building society or bank should be able to confirm the loan without a long waiting period. Similarly, it might be necessary to accept a low interest rate on savings in order to be able to withdraw the money at short notice.

In this diagram, three different ways of advertising the same repayment scheme for a loan are shown.

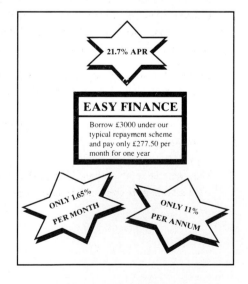

It is important that anyone considering borrowing should be able to compare interest rates such as those above, all of which are commonly seen. Each refers to the 'easy finance' payment described in the box. Notice that the customer must begin repaying the loan almost immediately.

1 .2F

11 per cent per annum
The customer repays

$$£277.50 \times 12 = £3330$$

and so has paid £330 in interest charges. Since

$$£3000 \times \tfrac{11}{100} = £330$$

the stated rate of 11 per cent is easy to understand.

The 11 per cent is called a flat rate and, although it is easy to understand, it is nevertheless misleading. The customer certainly pays 11 per cent interest on the £3000 but does *not* have the use of the full £3000 for a full year!

1 A loan of £800 is repaid by 12 monthly instalments of £100. What is the flat rate of interest?

1.65 per cent per month
This rate is also easy to understand. The customer pays 1.65 per cent interest on the amount owed during the month.

After one month the customer owes the original £3000 and interest of £3000×0.0165 = £49.50: a total of £3049.50. (A quick way of obtaining this total is to calculate £3000 × 1.0165.) Since the customer repays £277.50, the amount owing throughout the second month is £2772.

To find the amount owing after two months, the procedure is repeated. The outstanding debt after two months is (£2772 × 1.0165) − £277.50 = £2540.24.

2 Use either a spreadsheet or a calculator to continue the procedure for 12 months.

The debt is repaid after 12 months. Surprisingly, the flat rate of 11 per cent per annum and the rate of 1.65 per cent per month are equivalent!

21.7 per cent APR

The concept of APR or **annual percentage rate** is used to give consumers a simple way of comparing various methods of borrowing. Finance houses are currently obliged by law to quote the equivalent APR.

The APR corresponding to the rate of 1.65 per cent per month can be found by calculating the total interest on a year's loan, *assuming the entire repayment is at the end of the year*.

Suppose £100 is borrowed. After one month the amount outstanding is

$$£100 \times 1.0165 = £101.65$$

After two months, the amount has become

$$£101.65 \times 1.0165$$

and so on.

3 By finding the amount to be repaid after 12 months, show that the APR is 21.7 per cent.

Remarkably, the three rates of 21.7 per cent APR, 11 per cent per annum and 1.65 per cent per month are *all* equivalent! When considering ways of borrowing money, the APR enables sensible comparisons to be made.

4 Find the APR corresponding to monthly payments based on interest rates per month of:

(a) 1 per cent   (b) 2 per cent   (c) 5 per cent

5 Describe an algorithm or procedure for converting any monthly interest rate into an APR.

6 By trial and error using the method you found in question 5, find the monthly interest rate that corresponds to an APR of 100 per cent.

7 Use a computer or programmable calculator to show the amounts outstanding in successive months for any inputs of the initial loan, monthly interest rate and monthly repayments.

8 A loan of £800 is repaid by 5 monthly instalments of £200. Use your solution to question 7 and any appropriate method to find the monthly interest rate. Hence find the APR.

9

12.4% APR	
CAR PURCHASE FINANCED BY A HIRE PURCHASE AGREEMENT	
CASH PRICE (ON THE ROAD)	£7,292.86
DEPOSIT (30%)†	£2,187.86
BALANCE	£5,105.00
36 EQUAL MONTHLY PAYMENTS OF	£ 127.52*
1 TERMINAL RENTAL	£1,786.75
TOTAL PAYABLE	£8,565.33

*36 monthly payments of £127.52 is equivalent to approx £29.43 per week.   † MINIMUM DEPOSIT 20%

The figures in this car advertisement are the result of certain calculations. The 'terminal rental' is a final cash payment to clear any remaining debt.

(a) Explain how the figure of £2187.86 was obtained.

(b) How is the figure of £8565.33 obtained from the other figures?

(c) Show that £29.43 per week and £127.52 per month are equivalent.

(d) Find the monthly interest rate corresponding to an APR of 12.4 per cent.

1.2.5 Sigma notation

If you invest a sum of £1000 per year into a savings account which pays 8 per cent interest, then S_k, the sum of money in the account after k years, and S_{k+1} are related by

$$S_{k+1} = S_k \times 1.08 + 1000$$

This *inductive* definition is useful for programming a spreadsheet, but is *less* useful for generating a formula for total savings.

You can think of the savings over the ten-year period as being a set of ten investments – the first gaining interest for the full ten years, the second gaining interest for nine years, and so on.

.2G

1 How much is the first investment of £1000 worth after ten years?

2 How much is the second investment of £1000 worth at the end of the ten year period?

3 Explain why the total investment is worth

$$£1000(1.08 + 1.08^2 + 1.08^3 + \cdots + 1.08^{10})$$

after ten years.

Expressions such as $£1000(1.08 + 1.08^2 + 1.08^3 + \cdots + 1.08^{10})$ are cumbersome to handle. However, since each term is of the same form, you can write it more easily using a shorthand notation, known as **sigma notation**. Sigma, written Σ, is a Greek letter, which to mathematicians means 'the sum of'. Using this notation you can write the above series as

$$S = \sum_{i=1}^{10} 1000(1.08^i) \quad \text{or} \quad 1000 \sum_{i=1}^{10} 1.08^i$$

Sometimes this is written simply as $\sum_{1}^{10} 1000(1.08^i)$, where it is clear that the summation is taken over the range of values of i.

Stated fully, this reads:

> S is the sum of the series obtained by successively substituting the values of $i = 1$ to $i = 10$ in the general term $1000(1.08^i)$.

Note that the 1000, which multiplies each term, may be taken outside the summation as a common factor.

Example 4
Express the series $3 + 5 + 7 + 9 + \cdots + 99$ using Σ notation.

Solution
The general term of the series is $2i + 3$.

The first term, 3, corresponds to $i = 0$ and the last, 99, corresponds to $i = 48$.

Thus the series is $\sum_{i=0}^{48} (2i + 3)$. It could also be written as $\sum_{1}^{49} (2i + 1)$.

Example 5

Sum the arithmetic series:

(a) $\displaystyle\sum_{i=1}^{20}(3i+4)$ (b) $\displaystyle\sum_{i=1}^{n}(3i+4)$

Solution

(a) $\displaystyle\sum_{1}^{20}(3i+4) = 7 + 10 + 13 + \cdots + 64$ (20 terms)

$\qquad\qquad = \frac{20}{2}(7+64)$

$\qquad\qquad = 710$

(b) $\displaystyle\sum_{1}^{n}(3i+4) = 7 + 10 + \cdots + (3n+4)$ (n terms)

$\qquad\qquad = \frac{n}{2}\{7 + (3n+4)\}$

$\qquad\qquad = \frac{n}{2}(3n+11)$

1.2 Exercise 4

1 Write out the terms of the following series.

(a) $\displaystyle\sum_{i=1}^{5}\frac{1}{i}$ (b) $\displaystyle\sum_{i=3}^{7}i^2$ (c) $\displaystyle\sum_{i=1}^{5}\frac{1}{i(i+1)}$

(d) $\displaystyle\sum_{i=4}^{8}(-1)^i(2i+3)$ (e) $\displaystyle\sum_{i=0}^{5}(i+1)^3$ (f) $\displaystyle\sum_{i=1}^{6}i^3$

2 Rewrite each of these using Σ notation.

(a) $\sqrt{1}+\sqrt{2}+\sqrt{3}+\cdots+\sqrt{50}$

(b) $2^2 + 4^2 + 6^2 + \cdots + 100^2$

(c) $\frac{1}{3}+\frac{1}{5}+\frac{1}{7}+\cdots+\frac{1}{99}$

(d) $1^3 - 2^3 + 3^3 - 4^3 + \cdots + 19^3$

(e) $\frac{1}{2}+\frac{2}{3}+\frac{3}{4}+\frac{4}{5}+\cdots+\frac{99}{100}$

3 Calculate the sum of the following arithmetic series.

(a) $\displaystyle\sum_{i=5}^{24}(45-2i)$ (b) $\displaystyle\sum_{i=1}^{20}(2i-1)$

4 Use sigma notation to express the following.

(a) $20 + 25 + 30 + 35 + \cdots$ (25 terms)

(b) $10\,000 + 1000 + 100 + 10 + \cdots$ (10 terms)

(c) $1 + 1.1 + 1.21 + 1.331 + \cdots$ (15 terms)

(d) $\dfrac{1}{1+2} + \dfrac{1}{2+3} + \dfrac{1}{3+4} + \dfrac{1}{4+5} + \cdots$ (8 terms)

(e) $3 + 2 \times 3^2 + 3 \times 3^3 + 4 \times 3^4 + \cdots$ (20 terms)

5 Write out the following sums in full.

(a) $\displaystyle\sum_{1}^{6} i^2(i+1)$ (b) $\displaystyle\sum_{0}^{4} (-1)^i(i+1)$ (c) $\displaystyle\sum_{0}^{5} x^i$

(d) $\displaystyle\sum_{0}^{4} \dfrac{i}{i+1}$ (e) $\displaystyle\sum_{1}^{6} f(x_i)$

▷ 1.2 **Tasksheet E1 – Using sigma (page 540)**

1.2.6 Geometric series

An arithmetic series is a special type of series whose pattern enables a simple formula to be developed.

The series on page 32 which represented total savings in the account,

$$\pounds 1000(1.08 + 1.08^2 + 1.08^3 + \cdots + 1.08^{10})$$

can also be summed using a simple formula.

This series is an example of a **geometric progression (G.P.)**, in which each term increases by a constant multiple or **common ratio**, which in this case is 1.08.

Summing a geometric series is not as straightforward as summing an arithmetic series. To simplify matters ignore the 1000 and consider the sum of the series

$$S = 1.08 + 1.08^2 + 1.08^3 + \cdots + 1.08^{10} \qquad ①$$

The trick is to multiply by 1.08

$$1.08S = 1.08^2 + 1.08^3 + 1.08^4 + \cdots + 1.08^{11} \qquad ②$$

and then subtract the original series S, so that

$$0.08S = 1.08^{11} - 1.08 \qquad \text{(all of the middle terms cancel out)}$$

$$\Rightarrow S = \frac{1.08^{11} - 1.08}{0.08}$$

This method may be generalised for the general geometric series with first term a and common ratio r.

$$S = a + ar + ar^2 + ar^3 + \cdots + ar^{n-1} \qquad \left(\text{or } S = \sum_{i=1}^{n} ar^{i-1}\right)$$

Multiplying by the common ratio r,

$$rS = ar + ar^2 + ar^3 + \cdots + ar^n$$

Subtracting the two series gives

$$rS - S = ar^n - a$$

$$S(r - 1) = a(r^n - 1)$$

$$\Rightarrow S = \frac{a(r^n - 1)}{r - 1}$$

In general, for the G.P. with first term a and common ratio r

$$a + ar + ar^2 + \cdots + ar^{n-1}$$

$$\sum_{i=1}^{n} ar^{i-1} = a\left(\frac{r^n - 1}{r - 1}\right)$$

Example 6

Find the sum of the series:

(a) $3 + 6 + 12 + \cdots + 3072$

(b) $\displaystyle\sum_{i=2}^{10} \left(\tfrac{1}{3}\right)^i$

Solution

(a) The terms are $3,\ 3 \times 2,\ 3 \times 2^2,\ \ldots,\ 3 \times 2^{10}$.

The series is therefore a G.P. with first term 3, common ratio 2 and 11 terms. Its sum is

$$3 \times \frac{2^{11} - 1}{2 - 1} = 6141$$

(b) The series is a G.P. with first term $\tfrac{1}{9}$, common ratio $\tfrac{1}{3}$ and 9 terms. Its sum is therefore

$$\frac{1}{9} \times \frac{\left(\tfrac{1}{3}\right)^9 - 1}{\left(\tfrac{1}{3}\right) - 1} \approx 0.1667$$

1.2 Exercise 5

1 Calculate the sum of the series to the number of terms stated.

(a) $2 + 6 + 18 + 54 + \cdots$ (8 terms)

(b) $2 + 10 + 50 + 250 + \cdots$ (12 terms)

(c) $1 + 3 + 9 + 27 + \cdots$ (20 terms)

(d) $8 + 4 + 2 + 1 + \frac{1}{2} + \cdots$ (10 terms)

(e) $8 - 4 + 2 - 1 + \frac{1}{2} - \cdots$ (10 terms)

2 Calculate the sum of each series.

(a) $\displaystyle\sum_{i=1}^{5} 3^{i-1}$ (b) $\displaystyle\sum_{i=1}^{10} 8^{i-1}$ (c) $\displaystyle\sum_{i=1}^{7} 2^{i}$

(d) $\displaystyle\sum_{i=3}^{8} (\tfrac{1}{2})^{i}$ (e) $\displaystyle\sum_{i=1}^{20} (-\tfrac{3}{4})^{i-1}$

3 Legend tells that the Shah of Persia offered a reward to the citizen who introduced him to chess. The citizen asked merely for the number of grains of rice according to the rule:

    1 grain for the first square on the chessboard,

    2 grains for the second square,

    4 grains for the third square,

    8 grains for the fourth square, and so on.

(a) How many grains of rice did he request?

(b) If a grain of rice weighs 0.02 g, what weight of rice did he request?

4 Julius Caesar was born in 101 BC. If his mother had invested the Roman equivalent of 1p for him in a bank account which paid interest per annum of

(a) 1 per cent   (b) 5 per cent

how much would it have been worth in 1989?

5 The sum of £200 is invested annually at 5 per cent interest per annum. What is the total sum of money in the account at the end of 50 years?

6 Using a typical figure for a school leaver's salary and assuming that it will increase by 5 per cent annually, estimate a person's total earnings during their working life.

7 The sum of £1000 is invested annually at 7.5 per cent interest per annum.

(a) What is the total sum of money at the end of n years?

(b) How long will it take for the total sum of money to be twice the total amount invested?

1.2.7 Infinity

So far, when you have summed series you have taken a finite number of terms. On pages 19 and 20 you noticed that sequences show certain patterns of behaviour (for example convergence or divergence) as you take more and more terms. What happens to the sum as you take more and more terms in a series?

For a series with an infinite number of terms, the sum to infinity is the limit of the sum to n terms as n tends to infinity.

For example, the series $1 + \frac{1}{2} + \frac{1}{4} + \frac{1}{8} + \cdots + (\frac{1}{2})^{n-1}$ has sum

$$\frac{(\frac{1}{2})^n - 1}{\frac{1}{2} - 1} = 2\left(1 - \left(\frac{1}{2}\right)^n\right)$$

As $n \to \infty$, $(\frac{1}{2})^n \to 0$ and the sum of the series tends to 2.

On page 35 you found that, for a geometric series,

$$\sum_{i=1}^{n} ar^{i-1} = a\left(\frac{r^n - 1}{r - 1}\right)$$

For what values of r will the series have a 'sum to infinity'?

Clearly, if $|r| < 1$, then $r^n \to 0$ as $n \to \infty$ and so there is a 'sum to infinity'. (Recall that $|r| < 1$ means $-1 < r < 1$.)

The sum $\sum_{1}^{n} ar^{i-1} = a\left(\frac{r^n - 1}{r - 1}\right)$ can usefully be written as $a\left(\frac{1 - r^n}{1 - r}\right)$ for examples where $|r| < 1$. As $n \to \infty$, $r^n \to 0$ if $|r| < 1$ and so there is a 'sum to infinity' of $a\left(\frac{1}{1 - r}\right) = \frac{a}{1 - r}$.

If $|r| \geq 1$ then the series will not converge.

> An infinite G.P. can be summed providing the common ratio r satisfies $|r| < 1$.
>
> $$a + ar + ar^2 + \cdots = \frac{a}{1 - r}, \text{ for } |r| < 1$$

Example 7
Find the sum of the infinite series $1 + \frac{2}{3} + \frac{4}{9} + \frac{8}{27} + \cdots$

Solution
First term $a = 1$ Common ratio $r = \frac{2}{3}$

$\Rightarrow$ Sum to infinity $S_\infty = \dfrac{1}{1 - \frac{2}{3}} = 3$

▶ 1.2 **Tasksheet E2 – Zeno's paradox (page 542)**

1.2 Exercise 6

1 Where possible, calculate the sum of the infinite series:

(a) $\frac{9}{10} + \frac{9}{100} + \frac{9}{1000} + \cdots$ (b) $4 - 3 + \frac{9}{4} - \frac{27}{16} + \cdots$

(c) $1 - 2 + 4 - 8 + \cdots$ (d) $5 + \frac{5}{2} + \frac{5}{4} + \frac{5}{8} + \cdots$

2 Calculate the sum of:

(a) $\displaystyle\sum_{i=1}^{\infty} \frac{1}{3^{i-1}}$ (b) $\displaystyle\sum_{i=1}^{\infty} (0.25)^{i-1}$ (c) $\displaystyle\sum_{i=1}^{\infty} 2^{-i}$

3 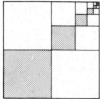 The diagram illustrates the infinite G.P.

$\frac{1}{4} + \frac{1}{16} + \frac{1}{64} + \frac{1}{256} + \cdots$

(a) Find the sum of the G.P.

(b) How could you see this result directly from the diagram?

4 Von Koch's 'snowflake' curve is shown below in its various stages of development. F_0 is an equilateral triangle; F_1 is derived from F_0 by trisecting each side and replacing the centre third of each side of the triangle by two sides of an equilateral triangle; F_2 is obtained in the same way from F_1 and so on.

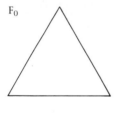 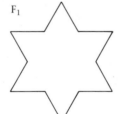 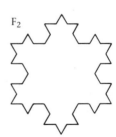

If each side of F_0 is of length 1 and P_n is the perimeter of the nth snowflake curve, write down:

(a) P_0 (b) P_1 (c) P_2 (d) P_n

What happens to the perimeter of the curve as $n \to \infty$?

5 How many terms of the series

$$2 + \frac{4}{5} + \frac{8}{25} + \frac{16}{125} + \cdots$$

must be taken before its sum to n terms differs from its sum to infinity by less than 0.01?

After working through section 1.2, you should:

1 know how to recognise, define and describe sequences;

2 be able to use Σ notation as a shorthand;

3 be able to recognise convergence to a limiting value;

4 be able to use the results:

(i) arithmetic progression:
   sum = number of terms × average of first and last terms,

(ii) geometric progression:

$$\sum_{i=1}^{n} ar^{i-1} = a\left(\frac{1-r^n}{1-r}\right) \quad \text{or} \quad a\left(\frac{r^n-1}{r-1}\right)$$

$$\sum_{i=1}^{\infty} ar^{i-1} = \frac{a}{1-r}, \quad \text{for } |r| < 1$$

1 Foundations

.3 Functions and graphs

1.3.1 Function notation

A scientist performs an experiment to investigate the absorption of light by a liquid. Light is shone through a coloured solution and the intensity of light emerging is measured.

She finds that if she varies the concentration of the solution her readings are as follows.

Concentration (mg cm^{-3}) c	0	0.2	0.4	0.6	0.8	1.0
Intensity (lux) L	20.0	17.4	15.2	13.2	11.5	10.0

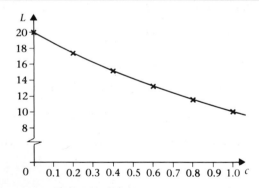

The two variables are related by the formula

$$L = \frac{20}{2^c}$$

This is known as Beer's law of absorption.

The formula can be used to calculate the value of L for any given value of c.

It is often helpful to consider an expression from a different point of view and think of it as a device which generates an **output** for any given **input**. In this case the input is c and the output is L.

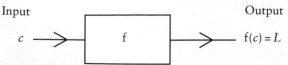

In other words, if the scientist inputs any value of c into her formula she will get a corresponding output which tells her the value of L. This dependence on c can be emphasised by use of the **function notation** $L = f(c)$, where the function f is given by

$$f(c) = \frac{20}{2^c}$$

This gives a convenient shorthand, since you can immediately write $f(0) = 20$, $f(1) = 10$ and so on.

Example 1

If $f(x) = 2x^2 - 3x$, then:

(a) find $f(1)$ and $f(2)$;

(b) find a simplified algebraic expression for $f(x+2)$;

(c) solve the equation $f(x) = 0$.

Solution

(a) $f(1) = 2 - 3 = -1, \quad f(2) = 8 - 6 = 2$

(b) $f(x+2) = 2(x+2)^2 - 3(x+2)$

$$= 2(x^2 + 4x + 4) - 3x - 6$$

$$= 2x^2 + 5x + 2$$

(c) $f(x) = 0$, so $\quad 2x^2 - 3x = 0 \quad \Rightarrow \quad x(2x - 3) = 0$

$$\Rightarrow x = 0 \quad \text{and} \quad x = \tfrac{3}{2} \quad \text{are solutions to } f(x) = 0$$

1.3 Exercise 1

1 If $f(x) = x^2 + 3$ for all values of x, find the values of:

(a) $f(0)$ (b) $f(1)$ (c) $f(\sqrt{2})$ (d) $f(-1)$

2 If $g(t) = \dfrac{5}{3^t}$ for all values of t, find:

(a) $g(2)$ (b) $g(1)$ (c) $g(0)$ (d) $g(-1)$ (e) $g(x)$

3 (a) If $f(x) = x^2 + 3x + 2$, find:

(i) $f(1)$ (ii) $f(-2)$ (iii) $f(0)$ (iv) $f(-1)$ (v) $f(n)$

(b) If $f(y) = y^2 + 3y + 2$, find:

(i) $f(1)$ (ii) $f(-2)$ (iii) $f(0)$ (iv) $f(-1)$ (v) $f(n)$

(c) Does $f(x)$ differ from $f(y)$?

4 If $g(x) = (x+1)^2$ and $h(x) = x^2 + 1$

(a) find simplified algebraic expressions for

(i) $g(x-3)$ (ii) $h(a+2)$

(b) solve the equation $g(x) = h(x)$

(c) solve the equation $g(x-3) = h(x-3)$

5 If $g(x) = x^2 + 2x + 1$ and $f(x) = x + 1$

(a) show that $\dfrac{g(x)}{f(x)} = x + 1$

(b) find simplified algebraic expressions for

(i) $g(2x)$ (ii) $g(x-1)$

1.3.2 Using function notation

The graphs of $f(x) = x^2$ and $y = x^2 + 6x + 5$ are given below.

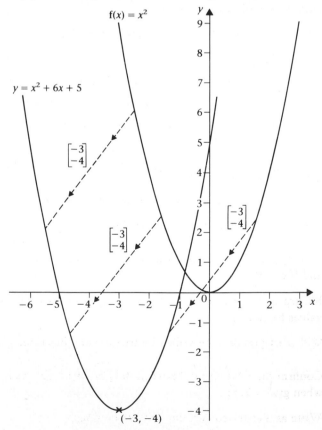

The expression for y can be written in completed squares form:

$$y = (x + 3)^2 - 9 + 5 = (x + 3)^2 - 4$$

Observe that this is the same as $f(x + 3) - 4$.

Considering the two graphs, you can see that the graph of $y = x^2 + 6x + 5$ is a translation of $\begin{bmatrix} -3 \\ -4 \end{bmatrix}$ of the graph of $f(x)$.

Function notation provides a convenient and useful way of describing the relationship between functions and their graphs. This idea is explored more fully in the following questions.

 .3A

1 (a) Sketch the graph of $f(x) = x^2$.

(b) Rearrange the expression for $f(x - 2) + 5$ into the form $ax^2 + bx + c$.

(c) Superimpose the graph of $f(x - 2) + 5$. How is this related to the graph of $f(x)$?

2 For each of the following functions:

(a) $g(x) = x^3$ (b) $g(x) = 2^x$ (c) $g(x) = \sqrt{x}$

(i) sketch the graph of $g(x)$;

(ii) write down the expression for $g(x - 2) + 5$;

(iii) what translation of the graph of $g(x)$ would you expect?

(iv) superimpose the graph of $g(x - 2) + 5$ and check your answer to part (iii).

3 (a) Sketch the graph of $f(x) = |x|$.

(b) Without using a graph plotter, sketch the graph of $|x + 3| - 4$.

(c) Check your answer using a graph plotter.

4 (a) For any function f, what is the relationship between the graph of $f(x)$ and $f(x + a) + b$?

(b) Illustrate your answer to (a) by choosing your own function and values for a and b.

(c) Will what you have described be true for any function?

5E (a) Confirm the relationship between the graphs of $g(x)$ and $g(x + a) + b$ when $g(x) = \sin x$.

(b) Write an illustrated account of your findings.

6E (a) Investigate the relationships between the graphs of

$$h(x) \quad \text{and} \quad ah(bx + c) + d$$

where h is any function, and a, b, c and d may take any values.

(b) Write an illustrated account of your findings.

Any function of the form $f(x + a) + b$ has a graph which is a translation by $\begin{bmatrix} -a \\ b \end{bmatrix}$ of the graph of $f(x)$.

1.3.3 Defining functions

You saw in section 1.3.1 that an example of Beer's law of absorption can be stated as

$$f(c) = \frac{20}{2^c}$$

It would not be sensible to calculate $f(-2)$, for example, because a concentration of $-2 \, \text{mg cm}^{-3}$ would have no meaning. When defining a function you must be specific about the values to which it applies.

The precise **definition** of a function consists of two parts.

The **rule** This tells you how values of the function are assigned or calculated.

The **domain** This tells you the set of values to which the rule may be applied.

For example, $f(x) = \sqrt{(x - 5)}$, $x \geq 5$ defines a function f, where

- the rule is $f(x) = \sqrt{(x - 5)}$

- the domain is $x \geq 5$

In describing the domain of a function, the following notation is a useful shorthand for defining important sets.

$\mathbb{N}$ – the natural numbers $1, 2, 3, \ldots$

$\mathbb{Z}$ – the integers $\ldots, -3, -2, -1, 0, 1, 2, 3, \ldots$

$\mathbb{Q}$ – the rational numbers (or fractions, including, for example, $\frac{6}{2}$)

$\mathbb{R}$ – the real numbers (both rational and irrational such as $\sqrt{2}$ and $-\pi$)

This notation can be extended using $^+$ and $^-$ signs. Thus $\mathbb{R}^+$ means the positive real numbers, $\mathbb{Z}^-$ means the negative integers.

You can also use the symbol $\in$ to mean 'belongs to'. Thus $x \in \mathbb{Q}^+$ means 'x belongs to the set of positive rationals'.

Note that $\mathbb{N}$ is a subset of $\mathbb{Z}$, which is itself a subset of $\mathbb{Q}$, which is a subset of $\mathbb{R}$.

When a function is written down, both the rule and the domain should be given. However, in practice the domain is often omitted and the function is assumed to be defined for all values that are valid in the rule. This is a common 'misuse' of the description of a function.

1.3 Exercise 2

1 If $f(x) = \dfrac{1}{x+2}$

(a) find:

    (i) $f(0)$ (ii) $f(-1)$ (iii) $f(a)$ (iv) $f(a-2)$ (v) $f(-2)$

(b) What is the largest possible domain for f?

(c) Sketch the graph of $f(x)$.

2 (a) If $h(x) = \sqrt{x}$, find the values of:

    (i) $h(2)$ (ii) $h(9)$ (iii) $h(\sqrt{2})$ (iv) $h(\pi)$ (v) $h(\pi^2)$

(b) What is the largest possible domain for h?

(c) Sketch the graph of $h(x-3)$.

3 Write down the largest possible domain for g in each of the following.

(a) $g(x) = \dfrac{1}{x+5}$ (b) $g(x) = \dfrac{1}{\sqrt{(x-3)}}$

(c) $g(x) = \sqrt[3]{x}$ (d) $g(x) = \dfrac{1}{\sqrt[3]{(x+2)}}$

4 The modulus function $|x|$, meaning 'the magnitude of x', is defined as

$$|x| = \begin{cases} x, & x \geq 0 \\ -x, & x < 0 \end{cases}$$

(On some calculators it is called abs(x), which is an abbreviation for 'the absolute value of x'.)

(a) Write down the value of:

    (i) $|5|$ (ii) $|-7|$ (iii) $|\sqrt{2}|$ (iv) $|-\pi|$ (v) $|0|$

(b) What is the largest possible domain for the function?

(c) Sketch the graph of:

    (i) $y = |x|$

    (ii) $y = |x - 2|$

    (iii) $y = |x - 2| + 4$

1.3.4 To plot or to sketch?

In 1.3.2 and 1.3.3 you looked at many different functions. Now you will investigate the general properties and techniques used for obtaining the graphs of functions. You will be *sketching* graphs rather than *plotting* them. You can illustrate why sketching is often better than plotting if you use the plotting method to draw the graph of the function

$$y = 4x + \frac{1}{2x - 5} \quad \text{for } x \in \mathbb{R}^+$$

This gives the table of values and plotted points as follows.

x	1	2	3	4	5
y	3.7	7.0	13.0	16.3	20.2

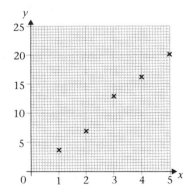

 .3B

1 What do you think the graph of $y = 4x + \dfrac{1}{2x - 5}$ looks like?

2 What are the values of y when $x = 2.45, 2.49, 2.499$?

3 What happens when $x = 2.5$?

4 Use the graph plotter to draw the graph for values of x from 0 to 5.

You have seen that drawing a 'smooth curve' through selected points can lead to major errors. In general, for functions it helps to have an idea of what the graph will look like before you attempt the sketch.

> Sketching a curve implies having a good overall impression of its shape without the need for detailed plotting of points.

To obtain the overall shape of a graph you only need to consider some of the major features.

 .3C

1 (a) Plot on the same screen and thus superimpose each of the following graphs.

   (i) $y = x^2$ (ii) $y = x^3$ (iii) $y = x^4$ (iv) $y = x^5$

   (b) What points do all the graphs have in common?

   (c) Which function increases most rapidly, and which increases least rapidly, as x becomes large?

   (d) What are the main differences between the graphs of the even powers of x and the graphs of odd powers of x?

2 (a) Plot on the same screen the following graphs.

   (i) $y = x^2$ (ii) $y = 4x$ (iii) $y = x^2 + 4x$

   (b) What do you notice about the graphs of $y = x^2$ and $y = x^2 + 4x$ when x is a large positive or negative number?

   (c) What do you notice about the graphs of $y = 4x$ and $y = x^2 + 4x$ when x is a small positive or negative number?

3 (a) Plot on the same screen the following graphs.

   (i) $y = x^3$ (ii) $y = -4x^2$ (iii) $y = x^3 - 4x^2$

   (b) What do you notice about the graphs of $y = -4x^2$ and $y = x^3 - 4x^2$ when x is a small positive or negative number?

   (c) What do you notice about the graphs of $y = x^3$ and $y = x^3 - 4x^2$ when x is a large positive or negative number?

4 (a) Plot the graph of the function

   $$y = x^3 + x^2 - 2x + 1$$

(b) Superimpose the graphs of:

    (i) $y = x^3$ (ii) $y = -2x + 1$

(c) Compare the three graphs for:

    (i) large positive and negative values of x,

    (ii) very small positive and negative values of x.

(d) Suggest a reason for ignoring the terms x^2, $-2x$ and 1 when considering the shape of the graph in part (a) for large values of x.

(e) Suggest a reason for ignoring the terms x^3 and x^2 when considering the shape of the graph in part (a) for very small values of x.

5 Plot the graph of the function $y = 3x + 2x^2 - x^3$.
What are the zeros of this function; that is, where does the graph cross the x-axis?
Which term do you think determines the shape for:

(a) large positive and negative values of x,

(b) very small positive and negative values of x?

6 (a) What term is suggested by the shape of this graph when x is large?

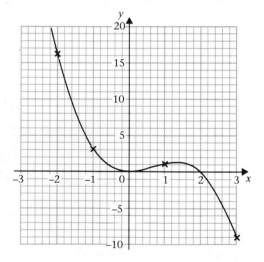

(b) What term is suggested by the shape of the graph when x is small?

(c) (i) Suggest an equation for the graph above.

    (ii) To confirm your suggestion, plot the graph of your equation.

(d) If necessary repeat (c) until you have found the equation of the graph.

In the questions in 1.3c, you developed some of the ideas that can be used to build up an impression of a graph of a polynomial function.

> For a general polynomial function of the form
>
> $$y = ax^m + \cdots + bx^n + c \quad (a, b \text{ are non-zero})$$
>
> where m is the highest power of x and n is the lowest non-zero power of x, the graph will look like $y = ax^m$ for very large x, look like $y = bx^n + c$ for very small x and will cross the y-axis at c.

Example 2

Sketch the graph of $f(x) = 4x^3 - 6x^2 - 11x + 18$.

Solution

(i) For large x the graph behaves like $y = 4x^3$. This is the **dominant** term.

(ii) For small x the graph behaves like $-11x + 18$.

Using just these features, you can draw part of the graph.

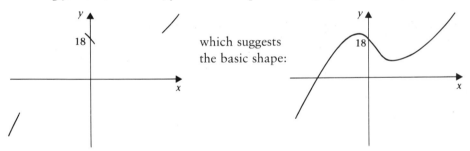

which suggests the basic shape:

However, the graph of example 2 might take any of these forms:

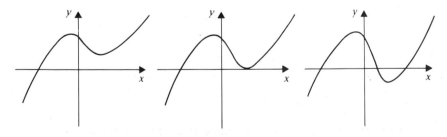

You need more information to establish which is the correct form. For example, you may be able to find the points of intersection with the x-axis, or the coordinates of the turning points (i.e. points where the gradient changes sign).

When a polynomial function is given in factorised form, the roots give you extra clues to help determine the shape of the graph.

Example 3
Sketch the graph of $f(x) = (x - 2)^2(2x + 7)$.

Solution

(i) $f(0) = 28$.

(ii) For large x, $2x^3$ is dominant.

(iii) The zeros of the function are at $x = 2$ (a repeated root) and $x = -3\frac{1}{2}$.

The available information is plotted as shown.

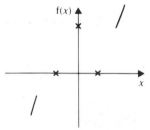   This suggests the graph: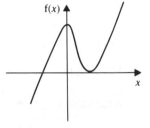

1 .3D

1 How can you obtain facts (i) and (ii) in the solution to example 3 *without* multiplying out the brackets?

2 Why is   not possible?

You can get a good idea of the main features of the graph of a polynomial function, $f(x)$, by:

(a) knowing the zeros, i.e. where it cuts the x-axis;

(b) knowing $f(0)$, i.e. where it cuts the y-axis;

(c) applying the principles of dominance.

It is only necessary to apply those principles which enable the essential features of the curve to be drawn.

1.3 Exercise 3

1 For the function $f(x) = (x - 2)(x + 3)(3x - 7)$, which in expanded form is

$$f(x) = 3x^3 - 4x^2 - 25x + 42$$

(a) on a partial sketch:

　(i) mark any zeros on a set of axes;

　(ii) mark the value of $f(x)$ when $x = 0$;

　(iii) sketch the dominant parts of the graph;

(b) complete the sketch.

2 For the function

$$f(x) = -5x^4 + 28x^3 - 33x^2 + 2x + 8 = -(x - 1)^2(x - 4)(5x + 2)$$

(a) sketch the dominant parts of the graph;

(b) complete the sketch.

3 Sketch the graph of the function

$$y = x^3(x + 4)(x - 7)$$

4 A girl standing on the edge of a cliff throws a stone. The height of the stone above the point of release, after t seconds, is given by

$$h = t(12 - 5t) \text{ metres}$$

(a) When is the stone level with the point of release again?

(b) The stone hits the sea after 4 seconds. Estimate the height of the cliff above sea level.

(c) Sketch a graph of height against time.

1.3.5 Rational functions

The idea of dominance may be applied to sketching the graphs of rational functions (i.e. algebraic fractions). However, your attention in rational functions must *always* be drawn first to the *denominator*.

For example, consider the function $\dfrac{x+1}{x+2}$.

This function is not defined for $x = -2$. The denominator of the fraction equals zero, and division by zero is not defined, so the function can have *no value at this point*. On the graph of the function this means that there can be *no y-value when* $x = -2$, and the graph will have a break where $x = -2$. Such a break in the curve is called a **discontinuity**.

Example 4
Sketch the graph of $\dfrac{x+1}{x+2}$.

Solution

(i) There is a discontinuity at $x = -2$.

(ii) As x becomes large positive, the function is approximately $\dfrac{x}{x} \approx 1$ and approaches 1 *from below*.

(iii) As x becomes large negative, the function is again approximately 1, but here approaches 1 *from above*.

(iv) To the right of the discontinuity at $x = -2$ (i.e. $x > -2$), the value of the function is very large and negative. Just to the left of the discontinuity (i.e. $x < -2$), the value of the function is very large and positive.

(v) When $x = -1$, $f(x) = 0$.

With this information you can complete the sketch.

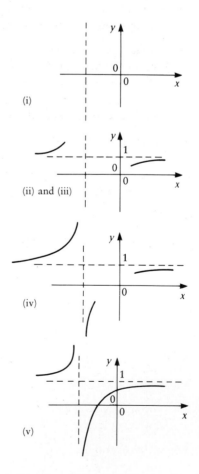

(i)

(ii) and (iii)

(iv)

(v)

Example 5

Sketch the graph of the function $f(x)$, where

$$f(x) = \frac{x+1}{x^2 + 5x + 6}$$

Solution

First try to factorise the denominator, so that $f(x)$ becomes

$$\frac{x+1}{(x+3)(x+2)}$$

Note:

(i) There are discontinuities at $x = -2$ and $x = -3$.

(ii) As x becomes large positive, the function is approximately $\frac{x}{x^2}$, i.e. $\frac{1}{x}$, and approaches 0 *from above*.

(iii) As x becomes large negative, the function is again approximately $\frac{1}{x}$, but here approaches 0 *from below*.

(iv) To the right of the discontinuity at $x = -2$ (i.e. $x > -2$), the value of the function is dominated by the value taken by $(x+2)$ in the denominator. $f(x)$ is very large and negative for values of x just greater than -2 (e.g. -1.9). Just to the left of the discontinuity (i.e. $x < -2$), the value of the function is very large and positive.

(v) To the right of the discontinuity at $x = -3$ (i.e. $x > -3$), the value of the function is dominated by the value taken by $(x+3)$ in the denominator. $f(x)$ is very large and positive here. Just to the left of the discontinuity (i.e. $x < -3$), the value of the function is very large and negative.

(vi) When $x = -1$, $f(x) = 0$. When $x = 0$, $f(x) = \frac{1}{6}$.

With this information you can complete the sketch.

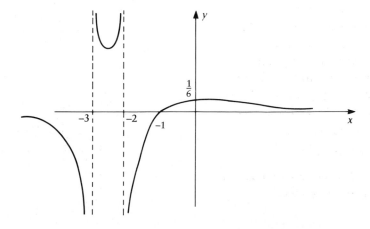

In example 5, the lines $x = -2$, $x = -3$, and $y = 0$ (the x-axis) are called **asymptotes** to the curve. The graph *approaches these lines* but does not (ever) touch them.

In example 4, the asymptotes are the lines $x = -2$ and $y = 1$.

> When sketching the graph of a function, it is helpful to consider the following.
>
> (i) Is the graph related to a standard graph by means of a simple transformation?
>
> (ii) Where does the graph cut the axes?
>
> (iii) How does the graph behave for large values of x, both positive and negative?
>
> (iv) Are there values of x for which the function is undefined? Given a value of x at which the graph is discontinuous, is y positive or negative each side of the vertical asymptote?

Example 6

Sketch the curve $y = 4x^2 + \dfrac{80\,000}{x}$.

Solution

(a) $y = 0$ when $4x^2 = -\dfrac{80\,000}{x}$

$\qquad$ so $x^3 = -20\,000$

$\qquad$ and $x = -27.1$

(b) When x is large, $\dfrac{80\,000}{x}$ is relatively small, and $y \approx 4x^2$. For instance, when $x = 100$, $4x^2 = 40\,000$ and $\dfrac{80\,000}{x} = 800$. When $x = 1000$, $4x^2 = 4\,000\,000$ and $\dfrac{80\,000}{x} = 80$.

(c) y is undefined when $x = 0$, so the y-axis is an asymptote.

$\qquad$ When x is small and positive, y is large and positive (for example $x = 0.1$ gives $y = 800\,000.04$); small negative values of x make y large and negative.

This information is plotted, together with the complete curve.

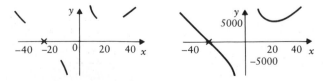

The shapes of the graphs of some simple functions are worth knowing, as they can be useful in sketching more complicated functions without the aid of a table of values. The graphs of some functions, all of which are simple powers of x, are shown below.

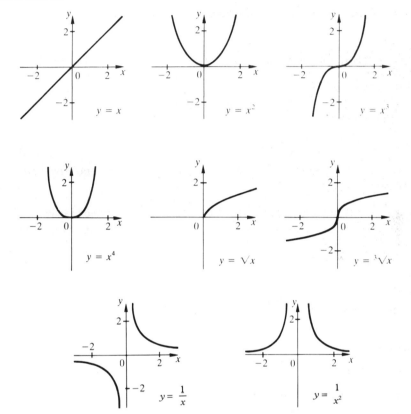

Notice that $y = \dfrac{1}{x}$ and $y = \dfrac{1}{x^2}$ are not defined when $x = 0$, and that $y = \sqrt{x}$ is not defined when $x < 0$.

1.3 Exercise 4

1 Sketch the graphs of:

(a) $\dfrac{x}{x+1}$

(b) $\dfrac{x^2}{x+1}$

(c) $\dfrac{x}{(x+1)(x-2)}$

(d) $\dfrac{x+2}{x^2-x-2}$

(e) $\dfrac{(x+1)(x-2)}{(x-3)}$

(f) $\dfrac{x^2+5x+6}{x^2-x-2}$

(g) $\dfrac{x}{x^2-1}$

(h) $x + \dfrac{1}{x}$

(i) $\dfrac{1}{(x-3)^2}$

2 A person who wishes to walk 20 km in 4 hours proposes to walk half the distance at v km h^{-1} and the remainder at u km h^{-1}. Show that $\dfrac{10}{v} + \dfrac{10}{u} = 4$, and hence that $v = \dfrac{5u}{(2u - 5)}$. Sketch the graph of v as a function of u, and comment on the result.

3 The total resistance R ohms of two resistors of R_1 and R_2 ohms in parallel is given by $\dfrac{1}{R} = \dfrac{1}{R_1} + \dfrac{1}{R_2}$. Sketch a graph of R as function of R_1, assuming that R_2 is fixed. Comment on the physical significance of very small and very large values of R_1.

4 The surface area of a cylinder is given by the expression $A = 2\pi r^2 + 2\pi rh$. Express h in terms of r, and hence sketch a graph of h as a function of r, assuming that A is constant.

5 Suggest possible functions for the graphs below.

(a)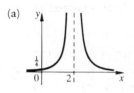

(b)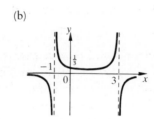

After working through section 1.3 you should:

1 understand the meaning of the term *function*;

2 be able to define and describe a function using the correct notation;

3 be able to sketch the graphs of functions using:

  (a) zeros,

  (b) dominance,

  (c) asymptotes.

1 Foundations

1.4 Expressions and equations

1.4.1 The language of algebra

The use of algebra in mathematics is extremely important. Many results are stated algebraically and many problems must be expressed algebraically before they can be solved – it is the **language** in which many mathematical ideas are expressed.

Letters appear in algebraic expressions in a variety of forms, and although you will have met all of these in earlier work you may not have reflected on the different uses of the letters in various cases.

Letters can stand for **variables** in expressions. In the quadratic expression

$$y = ax^2 + bx + c$$

x and y are variables, while a, b and c are **constants** for a *given* quadratic expression (although a, b and c may change for *different* quadratic expressions). Additionally, in the quadratic expression given, x is called the **independent variable**, while the variable y (which is calculated from the x-value) is the **dependent variable**. This has an important parallel in science, where in a scientific experiment the variable which you control is called the independent variable, while other variables are the dependent variables.

When plotting graphs, the independent variable is plotted along the horizontal (or x) axis.

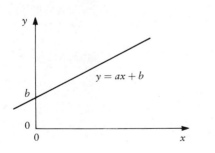
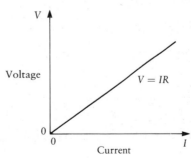

Letters can also stand for **unknowns** in expressions. For example, if five adults' tickets and three children's tickets for the cinema cost £20, then

$$5x + 3y = 20$$

where x is the price of an adult's ticket and y the price of a child's ticket.

As well as using letters to stand for unknowns, they may be used to express general results such as

$$1 + 2 + 3 + \cdots + n = \frac{n(n+1)}{2}$$

for the sum of a simple arithmetic progression, or to express general statements such as

Numbers of the form $2n + 1$, $\{n \in \mathbb{Z}\}$, are always odd.

The algebraic statement

$$x^2 - 4 = (x - 2)(x + 2)$$

is called an **identity**. Identities are also common in mathematics and differ from equations in that they are true for *any* value of the variable. An equation is only true for *specific* values of the variable, and these values are called the **solutions** of the equation.

$$x^2 - 4 = 0 \text{ is true } only \text{ for } x = \pm 2$$

Practice at setting up and solving equations is provided in the following exercise. If you need to revise some of the basic methods of solving equations then you should do tasksheet S1 first.

▶ 1.4 **Tasksheet S1 – Review of equations (page 530)**

1.4 **Exercise 1**

1 Solve the equations:

(a) $3x + 9 = 0$ (b) $x^2 = 25$ (c) $x^2 + 5x - 6 = 0$

(d) $x = \dfrac{4}{x}$ (e) $4(x + 3) = 6(2 - x)$ (f) $x(x - 4) = 0$

(g) $2x + 3y = 22$ (h) $2y - x = 2$ (i) $2x + 3y + 1 = 0$
    $3x + 2y = 23$ $6y + 5x = -2$ $y - x = 3$

2 The triangular numbers are defined as

$$T_1 = 1 \qquad T_2 = 1 + 2 \qquad T_3 = 1 + 2 + 3 \qquad \text{and so on}$$

If the nth triangular number is 210, formulate an equation for n and solve it to find n.

3 (a) Find the sum of three consecutive numbers. Repeat for several other sets of three consecutive numbers. What do you notice about the results?

(b) Any three consecutive numbers can be written algebraically as

$$n, (n + 1), (n + 2)$$

Find the sum of these three algebraic terms. How does this explain what you have observed about the numerical results?

4 'The difference between the squares of two consecutive odd numbers is always a multiple of 8.'

(a) Test this result in a few numerical cases. Is it true for the odd numbers 91 378 627 513 and 91 378 627 515?

(b) Prove the result algebraically.

5 'A bamboo 18 cubits high was broken by the wind. Its top touched the ground 6 cubits from the root. Tell the lengths of the segments of the bamboo.'

Solve this problem posed by Brahmagupta (Hindu mathematician c. AD 630).

From H. Eves, *Introduction to the History of Mathematics* (Saunders)

6 Four right-angled triangles with sides a, b and c are arranged as shown in the diagram.

Explain why the area of the large square can be given as both $(a + b)^2$ and $c^2 + 2ab$.

Use these two results to prove Pythagoras' theorem.

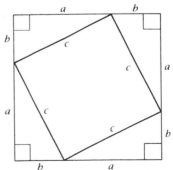

1.4.2 Quadratic equations

The path around a square lawn is 1 metre wide. If the area of the path is equal to the area of the lawn, the dimensions of the lawn may be found as follows.

Let x be the length of a side of the lawn.

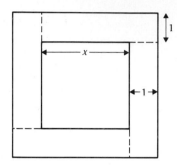

Area of lawn $= x^2$

Area of path $= 4(x + 1)$

So $x^2 = 4x + 4$

$x^2 - 4x - 4 = 0$

This equation does not factorise to give integer roots!

However, it may be solved using the method of completing the square developed earlier (section 1.1.4).

$$x^2 - 4x - 4 = 0$$
$$[(x - 2)^2 - 4] - 4 = 0$$
$$(x - 2)^2 - 8 = 0$$
$$(x - 2)^2 = 8$$
$$\Rightarrow x = 2 \pm \sqrt{8}$$

The negative solution $(2 - \sqrt{8})$ cannot be a solution in the context of this problem, so the only possible value for x is $2 + \sqrt{8}$.

The lawn is a square of side 4.83 m (to 3 s.f.).

Using the completed square form gives an alternative approach to solving a quadratic equation. It can also be used to derive an important formula that can be applied to any quadratic.

 .4A

1   Solve the equation $x^2 + 6x + 4 = 0$ using the method of completing the square.

The solution of the equation $x^2 + bx + c = 0$ depends entirely on the two numbers b and c. You can find a formula for the solutions in terms of these two letters using the method of completing the square.

$$x^2 + bx + c = 0$$

$$\left(x + \frac{b}{2}\right)^2 - \frac{b^2}{4} + c = 0 \qquad ①$$

$$\left(x + \frac{b}{2}\right)^2 = \frac{b^2}{4} - c \qquad ②$$

$$\left(x + \frac{b}{2}\right)^2 = \frac{b^2 - 4c}{4} \qquad ③$$

$$x + \frac{b}{2} = \frac{\pm\sqrt{(b^2 - 4c)}}{2} \qquad ④$$

$$x = \frac{-b \pm \sqrt{(b^2 - 4c)}}{2}$$

2 (a) Explain where the $\frac{b^2}{4}$ has come from in line ①.

(b) Why has the c in line ② become $4c$ in line ③?

(c) Why has the $\pm$ appeared in line ④?

3 Use the formula to solve:

(a) $x^2 + 6x + 4 = 0$ (b) $x^2 - 6x + 4 = 0$ (c) $x^2 = 5 - 3x$

By using a method similar to that above, the following result is obtained.

The formula for solving the general quadratic equation $ax^2 + bx + c = 0$, $a \neq 0$, is

$$x = \frac{-b \pm \sqrt{(b^2 - 4ac)}}{2a}$$

Example 1
Find (correct to 2 d.p.) the coordinates of the points of intersection of the straight line $y = 2x + 3$ with the parabola $y = 5x^2 - x - 1$.

Solution
The intersections occur when $5x^2 - x - 1 = 2x + 3$, i.e. when $5x^2 - 3x - 4 = 0$.

Using $x = \dfrac{-b \pm \sqrt{(b^2 - 4ac)}}{2a}$, where $a = 5$, $b = -3$, $c = -4$,

$$x = \frac{3 \pm \sqrt{(9 - 4 \times 5 \times (-4))}}{2 \times 5}$$

$$\Rightarrow x = \frac{3 \pm \sqrt{89}}{10}$$

$$\Rightarrow x = 1.24 \text{ or } x = -0.64 \quad \text{(to 2 decimal places)}$$

Note that the solution may be given in one of two forms.

$\dfrac{3 \pm \sqrt{89}}{10}$ are the **exact** solutions; 1.24 or −0.64 are the **approximate** solutions.

When $x = 1.24$, $y = 5.48$; when $x = -0.64$, $y = 1.72$. Hence the intersections occur at $(1.24, 5.48)$ and $(-0.64, 1.72)$.

Numbers such as $\dfrac{3 - \sqrt{89}}{10}$ are known as **surds**. Further practice at dealing with numbers written in surd form is provided on tasksheet S2.

▶ 1.4 **Tasksheet S2 – Working in surd form (page 532)**

Example 2
Solve the pair of simultaneous equations $x^2 + y^2 = 4$ and $x + y = 1$.

Solution
The problem is best solved by substitution, as follows.

$$y = 1 - x \qquad \text{(from the second equation)}$$
$$\therefore \quad x^2 + (1 - x)^2 = 4 \qquad \text{(substitute for } y \text{ in the first equation)}$$
$$\Rightarrow \quad 2x^2 - 2x - 3 = 0 \qquad \text{(expand and simplify)}$$
$$\Rightarrow \qquad x = \frac{2 \pm \sqrt{(4 - 4 \times 2 \times (-3))}}{4} = \frac{1 \pm \sqrt{7}}{2}$$

When $\quad x = \dfrac{1 + \sqrt{7}}{2}, \quad y = 1 - x = \dfrac{1 - \sqrt{7}}{2}$

When $\quad x = \dfrac{1 - \sqrt{7}}{2}, \quad y = \dfrac{1 + \sqrt{7}}{2}$

1.4 **Exercise 2**

1 Use the quadratic equation formula to solve the following, giving your answers (a) in exact form, and (b) to 2 decimal places.

(i) $x^2 + 5x + 3 = 0$ (ii) $3x^2 + 6x + 2 = 0$

(iii) $3x^2 + 4x - 1 = 0$ (iv) $5x^2 - 8x - 1 = 0$

(v) $x^2 + 2x = 4$ (vi) $6x^2 + 10x - 4 = x^2 + 7x - 3$

2 Find the coordinates of the points of intersection of the graphs of:

(a) $y = 5x^2$ and $y = 3x + 4$ (b) $y = x - x^2$ and $y = 8 - 6x$

(c) $xy = 4$ and $y - 2x = 1$

3 Solve the following equations where possible, giving your answers to 2 decimal places. Use factors, where appropriate, otherwise use either the formula or completing the square.

(a) $8x - x^2 = 0$ (b) $x^2 + 2x = 5x + 4$ (c) $x^2 + x - 1 = 0$

(d) $x^2 = 25$ (e) $x^2 + x + 1 = 0$ (f) $25 = 10x - x^2$

4 *Derive* the formula

$$x = \frac{-b \pm \sqrt{(b^2 - 4ac)}}{2a}$$

for the roots of the quadratic equation $ax^2 + bx + c = 0$.

5 Solve the following simultaneous equations.

(a) $y^2 = 4x$ (b) $y^2 = 4x + 1$ (c) $xy = 64$
    $y = x$ $y = x + 1$ $4x - y = 60$

6 Two numbers differ by 1 and have a product of 10. Let n be the smaller number. Form an equation in n and solve it. Hence find the two numbers exactly.

7 (a) Use the formula to solve, where possible, the equation $f(x) = 0$ for each of the functions:

(i) $f(x) = x^2 - 2x + 4$ (ii) $f(x) = x^2 - 4x + 4$ (iii) $f(x) = x^2 - 6x + 4$

(b) The graph of each of the functions is given below. Use the information about the roots that you found in part (a) to match each function to its graph.

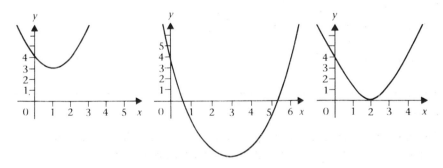

(c) Describe how the value of $b^2 - 4ac$ (known as the **discriminant** of the quadratic equation) relates to the number of roots.

▶ 1.4 **Tasksheet E1 – Regular pentagons and the Fibonacci sequence**
(page 544)

1.4.3 Inequalities

Some problems may not lead to an equation, but may give rise to an inequality. For example, what is the first triangular number greater than 50?

Trial and error may lead you to the result that $n = 10$, but if you were to take an algebraic approach you would have to solve

$$1 + 2 + 3 + \cdots + n > 50$$

$$\frac{n(n + 1)}{2} > 50$$

$$n^2 + n - 100 > 0$$

which is an example of a quadratic inequality.

We shall give two examples of how to handle inequalities. The first demonstrates how to solve a linear inequality.

Example 3
Find the solution set for the inequality $t + 2 > 6t + 7$.

> **Solution**
> $t + 2 > 6t + 7$
> $\Rightarrow -5t > 5$ Step 1: Gather together like terms.
> $\Rightarrow \quad t < -1$ Step 2: Divide both sides by a negative value
>   (note the change in the inequality sign).

The set of values of t which solve this inequality are known as the **solution set** for the inequality.

> When manipulating inequalities algebraically, normal algebraic rules are obeyed, except that when both sides are multiplied or divided by a negative number the inequality sign is reversed.

The following example demonstrates how a graphical approach is helpful in solving quadratic inequalities.

Example 4

Find the solution set for the following inequalities.

(a) $(x+1)(x-2) > 0$

(b) $(x+1)(x-2) > 4$

Solution

The graph of $y = (x+1)(x-2)$ is as shown.

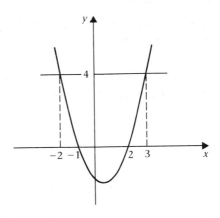

(a) From the graph you can see that $(x+1)(x-2) > 0$ implies

$$x > 2 \quad \text{or} \quad x < -1$$

(b) The graph of $y = (x+1)(x-2)$ crosses $y = 4$ at $x = -2$ and $x = 3$. So $(x+1)(x-2) > 4$ implies

$$x > 3 \quad \text{or} \quad x < -2$$

When you solve a quadratic inequality you are seeking the set of values for which it is true. It is usually simplest to solve the corresponding *equation* and refer to a sketch graph to find the ranges of values which satisfy the inequality.

Example 5

For what values of x is:

(a) $x^2 > 6 - x$

(b) $x^2 < 6 - x$?

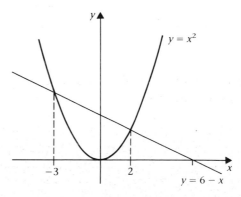

Solution

Solving $x^2 = 6 - x$:

$$x^2 + x - 6 = 0$$

$$(x+3)(x-2) = 0$$

$$x = -3 \quad \text{or} \quad x = 2$$

From the graph you can see that:

(a) $x^2 > 6 - x$ when *either* $x < -3$ or $x > 2$.

(b) $x^2 < 6 - x$ when *both* $x > -3$ *and* $x < 2$. This solution set is usually written as $-3 < x < 2$.

When dealing with algebraic fractions, the same ideas are employed but you must be careful that when you simplify the fractions you multiply by *positive* expressions. For example, to simplify $\dfrac{1}{x+1} > 1$ you might multiply by $x + 1$.

However, $x + 1$ may be either positive or negative, and this will cause problems with the inequality. It is better to multiply by $(x + 1)^2$, as $(x + 1)^2 > 0$ for *all* x (except -1, which cannot be part of the solution set anyway).

Example 6
Solve for x:

(a) $\dfrac{1}{x+1} > 1$ (b) $\dfrac{2x-1}{x} > 1$ (c) $\dfrac{x-1}{(x-2)(x+1)} > 0$

Solution

(a) $\dfrac{1}{x+1} > 1 \Rightarrow x + 1 > (x+1)^2$ [Multiply by $(x+1)^2$]

$$x + 1 > x^2 + 2x + 1$$

$$0 > x^2 + x$$

$$0 > x(x+1)$$

$f(x) = x(x+1) = 0$ when $x = 0$ and $x = -1$

when $x > 0$, $f(x) > 0$

when $-1 < x < 0$, $f(x) < 0$

when $x < -1$, $f(x) > 0$

So $\dfrac{1}{x+1} > 1 \Rightarrow -1 < x < 0$

(b) $\dfrac{2x-1}{x} > 1 \Rightarrow x(2x - 1) > x^2$

$$2x^2 - x > x^2$$

$$x^2 - x > 0$$

$$x(x-1) > 0$$

There are zeros at $x = 0$ and $x = 1$.

when $x > 1$, $x(x-1) > 0$ ✓

when $0 < x < 1$, $x(x-1) < 0$ ✗

when $x < 0$, $x(x-1) > 0$ ✓

So the solution set is $x > 1$ or $x < 0$.

(c) $\dfrac{x-1}{(x-2)(x+1)} > 0 \Rightarrow (x-2)(x-1)(x+1) > 0$

$\qquad f(x) = (x-2)(x-1)(x+1) = 0 \quad$ when $x = -1, 1, 2$

If $\qquad\qquad x > 2, \quad f(x) > 0 \qquad \checkmark$

$\qquad\qquad 1 < x < 2, \quad f(x) < 0 \qquad \times$

$\qquad\qquad -1 < x < 1, \quad f(x) > 0 \qquad \checkmark$

$\qquad\qquad x < -1, \quad f(x) < 0 \qquad \times$

So the solution set is $x > 2 \quad$ or $\quad -1 < x < 1$.

1.4 Exercise 3

1 Solve:

(a) $5x < -10$ (b) $1 - 2x < 3x + 6$

(c) $2(x - 3) < 8$ (d) $3(x + 5) < 2x + 3$

(e) $-3x < 6$

2 Find the range of possible values for x if $(2 - x)^2 > 0$.

3

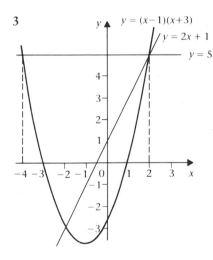

Use the graph to write down the solutions of:

(a) $(x - 1)(x + 3) \leq 0$

(b) $(x - 1)(x + 3) > 5$

(c) $(x - 1)(x + 3) < 2x + 1$

4 Use sketch graphs to help solve the inequalities:

(a) $(x + 5)(x - 2) > 0$ (b) $(x - 2)(3 - x) \leq 0$

(c) $(x + 2)(x - 2)(x - 5) \geq 0$ (d) $(x + 2)(x - 2)^2 \geq 0$

5 Solve the inequalities:

(a) $x^2 < 3x$ (b) $3x^2 + 2x \leq 2x^2 + 3x$

(c) $x(x - 3) < 10$ (d) $x^2 + x > 1$

6 Find the first triangular number which is greater than 1000.

7E Solve the following inequalities. You should use algebraic and not graphical methods in all cases.

(a) $\dfrac{1}{x} > 1$ (b) $\dfrac{3x+1}{x} > 0$ (c) $\dfrac{1}{x+1} > \dfrac{1}{x}$

(d) $\dfrac{x}{(x+1)(x+2)} > 0$ (e) $\dfrac{1}{(x+1)(x-1)} > 0$

1.4.4 Inventing new numbers: $\sqrt{-1}$

The quadratic equations we have met so far have either had no roots or two roots (counting equal or repeated roots as two roots). It would certainly be attractive and convenient if all quadratics had two roots.

Consider the equation $x^2 + 4 = 0$. There are no values of x among the real numbers that solve this equation. However, if we define a number $j = \sqrt{-1}$, then the equation has the two roots $\pm 2j$:

$$x^2 + 4 = 0$$
$$x^2 = -4$$
$$x = \pm \sqrt{-4}$$
$$= \pm \sqrt{(4 \times (-1))}$$
$$= \pm \sqrt{4} \times \sqrt{-1}$$
$$x = \pm 2j$$

It is clear that the roots of this equation are not real numbers (i.e. they are not numbers that have a place on the real number line); they are called **complex numbers**.

Extending the number system in this way has been a common feature of mathematics throughout its development over the past 2500 years or so. Problems associated with the solution of polynomial equations have absorbed the attention of mathematicians since the earliest times. The simplest equations such as $x - 7 = 0$ or $12x - 5 = 0$ could be solved in the positive integers or rationals, both of which were in common use by 1000 BC (although modern notation for fractions dates only from about AD 1500). In the 5th and 4th centuries BC, the Greeks made the first important extension to the number system by laying the foundations of irrational numbers, enabling equations like $x^2 - 5 = 0$ to be solved. Since their interest came principally from a geometric viewpoint, the Greeks did not appreciate that there might be *two* roots – indeed negative numbers in their present form were not fully established until the 16th century.

At about that time also, the modern system of classification of polynomial equations according to their degree was introduced and it was realised that there was no neat theory to account for the number of roots. A quadratic might have 0 or 2 roots (counting a repeated root as 2), a cubic might have 1 or 3 roots, a quartic might have 4, 2 or 0 and so on. Obviously, it would be ideal if *every* quadratic had exactly 2 roots, every cubic 3 roots and every equation of degree n had exactly n roots.

In 1545, Cardan was the first to attempt to deal with the solution of an equation like $x^2 + 4 = 0$, but it was more than 250 years later that the invention of complex numbers was completed by Gauss (who went on to show that no further numbers need be invented to solve equations of any degree).

In fact, only one *new* number is needed, denoted by j, such that $j^2 = -1$.

j is combined with the real numbers to form numbers of the form $z = a + bj$, the **complex numbers**. Notice that when $b = 0$, the complex numbers reduce to the familiar real numbers. In fact, the real numbers are simply a special set of the complex numbers. When $a = 0$, the complex numbers reduce to the form bj. Such numbers are said to be **imaginary numbers** and are again a special set of the complex numbers.

The arithmetic of the complex numbers is illustrated in the following example.

Example 7

If z_1 and z_2 are the complex numbers $z_1 = 2 + 3j$, $z_2 = 3 + j$, then find:

(a) $z_1 + z_2$ (b) $z_1 - z_2$ (c) $z_1 z_2$

Solution

(a) $z_1 + z_2 = 2 + 3j + 3 + j = 5 + 4j$

(b) $z_1 - z_2 = (2 + 3j) - (3 + j)$

$$= -1 + 2j$$

(c) $z_1 z_2 = (2 + 3j)(3 + j)$

$$= 2(3 + j) + 3j(3 + j)$$

$$= 6 + 2j + 9j + 3j^2$$

$$= 6 + 11j - 3 \qquad (j^2 = -1)$$

$$= 3 + 11j$$

Within the complex numbers, *every* quadratic will have exactly two roots. As described earlier, Gauss went on to show that every polynomial of degree n has exactly n roots. This is a considerable improvement on the previous position, and is a very important result.

Example 8

(a) Solve the equation $x^2 - 4x + 9 = 0$ (b) Factorise $x^2 + 4$

Solution

(a) $\qquad x^2 - 4x + 9 = 0$

$(x-2)^2 - 4 + 9 = 0$

$(x-2)^2 = -5 = -1 \times 5$

$x - 2 = \pm\sqrt{-1}\sqrt{5}$

$x - 2 = \pm j\sqrt{5}$

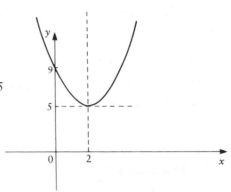

So $x = 2 + j\sqrt{5}$ and $x = 2 - j\sqrt{5}$ are the two solutions. The solutions are both complex numbers.

(b) $x^2 + 4 = (x + 2j)(x - 2j)$

You could factorise by finding the roots of $x^2 + 4 = 0$ (i.e. $x = \pm 2j$) and then writing the factorised form. This is often easier.

Introduction of the complex numbers is a crucially important extension of the number system. The study of complex numbers is most important as they may be applied to the solution of many problems, both within mathematics itself and its applications, especially in science and engineering.

1.4 Exercise 4

1 Work out the squares of:

   (a) $3j$ (b) $7j$ (c) $-4j$ (d) $-12j$ (e) $1 + j$ (f) $2 - 3j$

2 Write down the square roots of:

   (a) -9 (b) -16 (c) -12 (d) -20

3 If $z_1 = 2 - j$ and $z_2 = 4 + 2j$, find:

   (a) $3z_1 + 2z_2$ (b) $2(z_1 - z_2)$ (c) $z_1 z_2$

   (d) $z_1(z_1 + z_2)$ (e) $(z_1 + z_2)(z_1 - z_2)$

4 Solve the following quadratics by completing the square. Leave your answers in *exact* form.

(a) $x^2 - 6x + 10 = 0$ (b) $x^2 + 2x + 10 = 0$

(c) $x^2 + 4x + 20 = 0$ (d) $2x^2 - 2x + 1 = 0$

5 Find the real roots of the following equations.

(a) $x^2 - 6x + 6 = 0$ (b) $x^2 - 2x + 2 = 0$ (c) $x^2 + 6x + 9 = 0$

State how many real roots you find for each equation.

6E Factorise:

(a) $x^2 + 9$ (b) $x^2 + 2x + 5$ (c) $x^2 - 6x + 11$

7E Write down a quartic (fourth-degree) polynomial equation which has *no* real roots. Illustrate with a graph.

1.4.5 Polynomials

A **polynomial** is a function involving whole-number powers of a variable. In general, you can write

$$P(x) = a_n x^n + a_{n-1} x^{n-1} + \ldots + a_2 x^2 + a_1 x + a_0$$

where $a_0, a_1, a_2, \ldots, a_n$ are constants, referred to as **coefficients**. The highest power present is the **degree** of the polynomial. For example, a cubic polynomial is a polynomial of degree 3, such as

$$P(x) = x^3 + 3x^2 - 6x - 8$$

The zeros of $P(x)$ can be found by determining the values of x which make the **factors** zero.

$$P(x) = (x + 1)(x - 2)(x + 4)$$

The value $x = -1$ makes the first factor zero and so -1 is a root. The other roots are $+2$ and -4.

So $x^3 + 3x^2 - 6x - 8 = 0 \Rightarrow x = -1, 2, -4$

The next tasksheet will give you extra practice at expanding brackets if you need it.

▷ 1.4 **Tasksheet S3 – Expanding brackets (page 534)**

1 .4B

1 For the polynomial $P(x) = x^3 - 13x - 12$

(a) calculate the values of:

    (i) $P(1)$ (ii) $P(2)$ (iii) $P(3)$ (iv) $P(4)$

    (v) $P(-1)$ (vi) $P(-2)$ (vii) $P(-3)$ (viii) $P(-4)$

(b) write down three factors of $P(x)$;

(c) confirm your answers to (b) by multiplying the three factors together.

2 The cubic polynomial $P(x)$ is $x^3 - x^2 - 10x - 8$.

(a) To check whether $x + 2$ is a factor of $P(x)$, for which value of a should you choose to calculate $P(a)$?

(b) Is $x + 2$ a factor of $P(x)$?

3 (a) If $P(x) = (x - 2)(x^2 - x - 2)$, explain why $P(2) = 0$.

(b) More generally, if $P(x) = (x - a)Q(x)$, where $Q(x)$ is a polynomial, explain why $P(a) = 0$.

In question 3(b) you proved that:

If $x - a$ is a factor of $P(x)$, then $P(a) = 0$.

The converse, and more useful, result is:

If $P(a) = 0$, then $x - a$ is a factor of $P(x)$.

This is known as the **factor theorem**.

$P(x)$ can then be written as $(x - a)Q(x)$, where $Q(x)$ is a 'simpler' polynomial.

When you have found one linear factor, one approach to finding the remaining factor or factors is to use the process of algebraic division. This method, illustrated below, essentially evaluates the quotient function term by term. To divide $x^3 - 3x^2 - 10x + 24$ by $x - 2$, you would proceed as follows:

$$x^3 - 3x^2 - 10x + 24 = (x - 2)x^2 + 2x^2 - 3x^2 - 10x + 24 \quad \text{(match } x^3 \text{ terms)}$$

$$= (x - 2)x^2 - x^2 - 10x + 24$$

$$= (x - 2)x^2 - (x - 2)x - 2x - 10x + 24 \quad \text{(match remaining}$$

$$= (x - 2)x^2 - (x - 2)x - 12x + 24 \quad\quad\quad x \text{ terms)}$$

$$= (x - 2)x^2 - (x - 2)x - 12(x - 2)$$

$$= (x - 2)(x^2 - x - 12)$$

This process is more commonly set out in the style of numerical long division:

$$
\begin{array}{r}
x^2 - x\ - 12 \\
x - 2 \overline{\smash{\big)}\, x^3 - 3x^2 - 10x + 24} \\
-\ \underline{x^3 - 2x^2} \\
-x^2 - 10x \\
-\ \underline{-x^2 + 2x} \\
-12x + 24 \\
-\ \underline{-12x + 24} \\
0
\end{array}
$$

You should be able to see how this algorithm works by comparing it with the way it is set out earlier. It is usually easier to use the second of the two methods of setting out the work.

Example 9
Divide $x^3 + 2x - 1$ by $x - 2$.

Solution

$$
\begin{array}{r}
x^2 + 2x\ + 6 \\
x - 2 \overline{\smash{\big)}\, x^3 + 0x^2 + 2x - \ \ 1} \\
-\ \underline{x^3 - 2x^2} \\
2x^2 + 2x \\
-\ \underline{2x^2 - 4x} \\
6x -\ \ 1 \\
-\ \underline{6x - 12} \\
11
\end{array}
$$

$$\therefore\quad x^3 + 2x - 1 = (x^2 + 2x + 6)(x - 2) + 11$$

It helps the setting out of the division if you include the 'missing' term $0x^2$ – all missing terms should be included in this way. You should also check your final answer by expanding brackets, whichever method you use.

The factorised form of a polynomial $P(x)$ is very convenient for solving the equation $P(x) = 0$ and for sketching the graph of $P(x)$. The following example illustrates another method of finding the remaining factors once the factor theorem has provided the first. It can sometimes be used more easily than the method of long division described above.

Example 10

For the function $f(x) = x^3 - 3x^2 - 10x + 24$:

(a) find the factors of $f(x)$;

(b) find the roots of the equation $f(x) = 0$;

(c) sketch the graph of $f(x)$.

Solution

(a) The possible factors of 24 are ±1, ±2, ±3, ±4, ±6, ±8, ±12 and ±24. By trial,

$$f(2) = 8 - 12 - 20 + 24 = 0$$

so

$$x - 2 \text{ is a factor}$$

Instead of using algebraic division, you can proceed as follows. Write $x^3 - 3x^2 - 10x + 24$ as $(x - 2)(x^2 + ax - 12)$. **Comparing the coefficients** of x^2 gives

$$-3 = -2 + a$$
$$\Rightarrow a = -1$$

and so

$$f(x) = (x - 2)(x^2 - x - 12)$$
$$= (x - 2)(x + 3)(x - 4)$$

(b) $f(x) = 0$

$$\Rightarrow (x - 2)(x + 3)(x - 4) = 0$$
$$\Rightarrow x = -3, 2, 4$$

(c) The graph is a cubic which cuts the x-axis at -3, 2, 4 and the y-axis at 24 as shown.

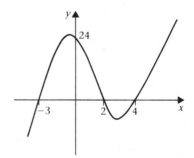

1.4 Exercise 5

1 Using algebraic division, find the quotient and remainder when:

(a) $x^3 + 2x^2 + 8x - 5$ is divided by $x + 1$

(b) $x^3 - 2x^2 + 3x - 5$ is divided by $x + 2$

(c) $2x^3 - 5x + 3$ is divided by $x - 1$

(d) $4x^3 + x^2 - 1$ is divided by $2x + 1$

(e) $x^4 + 2x^3 - 4x^2 - 2x + 1$ is divided by $x^2 - 1$

2 If $P(x) = x^3 - 2x^2 - 11x + 12$, show that $x + 3$ is a factor of $P(x)$, and find $Q(x)$ if $P(x) = (x + 3)Q(x)$.

3 If $P(x) = x^3 - 5x^2 + 2x + 8$
   (a) use the factor theorem to find one factor of $P(x)$;
   (b) factorise $P(x)$ completely;
   (c) write down the solutions of $P(x) = 0$;
   (d) sketch the graph of $P(x)$.

4 Solve the equation $x^3 + 5x^2 + 3x - 9 = 0$.

5 Solve the equation $x^3 + 4x^2 + 2x - 4 = 0$ by finding one simple factor and then solving a quadratic equation.

6 (a) Solve the equation $x^3 - 2x + 4 = 0$.
   (b) Sketch a graph of the function to explain the solution.

7 (a) Find all the zeros of, and hence factorise, the function
   $$P(x) = x^4 - x^3 - 7x^2 + x + 6$$
   (b) Sketch the graph of the function.
   (c) Solve the inequality $P(x) > 0$.

8 (a) What happens if you try to factorise these expressions completely?
   (i) $x^3 - 8$ (ii) $x^4 - 16$
   (b) Sketch the graphs of these functions and comment on their zeros.

After working through section 1.4 you should:

1 understand the terms identity, root, polynomial, coefficient;

2 understand that a letter can be used in algebra to generalise, to stand for a variable or a constant, or to represent an unknown quantity;

3 be able to formulate equations for a given problem;

4 be able to solve any quadratic equation, including those with complex roots;

5 be able to find the solution set for simple polynomial inequalities;

6 know how to use the factor theorem to help solve polynomial equations;

7 know how to do algebraic division.

1 Foundations

1.5 Numerical methods

1.5.1 The golden ratio

In section 1.4 you looked at techniques for solving polynomial equations. Although you found a formula that works for *all* quadratic equations, the method that you used for cubic and quartic equations will only work if the factors can be found easily. In fact there are general methods of solving both of these types of equation, but they are beyond the scope of this book.

Here we look at alternative ways of solving equations, using numerical techniques. These techniques do not give the *exact* solution to an equation, but will often give *good approximations* in cases where exact methods break down.

This section introduces two important numerical techniques for solving equations, a decimal search method and an iterative procedure.

Consider the following problem. Given a square, can a rectangle be 'added' ...

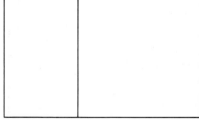

... so that the shape of the new rectangle is the same as that of the added rectangle, as shown below?

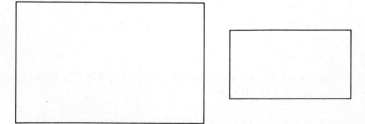

A rectangle with this shape is called a **golden rectangle** and the ratio of the lengths of its sides is called the **golden ratio**. Later you will see that there is only one possible value for this ratio. It is denoted by the Greek symbol ϕ (phi) in honour of the great sculptor Phidias who used it in his work. Like other famous mathematical constants such as π and e, ϕ is found in many situations. Many mythical and mystical properties were attributed to ϕ, which may explain the use of the term 'golden'.

How can you find the golden ratio? Comparing the added rectangle with the new rectangle,

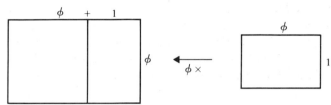

you can see that the ratio of the shorter sides is ϕ. The ratio of the longer sides must also be ϕ and so

$$\phi \times \phi = \phi + 1$$

ϕ therefore satisfies the quadratic equation

$$x^2 = x + 1$$

or, rearranging, $x^2 - x - 1 = 0$.

This equation can of course be solved using the formula, but in this instance you are going to see how it can be solved numerically.

If you put $x^2 - x - 1$ into the completed square form, $(x - \frac{1}{2})^2 - \frac{5}{4}$, the graph is easy to sketch.

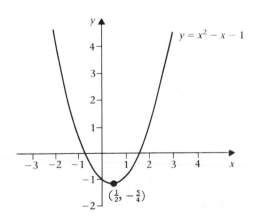

Possible values for ϕ occur at points where the graph cuts the x-axis. There is just one useful solution, between 1 and 2, because the negative solution cannot represent a length.

Now that you know an approximate value of ϕ you can find it more precisely by using the method of **decimal search**.

.5A

1 Begin the decimal search by considering values of x between 1 and 2 in steps of 0.1 and show that there is a solution between 1.6 and 1.7.

2 Continue the search in steps of 0.01, from 1.6 to 1.7.

The cold facts discussed so far have not done justice to the history of the golden ratio, from the serious school of Pythagoras to the fanciful theories of enthusiasts. Perhaps the most important work was done by Leonardo of Pisa (b.1175) otherwise known as Fibonacci. His study of natural phenomena led to the sequence of numbers which bears his name

$$1 \quad 1 \quad 2 \quad 3 \quad 5 \quad 8 \quad 13 \quad 21 \quad 34 \quad 55 \quad \ldots$$

which can be defined inductively by

$$u_1 = 1, \quad u_2 = 1,$$

$$u_i = u_{i-1} + u_{i-2}, \quad \text{for } i \geq 3.$$

Numbers from this sequence arise in many surprising contexts, including the structure of a beehive, the population of a rabbit warren and the white and black notes on a piano keyboard. Many plants have spiral patterns of petals or leaves and the number of spirals is invariably a number from the Fibonacci sequence. A detailed study shows that the sunflower head has 55 spirals in the clockwise direction and 34 in the anticlockwise, while the pine cone has 8 clockwise and 13 anticlockwise parts.

Another major contribution Fibonacci made to mathematics was his promotion of the Arabic system of numbers, which we use today.

What is the connection between the golden ratio and Fibonacci numbers?

Consider the ratio $\dfrac{u_{i+1}}{u_i}$, the values of which are plotted on the graph below.

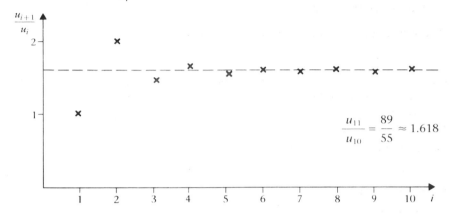

$$\frac{u_{11}}{u_{10}} = \frac{89}{55} \approx 1.618$$

This sequence converges to the golden ratio, ϕ, that is

$$\frac{u_{i+1}}{u_i} \to \phi \qquad \text{as } i \to \infty$$

As the shell of the chambered nautilus grows, the size of the chambers increases but their shape remains unchanged.

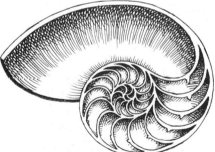

The same spiral shape can be constructed using golden rectangles.

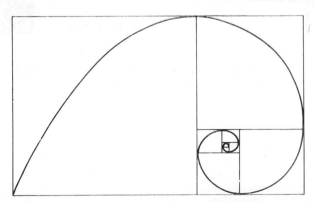

The convergence of the sequence of ratios suggests that an iterative method of solution could be used to evaluate the golden ratio. For such an approach, you need a **recurrence relation** or **iterative formula** to set up a sequence of values.

The equation $x^2 = x + 1$ can be written as $x = \sqrt{(x + 1)}$. (The root given by $x = -\sqrt{(x + 1)}$ is rejected as you are only interested in the positive root.)

If the sequence generated by the formula
$$x_{i+1} = \sqrt{(x_i + 1)}$$
converged, then the limiting value x would satisfy $x = \sqrt{(x + 1)}$ and would therefore satisfy $x^2 = x + 1$.

From the sketch of the graph on page 77, $x_1 = 1$ seems an appropriate choice for the first term of the sequence. Then

$x_2 = 1.414\,213\,6$	$x_8 = 1.617\,851\,3$
$x_3 = 1.553\,774\,0$	$x_9 = 1.617\,977\,5$
$x_4 = 1.598\,053\,2$	$x_{10} = 1.618\,016\,5$
$x_5 = 1.611\,847\,8$	$x_{11} = 1.618\,028\,6$
$x_6 = 1.616\,121\,2$	$x_{12} = 1.618\,032\,3$
$x_7 = 1.617\,442\,8$	

This sequence clearly converges to a solution for x which is 1.618 (to 3 decimal places). Using an 8-digit display calculator, the value $1.618\,034\,0$ is obtained after sixteen iterations and remains unchanged by any further iterations.

As well as fascinating mathematicians, the 'golden' property has also attracted the attention of philosophers, architects and artists over the centuries.

It has been claimed that the golden rectangle

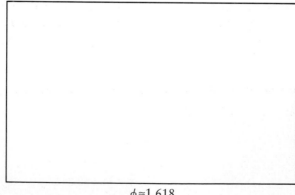

$\phi \approx 1.618$

is *the* most artistically pleasing rectangle.

An attempt to confirm or deny this was made by Gustav Fechner in 1876. His extensive experiments did confirm that the most aesthetically pleasing shape for a rectangle was something between that of a square and a rectangle with sides in the ratio 1:2.

Architecturally, some very famous and beautiful structures, for example the Parthenon, are said to be based on the golden ratio and golden rectangle.

It would be satisfying if an exact representation of the 'golden' number could be given. For this it is necessary to use the quadratic formula for the solution of $x^2 - x - 1 = 0$.

$$x = \frac{1 \pm \sqrt{(1+4)}}{2}$$

$$= \tfrac{1}{2} + \tfrac{1}{2}\sqrt{5} \quad \text{or} \quad \tfrac{1}{2} - \tfrac{1}{2}\sqrt{5}$$

$\sqrt{5}$ is a number written in **surd** form. This means that the square root sign remains, rather than replacing $\sqrt{5}$ with its decimal value of 2.236 068 (to 7 s.f), which would be clumsy to write out every time, and which of course has a small error associated with it.

As seen earlier, the negative value is discarded, so the golden ratio is

$$\phi = \tfrac{1}{2}(1 + \sqrt{5}) \approx 1.618\,034$$

We can link the golden ratio to the Fibonacci sequence algebraically, starting from the definition of the Fibonacci sequence.

$$u_{i+2} = u_{i+1} + u_i \qquad (u_2 = u_1 = 1)$$

$$\Rightarrow \frac{u_{i+2}}{u_{i+1}} = 1 + \frac{u_i}{u_{i+1}}$$

If we define $v_i = \dfrac{u_{i+1}}{u_i}$, then

$$v_{i+1} = 1 + \frac{1}{v_i}$$

With a suitable starting value, this gives ϕ iteratively and the limit satisfies $x = 1 + \dfrac{1}{x}$ or $x^2 = x + 1$, the equation for ϕ seen above.

If you would like to find out more about the golden ratio, many recreational mathematics books have chapters devoted to it. A very readable book is H. E. Huntley, *The Divine Proportion* (Dover, 1970).

1.5.2 Locating roots

Section 1.5.1 described two numerical methods for solving an equation – a decimal search and an iterative process. Both methods had the same first step of approximately locating any solutions by plotting a graph.

Two possible arrangements of the equation from section 1.5.1 are

$$x^2 = x + 1 \quad \text{and} \quad x^2 - x - 1 = 0$$

 1 .5B

1 In each arrangement:

(a) what graphs should you draw to solve the equation?

(b) which points give the solutions?

2 Sketch the graphs and find inequalities (**bounds**) for the roots.

3 Use the 'zoom' facility of a graph plotter to find the roots to 3 decimal places.

4 What are the advantages and disadvantages of the two arrangements?

Example 1

Find bounds for the solutions of

$$x^2 = 1 + \frac{1}{x+3}$$

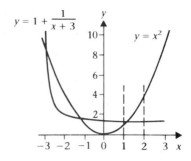

Solution

From the graph, it can be seen that roots lie between -3 and -2, between -2 and -1 and between 1 and 2.

Graphs can be drawn very easily using a graph plotter, but care is needed to ensure that all the solutions are displayed on the screen.

1.5 Exercise 1

1 For each of the following, sketch appropriate graphs and find bounds for all the possible solutions.

(a) $x^2 - 1 = 5\sqrt{x}$ (b) $x^3 + 3x^2 - 2x - 2 = 0$

(c) $2^x = 5 - x$ (d) $10 - x^2 = 2|x|$

2 Use decimal search to solve each equation correct to 2 decimal places.

1.5.3 Iterative formulas

One method of solving an equation is to use a 'zoom' facility on a graph plotter. An alternative method of reaching a solution was described in section 1.5.1. This iterative method consists of taking an initial value and using a formula to obtain a sequence of values which converges to the solution. Such formulas can be obtained by rearranging the equation into the form

$$x = g(x)$$

which suggests the iterative formula $x_{i+1} = g(x_i)$.

For example, to show that $x^2 - 3x + 2 = 0$ can be rearranged to give the iterative formula

$$x_{i+1} = \frac{x_i^2 + 2}{3}$$

proceed as follows.

$$x^2 - 3x + 2 = 0 \Rightarrow x^2 + 2 = 3x \Rightarrow x = \frac{x^2 + 2}{3}$$

A suitable iterative formula is $x_{i+1} = \dfrac{x_i^2 + 2}{3}$.

Alternatively, since the steps are reversible, it is sometimes easier to work backwards,

i.e.
$$x = \frac{x^2 + 2}{3}$$

$$\Rightarrow \qquad 3x = x^2 + 2$$

$$\Rightarrow \qquad x^2 - 3x + 2 = 0$$

Example 2

Find the positive root of the equation $x^3 - 8x - 7 = 0$ correct to 3 decimal places.

Solution

Step 1: Obtain the iterative formula

$$x^3 - 8x - 7 = 0$$

$$\Rightarrow x^3 = 8x + 7$$

$$\Rightarrow x = \sqrt[3]{(8x + 7)}$$

which suggests the iterative formula

$$x_{i+1} = \sqrt[3]{(8x_i + 7)}$$

Step 2: Sketch the graph to locate the roots.

Step 3: From the graph, choose a suitable value for x_1.

$x_1 = 3$ is nearest to the solution.

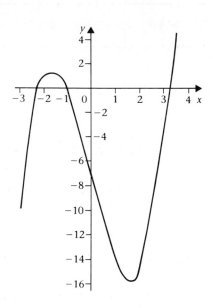

Step 4: Use the formula to generate the iterative sequence.

$$x_2 = \sqrt[3]{(8 \times 3 + 7)}$$

$$= 3.141\,380\,652$$

$$x_3 = 3.179\,129\,979$$

The solution to this problem can conveniently be obtained using a spreadsheet – the results are shown below.

Iteration number	Input (x_i)	Uutput (x_{i+1})
1	3	3.14138065
2	3.14138065	3.17912998
3	3.17912998	3.18905898
4	3.18905898	3.19166031
5	3.19166031	3.19234114
6	3.19234114	3.19251928
7	3.19251928	3.19256589
8	3.19256589	3.19257808
9	3.19257808	3.19258127
10	3.19258127	3.19258211

$x = 3.193$ (to 3 decimal places)

1.5 Exercise 2

1 For the equation

$$2x^2 - 5x + 1 = 0$$

find which of the following are possible iterative formulas and show how they can be obtained.

(a) $x_{i+1} = \sqrt{\left(\dfrac{5x_i - 1}{2}\right)}$

(b) $x_{i+1} = \dfrac{1 + 2x_i^2}{5}$

(c) $x_{i+1} = \dfrac{1}{2}\left(5 - \dfrac{1}{x_i}\right)$

(d) $x_{i+1} = \dfrac{1}{5 - 2x_i}$

(e) $x_{i+1} = \dfrac{1}{2}\sqrt{(1 - 5x_i)}$

(f) $x_{i+1} = 2x_i^2 - 4x_i + 1$

(g) $x_{i+1} = 1 + \dfrac{1}{2}\sqrt{(x_i + 1)}$

(h) $x_{i+1} = -\dfrac{1}{5}(1 - 2x_i^2)$

(i) $x_{i+1} = \sqrt{(5x_i - 1 - x_i^2)}$

(j) $x_{i+1} = 2 + \sqrt{\left(\dfrac{7 - 3x_i}{2}\right)}$

2 For the equation $x^3 = 10$

   (a) (i) show that the equation can be arranged into the form $x = \sqrt{\left(\dfrac{10}{x}\right)}$;

   (ii) by letting $x_1 = 2$, and using an iterative formula, obtain the positive solution for $x^3 = 10$, to 5 decimal places;

(b) (i) show that the equation can be rearranged to $x = \sqrt{(\sqrt{(10x)})}$;

   (ii) by letting $x_1 = 2$ and using an iterative formula, obtain the positive solution for $x^3 = 10$, to 5 decimal places.

3 Using an initial value of $x_1 = 3$ and an iterative formula, find a positive solution of $2^x = 3x$ to 4 decimal places.

4 (a) By sketching appropriate graphs, find an interval that contains the root of
$$x^2 - 1 = 6\sqrt{x}$$

   (b) Show that $x = \sqrt{(6\sqrt{x} + 1)}$ is a rearrangement of this equation.

   (c) By choosing an appropriate starting value, solve the equation giving your answer correct to 6 decimal places.

5 (a) Show that the equation $x^3 + 2x = 1$ has a root that lies between 0 and 1.

   (b) Show that $x = \dfrac{(1 - x^3)}{2}$ is a rearrangement of the equation.

   (c) Find the root between 0 and 1 correct to 5 decimal places using a starting value of: (i) 0   (ii) 1.

   (d) What happens if you take a starting value of 2?

6 This question concerns the equation $2x^2 - 5x + 1 = 0$ and three possible rearrangements given in question 1. All answers should be given to 6 decimal places.

   (a) Show that the equation $2x^2 - 5x + 1 = 0$ has one root in the interval $[0, 1]$ and another in the interval $[2, 3]$.

   (b) For the iterative formula $x_{i+1} = \sqrt{\left(\dfrac{5x_i - 1}{2}\right)}$:

      (i) explain why the starting value $x_i = 0$ cannot be used;

      (ii) solve the equation using starting values of 1, 2 and 10. Record the number of iterations used for each starting value.

   (c) Solve the equation using the iterative formula
$$x_{i+1} = \frac{1}{2}\left(5 - \frac{1}{x_i}\right)$$
   and starting values: (i) 1   (ii) 2   (iii) 10.
   Record the number of iterations used for each starting value.

   (d) Solve the equation using the iterative formula
$$x_{i+1} = \frac{1 + 2x_i^2}{5}$$
   and starting values: (i) 1   (ii) 2   (iii) 3.

   (e) Comment on the suitability of each formula.

1.5.4E Convergence

In exercise 2 of 1.5.3 you solved the equation $2x^2 - 5x + 1 = 0$ using a variety of formulas and starting points, of which some converged rapidly, some converged more slowly, some converged to a root in a different interval and some did not converge at all!

It is plain that the choice of an iterative formula is critical if you are to obtain a sequence which converges quickly.

 .5c

1 (a) Give a rough estimate for $\sqrt[3]{10}$.

   (b) Explain how the rearrangement $x = \dfrac{10}{x^2}$ is obtained from $x^3 = 10$.

   Use the iterative formula $x_{i+1} = \dfrac{10}{x_i^2}$, together with the starting value that you gave in part (a), to evaluate $x_2, x_3, \ldots, x_{10}$. What do you find?

It is helpful to know when a sequence is likely to converge *before* working out all the values. These questions show how a graphical approach can help to predict convergence.

2 Consider the rearranged equation $x = \dfrac{10}{x^2}$.

   This is equivalent to the two simultaneous equations

$$y = x \quad \text{and} \quad y = \frac{10}{x^2}$$

   and its solution lies at the intersection of the two graphs.

   (a) For $0 \le x \le 3$, plot $y = x$ and $y = \dfrac{10}{x^2}$ on the same graph. You can now illustrate the solution procedure for a particular starting value, say $x_1 = 2$.

$$x_1 = 2 \Rightarrow g(x_1) = \frac{10}{2^2} = 2.5$$

   Therefore $x_2 = 2.5$

   (b) On your graph, plot and join the points (x_1, x_1), (x_1, x_2) and (x_2, x_2). How could you have used your graph to locate the points (x_1, x_2) and (x_2, x_2) *without* doing any calculations?

(c) *Without* further calculation, plot and successively join up the points (x_2, x_3), (x_3, x_3), (x_3, x_4), (x_4, x_4).

The diagram you have obtained is called a **cobweb** diagram.

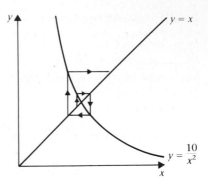

3 What does the cobweb diagram of question 2 illustrate about the iteration attempted in question 1?

4 (a) Draw a cobweb diagram for the function $g(x)$ illustrated. (It is not necessary to give $g(x)$ an equation – simply use the construction described in question 2.)

(b) What would happen in this case to the sequence defined by $x_{i+1} = g(x_i)$?

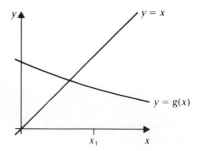

5 Draw similar diagrams for the following functions and describe their behaviour.

(a)
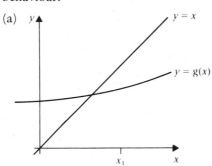

(b)
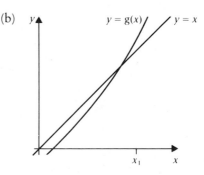

What happens in each case if x_1 is on the other side of the root?

6 In question 5, **staircase** diagrams should have been obtained. What property of $g(x)$ determines whether or not you get a staircase or a cobweb diagram?

7 By considering the staircase and cobweb diagrams above, explain how the gradient of g(x) determines whether an iteration based upon

$$x_{i+1} = g(x_i)$$

will converge or diverge.

8 For $x^3 = 10$

(a) show how to obtain the iterative formula

$$x_{i+1} = \frac{1}{3}\left(2x_i + \frac{10}{x_i^2}\right)$$

(b) using appropriate staircase or cobweb diagrams, investigate the convergence of the iterative sequence obtained for different initial values.

Example 3

Illustrate the convergence of the iterative formula

$$x_{i+1} = \sqrt{\left(\frac{10}{x_i}\right)}$$

with starting value $x_1 = 2$ using a cobweb diagram.

Solution

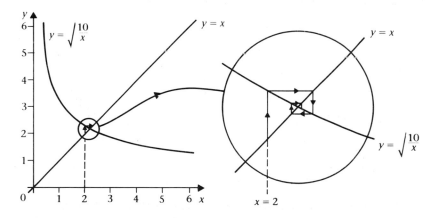

Convergence occurs here because, near the root, the graph is sufficiently flat.

The convergence of iterative sequences is of interest in various areas of mathematics. For example, the iterative process based upon the sequence $x_{i+1} = \lambda x_i(1 - x_i)$ is at the heart of the recently developed mathematical theory of **chaos**.

After working through section 1.5 you should:

1 know how to solve equations approximately by drawing graphs;

2 be able to obtain bounds for solutions of $f(x) = 0$ by looking for changes of sign of $f(x)$;

3 be able to use the iterative formula $x_{i+1} = g(x_i)$ to obtain a root to a given degree of accuracy;

4 be able to rearrange equations into the form $x = g(x)$;

5 appreciate that the iterative method based upon $x = g(x)$ may or may not converge.

1 Foundations

Miscellaneous exercise 1

1 Find the equation of the straight line which passes through the point $(2, 3)$ and is parallel to the line $y = 3x + 1$.

2 Find the point of intersection of the lines having equations $3x + 2y = 1$ and $2x + 3y = 5$.

3 *Without using a graph plotter*, sketch the graphs of:

   (a) $y = (x - 2)(x + 2)$ (b) $y = x(x + 2)$

   (c) $y = x^2(x - 5)$ (d) $y = (x - 1)(x + 2)(x + 3)$.

4 For a cylinder of radius r cm and height h cm, the volume V cm^3 and surface area A cm^2 are given by the formulas

$$V = \pi r^2 h, \qquad A = 2\pi r^2 + 2\pi rh.$$

   If the volume of a cylinder is given to be 500 cm^3, find h in terms of r, and hence A as a function of r. Then use a graph of this function to estimate to 2 s.f. the value of r which gives the smallest surface area.

5 Find the equation of the graphs obtained when the curve $y = x^3$ is translated:

   (a) through $\begin{bmatrix} 1 \\ 0 \end{bmatrix}$ (b) through $\begin{bmatrix} 0 \\ 2 \end{bmatrix}$ (c) through $\begin{bmatrix} 2 \\ 4 \end{bmatrix}$

6 What is the equation obtained from $y = x^2 - 6x$ by applying the following transformations to its graph?

   (a) A reflection in the x-axis   (b) A reflection in the y-axis

   (c) A translation $\begin{bmatrix} -3 \\ 2 \end{bmatrix}$

7 Find the sums of the following arithmetic and geometric progressions:

   (a) $7 + 15 + 23 + \ldots$ to 20 terms

   (b) $5 + (5 + x) + (5 + 2x) + \ldots$ to 20 terms

   (c) $3 + 6 + 12 + \ldots + 384$

   (d) $1 + 0.1 + 0.01 + \ldots$ to infinity

   (e) $16 - 4 + 1 - \frac{1}{4} + \ldots$ to infinity

8 Find the sum of n terms of the geometric progression

$$0.23 + 0.0023 + 0.000\,023 + \ldots$$

What happens to this sum as n becomes larger and larger? What fraction is equivalent to the recurring decimal $0.\dot{2}\dot{3}$ (i.e. $0.232\,323\,232\,323\ldots$)?

9 Evaluate:

(a) $\displaystyle\sum_{1}^{15} (i + 5)$ (b) $\displaystyle\sum_{10}^{20} (2i + 1)$ (c) $\displaystyle\sum_{i=1}^{n} (r + 3i)$ (d) $\displaystyle\sum_{i=1}^{n} (n - i)$

10 Evaluate:

(a) $\displaystyle\sum_{1}^{20} i + \sum_{1}^{20} (5 - i)$ (b) $\displaystyle\sum_{1}^{20} 2i + \sum_{1}^{20} (2i - 1) - \sum_{1}^{40} i$

11 Factorise:

(a) $x^2 + 5x + 4$ (b) $x^2 + 3x$ (c) $9x^2 + 9x - 4$

(d) $9x^2 - 4$ (e) $9x^2 - 9x - 4$

12 Solve the following quadratic equations by factorising:

(a) $x^2 - 5x + 6 = 0$ (b) $4x^2 - 4x + 1 = 0$

(c) $x^2 + 4.5x - 2.5 = 0$ (d) $(x - 2)(x - 3) + (x - 2)(x - 4) = 0$

13 The distance d metres fallen by a stone thrown down a vertical shaft in t seconds is given by $d = 5t^2 + 2t$. Find the time taken to fall 24 metres.

14 Express $x^2 - 4x + 2$ in the form $(x - p)^2 + q$. Hence sketch the curve $y = x^2 - 4x + 2$ and solve the quadratic equation $x^2 - 4x + 2 = 0$.

15 Find the solution sets of:

(a) $(x - 4)(x + 1) > 0$ (b) $x^2 - 4x + 3 < 0$

(c) $(x - 2)(x + 3)(5 - x) > 0$ (d) $x^3 - 9x^2 + 5x < 0$

16 Find the remainder when $A(x) = 2x^3 + 3x^2 - 5x - 6$ is divided by

(a) $x - 1$ (b) $x - 2$ (c) $x + 2$

Hence factorise $A(x)$ and find the values of x which make $A(x) = 0$.

17 What number must be added to $x^3 + 5x^2 + 10x + 1$ to make $x + 1$ a factor?

18 Use the factor theorem to investigate whether

  (a) $x - 2$ is a factor of $x^3 + 3x^2 - 7x - 6$,

  (b) $2x - 1$ is a factor of $4x^3 + 18x^2 + 6x - 5$,

  (c) $x - 1$ is a factor of $x^5 - 2x^3 + 11x^2 - 3x - 7$.

19 Express $f(x) = x^3 - 4x^2 + x + 6$ as the product of three linear factors. Hence solve $f(x) > 0$.

20 Show that $x - 5$ is a factor of $x^3 - 3x^2 - 9x - 5$. Hence solve $x^3 - 3x^2 - 9x - 5 = 0$.

21 Find the points of intersection of the curve $y = x^2 - x - 3$ and the straight line $y = x$.

22 The lengths in cm of the sides of a right-angled triangle are x, $2x + 1$ and $2x - 1$. Determine the lengths of the sides.

23 Sketch the curves:

  (a) $y = \dfrac{1}{x - 2}$ (b) $y = \dfrac{x}{x - 2}$ (c) $y = \dfrac{1}{2 - x}$

  (d) $y = \dfrac{x + 2}{x - 2}$ (e) $y = \dfrac{3(x - 2)}{x + 1}$ (f) $y = \dfrac{1 - 2x}{1 + x}$

2 Introductory calculus

.1 Rates of change

2.1.1 Introduction

Everything changes! Indeed, the rate at which things change may well be of very great significance – the rate at which populations grow, the rate at which a radioactive material decays or the temperature of an object cools are but a few examples where the study of **rates of change** is important.

The area of mathematics developed to deal with problems concerning and related to rates of change is known as the **calculus**. It is extremely important in mathematics and in many related disciplines and forms a considerable part of any study of mathematics at this and higher levels.

In this section we consider only rates of change for linear functions; we then extend these ideas to more general functions.

Rates of change do not always involve time; for example, a **conversion rate** (like the monetary exchange rate) enables us to convert from one unit to another.

For linear functions, a 'rate of change' is the gradient of a straight-line graph.

For example, you will be familiar with the conversion relationship between temperature in degrees fahrenheit (F) and in degrees celsius (C).

$$F = \tfrac{9}{5}C + 32$$

The graph of °F against °C is a **temperature conversion graph** with °F on the vertical axis and °C on the horizontal axis.

The gradient (slope) of the line is $\frac{72}{40} = \frac{9}{5}$.

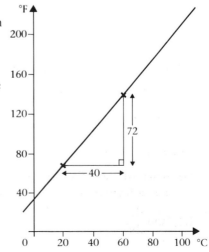

The gradient of any linear graph of y against x can be found by choosing any two points on the line and calculating

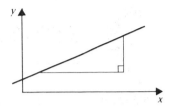

$$\frac{\text{the difference in } y\text{-coordinates}}{\text{the difference in } x\text{-coordinates}}$$

The symbol $\dfrac{dy}{dx}$ is used to represent the gradient of such a straight line. The gradient of the graph of fahrenheit against celsius would be written as $\dfrac{dF}{dC}$.

So $\quad F = \dfrac{9}{5}C + 32 \Rightarrow \dfrac{dF}{dC} = \dfrac{9}{5}$

Equally, if $s = 4t + 5$, for example, then $\dfrac{ds}{dt} = 4$.

$\dfrac{ds}{dt}$ is the rate of change of s with respect to t.

2.1 Exercise 1

1 For the line with equation $y = 3x + 2$, copy and complete these statements.

(a) gradient of line =   (b) $\dfrac{dy}{dx} =$

2 For the graph of $y = 6 - 3x$

(a) what are the 'difference in y-coordinates' and the 'difference in x-coordinates' from A to B?

(b) Find $\dfrac{dy}{dx}$.

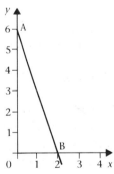

3 Write down the gradient, $\dfrac{dy}{dx}$, for each of the lines with equations

(a) $y = 5 - 7x$ (b) $y = 4 + x$

(c) $y = -2x$ (d) $y = \frac{1}{2}x - 1$

4 The graph of $2y + x = 4$ is as shown.

(a) What are the 'difference in y-coordinates' and the 'difference in x-coordinates' from A to B?

(b) Find $\dfrac{dy}{dx}$.

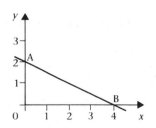

5 Write down the gradient, $\dfrac{dy}{dx}$, for each of the lines with equations:

(a) $2y = x + 4$ (b) $y + x = 7$

(c) $x - y = 6$ (d) $2y + x = 4$

6 The cost of electricity consists of a standing charge of 702p and a charge of 2.87p for each unit of electricity used.

(a) Write the total cost, C pence, in terms of the number of units, n.

(b) Find $\dfrac{dC}{dn}$ and explain what it means.

7 Copy and complete:

(a) $s = 3 - 8t \Rightarrow \dfrac{ds}{dt} =$

(b) $y = 4t + 2 \Rightarrow$

(c) $z = 2 - y \Rightarrow$

(d) $y = 5(2x + 1) \Rightarrow y = 10x + 5$

$$\Rightarrow \frac{dy}{dx} =$$

(e) $y = 4(3 - 5x) \Rightarrow$

8 The circumference, C, of a circle of radius r is given by the formula $C = 2\pi r$.

(a) Find $\dfrac{dC}{dr}$. Explain what this rate of change represents.

(b) A wire is placed taut around the Earth's equator. Approximately how much extra wire would be needed to enable the wire to be pulled 2 metres away from the surface at all points?

(c) Answer part (b) for a similar wire pulled taut around the Moon.

2.1.2 Linear functions

You know that, if, for example, $\dfrac{dy}{dx} = 4$ then the graph of y against x will be a straight line of slope 4.

Example 1

Find the equation of the straight line through $(5, 2)$ with $\dfrac{dy}{dx} = 2$.

Solution

$$\frac{dy}{dx} = 2 \Rightarrow y = 2x + c$$

As $(5, 2)$ is on this line, then $2 = 10 + c \Rightarrow c = -8$

So $y = 2x - 8$ is the equation of the line.

Many situations arise where variables are connected in some way, and you can now investigate how their rates of change are related. This problem is illustrated in the following example, and in the development section that follows it.

Example 2

A cylindrical water heater is 95 cm high and has a cross-sectional area of $2700\,\text{cm}^2$. It is initially full of water. Water is run out so that the height of water in the tank is reduced at 15 cm per minute.

(a) Find expressions for the height (h) and the volume (V) of water in the tank at time t.

(b) Write down $\dfrac{dh}{dt}$ and $\dfrac{dV}{dt}$ and explain how they are related.

Solution

(a) After t minutes

$$h = 95 - 15t$$

$$V = 2700(95 - 15t) \qquad \text{i.e.} \quad V = \text{cross-sectional area} \times \text{height}$$

(b) $\dfrac{dh}{dt} = -15 \qquad \dfrac{dV}{dt} = 2700 \times (-15)$

So $\dfrac{dV}{dt} = 2700 \times \dfrac{dh}{dt}$

The rate of change of the volume is equal to the area of cross-section times the rate of change of height. This idea is explored in the questions which follow.

 .1A

1 A handbook issued with a microwave oven gives the following guide for cooking a whole chicken from frozen.

'Thaw on a low setting for 15 minutes per kilogram, then stand in cold water for 30 minutes. Next cook on a high setting for 20 minutes per kilogram, then let it stand for 16 minutes.'

Consider a chicken of weight w kg, so that the time taken in minutes for the first stage is $u = 15w + 30$.

(a) Write down a similar formula for v, the time in minutes for the second stage.

(b) Hence find an expression for the total time taken, $T = u + v$, in terms of w.

(c) Write down the values of $\dfrac{du}{dw}$, $\dfrac{dv}{dw}$ and $\dfrac{dT}{dw}$. What do these rates of change represent?

(d) Explain why $\dfrac{dT}{dw} = \dfrac{du}{dw} + \dfrac{dv}{dw}$.

2 Let $u = 3x + 1$ and $v = 2x - 3$.

(a) Write down the values of $\dfrac{du}{dx}$ and $\dfrac{dv}{dx}$.

(b) By substituting for u and v, find an expression for y in terms of x for each of the following:

   (i) $y = u + v$ (ii) $y = 2u + v$
   (iii) $y = u - v$ (iv) $y = 4u - 3v$

(c) For each part of (b) write down the value of $\dfrac{dy}{dx}$.

(d) State the relationship between $\dfrac{du}{dx}$, $\dfrac{dv}{dx}$ and $\dfrac{dy}{dx}$ in each case.

(e) What would the relationship be if $y = au + bv$, where a and b are constants?

3 (a) A firm charges a basic fee of £12 plus £5 per hour for each engineer sent out on repair work. If one engineer is called out for t hours, write down an expression for u, the charge in £, in terms of t.

(b) A rival firm charges a basic fee of £9 plus £6 per hour for each engineer sent. Write down an expression for the charge £v if one engineer is called out for t hours.

(c) Comment on which firm is cheaper.

(d) Write down $\dfrac{du}{dt}$ and $\dfrac{dv}{dt}$ and explain their significance.

(e) In an emergency, a factory calls out three engineers from the first firm and two from the second. Write the total cost £c in terms of u and v.

(f) Deduce the value of $\dfrac{dc}{dt}$ and explain its meaning.

The work done so far should bring you to the following result.

If u and v are linear functions of x, and a and b are any constants, then $y = au + bv$ is also a linear function of x and

$$\frac{dy}{dx} = a\frac{du}{dx} + b\frac{dv}{dx}$$

The rates of change of the parts are combined in this way to give the rate of change of the whole.

2.1 **Exercise 2**

1 A linear graph has $\dfrac{dy}{dx} = 5$ and passes through the point $(-1, 2)$.

   Find its equation.

2 Find the equation of each of the following lines:

   (a) the line passing through $(3, 2)$ with $\dfrac{dy}{dx} = -2$;

   (b) the line passing through $(4, 3)$ with $\dfrac{ds}{dt} = \dfrac{1}{2}$;

   (c) the line passing through $(-6, -1)$ with $\dfrac{dp}{dx} = \dfrac{2}{3}$.

3 A line passes through the points $(1, 5)$ and $(4, 11)$. Find $\dfrac{dy}{dx}$ and the equation of the line.

4 (a) A plumber charges £5 for a call-out plus £7 per hour for labour.

       (i) Write the charge £C as a formula in terms of t, the number of hours taken to do the job.

       (ii) What is the value of $\dfrac{dC}{dt}$?

   (b) Another plumber charges £6 per hour for labour, and for a job lasting 3 hours the bill is £26.

       (i) Write down the value of $\dfrac{dC}{dt}$.

       (ii) Hence obtain the charge £C as a formula in terms of t, the number of hours taken to do the job.

5 The marks obtained in a test ranged from 25 to 50. They have to be rescaled to range from 0 to 100. Copy and complete this table.

Test mark, T	25	26		50
Rescaled mark, R	0		96	100

   (a) Find $\dfrac{dR}{dT}$.

   (b) Hence express R in terms of T.

6 The growth of the population of Britain in the first half of the twentieth century was approximately linear, rising from roughly 38 million in 1900 to 48 million in 1950.

(a) Find an expression for the population P millions of people t years after 1900.

(b) Find $\dfrac{dP}{dt}$. What does it represent?

(c) What does your formula give for the population in 1998? Comment on your answer.

7 Let $u = 4 + 2x$ and $v = 5 - 4x$.

(a) Write down $\dfrac{du}{dx}$ and $\dfrac{dv}{dx}$.

(b) Calculate $\dfrac{dy}{dx}$ for each of the following functions, *without* expressing y as a function of x.

   (i) $y = u + v$ (ii) $y = u - v$ (iii) $y = 3u + v$
   (iv) $y = u - 3v$ (v) $y = 3u + 2v$ (vi) $y = 2u - 3v$

(c) For each part of (b), substitute for u and v, then express y in terms of x. Hence check the value of $\dfrac{dy}{dx}$.

8 Making steamed puddings in a pressure cooker involves placing a basin containing a dough made from flour and suet into boiling water in a pressure cooker. To allow the raising agent to take effect, a short steaming time is allowed at low heat and then the cooker is brought to the appropriate pressure for the remaining cooking time.

One recipe for four portions recommends:

Amount of flour	Steaming time	Cooking time at pressure
200 grams	15 minutes	25 minutes

To adjust the recipe for other quantities, it is suggested that for every additional 15 grams of flour an extra 1 minute should be added to both the steaming time and the cooking time.

Let f grams be the amount of flour, s minutes the steaming time and p minutes the cooking time at pressure.

(a) Write s in terms of f. Hence find the value of $\dfrac{ds}{df}$ and describe the meaning in words of this rate of change.

(b) Write p in terms of f. Hence find the value of $\dfrac{dp}{df}$ and describe the meaning in words of this rate of change.

(c) Find T, the total cooking time in minutes. Hence find the value of $\dfrac{dT}{df}$ and describe the meaning of this rate of change.

After working through section 2.1 you should, for linear functions:

1 know that $\dfrac{dy}{dx}$ is the notation for the gradient of the graph of y against x;

2 for equations such as $y = 5 - 2z$, be able to write down the rate of change, $\dfrac{dy}{dz} = -2$;

3 be familiar with the result that, if u, v are linear functions of x with a, b any constants, then $y = au + bv$ is also a linear function and

$$\frac{dy}{dx} = a\frac{du}{dx} + b\frac{dv}{dx}$$

(i.e. the rates of change of the parts are combined in this way to give the rate of change of the whole);

4 be able to find and apply rates of change in simple problems.

2 Introductory calculus

.2 Gradients of curves

2.2.1 Locally straight curves

Examining what is meant by the gradient or slope of a curve is a rather more sophisticated problem than that of the straight line, although it is very closely related. Consider the curve sketched below.

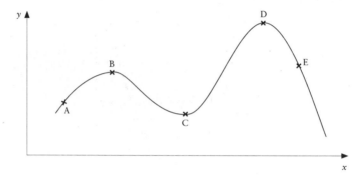

If you imagine moving along the curve *from left to right*, then the steepness of the curve is constantly changing (remember that for the straight line it was constant). Because the gradient changes continuously we talk about the **gradient at a point** on the curve. If you were to 'zoom' in more closely to the points labelled on the graph, then you would see the following.

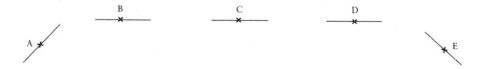

The gradient at A is positive, at B, C and D it appears to be zero, and at E it is negative. In every case the curve is **locally straight**.

Since you are already familiar with the gradients of straight lines, the fact that zooming in on the curve shown gives straight lines is an idea worth exploring when trying to find the gradient of a curve at a point. The questions of 2.2A consider what happens when you zoom in at various points on a number of different curves.

.2A

These questions require the use of a computer or graphical calculator to enlarge and zoom in on part of a graph.

1 (a) Input the graph of $y = x^3 - 7x^2 + 8x + 7$ for $0 \le x \le 5$.

(b) Zoom in to the point with $x = 2$ and redraw.

(c) Repeat, increasing the magnification. What do you notice?

(d) Zoom in at $x = 4$. Note your observation.

When you zoom in at some point on a sufficiently smooth curve, the curve starts to look more and more like a straight line. The diagram below shows this for the graph $y = x^2 - 2$.

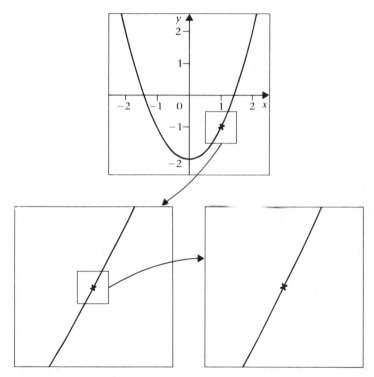

2 (a) What would you expect to see if you zoomed in at $(0, -2)$ on the graph $y = x^2 - 2$?

(b) Check your answer on the graph plotter.

3 Investigate the local straightness of the following graphs.

(a) $y = |x|$ ($|x|$ is entered on some graph plotters as ABS(x).)

(b) $y = 100x^2$ (c) $y = \text{Int}\,(x)$ (d) $y = |x^2 - 4|$

4E (a) Use the graph plotter to obtain the graph of $y = \frac{1}{5}\sin 3x$. Describe fully in words the transformations from the graph of $y = \sin x$ to that of $y = \frac{1}{5}\sin 3x$.

(b) Use the graph plotter to obtain the graph of:

(i) $y = \sin x + \frac{1}{5}\sin 3x$

(ii) $y = \sin x + \frac{1}{50}\sin 100x$

(c) Can you invent a function whose graph looks just like that of $y = \sin x$ under normal magnification but not under magnification $\times 1000$?

> If a curve appears to be a straight line when you zoom in at a point, then it is 'locally straight' at that point.

When you zoomed in on some of the graphs in 2.2A, you found that some functions, such as $y = |x|$, were not 'locally straight' everywhere. For example, the graph of $y = |x^2 - 4|$ is locally straight at all points *except* $(2, 0)$ and $(-2, 0)$.

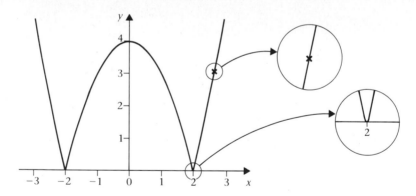

However, the cubic graph *was* locally straight everywhere. In fact, so are *all* polynomial graphs. Suppose you could superimpose the 'zoom' view onto the graph at a particular point; you would see the following.

The line AB is called a **tangent** to the curve at P.

> The gradient of a curve at a point is defined as the gradient of the tangent to the curve at that point.

2.2.2 Gradient graphs

The previous section showed that the value of the gradient may be different for different points on a graph. On the graph shown below, if you imagine moving from left to right, you would experience:

- a numerically large negative gradient which increases to zero at A;

- a positive gradient which increases from A to B and then decreases to zero at C;

- a gradient which finally decreases through numerically larger and larger negative values.

If you plot the gradient at each point against x, you obtain (very roughly) a **gradient graph** as shown.

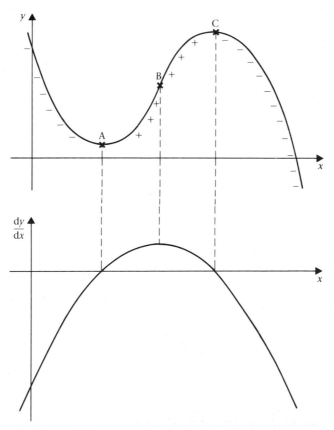

A, B and C are special points; A and C are the only points where the gradient is zero and B is the point where the gradient is maximum.

> Points of a graph where the curve has zero gradient are called **stationary points**.
>
> Points where a graph is locally a maximum or minimum are called **turning points**.

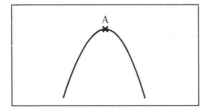

This **local maximum** is both a stationary point and a turning point.

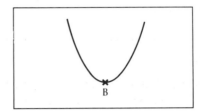

This is a **local minimum**.

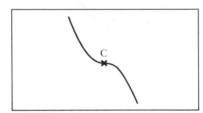

This is a stationary point but not a turning point.

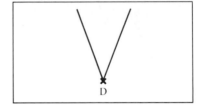

This is a turning point but not a stationary point.

Note that the point at D is not a stationary point because the graph at D is not locally straight, and therefore the gradient is not defined at this point. At a stationary point the gradient must be equal to zero.

The maximum and minimum points are generally described as *local* maximum or *local* minimum points, because they are not generally the maximum or minimum values of the function itself, simply the maximum or minimum value around the particular point on the function.

Also note carefully the distinction between stationary points and turning points, as illustrated at points B and C, for example.

Example 1

Find the stationary points and/or turning points on the graph of

$$y = |x^2 - 4|$$

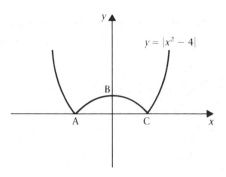

Solution

A and C are turning points (local minima) but are not stationary points. B is both a stationary point and a turning point (a local maximum).

2.2 Exercise 1

1   Copy each of these graphs. Directly beneath each one, sketch the corresponding gradient graph, using the same scale for x.

Mark any points you think are special and state the important features of each graph.

(a)

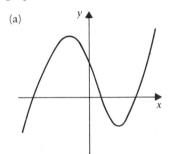

(b)

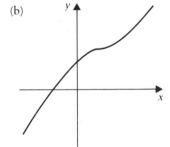

(c)

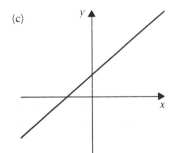

(d)

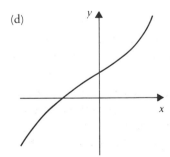

(e)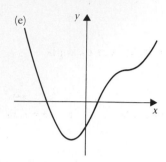

(f)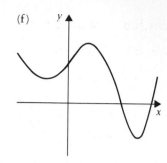

2   Sketch each of these graphs and its gradient graph. Start by deciding what happens to each gradient graph when x is near zero and also when x is numerically large (either positive or negative).

(a)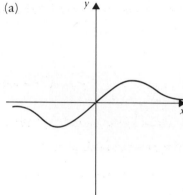

(b)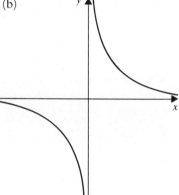

3   Two gradient graphs are sketched below.

(a) For each of them sketch a possible (x, y) graph.

(i)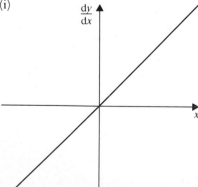

(ii)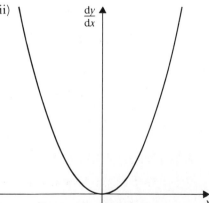

(b) How many other possible (x, y) graphs are there for each of them?

2.2.3 Obtaining a gradient

You are already able to state some gradients *exactly*. For example,

$$y = 5x + 4 \Rightarrow \frac{dy}{dx} = 5$$

For non-linear graphs the notation $\frac{dy}{dx}$ is still used, but now this represents the gradient along the tangent at the point P.

> The process of obtaining $\frac{dy}{dx}$ for a given function y of x is called **differentiation.**

A practical method for obtaining $\frac{dy}{dx}$ at any point on a curve is introduced below.

 .2B

1 On a sheet of graph paper, draw accurately the graph of $y = \frac{1}{2}x^2$ for values of x between -3 and 3, using the same scale for both axes.

   (a) Draw, as accurately as possible, the tangent at the point $(1.5, 1.125)$, and hence measure the gradient $\frac{dy}{dx}$ of the curve at this point.

   (b) By repeating this process as necessary, and using the symmetry of the graph, copy and complete the following table.

x	-2	-1.5	-1	0	1	1.5	2
Gradient $\frac{dy}{dx}$							

   (c) Plot all the points $\left(x, \dfrac{dy}{dx} \right)$ to obtain the gradient graph for $y = \frac{1}{2}x^2$.

   Your points should be approximately on a straight line through the origin (the line $y = x$). So,

   $$y = \tfrac{1}{2}x^2 \Rightarrow \frac{dy}{dx} = x$$

2 Plot the graph of $y = 21 + 4x - x^2$.

   (a) Find the gradient at a number of different points on the curve.

   (b) Check that your answers satisfy the equation of the gradient graph
   $$\frac{dy}{dx} = 4 - 2x.$$

You found that the graph of $y = \frac{1}{2}x^2$ has a gradient graph with $\dfrac{dy}{dx} = x$ as its equation.

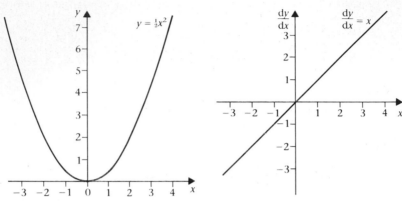

In the following questions you will investigate, by drawing graphs, the gradient functions for various quadratic functions.

 .2c

1 (a) Plot the graph $y = \frac{1}{2}x^2 + 1$, letting 1 unit be represented by 2 cm on each axis.

  (b) By drawing an accurate tangent, confirm that $\dfrac{dy}{dx} = 2$ at the point $(2, 3)$.

  (c) Find sufficient gradients to sketch the gradient graph, and state its equation.

  (d) How are the graphs of $y = \frac{1}{2}x^2 + 1$, $y = \frac{1}{2}x^2 - 2$ and, generally, $y = \frac{1}{2}x^2 + c$ all related to that of $y = \frac{1}{2}x^2$?

  (e) What can be deduced about the gradient graph for any curve of the form $y = \frac{1}{2}x^2 + c$?

2 (a) Plot the graph of $y = x^2$, letting 1 unit be represented by 4 cm on each axis.

  (b) Find sufficient gradients to sketch the gradient graph, and state its equation.

  (c) Carefully explain why the gradient of $y = x^2$ is twice that of $y = \frac{1}{2}x^2$ for corresponding values of x.

  (d) What would you expect the gradient graph for $y = 3x^2$ to be?

  (e) What can be deduced about the gradient graph for any curve of the form $y = ax^2$?

3 What is the equation of the gradient graph of $y = ax^2 + c$?

You have seen some justification for the following result:

$$y = ax^2 + c \Rightarrow \frac{dy}{dx} = 2ax$$

Example 2

Find the gradient of the graph of $y = 3x^2 + 1$ when $x = 2$.

Solution

$$y = 3x^2 + 1 \Rightarrow \frac{dy}{dx} = 6x$$

At $x = 2$, the gradient is 12.

The gradient of a curve at a point may be found very accurately and much more quickly by using the zoom facility on a calculator or computer, or by obtaining its value numerically in the following way.

You have seen that when you zoom in on the graph of $y = x^2$ the curve is everywhere locally straight.

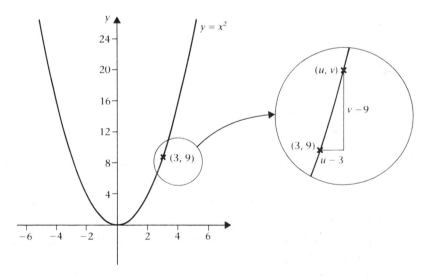

If you zoom in at $(3, 9)$, you know the property of local straightness will mean that the graph looks increasingly like a straight line which becomes more and more like the tangent to the graph at $(3, 9)$. So, to find the gradient of the tangent, you can use the curve itself.

Using the point (u, v) you will get an approximate gradient for $y = x^2$ at $x = 3$ by calculating

$$\text{approximate gradient} = \frac{v - 9}{u - 3}$$

You could take the point (u, v) to be $(3.1, 9.61)$, for example, and this would give an estimate of the gradient of the tangent at $(3, 9)$. You could get a more accurate value for the slope by taking u even closer to $x = 3$, for example, 3.01.

 .2D

Find estimates for the gradient of $y = x^2$ at $x = 3$ by taking $u = 3.2$, 3.1, 3.01, 3.001 and so on. Describe what is happening to the estimate as you move u closer to $x = 3$. State the gradient at $x = 3$.

It is often convenient to use function notation when finding gradients numerically.

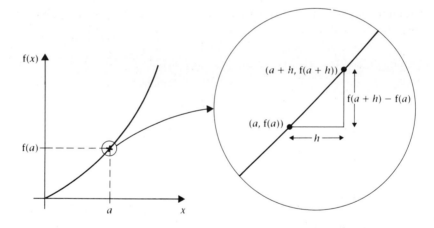

The gradient of the graph of a function $f(x)$ at a point $(a, f(a))$ is given the symbol $f'(a)$, and can be estimated numerically as

$$f'(a) \approx \frac{f(a + h) - f(a)}{h}$$

where h, the difference in x, is small.

Example 3

Find the gradient of the graph of $f(x) = 2x^3 - 3x^2$ at $(2, 4)$.

Solution

$$f(2) = 4 \quad \text{and} \quad f(2.00001) = 4.000\,120\,001\ldots$$

and so the gradient of the graph is approximately

$$f'(2) \approx \frac{4.000\,120\,001 - 4}{0.00001} = 12.0001$$

Using smaller differences in x will result in values closer and closer to 12. This limit is the gradient of the graph.

If $f(x) = 2x^3 - 3x^2$ then $f'(2) = 12$.

2.2 **Exercise 2**

Calculate numerical estimates of the gradients of the functions at the point indicated.

1   $y = x^3$ at $(2, 8)$

2   $y = 2x^2 + 3$ at $(3, 21)$

3   $y = x^2 + 4x$ at $(1, 5)$

4   $y = x^3 - x^2$ at $(2, 4)$

5   $y = x^4 + 5x$ at $(1, 6)$

6   $y = x^2$ at the points with x-coordinates:

    (a) 3   (b) 5   (c) 0   (d) −2

    Use your results, together with that for $x = 1$, to predict the gradient when the x-coordinate is (e) 15, (f) 3.6, and confirm these guesses by calculation.

2.2.4 Gradient functions

The great speed and accuracy of numerical methods, compared for example with the use of a gradient measurer, enables you to construct many gradient functions.

.2E

1 (a) Draw a rough sketch of what you would expect for the gradient graph of $y = x^3$.

(b) Use a numerical method to calculate the gradient at $x = 0, 1, -2$ and 3.

(c) What is the gradient function?

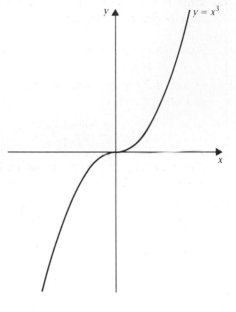

Many graph plotters will calculate gradients numerically for several values of x and plot them on the graph. This gives you an accurate picture of the gradient graph. You can then make a sensible guess at the equation of the gradient graph and check your conjecture by superimposing. Use a graph plotter with this facility to check your answer to question 1(c) and to answer the rest of these questions.

2 For a function of the form

$$y = ax^3$$

what does the gradient function appear to be?

A general polynomial is built up from multiples of simple powers of x. For example, $x + x^2$ is built up as shown below.

x	0	1	2	3
x^2	0	1	4	9
$x + x^2$	0	2	6	12

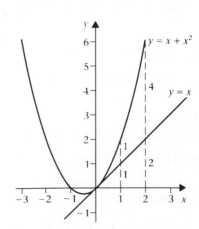

When x increases from 1 to 2, x increases by 1, x^2 increases by 3 and $x + x^2$ increases by both amounts, i.e. 4.

Does this remind you of a result you discovered in section 2.1?

In section 2.1 you found that if $y = au + bv$, where u, v are linear functions of x, then

$$\frac{dy}{dx} = a\frac{du}{dx} + b\frac{dv}{dx}$$

You might expect functions that are locally straight to behave in a similar way to linear functions.

3 If $y = ax + bx^2$, check that $\dfrac{dy}{dx} = a + 2bx$ for various values of a and b.

4 If $y = a + bx + cx^2 + dx^3$, find the equation of the gradient graph.

5E If $y = ax^n + bx^m$, find the gradient function.

The questions of 2.2E above have provided considerable evidence for the following result.

A polynomial graph with equation of the form

$$y = a + bx + cx^2 + dx^3$$

has a gradient graph with equation

$$\frac{dy}{dx} = b + 2cx + 3dx^2$$

$\dfrac{dy}{dx}$ is called the **derivative** of y with respect to x and $b + 2cx + 3dx^2$ is called the **derived function**.

Example 4

(a) Find the gradient of the graph of $y = 1 - 3x + 2x^2$ at the point $(2, 3)$.

(b) Hence find the equation of the tangent at $(2, 3)$.

Solution

(a) $\dfrac{dy}{dx} = -3 + 4x$. At the point $(2, 3)$, $\dfrac{dy}{dx} = -3 + 4 \times 2 = 5$

(b) The tangent has gradient 5 and passes through $(2, 3)$. If (x, y) is any other point on the tangent, then

$$\frac{y - 3}{x - 2} = 5 \Rightarrow y - 3 = 5x - 10 \Rightarrow y = 5x - 7$$

The equation of the tangent is $y = 5x - 7$.

2.2 Exercise 3

1   Use the rules you have discovered to find the equation of the gradient graph for each of the following.

   (a) $y = 3x^2 + 4$ (b) $v = 5u^3 - 2u^2$
   (c) $y = 6 - x^2$ (d) $s = 4t - t^2$

2   For the graph whose equation is $y = 2 + 5x^2$

   (a) write down the equation of the gradient graph;

   (b) write down the gradients of the graph at:

       (i) $(1, 7)$ (ii) $(2, 22)$ (iii) the point where $x = -1$.

3   Find the gradients of each of the following graphs at the given points.

   (a) $y = 3 - 2x^3$ at $(0, 3)$ and $(2, -13)$ (b) $y = 5x - x^2$ at $(2, 6)$ and $(4, 4)$

4   Find the equations of the tangents to each of the following graphs at $(2, 3)$.

   (a) $y = 3 + 2x - x^2$
   (b) $y = x^3 - 5$
   (c) $y = 7 + x^2 - x^3$

5   Find the equation of the tangent to $y = x + 2x^2$ at the point whose x-coordinate is 3.

6   Find the equations of the tangents to each of the following graphs at $(0, 5)$.

   (a) $y = 5 + x - x^3$
   (b) $y = 5 - 3x + 2x^3$
   (c) $y = 5 + 4x^2 + 3x^3$

▶ 2.2 **Tasksheet E1 – Tangents and normals (page 551)**

2.2.5 Differentiation from first principles

The introductory study of calculus so far has been based upon the idea of local straightness. When you zoom in at a point on a locally straight curve, the curve appears to be a straight line and this enables you to find the gradient.

However, zooming in does not always make a curve appear straight. From a spaceship, the Earth appears to have a smooth, spherical surface, but from a closer vantage point, enormous imperfections in the surface are apparent.

To be able to differentiate a function you require the graph of the function to be locally straight, but so far you have no way of knowing whether a graph *really is* locally straight.

One important aspect of mathematics concerns giving rigorous arguments to prove results indisputably. It seems that you would have to zoom in forever in order to confirm that graphs of relations such as $y = \sin x$ or $y = x^2$ really *are* locally straight. We now consider the mathematical technique for doing this.

To be able to find the numerical gradient of $y = x^2$ at the point $(3, 9)$ you have previously considered the gradients of lines joining $(3, 9)$ to nearby points on the graph.

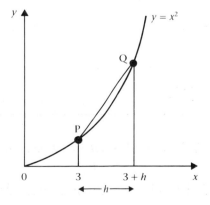

P is the point $(3, 3^2)$. Q, a nearby point, has coordinates $(3 + h, (3 + h)^2)$.

The gradient of the chord PQ is

$$\frac{y_Q - y_P}{x_Q - x_P} = \frac{(3 + h)^2 - 3^2}{(3 + h) - 3} = \frac{6h + h^2}{h}$$

$$= 6 + h$$

As h becomes smaller and smaller the gradient of PQ becomes closer and closer to 6. The chord PQ becomes closer and closer to the tangent at P.

You can see that for *any* small h, the gradient is close to 6. You therefore know that zooming in further (by taking smaller values of h) cannot cause any change in this result: *the graph is locally straight at x = 3 and has gradient 6 at that point.*

Making the value of h smaller and smaller is termed 'letting h tend to zero' and the notation for this is

$$h \to 0$$

Finding the value of $6 + h$ as h tends to zero is termed 'finding the limit of $6 + h$ as h tends to zero' and the notation for this is

$$\lim_{h \to 0} (6 + h)$$

> The limit of $6 + h$ as h tends to zero is
>
> $$\lim_{h \to 0} (6 + h) = 6$$

This idea is explored in the questions which follow.

.2F

1 Evaluate:　(a) $\displaystyle\lim_{h \to 0} (5h - 2)$　　(b) $\displaystyle\lim_{h \to 0} (3 + 2h)$

Limits can be obtained for h tending to values other than 0.

The limit of $\dfrac{h(h - 2)}{h - 2}$ as h tends to 2 is written as $\displaystyle\lim_{h \to 2} \dfrac{h(h - 2)}{h - 2}$.

This limit *cannot* be evaluated simply by putting h equal to 2, because $\frac{0}{0}$ is undefined. However, for $h \neq 2$, the factor $h - 2$ can be cancelled.

$$\lim_{h \to 2} \frac{h(h - 2)}{h - 2} = \lim_{h \to 2} h = 2$$

2 Use this method to evaluate:

(a) $\displaystyle\lim_{h \to 0} \frac{h(h - 2)}{h}$　　(b) $\displaystyle\lim_{h \to 0} \frac{5h^2 - 2h}{h}$　　(c) $\displaystyle\lim_{h \to 0} \frac{4h^2 - h^3}{h}$

(d) $\displaystyle\lim_{h \to 2} \frac{(h - 2)(h + 2)}{h - 2}$　　(e) $\displaystyle\lim_{h \to -3} \frac{2h^2 - 18}{h + 3}$

You have found a number of limits of the type

$$\lim_{h \to 0} 2(h + 3) = 6$$

A limit of the form

$$\lim_{h \to 0} \frac{3 + h}{2 + h} = \frac{3}{2}$$

can be found simply by substituting zero for h in both numerator and denominator. However, this method cannot be applied if the denominator is zero when h is zero.

Example 5

Find $\lim\limits_{h \to 0} \dfrac{4h - h^3}{9h + h^2}$

Solution

For $h \neq 0$, $\quad \dfrac{4h - h^3}{9h + h^2} = \dfrac{(4 - h^2)h}{(9 + h)h} = \dfrac{4 - h^2}{9 + h}$

$\Rightarrow \lim\limits_{h \to 0} \dfrac{4h - h^3}{9h + h^2} = \dfrac{4}{9}$

The notation developed for limits can be used to give a general definition for the gradient of the graph of a function.

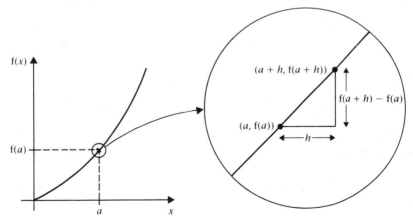

> The gradient of the graph of the function f at the point $(a, f(a))$ is given by
>
> $$f'(a) = \lim_{h \to 0} \frac{f(a+h) - f(a)}{h}$$
>
> (If the limit does not exist, then the function is *not* locally straight and does not have a gradient at $x = a$.)

Finding a gradient by means of the limit is called **differentiating from first principles**.

Example 6

Differentiate $y = 3x^2 - 4x$ at $(3, 15)$ from first principles.

Solution

$$f(3 + h) = 3(3 + h)^2 - 4(3 + h)$$

$$= 3(9 + 6h + h^2) - 12 - 4h$$

$$= 15 + 14h + 3h^2$$

The gradient is $\displaystyle \lim_{h \to 0} \frac{15 + 14h + 3h^2 - 15}{h} = \lim_{h \to 0} (14 + 3h) = 14$

For any function f, a general formula for $f'(x)$ can be found from first principles using the definition

> $$f'(x) = \lim_{h \to 0} \frac{f(x + h) - f(x)}{h}$$

Example 7

If $y = x^2$, find $\dfrac{dy}{dx}$ from first principles.

Solution

$$\frac{dy}{dx} = \lim_{h \to 0} \frac{(x + h)^2 - x^2}{h}$$

$$= \lim_{h \to 0} \frac{x^2 + 2xh + h^2 - x^2}{h}$$

$$= \lim_{h \to 0} (2x + h) = 2x$$

Example 8

If $y = \dfrac{1}{x}$, find $\dfrac{dy}{dx}$ from first principles.

Solution

$$\frac{dy}{dx} = \lim_{h \to 0} \left[\frac{\dfrac{1}{x+h} - \dfrac{1}{x}}{h} \right]$$

$$= \lim_{h \to 0} \left[\frac{x - (x+h)}{hx(x+h)} \right]$$

$$= \lim_{h \to 0} \left[\frac{-h}{hx(x+h)} \right] = \lim_{h \to 0} \left[\frac{-1}{x(x+h)} \right] = -\frac{1}{x^2}$$

$$y = \frac{1}{x} \Rightarrow \frac{dy}{dx} = -\frac{1}{x^2}$$

The method of differentiating from first principles is important, since it is the way in which mathematicians have proved all the known derivatives. It can also be used to **prove** the correctness of the various rules of differentiation.

2.2 Exercise 4

1 Suppose $y = 3x^2$.

    (a) Find the gradient at $(1, 3)$ from first principles.

    (b) Find a general formula for $\dfrac{dy}{dx}$ from first principles.

2 Differentiate $5x^2 + 3x$ with respect to x, from first principles.

3 Differentiate $4x^2 - 2x + 7$ with respect to x, from first principles.

4E Show, from first principles, that if $y = \dfrac{1}{2t + 5}$, then $\dfrac{dy}{dt} = \dfrac{-2}{(2t + 5)^2}$.

5E Differentiate x^3 from first principles.

2.2.6 Leibniz notation

Calculus is the study of the changes of a continuously varying function. In section 2.2, you have looked at the gradients of locally straight curves and, in particular, the gradients of graphs of polynomial functions. At any point, the gradient of a locally straight curve is the same as the gradient of its tangent at that point. The concept of a derivative arose chiefly as the result of many centuries of effort spent in drawing tangents to curves and finding the velocities of bodies in non-uniform motion.

Isaac Newton was born in 1642 and entered Cambridge University in 1660, quickly mastering all the mathematics known at that time. In 1665, the year of the Great Plague, he invented his 'method of fluxions', which was a method of dealing with varying quantities. If a quantity, say x, was a function of time t, then Newton used the notation $\dot{x}$ to represent $\dfrac{dx}{dt}$. In mechanics, the notations $\dot{x}$ and $\dot{y}$ are still used to represent velocities in the x and y directions respectively. During the Great Plague, Newton retired from Cambridge to his home in Lincolnshire. Here, he investigated various applications of his method, including finding the equations of tangents. His treatise on calculus was written in 1671 but its publication did not take place until 1736, nine years after his death. It is interesting that in his *Principia* of 1687, in which he dealt with both terrestrial and celestial mechanics, he relied on geometry and did not use fluxions.

Because Newton's results were published so late, a bitter controversy arose between the supporters of Newton and of the German mathematician and philosopher, Leibniz. Gottfried Leibniz (1646–1716) had not yet started his study of mathematics in 1671 and it was not until 29 October 1675 that the first mention of the calculus notation in use today appeared in his notes. Having noticed that differentiation reduced the degree of a polynomial, he used the notation $\dfrac{x}{d}$ but soon changed this to dx. In 1676, in correspondence with the Royal Society, Leibniz learnt that Newton had produced some important results. Newton supplied him with a variety of theorems but referred to his method of fluxions by means of two anagrams from which Leibniz deduced nothing. In a reply he gave his rules for dy and dx. Newton, in his *Principia*, mentioned that Leibniz had discovered independently a method 'which hardly differed from mine except in words and symbols'.

The greatest merit of Leibniz's work was his creation of a mathematical symbolism. Besides his introduction of dx, he invented the notations $\dfrac{dy}{dx}$ and $\dfrac{d}{dx}$. In the text you have seen that $\dfrac{dy}{dx}$ represents

$$\dfrac{\text{the difference in } y\text{-coordinates}}{\text{the difference in } x\text{-coordinates}}$$

along the tangent to the curve. Using the notation invented by Leibniz,

$$y = 2x^3 \Rightarrow \frac{dy}{dx} = 6x^2 \quad \text{or} \quad \frac{d}{dx}(2x^3) = 6x^2$$

Leibniz also adopted a useful notation for the second derivative – the function obtained when you differentiate the first derivative. In mechanics, the second derivative of displacement with respect to time (which is the acceleration) is often written as $\ddot{x}$ or $\dfrac{d^2x}{dt^2}$. Using this notation,

$$x = ut + \tfrac{1}{2}at^2 \;\Rightarrow\; \dot{x} = u + at \;\rightarrow\; \ddot{x} = a$$

or $\qquad x = ut + \tfrac{1}{2}at^2 \;\Rightarrow\; \dfrac{dx}{dt} = u + at \;\Rightarrow\; \dfrac{d^2x}{dt^2} = a$

A further adaptation of this notation, extensively used later in the text, refers to the first and second derivatives $f'(x)$ and $f''(x)$ of a function $f(x)$. For example,

$$f(x) = x^3 - 2x^5$$

$$\frac{df}{dx} = f'(x) = 3x^2 - 10x^4$$

$$\frac{d^2f}{dx^2} = f''(x) = 6x - 40x^3$$

All of these notations are in common use.

After working through section 2.2 you should:

1 be able to sketch the gradient graph for a given graph;

2 know that

$$y = a + bx + cx^2 + dx^3 \;\Rightarrow\; \frac{dy}{dx} = b + 2cx + 3dx^2$$

3 recognise the rule above for differentiating cubics as a particular case of a general rule (not yet proved) that if a, b are constants and u, v are functions of x, then

$$y = au + bv \;\Rightarrow\; \frac{dy}{dx} = a\frac{du}{dx} + b\frac{dv}{dx}$$

4 be able to find the equation of a tangent to a graph at a given point;

5 appreciate that you need the algebraic limit process to determine whether the graph of a function really is locally straight;

6 understand the notation $\lim\limits_{h \to 0} f(h)$;

7 be able to evaluate simple limits;

8 know how to obtain derivatives from first principles using the expression $\lim\limits_{h \to 0} \dfrac{f(x+h) - f(x)}{h}$.

2 Introductory calculus

.3 Optimisation

2.3.1 Graphs and gradient graphs

Optimisation is the process of producing the most favourable outcome: the greatest food supply or the least pollution, for example. Decision-making can sometimes depend upon an analysis using calculus and stationary points. Before tackling such optimisation problems we shall review the use of stationary points in graph sketching.

 .3A

Part of the graph of
$$y = x^3 - 2x^2 + x + 1$$
is as sketched.

1 (a) Explain how the details of the graph shown above are obtained.

(b) What features of the $\left(x, \dfrac{dy}{dx} \right)$ gradient graph sketched below can you relate to the shape of the (x, y) graph?

The graph of
$$\frac{dy}{dx} = 3x^2 - 4x + 1$$
is shown here.

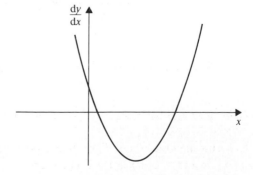

(c) Complete the gaps in the original (x, y) graph.

How can you be certain that your sketch is roughly correct?

2 Make a copy of this sketch graph and indicate on it:

(a) the parts of the graph where $\dfrac{dy}{dx}$ is positive;

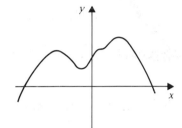

(b) the parts of the graph where $\dfrac{dy}{dx}$ is negative;

(c) the points on the graph where $\dfrac{dy}{dx}$ is zero;

(d) any local maxima or minima.

3 The points shown on an (x, y) graph and corresponding $\left(x, \dfrac{dy}{dx}\right)$ graph have the same x-coordinate.

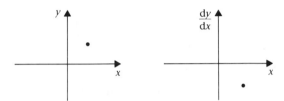

Sketch a possible shape for the part of the (x, y) graph *near* the point shown, carefully explaining your answer.

4 One point of an (x, y) graph and a segment of the corresponding $\left(x, \dfrac{dy}{dx}\right)$ graph are shown.

Sketch the (x, y) graph *near* $x = 0$, carefully explaining your answer.

The values and behaviour of $\dfrac{dy}{dx}$ can be used to help sketch graphs.

Knowing the gradient of a graph at a point tells you what the graph is like *near the point* and not just at the point itself.

Finding the stationary points (where $\dfrac{dy}{dx} = 0$) can help you to determine quickly the overall shape of the graph.

For a local minimum at a point,

$$\frac{dy}{dx} = 0$$

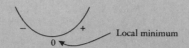

and the sign of $\frac{dy}{dx}$ changes from negative, through zero to positive as x increases *through* the stationary point.

For a local maximum at a point,

$$\frac{dy}{dx} = 0$$

and the sign of $\frac{dy}{dx}$ changes from positive, through zero to negative as x increases *through* the stationary point.

Example 1

(a) Sketch the graph of $y = x^2 - 5x$.

(b) Indicate on your sketch where $\frac{dy}{dx}$ is positive and where it is negative.

(c) For what value of x does $\frac{dy}{dx} = 0$?

(d) Is this point a maximum or a minimum? State its coordinates.

Solution

(a) $y = x^2 - 5x$ or $y = x(x - 5)$

(b) $+, -$, as on the graph

(c) $y = x^2 - 5x \Rightarrow \frac{dy}{dx} = 2x - 5$

$\frac{dy}{dx} = 0 \Rightarrow 2x - 5 = 0 \Rightarrow x = 2.5$

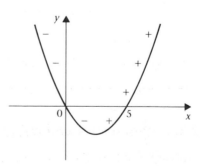

(d) It is clear from the graph that it is a minimum. When $x = 2.5$,
$y = 2.5^2 - 5 \times 2.5 = -6.25$.
The coordinates are $(2.5, -6.25)$.

2.3 Exercise 1

1 Sketch $y = (x - 1)(x - 2)(x - 4)$. What extra information about the graph could be obtained using calculus? (There is no need to find this extra information!)

2 Three cubic graphs are sketched below.

(a)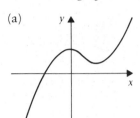

(b)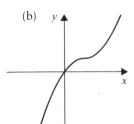

(c)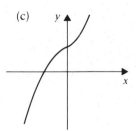

Sketch the corresponding $\left(x, \dfrac{dy}{dx}\right)$ graphs and relate features of the gradient graphs to the shape of the (x, y) graphs.

3 A cubic graph passes through $(0, 2)$ and has gradient graph as shown.

Sketch the (x, y) graph.

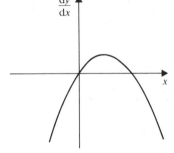

4 The distance travelled by an object in time t is given by

$$s = t^3 - 6t^2 + 12t$$

(a) Find $\dfrac{ds}{dt}$ and sketch the graph of $\dfrac{ds}{dt}$ against t.

(b) Sketch the graph of s against t.

(c) By considering the two graphs, describe the motion of the object.

2.3.2 Quadratics and cubics

It is easy to differentiate quadratic and cubic functions and hence to find the stationary points.

 .3B

1 For $y = x^3 - 12x + 2$, find $\dfrac{dy}{dx}$ and solve the equation $\dfrac{dy}{dx} = 0$.

Hence find the stationary points and complete the graph.

2 For $u = 3x^2 + 6x + 5$, solve the equation $\dfrac{du}{dx} = 0$.

Hence find the stationary point and sketch the quadratic graph.

3 Use your sketch graph for question 2 to show that $y = x^3 + 3x^2 + 5x + 7$ has *no* stationary points. Hence sketch the cubic graph.

4 Use a graph plotter to obtain cubic graphs with equations of the form $y = x^3 + ax$ for various values of a. Describe how the value of a affects the shape of the curve.

Relate what you discover to $\dfrac{dy}{dx}$ and stationary points.

The graphs of quadratics and cubics can be sketched rapidly by:

1 finding the y-intercept;

2 considering the sign of the highest power of x to determine their shape for large $|x|$;

3 finding the x-coordinates of any stationary points by solving the equation

$$\frac{dy}{dx} = 0$$

Example 2
Sketch $y = -x^3 + 27x - 2$.

Solution
For large x, the graph has roughly the same shape as that of $-x^3$.

At the stationary points,

$$\frac{dy}{dx} = 0$$

$$-3x^2 + 27 = 0$$

$$3(9 - x^2) = 0$$

$$x = 3 \text{ or } -3$$

When $x = 3$

$$y = -3^3 + 27 \times 3 - 2 = 52$$

When $x = -3$

$$y = -(-3)^3 + 27 \times (-3) - 2 = -56$$

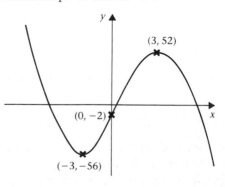

2.3 Exercise 2

1 Find the stationary points on the graph of $y = x^3 - 12x + 5$. Hence sketch the graph.

2 Repeat question 1 if the graph is that of $y = 2x^3 - 9x^2 + 12x - 7$.

3 For each function (a) to (f) given below:

(i) find all the values of x, if any, for which $\dfrac{dy}{dx} = 0$ and hence find the coordinates of all the local maximum and minimum points;

(ii) sketch carefully the graphs of the functions below and indicate on your sketch the parts of the graphs where $\dfrac{dy}{dx}$ is positive and the parts where $\dfrac{dy}{dx}$ is negative.

(a) $y = 5x - x^2$ (b) $y = (1 - x)^2$

(c) $y = x^3 - 3x^2 + 5$ (d) $y = 4x - x^2 - 4$

(e) $y = 2x^3 - 9x^2 + 12$ (f) $y = x^4 - 8x^2 + 12$

4 The sketch graphs below are those of $y = x^2 - 6x$ and $y = x^3 - 6x^2$.

(a) Find the x-coordinates of A, B and C. Explain the relationship between the x-coordinate of B and the other two x-coordinates.

(b) Find the x-coordinates of D, E and F. Does the relationship you noticed in (a) hold for this graph?

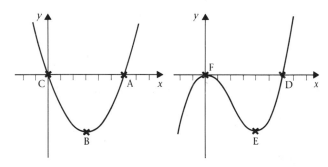

2.3.3 Maxima and minima

Decision-making often depends upon choosing the value of one variable so as to maximise or minimise another variable. For example, it might involve maximising profits, minimising the amount of material used in a design, maximising the number of customers served each hour and so on. Calculus can be of great help in this decision-making process. The stages in such a process can be seen in the following simple example.

A circular piece of paper is folded into a cylindrical paper case for a cake. Where should the paper be folded to create the container of greatest volume?

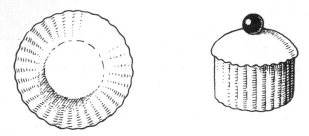

What do you think happens to the volume of the cylinder as it changes from a tall thin cylinder to a short fat cylinder as shown below?

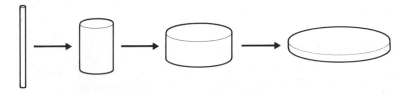

To use calculus methods to solve this problem you can express the volume, V, in terms of a suitable variable length.

Consider a circle of paper of fixed radius R, folded at radius r. The paper folds up to form a cylinder, of volume V.

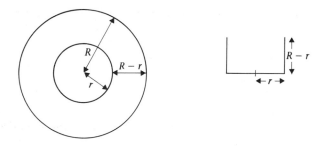

Volume = area of base × height

$$V = \pi r^2(R - r)$$

$$= \pi R r^2 - \pi r^3$$

$$\frac{dV}{dr} = 2\pi R r - 3\pi r^2 \quad \text{(Note that } R \text{ is fixed and does not vary with } r.\text{)}$$

$$= \pi r(2R - 3r)$$

$\dfrac{dV}{dr} = 0$ when $r = 0$ (zero volume) and when $r = \frac{2}{3}R$ (maximum volume). The maximum volume is therefore

$$\pi(\tfrac{2}{3}R)^2(R - \tfrac{2}{3}R) = \tfrac{4}{27}\pi R^3$$

V can, of course, be expressed in terms of other lengths, for example fixed diameter D and variable height h. It could also be expressed in terms of an area, such as the area of the base of the cake case. It is important to choose quantities which make the calculations reasonably easy.

The questions below further illustrate the method.

 .3c

The population density (number of residents per unit area) of many cities depends roughly on the distance from the city centre.

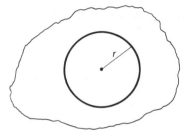

For a particular city, the population density P in thousands of people per square kilometre at a distance r kilometres from the centre is given approximately by

$$P = 5 + 30r - 15r^2$$

1 What is the population density in the centre of the city?

2 Sketch a graph of P against r. For what values of r is the formula definitely not valid?

3 Find $\dfrac{dP}{dr}$ and calculate the rate of change of population density at a radius of

    (a) 0.5 km   (b) 1 km   (c) 2 km from the city centre.

Sketch a graph of $\dfrac{dP}{dr}$ against r.

4 Use the two graphs to describe in words how population density varies with distance from the centre.

Example 3
During a promotion drive, an electrical retailer sells a particular make of television at cost price. She finds that, at this price, she sells twenty televisions a week. However, according to a market survey the demand would fall to zero if the price were increased by £40.

By what amount should the retailer increase the price to make the maximum weekly profit?

Solution

For a price increase of £I you can model the number sold by

$$N = 20 - \tfrac{1}{2}I$$

£I is the increase above cost price and so the profit (in £) is

$$P = NI$$
$$= (20 - \tfrac{1}{2}I)I$$
$$= 20I - \tfrac{1}{2}I^2$$

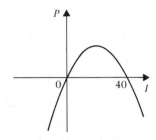

P is maximum when $\dfrac{dP}{dI} = 0$.

Since $\dfrac{dP}{dI} = 20 - I$, $\dfrac{dP}{dI} = 0$ when $I = 20$

The retailer should increase the price by £20.

2.3 Exercise 3

1 The fuel economy of a new car was measured when it was test driven at various speeds in top gear. For a speed of v miles per hour, the fuel consumption, F miles per gallon, was found to be roughly modelled, for $30 \leq v \leq 80$, by the formula $F = 25 + v - 0.012v^2$.

(a) Find F and $\dfrac{dF}{dv}$ when $v = 35$ and when $v = 60$. What do these results indicate about fuel economy?

(b) What speed is most economical for this car?

2 As a result of a survey, the marketing director of a company found that the demand for its product was given approximately by the linear equation $n = 30 - 2P$ where n is the demand, or the number of items that will be sold (in millions), at a price £P.

If n million are sold at £P each then the revenue (money taken) will be £R million where

$$R = nP = (30 - 2P)P = 30P - 2P^2$$

(a) Find $\dfrac{dR}{dP}$ and explain what it means. What is the best selling price?

(b) Calculate the value of $\dfrac{dR}{dP}$ when $P = 5$ and when $P = 10$.

(c) For what range of selling prices would the revenue rise if the price were increased a little?

3 A rectangular strip of plastic of width 20 cm is folded into a length of guttering as shown.

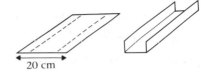

20 cm

Where should the folds be located to enable the gutter to carry as much water as possible?

4 A new housing estate started with a population of approximately 500 people.

(a) It was planned that it should grow by roughly 100 inhabitants each year. Find an expression for the intended population P of the estate t years after its opening. Find $\dfrac{dP}{dt}$ and explain what it represents.

(b) For various reasons, the new estate did not grow as planned and the population was better modelled by the quadratic expression

$$P = 100(5 + t - 0.25t^2)$$

What was the rate of change of the population after 1, 2 and 3 years? What was the maximum population of the estate? What happened to the estate?

5 To express 10 as a product of two numbers which have the least possible sum you can take the two numbers to be x and $\dfrac{10}{x}$ and try to minimise $x + \dfrac{10}{x}$.

(a) Use a graph plotter to sketch $x + \dfrac{10}{x}$.

(b) From the graph, estimate some possible answers to this minimising problem, depending upon what types of numbers are allowed.

2.3.4 Graphical optimisation

Calculus has been described as the most powerful and useful invention of mathematics. Applications of calculus range over many areas of mathematics, physical science, engineering and the social sciences. Section 2.3 has concentrated upon just one type of application – optimisation.

Calculus can be used to find the local maximum and minimum values of a quantity. The quantity must first be expressed in terms of another simpler variable. You can then consider the graph of the relationship between the two variable quantities and, in particular, its stationary points.

When tackling real problems, the expressions obtained may be difficult to optimise algebraically. In such cases you can use a graph plotter to observe the overall shape of the curve and hence obtain from the graph the approximate positions of any local maxima and minima.

In question 3 of exercise 3 you should have obtained proportions for the rectangular guttering of

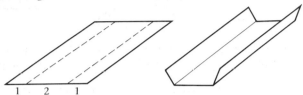

Gutters can, however, have splayed sides. Intuitively, do you think that the amount of water which the gutter is able to carry can be increased by splaying its sides while keeping the 1:2:1 ratio as above?

 .3D

Find an expression for the cross-sectional area of the splay-sided gutter in terms of some chosen variable quantity. Use a graph plotter to check if your intuition was correct.

2.3 Exercise 4

1

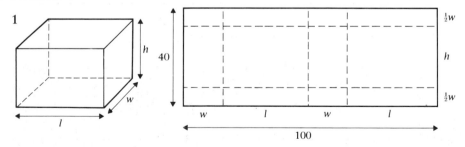

A cardboard box is to be made from a rectangular piece of card, 100 cm by 40 cm, by cutting and folding as necessary along the dashed lines shown in the right-hand diagram. The problem is to find the values of l, w and h which maximise the volume, V cm^3.

(a) Explain why $2l + 2w = 100$. Hence express l in terms of w.

(b) Similarly, find h in terms of w.

(c) The volume of the box is given by $V = whl$. Use your answers to (a) and (b) to show that $V = w(40 - w)(50 - w)$.

(d) Find, approximately, the value of w corresponding to the maximum possible volume. What approximate dimensions will the box then have?

2 Small open-topped boxes are to be made out of sheet steel. Each box is to be made from a 6 cm by 4 cm rectangular piece of steel. A square will be cut from each corner, as shown in the diagram, and the remainder made into the box by bending along the dashed lines and welding.

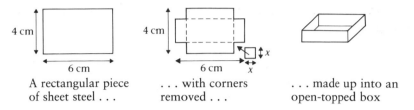

A rectangular piece of sheet steel . . .   . . . with corners removed . . .   . . . made up into an open-topped box

(a) If the squares cut out have side x cm, show that the volume of the box is V cm^3, where $V = x(4 - 2x)(6 - 2x)$.

(b) What should be the approximate dimensions if the volume of the box is to be as large as possible?

3 A box with a lid has a square base of side x cm and height h cm. If its total surface area is 2040 cm^2 write down a formula for its volume V cm^3 and eliminate h to show that $V = 510x - \frac{1}{2}x^3$. Hence find the dimensions giving the maximum possible volume, and calculate this volume.

4 The height, in metres, of a rocket t minutes after blast-off is given by

$$h = \tfrac{1}{4}t(36 - 24t + 10t^2 - t^3)$$

Calculate the maximum velocity and maximum acceleration attained.

▶ 2.3 **Tasksheet E1 – Optimisation problems (page 553)**

After working through section 2.3 you should be able to:

1 recognise and interpret rates of change in various contexts;

2 use the derived function as an aid in graph-sketching;

3 sketch quadratics and cubics rapidly;

4 use sketches as an aid in optimisation problems;

5 use the derived function as an aid in optimisation problems.

Introductory calculus

.4 Numerical integration

2.4.1 Areas under graphs

Suppose that water flows from a tap at a constant rate of 15 litres per minute. This can be represented graphically.

Rate (litres per minute)

15

0   20   Time (minutes)

The area under the graph represents the actual volume of water that has passed in a given time interval. In the first 20 minutes, $15 \times 20 = 300$ litres flow from the tap.

In this section we start to develop methods for finding the area under a graph, an important problem with many applications. We shall consider two of the possible methods for calculating such areas.

However, calculating an area is only part of the problem; knowing what quantity that area represents is also very important. You have probably met the idea of distance travelled being represented by the area under a (time, speed) graph. In the example above the fact that the area represents a volume of water in litres can be deduced by considering the units of the axes of the graph.

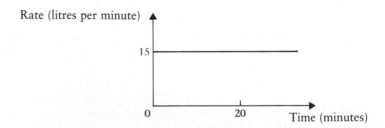

litres per minute

minutes

Area is calculated by multiplying a height by a width, so the units of the area in this case are

$$\frac{\text{litres}}{\text{minutes}} \times \text{minutes} = \text{litres}$$

Using the units of the axes of a graph in this way is an essential step in solving many problems.

.4A

1 State the dimensions of area for each of these sets of axes.

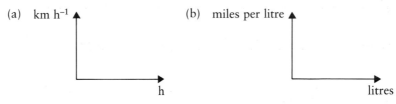

(a)   km h⁻¹

(b)   miles per litre

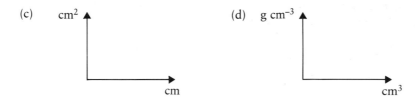

(c)   cm²

(d)   g cm⁻³

2 A graph shows how the speed of a turntable, recorded in revolutions per minute (r.p.m.), varies with time (seconds). What would one unit of area under such a graph represent?

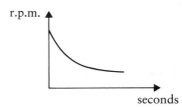

We now consider specific methods for estimating area which will be useful in later work.

.4B

Suppose the driver of a car leaving the motorway allows the car to decrease in speed gradually over a 60-second time period. The speed is recorded at 10-second intervals to give the table below.

Time (s)	5	15	25	35	45	55
Speed (m s⁻¹)	29.9	23.1	19.2	17.0	15.7	15.0

1 Plot the (time, speed) coordinates from the table on graph paper and draw the graph for times ranging from 0 to 60 seconds. What does the area under the graph represent?

You need to use the information in the table to estimate the distance the car travels during the 60 seconds. Although common sense may tell you that the speed of the car is continuously changing with time, you can approximate the motion in the following way. Suppose the car travels at a constant $29.9 \, \mathrm{m \, s^{-1}}$ during the time interval $0 \to 10$ seconds, then instantly changes speed and travels at $23.1 \, \mathrm{m \, s^{-1}}$ during the time interval $10 \to 20$ seconds, and so on (call this the 'constant speed' model).

2 Use this model to estimate the distance the car travels during the 60 seconds.

3 Superimpose the 'constant speed' model graph on the graph you drew for 1.

4 Shade in the area of the graph which corresponds to your answer to 2, and, by considering this area, explain why your answer is a good estimate of the actual distance travelled.

5 Do you think your answer to 2 over-estimates or under-estimates the actual distance travelled? Explain why.

The method of estimation used above is called the **mid-ordinate rule**.

The mid-ordinate rule uses a series of rectangles to estimate the area under a graph. The height of each rectangle is determined by the height of the curve at the mid-point of the interval.

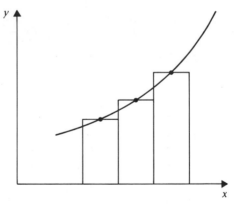

The diagram illustrates the mid-ordinate rule with three strips. It is customary to keep all strip widths the same. This makes the calculation of the area much simpler.

We now consider an alternative numerical method, known as the **trapezium rule**.

 .4C

Suppose readings of the speed of the car considered in 2.4B were taken at different times, with results as follows.

Time (s)	0	10	20	30	40	50	60
Speed (m s^{-1})	35.0	26.0	20.9	18.0	16.3	15.3	14.7

1 Draw the (time, speed) graph for times ranging from 0 to 60 seconds.

Although the graph is obviously curved, you can approximate it with a series of six straight line segments by joining the known points on the graph. In this model of the car's motion you assume that the car's speed decreases uniformly during each 10-second interval.

2 Superimpose this model as a graph on the (time, speed) graph you have just drawn.

3 Use the model to estimate the distance travelled by the car during the 60 seconds.

4 Does the method over-estimate or under-estimate the actual distance travelled?

The trapezium rule uses a series of trapezia to estimate the area under a graph.

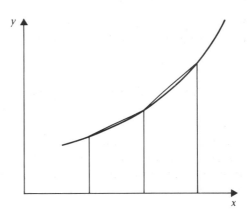

Example 1

A research firm has a circuit which is used to evaluate the performance of engines. A test car is fitted with a computer to record various information, and in one trial it is driven for 8 km around the circuit, gradually increasing in speed. The fuel consumption in $cm^3 \, km^{-1}$ is recorded at each kilometre.

Distance driven (km)	0	1	2	3	4	5	6	7	8
Fuel consumption $(cm^3 \, km^{-1})$	95	70	62	57	55	60	72	87	109

(a) Sketch the graph, explain briefly the characteristics of the graph and state what the area under the graph represents.

(b) Calculate the area under the graph using:
  (i) the mid-ordinate rule with four strips,
  (ii) the trapezium rule with four strips.

Solution

(a)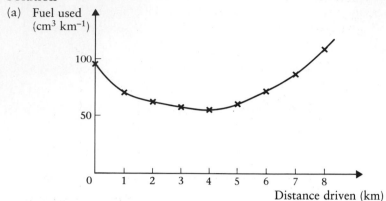

At low speed and at high speed the engine is less economical. As the speed increases from the start, the fuel consumption, in $cm^3 \, km^{-1}$, decreases until the most economical speed is reached (after about 4 km); then the fuel consumption increases again.

The area under the graph represents the volume of fuel, in cm^3, used during the 8 km circuit.

(b) (i) Mid-ordinate rule

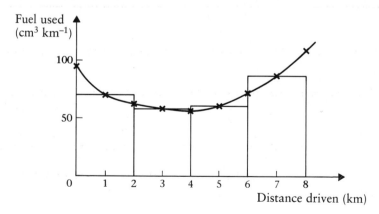

$$\text{Area} = 2 \times 70 + 2 \times 57 + 2 \times 60 + 2 \times 87$$

$$= 548$$

$$\text{Fuel used} = 548 \, cm^3$$

(ii) Trapezium rule

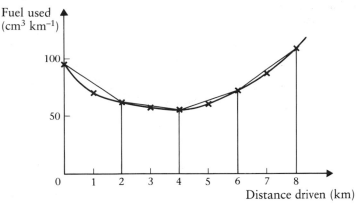

$$\text{Area} = \tfrac{1}{2} \times 2 \times (95 + 62) + \tfrac{1}{2} \times 2 \times (62 + 55) + \tfrac{1}{2} \times 2 \times (55 + 72)$$
$$+ \tfrac{1}{2} \times 2 \times (72 + 109)$$
$$= 582$$

Here, the trapezium rule over-estimates the area while the mid-ordinate rule under-estimates the area. The actual amount of fuel used is somewhere between the two values calculated.

2.4 Exercise 1

1 Depth readings are taken across a river of width 18 metres. Depths at various distances from the left bank are shown in the table.

Distance (m)	0	2	4	6	8	10	12	14	16	18
Depth (m)	0	0.2	1	2	3.1	3.8	3.8	3.9	3.5	0

Use the trapezium rule with nine strips to calculate an estimate of the cross-sectional area.

2 A geologist does a survey of stalactites and stalagmites in a cave. In order to estimate their volumes, she measures their circumferences at different points along their lengths.

Her measurements for one particular stalagmite are shown in the following table.

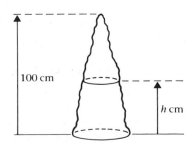

Height (cm)	10	30	50	70	90
Circumference (cm)	50	40	30	20	10

(a) Estimate the cross-sectional area of the stalagmite at each height and draw a graph which shows how the cross-sectional area changes with the height of the stalagmite. What assumptions have you made?

(b) Use the mid-ordinate rule to estimate the area under the graph. What does this area represent?

3 A train is travelling at $20 \, \text{m s}^{-1}$ when the brakes are applied; t seconds later the speed of the train is given by $20 - 0.2t^2 \, \text{m s}^{-1}$. Sketch the (time, speed) graph and use the trapezium rule, with two-second intervals, to estimate the distance travelled by the train before it comes to rest.

2.4.2 Integration

You have already seen that to solve some problems it is necessary to find areas under curves.

The *precise* value of the area under an (x, y) graph from $x = a$ to $x = b$ is denoted by

$$\int_a^b y \, dx$$

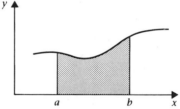

The notation may look complicated but it is very useful. It was introduced by Leibniz in 1684 and is one of the reasons why Leibniz's version of the calculus was more popular than Newton's.

The symbol $\int$ is an old-fashioned form of the letter 's' and indicates that Leibniz thought of the area under a curve as being obtained by $\int$umming areas of lots of very thin rectangles.

The area under the graph of $y = x^2 + 4$ is shown in the diagram. The *precise* value of this area is written as

$$\int_1^3 (x^2 + 4) \, dx$$

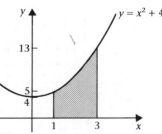

The process of finding the area under a graph is called **integration** because it is, in essence, a process of combining many small parts to form a whole.

The symbol $\int_a^b f(x)\,dx$ denotes the *precise* value of the area underneath the graph of $y = f(x)$, between $x = a$ and $x = b$.

It is known as the **integral** of y with respect to x over the interval from a to b.

The integral can be found *approximately* by various numerical methods.

Example 2

Consider the function $y = \sqrt{(4 - x^2)}$.

(a) Draw a diagram to illustrate the area represented by

$$\int_0^2 \sqrt{(4 - x^2)}\,dx$$

(b) What is the precise value of this integral?

(c) Use the mid-ordinate rule with two strips to estimate this integral.

Solution

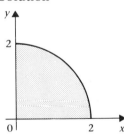

(a) The shaded area under the graph of $y = \sqrt{(4 - x^2)}$ is one quarter of the area of the circle with equation $x^2 + y^2 = 4$. The radius is 2.

(b) The area of the circle is 4π. So

$$\int_0^2 \sqrt{(4 - x^2)}\,dx = \pi.$$

(c)

When $x = 0.5$, $y = \sqrt{3.75} = 1.936$ (to 4 s.f.)

When $x = 1.5$, $y = \sqrt{1.75} = 1.323$ (to 4 s.f.)

$$\int_0^2 \sqrt{(4 - x^2)}\,dx \approx (1 \times 1.936) + (1 \times 1.323) \approx 3.26 \quad \text{(to 3 s.f.)}$$

This method could be used to find an approximate value for π.

2.4 Exercise 2

1 Draw the graph of $y = x$ and indicate the area represented by the integral $\int_0^3 x \, dx$. Find the precise value of this integral.

2 Calculate: (a) $\int_1^4 x \, dx$ (b) $\int_1^3 5 \, dx$ (c) $\int_1^4 (2x + 3) \, dx$

3 To estimate, for example, the depth of a well or the height of a cliff, you can use the fact that the downward speed of a dropped stone increases by approximately $10 \, \text{m s}^{-1}$ each second.

From the top of a particular cliff, a stone takes 5 seconds to reach the sea.

(a) Find the speed of the stone t seconds after being dropped.

(b) Express the height of the cliff as an integral.

(c) Find the height of the cliff.

4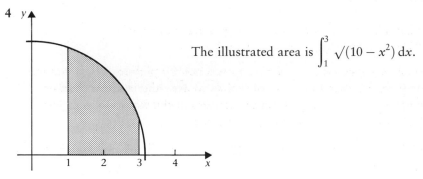

The illustrated area is $\int_1^3 \sqrt{(10 - x^2)} \, dx$.

Copy the diagram and draw in the two strips you use to estimate the area.

Calculate this area approximately using the mid-ordinate rule with two strips.

2.4.3 Numerical methods

In the previous section we obtained an approximation for π using the mid-ordinate rule with just two strips. You can improve this estimate by using more (thinner) strips.

To get a very accurate estimate of the integral you might have to use a very large number of strips.

The diagram shows the area represented by $\int_0^2 \sqrt{(4 - x^2)}\, dx$ divided into ten strips. (Only a few of the strips are shown.)

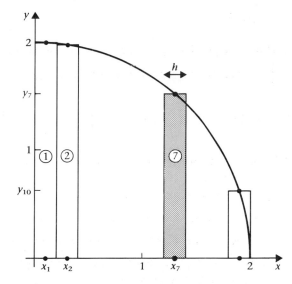

The width of each strip $= h = \dfrac{2}{\text{no. of strips}} = 0.2.$

Strip ① has a height of $\sqrt{(4 - 0.1^2)} = 1.9975$ and an area of $0.2 \times 1.9975 = 0.3995$ (to 4 decimal places).

To obtain an accurate estimate of an area you need to perform a large number of calculations. It is therefore very convenient to use either a spreadsheet or a programmable calculator to perform calculations of this kind and to explore, for example, the effect of using more and more strips.

The following are the results of using a spreadsheet to obtain an estimate for the area with 10 strips.

Number of strips = 10

Width of strip	Mid value (x)	y	Area of strip	Cumulative area
0.2	0.1	1.99750	0.3995	0.3995
0.2	0.3	1.97737	0.3955	0.7950
0.2	0.5	1.93649	0.3873	1.1823
0.2	0.7	1.87350	0.3747	1.5570
0.2	0.9	1.78606	0.3572	1.9142
0.2	1.1	1.67033	0.3341	2.2483
0.2	1.3	1.51987	0.3040	2.5523
0.2	1.5	1.32288	0.2646	2.8169
0.2	1.7	1.05357	0.2107	3.0276
0.2	1.9	0.62450	0.1249	3.1525

Estimate of area = 3.1525

.4D

The mid-ordinate rule

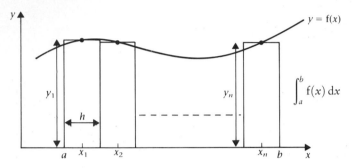

Consider the area represented by the integral above to be split up into n strips of equal width, h. Using the mid-ordinate rule to approximate the integral, the area of the first strip would be calculated as hy_1, the second strip would be hy_2, and so on.

1 (a) Express h in terms of a, b and n.

   (b) Express x_1 in terms of a and h.

   (c) By how much do you increase x each time you move up a strip?

The trapezium rule

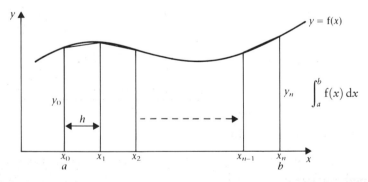

Again, consider the area represented by the integral above to be split up into n strips of equal width, h. Using the trapezium rule, the area of the first strip would be $\frac{1}{2}h(y_0 + y_1)$, the area of the second strip would be $\frac{1}{2}h(y_1 + y_2)$, and so on.

2 Derive a formula for the total area of the n strips shown.

The trapezium and the mid-ordinate rules with n strips both involve the sum of n areas.

The mid-ordinate rule

$$\int_a^b \mathrm{f}(x)\,\mathrm{d}x \approx \sum_{r=1}^{n} hy_r$$

where

$$h = \frac{b-a}{n}$$

$$x_1 = a + \tfrac{1}{2}h$$

$$x_{r+1} = x_r + h$$

$$y_r = \mathrm{f}(x_r)$$

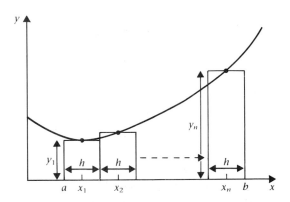

The trapezium rule

$$\int_a^b \mathrm{f}(x)\,\mathrm{d}x \approx \sum_{r=1}^{n} \tfrac{1}{2}h(y_{r-1} + y_r)$$

where

$$h = \frac{b-a}{n}$$

$$x_0 = a$$

$$x_{r+1} = x_r + h$$

$$y_r = \mathrm{f}(x_r)$$

The two rules can be summarised as follows.

The mid-ordinate rule

$$\int_a^b y\,\mathrm{d}x \approx hy_1 + hy_2 + hy_3 + \cdots + hy_n = h(y_1 + y_2 + \cdots + y_n)$$

The trapezium rule

$$\int_a^b y\,\mathrm{d}x \approx \tfrac{1}{2}h(y_0 + y_1) + \tfrac{1}{2}h(y_1 + y_2) + \cdots + \tfrac{1}{2}h(y_{n-1} + y_n)$$

$$= \tfrac{1}{2}h(y_0 + 2y_1 + 2y_2 + \cdots + y_n)$$

As you take more and more strips, the effect near the mid-point of any strip is similar to the effect you observe when a computer or calculator is used to zoom in on a small part of a graph.

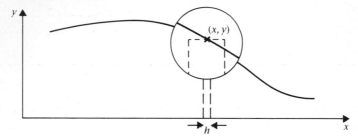

The area estimate given by either the trapezium or the mid-ordinate rule will become closer and closer to the true value, at least for all locally straight graphs.

For the graph of $y = \sqrt{(4 - x^2)}$ you may have noticed that the trapezium rule consistently under-estimates the true area whereas the mid-ordinate rule always over-estimates it.

The trapezium rule approximates a graph with a series of chords and it is easy to tell whether it will over- or under-estimate the area.

Over-estimate   Under-estimate

To predict if the mid-ordinate rule will over- or under-estimate an area, it is helpful to think of it as producing trapezia rather than rectangles!

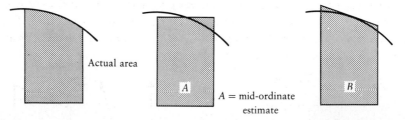

Actual area A = mid-ordinate
A estimate

The area of trapezium B is precisely the same as the area of rectangle A. (Can you see that this is so?)

Thus, you can think of the mid-ordinate rule as approximating a graph with a series of tangents to the graph.

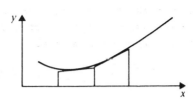

2.4 Exercise 3

1 State, where it is clear, whether a mid-ordinate rule estimate of each of the following areas will be too large or too small.

(a)
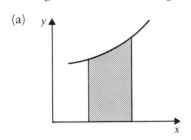

(b)
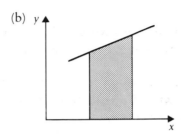

(c)
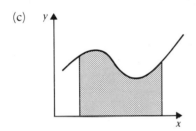

(d)
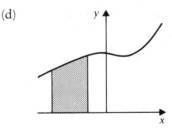

2 Repeat question 1 for the trapezium rule.

3 Among other things, a firm manufactures two types of metal alloy casting which will be machined into components for use in the car industry. The castings are in the form of prisms whose cross-sectional areas are shown below. (Measurements are in centimetres.)

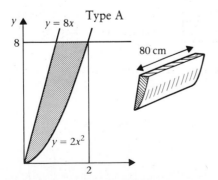

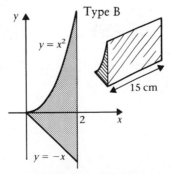

The firm received an order for 12 000 castings of type A and 8000 of type B. The production manager needs to calculate how much alloy to prepare. He does this by calculating the combined volume of all the castings and then adding on 5% for wastage. Calculate this volume and give your answer in cubic metres.

4 Evaluate $\displaystyle\int_0^1 \frac{1}{1+x^2}\,dx$ using the mid-ordinate rule with five strips.

2.4.4 'Negative' areas

When calculating areas, note that the mid-ordinate rule assigns positive values to areas above the x-axis and negative values to areas below the x-axis. This is because it uses sums of terms, each of the form yh.

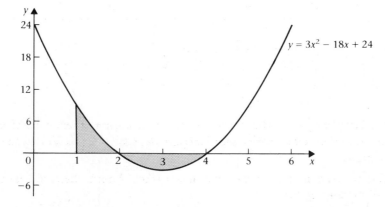

yh is positive
if y is positive

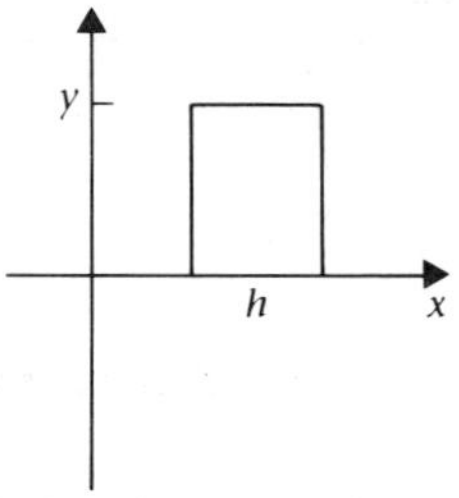

yh is negative
if y is negative

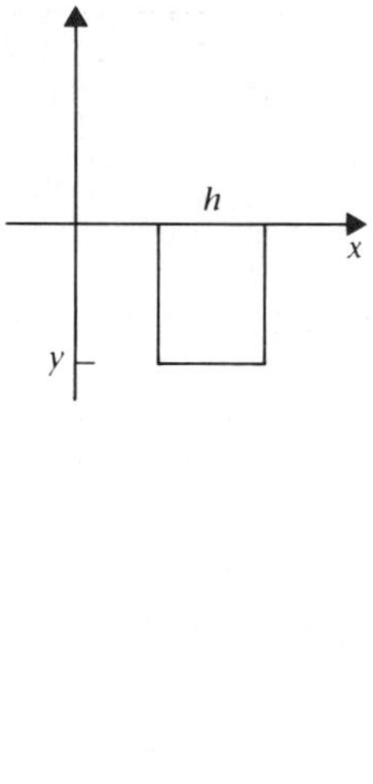

For example, consider

$$\int_a^b (3x^2 - 18x + 24)\,dx$$

for intervals given by

$$a = 1, b = 2; \quad a = 2, b = 4; \quad a = 1, b = 4$$

The graph of the function $3x^2 - 18x + 24$ is shown below.

$$y = 3x^2 - 18x + 24$$

Using a numerical method (either the mid-ordinate or trapezium rule) we obtain the following.

$$\int_1^2 (3x^2 - 18x + 24)\,dx = 4$$
Between $x = 1$ and $x = 2$ the graph is above the x-axis and the integral is positive.

$$\int_2^4 (3x^2 - 18x + 24)\,dx = -4$$
Between $x = 2$ and $x = 4$ the graph is below the x-axis and the integral is negative.

$$\int_1^4 (3x^2 - 18x + 24)\,dx = 0$$
The area below the x-axis is equal to the area above.

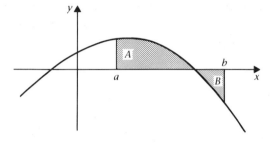

$$\int_a^b y\,dx = A - B$$

Note that **area** is always positive. The areas A and B indicated are both *positive*.

2.4 Exercise 4

1 In a balanced aquarium, the rate of change of the amount of carbon dioxide dissolved in a litre of water is found to have the following daily pattern.

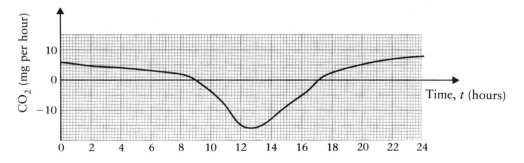

(a) During what part of the day is the amount of carbon dioxide dissolved in the aquarium water increasing? Estimate the total increase during this part of the day.

(b) Estimate the increase in the amount of carbon dioxide dissolved during a full 24-hour cycle.

2 (a) Sketch the graph of $y = x^2 - x - 2$.

(b) Estimate:

(i) $\displaystyle\int_{-4}^{4} y\,dx$ (ii) $\displaystyle\int_{-4}^{-1} y\,dx$ (iii) $\displaystyle\int_{-1}^{2} y\,dx$ (iv) $\displaystyle\int_{2}^{4} y\,dx$

(c) Estimate the area enclosed between the graph and the x-axis.

3 Water flows both into and out of a tank. The flow out is at a constant rate of 3 litres per minute, whereas the flow in starts off at 15 litres per minute but then decreases with time. The supervising engineer decides that the flow in at time t minutes may be modelled by

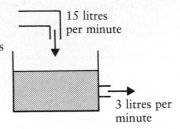

$$\frac{15}{t^2 + 1} \text{ litres per minute}$$

The tank initially contains 50 litres of water.

(a) The net flow into the tank is given by the expression

$$\frac{15}{t^2 + 1} - 3$$

Use a graph plotter to show the graph of this (time, flow) function. Why is $t = 2$ an important point on the graph?

(b) What does area under the (time, flow) graph represent and what is the significant difference between the areas above and below the axes?

(c) Estimate

$$\int \left(\frac{15}{t^2 + 1} - 3 \right) dt$$

over the time intervals:

(i) $t = 0$ to $t = 2$ (ii) $t = 2$ to $t = 5$ (iii) $t = 0$ to $t = 5$.

Explain the meaning of your answer in each case.

(d) How much water is there in the tank after 2 minutes and after 5 minutes? About how long will it take to empty the tank completely?

4 An alloy casting is in the form of a prism with cross-sectional area as shown.

Calculate $\displaystyle\int_{0}^{5} x\,dx$ precisely and use

the mid-ordinate rule to estimate

$$\int_{0}^{4} (x^2 - 4x)\,dx \quad \text{and} \quad \int_{4}^{5} (x^2 - 4x)\,dx.$$

Explain how you can use these integrals to evaluate the shaded area.

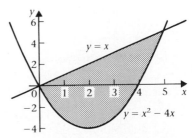

5 An alternative 'profile' for the prism in question 4 is obtained by translating the graphs up 5 units, so that they become the graphs of

$$y = x + 5 \quad \text{and} \quad y = x^2 - 4x + 5$$

(a) Sketch the graphs of these two functions on the same axes and shade in the area representing the cross-section of the alloy casting.

(b) Evaluate $\int_0^5 (x + 5)\,dx$ precisely, estimate $\int_0^5 (x^2 - 4x + 5)\,dx$ and use your answers to calculate the shaded area, confirming your answer to question 4.

After working through section 2.4 you should:

1 know what the area under a graph represents;

2 understand the process of estimating areas under graphs using the mid-ordinate rule and the trapezium rule;

3 understand the notation $\int_a^b y\,dx$ used to denote the *precise* area under a graph;

4 understand why increasing the number of strips increases the accuracy of the mid-ordinate and the trapezium rules;

5 understand why areas below the x-axis are calculated as being negative and areas above the x-axis are positive.

2 Introductory calculus

.5 Algebraic integration

2.5.1 The integral function

In section 2.4, you used the mid-ordinate rule with two strips to obtain the approximation to the area under the graph of $y = \sqrt{(4 - x^2)}$ given below.

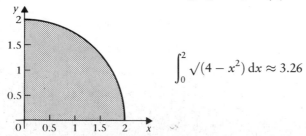

$$\int_0^2 \sqrt{(4 - x^2)}\, dx \approx 3.26$$

This is a value for the area of a quarter of a circle of radius 2 units, which you could use to estimate the area of the whole circle. While this is one way of finding the area of the circle, it is unlikely to be the way you would choose because you already know the formula

$$A = \pi r^2$$

for the area of a circle of radius r units.

The formula $A = \pi r^2$ for the area of a circle was known in classical times. In the seventeenth century, the calculus developed by Leibniz and Newton enabled formulas to be obtained for various areas. Today, calculators and computers can be used to work out such areas by numerical methods but there are still advantages in knowing simple formulas. This section will look at formulas for the areas under the graphs of a few simple functions, starting with $f(x) = x$.

Example 1

(a) Explain why $\int_0^u x\, dx = \frac{1}{2}u^2$.

(b) Use this formula to evaluate the integral

$$\int_3^7 x\, dx$$

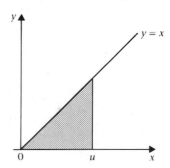

Solution

(a)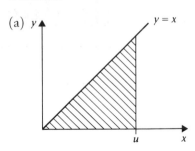

$$\int_0^u x\,dx = \text{area of shaded triangle}$$
$$= \tfrac{1}{2} \times \text{base} \times \text{height}$$
$$= \tfrac{1}{2} \times u \times u$$
$$= \tfrac{1}{2}u^2$$

(b)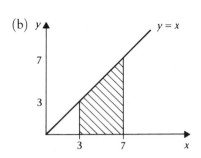

$$\int_3^7 x\,dx = \int_0^7 x\,dx - \int_0^3 x\,dx$$
$$= \tfrac{1}{2} \times 7^2 - \tfrac{1}{2} \times 3^2$$
$$= 24.5 - 4.5$$
$$= 20$$

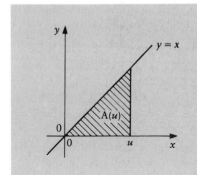

For areas measured from $x = 0$

$$f(x) = x \Rightarrow A(u) = \tfrac{1}{2}u^2 = \int_0^u x\,dx$$

The following examples investigate the integral function for $f(x) = x^2$.

 .5A

$A(u) = \displaystyle\int_0^u x^2\,dx$ is the area shaded.

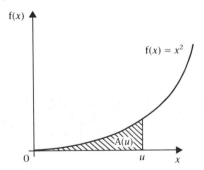

1

u	0	1	2	3	4	5	6
$A(u)$	0	?	$2\frac{2}{3}$	9	$21\frac{1}{3}$	$41\frac{2}{3}$	72

Using the mid-ordinate rule, calculate an estimate of the value of $A(u)$ missing from the table above.

2 Use the completed table of question 1 to estimate:

(a) $\displaystyle\int_{2}^{4} x^2 \, dx$ (b) $\displaystyle\int_{1}^{3} x^2 \, dx$

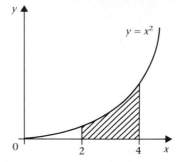

3 (a) Use the completed table from question 1 to draw the graph of $A(u)$ against u.

(b) Use suitable values from your graph to estimate:

(i) $\displaystyle\int_{2.5}^{3.1} x^2 \, dx$ (ii) $\displaystyle\int_{0.7}^{3.8} x^2 \, dx$

(c) Suggest a formula for $A(u)$ in terms of u.

You have some numerical evidence for the result that

$$f(x) = x^2 \Rightarrow A(x) = \tfrac{1}{3}x^3$$

This result, although true, has *not* of course been *proven* here, only suggested. You can now use these area functions, called **integral functions**, to evaluate integrals precisely and easily.

Example 2
Sketch the graph of $y = x^2$. Calculate the area given by

$$\int_{2.5}^{4} x^2 \, dx$$

Solution
For $f(x) = x^2$, $A(x) = \tfrac{1}{3}x^3$.

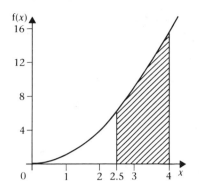

So

$$\int_{2.5}^{4} x^2 \, dx = A(4) - A(2.5)$$
$$= \tfrac{1}{3} \times 4^3 - \tfrac{1}{3} \times 2.5^3$$
$$= 16.125$$

A special notation is used when writing out the evaluation of integrals. For example,

$$\int_{2.5}^{4} x^2 \, dx = \left[\tfrac{1}{3} x^3 \right]_{2.5}^{4}$$

where the new notation on the right-hand side shows the integral function, $\tfrac{1}{3}x^3$, and also shows the limits, 2.5 and 4. The full solution to example 2 would therefore be written

$$\int_{2.5}^{4} x^2 \, dx = \left[\tfrac{1}{3} x^3 \right]_{2.5}^{4} = \tfrac{1}{3} \times 4^3 - \tfrac{1}{3} \times 2.5^3 = 16.125$$

Example 3

An object starts from rest and its speed $v \, \mathrm{m\,s^{-1}}$ at time t seconds is given by $v = t^2$. Calculate the distance travelled in the third second of its motion.

Solution

The (time, speed) graph shows that the distance travelled in the third second, as represented by the shaded area, will be given by

$$\int_{2}^{3} t^2 \, dt = \left[\tfrac{1}{3} t^3 \right]_{2}^{3}$$
$$= \tfrac{27}{3} - \tfrac{8}{3}$$
$$= \tfrac{19}{3}$$

The distance travelled is $6\tfrac{1}{3}\,\mathrm{m}$.

 .5B

1 (a) Sketch the graph of $y = x^2$.

(b) Use the symmetry of the quadratic graph in part (a) to explain why

$$\int_{2}^{4} x^2 \, dx = \int_{-4}^{-2} x^2 \, dx$$

(c) Use the formula for the integral function to confirm that

$$\int_2^4 x^2\,dx = \int_{-4}^{-2} x^2\,dx$$

2 (a) Using the integral function, evaluate:

(i) $\displaystyle\int_{-3}^{-1.5} x^2\,dx$ (ii) $\displaystyle\int_{-1.5}^{1.5} x^2\,dx$ (iii) $\displaystyle\int_{1.5}^{3} x^2\,dx$ (iv) $\displaystyle\int_{-1.5}^{3} x^2\,dx$

(b) Write down any relationships which connect two or more of these integrals. Explain, with the aid of a sketch graph, why these relationships are true.

3 (a)

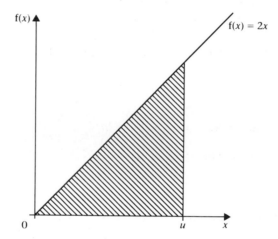

Calculate the shaded area in terms of u.

(b) What is the formula for the integral function?

4 For the function $f(v) = 3v$:

(a) sketch and shade the area between the graph and the horizontal axis, between the limits $v = 0$ and $v = u$;

(b) calculate the shaded area in terms of u.

5 Repeat question 4 using the following functions.

  (i) $f(x) = 2$ (ii) $g(t) = -3$

(iii) $f(t) = 2t$ (iv) $g(v) = -3v$

6 Write down the integral function for:

(a) $f(x) = m$ (b) $g(x) = mx$

when m is any constant and areas are measured from $x = 0$.

2.5.2 Integrals of polynomials

So far, you have met the following integral functions:

(a) If $f(x) = m$, then $A(x) = mx$

(b) If $f(x) = mx$, then $A(x) = \frac{1}{2}mx^2$

(c) If $f(x) = x^2$, then $A(x) = \frac{1}{3}x^3$

This might suggest that if, for example, $f(x) = 2x^2$, then the integral function would be $A(x) = \frac{2}{3}x^3$.

What about $A(x)$ if $f(x) = x^3$? The results for $f(x) = x$ and $f(x) = x^2$ might suggest that, if $f(x) = x^3$, then $A(x) = \frac{1}{4}x^4$.

These possibilities are explored in the questions which follow.

 .5C

1 (a) Sketch the graphs of $y = x^2$ and $y = 2x^2$.

(b) Shade the areas represented by the integrals:

$$\int_0^5 x^2\,dx \quad \text{and} \quad \int_0^5 2x^2\,dx$$

(c) What simple geometrical transformation connects the two regions?

(d) What will be the connection between $\displaystyle\int_a^b kx^2\,dx$ and $\displaystyle\int_a^b x^2\,dx$?

2 (a) Explain, with the aid of a copy of the graph of $y = 2x + 3$, and considering the areas A_1 and A_2, why

$$\int_0^u (2x + 3)\,dx = \left[x^2 + 3x\right]_0^u$$

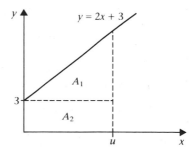

(b) Sketch the graph of $y = x^2 + 4$ and use it to explain, by considering suitable areas, why

$$\int_0^u (x^2 + 4)\,dx = \left[\tfrac{1}{3}x^3 + 4x\right]_0^u$$

3 Choose two functions of the form $ax^2 + bx + c$, where a, b and c are constants. (Do not always choose positive values for a, b and c.) Write down probable integral functions and check these either with a graph plotter, or by numerical integration with suitable limits.

4 Suggest a general formula for the integral function of any quadratic.

5 Repeat question 3 for a function of the form $ax^3 + bx^2 + cx + d$.

6 Suggest a general formula for the integral function of any cubic.

You now have the following rule for integrating:

> A polynomial function of the form $f(x) = a + bx + cx^2 + dx^3$ has integral function $A(x) = ax + \frac{1}{2}bx^2 + \frac{1}{3}cx^3 + \frac{1}{4}dx^4$.

Example 4

(a) Evaluate the integral $\displaystyle\int_0^3 (x - 4)(x - 2)(x + 1)\,dx$.

(b) Use a suitable sketch to interpret your answer.

Solution

(a) $\displaystyle\int_0^3 (x - 4)(x - 2)x + 1)\,dx = \int_0^3 (x^3 - 5x^2 + 2x + 8)\,dx$

$$= \left[\frac{x^4}{4} - \frac{5x^3}{3} + \frac{2x^2}{2} + 8x\right]_0^3 = 8.25$$

(b) The integral is the sum of a positive part from $x = 0$ to $x = 2$ and a negative part from $x = 2$ to $x = 3$.

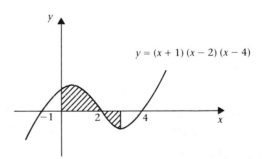

$y = (x + 1)(x - 2)(x - 4)$

2.5 Exercise 1

1 (a) Write down the integral which represents the shaded area.

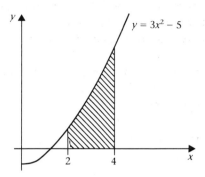

(b) Calculate this area.

2 (a) Evaluate $\int_{-2}^{1} (t^3 + 2t^2 - 3)\, dt$.

(b) Using a suitable sketch, explain why your answer is negative.

3 (a) Sketch the graph of $y = x^3 - 2x^2 - 5x + 6$, showing clearly where the curve cuts the x-axis.

(b) Calculate the total area enclosed by the curve and the x-axis.

4 A stone is projected vertically upwards such that its speed $(v\,\mathrm{m\,s^{-1}})$ after t seconds is given by

$$v = 5(5 - 2t)$$

(a) How far does the stone travel in the first two seconds?

(b) After how many seconds does it reach its maximum height?

(c) Calculate the maximum height the stone will reach.

5 Evaluate:

(a) $\int_{0}^{1} (x^3 - x)\, dx$ (b) $\int_{-4}^{2} (x + 1)\, dx$ (c) $\int_{-2}^{-1} x^2\, dx$

(d) $\int_{0}^{1} (x^2 - 2x + 1)\, dx$ (e) $\int_{1}^{2} (x^3 - 2x + 1)\, dx$ (f) $\int_{0}^{1} (x + 1)(x + 2)\, dx$

6 Sketch the graph of $y = 3x - x^2$, and then find the total area between the graph and the x-axis over the interval $[0, 5]$.

7 Find the values of a for which $\int_{1}^{a} (5 - 2x)\, dx = 0$.

8 The velocity, in $\mathrm{m\,s^{-1}}$, of a particle is given by $v = 4t - t^2$. Find the total distance travelled in the first 6 seconds.

2.5.3 Numerical or algebraic integration?

Many problems of integration can be solved easily using an appropriate algorithm on a hand-held calculator. So why have a formula for integral functions?

If you just want a numerical answer then numerical integration is fine. But in this section you will see that if you want to understand what is going on in a problem, then having a formula can be very helpful.

Example 5

A fruit farmer estimates that the average apple tree yields 45 kg of fruit and that it takes about 3 hours to pick all the apples. The fruit pickers are paid at a rate of £6 per hour and the farmer sells the apples for 60p per kg. Productivity decreases with time; in other words a person can pick more apples during the first half hour than during the last as the apples become harder to reach. The farmer assumes productivity decreases linearly with time.

(a) What weight of apples can be picked from the tree in t hours?

(b) What is the maximum profit that the farmer can make?

Solution

(a)

Area represents $\dfrac{\text{kg}}{\text{h}} \times \text{h} = \text{kg}$.

As 45 kg can be picked in 3 hours, the area shown is 45 and the height of the triangle must be 30.

Hence the formula for productivity is:

$$p = 30 - 10t$$

Then the weight of apples picked in t hours is

$$\int_0^t (30 - 10t) = \left[30t - 5t^2 \right]_0^t$$

$$= 30t - 5t^2$$

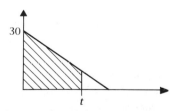

(b) If all the apples on a tree are picked, the farmer makes a profit of £9 (45 kg at 60p less 3 hours at £6). If, however, the person picking the apples stops after t hours, then the profit, £P, is obtained by calculating $(30t - 5t^2)$ kg at £0.60 less t hours at £6.

$$P = 0.6(30t - 5t^2) - 6t = 12t - 3t^2 \quad (0 \le t \le 3)$$

You can see that the farmer can increase the profit to £12 per tree by instructing the workers to spend only 2 hours on each tree and leave the last few apples for the birds.

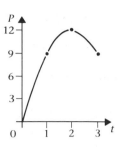

The following extended example provides further illustration of the usefulness of algebraic integration, this time in the industrial process of 'catalyst renewal'.

 .5D

You may know that a catalyst is often necessary to promote a chemical reaction. As the reaction goes on, the efficiency of the catalyst diminishes, until eventually it has to be renewed.

Suppose a chemical plant can produce a desired chemical at a rate of 100 kg per hour when the catalyst is fresh but that this productivity gradually decreases in such a way that after t hours the productivity has fallen to a value p kg per hour, where

$$p = 4(t - 5)^2$$

After 5 hours the catalyst has no effect whatsoever, so the graph does not apply beyond this point.

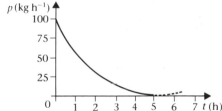

Maximising production

Clearly, what is important is the total amount of chemical produced in a given period of time and not the rate at which it is being produced (the productivity) at any particular time.

Suppose the catalyst is renewed after 3 hours. The production manager would want to know how much chemical is produced in this time. You can see that as one axis of the graph represents time in hours and the other represents productivity in kg hour^{-1}, the area under the graph will represent amount in kilograms.

$$\frac{\text{kg}}{\text{hour}} \times \text{hour} = \text{kg}$$

The total production of chemical is therefore given by the area under the graph.

The amount of chemical produced during the first 3 hours is

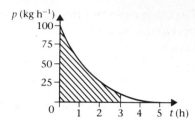

$$\int_0^3 4(t - 5)^2 \, dt$$

$$= 4 \int_0^3 (t^2 - 10t + 25) \, dt$$

1 Integrate algebraically to find the amount of chemical produced in the first 3 hours.

When the catalyst is renewed the whole plant is shut down. Suppose it takes 30 minutes to change the catalyst. In this case, the plant works on a 3.5-hour production cycle which can be shown graphically.

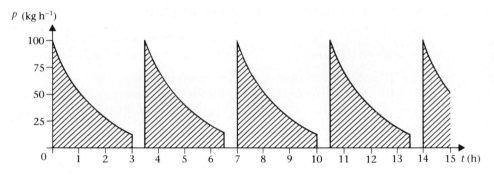

2 (a) What is the average output per hour (average productivity) for a complete production cycle?

(b) Suppose the catalyst is changed after 1.5 hours (i.e. the plant works on a 2-hour production cycle as it still takes 30 minutes to change the catalyst). Use the integral function you obtained in question 1 to find the average productivity.

(c) Suppose the catalyst is changed after 40 minutes. What would the average productivity be now?

3 The production manager wants to maximise production (i.e. run the plant so that as much chemical as possible is produced). Investigate different time intervals and determine the frequency with which the catalyst should be changed. Give your answer to the nearest minute.

Maximising profit

Suppose that the chemical is sold at a fixed price of £3 per kg and that there is a cost of £150 each time the catalyst is renewed, with other production costs more or less fixed at £50 per hour.

The company is not sure that maximising production is necessarily the same as maximising profit.

4E (a) If the catalyst is renewed every 3 hours, what profit does the company make on each kilogram of chemical sold?

(b) How much profit does the company make per hour in this case?

5E Investigate the profit per kilogram and profit per hour for other time intervals between catalyst renewal. To maximise annual profit, should the company maximise production, profit per kilogram, or profit per hour?

2.5.4 The fundamental theorem of calculus

You have been able to calculate some integrals precisely by first finding an integral function. For example, $x^3 + x$ is an integral function for $3x^2 + 1$ and so

$$\int_3^5 (3x^2 + 1)\, dx = \left[x^3 + x \right]_3^5$$

There is a simple relationship between a function and its integral function. The table below may help you to spot the connection.

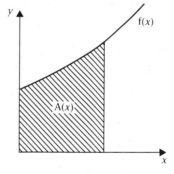

f(x)	1	x	$3x^2$	$3x^2 + 1$
A(x)	x	$\frac{1}{2}x^2$	x^3	$x^3 + x$

It is clear that if you differentiate the integral function, you obtain the function you are integrating, that is,

$$\frac{d}{dx}(A(x)) = f(x)$$

The process of differentiation (e.g. finding gradients) is an inverse process to that of integration (e.g. finding areas).

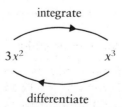

This remarkable relationship is called the **fundamental theorem of calculus**.

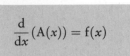

$$\frac{d}{dx}(A(x)) = f(x)$$

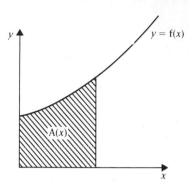

The graphs of all differentiable functions are locally straight, so it is sensible to investigate the connection between differentiation and integration by first considering linear functions.

The gradient of a line segment joining two points is constant. For example:

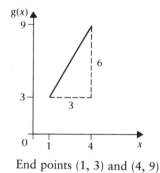

End points (1, 3) and (4, 9)

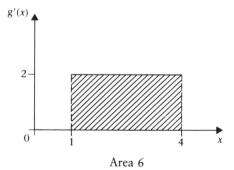

Area 6

 .5E

1 Draw diagrams similar to those above for line segments joining the points:

(a) $(1, 2), (5, 6)$ (b) $(4, 8), (6, 2)$ (c) $(3, 5), (6, 5)$

Can you spot a connection between the y-coordinates of the end points of the function and the area under the graph of the derived function?

Explain this connection by considering the definition of the gradient of a straight line.

When the graph of $g(x)$ is a *series* of connected line segments, the diagrams obtained are like those below.

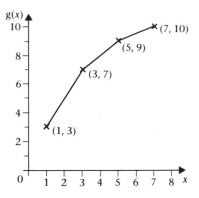

End points $g(1) = 3$ and $g(7) = 10$

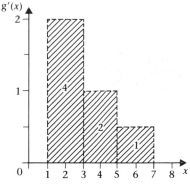

Area $\displaystyle\int_1^7 g'(x)\, dx = 4 + 2 + 1 = 7$

2 The following diagrams show two further ways of joining the end points $(1, 3)$ and $(7, 10)$ with three line segments.

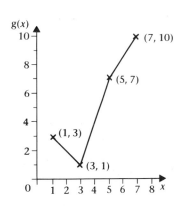

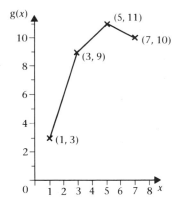

Sketch the graph of the function $g'(x)$ for each of the examples shown above, or any two similar examples of your own invention.

In each case, find $\displaystyle\int_1^7 g'(x)\, dx$. Is it always true that

$$\int_1^7 g'(x)\, dx = g(7) - g(1)?$$

3 Is it always true that $\displaystyle\int_a^b g'(x)\, dx = g(b) - g(a)$? Test this conjecture with *any* similar type of function of your own choice consisting of several line segments.

4E (a) The graph shows a derived function $g'(x)$. Construct a possible graph of the original function $g(x)$.

(b) Explain why your answer to (a) is not unique. Construct another possible graph of $g(x)$.

(c) In each case, check that

$$\int_1^6 g'(x)\,dx = g(6) - g(1).$$

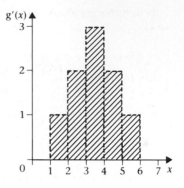

You have seen that, for a graph made up of connected straight-line segments,

$$\int_a^b g'(x)\,dx = g(b) - g(a)$$

Any differentiable function g is locally straight and so can be approximated by a series of straight-line segments.

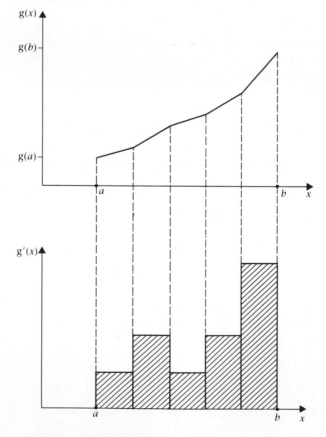

The gradient function g' can then be approximated by a step-graph.

This does not *prove* the fundamental theorem of calculus but at least indicates why:

> for any differentiable function f,
>
> $$\int_a^b f'(x)\,dx = f(b) - f(a)$$

The fact that integration and differentiation are inverse operations should not come as a surprise when you think about the way in which (time, speed) and (time, distance) graphs are related. Given a (time, distance) function you differentiate to find speed, and given a (time, speed) function you integrate to find distance.

The fundamental theorem gives a method of integrating which is easy to use. You must find a function which, when differentiated, gives the function you wish to integrate!

2.5 **Exercise 2**

1 (a) Evaluate:

   (i) $\displaystyle\int_{-1}^{1} (x^3 - 3x^2 - x + 3)\,dx$ (ii) $\displaystyle\int_{-1}^{3} (x^3 - 3x^2 - x + 3)\,dx$

   (b) Sketch the graph of $y = x^3 - 3x^2 - x + 3$. Hence explain the connection between your answers to (a) and the value of $\displaystyle\int_1^3 (x^3 - 3x^2 - x + 3)\,dx$.

2 Find $\displaystyle\int_1^2 (3x^2 - 10x)\,dx$.

3 (a) If $\displaystyle\int_c^d g(x)\,dx = \left[5x^2 + 3x\right]_c^d$, write down g(x).

   (b) If $\displaystyle\int_a^b h(t)\,dt = \left[2t^3 - 7\right]_a^b$, write down h(t).

4 Some areas which cannot be calculated directly can be obtained by considering a combination of integrals.

(a)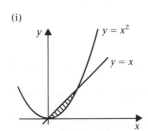

(i) Explain why the shaded area is given by

$$A = \int_0^a x^2 \, dx + \int_a^b (8 - x^2) \, dx$$

where a and b are to be found.

(ii) Find the shaded area A.

(b) Find the shaded areas illustrated in (i), (ii) and (iii) below.

(i)

(ii)

(iii)

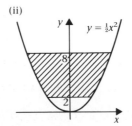

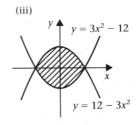

5 Find c if the shaded area is 6 square units.

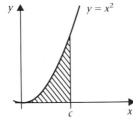

6E

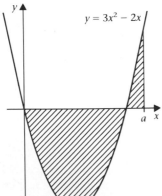

Find a such that

$$\int_0^a (3x^2 - 2x) \, dx = 0$$

2.5.5 The indefinite integral

Since $\dfrac{d(x^2 + 5x)}{dx} = 2x + 5$ you know that

$$\int_1^2 (2x + 5)\, dx = \left[x^2 + 5x\right]_1^2 = 8$$

 .5F

Differentiate each of:

$$x^2 + 5x + 1, \quad x^2 + 5x + 4, \quad x^2 + 5x - 3.$$

Explain why each of these functions could be used as an integral function for $2x + 5$ and why each gives the same answer for

$$\int_1^2 (2x + 5)\, dx$$

To evaluate an integral such as $\displaystyle\int_3^5 (2x)\, dx$ you can use *any* integral function of the form $x^2 + c$ where c is a constant, known as the **constant of integration**.

A general integral function such as $x^2 + c$ is called an **indefinite integral**.

An integral sign without any limits is used to denote indefinite integrals. A constant term '$+c$' should always be included, for example

$$\int (2x)\, dx = x^2 + c,$$

$$\int x^2\, dx = \tfrac{1}{3}x^3 + c$$

Integrals between limits, for example

$$\int_3^5 (2x)\, dx = 16$$

are called **definite integrals**. A definite integral has a (definite) numerical value.

For definite integrals, there is no need to include the constant of integration because it cancels out as shown in the following example.

$$\int_1^3 x^2\, dx = \left[\tfrac{1}{3}x^3 + c\right]_1^3$$
$$= (9 + c) - (\tfrac{1}{3} + c)$$
$$= 8\tfrac{2}{3} \quad \text{(irrespective of the value of } c\text{)}$$

You can therefore simply write

$$\int_1^3 x^2\, dx = \left[\tfrac{1}{3}x^3\right]_1^3 = 9 - \tfrac{1}{3} = 8\tfrac{2}{3}$$

Example 6

Find y as a function of x given that $y = 10$ when $x = 1$ and that

$$\frac{dy}{dx} = (3x - 1)(x + 3)$$

Solution

$$y = \int (3x - 1)(x + 3)\, dx$$

$$= \int (3x^2 + 8x - 3)\, dx$$

$$= x^3 + 4x^2 - 3x + c$$

But $y = 10$ when $x = 1$

$$\Rightarrow 10 = 1 + 4 - 3 + c$$

$$\Rightarrow \quad c = 8$$

$$\Rightarrow \quad y = x^3 + 4x^2 - 3x + 8$$

2.5 Exercise 3

1 Find the following:

(a) $\displaystyle\int (x^3 - 1)\, dx$ (b) $\displaystyle\int_1^3 (x + 1)(x - 2)\, dx$

2 Find y as a function of x, if:

(a) $\dfrac{dy}{dx} = x - 4$ (b) $\dfrac{dy}{dx} = 3x^2 + x$

(c) $\dfrac{dy}{dx} = x^2 + x + 1$ (d) $\dfrac{dy}{dx} = (x + 1)(x - 2)$

3 Express y as a function of x if:

(a) $\dfrac{dy}{dx} = 3x^2 + 4x$ and the (x, y) graph passes through $(1, 5)$.

(b) $\dfrac{dy}{dx} = x^2 + x + 1$ and the (x, y) graph passes through $(0, 3)$.

4 (a) If $\displaystyle\int_a^b (3x^2 - 2x + 5)\, dx = \Big[f(x) \Big]_a^b$, write down a possible $f(x)$.

(b) If $\displaystyle\int_c^d (2t + 1)(t - 4)\, dt = \Big[k(t) \Big]_c^d$, find a suitable $k(t)$.

5 The population of a certain country increases by approximately 0.2 million per year. Find an expression for the population P million in year t, remembering to include the constant of integration.

Given that the population was roughly 38 million in 1900, estimate the population in 2000.

6 A ball is released from rest on a ramp. Its speed t seconds later is $4t\,\mathrm{m\,s}^{-1}$.

(a) Show that $s = 2t^2 + c$, where c is the constant of integration. What information is provided by the value of c in this case?

(b) Write s in terms of t if the ball is released 0.5 m from the top of the ramp. Find the length of the ramp if the ball then takes 1 second to reach the bottom.

(c) Write s in terms of t if the ball is released 1 m from the top of the ramp. How long will it then take to reach the bottom of the ramp?

▶ 2.5 **Tasksheet E1 – Traffic (page 555)**

After working through section 2.5 you should:

1 understand what is meant by a definite integral;

2 understand what is meant by an indefinite integral and the need for a constant of integration;

3 be able to integrate polynomial functions and know that

$$\int (a\mathrm{f}(x) + b\mathrm{g}(x))\,\mathrm{d}x = a\int \mathrm{f}(x)\,\mathrm{d}x + b\int \mathrm{g}(x)\,\mathrm{d}x$$

4 be able to find areas by using combinations of appropriate integrals;

5 be able to integrate algebraically by using the fact that integration is the inverse process of differentiation:

$$\int_a^b \mathrm{f}'(x)\,\mathrm{d}x = \mathrm{f}(b) - \mathrm{f}(a)$$

2 Introductory calculus

Miscellaneous exercise 2

1 Find the derivative of each of the following:

(a) $y = x^2 + 7$ (b) $y = 2x^4 + 3x$ (c) $y = -4x^3 + 3$

(d) $y = 6x - 11$ (e) $y = 5x^2 - x - 8$ (f) $y = x - x^5$

2 Find the gradients of each of the following curves at the given points:

(a) $y = 2x^3 - x$ at $(1, 1)$ (b) $y = \frac{1}{2}x^4 + 3$ at $(-2, 11)$

(c) $y = 3 - x - x^3$ at $(2, -7)$

3 Find the equation of the tangent to the curve at the point given. Then sketch both curve and tangent on the same diagram.

(a) $y = x^2 + 4$ at $(-1, 5)$ (b) $y = 4x^3$ at $(1, 4)$

(c) $y = 3x^5 - 1$ at $(0, -1)$

4 Sketch the curve $y = 2x^2 + 3$. Calculate the points where the gradient is:

(a) 2   (b) 6   (c) 0

5 Find the point on $y = x^2 - 2x + 8$ where the tangent is parallel to the straight line $y = 4x + 1$.

6 Show that at $(0, 8)$ the gradient of the curve $y = x^3 - 3x^2 + 8$ is zero. Find another point on the curve where the gradient is also zero.

7 Find the equations of the tangents to $y = x^2$ at the points $(2, 4)$ and $(-1, 1)$. Verify that the tangents intersect at $(\frac{1}{2}, -2)$, and illustrate with a sketch.

8 Find the equations of the tangents to $y = x^3 - 1$ at $(1, 0)$ and $(2, 7)$. By solving simultaneous equations, find where the tangents intersect.

9 A particle moves along a straight line so that after t seconds its position in metres relative to a fixed point is given by

$$x = t^3 - 3t^2 + 10$$

(a) What is the formula for the velocity?

(b) When is the particle stationary?

(c) In which direction is the particle moving at time $t = 1$? For how long overall is it moving in this direction?

10 A ball is thrown vertically upwards so that its height after t seconds is $(30t - 5t^2)$ metres.

(a) What is its initial velocity?

(b) When is its velocity zero?

(c) How high does the ball go?

11 A stone is projected vertically upwards from the surface of the Moon, and its height after t seconds is $(20t - 0.8t^2)$ m.

(a) What is its initial speed?

(b) To what height does the stone rise?

(c) After how long will the stone be descending at $5\,\mathrm{m\,s}^{-1}$?

12 The curve $y = x + \frac{1}{50}x^3$ for $0 \le x \le 10$ is used to model the vertical cross-section of a sea wall, the units being metres.

(a) Draw a sketch of the wall, and find its height.

(b) Find the gradient of the wall at the base and at the top.

13 Find the stationary points of each of the following:

(a) $f(x) = x^2 - 4x + 3$ (b) $h(x) = 4 + x - x^2$

(c) $z = x^4 - 32x + 50$ (d) $q = 8t + 5t^2 - t^3$ for $t > 0$

14 A faulty firework moves so that its displacement s metres from a fixed point is given by $s = \frac{1}{4}t^3 - \frac{3}{4}t^2 + 1$ where t is the time in seconds and $0 \le t \le 4$. Find an expression for the velocity and hence find the two values of t at which the firework is stationary. Make a rough sketch of the graph of s against t, marking in clearly the stationary points.

15 Find all stationary points of the following. Hence sketch their graphs.

(a) $y = 7 - 8x + 2x^2$ (b) $y = x^4 - 2x^3$ (c) $y = \frac{1}{3}x^3 - x^2 - 3x + 1$

16 A flower bed is to be L-shaped as shown, and its perimeter is 36 m. Write down a formula for its area A m^2 and eliminate x to show that

$$A = 36y - 6y^2.$$

Hence find the values of x and y giving maximum area.

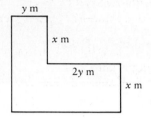

17 A body moves in a straight line such that its displacement in metres from a fixed point O is related to the time t seconds by $s = 12t^2 - t^3$ for $0 \le t \le 10$. Find

(a) when the body is stationary,

(b) when its velocity is 36 m s^{-1},

(c) the maximum velocity.

18 Find the areas under the graphs of the following
   (i) using the trapezium rule with six trapezia,
   (ii) by algebraic integration.

(a) $y = 30 + 2x - x^2$ from $x = 1$ to $x = 4$

(b) $y = 1 + 10x - x^3$ from $x = 0$ to $x = 3$

19 Find the areas of the regions bounded by the x-axis and the graphs of the following:

(a) $y = x^2 - 3x$ (b) $y = (x + 1)(6 - x)$ (c) $y = x(6 - x)^2$

20 Find the areas bounded by parts of the graphs of $y = 3x + 5$ and $y = x^2 + 1$.

21 The following definite integrals clearly have a meaning, yet their values cannot be found by the algebraic methods you have met so far. Find their approximate values, to 3 s.f.:

(a) $\displaystyle\int_1^2 \frac{1}{x}\,dx$ (b) $\displaystyle\int_{-1}^1 \frac{1}{1+x^2}\,dx$ (c) $\displaystyle\int_{-3}^0 2^x\,dx$

22 Determine the values of $\displaystyle\int_2^5 x^2\,dx$ and $\displaystyle\int_1^4 (x^2 + 2x + 1)\,dx$, and explain why your answers are related.

23 Find these indefinite integrals:

(a) $\int (x^3 + 6x^2)\,dx$ (b) $\int x(x^2 + 1)\,dx$ (c) $\int (ax^2 + bx + c)\,dx$

24 The velocity (in $m\,s^{-1}$) of a particle moving along the x-axis is given by $v = 5t - 3t^2$. Find an equation for the displacement x in terms of t, given that $x = 2$ when $t = 0$. When is x greatest? When is v greatest?

25 The rate at which water was flowing in a stream was measured at hourly intervals with the following results:

Time	12 a.m.	1 p.m.	2 p.m.	3 p.m.	4 p.m.
Rate (m^3/min)	8	10	11	9.5	9

(a) Plot these points on a graph. Join the points with straight lines. What does the area under the graph represent?

(b) Find a trapezium rule approximation for the volume of water flowing in the stream between 12 noon and 4 p.m.

26 Sketch graphs to illustrate the following integrals, and find their values:

(a) $\int_1^3 x\,dx$ (b) $\int_1^4 x^2\,dx$ (c) $\int_1^2 x^3\,dx$

27 Sketch graphs to illustrate the following definite integrals, and find expressions for their values:

(a) $\int_t^{2t} x^3\,dx \quad (t > 0)$ (b) $\int_{t+3}^{t+5} x\,dx \quad (t > -3)$

28 Find b in the following:

(a) $\int_2^b x^3\,dx = 60$ (b) $\int_3^b x^2\,dx = 63$ (c) $\int_b^{3b} x\,dx = 0.5 \quad (b > 0)$

3 Functions

.1 Algebra of functions

3.1.1 Composition of functions

Temperatures are often measured in degrees celsius or degrees fahrenheit. On the fahrenheit scale, water freezes at 32 °F and boils at 212 °F. The celsius scale is such that water freezes at 0 °C and boils at 100 °C.

The function f, given by

$$f(t) = \tfrac{5}{9}(t - 32)$$

converts a temperature of t degrees fahrenheit to celsius.

Temperature is a measure of the vibration of molecules and at -273 °C molecules are no longer vibrating, so -273 °C is the lowest temperature that can be obtained. This temperature is called 0 on the kelvin scale, or 0 K.

In order to convert from celsius to kelvin the function g is used.

$$g(t) = t + 273$$

To convert a temperature measured on the fahrenheit scale to one on the kelvin scale would require conversion to the celsius scale first – using $f(t)$ – then to the kelvin scale – using $g(t)$. It would be helpful to have a function which does this conversion directly.

The rule for converting from °F directly into K can be illustrated by using an arrow graph or a flow diagram.

	f		g	
°F	$\longrightarrow$	°C	$\longrightarrow$	K
212	$\longrightarrow$	100	$\longrightarrow$	373
122	$\longrightarrow$	50	$\longrightarrow$	323
32	$\longrightarrow$	0	$\longrightarrow$	273
t	$\longrightarrow$	$\tfrac{5}{9}(t - 32)$	$\longrightarrow$	$\tfrac{5}{9}(t - 32) + 273$

$$t \longrightarrow \boxed{f} \xrightarrow{\tfrac{5}{9}(t-32)} \boxed{g} \xrightarrow{\tfrac{5}{9}(t-32)+273}$$

The resulting function is the **composition** of the two functions f and g.

Note that, since $f(122) = 50$, you can write $g(50)$ as $g(f(122))$ or, with fewer brackets, as $gf(122)$. So, contrary to what might be expected, the notation for f followed by g is gf.

$$x \longrightarrow \boxed{f} \longrightarrow \boxed{g} \longrightarrow gf(x)$$

For $fg(x)$, x is first put through the function g, and the output from g is fed through f.

$$x \longrightarrow \boxed{g} \longrightarrow \boxed{f} \longrightarrow fg(x)$$

Example 1

If f and g are the functions given by $f(x) = x^2$ and $g(x) = 2x + 3$, then find the functions fg, gf and gg.

Solution

$$fg(x) = f(g(x)) = f(2x + 3) = (2x + 3)^2$$

$$gf(x) = g(f(x)) = g(x^2) = 2x^2 + 3$$

$$gg(x) = g(g(x)) = g(2x + 3) = 2(2x + 3) + 3$$

$$= 4x + 9$$

Tasksheet S1 gives further practice in working with functions, should you need it.

▶ 3.1 **Tasksheet S1 – Functions of functions (page 535)**

3.1 **Exercise 1**

1 For each of the functions f and g defined below, evaluate   (i) $fg(x)$,   (ii) $gf(x)$.

(a) $f(x) = 2x + 3$, $g(x) = x^3$

(b) $f(x) = 2x + 1$, $g(x) = \dfrac{1}{x}$

(c) $f(x) = 3x + 2$, $g(x) = 5 - x$

(d) $f(x) = 1 - x^2$, $g(x) = 1 - 2x$

2 On a gas bill, the cost of x therms of gas used by a consumer is given by £c, where

$$c(x) = 9 + 0.4x$$

A gas meter indicates the amount of gas in cubic feet used by a consumer. The number of therms of heat from x cubic feet of gas is given by the function t:

$$t(x) = 1.034x$$

(a) Find the function ct.

(b) What does ct(x) represent?

3 Each of the following is of the form fg(x). Identify f(x) and g(x).

(a) $\dfrac{1}{x+2}$ (b) $\dfrac{1}{x}+2$ (c) $\dfrac{1}{2x+3}$ (d) $2\sqrt{x}-1$

(e) $\dfrac{1}{x^2}+3$ (f) $(2x+1)^4$ (g) $x^8 - 4x^4 - 3$

4 ff(x) means the function f applied twice to x; this is often written as $f^2(x)$.

If each of the expressions below is f(x), write down an expression for $f^2(x)$ in each case.

(a) $x+2$ (b) x^2 (c) $2x-3$ (d) x (e) $\sin x$ (f) $\dfrac{1}{x}$

5 If $f(x) = x - 3$ and $g(x) = x^2$, it is possible to combine these functions in many ways.

(a) Explain why $(x - 3)^2 - 3 = \text{fgf}(x)$.

(b) Express each of the following as combinations of f and g.

    (i) $x^2 - 3$ (ii) $(x^2 - 3)^2$ (iii) $x - 6$ (iv) $x^8 - 3$ (v) $(x - 3)^4 - 6$

6 Using $s(x) = \sin x$ and $q(x) = x^2$, distinguish clearly between:

(a) $\sin^2 x$, i.e. $(\sin x)^2$ (b) $\sin x^2$, i.e. $\sin(x^2)$ (c) $\sin \sin x$, i.e. $\sin(\sin x)$

7 In each case, find fg(x) and gf(x), and then determine the set of values for which fg$(x) = \text{gf}(x)$.

(a) $f(x) = x^2$, $g(x) = x + 3$ (b) $f(x) = x - 5$, $g(x) = x + 2$

(c) $f(x) = 2x - 1$, $g(x) = 3x + 1$ (d) $f(x) = \dfrac{1}{x}$, $g(x) = x^3$

(e) $f(x) = 2x + 1$, $g(x) = \frac{1}{2}(x + 1)$ (f) $f(x) = \sqrt{x}$, $g(x) = x - 1$

8 Four functions, e, f, g and h, are defined by

$$e(x) = x \qquad f(x) = -x \qquad g(x) = \frac{1}{x} \qquad h(x) = -\frac{1}{x}$$

Then $fg(x) = f\left(\frac{1}{x}\right) = -\frac{1}{x} \Rightarrow fg = h$

Complete the following table, where each entry is one of e, f, g or h.

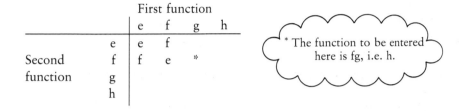

		First function			
		e	f	g	h
	e	e	f		
Second	f	f	e	*	
function	g				
	h				

* The function to be entered here is fg, i.e. h.

3.1.2 Range and domain

You have seen that the function $f(t) = \frac{5}{9}(t - 32)$ converts °F to °C.

The lowest attainable temperature is $-273\,°C$ and this places a corresponding restriction on temperatures in °F.

> The set of values for which a function is defined is called the **domain** and the set of values which the function can take is called the **range**.

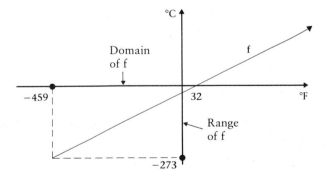

In a Cartesian graph of a function, the domain is all or part of the x-axis and the range is all or part of the y-axis.

For example, the function

$$f(x) = x^2 - 2x$$

has domain all real numbers but the range consists only of the real numbers greater than or equal to -1, that is $\{y \in \mathbb{R} : y \geq -1\}$.

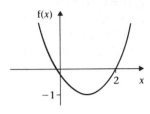

The function

$$f(x) = \sqrt{(x - 4)}$$

has domain $\{x \in \mathbb{R} : x \geq -4\}$ and range $\{y \in \mathbb{R} : y \geq 0\}$.

When only the formula for a function is given, it is usual to take as the domain *all* the numbers for which the formula can be worked out; for example, given the function g such that

$$g(x) = \frac{1}{x - 1}$$

you would assume that the domain is all numbers except 1. The range is then all numbers except 0, as can be seen from the graph.

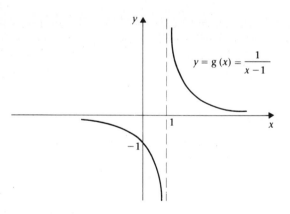

 .1A

Give the natural domain and find the corresponding range for the function h such that

$$h(x) = \frac{1}{x^2}$$

Sketch the graph of $y = x^2$ and deduce the sketch for $y = \frac{1}{x^2}$.

Two or more values in the domain of a function can correspond to the same value in the range. Such a function is said to be **many-to-one**. For example, the function $y = x^2$ is many-to-one.

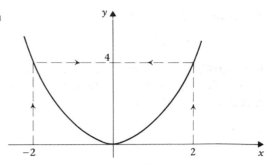

The function $y = x^3$ is an example of a **one-to-one** function.

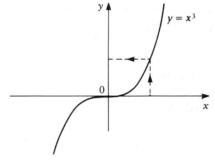

However, it is a requirement that a value in a function's domain *must correspond to only one value in the range*. Functions, therefore, cannot be one-to-many (although they can be many-to-one). So, for example, $x = y^2$ does not define y as a function of x because, if $x = 9$, $y = \pm 3$ (i.e. there are *two* values in the range).

3.1.3 Inverse functions

To return to the example of temperature, the **inverse** function reverses what was done by f – in other words it converts °C to °F. In building up the function f, two functions were used.

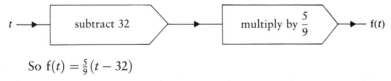

So $f(t) = \frac{5}{9}(t - 32)$

To find the inverse function you need to 'undo' this.

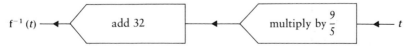

The inverse of f is denoted by f^{-1}. The flow diagram above shows that
$$f^{-1}(t) = \tfrac{9}{5}t + 32$$

As a quick check, note that
$$f(212) = 100 \qquad \text{and} \qquad f^{-1}(100) = 212$$

As noted in the last section, if $f(x) = x^2$ then both $f(3)$ and $f(-3)$ give $f(x) = 9$ and consequently $f^{-1}(9)$ is ambiguous, since it could mean both -3 and $+3$. A function must be unambiguous – a single input must give rise to a *unique* output. Thus f does not have an inverse function if its domain is unrestricted.

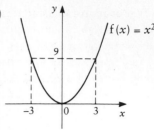

The inverse function, $f^{-1}(x)$, does exist if the domain is restricted to non-negative numbers, that is if $f(x) = x^2$ $\{x \geq 0\}$, then $f^{-1}(x) = \sqrt{x}$.

In general, a function must be one-to-one in order to have an inverse.

In order to avoid ambiguity, mathematicians take $\sqrt{x}$ to mean the *positive* square root of x, and $\sqrt[4]{x}, \sqrt[6]{x}, \sqrt[8]{x}, \ldots$, to mean the positive fourth, sixth, eighth, ... roots of x.

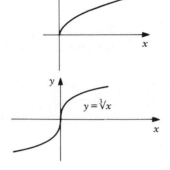

The same problem does not arise with $\sqrt[3]{x}$ because $x \rightarrow x^3$ is a one-to-one function.

Example 2

Find the inverse of $f(x) = \dfrac{1}{1 - x}$ $\{x \neq 1\}$

Solution

Flow chart for f

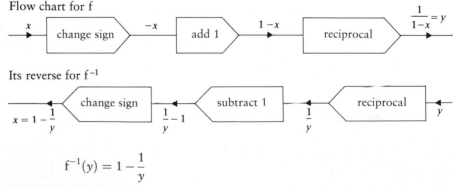

$$f^{-1}(y) = 1 - \frac{1}{y}$$

As a quick check, note that $f(3) = -0.5$, $f^{-1}(-0.5) = 3$.

The letter y can be changed for any other and it is usual to write

$$f^{-1}(x) = 1 - \frac{1}{x}.$$

If a function f is to have an inverse function, the situation must be as follows.

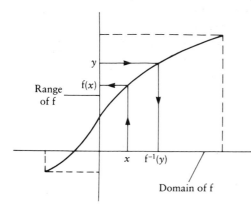

Since f is a function, any vertical line cuts the graph once only.

f^{-1} is a function: any horizontal line from a value on the range of f cuts the graph once only.

The following examples investigate the relationship between the graph of a function f, and the graph of its inverse function f^{-1}.

 .1B

1 (a) What is $f^{-1}(f(x))$?

(b) Explain why the domain of f is the range of f^{-1}.

(c) Sketch the graph of a function with no inverse function.

(d) If both f and f^{-1} are functions, explain why f must be a one-to-one function.

2 For each function given below, choose a suitable domain so that the function has an inverse function and plot on the same axes (which should have equal scales) the graphs of the function, its inverse and $y = x$. Define the inverse function in each case.

(a) $f(x) = 3x + 5$ (b) $g(x) = x^2 - 7$

(c) $h(x) = (x - 7)^2$ (d) $r(x) = \sqrt{x + 6}$

3 What simple transformation will map the graph of $y = f(x)$ onto the graph of $y = f^{-1}(x)$?

4 The graph of:

(a) $f(x) = (x + 5)^2 - 3$ (b) $f(x) = 3(2x - 1)$

is reflected in the line $y = x$. Find the equation of the image.

5 (a) Investigate the sequences:

   (i) $x_{n+1} = \dfrac{1}{x_n}$ (ii) $x_{n+1} = -x_n$

   for various different values of x_1 in each case.

(b) What is the inverse of:

   (i) $f(x) = \dfrac{1}{x}$, the reciprocal function, and

   (ii) $f(x) = -x$, the 'change sign' or 'multiply by -1' function?

   Why do you think these functions are called **self-inverse**? Sketch the graphs of the two functions and explain how they are related to what you observed in question 3.

6 Find the inverse of each of the functions f defined as follows.

   (a) $f(x) = \dfrac{1}{2x + 1}$ $\{x \neq -\frac{1}{2}\}$ (b) $f(x) = 12 - x$ (or $-x + 12$) $\{x \in \mathbb{R}\}$

   (c) $f(x) = \dfrac{1}{x} - 1$ $\{x \neq 0\}$ (d) $f(x) = \dfrac{8}{(x + 1)^2}$ $\{x > -1\}$

   (e) $f(x) = \sqrt{(1 - x^2)}$ $\{0 \leq x \leq 1\}$ (f) $f(x) = 4 - (x - 2)^2$ $\{x \geq 2\}$

   Which of these functions are self-inverse? What are the equations of the lines of symmetry of the graphs of the self-inverse functions?

The graphs of a function and its inverse have reflection symmetry in the line $y = x$.

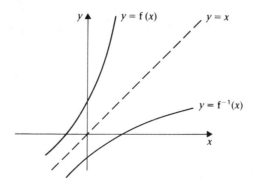

A function f has an inverse function only if f is one-to-one.

Example 3

If $f(x) = (x - 3)^2 + 4 \{x \geq 3\}$, find $f^{-1}(x)$. Sketch the graphs of $f(x)$ and $f^{-1}(x)$.

Solution

To find the inverse function, represent f by a flow chart showing the simpler functions which compose it.

Then reverse the flow chart.

$$f^{-1}(x) = \sqrt{(x - 4)} + 3 \quad \{x \geq 4\}$$

Note that x is usually chosen to represent the input variable for the inverse function as well as the original function.

The graphs of the function and the inverse function are sketched below.

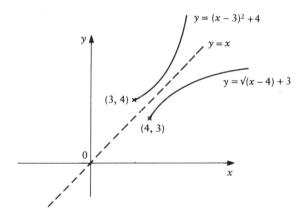

3.1.4 Rearranging formulas

The process of finding an inverse function is identical to that of rearranging a formula. In the temperature example,

$$f(t) = \tfrac{5}{9}(t - 32)$$

converts °F to °C, which could be written as

$$C = \tfrac{5}{9}(F - 32)$$

$$f^{-1}(t) = \tfrac{9}{5}t + 32$$

converts °C to °F, which could be written as

$$F = \tfrac{9}{5}C + 32$$

The formula for C in terms of F has been rearranged to give F in terms of C. The process can be seen as applying the same function to both sides of the formula and is often set out in this way.

$$C = \tfrac{5}{9}(F - 32) \qquad \text{Multiply both sides by } \tfrac{9}{5}$$

$$\tfrac{9}{5}C = F - 32 \qquad \text{Add 32 to both sides}$$

$$\tfrac{9}{5}C + 32 = F$$

This approach may be used for finding inverse functions and is equivalent to the flow diagram as shown below:

$$C = \tfrac{5}{9}(F - 32)$$
$$\tfrac{9}{5}C = F - 32$$
$$\tfrac{9}{5}C + 32 = F$$

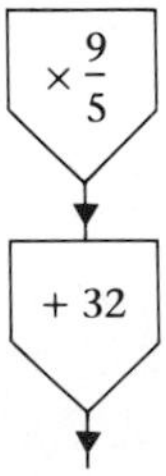

$$\times \tfrac{9}{5}$$

$$+\,32$$

Example 4

Make x the subject of the formula $y = (3x + 1)^2$.

Solution

$$y = (3x + 1)^2 \qquad \text{Take the square root of each side.}$$

$$\pm\sqrt{y} = 3x + 1 \qquad \text{Subtract 1 from both sides.}$$

$$\pm\sqrt{y} - 1 = 3x \qquad \text{Divide both sides by 3.}$$

$$\frac{\pm\sqrt{y} - 1}{3} = x$$

The '$\pm$' is appropriate here as we are not defining functions, simply changing the subject of the formula.

There is more practice on rearranging formulas on tasksheet S2.

▶ **3.1 Tasksheet S2 – Rearranging formulas (page 536)**

A particular difficulty arises with the flow chart method when the letter that is to be the subject of the formula appears more than once. A different strategy is then required, which is illustrated by the next example.

Example 5

Find the inverse of the function

$$f(x) = \frac{x+1}{x+2} \quad \{x \neq -2\}$$

Solution

Let $y = f(x)$, then rearrange to find x in terms of y.

$$y = \frac{x+1}{x+2}$$ Multiply both sides by $x + 2$.

$$y(x+2) = x+1$$ Multiply out the brackets.

$$yx + 2y = x + 1$$ Collect x terms together by subtracting $2y$ and then subtracting x from both sides.

$$yx - x = 1 - 2y$$ Factorise the left-hand side.

$$x(y-1) = 1 - 2y$$ Divide both sides by $y - 1$.

$$x = \frac{1 - 2y}{y - 1}$$

Thus the inverse of the function which maps x to $\dfrac{x+1}{x+2}$ is

$$f^{-1}(y) = \frac{1 - 2y}{y - 1}$$

x is conventionally chosen as the input variable and so it is usual to write

$$f^{-1}(x) = \frac{1 - 2x}{x - 1} \quad \{x \in \mathbb{R}, \quad x \neq 1\}$$

3.1 Exercise 2

1 Make x the subject of the following formulas.

(a) $y = \dfrac{5x - 3}{2}$ (b) $y = \dfrac{3}{4}(x - 5)$

(c) $y = (x - 5)^2 + 4$ (d) $y = \dfrac{1}{x - 3}$

2 Taking the formulas in question 1 as of the form $y = f(x)$, write down in each case the formula for $f^{-1}(x)$, stating also the greatest possible domain and range of f for which f^{-1} can be defined.

3 A major chemical company researching crop yields tries out a new pesticide. The results indicate that, per hectare, for a kg of pesticide the extra yield y kg of a crop is given by

$$y = \frac{900a}{2 + a}$$

(a) What is the formula which gives the amount, a kg, of pesticide needed to return an extra yield of y kg?

(b) Explain why the values of y will lie between 0 and 900.

4 Make x the subject of the formulas:

(a) $y = \dfrac{x-1}{x+1}$ (b) $y = \dfrac{2-x}{x+3}$

5 The graph of

$$y = \dfrac{x}{2x+1}$$

is reflected in the line $y = x$. Find the equation of the image and use a graph plotter to check your answer.

(Hint: how are the graphs of $y = f(x)$ and $y = f^{-1}(x)$ related?)

6 If $f(x) = \dfrac{1+x^2}{1-x^2}$ $\{x < -1\}$, find $f^{-1}(x)$.

3.1.5 Parameters and functions

If a holidaymaker takes £x into her local bank, which offers an exchange rate of 8 francs to £1 and charges a commission of £4, the formula

$$y = 8(x-4)$$

gives y, the number of francs that she will receive.

The formula for an exchange rate of a francs to £1 and a commission of £b would be $y = a(x-b)$.

The formula $y = a(x-b)$ is of a more general kind than those met in 3.1.4, and the roles of a and b are different from those of x and y. a and b can vary, but for any given function mapping x onto y they will act as constants. They are called **parameters**.

$y = 8(x-4)$ gives the value of £x in francs, at the exchange rate given above. To find the number of pounds required to buy y francs you first need to rearrange the formula, giving

$$x = \dfrac{y}{8} + 4$$

Using the more general formula, the value of y francs in pounds is found by rearranging $y = a(x-b)$ to give

$$x = \dfrac{y}{a} + b$$

The same techniques used in finding the inverse of a function will be suitable if parameters replace numbers.

Example 6

Make a the subject of the formula $s = ut + \frac{1}{2}at^2$.

Solution

$$s - ut = \frac{1}{2}at^2 \qquad \text{subtracting } ut \text{ from both sides}$$

$$2s - 2ut = at^2 \qquad \text{multiplying both sides by 2}$$

$$\frac{2s}{t^2} - \frac{2u}{t} = a \qquad \text{dividing both sides by } t^2$$

So $\quad a = \dfrac{2s}{t^2} - \dfrac{2u}{t}$

3.1 **Exercise 3**

1 Make the variable shown in brackets the subject of the formula.

(a) $P = aW + b$ $\quad$ (W) $\qquad$ (b) $C = 2\pi r$ $\quad$ (r) $\qquad$ (c) $s = \dfrac{n}{2}(a + l)$ $\quad$ (l)

(d) $s = \dfrac{a}{1 - r}$ $\quad$ (r) $\qquad$ (e) $\dfrac{1}{R} = \dfrac{1}{x} + \dfrac{1}{y}$ $\quad$ (x)

2 The driver of a car travelling at v m.p.h. sees an obstruction ahead of him and immediately applies the brakes. The distance, d feet, that the car travels from the time that the driver sees the obstruction until the car stops is given by

$$d = \frac{(v + 10)^2}{20} - 5$$

(a) Find the stopping distance for a car travelling at:

(i) 30 m.p.h. $\qquad$ (ii) 50 m.p.h. $\qquad$ (iii) 70 m.p.h.

(b) Rearrange the formula to find v in terms of d.

(c) The driver sees an obstruction 250 feet ahead of him. What is the greatest speed at which he can be driving if he is to pull up before he reaches the obstruction?

3 If a metal rod is heated, the length increases according to the equation

$$l = l_0(1 + \alpha t)$$

where l is the final length, l_0 is the initial length, t is the increase in temperature and α is the coefficient of expansion of the rod.

Find α if a steel rod of length 1 metre expands to a length of 1.004 m when heated through 230 °C.

4 Einstein's famous equation $E = mc^2$ gives the energy equivalent to a mass m, where c is the speed of light. Rearrange this equation to find c in terms of E and m.

5 If a body of mass m moving with velocity u is later observed to be moving with velocity v then the change in kinetic energy of the body is given by

$$E = \tfrac{1}{2}mv^2 - \tfrac{1}{2}mu^2$$

Rearrange this formula to give v in terms of E, m and u.

6 A pendulum consists of a light steel rod with a heavy metal disc attached to the end. The time, T, taken for the pendulum to swing through a complete cycle is given by

$$T = 2\pi\sqrt{\left(\frac{l}{g}\right)}$$

where l is the length of the pendulum and g is a constant.

Complete the following steps to find l in terms of T and g.

$$\_\ \_\ \_\ \_\ \_ = \sqrt{\left(\frac{l}{g}\right)} \qquad \text{[square both sides]}$$

$$\Rightarrow \_\ \_\ \_\ \_\ \_ = \frac{l}{g}$$

$$\Rightarrow \_\ \_\ \_\ \_\ \_ = l$$

For a grandfather clock, $T = 2$ and $g = 9.81$ in SI units. The equation then gives a value for l in metres. Find this value.

7 (a) Show that the surface area of a solid cylinder of radius r and height h is

$$S = 2\pi r(r + h)$$

(b) Rearrange the formula $S = 2\pi r(r + h)$ to give h in terms of S and r.

8 In rearranging formulas a student proceeds as follows. Simplify her working in order to arrive at more elegant solutions.

(a) The volume V of a cone of radius r and height h is

$$V = \tfrac{1}{3}\pi r^2 h \Rightarrow \frac{V}{\frac{1}{3}\pi} = r^2 h$$

$$\Rightarrow \quad r = \sqrt{\left(\frac{\left(\frac{V}{\frac{1}{3}\pi}\right)}{h}\right)}$$

(b) The total interest $£I$ on $£P$ invested at $r\%$ for n years is given by

$$I = \frac{Prn}{100} \Rightarrow I \times 100 = Prn$$

$$\Rightarrow r = \frac{\left(\dfrac{I \times 100}{P}\right)}{n}$$

9 Locate and correct the errors in the following.

(a) The current I flowing in a circuit consisting of a resistance R and n batteries of voltage E each and internal resistance r each is given by

$$I = \frac{nE}{R + nr} \Rightarrow IR = \frac{nE}{nr} \Rightarrow R = \frac{E}{Ir}$$

(b) The kinetic energy E of a body of mass m moving with speed v is

$$E = \tfrac{1}{2}mv^2$$

$$\Rightarrow v = \frac{\sqrt{(\tfrac{1}{2}m)}}{E}$$

3.1.6 Functions and transformations of graphs

You have seen that the graph of the inverse of a function is obtained by reflecting the graph of that function in the line $y = x$. You can now look at other transformations of graphs and find how the equations of the resulting graphs relate to those of the original graphs.

 .1c

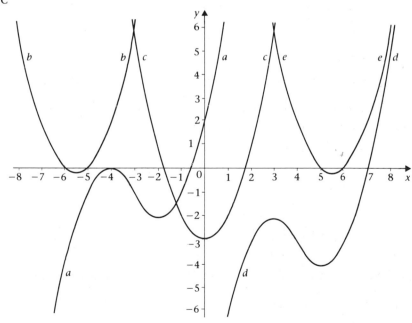

1 Which of these graphs can be mapped onto other graphs in the diagram?

2 What transformations would map:

(a) graph b onto graph c,

(b) graph a onto graph d,

(c) graph b onto graph e?

3 Is there more than one possible answer to any of parts (a) to (c)?

In chapter 1 you saw that the image of the graph of $y = x^2$ under the translation $\begin{bmatrix} -2 \\ 3 \end{bmatrix}$ is the graph of $y = (x + 2)^2 + 3$. Using function notation, this can be expressed as

$$\text{the image of } y = f(x) \text{ under a translation } \begin{bmatrix} -2 \\ 3 \end{bmatrix} \text{ is } y = f(x + 2) + 3$$

In general:

> The image of $y = f(x)$ under a translation $\begin{bmatrix} -p \\ q \end{bmatrix}$ is $y = f(x + p) + q$.

 3 .1D

1 The function f is defined by $f(w) = w^4$.

(a) Write down the expressions $f(x)$, $f(x) + 2$ and $f(x + 3)$, then plot the graphs of $y = f(x)$, $y = f(x) + 2$ and $y = f(x + 3)$ on the same screen.

(b) What translation would transform the graph of $y = f(x)$ onto the graph of:

(i) $y = f(x) + 2$ (ii) $y = f(x + 3)$?

2 The function g is defined by $g(u) = \dfrac{1}{u}$.

(a) Write down the expressions $g(x)$, $g(x + 4)$ and $g(x + 4) + 3$, then plot the graphs of $y = g(x)$, $y = g(x + 4)$ and $y = g(x + 4) + 3$ on the same screen.

(b) What translation transforms the graph of $y = g(x)$ onto the graph of:

(i) $y = g(x + 4)$ (ii) $y = g(x + 4) + 3$?

3

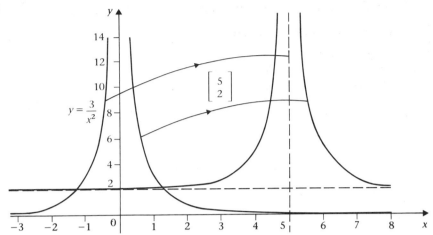

The graph of $y = \dfrac{3}{x^2}$ is translated through $\begin{bmatrix} 5 \\ 2 \end{bmatrix}$ as shown above. Suggest an equation for the new curve. Check your answer by plotting the graph of your equation.

4 By completing the square, rewrite $y = x^2 + 4x + 3$ in the form $y = (x + p)^2 + q$.

What translation will map the graph of $y = x^2$ onto the graph of $y = x^2 + 4x + 3$? Check your answer by plotting both graphs on the same screen.

Example 7

Find the image of the graph of $y = 5\sqrt{x}$ under a translation $\begin{bmatrix} 4 \\ 3 \end{bmatrix}$.

Solution
Taking

$$f(x) = 5\sqrt{x} \quad \text{and} \quad p = -4, q = 3$$

then

$$f(x + p) + q = f(x - 4) + 3 = 5\sqrt{(x - 4)} + 3$$

so the image of

$$y = 5\sqrt{x}$$

is

$$y = 5\sqrt{(x - 4)} + 3$$

3.1 **Exercise 4**

(Do *not* use a calculator in this exercise.)

Use translations of simple graphs to sketch the graphs of the following. In each case give the equation of the basic graph and the translation used.

1 $y = x^2 + 9$ **4** $y = x^3 - 2$

2 $y = (x - 1)^2$ **5** $y = 5(x - 3)^2 + 6$

3 $y = \dfrac{3}{x + \frac{1}{2}}$ **6** $y = x^2 + 2x$

3.1.7 **Combining transformations of graphs**

In 3.1.6 you saw how translations of graphs changed their equations. Here, we shall consider other transformations and combinations of transformations of graphs, together with their effect on the general equation $y = f(x)$.

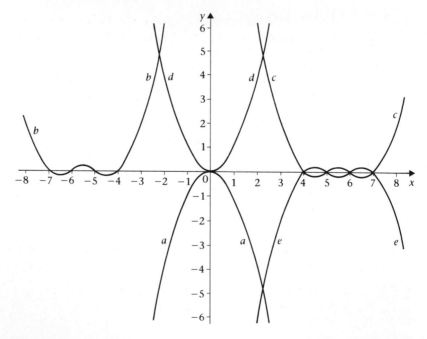

Graphs b, c and e can be mapped onto each other by translations, reflections or rotations. Graphs a and d can be mapped onto each other by a reflection or a half-turn. Some of the graphs can be mapped onto each other by a combination of transformations.

Graph b maps to c by a translation through $\begin{bmatrix} 11 \\ 0 \end{bmatrix}$ or a reflection in the y-axis.

Graph a maps to d by a reflection in the x-axis or a half-turn about the origin.

Graph c maps to e by a half-turn about the point $(5\frac{1}{2}, 0)$ or a reflection in the x-axis.

Graph b maps to e by a half-turn about the origin or reflections in the x-axis and in the y-axis.

These ideas are explored below.

 .1E

1 (a) If $f(w) = w^2 - w$, write down expressions for $f(x)$, $f(-x)$ and $-f(x)$ and draw their graphs.

(b) (i) What transformation will map $y = f(x)$ onto $y = f(-x)$?

(ii) What transformation will map $y = f(x)$ onto $y = -f(x)$?

(c) For any function f, will the transformations found in (b) always be the same? Give reasons for your answer.

2 (a) $f(x) = x^4 - 2x^3$. The graph of $y = f(x)$ is reflected in the x-axis. Use the ideas of question 1 to find the equation of the new graph. Plot both graphs to check your answer.

(b) The original graph is now reflected in the y-axis. Write down the equation of the new graph. Plot the graph of your equation to check your answer.

3 (a) If $f(x) = 3x^2 - x^4$, write down $f(-x)$. Plot the graphs of $f(x)$ and $f(-x)$. Explain what occurs.

(b) If $f(x) = x^3 - 5x$, write down $f(-x)$ and $-f(x)$. Plot the graphs of $f(x)$, $f(-x)$ and $-f(x)$. Explain what occurs.

If $f(-x) = f(x)$, then f is called an **even** function and its graph has line or reflection symmetry in the y-axis.

If $f(-x) = -f(x)$, then f is called an **odd** function and its graph has rotational (half-turn) symmetry about the origin.

4 Classify the following functions f as odd, even or neither.

(a) $f(x) = \dfrac{3}{x^2}$ (b) $f(x) = 2x^5 - 3x^3$ (c) $f(x) = x^3 + 2$

5 Classify the following functions f as odd, even or neither.

(a)

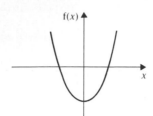

(b)

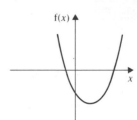

(c)

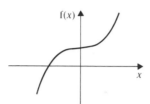

(d)

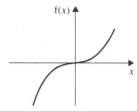

(e)

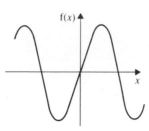

(f)

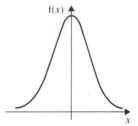

6 $f(x) = x^2 + 3x - 2$. The graph of $y = f(x)$ is first reflected in the x-axis and then the new curve is reflected in the y-axis.

(a) Find the equations of these two new curves and plot the three graphs to check your answers.

(b) How could you have transformed the first curve onto the third using a single transformation?

7 $f(x) = 2x^2 - \dfrac{1}{x}$. The graph of $y = f(x)$ is first reflected in the y-axis

and then translated through $\begin{bmatrix} 4 \\ 3 \end{bmatrix}$. Find the equation of the final curve.

Check your answer by using the graph plotter.

Example 8

Find the image of $y = \dfrac{x^3}{4}$ after a translation of $\begin{bmatrix} -2 \\ -7 \end{bmatrix}$ followed by a reflection in the x-axis.

Solution

Under a translation of $\begin{bmatrix} -2 \\ -7 \end{bmatrix}$, the image of $y = f(x)$ is $y = f(x + 2) - 7$. So the image of $y = \dfrac{x^3}{4}$ is

$$y = \frac{(x + 2)^3}{4} - 7$$

Under a reflection in the x-axis, the image of $y = f(x)$ is

$$y = -f(x)$$

So the image of $y = \dfrac{(x + 2)^3}{4} - 7$ is

$$y = -\left\{ \frac{(x + 2)^3}{4} - 7 \right\}$$

i.e.

$$y = 7 - \frac{(x + 2)^3}{4}$$

You have now seen the effects of translations and reflections in the axes. The general rules for these transformations are summarised below.

- **Translations**

  The graph of $y = f(x + p) + q$ is the image of the graph of $y = f(x)$ after translation through $\begin{bmatrix} -p \\ q \end{bmatrix}$.

- **Reflections in the axes**

  The graph of $y = f(-x)$ is the image of the graph of $y = f(x)$ after it has been reflected in the y-axis. The graph of $y = -f(x)$ is the image of the graph of $y = f(x)$ after it has been reflected in the x-axis.

3.1 **Exercise 5**

1 For each of the following pairs of graphs, the equation of one graph is given.
Find the equation of the other.

Use the graph plotter to check your answers.

(a)

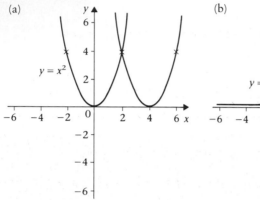

(b)

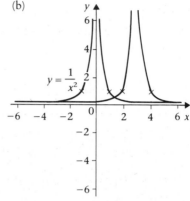

(c)

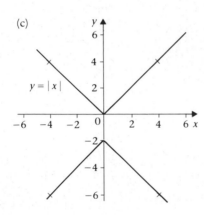

(d)

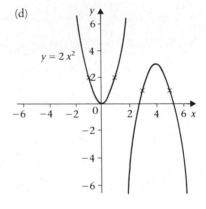

(e)

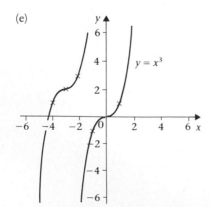

(f)

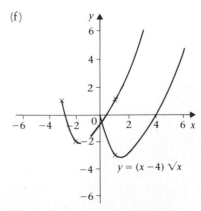

2 Find the images of the graphs of the following functions under the transformations given.

(a) $y = \dfrac{1}{x}$

reflection in the x-axis followed by a translation through $\begin{bmatrix} -6 \\ -7 \end{bmatrix}$

(b) $y = 3x - 7$

reflection in the y-axis followed by a reflection in the x-axis

(c) $y = \dfrac{1}{x^2}$

translation through $\begin{bmatrix} 2 \\ -3 \end{bmatrix}$ followed by a reflection in the x-axis

---

After working through section 3.1 you should:

1 understand the terms domain, range, one-to-one, even, odd, as applied to functions;

2 be able to combine functions;

3 be able to find the inverse of a function;

4 be able to rearrange formulas;

5 be able to find the images of graphs after:

(a) translation,

(b) reflections in the axes,

(c) reflection in the line $y = x$;

6 be able to use your knowledge of transformations to help you sketch graphs.

3 Functions

.2 Circular functions

3.2.1 Rotation

The mathematics of the circular functions describes the behaviour of many physical systems. Those illustrated below are but a few examples; others include the motion of the tides and the current flow in an electric circuit. There are many more.

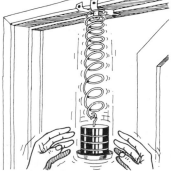

Although some of these movements are obviously circular (the rotation of the big wheel, for example), others are not (for example, tidal movements). However, the same mathematics is used to describe their behaviour. This is the mathematics of the elementary trigonometric functions – the sine, cosine and tangent functions.

Our study begins with definitions of the functions themselves. Initially, we shall concentrate on the sine and cosine functions.

Consider a point rotating around a unit circle (a circle of radius 1 unit) as shown.

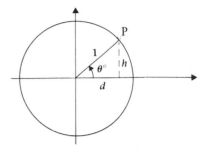

Define $(\cos\theta°, \sin\theta°)$ to be the coordinates of P.

So $h = \sin\theta°$ and $d = \cos\theta°$, where $\theta°$ is the angle through which the point has turned from the horizontal position.

The values for d and h are obtained from the elementary ratios in a right-angled triangle.

In a right-angled triangle for which the hypotenuse is of length 1,

$$\sin\theta° = \frac{h}{1} \quad \text{and} \quad \cos\theta° = \frac{d}{1}$$

i.e. $\sin\theta° = h$ and $\cos\theta° = d$

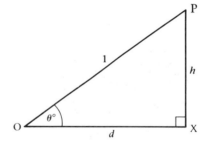

The definition of the sine and cosine in terms of the coordinates of a point rotating around the unit circle apply for *all* values of the angle $\theta°$. If the point P moves in an anticlockwise direction then the angle generated is taken to be positive. In a clockwise direction the angle is negative.

By considering the height h of the point P above the horizontal as θ varies, the sine curve can be obtained. The cosine curve is obtained by considering the horizontal distance, d metres, from the origin O.

A few values are calculated below.

$$h = \sin 30°$$
$$(\theta, h) = (30, 0.5)$$
$$d = \cos 30°$$
$$(\theta, d) = (30, 0.866)$$

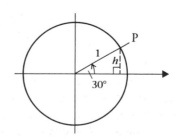

$$h = \sin 120°$$
$$(\theta, h) = (120, 0.866)$$
$$d = \cos 120°$$
$$(\theta, d) = (120, -0.5)$$

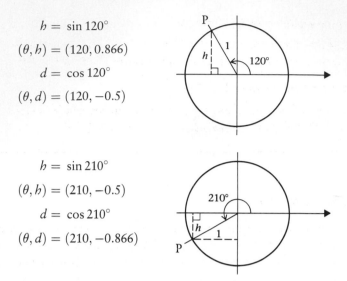

$$h = \sin 210°$$
$$(\theta, h) = (210, -0.5)$$
$$d = \cos 210°$$
$$(\theta, d) = (210, -0.866)$$

The sine and cosine functions are both **periodic** – that is, they repeat themselves after a certain interval known as the **period**. In the case of both sine and cosine the period is 360°.

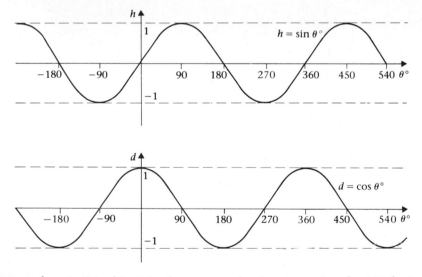

Observe that sin ('anything') is *always* a number between +1 and −1 inclusive (the range of the function); similarly, for cos ('anything').

3.2 **Exercise 1**

1   (a) Use your calculator to give the value of sin 50°.

(b) Write down, from the sine graph, six other angles which have the same sine as 50°.

2 (a) Use your calculator to find cos 163°.

(b) Write down, from the cosine graph, five other angles which have the same cosine as 163° and which lie in the range $-360 \le \theta \le 720$.

3 (a) Use your calculator to find sin 339°.

(b) Write down, from the sine graph, five other angles which have the same sine as 339° and which lie in the range $-360 \le \theta \le 720$.

3.2.2 Transformations

In this section we consider the effect of various transformations on the graphs of the sine and cosine functions. This will help when you sketch graphs of related functions, such as $\cos(2x + 60)°$, for example. Consider first the sine and cosine functions themselves.

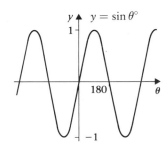 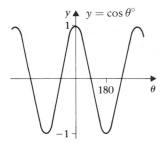

- $\sin \theta°$ is an odd function whose graph has rotational symmetry about the origin.

$$\sin(-\theta°) = -\sin \theta°$$

so that $\sin(-50°) = -\sin 50° = -0.766$

- $\cos \theta°$ is an even function, as the graph has reflection symmetry in the y-axis.

$$\cos(-\theta°) = \cos \theta°$$

so that $\cos(-50°) = \cos 50° = 0.643$

- The graph of $\cos \theta°$ may be obtained by a translation of $\begin{bmatrix} -90° \\ 0° \end{bmatrix}$ of the $\sin \theta°$ graph.

$$\sin(\theta + 90)° = \cos \theta°$$

so that $\sin 120° = \cos 30° = 0.866$

Further relationships are explored in 3.2A, which follows.

.2A

1 Use a graph plotter, working in degrees, to plot the graph of
$$y = \sin \theta°$$
Investigate the graph of $y = a \sin \theta°$ for various values of a, including negative values, and describe the transformations involved. a is called the **amplitude** of the function.

2 (a) Investigate $y = \sin b\theta°$ for various values of b and comment on the significance of the factor b.

(b) What is the period of $\sin b\theta°$ in terms of b?

3 Investigate $y = \sin (\theta + c)° + d$ for various values of c and d and describe the transformations involved.

4 Investigate:
(a) $y = \cos b\theta°$ (b) $y = \cos (b\theta + c)°$
for various values of b and c and describe carefully the transformations involved.

5

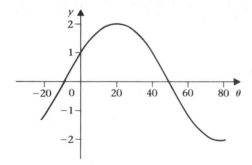

The diagram shows a part of the graph of
$$y = a \sin (b\theta + c)°$$
Find a, b and c.

6 Describe fully a sequence of transformations which maps the graph of
$$y = \cos \theta°$$
onto the graph of
$$y = a \cos (b\theta + c)° + d$$
where a, b, c and d may take any values. Illustrate your conclusions with appropriate diagrams.

You should have noted the following results.

Starting with $y = \sin x°$,

$y = \sin(x + c)° + d$ is obtained by a translation of $\begin{bmatrix} -c \\ d \end{bmatrix}$.

$y = a \sin x°$ is obtained by a one-way stretch parallel to the y-axis which changes the **amplitude** of the function from 1 to a.

$y = \sin bx°$ is obtained by a one-way stretch parallel to the x-axis which changes the **period** of the function from 360° to $\left(\dfrac{360}{b} \right)°$.

$y = \sin(bx + c)°$ can be obtained by a stretch of $\dfrac{1}{b}$ followed by a translation of $\dfrac{-c}{b}$, called a **phase shift** of $\dfrac{-c}{b}$.

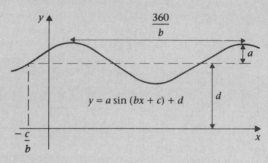

These results are entirely consistent with the results for the polynomial functions with which you are familiar. This is an important observation and one we will meet again.

Example 1
(a) For $y = 3 \cos(6\theta + 180)°$, what are the amplitude, period and phase shift? Sketch the graph.
(b) Describe a sequence of transformations which maps the graph of $y = \cos \theta°$ onto that of $y = 3 \cos(6\theta + 180)°$.

Solution

(a)

Amplitude 3.
Period 60.
Phase shift $-30°$.

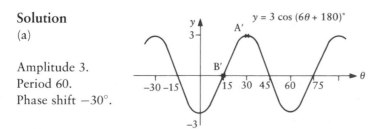

(b) The transformations are:

- a one-way stretch, parallel to the x-axis, of scale factor $\frac{1}{6}$, followed by
- a one-way stretch, parallel to the y-axis, of scale factor 3, followed by
- a translation $\begin{bmatrix} -30 \\ 0 \end{bmatrix}$.

It is informative to track some of the points from the graph of $y = \cos\theta°$ to $y = 3\cos(6\theta + 180)°$.

For example, point A $(360°, 1)$

$$(360°, 1) \rightarrow (60°, 1) \rightarrow (60°, 3) \rightarrow (30°, 3) = A'$$

point B $(270°, 0)$

$$(270°, 0) \rightarrow (45°, 0) \rightarrow (45°, 0) \rightarrow (15°, 0) = B'$$

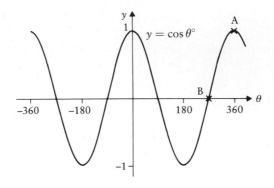

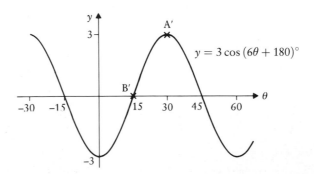

3.2 Exercise 2

1 Suggest suitable equations for the following graphs. Check your answers using a graph plotter.

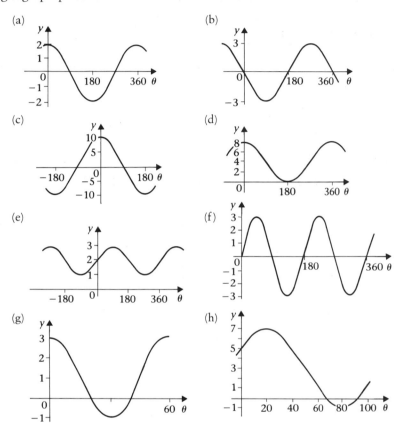

2

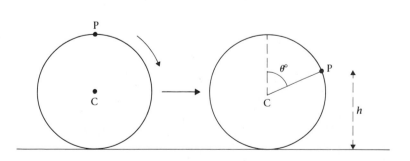

A wheel of radius 0.2 metres rolls along a straight horizontal line. Initially, a spot P on the rim is directly over the centre C. After turning through $\theta°$, the height of the spot P is h metres. Find an equation for h in terms of θ and sketch the graph of h against θ.

3   (a) Describe a sequence of transformations that maps the graph of $y = \sin x°$
        to $y = 2 \sin (3x + 60)°$.

    (b) Find the image point of   (i) (180°, 0)   (ii) (90°, 1)
        under the transformations in (a).

3.2.3 Modelling periodic behaviour

The sine and cosine functions are ideal for modelling many situations which are
periodic. As you will see, the input to a sine or cosine function need not be an
angle.

3 .2B

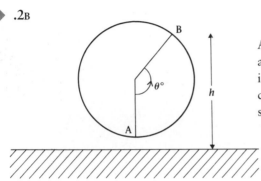

A big wheel has a radius of 4.8 m
and a seat in the lowest position
is 0.8 m above ground level. One
complete revolution takes 60
seconds.

1 If a seat starts from the bottom in position A, and if after t seconds it has
   turned through an angle $θ°$, express $θ$ in terms of t.

2 Draw a rough sketch to show how the height in metres, h, will vary
   with   (a) $θ$,   (b) t.
   (There is no need to perform any detailed calculations.) In each case,
   suggest a possible formula for h.

3 Plot a graph of the first part of the motion by completing the following
   table of values of h for various values of $θ$.

$θ$	0	30	60	90	120	150	180
h							

4 Repeat question 3, but this time using t as the variable.

t	0	5	10	15	20	25	30
h							

You may have noticed that a subtle change has occurred in this example. Until now sine and cosine have been used exclusively with *angles* as input. In part (d), however, the input to the function was *t*. There is no reason why, having drawn the basic graphs of the circular functions, you should not use *any variable* you choose as input.

Example 2

When a particular tuning fork is struck, each prong vibrates at a frequency of 256 Hz (hertz, i.e. cycles per second) with a maximum displacement at the tip of 0.3 mm.

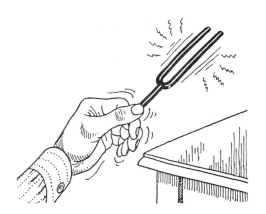

(a) Sketch a graph to show the displacement of the tip of a prong with time.

(b) Assuming that this is a sine graph, express *d*, the displacement in millimetres, as a function of *t*, the time in seconds from the start of the motion.

Solution

(a) Assume the initial displacement is 0.3 mm.

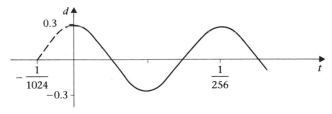

(b) $d = a \sin (bt + c)^\circ$

Amplitude: $a = 0.3$

Period: $\dfrac{360}{b} = \dfrac{1}{256} \Rightarrow b = 92\,160$

Phase shift: $\dfrac{-c}{b} = -\dfrac{1}{1024} \Rightarrow c = 90$

So $d = 0.3 \sin (92\,160t + 90)^\circ$

Example 3

(a)

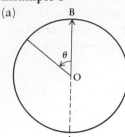

A wave machine in a swimming pool comprises a cylinder of radius 2 m which rotates at 1 revolution every 10 seconds. The cylinder starts with the bar, B, uppermost and has rotated through an angle $\theta°$ after t seconds. A is a fixed point just beneath the cylinder. Express θ in terms of t.

(b) Hence write down the height, after t seconds, of the bar above

(i) O,   (ii) A

Solution

(a) There is a rotation of $36°$ in 1 second

So $\theta = 36t$

(b) (i) Height $= 2\cos(36t)°$ (ii) Height $= 2 + 2\cos(36t)°$

3.2 Exercise 3

1 As the Moon circles the Earth, its gravitational force causes tides. The height of the tide can be modelled by a sine or cosine function.

(a) Assuming an interval of 12 hours between successive high tides:

    (i) sketch the graph of the height if it is 5.7 metres at low tide and 7.3 metres at high tide;

    (ii) use the graph to help express the height of the tide, h metres, as a function of the time t hours after high tide.

(b) Express h as a function of t if h is 3.6 at low tide and 4.9 at high tide.

2 The times for sunset at four-weekly intervals over a year are as follows.

Jan. 2	16:03	July 16	21:10
Jan. 30	16:45	Aug. 13	20:27
Feb. 27	17:36	Sep. 10	19:26
Mar. 26	18:24	Oct. 8	18:22
Apr. 23	20:11	Nov. 5	16:26
May 21	20:55	Dec. 3	15:54
June 18	21:21		

Plot these data on a graph and, making any necessary adjustments, find a suitable function to model the data approximately.

3

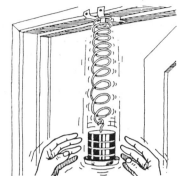

A mass oscillates up and down at the end of a spring. The unstretched length of the spring is 12 cm, and it is extended to 14.5 cm and released. One complete oscillation takes one second. Sketch a graph to show the length of the spring as a function of time. Assuming that this is a cosine graph, express l, the length in centimetres, as a function of t, the time in seconds from the start of the motion.

4E The 'science' of bio-rhythms is based on the belief that an individual's behaviour is governed by three cycles which begin at birth. The physical cycle (P), with a period of 23 days, governs such things as strength, confidence and aggression; the emotional cycle (E), with a period of 28 days, affects feelings, creativity and cooperation; and the intellectual cycle (I), period 33 days, covers intelligence, concentration, memory and quickness of mind.

Critical days in an individual's behaviour occur when the graph of a cycle crosses the time axis.

Each cycle of the physical curve may be modelled by a sine wave using the equation

$$P = \sin\left(\frac{360t}{23}\right)^\circ$$

(a) Suggest suitable models for the other two cycles.

(b) Calculate your current values for P, E and I.

(c) When is your next critical day for each of the three cycles?

(d) On what days of your life are all three cycles critical?

3.2.4 Inverse trigonometric functions

In studying periodic behaviour it is often useful to be able to solve problems involving the inverse functions. For example, a student who believes that his intellectual bio-rhythm is governed by the equation

$$I = \sin \left(\frac{360t}{33} \right)^{\circ}$$

may wish to know on what days his value for I is greater than 0.9. In order to do this he would need to solve the equation

$$\sin \left(\frac{360t}{33} \right)^{\circ} = 0.9$$

Before you can solve equations like this, you need to be able to solve equations of the form $\sin x^{\circ} = a$.

 .2c

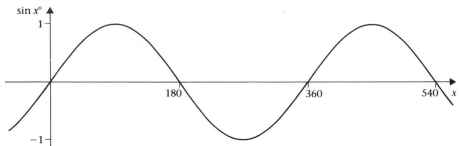

1 (a) Use your calculator to find a solution of $\sin x^{\circ} = 0.4$.

(b) Use the graph above to find three more solutions in the range $0 \leq x \leq 540$.

(c) Write down two solutions in the range $3600 \leq x \leq 3960$.

(d) Write down two solutions in the range $360n \leq x \leq 360(n+1)$.

(e) Does your formula apply if n is negative?

Your solution to question 1(d) is known as the **general solution** of the question. It is possible to write the general solution in a rather more elegant form, as question 2 demonstrates.

2 (a) Find a solution, p, of $\sin x° = 0.5$ in the range $0 \leq x \leq 90$.

 (b) Two more solutions are $180 - p$ and $360 + p$. Write down the next two in the same form.

 (c) Write down the 20th and 21st terms of the sequence starting $180 - p$, $360 + p$.

 (d) Write down the nth term. (Hint: $(-1)^n$ equals $+1$ if n is even, -1 if n is odd.)

3 Find the general solutions of:

 (a) $\sin x° = 0.7$ (b) $\sin x° = -0.7$ (c) $\cos x° = 0.7$

Example 4
Solve the equation $\sin x° = 0.6$ where $0 \leq x \leq 360$.

Solution
The calculator gives a single value of $x = 36.9$.

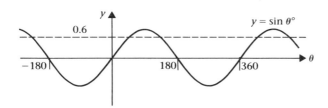

However, from the graph there is clearly an infinite number of solutions. They include

$$180 - 36.9 = 143.1, \quad 360 + 36.9 = 396.9, \quad 360 + 143.1 = 503.1,$$

$$36.9 - 360 = -323.1, \quad 143.1 - 360 = -216.9$$

The *general solution* is $180n + (-1)^n 36.9$.

The solutions in the given range are

$$39.9°, \quad 143.1° \quad \text{(when } n = 0 \text{ and } n = 1)$$

When considering the inverse function of $\sin x°$ ($x \in \mathbb{R}$), you should recall that, in general, a mapping from a set A to a set B is a function if and only if every element a of set A has a unique image in set B. For continuous functions of real numbers, this means that a vertical line drawn on the graph must cut the graph at exactly one point.

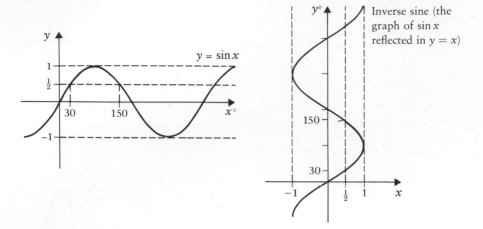

$\sin x$ *is* a function. It is a many-to-one mapping.

From the graph you can see that inverse sine x is *not* a function. For example, the image of $\frac{1}{2}$ under inverse sine includes 30, 150, 390, ... It is a one-to-many mapping.

The function called $\sin^{-1}$ below is sometimes called arcsin to avoid confusion with the one-to-many mapping.

> If $\sin a° = b$, then $a° = \sin^{-1} b$, where $\sin^{-1} b$ means 'the angle whose sine is b'.
>
> In order to ensure that $\sin^{-1}$ is a function, you need to restrict the image set to those values given by a calculator. These values are known as the **principal values**.
>
> For $\sin^{-1} x$ the principal values lie in the range $-90° \le \sin^{-1} x \le 90°$.

The graphs of $\sin^{-1} x$ and $\cos^{-1} x$ are shown below.

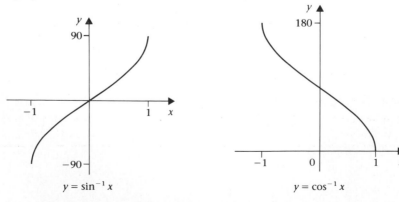

Example 5

(a) Find the value of $\cos^{-1}(-0.25)$.

(b) Solve $\cos x° = -0.25$ for $-360 \leq x \leq 360$.

Solution

(a) A calculator gives $\cos^{-1}(-0.25)$ as $104.5°$, which is the principal value.

(b) A graph shows there are four solutions. Angles having the same cosine are found using the symmetry of the graph. They are:

A $-360 + 104.5 = -255.5°$

B $-104.5°$

C $104.5°$

D $360 - 104.5 = 255.5°$

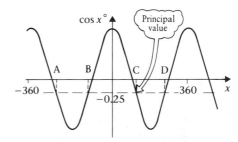

$\sin^{-1}$ and $\cos^{-1}$ both have domain $\{x \in \mathbb{R} : -1 \leq x \leq 1\}$.

Their ranges are restricted to the sets of principal values

$$-90° \leq \sin^{-1} x \leq 90° \quad \text{and} \quad 0° \leq \cos^{-1} x \leq 180°$$

3.2 **Exercise 4**

1   Give the (principal) values of the following.

(a) $\sin^{-1} 0.2$ (b) $\cos^{-1} 0.9$ (c) $\sin^{-1}(-0.36)$

(d) $\cos^{-1}(-0.74)$ (e) $\sin^{-1}(1)$ (f) $\cos^{-1}(-1)$

2   Solve the following equations, giving solutions in the range $-360 \leq x \leq 720$.

(a) $\sin x° = 0.3$ (b) $\cos x° = 0.8$ (c) $\cos x° = -0.3$

(d) $\sin x° = -0.5$ (e) $\cos x° = -1$ (f) $3 \sin x° = 1$

3   Find general solutions to the equations

(a) $3 \sin x° = 0.6$ (b) $\cos x° = -0.8$

3.2.5 Solving equations

 .2D

Suppose that the height of the tide, h metres, at a harbour entrance is modelled by the function

$$h = 2.5 \sin 30t° + 5$$

where t is the number of hours after midnight.

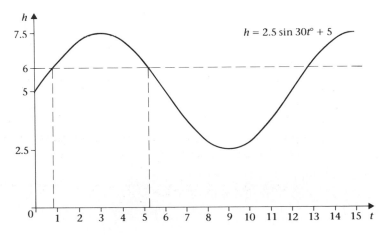

$h = 2.5 \sin 30t° + 5$

1 When is the height of the tide 6 m?

2 If a boat can only enter and leave the harbour when the depth of water exceeds 6 m, for how long each day is this possible?

Example 6

A girl is sitting on a big wheel which rotates once every 30 seconds. When the wheel begins to rotate for the ride, she is sitting in the position marked A on the diagram. The diameter of the wheel is 16 m.

(a) Show that her height y metres above the lowest point of the wheel t seconds later is given by

$$y = 8 + 8 \sin(12t + 30)°$$

(b) At what times is she

   (i) 15 metres above the ground,

   (ii) at the highest point?

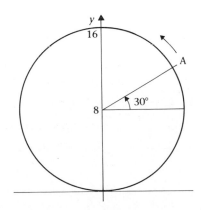

Solution

(a) $AN = 8 \sin (12t + 30)°$

So height of A $= y = 8 + 8 \sin (12t + 30)°$

(b) (i) When $y = 15$, you need to solve the equation

$$8 + 8 \sin (12t + 30)° = 15$$

$$\Rightarrow \quad 8 \sin (12t + 30)° = 7$$

$$\Rightarrow \quad \sin (12t + 30)° = 0.875$$

Now solve $\sin x° = 0.875$, where $x = 12t + 30$.

The calculator gives $x = 61.0$ so the possible solutions are

$$x = 61.0, \quad 180 - 61.0, \quad 360 + 61.0, \ldots$$

$$\Rightarrow 12t + 30 = 61.0, \quad 119.0, \quad 421.0, \quad 479.0, \ldots$$

$$\Rightarrow \quad t = 2.6, \quad 7.4, \quad 32.6, \quad 37.4, \ldots$$

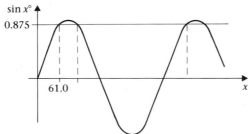

(ii) At the highest point, $y = 16$, so you have to solve the equation

$$8 + 8 \sin (12t + 30)° = 16$$

$$\Rightarrow \quad 8 \sin (12t + 30)° = 8$$

$$\Rightarrow \quad \sin (12t + 30)° = 1$$

Now solve $\sin x° = 1$, where $x = 12t + 30$.

This time there is only a single solution for each cycle and you do not need a calculator to tell you that the basic solution is $x = 90$. So the possible solutions are

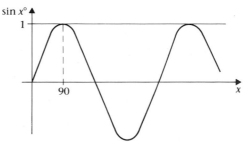

$$x = 90, \quad 360 + 90, \quad 720 + 90, \quad 1080 + 90, \ldots$$

$$\Rightarrow 12t + 30 = 90, \quad 450, \quad 810, \quad 1170, \ldots$$

$$\Rightarrow \quad t = 5, \quad 35, \quad 65, \quad 95, \ldots$$

The function $\sin(12t + 30)°$ has a period of $\dfrac{360}{12} = 30$, so if $t = a$ is a solution then so is $t = 30n + a$, where n is any integer.

The following tasksheet provides further practice at solving simple trigonometric equations.

▶ 3.2 **Tasksheet S1 – Solving equations (page 537)**

3.2 **Exercise 5**

1   Find the values of t in the range $0 \leq t \leq 60$ which satisfy the following equations.

   (a) $8 \sin 10t° = 5$ (b) $4 - 7 \cos(t + 35)° = 0$

   (c) $3 + 4 \sin(8t - 21)° = 0$ (d) $10 \cos \frac{1}{2}t° = 9$

2   The height above ground of a chair in a big wheel is given by

   $$h = 5.6 - 4.8 \cos 6t°$$

   where t is the time measured in seconds from the instant when the chair is at the lowest point. For how many seconds during one complete revolution is the chair more than 9 metres above ground level?

3   If the height of the tide is h metres at time t hours, where

   $$h = 5 + 2.5 \sin 30t°$$

   find all the times in the first 24 hours when the height is:

   (a) 6.7 metres   (b) 4.5 metres

4   A cowboy ties a handkerchief to a lasso which he then spins so that the height in metres of his handkerchief above the ground after t seconds is given by

   $$h = 2 + 1.5 \sin 500t°$$

   Find at what times the height of the handkerchief above the ground is:

   (a) 2.75 metres   (b) 2 metres   (c) 3.5 metres

3.2.6 tan $\theta°$

While sine and cosine are the most commonly used, they are certainly not the only periodic functions. Another important periodic function is the tangent function.

 .2E

A tennis umpire, U, is watching a rally between two players. The ball, B, is hit straight down the court from P to Q over the centre of the net, C.

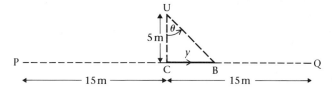

1 What is   (a) length y (b) angle CUQ?

2 Sketch a graph to show how y varies with θ as the ball travels
   (a) from C to Q   (b) from P to Q.

3 Using the sides of a right-angled triangle, show that if $0 \leq \theta < 90$ then

$$\tan \theta° = \frac{\sin \theta°}{\cos \theta°}$$

4 What is the greatest possible domain for tan?

5 Find a suitable set of principal values for $\tan^{-1} x$.

$$\tan x° = \frac{\sin x°}{\cos x°} \quad \{\cos x° \neq 0\}$$

$\tan x°$ is an odd function; $\tan (-x)° = -\tan x°$

$\tan^{-1}(x)$ has domain $\{x \in \mathbb{R}\}$, range $-90° < \tan^{-1} x < 90°$.

Although these results were illustrated for $0 \leq x < 90$, they are true for values of x outside this range.

The graph of $y = \tan x°$ can be transformed into the graph of $y = a \tan (bx + c)° + d$ in the same way as the graph of $y = \sin x°$ is transformed into the graph of $y = a \sin (bx + c)° + d$.

The graph of the tangent function is shown.

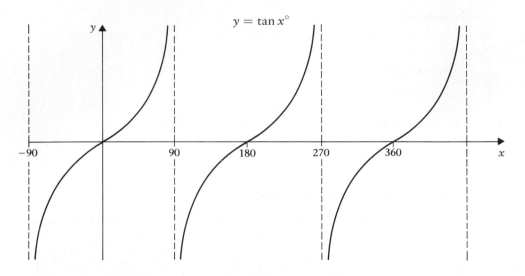

$$y = \tan x^\circ$$

The inverse tangent function has the following graph.

$$y = \tan^{-1}(x)$$

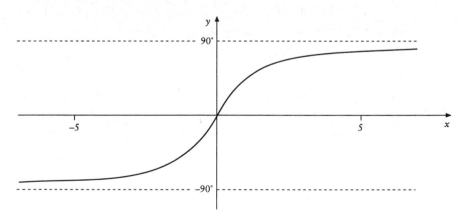

Example 6
State the general solution to the equation $\tan x^\circ = 0.8$.

Solution
The calculator gives $x = 38.66$. However, it is clear from the graph above that there is an infinite number of solutions. The solutions occur every 180°, so the general solution to the equation is

$$x = 38.66 \pm 180n \qquad (n = 0, \pm 1, \pm 2, \ldots)$$

3.2 **Exercise 6**

1   Find the values of

(a) $\tan^{-1} 1$ (b) $\tan^{-1}(-6)$ (c) $\tan^{-1} 0$

2   Sketch the graph of

(a) $y = \tan 2x^\circ$ (b) $y = \tan(x + 45)^\circ$

3   Solve the equations for values of x in the ranges $0 \le x \le 360$.

(a) $\tan x^\circ = 3$ (b) $5 \tan(2x + 30)^\circ = 4$

(c) $\tan^2 x^\circ = 1$ (d) $4 \sin x^\circ = 3 \cos x^\circ$

4   State the general solutions to the equations in 3(a) and 3(b).

After working through section 3.2 you should be able to:

1 define sin, cos, tan and their inverses;

2 sketch the graph of a circular function such as

$$y = a \sin(bx + c)^\circ$$

3 obtain solutions to equations of the form

$$a \cos(bx + c)^\circ = d$$

in a specified range;

4 apply circular functions in modelling periodic behaviour;

5 obtain general solutions to trigonometric equations.

3 Functions

.3 Growth functions

3.3.1 Exponential growth

Under favourable circumstances some organisms exhibit a particular type of unrestricted growth. The graph shows the growth of a number of bacteria starting with roughly 3000 at time $t = 0$ (hours).

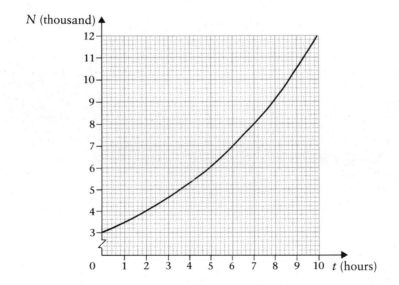

From the graph, there were 4000 bacteria after approximately 2 hours and 8000 after 7 hours. There were 5000 bacteria after approximately 3.7 hours and 10 000 after 8.7 hours.

Notice that in each of the cases above it takes 5 hours to double the number of bacteria. If the number of bacteria doubles in any period of 5 hours, you could use this to estimate the time for 24 000 bacteria. Doubling does appear to take place in all 5-hour intervals. Since there are 12 000 bacteria after 10 hours it is reasonable to suggest that there will be 24 000 after 15 hours. Similarly, since there are 3000 bacteria after 0 hours, there would have been 1500 bacteria 5 hours earlier, when $t = -5$.

It can also be seen that the number of bacteria trebles approximately every 8 hours – for example, 3000 after 0 hours, 9000 after 8 hours; 4000 after 2 hours,

12 000 after 10 hours. Given any fixed time period, the number of bacteria *increases by the same factor during that time*, independent of the number at the start of the period.

> Growth is called **exponential** when there is a constant, called the **growth factor**, such that during each unit time interval the amount present is multiplied by this factor.

Example 1

The graph shows the growth of world population from 1650 to 1950. Is the growth exponential?

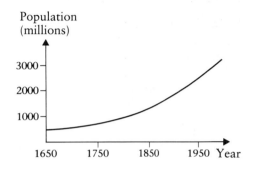

Solution

The populations in 1650, 1750, 1850 and 1950 were approximately 500 million, 700 million, 1300 million and 2500 million.

The growth factors over successive hundred-year intervals are:

Time interval	Growth factor
1650–1750	$\frac{700}{500} = 1.4$
1750–1850	$\frac{1300}{700} = 1.857$
1850–1950	$\frac{2500}{1300} = 1.923$

The growth factors for successive equal time intervals are not constant, so the growth is not exponential.

Exponential decay occurs when the growth factor is less than 1.

Example 2

A scientist was analysing the decay of a radioactive form of lead, lead-214. The mass of lead-214 remaining in a particular sample of lead was as follows:

Time (minutes)	0	1	2	3	4	5	6	7	8
Mass (kg)	3.127	3.047	2.969	2.894	2.820	2.748	2.678	2.609	2.542

Was the radioactive lead decaying exponentially?

Solution

In the first minute, the growth factor was $\dfrac{3.047}{3.127} = 0.974$.

As you can verify, the growth factors in succeeding minutes were all 0.974.

The lead decayed exponentially (the constant growth factor was less than 1).

3.3 Exercise 1

1 To attract new investors, a construction company publishes its pre-tax profit figures for the last ten years.

Profit before tax
(millions of pounds)

Year	Profit
1988	27.0
1989	32.4
1990	38.9
1991	46.7
1992	56.0
1993	67.2
1994	80.6
1995	96.7
1996	116.1
1997	139.3

Was the growth of profits exponential?

2 £5000 is deposited in a fixed interest building society account. The amount in the account increases as shown below.

End of year	1	2	3	4	5
Amount	£5450	£5940.50	£6475.15	£7057.91	£7693.12

What is the interest rate? Is the growth exponential?

3 A girl's annual pocket money is £50 plus £10 for each year of her age. Does her pocket money increase exponentially with age?

4 The following table shows the population of Latin America over a period of 24 years.

Year	1950	1954	1962	1966	1974
Population (millions)	164	183	227	254	315

Is this exponential growth? Justify your answer.

5 A capacitor is an electronic component which can store charge.

(a) A capacitor is initially charged to 9 volts. It is discharged across a particular circuit, the voltage dropping by one volt each second.

(b) In another circuit, the voltage would have dropped by one quarter of its value each second.

Are either of the above examples of exponential decay? Find the growth factors, if appropriate.

3.3.2 Indices

1 week ago   Now   In 1 week   In 1½ weeks   In 2 weeks

A culture of algae doubles in area each week. Now it covers $1\,\text{cm}^2$, so in a week it will cover $2\,\text{cm}^2$, in a fortnight $4\,\text{cm}^2$, and so on. The growth of algae is exponential with growth factor 2. In t weeks the area, A, will be

$$A = 2^t$$

The number 2 is called the **base** and t the **index** (plural: indices).

The following examples introduce definitions and laws for powers of 2 and for other base numbers.

 .3A

The area, A, covered by an algal growth is initially $1\,\text{cm}^2$. The growth increases exponentially with time, t, in such a way that $A = 2^t$, where t is measured in weeks.

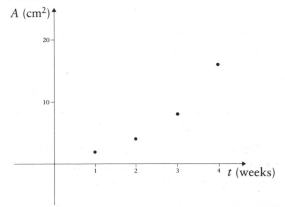

So far 2^t has been defined only when t is a positive whole number. It is nevertheless sensible to join the points on the graph with a smooth curve.

1 (a) Explain why, for whole number powers,

      (i) $2^m 2^n = 2^{m+n}$ (ii) $2^m \div 2^n = 2^{m-n}$

  (b) Simplify $(2^m)^n$.

2 From your graph, find 2^0 and interpret 2^0 in terms of growth of algae.

3 (a) What was the area of algae a week before measurements started? How would you define 2^{-1}?

  (b) Use the same approach to define

      (i) 2^{-2} (ii) 2^{-3} (iii) 2^{-n}

4 You do not have to restrict yourself to doubling. Suggest values for:

  (a) 3^{-2} (b) 5^0 (c) 10^{-6} (d) a^0 (e) a^{-n}

You need to check that the laws of question 1 are still being obeyed.

5 (a) Use the laws to simplify $2^{-4} \times 2^{-3}$.

  (b) Express 2^{-4} and 2^{-3} as fractions.

  (c) Multiply the two fractions in (b) to check that the answer in (a) fits in with the laws of indices.

  (d) Verify that the laws hold for:

      (i) $2^{-3} \times 2^0$ (ii) $2^{-1} \times 2$ (iii) $2^{-4} \div 2^{-3}$ (iv) $2 \div 2^{-3}$

6 Decide which of the following are equal.

  (a) $\left(\dfrac{1}{2}\right)^3$ (b) $\dfrac{1}{2^3}$ (c) 8 (d) 2^{-3} (e) $\dfrac{1}{8}$ (f) 3^{-2}

7 (a) If $2^{\frac{1}{2}}$ is to obey the laws, what must $(2^{\frac{1}{2}})^2$ equal?

  (b) What is $(\sqrt{2})^2$?

    How will you define $2^{\frac{1}{2}}$, $2^{\frac{1}{3}}$, $2^{\frac{1}{n}}$, $a^{\frac{1}{n}}$?

8 Find: (a) $9^{\frac{1}{2}}$ (b) $8^{\frac{1}{3}}$ (c) $64^{\frac{1}{4}}$ (d) $81^{0.5}$

9 (a) Explain why $4^{\frac{p}{q}} = (4^{\frac{1}{q}})^p = (4^p)^{\frac{1}{q}}$

  (b) Find the value of: (i) $8^{\frac{2}{3}}$ (ii) $16^{\frac{3}{4}}$

10 Check the laws of indices using the graph and your calculator. For example, on your calculator find $\sqrt{2}$ and $2^{0.5}$.

Read off from your graph the value of A when $t = 0.5$.

You should experiment with various bases and both signs of indices.

For any *positive* number a and *any* numbers p, q:

$$a^0 = 1$$

$$a^{-p} = \frac{1}{a^p}$$

$$a^p \times a^q = a^{p+q}$$

$$a^p \div a^q = a^{p-q}$$

$$(a^p)^q = a^{pq}$$

If n is a positive integer,

$$a^{\frac{1}{n}} = \sqrt[n]{a}$$

We can use these laws for $a < 0$, *where it is meaningful to do so*. Note that, while $a^0 = 1$, *no* value is assigned to 0^0, which is undefined. Equally, 0^{-x} is undefined.

Example 3

By using a combination of several laws of indices, evaluate $8^{-\frac{2}{3}}$.

Solution

$$8^{-\frac{2}{3}} = \frac{1}{8^{\frac{2}{3}}} = \frac{1}{(8^{\frac{1}{3}})^2}$$

$$= \frac{1}{(\sqrt[3]{8})^2} = \frac{1}{2^2}$$

$$= \tfrac{1}{4}$$

3.3 Exercise 2

1 Express the following as single powers of 2.

(a) $2^2 \times 2^3$ (b) 2×2^9 (c) $2^{12} \div 2^7$ (d) $(2^5)^3$

2 Simplify the following.

(a) $x^2 \times x^3$ (b) $a \times a^9$ (c) $d^{12} \div d^7$ (d) $(b^5)^3$

3 Evaluate:

(a) 3^{-2} (b) 10^{-3} (c) $3^{-2} \times 3^5$ (d) $5^2 \div 5^{-1}$

4 Simplify:

(a) $y^3 \times y^{-5}$ (b) $c^3 \div c^{-2}$ (c) $x^{-5} \times x^5$ (d) $(x^{-2})^{-3}$

5 Evaluate these, checking your answers using the x^y or $x^{\frac{1}{y}}$ key on your calculator.

(a) $4^{\frac{1}{2}}$ (b) $25^{-\frac{1}{2}}$ (c) $25^{-\frac{3}{2}}$ (d) $1\,000\,000^{\frac{1}{3}}$ (e) $0.01^{\frac{1}{2}}$

6 Use your calculator to solve the equation $2^t = 10$ by trial and improvement, correct to two decimal places.

Further practice in using the laws of indices can be found on tasksheet S1.

▷ 3.3 **Tasksheet S1 – Laws of indices (page 538)**

3.3.3 Growth factors

In 3.3.2 you considered the growth function with equation $y = 2^x$. In many fields of study it can be useful to find equations which closely model given data. For example, the population figures for England and Wales from 1841 to 1901 are as follows.

Year	1841	1851	1861	1871	1881	1891	1901
Population, P millions	15.9	17.9	20.1	22.7	26.0	29.0	32.5

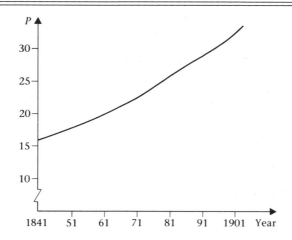

If you could fit an equation to such data, then you could make reasonable estimates for populations in years when a census was not taken, and you could also project the figures beyond the years for which data are available. However, great care must be taken in making such projections because changes in conditions dramatically alter population trends.

The table gives the data in 10-yearly intervals. To find out whether it is suitable for modelling using a growth function, you can check to see if the 10-yearly growth factor is approximately constant.

Year	Population	Growth factor
1841	15.9	
1851	17.9	1.13
1861	20.1	1.12
1871	22.7	1.13
1881	26.0	1.15
1891	29.0	1.12
1901	32.5	1.12

The 10-yearly growth factor is roughly constant, so the data can be modelled using a growth function. To do this, it is necessary to find an estimate for the yearly growth factor.

In the sixty years from 1841 to 1901 the population grows by a factor of $\frac{32.5}{15.9} = 2.044$. If the yearly growth factor is a, this means that

$$a^{60} = 2.044 \Rightarrow a = 2.044^{\frac{1}{60}} = 1.012$$

Some of the properties of the equations and graphs of growth functions are investigated in the following questions.

 .3B

You have seen that $y = a^x$ may be used as a model for exponential growth. Here you will see how, by changing the function to Ka^x, you can model *any* exponential data.

1 (a) Investigate the graph of $K \times 2^x$ for various values of K. What is the significance of the factor K?

  (b) What is the significance of K if $y = K \times a^x$?

2 (a) If $y = a^t$, what is the **initial** value of y, i.e. the value of y when $t = 0$?

  (b) If $y = K \times a^t$ what is the initial value of y?

3 Investigate the graph of $K \times \left(\frac{1}{2}\right)^x$ for various values of K. What is the significance of the factor K?

4 Use the ideas developed in questions 1–3 to sketch the graphs of:

  (a) $y = 5 \times 3^t$ (b) $y = 2 \times \left(\frac{1}{3}\right)^t$ (c) $y = \frac{1}{2} \times 5^t$ (d) $y = 2 \times \left(\frac{1}{5}\right)^t$

Check your answers using a graph plotter.

5 The population P of Great Britain has been estimated at 1.5 million in 1066 and 6.1 million in 1700. Assume that an exponential growth model is appropriate and that t years after 1066, $P = Ka^t$.

  (a) Write down the value of K.

  (b) Use the data for the population in 1700 to explain why

$$a = \left(\frac{6.1}{1.5}\right)^{\frac{1}{634}}$$

    Evaluate this to 5 decimal places.

  (c) Use this model to estimate the population of the UK in 1990.

  (d) Comment on the model.

> The general growth function has an equation of the form $y = Ka^x$, where K and a are constants. K is the value of y when x is zero and a is the growth factor.

Example 4

Model the population data for England and Wales given on page 231 with an equation for P in terms of t, the number of years after 1841.

Solution

Assuming the growth is exponential, $P = K \times a^t$. $K = 15.9$, the initial value and, since $32.5 = 15.9 \times a^{60}$ the annual growth factor can be estimated by

$$\left(\frac{32.5}{15.9}\right)^{\frac{1}{60}} \approx 1.012$$

The equation is then

$$P = 15.9 \times 1.012^t$$

A check on the suitability of this model can be made by comparing tabulated values of the original data and populations predicted by the equation.

t	0	10	20	30	40	50	60
P	15.9	17.9	20.1	22.7	26.0	29.0	32.5
15.9×1.012^t	15.9	17.9	20.2	22.7	25.6	28.9	32.5

Although there is some variation, this model gives results close to the true values.

The model predicts that the population in 1990 would be 15.9×1.012^{149}, that is, 94.0 million. This figure is much higher than the true value of about 49 million. Many factors have affected this, including the world wars, family planning and a different social structure (mothers working outside the home, and so on).

3.3 Exercise 3

1 A colony of bacteria has a growth factor of 6 per hour. Initially there are 400 bacteria.

(a) After how many hours will there be 14 400 bacteria?

(b) When will there be 1 000 000 bacteria?

(c) Write down an expression for the number of bacteria t hours after the start.

2 The compound interest on a savings account is 8% per annum.

(a) What is the growth factor?

(b) Explain why the number, n, of years before an initial investment of £4000 grows to £5000 is given by $1.08^n = 1.25$.

(c) Find an approximate value for n.

3 A radioactive element, bismuth-210, was observed every few days, and the mass remaining was measured.

The following figures were obtained.

No. of days from start of experiment	0	2	3	6	7	10
Mass (kg)	10	7.57	6.57	4.34	3.77	2.48

(a) Estimate the growth factor.

(b) Write down an equation for M, the mass of bismuth remaining, in terms of t, the number of days from the start of the experiment.

(c) Check how well your equation models the data.

(d) How much will remain after 3 weeks?

(e) What is the half-life of bismuth-210 (i.e. after how many days does only half of the original amount remain), to the nearest whole day?

4 In an electronic circuit, the voltage V across a capacitor drops from 15 volts to 6 volts in 12 seconds. Assuming that the process is one of exponential decay, find a formula for V in terms of t, the time in seconds from the start.

3.3.4 Logarithms

The graph shows the growth of aquatic plants starting with an initial surface coverage of $1\,m^2$.

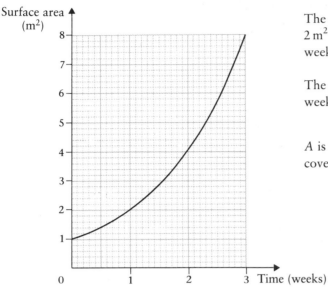

The time taken to reach $2\,m^2$ and $4\,m^2$ are 1 and 2 weeks respectively.

The growth factor is 2 per week.

$$Area\ (A) = 2^t$$

A is the surface area covered after t weeks.

The exponential equation expresses A as a function of t. Often though, you require the *inverse function*, i.e. t in terms of A. This inverse function is called the **logarithm of A to base 2**, written as $\log_2 A$.

From the graph, the area is $8\,m^2$ after 3 weeks, i.e. $8 = 2^3$. Conversely, it takes 3 weeks before the area is $8\,m^2$, i.e. $3 = \log_2 8$.

Since $\log_2 x$ is the inverse function of 2^x, the graph of $\log_2 x$ is the reflection of the graph of 2^x in the line $y = x$. Since $\log_2 1 = 0$, the graph cuts the x-axis at $x = 1$.

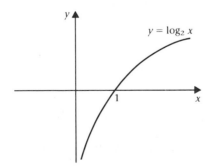

Note that $\log_2 x$ is not defined for $x \leq 0$.

Example 5

Write down the values of:

(a) $\log_2 32$ (b) $\log_5 25$ (c) $\log_{10} 1000$ (d) $\log_3 27$

Solution

(a) Since $32 = 2^5$, 5 is the logarithm of 32 to base 2, i.e. $\log_2 32 = 5$.

(b) Since $5^2 = 25$, $\log_5 25 = 2$.

(c) $10^3 = 1000 \Rightarrow \log_{10} 1000 = 3$

(d) $3^3 = 27 \Rightarrow \log_3 27 = 3$

Properties of the 'log' function are developed in the questions which follow.

 .3c

You know that

$$y = 2^x \Leftrightarrow x = \log_2 y$$

1 Use this result to find:

(a) $\log_2 64$ (b) $\log_2 \frac{1}{8}$ (c) $\log_2 2$ (d) $\log_2 \sqrt{2}$

Just as you can find the logarithm of a number to base 2, you can find logarithms to any positive base. The power of a which equals y is called $\log_a y$. So,

$$y = a^x \Leftrightarrow x = \log_a y$$

2 Use this definition to find:

(a) $\log_3 9$ (b) $\log_5 125$ (c) $\log_5 \frac{1}{25}$ (d) $\log_7 1$ (e) $\log_6 \frac{1}{216}$

(f) $\log_3 \sqrt[4]{3}$ (g) $\log_4 2$ (h) $\log_{11} 11$ (i) $\log_3 -3$

3 Find: (a) $\log_a 1$ (b) $\log_a a$ (c) $\log_a \dfrac{1}{a}$ (d) $\log_a a^2$

4 Use your calculator to find: (a) $\log_{10} 10^{3.7}$ (b) $10^{\log_{10} 3.7}$
Explain your findings.

5 (a) Write down: (i) $\log_2 8$ (ii) $\log_2 16$ (iii) $\log_2 128$

(b) Since $8 \times 16 = 128$, you can write this as $2^a \times 2^b = 2^c$. What are a, b and c? How is c related to a and b?

(c) Use this to explain why $\log_2 8 + \log_2 16 = \log_2 (8 \times 16)$.

6 $3^2 \times 3^3 = 3^5$

Explain how this verifies that $\log_3 9 + \log_3 27 = \log_3 (9 \times 27)$.

7 (a) Use your calculator to verify that $3 \approx 10^{0.4771}$, $\quad 5 \approx 10^{0.6990}$.

(b) What is: (i) $\log_{10} 3$ (ii) $\log_{10} 5$?

(c) Use these results to find $\log_{10} 15$.

8 Use your calculator to verify that $\log_{10} 9 + \log_{10} 8 = \log_{10} 72$.

Questions 5–8 suggest that logs are related by the law

$$\log_a m + \log_a n = \log_a mn$$

In fact, it is possible to prove that this result is true for any positive base a by using the result

$$a^{\log_a x} = x$$

The proof is as follows.

$$a^{\log_a m + \log_a n} = a^{\log_a m} \times a^{\log_a n} \quad \text{(law of indices)}$$

$$= m \times n$$

$$= a^{\log_a (mn)}$$

$$\Rightarrow \log_a m + \log_a n = \log_a (mn)$$

Question 9 extends this result to logs of quotients.

9 In the law above, replace n by $\dfrac{l}{m}$. Hence show that

$$\log_a l - \log_a m = \log_a \frac{l}{m}$$

Verify that this holds by choosing two arbitrary numbers for l and m.

10 $\log_{10} 2 = 0.3010 \qquad \log_{10} 3 = 0.4771$

Use the properties of logs and the result that $\log_{10} 10 = 1$ to find (in any order):

$\log_{10} \frac{1}{2}, \quad \log_{10} 1.5, \quad \log_{10} 2.5, \quad \log_{10} 4, \quad \log_{10} 5,$
$\log_{10} 6, \quad \log_{10} 8, \quad \log_{10} 9$

You have obtained the following results.

> The power of a which equals y is called $\log_a y$, i.e.
>
> $$y = a^x \Leftrightarrow x = \log_a y$$
>
> Logarithms have the following properties for any positive base a.
>
> $$\log_a a = 1$$
>
> $$\log_a 1 = 0$$
>
> $$\log_a \left(\frac{1}{a} \right) = -1$$
>
> $$\log_a mn = \log_a m + \log_a n$$
>
> $$\log_a \left(\frac{m}{n} \right) = \log_a m - \log_a n$$
>
> $$\log_a a^x = x; \quad a^{\log_a x} = x$$

In pre-calculator days, tables of logarithms were used to help perform various calculations. Part of a table of logarithms to base 10 is given below. From the table, $\log_{10} 1.351 = 0.1306$ and so on.

	0	1	2	3	4	5	6	7	8	9	1	2	3	4	5	6	7	8	9
1.0	.0000	0043	0086	0128	0170	0212	0253	0294	0334	0374	4	8	12	17	21	25	29	33	37
1.1	.0414	0453	0492	0531	0569	0607	0645	0682	0719	0755	4	8	11	15	19	23	27	30	34
1.2	.0792	0828	0864	0899	0934	0969	1004	1038	1072	1106	3	7	10	14	17	21	24	28	31
1.3	.1139	1173	1206	1239	1271	1303	1335	1367	1399	1430	3	6	10	13	16	19	23	26	29
1.4	.1461	1492	1523	1553	1584	1614	1644	1673	1703	1732	3	6	9	12	15	18	21	24	27
1.5	.1761	1790	1818	1847	1875	1903	1931	1959		2014	3	6	8	11	14	17	20	22	25
1.6	.2041	2068	2095	2122	2148	2175	2201				3	5	8	11			18	21	24

In 1615, the Scottish mathematician John Napier discussed the idea of using logarithms with the Oxford professor Henry Briggs. Two years later, Briggs published his first table of logarithms (to 14 decimal places!) and after much further work published his *Arithmetica Logarithmica* in 1624.

Nowadays logarithms can be found using a calculator but originally their calculation involved considerable hard work and ingenuity. 'Log' is by convention usually taken to mean $\log_{10}$, and you will therefore find that the $\boxed{\log}$ key on calculators evaluates logarithms to the base 10.

3.3 **Exercise 4**

1 You have seen that

$$2^3 = 8 \Rightarrow \log_2 8 = 3$$

From these equations with indices, form equations using logarithms.

(a) $3^2 = 9$ (b) $4^{-3} = \frac{1}{64}$ (c) $(0.5)^{-2} = 4$

(d) $\left(\frac{1}{8}\right)^{-\frac{1}{3}} = 2$ (e) $27^{\frac{2}{3}} = 9$

2 Write down the values of:

(a) $\log_2\left(\frac{1}{4}\right)$ (b) $\log_5 125$ (c) $\log_7\left(\frac{1}{7}\right)$ (d) $\log_8\left(\frac{1}{4}\right)$

3 Simplify:

(a) $\log_3 9 + \log_3 27 - \log_3 81$ (b) $\log_5 15 - \log_5 3$ (c) $2\log_7 \sqrt{7}$

4 Sketch, on the same axes, $y = \log_{10} x$, $y = \log_{10} 2x$ and $y = \log_{10} 3x$. How are the graphs related? Use the laws of logs to explain this relationship.

5 (a) Use the log tables given earlier to calculate 1.05×1.267.

    (b) Use the properties of logs to write down $\log_{10} 10.5$ and $\log_{10} 1267$. Hence use log tables to find 10.5×1267.

6 The notation 4! means $4 \times 3 \times 2 \times 1$ and is read as '4 factorial'. If $\log_5 4! = 1.9746$, write down $\log_5 5!$.

7 A colony of bacteria doubles every hour. Explain why the time t hours for the colony to increase in size 1000-fold is given by $2^t = 1000$. Express t as a logarithm to base 2 and explain why $9 < t < 10$. Use a numerical method to find t to two decimal places.

3.3.5 The equation $a^x = b$

In answering the problem in exercise 4 about a colony of bacteria you used a numerical method to solve the equation

$$2^t = 1000$$

Problems concerning growth often lead to such equations, in which the unknown occurs as an index.

Example 6
Suppose that a radioactive isotope decays by 10% each year.

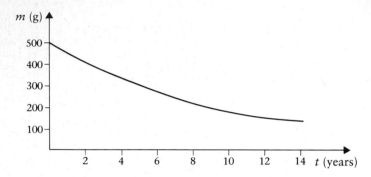

(a) Initially there is 500 g of the isotope. Find an expression for the amount t years later.

(b) The half-life of the isotope is the time taken for the amount present to decrease by 50%. Use the graph to estimate this half-life.

(c) What equation must be solved to find the half-life more precisely?

(d) Use a decimal search to solve the equation in (c).

Solution
(a) If 10% of the isotope decays each year then 90% will remain, so the growth factor must be 0.9. After t years, 500×0.9^t will remain.

(b) The half-life will be the time taken for the amount to drop to 250 grams. From the graph, this is approximately 6.3 years.

(c) To find the half-life more precisely, the equation

$$500 \times 0.9^t = 250$$

must be solved. This simplifies to

$$0.9^t = 0.5$$

(d)

t	6	7	6.5	6.6	6.58
0.9^t	0.531	0.478	0.504	0.499	0.499 94

Equations of the form

$$a^x = b$$

can be solved by a numerical method. There is, however, a more direct way of solving such equations, which is explored in the following questions.

.3D

1 (a) Use your calculator to find the relationship between

    (i) $\log_{10} 49$ and $\log_{10} 7$ (ii) $\log_{10} 64$ and $\log_{10} 2$

    (iii) $\log_{10} 125$ and $\log_{10} 5$

  (b) What is the relationship between $\log_{10} m^p$ and $\log_{10} m$?

2 (a) Use the result $\log_a mn = \log_a m + \log_a n$ to explain why $\log_a m^2 = 2 \log_a m$.

  (b) Generalise this method to explain the law that you found in question 1(b).

3 What is the relationship between $\log 2^x$ and $\log 2$? By taking logs of both sides, use this relationship to solve the equation

$$2^x = 7$$

4 £1000 is invested in an account which earns 1% interest per month, all interest being reinvested.

  (a) Explain why the number m of months taken for the total investment to reach £2000 is given by the equation

$$1.01^m = 2$$

  (b) Find m.

5 The half-life, t days, of bismuth-210 is given approximately by the equation

$$10 \times (0.87)^t = 5$$

Find its half-life in days, correct to 2 significant figures.

> If $a > 0$,
>
> $$\log a^p = p \log a$$

Example 7
Find the half-life of the radioactive isotope considered in example 6.

Solution

$$500 \times 0.9^t = 250$$

$$\Rightarrow \qquad 0.9^t = 0.5 \qquad \text{(divide both sides by 500)}$$

$$\Rightarrow \qquad \log 0.9^t = \log 0.5 \qquad \text{(take logs of both sides)}$$

$$\Rightarrow \qquad t \log 0.9 = \log 0.5 \qquad \text{(using the property of logs above)}$$

$$\Rightarrow \qquad t = \frac{\log 0.5}{\log 0.9} \approx 6.58 \qquad \begin{array}{l}\text{(You may use \textit{either} of the} \\ \text{logarithm buttons on your} \\ \text{calculator here.)}\end{array}$$

The half-life is approximately 6.58 years.

3.3 Exercise 5

1 Solve for x:

(a) $2^x = 32$ (b) $9^x = 243$ (c) $8^x = 256$

(d) $3^x = 10.05$ (e) $5^x = 9.2$ (f) $2.073^x = 7.218$

2 Explain how you could have obtained the answers to 1(a), 1(b) and 1(c) without using a calculator.

3 A colony of bacteria has a growth factor of 3.7 per hour and initially there are 250 bacteria.

(a) Write down an expression for the number of bacteria after t hours.

(b) Find the time (to the nearest minute) after which there are 10 000 bacteria.

4 A capacitor is discharging with a growth factor of 0.9 per second. After how long will there be $\frac{1}{5}$ of the original charge? (Give your answer in seconds, to 2 d.p.)

5 The number, n, of years needed for an investment of £4000 to grow to £5000 at 8% per annum compound interest is given by $1.08^n = 1.25$. Find n using logarithms.

6 In 1980, the population of Africa was 470 million and growing at a rate of 2.9% per annum. In what year will its population reach one thousand million according to this model?

7 In 1980, the population of China was 995 million and growing at a rate of 1.4% per annum. After how many years will the population of China equal that of Africa?

3.3.6 Using logarithms in experimental work

A very important practical use of logarithms is in experimental work, and you may have the opportunity in your other studies to employ the following procedure.

Suppose that you obtained the following results while investigating the relationship between the time of swing of a pendulum and its length.

Length of pendulum, l (m)	0.6	1.0	1.4	1.8	2.2
Average time of swing, t (s)	1.54	2.03	2.39	2.67	2.97

It would be natural to plot the graph of t against l.

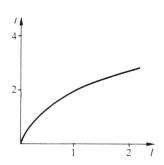

The shape of the graph does not make it easy to predict what the relationship is, although it clearly indicates a definite relationship which would be convenient to represent algebraically.

If either the shape of the graph or other considerations lead you to suspect that the relationship is that t is proportional to some power of l, then you can test this with the help of logarithms.

$$t = kl^n$$

$$\log t = \log (kl^n)$$

$$\log t = n \log l + \log k$$

Comparing this with the equation of the straight line, $y = mx + c$, indicates that, if the power relationship is correct, then the graph of **log t** (the 'y' variable) against **log l** (the 'x' variable), should be a straight line having gradient n and intercept on the log t-axis of log k.

For convenience (calculators have an appropriate button!), we have taken the logs to base 10 and tabulated the values below.

$\log_{10} l$	-0.222	0.000	0.146	0.255	0.342
$\log_{10} t$	0.187	0.307	0.387	0.426	0.473

The graph is plotted here. You can read off the values for n and $\log k$.

$$\log_{10} k \approx 0.30$$

$$\Rightarrow k = 10^{0.30} = 2 \quad \text{(to 2 s.f.)}$$

$$n = 0.50$$

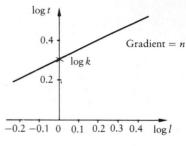

Hence the relationship is

$$t = 2.0 l^{0.5}$$

or $\quad t = 2\sqrt{l}$

A very similar method is employed if the relationship is thought to be a power function. If

$$y = kb^x$$

then taking logs of both sides of this equation gives

$$\log y = \log(kb^x)$$

$$= \log(b^x) + \log k$$

$$\log y = x \log b + \log k$$

A graph of $\log y$ against x would be a straight line of gradient $\log b$ and intercept $\log k$.

3.3 Exercise 6

1 In an experiment to determine how the sag of a beam varies with the distance between its supports the following results were obtained

d (cm)	500	540	580	620	660	700
z (cm)	1.1	1.3	1.7	2.0	2.4	2.8

where d is the distance between the supports and z is the sag.

By drawing the graph of $\log z$ against $\log d$, determine the power of d to which z is proportional.

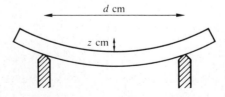

2 The charge on a capacitor, t milliseconds after a switch is closed, is believed to decay exponentially. The results of a set of measurements are as follows.

Time, t	2	3	4	5	6
Charge, Q	7.6	2.8	1.0	0.4	0.1

If $Q = kb^t$, by taking logs and plotting an appropriate straight line graph, find the relationship between Q and t.

3 The period of oscillation, P seconds, for bars of uniform material is thought to be proportional to some power of their length, L metres $(P = kL^n)$. One set of measurements is given in the table below.

L	2	3	4	5	6
P	4.5	5.5	6.4	7.2	8.7

However, one result has been incorrectly copied. Plot an appropriate straight line graph. Give the corresponding formula connecting P and L and state what you think the incorrect result might have been.

4 The rate of decay of a radioactive substance is usually measured in terms of its half-life.

Suppose that the formula for its mass at time t is $m = m_0 e^{-kt}$ where m_0 is the initial mass, e = 2.718 and k is a constant with a value particular to these circumstances.

If $m = 0.9m_0$ when $t = 2$, show that $k = 0.0527$; hence find the value of t when $m = 0.5m_0$.

After working through section 3.3 you should:

1 recognise data which exhibits exponential growth;

2 understand the relationship between logarithms and indices;

3 be able to draw the graph of a logarithmic function;

4 be able to use the laws of indices and logarithms;

5 be able to model data using the equation $y = Ka^x$;

6 be able to solve equations of the form $a^x = b$;

7 be able to use the logarithmic function when investigating experimental data.

3 Functions

.4 The number e

3.4.1 e^x

You saw in section 3.3 how functions given by equations of the form $y = Ka^x$ can be used to model growth. In this section we shall look in detail at *rates* of growth for these functions and see how all functions of this kind are very closely related.

In the following questions you will investigate the gradient function for $y = a^x$.

 .4A

You will need a graph plotter which can plot the gradient graph of a function, so that you can check your results.

1 (a) Sketch the graphs of $y = 2^x$ and $\dfrac{dy}{dx}$, the gradient function.

(b) Suggest an equation for the function $\dfrac{dy}{dx}$, and check your answers using a graph plotter.

2 Repeat question 1 for each of the following functions.

(a) $y = 3^x$ (b) $y = 1.5^x$ (c) $y = 10^x$

3 Suggest a value for a for which $\dfrac{d}{dx}(a^x) = a^x$. Check your answer by sketching appropriate graphs.

4 Suggest an appropriate gradient function for ke^x, where e is the value for a that you suggested in question 3.

The gradient function for $y = 2^x$ can be found by 'zooming-in' at any point $P(x, y)$ on the graph of $y = 2^x$ until the curve looks straight.

The gradient of the graph at P is approximately equal to the gradient of PQ, where Q is a nearby point on the graph.

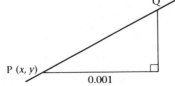

5 (a) Explain why the y-coordinate of Q is $2^{0.001}2^x$.

(b) Explain why the gradient PQ is $\dfrac{2^{0.001}2^x - 2^x}{0.001}$.

(c) Show how the expression in (b) can be simplified to 0.693×2^x.

(d) You have seen that $y = 2^x \Rightarrow \dfrac{dy}{dx} \approx 0.693 \times 2^x$. How could you increase the accuracy of this result?

6 Adapt the method of question 5 to find $\dfrac{dy}{dx}$ when $y = 5^x$.

The gradient of an exponential function at any point is proportional to its value at that point.

$$y = 2^x \Rightarrow \frac{dy}{dx} = 0.69 \times 2^x$$

$$y = 3^x \Rightarrow \frac{dy}{dx} = 1.10 \times 3^x$$

$$y = 10^x \Rightarrow \frac{dy}{dx} = 2.30 \times 10^x$$

Generally, $y = a^x \Rightarrow \dfrac{dy}{dx} = k \times a^x$, where k is a constant.

The value of a for which $k = 1$ is denoted by the letter e. This gives the important results

$$\frac{d}{dx}(e^x) = e^x$$

$$\int e^x \, dx = e^x + c$$

e = 2.718 281 828 4 to ten decimal places.

Like π, e is an irrational number. The Swiss mathematician Leonhard Euler (1707–1783) first used the letter e to represent this number. Euler introduced several other mathematical notations, including that for functions, f(x). He was also the first to use the summation sign $\sum$, the letter π for the ratio of circumference to diameter of a circle and i for $\sqrt{-1}$ (both i and j are in common use today). He continued to work actively after becoming totally blind in 1768.

The shapes of the graphs of $y = e^x$ and $y = e^{-x}$ are typical of exponential growth and decay respectively. Some calculators and textbooks express e^x as $\exp x$. This notation is also used in some computer languages.

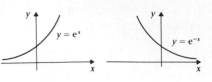

Notice that $\dfrac{dy}{dx} > 0$ for all x for the exponential function $y = e^x$. Such a function is called an **increasing function** of x.

> If $f'(x) > 0$ for all x, then $f(x)$ is an increasing function of x.
>
> $f'(x) < 0$ for all $x \Rightarrow f(x)$ is a decreasing function of x.

Clearly e^x is an increasing function of x, while e^{-x} is a decreasing function.

3.4 Exercise 1

1 (a) Use your calculator to find:

   (i) e^3 (ii) $\exp(5.1)$ (iii) e^{-2} (iv) $\dfrac{5}{e^3}$ (v) $\exp(0.5)$

   (b) What is the largest power of e that your calculator can evaluate, and why?

2 Make tables of values for $-4 \le x \le 4$ and draw the graphs of:

   (a) $y = e^{2x}$ (b) $y = e^{-x}$

3 Draw the graph of
$$y = 5(1 - e^{-x})$$
for $0 \le x \le 5$. Check the shape using a graph plotter.

4 (a) When certain drugs are injected into the body, the amount remaining in the bloodstream decays exponentially. The amount of one drug in the bloodstream is modelled by the equation
$$y = 5e^{-0.2t}$$
where t is the time in hours after the dose is administered, and y is the amount remaining, in milligrams.

   (i) What is the initial value of y?
   (ii) What is the value of y when $t = 10$?
   (iii) Sketch the graph of y against t.

   (b) The amount of a second drug is modelled by the equation $y = 5e^{-0.5t}$. Does it decay more or less rapidly than the first drug?

5 A colony of bacteria grows according to the law $y = 4e^t$, where t is measured in hours and y is the population.

By differentiating, show that $\dfrac{dy}{dt} = y$. What does this tell you about the rate of growth of the bacterial colony?

How rapidly is the colony growing at a time when it contains 500 bacteria?

6E Show by a numerical method that $\lim\limits_{h \to 0} \left(\dfrac{e^h - 1}{h} \right) = 1$. Hence show, using

differentiation from first principles, that $\dfrac{d}{dx}(e^x) = e^x$.

3.4.2 e^{ax}

One of the great benefits of introducing e as a base for the growth function is that it can replace all the other bases. This simplifies subsequent work, particularly in calculus.

Example 1
(a) Find alternative expressions of the form 2^{at} for   (i) 8^t (ii) 5^t

(b) Is it *always* possible to express b^t in the form 2^{at}?

Solution
(a)   (i) $8^t = (2^3)^t = 2^{3t}$

(ii) $5^t = 2^{at} \Rightarrow 5 = 2^a$, i.e. $a = \dfrac{\log 5}{\log 2} = 2.32$. Therefore $5^t = 2^{2.32t}$

(b) When $b > 0$, it is clear that you can always write b^t in the form 2^{at}, since you can always solve the equation $b = 2^a$. As has been noted already, when $b < 0$ the meaning of b^t is not defined for some values of t (for example, $t = \frac{1}{2}$).

This idea of changing the base of an exponential function is explored below.

 .4B

1 (a) Use a graph plotter to verify that the graphs of 9^x and 3^{2x} coincide.

(b) Find the value of a so that the following pairs of graphs coincide.

(i) 5^x and 3^{ax} (ii) 7^x and 3^{ax} (iii) 2^x and 3^{ax}

It appears that, for any positive value of b, you could replace b^x by 3^{ax}. In other words, only one base is needed for all exponential functions. The base used in practice is not 3 but e.

2 (a) Use a graph plotter to sketch the family of curves $y = e^{ax}$

 (i) for a few positive values of a, of your own choice,

(ii) for a few negative values of a.

What shape is the graph if $a = 0$?

(b) If $a > b > 0$, describe the relationship of the graph of e^{ax} to that of e^{bx}. For what values of x is $e^{ax} > e^{bx}$?

3 Using the same method as in question 1, find the value of a so that the following pairs of graphs coincide.

(a) 5^x and e^{ax} (b) 8^x and e^{ax} (c) 2^x and e^{ax}

4 (a) You know from section 3.4.1 that, if $y = 2^x$, $\dfrac{dy}{dx} \approx 0.69 \times 2^x$ and, from question 3, that $2^x \approx e^{0.69x}$. Explain how these results can be combined to show that

$$\frac{d}{dx}(e^{0.69x}) = 0.69e^{0.69x}$$

(b) Suggest a possible derivative for e^{5x}.

The previous question suggests that $\dfrac{d}{dx}(e^{ax}) = ae^{ax}$. In the next question you investigate how this result arises.

5

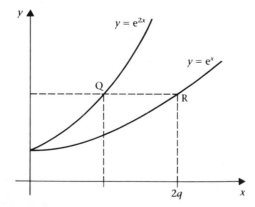

(a) In the diagram, Q and R have the same y-coordinate. What is it?

(b) What is the x-coordinate of Q?

(c) The graph of $y = e^{2x}$ can be obtained from the graph of $y = e^x$ by squashing by a factor of 2 in the x-direction. What effect does this have on the gradient of the graph?

(d) If the gradient at R is g, what is the gradient at Q?

(e) Write down, in terms of q, the gradient of $y = e^x$ at the point R. Hence write down the gradient of $y = e^{2x}$ at the point Q.

(f) Complete

$$\frac{d}{dx}(e^{2x}) = \ldots \times e^{2x}$$

You have seen that, if $b > 0$, you can express b^x in the form e^{ax} and that

$$\frac{d}{dx}(e^{ax}) = ae^{ax}$$

3 .4c

(a) What is $\int e^{ax} \, dx$?

(b) In general, if $\frac{d}{dx}(f(x)) = g(x)$, what are:

(i) $\frac{d}{dx}(f(ax))$ (ii) $\int g(ax) \, dx$?

Example 2

If $y = 5\left(\dfrac{e^{2x} + 1}{e^{2x}}\right)$, show that y is a decreasing function of x.

Solution

$$y = 5\left(\frac{e^{2x} + 1}{e^{2x}}\right) = 5 + 5e^{-2x}$$

$$\frac{dy}{dx} = 5(-2)\,e^{-2x} = -10e^{-2x}$$

Since $e^{-2x} > 0$ for all x, $\dfrac{dy}{dx} = -10e^{-2x} < 0$ for all x, so y is a decreasing function of x.

3.4 **Exercise 2**

1 Differentiate:

(a) e^{4x} (b) e^{-2x} (c) $(e^x)^5$ (d) $\dfrac{1}{e^{3x}}$

(e) $5e^{4x}$ (f) $e^x + \dfrac{1}{e^x}$ (g) $\sqrt{e^x}$ (h) $\dfrac{5}{e^{9x}}$

2 Integrate the functions of x in question 1.

3 Sketch the graphs of:

(a) $y = e^{-4x}$ (b) $y = 3(1 - e^{-2x})$ (c) $y = e^x + \dfrac{1}{e^x}$

4 When a drug such as penicillin is prescribed, it is usual to take it 3 or 4 times a day. One or two days may elapse before the drug starts to take effect. A simple model of this process is known as the 'Rustogi' drug model.

Suppose that for a certain drug, the amount in milligrams in the bloodstream t hours after taking a dose of size A mg is given by

$$x = Ae^{-\frac{1}{8}t}$$

and that a dose of 10 mg is administered at 8-hourly intervals. On graph paper, using a scale of 1 cm to 2 hours on the t-axis and 1 cm to 2 mg on the x-axis, plot the drug level in the body over the first 32 hours as follows:

(a) For the first 8 hours calculate the drug level for $t = 0, 2, 4, 6, 8$ and plot these values.

(b) Add the next dose of 10 mg and plot this point, also at $t = 8$.

(c) This gives the 'effective dose' at this time, i.e. the new value for A. Recalculate the drug level for the next 8-hour period, again taking $t = 0, 2, 4, 6, 8$.

(d) Repeat steps (b) and (c) to show how the drug level varies in the body for the remainder of the period.

What value does the maximum drug level in the body approach?

5 In hospitals, when it is necessary for a patient to respond rapidly to treatment, a doctor will often give a 'booster' dose, equivalent to 1.6 times the initial dose. Repeat question 4, but with an initial dose of 16 mg and subsequent doses of 10 mg. [It should only be necessary to consider the first 8 hours.]

Note: this method is not used for drugs available on prescription to the general public; if subsequent doses of 16 mg were taken in error the drug level would rise to $1.6 \times 16 = 25.6$ mg, with potentially dangerous consequences.

3.4.3 The natural log

You saw in 3.3.4 that the power of 2 that was equal to y was called $\log_2 y$, i.e.

$$\text{if } 2^x = y, \quad \text{then } x = \log_2 y$$

You also saw how this idea can be extended to other bases, so that, for example, if $10^x = y$ then $x = \log_{10} y$.

Since e was chosen as the base for exponential functions in order to simplify results in calculus, it is useful to consider e as a base for logarithms. Logarithms to base e are called **natural logarithms** and $\log_e x$ may be written as $\ln x$ (n for 'natural'). Some older texts simply use $\log x$ for $\ln x$.

By analogy with base 2, $\ln x$ is defined so that, if $y = \ln x$, then $x = e^y$. $\ln x$ and e^x are therefore inverse functions.

Since $\ln x$ and e^x are inverse functions, the application of one followed by the other restores the original value.

At this stage you may find it useful to recall the laws of logarithms, as applied to logarithms with base e.

$$\ln e = 1 \qquad \ln 1 = 0$$

$$\ln(ab) = \ln a + \ln b \qquad \ln\left(\frac{a}{b}\right) = \ln a - \ln b$$

$$\ln(a^n) = n \ln a$$

Example 3
Express in terms of $\ln x$: (a) $\ln 4x^5$ (b) $\ln\left(\dfrac{1}{\sqrt{x}}\right)$

Solution
(a) $\ln 4x^5 = \ln 4 + \ln x^5 = \ln 4 + 5\ln x$

(b) $\ln\left(\dfrac{1}{\sqrt{x}}\right) = \ln 1 - \ln \sqrt{x} = 0 - \ln x^{\frac{1}{2}} = -\frac{1}{2}\ln x$

or

$\ln\left(\dfrac{1}{\sqrt{x}}\right) = \ln(x^{-\frac{1}{2}}) = -\frac{1}{2}\ln x$

Natural logarithms are sometimes called Napierian logarithms, after John Napier. However, this is a misnomer as they are not the logarithms originally developed by Napier.

Some of the properties of $\ln x$ are explored in 3.4D, especially its gradient function.

.4D

The graph of ln x

1 (a) $\ln y \, (= \log_e y)$ is the power of e that equals y, that is $y = e^x \Leftrightarrow x = \ln y$.
Use this result to find:

    (i) $\ln 1$ (ii) $\ln e$ (iii) $\ln e^2$

    (iv) $\ln \dfrac{1}{e}$ (v) $\ln \dfrac{1}{e^5}$ (vi) $\ln(-1)$

  (b) Use your results to sketch the graph of $\ln x$.

Derivative of ln x

The graphs of e^x and of $\ln x$ are sketched below. Since they are inverse
functions, the graph of $\ln x$ is a reflection of that of e^x in the line $y = x$. You
can use this idea to find the derivative of $\ln x$.

2

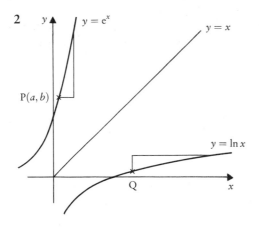

The figure shows the graph of
$y = e^x$ and $y = \ln x$. Q is the
reflection of P (a, b) in the line
$y = x$.

You can use the relationship
between the two graphs to
find the gradient of $y = \ln x$
at Q.

(a) Express b in terms of a.

(b) Write down the coordinates of Q.

(c) Use the fact that the triangle at Q is a reflection of the triangle at P to
explain why the gradient of the curve at Q is $\dfrac{1}{\text{gradient of } y = e^x \text{ at P}}$.

(d) Since P lies on the curve $y = e^x$, you know that the gradient at P (a, b)
is e^a. What is the gradient of $y = \ln x$ at Q?

(e) Explain why $\dfrac{d}{dx}(\ln x) = \dfrac{1}{x}$.

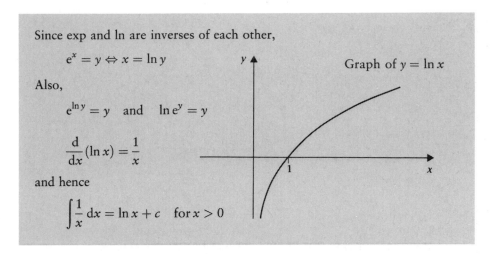

Since exp and ln are inverses of each other,

$$e^x = y \Leftrightarrow x = \ln y$$

Also,

$$e^{\ln y} = y \quad \text{and} \quad \ln e^y = y$$

$$\frac{d}{dx}(\ln x) = \frac{1}{x}$$

and hence

$$\int \frac{1}{x}\,dx = \ln x + c \quad \text{for } x > 0$$

Graph of $y = \ln x$

As you have seen, physical situations involving growth are often modelled using exponential functions. In solving the model, a useful step is that from an equation of the form $e^A = B$ to one of the form $A = \ln B$. An example of this is in the use of the logistic curve, a model that is appropriate when growth is limited by fixed resources. Its general equation is

$$y = \frac{A}{1 + Ke^{-\lambda x}}$$

where A, K and λ are constants, and its graph is as shown.

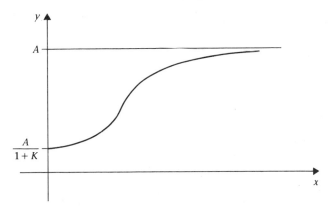

Example 4

A highly infectious disease is introduced into a small isolated village, of population 200. The number of individuals, y, who have contracted the disease t days after the outbreak begins is modelled by the logistic equation

$$y = \frac{200}{1 + 199e^{-0.2t}}$$

After what time has half the population been infected?

Solution

When half the population has been infected $y = 100$.

$$100 = \frac{200}{1 + 199e^{-0.2t}} \qquad \Rightarrow \qquad 1 + 199e^{-0.2t} = 2$$

$$\Rightarrow \qquad e^{-0.2t} = \tfrac{1}{199}$$

$$\Rightarrow \qquad -0.2t = \ln\tfrac{1}{199}$$

$$\Rightarrow \qquad t = -\tfrac{1}{0.2}\ln\tfrac{1}{199} = 26.5 \,(\text{days})$$

3.4 Exercise 3

1 Use your calculator to evaluate: (a) $\ln 3.5$ (b) $\ln 0.35$ (c) $\ln 7$

2 Use the laws of logarithms to prove that:
  (a) $\ln 3 + \ln 4 = \ln 12$ (b) $\ln 10 - \ln 2 = \ln 5$

  (c) $3\ln 5 = \ln 125$ (d) $\dfrac{\ln 20}{\ln 4} \neq \ln 5$

3 Use the laws of logarithms to express the following in terms of $\ln x$.
  (a) $\ln x^3$ (b) $\ln 4x$ (c) $\ln \tfrac{1}{3}x$

4 Find: (a) $\dfrac{d}{dx}(4\ln x)$ (b) $\dfrac{d}{dx}(\ln x^3)$ (c) $\dfrac{d}{dx}(\ln 4x)$

5 Use the population model of example 4 to find how long it takes for 90% of the population to become infected.

6 A cup of coffee, initially at boiling point, cools according to Newton's law of cooling, so that after t minutes its temperature, $T\,°C$, is given by

$$T = 15 + 85e^{-t/8}$$

Sketch the graph of T against t. How long does the cup take to cool to $40\,°C$?

7 In the process of carbon dating, the level of the isotope carbon-14 (^{14}C) is measured. When a plant or animal is alive the amount of ^{14}C in the body remains at a constant level, but when it dies the amount decays at a constant rate according to the law $m = m_0 e^{-Kt}$, where m_0 is the initial mass and m the mass after t years.

  (a) If the half-life of ^{14}C is 5570 years, find the decay constant K.

  (b) A piece of oak from an old building contains $\tfrac{9}{10}$ of the level of ^{14}C that is contained in living oak. How old is the building?

After working through section 3.4 you should:

1 understand the reason for the choice of e as base for exponential and logarithmic functions;

2 be able to sketch graphs of exponential growth and decay and of logarithmic functions;

3 be able to differentiate e^{ax} and $\ln ax$, and to integrate e^{ax} and $\frac{1}{x}$;

4 appreciate that exp and ln are inverse functions;

5 be able to solve problems involving e^x and $\ln x$ by using appropriate algebraic manipulation;

6 be able to show whether a function is increasing or decreasing by considering its derivative.

3 Functions

.5 Radians

3.5.1 Rates of change

This section considers the rates of change of the sine and the cosine functions and introduces an important new measure of angle. Consider first the graph of $y = \sin \theta°$.

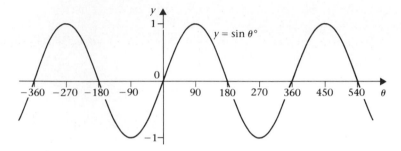

The graph of $y = \sin \theta°$ has gradient $\dfrac{dy}{d\theta}$.

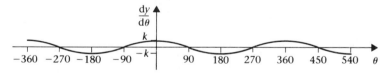

You should be able to sketch this graph from the graph of $\sin \theta°$ by noting the points on $\sin \theta°$ where the gradient is zero ($-270°$, $-90°$, $90°$), where it is at its greatest value (at $-360°$, $0°$, $360°$) and at its least value ($-180°$, $180°$, ...). The value of k is the gradient of the graph $y = \sin \theta°$ at the origin.

Zooming in to the origin on the graph of $y = \sin \theta°$ and using the principle of local straightness, the gradient of $y = \sin \theta°$ at the origin is

$$\frac{dy}{d\theta} \approx \frac{\sin \theta°}{\theta}$$

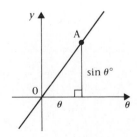

Observe that:

- the gradient graph appears to be a cosine curve, with amplitude k. It has equation

$$\frac{dy}{d\theta} = k \cos \theta^\circ;$$

- k is the gradient of $y = \sin \theta^\circ$ at 0. Thus, from the diagram and argument above

$$k \approx \frac{\sin \theta^\circ}{\theta} \quad \text{for small } \theta$$

- you can obtain a sequence of values which approaches k by taking smaller and smaller values of θ. This is explored further in 3.5A below.

 .5A

For these questions you will need a graph plotter which can plot the gradient graph of a function.

1 (a) (i) Calculate the values of $\dfrac{\sin \theta^\circ}{\theta}$ for $\theta = 10, 5, 2, 1$ and 0.1.

    (ii) To what value (to 5 d.p.) does your sequence of values of $\dfrac{\sin \theta^\circ}{\theta}$ converge, as θ approaches zero?

  (b) Use a graph plotter to obtain the gradient graph of $y = \sin \theta^\circ$. Does this give a value of k which agrees with your solution to part (a)? You will need to be careful with the vertical scale.

2

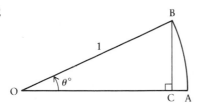

Consider a sector AOB of a circle of unit radius with angle θ° at the centre. BC is the perpendicular from B to OA.

  (a) For $\theta = 10, 5, 2, 1$ and 0.1 calculate:

    (i) the length of BC   (ii) the length of the arc BA

  (b) What do you notice about the results?

3 Express the length BC and the length of arc BA as functions of θ.

From the previous question it is evident that these two lengths are approximately equal for small values of θ. Use this fact to explain why

$$\frac{\sin \theta^\circ}{\theta} \approx \frac{\pi}{180}$$

for small values of θ.

4 Calculate the value of $\dfrac{\pi}{180}$ and compare it with the answer to question 1(a)(ii).

5 What is the gradient of $y = \sin\theta°$ at the origin?

6 Suggest a suitable expression for $\dfrac{dy}{d\theta}$, if $y = \sin\theta°$.

The questions of 3.5A demonstrate the result

$$\frac{d}{d\theta}(\sin\theta°) = \frac{\pi}{180}\cos\theta°$$

At $(0, 0)$,

$$\text{gradient} = \frac{\pi}{180}$$

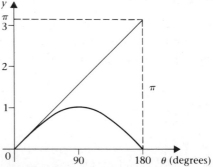

If angles were measured in units other than degrees, with π of these new units equivalent to $180°$, then the diagram above would look like this:

At $(0, 0)$,

$$\text{gradient} = \frac{\pi}{\pi} = 1$$

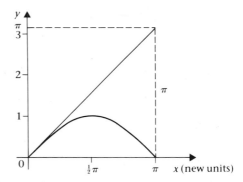

The new units would then give the simple result

$$y = \sin x \Rightarrow \frac{dy}{dx} = \cos x$$

Scientific calculators provide the option of using these new units, which are called **radians** and are defined by the relationship

$$\pi \text{ radians} = 180°$$

.5B

(a) Sketch the gradient graph for $y = \cos x°$.

(b) What do you think is the derivative of:

(i) $\cos x$ (x in radians)   (ii) $\cos x°$?

3.5.2 Radian measure

In most of the subsequent work on circular functions you will be using radians. It is often convenient to express radians as multiples of π, because the key relationship between radians and degrees is

π radians $= 180°$

The symbol for a radian is 1^c ('c' suggests *circular* measure); thus $\pi^c = 180°$. Except when the radian unit is being stressed, the c is usually omitted.

Calculators will accept either degrees or radians as input for circular functions. The following questions allow you to explore the different modes on your calculator.

 .5C

1 Use your calculator in appropriate mode to find:

(a) $\sin 1^c$ (b) $\sin 1°$ (c) $\cos -5°$ (d) $\cos -5°$

(e) $\tan \frac{1}{4}\pi^c$ (f) $\tan \frac{1}{4}\pi°$

2 (a) Find: (i) $\sin 30°$ (ii) $\sin \frac{1}{6}\pi^c$

What do you notice?

(b) You know π radians are equal to $180°$. This can be used to establish a number of other reference points between the two scales. Complete the following table.

Radians		$\frac{1}{2}\pi$			$\frac{1}{6}\pi$	$\frac{3}{2}\pi$	
Degrees	180		60	45			360

(c) What formula will convert $\theta°$ to radians?

(d) What formula will convert θ^c to degrees?

3 It is very easy to leave your calculator in the wrong mode! Suppose you are asked to find $\sin \frac{1}{3}\pi$ and you have your machine in degree mode.

(a) What is $\frac{1}{3}\pi$ to 3 decimal places?

(b) What is $\sin \frac{1}{3}\pi$ (taking $\frac{1}{3}\pi$ in radians)?

(c) What answer does your calculator give if left in degree mode?

4 Suppose you try to evaluate $\sin 60°$, but leave your calculator in radian mode. What should you get in degree mode? What in fact do you get?

5 Working in radians, plot on graph paper the graph of $y = \sin x$ for values of x from 0 to 7, increasing in steps of 0.5. In addition, mark on the x-axis the numbers $\frac{1}{4}\pi, \frac{1}{2}\pi, \frac{3}{4}\pi, \pi, \frac{3}{2}\pi, 2\pi$.

3.5 Exercise 1

1 Express these angles, measured in degrees, in radians.
   (a) $90°$ (b) $360°$ (c) $45°$ (d) $120°$
   (e) $60°$ (f) $720°$ (g) $-30°$ (h) $135°$

2 Express these angles, measured in radians, in degrees.
   (a) $\frac{1}{4}\pi$ (b) 3π (c) $-\pi$
   (d) $\frac{3}{2}\pi$ (e) -2π

3 If the period of $y = \cos \theta°$ is 360, what is the period of $y = \cos \theta^c$?

4 What are the periods of the functions with these equations?
   (a) $y = \sin t$ (b) $y = \sin \pi t$ (c) $y = \sin \omega t$

3.5.3 Area and arc lengths

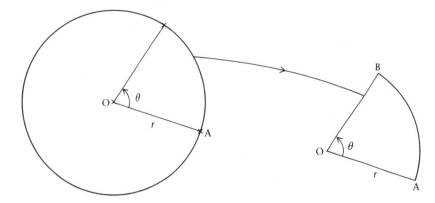

The angle θ shown is measured in radians.

Since the circumference of a full circle of radius r is $2\pi r$ units and the arc AB is $\dfrac{\theta}{2\pi}$ of the full circle, the length of arc AB is $\dfrac{\theta}{2\pi} \times 2\pi r = r\theta$.

This gives rise to the alternative definition of a radian as that angle which is subtended at the centre by an arc of length 1 in a circle of radius 1. Observe that 1 radian is a little less than 60°.

The area of the sector OAB is $\dfrac{\theta}{2\pi}$ of the area of the full circle. For a circle of radius r, then, the sector of angle θ radians has area

$$\frac{\theta}{2\pi} \times \pi r^2 = \tfrac{1}{2}r^2\theta$$

Radian measure for angles can be directly related to circles, and is therefore often called circular measure.

A radian is the angle subtended by an arc of unit length at the centre of a circle of unit radius.

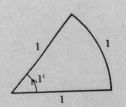

For a sector of a circle radius r, with angle θ radians,

arc length $l = r\theta$

area $A = \tfrac{1}{2}r^2\theta$

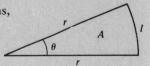

3.5 Exercise 2

1 The wedge OAB is cut from a circle of radius 2 cm.

(a) What is the area of the wedge?

(b) What is the length of arc AB?

(c) What is the perimeter of the wedge?

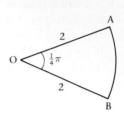

2

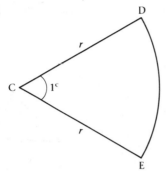

If the perimeter of sector CDE is numerically equal to the area of sector CDE, find r.

3 An area is to be fenced off for a crowd at a pop concert.

(a) Calculate the length required to fence off the perimeter.

(b) Calculate the maximum crowd if the police decide that the crowd density should not exceed 1 person per 2 square metres.

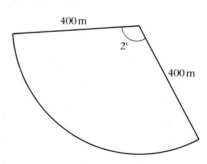

4 OAB is a sector of a circle of radius r. Find in terms of r and θ:

(a) the length BC

(b) the area of triangle OAB

(c) the area of the sector OAB

(d) the area of the shaded segment

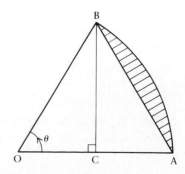

5 A circular cake of diameter 20 cm is cut along AB, half-way from the centre to the rim. Show that the angle θ is 120°. Calculate the areas of the sector OAB, the triangle OAB, and hence the area of cake cut off.

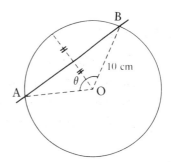

6E In the diagram show that the ratio of the area of the triangle OAB to the area of the sector OAB is $\dfrac{\sin\theta}{\theta}$. Deduce that $\dfrac{\sin\theta}{\theta}$ tends to 1, and is always less than 1, as θ tends to 0. (Use the area formula $\frac{1}{2}bc\sin A$ for a triangle.)

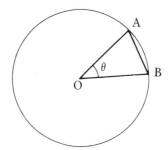

3.5.4 More about derivatives

You have seen evidence to suggest that, when x is measured in radians,

$$y = \sin x \Rightarrow \frac{dy}{dx} = \cos x \qquad y = \cos x \Rightarrow \frac{dy}{dx} = -\sin x$$

These results will be *proved* when we do more work on these functions later in the text. The results, however, *are* true and we can use them to find derivatives of functions such as $\sin 2x$, $5\cos x$ and $10\sin 0.1\pi x$. The graphs of such functions are related to those of $\sin x$ and $\cos x$ by means of stretches in the x- and y-directions. You have seen that a stretch of factor $\dfrac{1}{b}$ in the x-direction and a stretch of a in the y-direction maps $y = \sin x$ onto $y = a\sin bx$.

In the following questions you can use these ideas to find the derivative of $y = a\sin bx$.

 .5D

It is important to remember that x is measured in *radians* throughout. You will need a graph plotter which can plot the gradient graph of a function, to check your findings.

1 On the same axes sketch the graphs of $y = \sin x$ and $y = 5 \sin x$ for $0 \le x \le 2\pi$.

(a) Describe the stretch which maps $y = \sin x$ onto $y = 5 \sin x$.

(b) What is the effect of this stretch on the gradient of the graph of $y = \sin x$?

(c) Suggest what the derivative of $y = 5 \sin x$ might be.

(d) Check your answer to (c) by using a graph plotter to obtain the gradient graph for $y = 5 \sin x$.

2 On the same axes, sketch the graphs of $y = \sin x$ and $y = \sin 3x$ for $0 \le x \le 2\pi$.

(a) Describe the stretch which maps $y = \sin x$ onto $y = \sin 3x$.

(b) What is the effect of this stretch on the gradient of the graph of $y = \sin x$?

(c) Suggest what the derivative of $y = \sin 3x$ might be. Check your answer by using a graph plotter.

3 Investigate the derivative of $y = 5 \sin 3x$ in a similar way.

4 Using the ideas of the previous questions, find the derivatives of:

(a) $y = \cos 2x$ (b) $y = 10 \sin 2x$ (c) $y = \sin 0.5x$

5 (a) Sketch graphs of $y = 3 \cos 2x$, $y = 3 \cos 2x + 4$ and $y = 3 \cos 2x - 1$.

(b) What are the derivatives of each of these functions?

6 (a) What are the derivatives of:

(i) $y = a \sin x$ (ii) $y = \sin bx$ (iii) $y = a \sin bx$?

(b) Write down the corresponding result for cosine functions for part (iii).

You have now seen that:

With x in radians,

$$y = a \sin bx \Rightarrow \frac{dy}{dx} = ab \cos bx$$

$$y = a \cos bx \Rightarrow \frac{dy}{dx} = -ab \sin bx$$

3.5 **Exercise 3**

1 Find $\dfrac{dy}{dx}$ when:

(a) $y = \frac{1}{2}\sin x$ (b) $y = 5\cos x$ (c) $y = 0.1\sin x + 0.5$

(d) $y = \sin 4x$ (e) $y = \cos 2\pi x$ (f) $y = \sin 0.2x$

(g) $y = 3\cos 2x$ (h) $y = 6\sin\frac{1}{2}\pi x$ (i) $y = 4 + 3\sin\frac{1}{3}x$

2 (a) If $y = \cos 2x$, what is $\dfrac{dy}{dx}$?

(b) Find $\displaystyle\int \sin 2x \, dx$.

(c) Find $\displaystyle\int \cos 3x \, dx$.

▶ 3.5 **Tasksheet E1 – Derivative of $\sin^2 x$ (page 556)**

3.5.5 Applications

You can formulate many problems in terms of radians so that it is easier to answer questions about rates of change. For example, suppose the height of the tide in a harbour at time t is as shown.

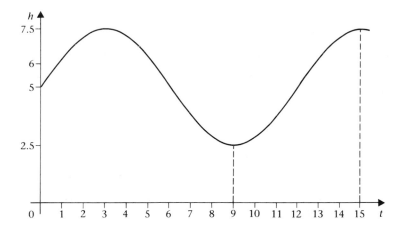

In building up the equation which links h and t, observe that the graph could be a sine function stretched by scale factor 2.5 in the direction of the y-axis and translated $\begin{bmatrix} 0 \\ 5 \end{bmatrix}$.

$$h = 2.5 \sin(\omega t) + 5$$

Since the period of $y = \sin \omega t$ is $\dfrac{2\pi}{\omega}$,

$$\frac{2\pi}{\omega} = 12 \Rightarrow \omega = \tfrac{1}{6}\pi$$

The amplitude is 2.5 and the mean height is 5 and so

$$h = 2.5 \sin \tfrac{1}{6}\pi t + 5$$

Differentiating to find the rate at which the tide is changing at any time,

$$\frac{dh}{dt} = \tfrac{5}{12}\pi \cos \tfrac{1}{6}\pi t$$

When $t = 0$, $\dfrac{dh}{dt} = \tfrac{5}{12}\pi = 1.3$ (to 2 s.f.)

The tide is rising most rapidly when $t = 0$ (and also when $t = 12, 24, \ldots$), and the rate of rise is 1.3 metres per hour. You can use the formula for $\dfrac{dh}{dt}$ to find the rate of change at any time.

Example 1

A pendulum is pulled to one side and then released from rest, after which its displacement x cm from the central position after t seconds is given by $x = 1.5 \cos \pi t$. Write down the period and amplitude of the motion, and calculate the first two times when $x = 1$, and its velocity at these times.

Solution

By inspection of the function, period $= \dfrac{2\pi}{\pi} = 2$ seconds and amplitude $= 1.5$ cm.

$$x = 1 \text{ when } \cos \pi t = \frac{1}{1.5} = 0.666 \ldots,$$

$$\pi t = 0.8410, \quad 2\pi - 0.8410 \ldots$$

So $t = 0.268$ and $t = 1.732$ are the first two times, to 3 d.p.

The velocity $v = \dfrac{dx}{dt} = -1.5\pi \sin \pi t$.

Substituting,

$$\text{when } t = 0.268 \ldots, \quad v = -3.52 \text{ cm s}^{-1},$$

$$\text{when } t = 1.732 \ldots, \quad v = 3.52 \text{ cm s}^{-1}.$$

The negative sign in the first velocity indicates that the pendulum is then moving in the opposite direction to that in which x is increasing.

3.5 **Exercise 4**

1   A mass oscillates up and down at the end of a spring. The length of the spring in centimetres after time t seconds is given by the equation

$$L = 12 + 2.5 \cos 2\pi t$$

(a) Find the derivative, $\dfrac{dL}{dt}$. Sketch the graphs of L and $\dfrac{dL}{dt}$ against t.

(b) Calculate, when $t = 0, 0.1, 0.25, 0.4$ and 0.5,

(i) the length of the spring,   (ii) the velocity of the mass.

Comment on the results.

2   The height in metres of the tide at a harbour entrance is given by

$$h = 0.8 \cos \tfrac{1}{6}\pi t + 6.5$$

where t is the time in hours measured from high tide.

(a) Find the derivative, $\dfrac{dh}{dt}$. Sketch graphs of h and $\dfrac{dh}{dt}$ against t for a 24-hour interval.

(b) Calculate the two times during the first 12 hours when the height of the tide is 6 metres. Find the rate of change of height at both these times and comment on the results.

(c) When is the tide falling most rapidly during the first 12 hours? Find the rate at which it is then falling.

(d) When is the speed of the tidal current least and when is it greatest? What factors are important in deciding when it is safe to enter or leave the harbour?

3   The height in metres above ground level of a chair on a big wheel is given by

$$h = 5.6 - 4.8 \cos \tfrac{1}{30}\pi t$$

where t is the time measured in seconds.

(a) Find the derivative, $\dfrac{dh}{dt}$, and sketch graphs of h and $\dfrac{dh}{dt}$ against t for a two-minute interval.

(b) Between what times is the chair descending at a rate greater than 0.4 metre per second? When is the chair descending most rapidly and at what speed?

4   (a) The heights of the tide at Sheerness on a certain September day were 4.6 m at high water and 1.7 m at low water.

(i) Assuming a period of 12 hours and measuring the time in hours from high tide, sketch a graph of the height from 6 hours before to 6 hours after high water.

(ii) Suggest a suitable formula for h, the height in metres, in terms of t, the time in hours.

(b) The currents in the Thames estuary near to Sheerness are given in the following table.

Hours before high water	5	4	3	2	1
Current in knots	0.7	0.9	1.1	1.0	0.7

   (i) Assuming that the currents after high water are the same, but in the opposite direction, sketch the graph of current against time from 6 hours before to 6 hours after high water.

   (ii) Suggest a suitable formula for the current in knots in terms of the time in hours.

   (iii) How is this related to the height equation found in part (a)?

(c) (i) Find the rate of change of h and sketch a graph of $\dfrac{dh}{dt}$ against t for the same values as those in the previous graphs.

   (ii) Comment on the relationship between this and the graph of the current.

After working through section 3.5 you should:

1 be able to understand and use radian measure;

2 know that the period of $y = \sin \omega t$ is $\dfrac{2\pi}{\omega}$;

3 know that for a sector of angle θ radius r,

   arc length $= r\theta$

   area $= \frac{1}{2}r^2\theta$

4 be able to differentiate circular functions and know that, for x in radians,

$$\frac{d}{dx}(a \sin bx) = ab \cos bx$$

$$\frac{d}{dx}(a \cos bx) = -ab \sin bx$$

3 Functions

.6 Transformations

3.6.1 Graph sketching

You will have noticed that the transformations of graphs have formed a central theme throughout the text. You have seen several examples where a simple algebraic transformation of the equation of a function has brought about a geometric transformation of the graph.

 .6A

If the equation $y = x^2 - 4x$ is transformed by replacing y with $3y$, the new equation is $3y = x^2 - 4x$ or $y = \frac{1}{3}x^2 - \frac{4}{3}x$. By plotting the graphs of $y = x^2 - 4x$ and $y = \frac{1}{3}x^2 - \frac{4}{3}x$ you can observe the geometric effect of this algebraic transformation.

1 Choose various values for k and describe what geometrical transformation of the graph is produced by each of the four algebraic transformations described by:

(a) replacing x with $x + k$ or $x - k$

(b) replacing y with $y + k$ or $y - k$

(c) replacing x with kx or $\dfrac{x}{k}$

(d) replacing y with ky or $\dfrac{y}{k}$

for the graph of:

(i) $y = \frac{1}{2}x^2 - 4x$ (ii) $y = \sin x$ (iii) $y = e^x$ (iv) $x^2 + y^2 = 1$

(You may need to plot both $y = \sqrt{(1 - x^2)}$ and $y = -\sqrt{(1 - x^2)}$ for (iv).)

2 What is the geometrical transformation of a graph when:

(a) x is replaced with $-x$;

(b) y is replaced with $-y$;

(c) x and y are interchanged?

3 Describe the transformations which map the graphs of:

(a) $|x|$ to: (i) $|x + 1|$ (ii) $|2x + 1|$ (iii) $2|x + 1|$

(Illustrate each function with sketch graphs.)

(b) $\dfrac{1}{x}$ to: (i) $\dfrac{1}{x + 1}$ (ii) $\dfrac{1}{2x + 1}$ (iii) $\dfrac{2}{x + 1}$

Algebraic transformation of the equation	Geometric transformation of the graph
Replace x with kx	One-way stretch from the y-axis, scale factor $\dfrac{1}{k}$
Replace y with ky	One-way stretch from the x-axis, scale factor $\dfrac{1}{k}$
Replace x with $x + k$	Translation $\begin{bmatrix} -k \\ 0 \end{bmatrix}$
Replace y with $y + k$	Translation $\begin{bmatrix} 0 \\ -k \end{bmatrix}$
Replace x with $-x$	Reflection in the y-axis
Replace y with $-y$	Reflection in the x-axis
Interchange x and y	Reflection in $y = x$

Combining transformations can produce interesting effects. Suppose the equation $y = x^2 - 6x + 11$ has the algebraic transformation 'x is replaced with $-x$' followed by 'y is replaced with $-y$' applied to it. The new equation is

$$(-y) = (-x)^2 - 6(-x) + 11$$

$$\Rightarrow \quad -y = x^2 + 6x + 11$$

$$\Rightarrow \quad y = -x^2 - 6x - 11$$

Understanding the relationship between algebraic and geometric transformations can help you sketch the graphs of quite complicated functions.

Example 1

Describe the transformations which map the graph of $y = e^x$ onto $y = 2e^{3x+1}$

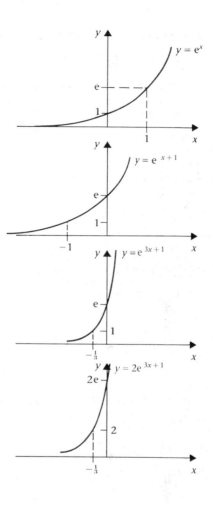

Solution

Replace x with $x + 1$.

Translate $\begin{bmatrix} -1 \\ 0 \end{bmatrix}$.

Replace x with $3x$.
One-way stretch from the y-axis, scale factor $\frac{1}{3}$.

Replace y with $\frac{1}{2}y$.
One-way stretch from the x-axis, scale factor 2.

3 .6B

In example 1 above, what would happen if you replaced x with $3x$ *before* you replaced x with $x + 1$?

3.6.2 Stretching a circle

$x^2 + y^2 = 1$ is the equation of a circle, centre $(0, 0)$, radius 1.

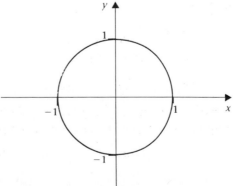

Rearranging the equation gives $y = \pm\sqrt{(1 - x^2)}$, and plotting $y = \sqrt{(1 - x^2)}$ followed by $y = -\sqrt{(1 - x^2)}$ gives the graph of the full circle. Make sure that the same scale is used on both axes so that your graph will look like a circle.

Note that $x^2 + y^2 = 1$ is *not* the equation of a function. If x is 0.6, for example, then $y = \pm 0.8$. A function can have only one output for any given input.

Example 2

(a) Describe what effect replacing x with $\frac{1}{3}x$ and y with $(y - 2)$ has on the graph of $x^2 + y^2 = 1$.

(b) Sketch the graph of $(\frac{1}{3}x)^2 + (y - 2)^2 = 1$.

(c) Rearrange the equation into the form $y = \ldots$ so that you can plot the graph.

Solution

(a) Replacing x with $\frac{1}{3}x$ and y with $(y - 2)$ gives $(\frac{1}{3}x)^2 + (y - 2)^2 = 1$. The unit circle, $x^2 + y^2 = 1$, is stretched by a factor 3 from the y-axis and then the resulting ellipse is translated through $\begin{bmatrix} 0 \\ 2 \end{bmatrix}$.

(b)

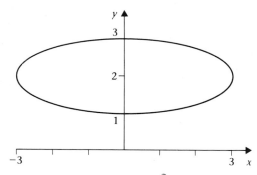

(c) $\frac{1}{9}x^2 + (y - 2)^2 = 1 \Rightarrow (y - 2)^2 = 1 - \frac{1}{9}x^2 \Rightarrow y = 2 \pm \sqrt{(1 - \frac{1}{9}x^2)}$

.6c

1 What is the equation of a circle, radius r, centre $(0, 0)$?

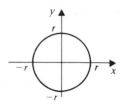

2 What is the equation of the ellipse shown in the diagram?

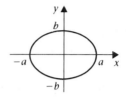

3 What is the equation of a circle, radius r, centre (p, q)?

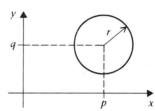

The shape of an ellipse is defined by the lengths of its major and minor axes. You can obtain the shape of an ellipse by stretching a unit circle along the x- and y-axes. You can then translate the shape to any location on the grid.

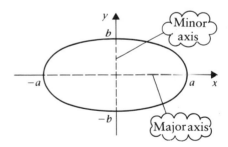

Example 3

Give the equation of the ellipse shown in the diagram.

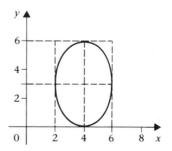

Solution

The unit circle, $x^2 + y^2 = 1$, can be transformed onto the ellipse by a one-way stretch factor 2 along the x-axis and a one-way stretch factor 3 along the y-axis (replace x with $\frac{1}{2}x$ and y with $\frac{1}{3}y$), giving

$$\left(\tfrac{1}{2}x\right)^2 + \left(\tfrac{1}{3}y\right)^2 = 1$$

This is followed by a translation $\begin{bmatrix} 4 \\ 3 \end{bmatrix}$ (replace x with $x - 4$ and y with $y - 3$). The equation of the ellipse is $\left[\tfrac{1}{2}(x - 4)\right]^2 + \left[\tfrac{1}{3}(y - 3)\right]^2 = 1$.

The technique of taking a basic graph and transforming it to fit another has been used several times throughout this chapter. You have, for example, seen how both stretches and translations are used to fit the graph of $y = \sin x$ to the graph of $y = a \sin(bx + c) + d$. You will also recall that it was understanding the effect a stretch has on the gradient of a graph that enabled you to differentiate $y = a \sin x, y = \sin bx$ and $y = e^{ax}$.

You have also seen how transformations can be used to enhance your understanding of some functions. Understanding how two distinct transformations can be used to map the graph of $y = \ln x$ onto the graph of $y = \ln ax$ should, for example, have given you a greater insight into the log function.

3.6 Exercise 1

1 The graph of $y = \ln x$ can be fitted to the graph of $y = \ln 3x$ by either a one-way stretch or a translation. Describe the transformation in each case.

2 The graph of $y = x^2$ can be fitted to the graph of $y = 4x^2$ by either:

    (a) a one-way stretch along the x-axis from $x = 0$

or (b) a one-way stretch along the y-axis from $y = 0$

What is the stretch factor in each case?

3 The equation of the ellipse shown in the diagram can be obtained by transforming the unit circle. The unit circle can be fitted to the ellipse in two ways:

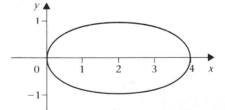

(a) a stretch followed by a translation

(b) a translation followed by a stretch

Specify the transformations in each case and hence obtain the equation of the ellipse in two different ways.

After working through section 3.6 you should:

1 have a clear understanding of how simple algebraic transformations on the equation of a graph bring about geometric transformations of the graph;

2 know how to apply these transformations to a variety of basic graphs, particularly the unit circle.

3 Functions

Miscellaneous exercise 3

1 The functions f and g are defined by $f(x) = 3x - 2$, $g(x) = 2 - \dfrac{3}{x}$.

    (a) Write down formulae for (i) $g^{-1}(x)$, (ii) $g^{-1}f(x)$.

    (b) Find a value of x for which $ff(x) = -f(x)$.

2 Given the functions $f(x) = 2x - 3$, $g(x) = 4 - 3x$, find

$$f(5), \quad gf(5), \quad fg(5), \quad fg(x), \quad gf(x), \quad f^{-1}(5), \quad g^{-1}(5),$$
$$g^{-1}f^{-1}(x), \quad f^{-1}g(x), \quad g^{-1}f(x)$$

3 Find inverse functions of

    (a) $f(x) = 7x + 10$ (b) $f(x) = \dfrac{6 - 8x}{3}$

    (c) $f(x) = \dfrac{x + 1}{4x - 5}$ (d) $f(x) = 4 - x^2$

    State any restrictions on the domains.

4 Give the equation of the image of the graph of $y = \sqrt{x}$ under each of the following transformations:

    (a) the translation $\begin{bmatrix} 2 \\ 0 \end{bmatrix}$ (b) the translation $\begin{bmatrix} -1 \\ 5 \end{bmatrix}$

    (c) reflection in the y-axis   (d) reflection in the x-axis

    (e) reflection in $y = x$

    Write down the image of $(25, 5)$ under each of these transformations, and hence check your equations.

5 Express $\dfrac{x - 4}{x^2 + 4x} - \dfrac{x - 2}{(x + 3)(x + 4)}$ as a single fraction in its simplest form.

6 (a) Sketch a cosine graph with amplitude 3 and period $90°$.

    (b) Write down the equation of the graph you have sketched.

7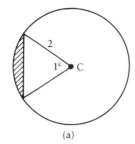

(a) (b)

(a) Calculate the shaded area in (a). (C is the centre of the circle.)

(b) Two circular ripples with centres C and D, each with radius 2 m, intersect at L and M (b). Angle LCM is θ radians.

   (i) Show that the area of the common region is $(4\theta - 4\sin\theta)$.

   (ii) Hence show that all three regions will have the same area when
$$\theta - \sin\theta = \tfrac{1}{2}\pi.$$

   (iii) Show that this occurs when angle LCM is approximately $132°$.

8 Calculate the gradient of each of the following graphs at the given point:

(a) $y = 3\sin\theta$ at $\theta = 1$ (b) $y = \cos 2\theta$ at $\theta = \tfrac{1}{4}\pi$

(c) $y = 2\sin 3\theta$ at $\theta = 2$ (d) $y = 5\cos\tfrac{1}{2}\theta$ at $\theta = \tfrac{3}{4}\pi$

9 The height of the water level at a jetty is shown on a post, marked in metres above the mud bottom. One day the height h metres is given by the formula
$$h = 5.5 + 4\sin\frac{\pi t}{6},$$

where t is the number of hours after midnight.

(a) At what time during the day is the first high tide?

(b) Write down the values of h at high tide and low tide, and show that there are 6 hours between them.

(c) Sketch the graph of h against t for the whole 24 hours.

(d) Calculate the rate at which the water is rising at 10 a.m.

10 Solve the following, giving solutions to the nearest degree in the range $0 \le x \le 180$.

(a) $\cos x° = 0$ (b) $\cos 2x° = 0$ (c) $\cos 5x° = 0$

(d) $1 + 2\cos x° = 0$ (e) $1 + 2\cos 3x° = 0$

11 The height above the road, y cm, of the pedal of a child's cycle t seconds after an instant when it is at its highest point is given by $y = 20 + 10\cos 180t°$

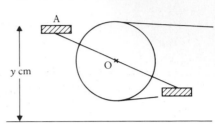

(a) What is the height of the bottom bracket O above the road?

(b) What is the length of the crank AO?

(c) How long does it take to complete one revolution of the pedals?

Rewrite the equation connecting y and t if

(d) the cyclist speeds up so that the pedal rotates once every second,

(e) she changes gear so the pedal rotates once every 3 seconds.

12 For the following graphs, state their period and amplitude, and sketch them for $-360 \leq x \leq 360$:

(a) $y = 2\sin x°$ (b) $y = 2 + 3\cos x°$ (c) $y = 0.5\sin 2x°$

(d) $y = -5\cos\frac{1}{3}x°$ (e) $y = 6 - 3\sin\frac{2}{3}x°$

13 Write sine functions (angles in degrees) with

(a) period 90, amplitude 1   (b) period 720, amplitude 2.5

(c) period 60, amplitude 3   (d) period 1440, amplitude $\frac{1}{2}$

14 Solve for x: (a) $3^x = 4$ (b) $x^4 = 3$ (c) $x = \log_3 4$

15 2% of a radioactive substance decays every hour. Give a formula for the percentage remaining after T hours. Calculate

(a) the percentage which decays in one day,

(b) the half-life of the substance.

16 The stress y in a joint is believed to be proportional to some power p of the strain x applied to it. Write down the form of equation connecting x and y. In an experiment, the corresponding values of y are measured for five different values of x. State what should be plotted against what to obtain a straight line graph. How can the value of p and of the constant of proportion be found from this graph?

17 The temperature of a cooling liquid falls exponentially. The table shows, to the nearest degree, its temperature, $\theta\,°C$, above its surroundings at 5 minute intervals.

T (min)	0	5	10	15	20	25	30
$\theta\,(°C)$	83	68	55	45	37	30	24

Plot a suitable straight line graph, and hence find the relation between θ and T.

18 Show that $x = e^{7t}$, $x = 3\,e^{7t}$ and $x = A\,e^{7t}$ all satisfy $\dfrac{dx}{dt} = 7x$.

19 Show that $x = e^{-t}$, $x = 5\,e^{-t}$ and $x = A\,e^{-t}$ all satisfy $\dfrac{dx}{dt} = -x$.

20 Show that $x = A\,e^{5t}$ satisfies $\dfrac{dx}{dt} = 5x$ and find A if $x = 33$ when $t = 0.1$.

21 A bacteriologist finds that the rate of growth of a culture of a certain type of bacteria is described by the differential equation

$$\frac{dm}{dt} = 0.4m$$

where m grams is the total mass of the culture at time t hours after observations began.

(a) Show that $m = m_0 \exp(0.4t)$ (where m_0 is a constant) satisfies the differential equation.

(b) Find m_0 if $m = 10$ when $t = 0$.

(c) With this value of m_0 find the mass at (i) $t = 1$, (ii) $t = 2$.

(d) Find the percentage increase in the mass during
    (i) the first hour,   (ii) the second hour.

22 The mass m kg of radioactive lead remaining in a sample t hours after observations began is given by $m = 2 \exp(-0.2t)$.

(a) Find the mass left after 12 hours.

(b) Find how long it takes for the mass to fall to half its value at $t = 0$ (the half-life).

(c) Find how long it takes for the mass to fall to
    (i) one-quarter,   (ii) one-eighth of its value at $t = 0$.

(d) Express the rate of decay as a function of m.

23 The velocity of a particle at time t seconds is $v \, \text{m s}^{-1}$, where $v = 4t - t^2$.

  (a) Sketch the graph of v against t for $0 \le t \le 4$.

  (b) Calculate the acceleration when $t = 1$.

  (c) Find the distance travelled between $t = 1$ and $t = 2$.

24 (a) Simplify $(x^{-1}y)^{\frac{1}{2}} \div (x^{\frac{1}{2}}y^{-\frac{1}{2}})^3$.

  (b) Express as single fractions in their simplest form:

  (i) $\dfrac{1}{4x} + \dfrac{1}{6x^2}$ (ii) $\dfrac{1}{x}\left(\dfrac{1}{2-x} - \dfrac{1}{2+x}\right)$

25 (a) Sketch the curve with the equation $y = x + \dfrac{1}{x^2}$.

  (b) Suggest a suitable equation for the graph shown.

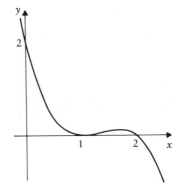

4 Problem solving

.1 Mathematical enquiries

4.1.1 Introduction

In this chapter we try to unravel some of the processes of mathematical activity. Considerable independence of thought is necessary if you are to be able to tackle unfamiliar problems with confidence. To develop an investigative attitude to mathematics you must always pursue your own ideas!

The three problems below (4.1A) may be attempted in any order. As you work through them note the strategies you use – what methods you have of setting out to crack an unfamiliar puzzle or investigating a new situation. The problems will be referred to later, so keep a record of your solutions. All the extensions should be attempted but they are quite demanding and you should feel satisfied if you manage just one in depth.

It may be helpful to work with a small group of fellow students on some stages of discussion or investigation. It is important that you should then write an individual account and attempt to extend the work on your own.

 .1A

1 Eleven players enter for a singles knockout tennis tournament. The two organisers decide not to attempt any seeding but to pair at random. They disagree about byes; one wants all byes to be in the first round but the other insists that in each round as many players as possible should be involved. (A player given a 'bye' in a round of a tournament is not required to play in that round but carries straight on to the next round.)

Make a full analysis of the two suggestions, including in each case:

(a) the number of byes,

(b) the number of rounds,

(c) the total number of matches played.

Extend your investigation by considering numbers other than 11.

2 Think of a three-digit number, i.e. a whole number between 100 and 999. Reverse its digits and find the difference between the 'reversed' number and the original number. Check that it is a multiple of 99. Try one or two more examples.

Now try following the same procedure with numbers with two, four and five digits. Comment on your findings.

Extend your investigation so that you can make and explain a general statement about your findings.

3 'Everybody knows' that equilateral triangles and squares will tessellate. What exactly is meant by this?

Show that:

(a) a tessellation can be made using any parallelogram;

(b) a tessellation can be made using any triangle;

(c) no tessellation can be made using a regular pentagon.

Extend your investigation by considering other shapes. Is there *any* pentagon which will tessellate? Can *all* quadrilaterals tessellate?

In attempting these problems you may have felt in turn frustrated, bored, then interested and (it is hoped) finally satisfied that you had reached a pretty good understanding. In this section, the mathematical activities which accompanied these various emotions are analysed. A vocabulary is introduced which you should use in future solutions.

The analysis will not be exhaustive; for example there is no specific mention of the skill of using iterative techniques. This is because the text concentrates on features common to many problems. Of course, you can use any method you like to solve problems. The analysis of processes is there to help, not to constrain.

You should read with pencil and notebook at the ready; to check the various assertions made, work through the exercises and make notes. For each process a brief explanation is given, followed by a few exercises. Do not get too carried away by these exercises: just deal with the particular process under discussion. In certain cases you will meet a problem more than once because it gives a good illustration of more than one process.

The first example illustrates the use of mathematical processes which seem to be particularly important. They are:

- investigating particular cases;
- finding patterns;
- generalising.

Example 1
Investigate:

$$1^3 =$$

$$1^3 + 2^3 =$$

$$1^3 + 2^3 + 3^3 =$$

$$1^3 + 2^3 + 3^3 + 4^3 =$$

Solution
A first reaction might be to work out these **particular cases** and **look for a pattern**. You might then predict the next line in the sequence:

$$1^3 + 2^3 + 3^3 + 4^3 + 5^3 =$$

Investigating further particular cases seems to confirm the general pattern:

$$1^3 + 2^3 + 3^3 + 4^3 + 5^3 \qquad = 225 = 15^2$$

$$1^3 + 2^3 + 3^3 + 4^3 + 5^3 + 6^3 = 441 = 21^2$$

The numbers on the right-hand side are squares of

$$1, 3, 6, 10, 15, 21, \ldots$$

You need to look for a connection between the numbers on the left-hand side and the resulting square number on the right-hand side.

$$1 + 2 \qquad\qquad = 3$$

$$1 + 2 + 3 \qquad\qquad = 6$$

$$1 + 2 + 3 + 4 \qquad = 10$$

$$1 + 2 + 3 + 4 + 5 \quad = 15$$

$$1 + 2 + 3 + 4 + 5 + 6 = 21$$

In symbols, the pattern can be expressed as the **generalisation**

$$1^3 + 2^3 + 3^3 + \cdots + n^3 = (1 + 2 + 3 + \cdots + n)^2$$

It still remains to verify or **prove** that this general result holds for all possible particular cases. The important process of proof is discussed later (in section 4.2).

The two processes of **investigating particular cases** and **finding patterns** both appear in this example but in no obviously systematic way. The processes are like tools used as and when the need arises. For the problem just considered, the process of mathematical enquiry has appeared to be:

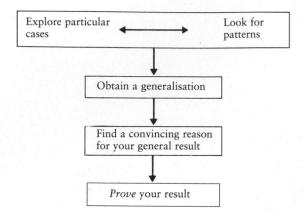

Often a problem asks for a **general result**, for example the number of byes in a tournament with n players. If no solution immediately suggests itself then you might decide to experiment with particular values of n. In the tennis tournament problem of 4.1A, you were invited to start with $n = 11$ and then try other particular cases. Perhaps you tried the case of 12 players, or a number chosen at random. Similarly, in the tessellation problem, a particular kind of quadrilateral – a parallelogram – was considered initially. Although none of these particular cases may have led directly to a general solution they can give you a hint on how to approach the general case.

It is often (though not always) best to consider particular cases methodically in some sort of order. Very often the smallest possible case is important but sometimes particular cases are chosen for other reasons.

 .1B

1 In discussing the solution of equations of the form

$$x^3 + ax + b = 0$$

for various values of a and b, which particular values might you dispose of before treating the general case?

2 In teaching a young child how to find the area of a triangle, which special kind of triangle would you first consider?

3 In sketching the graph of $y = x + \dfrac{1}{x}$, which particular values of x would you first consider?

4 (a) Find a particular set of values of the numbers a, b, c, d, e and f for which the simultaneous equations

$$ax + by = c$$
$$dx + ey = f$$

have no solutions in x and y.

(b) Find another set for which the equations have an infinity of solutions.

In original mathematical investigations, guesswork can loom large, though this is not always apparent in the final written account. At this level a guess is often given the more respectable name of **conjecture**; for example, 'conjecture – knockout tournaments with 2^n players have no byes'. If this is not immediately obvious you can verify it in particular cases by drawing up tournament tables for (1, 2,) 4, 8, 16, ... players.

Just because a conjecture can be verified for some particular values of n, it is not necessarily true for all values of n. Having shown the results to be true in a few cases you should then try to give a convincing argument that the conjecture is true for *all* possible values of n; that is, you need to prove the result. The process of proof will be discussed later.

The patterns formed in your investigations need not be of numbers; they may be actual geometrical patterns, such as you made in answering the tessellation problem of 4.1A. Such patterns can give rise to further interesting problems.

 .1c

1 (a) Investigate:

$$(1 \times 2 \times 3 \times 4) + 1 =$$
$$(2 \times 3 \times 4 \times 5) + 1 =$$
$$(3 \times 4 \times 5 \times 6) + 1 =$$
$$\vdots \qquad\qquad \vdots$$

(b) Hence, find consecutive integers a, b, c and d such that

$$(a \times b \times c \times d) + 1 = 43\,681$$

2 The first seven terms of the Fibonacci sequence are 1, 1, 2, 3, 5, 8, 13.

(a) What are the next two terms?

(b) Continue the sequence

$$2^2 = (3 \times 1) + 1, \qquad 3^2 = (5 \times 2) - 1, \qquad 5^2 = (8 \times 3) + 1, \ldots$$

(c) The 3rd, 6th, 9th, 12th, ... terms are all even. List the 4th, 8th, 12th, ... terms. What do you notice?

(d) Make a conjecture about the 5th, 10th, 15th, ... terms and check it by working them out.

Very often the aim of an investigation is to arrive at a general result, commonly (though not always) expressed in a formula. You may have had the satisfaction of finding that in a knockout competition with n players the minimum number of byes, number of rounds and number of matches played can all be given by formulas.

The statement 'no tessellation is possible using only a regular polygon with more than six sides' contains no formula but, being about a whole class of objects, is still a generalisation.

4.1 **Exercise 1**

1 Generalise on this sequence of equations

$$
\begin{aligned}
1 &= 1 \\
1 + 3 &= 4 \\
1 + 3 + 5 &= 9 \\
1 + 3 + 5 + 7 &= 16
\end{aligned}
$$

(a) in symbols, (b) in words.

2 The sum of two consecutive odd numbers is divisible by 4.

(a) Can you make similar statements about the sum of three consecutive odd numbers and of four consecutive odd numbers?

(b) Generalise your findings.

3 How many diagonals has a quadrilateral? A pentagon? A hexagon? A polygon with n sides?

4 (a) Of all triangles of equal perimeter, the equilateral triangle has the greatest area.

(b) Of all quadrilaterals of equal perimeter, the square has the greatest area.

Make a general statement of which (a) and (b) are particular cases.

4.1.2 Organising your work

Organising your work is very important in rendering a problem manageable – and its solution readable! Here, we consider the processes of **choosing a notation** and **classifying**. In section 4.1.3 we focus on **tabulation**.

The choice of notation in problem-solving is often routine. In the tennis
tournament problem of 4.1A you probably used the standard tournament table.

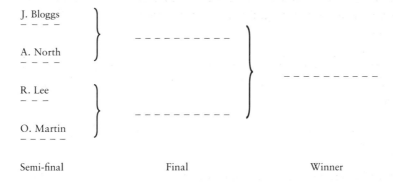

| Semi-final | Final | Winner |

In the digit-reversing problem of 4.1A you probably used letters to represent
the digits of a general three-digit number, the number looking like *ABC* having
the value $100A + 10B + C$. This would have allowed you to tackle the problem
algebraically.

 .1D

1 How good are you at describing objects or giving clear directions without
using a street plan?

Suppose you have to describe a diagram, such as the one below, over the
telephone. How could you do it?

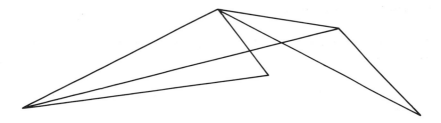

2 A journey in a US city is described by the notation R S S R S L,
where

R means turn right
S means go straight on $\Big\}$ at the next intersection.
L means turn left

How would you describe the inverse (return) journey?

3 Three tumblers are arranged with just one upside-down.

Take any pair and turn them over, and continue doing this, a pair at a time, in an effort to finish with all three right way up. Invent a simple notation to explain why this is impossible.

Sometimes an investigation is simplified if you deal with separate classes one at a time. In the digit-reversing problem of 4.1A, the class of numbers with an odd number of digits behaves differently from that with an even number of digits. An important class in the tessellation problem of 4.1A is that of pentagons with a pair of parallel sides. The process of classifying can help in the solution of a problem, or provide a good structure for an investigation.

4.1 Exercise 2

1 Name at least three different classes of:

(a) angle   (b) triangle   (c) solid shape

2 A strategy for the game of noughts and crosses hinges on the first move made. How many essentially different first moves are possible?

3 Which classes of quadrilateral have exactly two lines of symmetry?

4 By classifying the integers a and b as being odd or even and by considering the different combinations, show that the equation

$$a^2 + b^2 = 4c + 3$$

has no solution in integers a, b and c.

5 Your friend has a pack of eight cards and invites you to choose one at random.

He then asks three questions to which you answer 'yes' or 'no', after which he identifies the card chosen. It later turns out that he can always do this by asking the same three questions, in the same order. What might the questions be?

4.1.3 Tabulation

You sometimes explore particular cases in a more or less haphazard way as you feel your way into an investigation. To make progress you then need to display your findings in a more orderly fashion. At this stage a table may suggest a way ahead. Tables are important, too, in communicating information clearly to a reader of your work. For both these reasons, in solving the tennis tournament problem you may have felt the need to draw up a table like this.

No. of players	1	2	3	4	. . .
No. of byes	0	0	1	0	. . .
No. of rounds	0	1	2	2	. . .
No. of matches	0	1	2	3	. . .

Though there are other kinds of table, of properties of shapes for example, a table is often useful when building up a sequence of numbers. In trying to find the pattern in a sequence, a **table of differences** sometimes helps. Consider the problem: what is the greatest number of points of intersection given by n lines? Starting with small values of n you can quickly draw up a table.

No. of lines	1	2	3	4	5
No. of points	0	1	3	6	10

Perhaps you do not remember the sequence in the second line. Or perhaps you vaguely recognise the triangular numbers but do not find this particularly helpful. But if you subtract each number from the one on its right, the pattern becomes clear.

$$0 \underset{1}{\top} 1 \underset{2}{\top} 3 \underset{3}{\top} 6 \underset{4}{\top} 10$$

First differences 1 2 3 4

This enables you to extend the table easily – the next 'first difference' is probably 5, so the next entry above will be 15, and so on. As a result the problem is replaced by a much simpler one; the number required appears to be

$$1 + 2 + 3 + \cdots + (n - 1)$$

Looking at differences can be extended into a useful method for finding a **generating formula** for a polynomial sequence.

For example, to find the sequence generated by the quadratic expression

$$2n^2 - n + 3$$

you can calculate its value for $n = 1, 2, 3, \ldots$ to obtain

$$4, \quad 9, \quad 18, \quad 31, \quad 48, \quad \ldots$$

The **first differences** are found by subtracting each term from the one to its right.

$$4 \underset{5}{\top} 9 \underset{9}{\top} 18 \underset{13}{\top} 31 \underset{17}{\top} 48 \ldots$$

The process may be repeated to find **second differences**.

$$5 \underset{4}{\top} 9 \underset{4}{\top} 13 \underset{4}{\top} 17 \ldots$$

You will see that the **third differences** would all be zero. This is investigated further in the examples below.

 .1E

1 Choose another quadratic sequence, i.e. one generated by an expression of the form

$$an^2 + bn + c$$

where a, b and c are integers. Find first and second differences.

2 Use a cubic sequence, generated by an expression of the form

$$an^3 + bn^2 + cn + d$$

and find first, second and third differences.

3 Use the method of differences to make a conjecture about the sequence

$$-1, \quad -6, \quad 3, \quad 68, \quad 255, \quad 654, \quad 1379, \quad \ldots$$

4 Find the tables of differences given by sequences generated by the expressions:

(a) n (b) n^2 (c) n^3 (d) n^4

5 If the fifth differences given by a sequence are all 30, how do you think the sequence was generated? (Answer in as much detail as you can.)

4.1 **Exercise 3**

1 Make a table showing the number of diagonals of an n-sided polygon for values of n from 3 to 6. By finding first differences, conjecture the number of diagonals of a decagon. Check your conjecture.

2 Devise a table showing the properties of bilateral and rotational symmetry for parallelograms, rhombi, rectangles, kites and squares.

3

n	1	2	3	4	5
$r(n)$	1	2	2	3	3
$s(n)$	1	2	3	5	8

In the table, $r(n)$ is the number of ways of representing the number n as a sum, using only the terms 1 and 2, the order of the terms not being significant; for example

$$4 = 1 + 1 + 1 + 1 = 1 + 1 + 2 = 2 + 2$$

$s(n)$ is the number of ways when the order *is* significant; for example

$$4 = 1 + 1 + 1 + 1 = 1 + 1 + 2 = 1 + 2 + 1 = 2 + 1 + 1 = 2 + 2$$

Check the entries in the table, find $r(6)$ and $s(6)$, and conjecture a formula for $r(n)$ and a rule for generating the sequence $s(n)$.

4.1.4 Starting points

The following is a list of possible starting points for investigations of your own. In considering these problems, you should use the ideas met in this section where appropriate, and other ideas – especially that of proof – as you progress through this chapter.

1 Chains – Divisors
The numbers which divide 12, and are smaller than 12, are 1, 2, 3, 4 and 6.
Add these divisors: $1 + 2 + 3 + 4 + 6 = 16$. Write $12 \rightarrow 16$.

Repeat the procedure for 16. Its divisors are 1, 2, 4, 8.
Add: $1 + 2 + 4 + 8 = 15$. Write $12 \rightarrow 16 \rightarrow 15$.

Repeat the procedure until you have

$$12 \rightarrow 16 \rightarrow 15 \rightarrow 9 \rightarrow 4 \rightarrow 3 \rightarrow 1$$

Investigate with other numbers.

(a) Some numbers go to bigger numbers: for example $12 \rightarrow 16$. These are called **abundant** numbers. Can you find more abundant numbers, and a pattern within them?

(b) Numbers which go to smaller numbers are called **deficient** numbers (for example $9 \rightarrow 4$). Investigate these.

(c) Note that $6 \rightleftarrows 6$ and $28 \rightleftarrows 28$. These are called **perfect** numbers. Investigate.

(d) $220 \rightleftarrows 284$. Can you find smaller pairs? (Pairs such as 220 and 284 are called **friendly** numbers.)

2 Triangle-square numbers
The triangular numbers are $1, 3, 6, 10, \ldots, \frac{1}{2}n(n+1), \ldots$

The square numbers are $1, 4, 9, 16, \ldots, m^2, \ldots$

Which numbers are both triangular and square? The first two are 1 and 36.

3 Chains – Reordering digits
Any four-digit number is rewritten with its digits arranged in ascending and descending order of size. The smaller is then subtracted from the larger and the process is repeated.

$$\text{Example:} \quad 7345 \text{ gives } 7543 - 3457 = 4086$$

$$4086 \text{ gives } 8640 - 0468 = 8172$$

$$\text{Then write } 7543 \rightarrow 8640 \rightarrow 8721 \rightarrow \ldots$$

Complete this chain and then try again with other four-digit numbers.

Now try with three or five or six or n digits.

4 Stamps
A small mail-order firm finds that it is constantly running out of stamps of the right denomination, so it calls on Professor Schomp for help. 'Buy lots of 3p and 5p stamps' is his advice.

Examine this reply and consider related situations.

5 Solution in integers
In the equation

$$x^2 - y^2 = m^n$$

x, y, m and n are all integers. Investigate the possibility of solutions in the cases

(a) $m = 1$ (b) $m > 1, \quad n > 2$ (c) $m > 1, \quad n = 2$

6 Cyclic arrangements of digits
Take any three-digit multiple of 37, for example $7 \times 37 = 259$.

Arrange the digits of 259 in a cycle:

and construct the other two numbers having the same three digits in the same cyclic order, 592 and 925.

Both of these are also multiples of 37:

$$592 = 16 \times 37 \quad \text{and} \quad 925 = 25 \times 37.$$

Explain why this happens and construct similar examples.

7 Recurring decimals

$$\tfrac{1}{7} = 0.\dot{1}4285\dot{7}$$

$$\tfrac{2}{7} = 0.\dot{2}8571\dot{4}$$

$$\tfrac{3}{7} = 0.\dot{4}2857\dot{1}$$

Starting with some observations on these and other particular cases, write an account of recurring decimals.

8 Integral part
For positive integers n, let

$$p(n) = [n + \sqrt{n} + \tfrac{1}{2}]$$

where the square brackets represent the integral part (written INT in computer language).

Which values does $p(n)$ not take, and why?

9 Divisors of N
12 can be written as the product of two positive divisors (factors) in six different ways:

$$12 = 1 \times 12 = 2 \times 6 = 3 \times 4 = 4 \times 3 = 6 \times 2 = 12 \times 1$$

You can look at it in a slightly different way and say that 12 has six divisors, 1, 2, 3, 4, 6 and 12.

Define $d(N)$ to be the number of positive integers dividing N. So

$$d(12) = 6$$

What can you say about $d(N)$ for different integers N? Justify any statements you make.

10 Average number of divisors

Let $d(N)$ be the number of divisors of N, defined above. Now define $D(N)$, the average number of divisors for numbers up to N, by

$$D(N) = \frac{1}{N}\sum_{n=1}^{N} d(n)$$

By relating $D(N)$ to the number of lattice points on or under the graph of $y = \dfrac{N}{x}$, find the limit of $D(N)$ for large N. (A lattice point is a point with integer coordinates.)

11 Railway layouts

A railway set contains a large number of pieces of rail, each in the form of a quadrant of a circle. These can be joined together to make **layouts**:

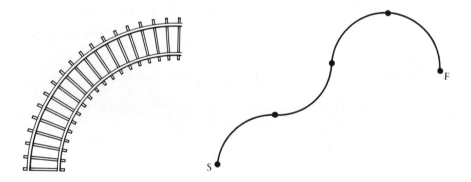

The layouts can be described by 'words' consisting of R for right and L for left. If the layout above starts at S and finishes at F its word is R L R R.

Some layouts are closed.

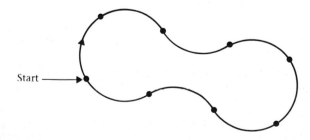

These are called **circuits**. The diagram above shows the circuit R R L R R R L R.

Given a word consisting of a large number of Rs and Ls, how would you tell (without drawing the layout) whether or not it represented a circuit?

12 Wrong deliveries

A postman has 4 letters to deliver, one for each of 4 flats. In how many ways can he deliver them so that each is in a wrong box (and no two go into the same box)?

Try the same problem for 5 letters for 5 flats and explore the possibility of obtaining a general result.

13 Garden path

A garden path is to be laid with rectangular slabs, each of width 1 unit and length 2 units. If the length of the path is n units, in how many ways can this be done? (Consider various widths of path.)

14 Cubic graphs

What 'different' graphs are possible for the cubic function

$$y = a + bx + cx^2 + dx^3?$$

Explain how the shape is related to the values of the coefficients a, b, c, d.

Investigate possible shapes of graphs of polynomial functions of degree more than 3.

15 Pebbles

Fifteen pebbles are placed on the table; two players, in turn, take one, two or three pebbles until all pebbles are taken. The player who then holds an odd number of pebbles wins. Investigate winning strategies and extend the problem.

After working through section 4.1 you should:

1 feel confident about starting a mathematical enquiry;

2 be ready to adopt an investigative attitude to mathematics;

3 be familiar with the use and meaning of the terms particular cases, conjecture and generalisation;

4 appreciate the need for orderly procedures and presentation;

5 be familiar with the use and meaning of the terms classification and tabulation;

6 know how to use a table of differences;

7 be able to find the degree of the polynomial generating a given sequence;

8 have experience of problem solving which will be of use in your later work.

4 Problem solving

.2 Proof

4.2.1 Introduction

Proof has been described as the very essence of mathematics. It gives permanence to a result or theorem. It is proof, or the nature of mathematical proof, that distinguishes mathematics from most other fields of human endeavour. It is an area where great creativity, elegance and beauty in mathematics can be seen. Some of the great proofs, for example those made by the Greek mathematicians, are still regarded as classics. Euclid's proof of the Theorem of Pythagoras, or his proof that there are infinitely many prime numbers, are proofs of great beauty which demonstrate conciseness, creativity and elegance, and have not been improved upon. There is simply no doubt about the theorems they prove – they are permanent, fixed for all time.

A major reason for studying mathematics is to understand something of mathematical proof and the process of mathematical thought. Proof provides a framework within which you are able to present a reasoned argument logically, with clarity and precision, whether within mathematics or more generally.

Proof is often such a complicated process that whole books can be written about it. Disproof, however, is often a very short and simple matter, as the following example shows.

Suppose that a friend, having tried many particular pentagons, is convinced that no pentagon will tessellate. To refute this generalisation, all you have to do is produce a single **counter-example**.

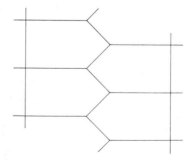

An excellent book, which explores many of the great theorems of mathematics, is *Journey Through Genius* by William Dunham (John Wiley, 1990; ISBN 0 471 50030 5).

4.2 **Exercise 1**

1   Disprove, by finding a suitable counter-example, the statement

$$x^2 > y^2 \Rightarrow x > y$$

2   If two lines are perpendicular to a third line then they must be parallel to each other – true or false?

3    $1 = 0^2 + 1^2$, $5 = 1^2 + 2^2$, $9 = 0^2 + 3^2$, ... $97 = 4^2 + 9^2$

All numbers of the form $(4n + 1)$ may be expressed as a sum of two squares – true or false?

4   Find the first four terms, t_1, t_2, t_3 and t_4 for the sequence defined by

$$t_n = (n - 1)(n - 2)(n - 3)(n - 4) + n$$

What might you expect t_5 to be? Is it?

4.2.2 Making a proof

In the previous section, you considered several conjectures which could be *disproved* by finding counter-examples.

Simply spotting a pattern is not the end of a mathematical investigation. You then need *either* to look for a convincing reason for the pattern *or* to find a counter-example.

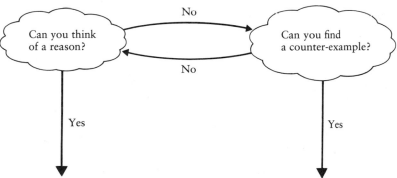

No

Can you think of a reason?   Can you find a counter-example?

No

Yes   Yes

Write out the reason so as to convince someone else. The written reasoning is called a **proof**.

Further investigation is needed so that you can make another conjecture.

The real challenge of a mathematical investigation is to break out of the potentially endless 'no–no' cycle of not being able to find *either* a convincing reason *or* a counter-example!

Amassing particular cases, no matter how many, does not establish a general result. To complete your investigation you must normally find convincing reasons for any patterns or results you have discovered.

Example 1

Prove that $(1 + 2 + 3 + \cdots + n)^2 = 1^3 + 2^3 + 3^3 + \cdots + n^3$.

Solution

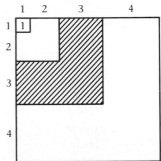

Building up the left side of the equation above by adding 'shells' provides a geometrical approach. The area of the shaded shell is:

$$(1 + 2 + 3)^2 - (1 + 2)^2 = 6^2 - 3^2$$

$$= 27 \text{ sq. units}$$

The three L-shaped shells have areas 8, 27 and 64 square units respectively.

The diagram demonstrates that

$$(1 + 2 + 3 + 4)^2 = 1^3 + 2^3 + 3^3 + 4^3$$

You need to show that, in general, the kth shell has area k^3. For this, use the result

$$1 + 2 + 3 + \cdots + (k - 1) = \tfrac{1}{2} k(k - 1)$$

For instance, as you can see in the top diagram, the fourth shell has an 'inside arm' measurement of $1 + 2 + 3 = \tfrac{1}{2} \times 4 \times 3$.

The kth shell looks like this when divided into three parts.

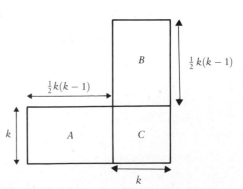

Consider the areas A, B and C.

$$A = k \times \tfrac{1}{2}k(k-1) = \tfrac{1}{2}k^2(k-1)$$

$$B = \tfrac{1}{2}k^2(k-1)$$

$$C = k^2$$

So $\quad A + B + C = \tfrac{1}{2}k^2(k-1) + \tfrac{1}{2}k^2(k-1) + k^2$

$$= k^2(k-1) + k^2 = k^3$$

The area of a square of side $(1 + 2 + \cdots + n)$ is the sum of the areas of n shells. So

$$(1 + 2 + \cdots + n)^2 = 1^3 + 2^3 + \cdots + n^3$$

and the proof is complete.

The next example illustrates a very powerful and useful method of proof known as **proof by contradiction**. It has been used by mathematicians for centuries and is at the heart of many classic and beautiful proofs.

Example 2

Prove that the product of two integers whose sum is 1001 cannot be divided by 1001.

Solution

Let the two numbers be n and m.

You want to prove that nm is *not* divisible by 1001.

The essence of this proof is to suppose nm *is* divisible by 1001 and to show that this leads to a **contradiction**.

Suppose nm is divisible by 1001, i.e. $nm = 1001k$ (k being an integer)

$$nm = 1001k$$

$$= 7 \times 11 \times 13k$$

$\Rightarrow n$ (or m or both) has a factor of 7.

But $n + m = 1001$ (given)

$$n + m = 7 \times 11 \times 13$$

$\Rightarrow n + m$ has a factor of 7

$\Rightarrow$ *both* n and m have a factor of 7

An identical argument applies to 11 and 13.

So n and m have factors of 7, 11 and 13.

$$\Rightarrow n \geq 1001 \quad (\text{i.e. } n \geq 7 \times 11 \times 13)$$

$$\text{and} \quad m \geq 1001$$

$$\Rightarrow n + m \geq 2002$$

So *if nm is* divisible by 1001, then $n + m$ must be *greater* than 1001.

But $n + m = 1001$ (given) and so the product nm *cannot* be divisible by 1001 if $n + m = 1001$.

4.2 Exercise 2

1 (a) Explain why $2n$ is always even for all integer values of n.

   (b) Write down a number, in terms of n, which you know is odd. Explain *how* you know.

   (c) 'The sum of three consecutive odd numbers is always divisible by 3.' Check this conjecture by considering a number of cases. Prove that the statement is true.

2 Take any two-digit number, reverse its digits and add to the original number. For example:

$$\begin{array}{r} 34 \\ +43 \\ \hline 77 \end{array} = 11 \times 7$$

A convincing explanation that the result will always be divisible by 11 might start by letting the two digits be a and b, so that the original number is $10a + b$.

   (a) Write down the value of the 'reversed' number.

   (b) Find the sum of the numbers and show that the sum *is* always divisible by 11.

   (c) Discover if the rule applies to three- or four-digit numbers. Explain your findings.

3 A neat party trick is the following rule for multiplication by 11, illustrated by $11 \times 321 = 3531$.

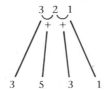

For 11×1325 you can therefore proceed by:

$$
11 \ \times \ \overset{+\ \ +\ \ +}{\overset{\frown\frown\frown}{1 \quad 3 \quad 2 \quad 5}} \ = \ 14\,575
$$

(a) Check that this method always seems to work.

(b) Using the method of expressing a two-digit number used in question 2 (i.e. 'ab'$= 10a + b$), explain how this method for multiplying by 11 works.

(c) Explain carefully how the method works for 11×392.

4   What is wrong with the following demonstration that the area of an 8×8 square is the same as the area of a 5×13 rectangle?

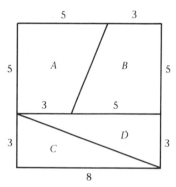
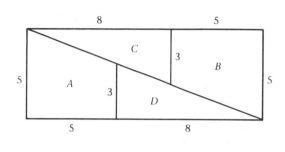

5   (a) Prove that the sum of two consecutive odd numbers is divisible by 4.

   (b) Prove that the sum of n consecutive odd numbers is divisible by n if n is odd, and by $2n$ if n is even.

6E Using the method of 'proof by contradiction', show that $\sqrt{2}$ is an irrational number (i.e. it cannot be written as $\dfrac{a}{b}$, where a and b are whole numbers).

4.2.3 Fermat and proof

In question 3 of exercise 1 you may have discovered that 21 cannot be expressed as the sum of two squares. The seventeenth-century amateur mathematician Pierre de Fermat (1601–1665) studied a refinement of the conjecture that you looked at in exercise 1.

All primes of the form $(4n + 1)$ *can be expressed as the sum of two squares.*

Of his attempts to prove this conjecture, Fermat wrote (*Diophantus*, page 268):

'*... when I had to prove that every prime number of the form* $(4n + 1)$ *is made up of two squares, I found myself in a pretty fix.*'

Fermat was in the 'no–no' cycle. However,

> *'But at last a certain reflection many times repeated gave me the necessary light, and affirmative questions yielded to my method, with the aid of some new principles by which sheer necessity compelled me to supplement it.'*

Another problem with which Fermat wrestled is known as 'Fermat's last theorem'. The problem is to prove that there are no positive integers x, y, z such that, for some integer m greater than 2,

$$x^m + y^m = z^m$$

There are certainly positive integers satisfying $x^2 + y^2 = z^2$.

$$x = 3, y = 4, z = 5 \quad \text{and} \quad x = 5, y = 12, z = 13$$

are well-known cases. Fermat's theorem is that $x^3 + y^3 = z^3$, $x^4 + y^4 = z^4$, and so on, *cannot* be solved for positive integers x, y and z.

Of this problem, Fermat wrote (*Diophantus*, page 145):

> *'I have discovered a truly marvellous proof of this, which however the margin is not large enough to contain.'*

Although it was demonstrated for many values of m, the full result remained unproved from Fermat's time and was regarded as one of the great unsolved problems of mathematics until, in 1993, it was announced that a complete (and very long) proof had been made by Professor Andrew Wiles of Princeton University, USA. The story does not end even here, however; a tiny but crucial gap in the proof, unnoticed until after the announcement, took a further year's work to repair and the proof is now accepted as correct.

Other attempts on this problem have stimulated many important advances in number theory. When you are in the 'no–no' cycle, the ideas you think of and try may be far more important than any eventual solution to the problem!

You may feel that proof is not really a part of problem-solving as such. After all, you may argue, the problem has really been solved when you reach the point of 'knowing', and proving is then no more than icing on the cake. The trouble is that you often do not 'know' until a proof has been found.

The following problem illustrates this point.

How many regions are formed when n points on the circumference of a circle are joined?

It can be tackled step by step as follows:

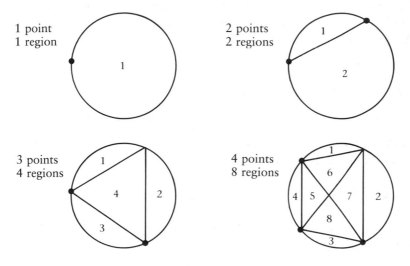

1 point
1 region

2 points
2 regions

3 points
4 regions

4 points
8 regions

 .2A

1   Tabulate this information, guess a pattern and write a general formula based on your conjecture.

2   Check your formula in the cases $n = 5$ and $n = 6$.

   You must draw the diagram for $n = 6$ *very* carefully if you are not to miscount the number of regions. To obtain the greatest number of regions for $n = 6$, you must *not* draw, for example, a regular hexagon.

3   At this stage, after a recount, your investigation will need to take a fresh direction. Extend your table up to 7 points.

4   Make a table of differences.

5   Make a final conjecture.

 4.2 **Tasksheet E1 – Prime number formulas (page 557)**

A simplified outline for the process of solving a problem can be represented by a loop:

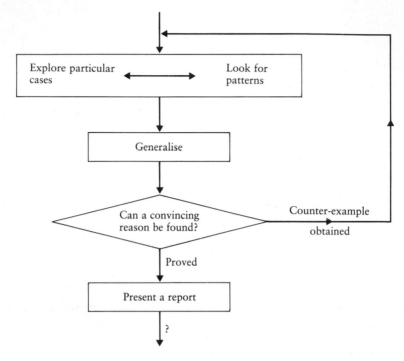

Even when you have written up your findings, the investigation may not be over.

For example, suppose you had solved the problem of finding how many squares of various sizes are bounded by the lines in a 4 × 4 grid. You might then go on to look at what is essentially another particular case, say that of the 5 × 5 grid. This is a fairly trivial form of extension of a problem, though it might lead ultimately to a generalisation. On the other hand you might ask yourself the question: *what would happen if* a triangular grid had been used?

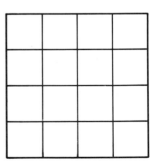

 .2B

1 How many different sizes of square may be seen in the 4 × 4 square grid?

2 What is the total number of squares?

3 How many squares would there be in an $n \times n$ square grid? You will need the result for the sum of the squares of integers here, i.e.

$$\sum_{i=1}^{n} i^2 = \frac{n}{6}(n+1)(2n+1)$$

4 Find the total number of triangles in the $4 \times 4 \times 4$ triangular grid.

5 Find the total number of triangles in:

(a) a $3 \times 3 \times 3$ grid,

(b) a $5 \times 5 \times 5$ grid.

6 Find a useful way of dividing the triangles in $n \times n \times n$ grids into two classes and hence conjecture the number of triangles in a $6 \times 6 \times 6$ grid.

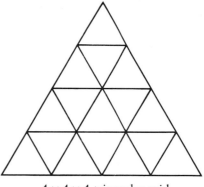

$4 \times 4 \times 4$ triangular grid

The original problem of finding the number of squares on a 4×4 grid can be extended in a variety of ways:

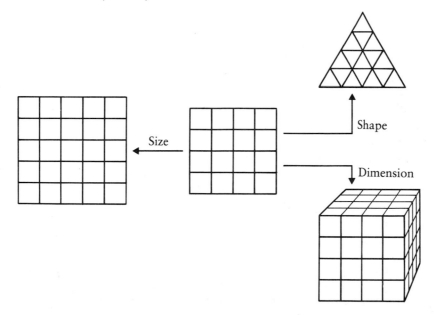

An extension into an analogous problem is more interesting when the new situation, though related, is really different from the old one.

The square and cubical grids also have a one-dimensional analogue – five equally spaced points in a straight line. So there is a chain of analogous problems.

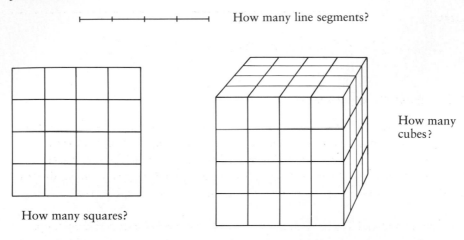

How many line segments?

How many squares?

How many cubes?

There are 10 line segments, but to see the analogy clearly you can write this as

$$1 + 2 + 3 + 4$$

Then the number of squares is

$$1^2 + 2^2 + 3^2 + 4^2$$

and the number of cubes is

$$1^3 + 2^3 + 3^3 + 4^3$$

After working through section 4.2 you should:

1 be aware that a general result cannot be established simply by considering a large number of particular cases;

2 appreciate that mathematical advances sometimes occur when mathematicians have been unable to find either a proof or a counter-example;

3 be more difficult to convince;

4 be better at convincing others by improving the standards of rigour in your arguments;

5 appreciate that all investigations have scope for extension.

4 Problem solving

.3 Mathematical modelling

4.3.1 Modelling processes

Modelling is concerned with using pure mathematical techniques and processes to solve 'real' problems. There are several important stages concerned with deciding what mathematical techniques need to be applied and making sense of the answers obtained. In attempting to solve 'real' problems, we go from the real world into the theoretical world of mathematics and back again.

The process of modelling can be represented by the following modelling loop.

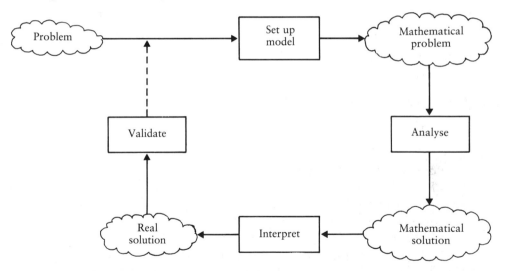

Set up model	Define the real problem. Formulate the mathematical problem. (This often involves deciding what variables are relevant and what connecting relationships can be assumed.)
Analyse	Solve the mathematical problem.
Interpret	Interpret the solution in real terms.
Validate	Compare the solution with reality. If the solution does not compare well with reality, then you must go around the loop again, refining the model.

4.3.2 An extended example – solar eclipses

Partial and total eclipses of the Sun have long both terrified and fascinated humanity. We now know that an eclipse occurs when the Earth, Moon and Sun are in a straight line with the Moon between the Earth and the Sun.

During a total eclipse, all that is visible of the Sun is a bright ring (called the corona) surrounding a black disc (the Moon). The diagram below shows successive stages in a total eclipse of the Sun. The difference in apparent size of the discs representing the Sun and Moon is exaggerated.

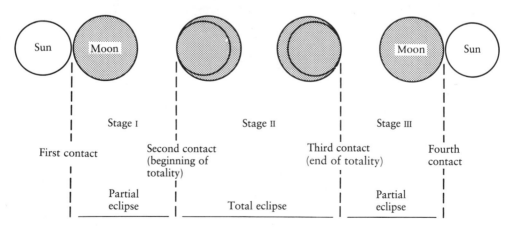

The period of total eclipse is in stage II. During stages I and III, a partial eclipse is observed.

The total eclipse is only seen on a narrow band of the Earth's surface known as the **zone of totality** or the **umbra**.

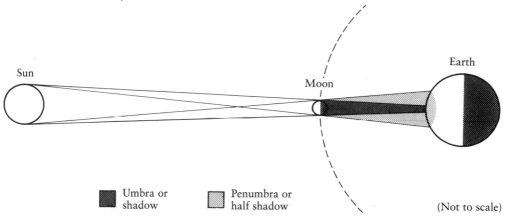

To an observer standing in the **penumbra**, the Moon passes in front of the Sun but never completely obscures it and only a partial eclipse is observed.

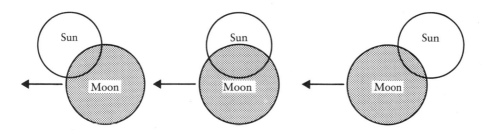

The last total eclipse visible from Britain was in 1927 and the next one is due in 1999!

Mathematics has a vital role to play in our attempts to explain and understand events we observe in the world. Mathematical tools enable us to predict that there *will* be a total eclipse in 1999, to determine its duration and to pick the best observation point.

Consider the following problem.

How long does a total eclipse last?

This is *not* an easy problem. To obtain an estimate for the total time for an eclipse you need to make a number of simplifying assumptions. These are considered in the various models discussed below.

The main dimensions needed are (from *Encyclopedia Britannica*):

Diameters in km:

	Sun	1.39×10^6
	Earth	1.28×10^4
	Moon	3.48×10^3

Mean distances from Earth in km:

	Sun	1.50×10^8
	Moon	3.82×10^5

The Moon orbits the Earth in 27.3 days, a lunar month.

First model

In a simple model, you might consider the Sun and Earth to be stationary and the Moon's orbit around the Earth to be circular. You can define an eclipse as total when, for some time, the Moon completely obscures the main disc of the Sun from some observer O on Earth.

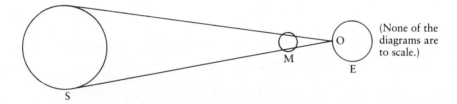

(None of the diagrams are to scale.)

A partial eclipse begins with the Moon in position M_1 and ends in position M_4. The total eclipse is between positions M_2 and M_3.

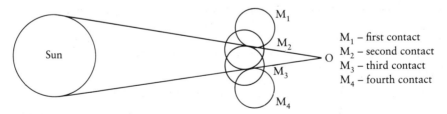

M_1 – first contact
M_2 – second contact
M_3 – third contact
M_4 – fourth contact

To make further progress, you can simplify your model by assuming that the Moon's orbit is locally straight.

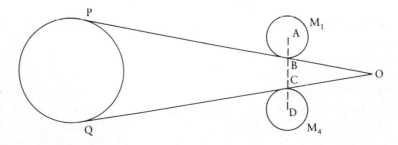

You may also make the assumption that PQ is the Sun's diameter and BC is part of the Moon's orbit.

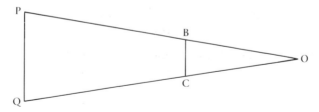

Triangle OPQ is an enlargement of triangle OBC with centre O, scale factor $\dfrac{OP}{OB}$ and so

$$BC = PQ \times \frac{OB}{OP} = 1.39 \times 10^6 \times \frac{3.82 \times 10^5}{1.50 \times 10^8}$$

$$= 3.54 \times 10^3 \, \text{km}$$

The diameter of the Moon is 3.48×10^3 km so, according to the model, total eclipses do not occur! Since $3.48 < 3.54$, the Moon never completely obscures the Sun. So you must refine the model in some way.

Second model
One simplification you made was that the orbits of the Earth around the Sun and of the Moon around the Earth are circular. In fact, both are roughly elliptical; instead of using mean distances, you should consider a range of distances.

	Moon	Sun
Nearest distance from Earth (km)	3.63×10^5	1.47×10^8
Farthest distance from Earth (km)	4.06×10^5	1.52×10^8

The eclipse of maximum duration will occur when the Moon is nearest the Earth and the Sun farthest away. Applying the model in this case,

$$BC = 1.39 \times 10^6 \times \frac{3.63 \times 10^5}{1.52 \times 10^8} = 3.32 \times 10^3 \, \text{km}$$

The eclipse is total only when BC falls within the diameter of the Moon, for a distance of

$$(3.48 - 3.32) \times 10^3 = 1.6 \times 10^2 \, \text{km}$$

The Moon's speed is

$$\frac{\text{circumference of total circular orbit}}{\text{lunar month}} = \frac{2\pi \times 3.82 \times 10^5}{27.3 \times 24 \times 60}$$

$$= 61.1 \, \text{km per minute}$$

(The elliptical orbit has a length about equal to that of a circle with radius the mean distance.)

Using the relation

$$\text{time} = \frac{\text{distance}}{\text{speed}}$$

$$\text{time of total eclipse} = \frac{1.6 \times 10^2}{61.1}$$

$$= 2.6 \, \text{minutes}$$

The maximum duration of total eclipse is observed to be about 7 minutes. The model can be amended further to account for this.

Third model
Another main assumption made at the outset was that the Earth could be regarded as stationary. In fact the observer O is moving because of the spin of the Earth on its axis. The speed of an observer is greatest on the equator, being

$$\frac{\text{circumference of Earth}}{\text{day length}} = \frac{\pi \times 1.28 \times 10^4}{24 \times 60}$$

$$= 27.9 \, \text{km per minute}$$

Since the observer and the Moon move in the same direction, the speed of the Moon relative to the observer is

$$\text{Moon's speed in orbit} - \text{observer's speed} = 61.1 - 27.9$$

$$= 33.2 \, \text{km per minute}$$

Using this figure, you will find that the time of total eclipse is

$$\frac{1.6 \times 10^2}{33.2} = 4.8 \, \text{minutes}$$

You still have not reached the target and a dutiful modeller would check assumptions and consider other refinements.

You should at least consider the following relevant observations.

• Over a series of calculations, a considerable rounding error accumulates.

• The distances between bodies are probably 'centre-to-centre'; this is not always made clear in reference books.

• The Moon's speed in elliptical orbit is not constant.

• Orbits are not quite elliptical anyway! In particular, the Sun perturbs the orbit of the Moon.

• In observations not made from the equator, you must take into account the latitude in calculating the speed of the observer.

Since 1963, scientists have used specially equipped aircraft or observation platforms above the clouds. Supersonic machines flying at 2000 km per hour in the direction of the Moon's shadow prolong the period of total eclipse to an hour or more.

For the eclipse problem, the various stages in the modelling cycle can be identified as follows.

Set up model
The stage of setting up a model is at the heart of the mathematical modelling process. It is important to choose suitable simplifying assumptions which preserve the key features of the real situation but which avoid an unnecessarily complicated model. Essentially, there are two key stages in setting up a model.

- Decide on the relevant variables, keeping your list as short and simple as possible.
- Look for relations connecting the variables on your list.

For the total eclipse problem, initial models were chosen in which the relevant variables were the distances on the diagram below, together with the orbital speed of the Moon and time of the eclipse.

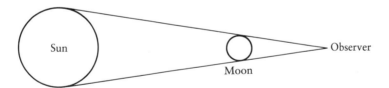

In this case, a relationship between the distances can be obtained from the diagram and a further relationship is

$$\text{distance} = \text{speed} \times \text{time}$$

Analyse
For the eclipse problem a further simplification was made, producing the similar triangles shown below.

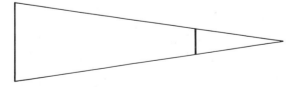

The mathematical analysis was then simply the use of similar triangles, followed later by a use of the distance–speed relationship.

Interpret
When modelling 'real' problems it is important to remember that 'real' answers are required. If you are trying to estimate the annual cost of running the family car, then an answer such as £4000 is required and not an algebraic formula.

An analysis of the initial eclipse model had a very simple interpretation – total eclipses cannot occur!

Validate
It will be possible to check the solutions to many problems by direct comparison with reality.

You know that total eclipses do occur and so the initial model needed refining. Even after two successive refinements the eclipse model still predicted a much shorter eclipse than can actually occur.

The acid test of a model is always how well it represents reality but, generally, over-elaboration should be avoided.

Normally a model will need improvement and you will have to go around the loop in the flow chart a second or even a third time. At some point, however, the model will be judged to be good enough and you stop.

Mathematical modelling occurs when solving pure problems as well as 'real' ones.

Example 1
The product of the ages of Ann and Mike is 300. Find their ages if Ann is 20 years older than Mike.

Solution
Let Mike be m years old; then Ann is $m + 20$ years old.

Set up model   Appropriate notation is introduced for the variables.

$$m(m + 20) = 300$$

Relationships are listed.

$$\Rightarrow m^2 + 20m - 300 = 0$$
$$\Rightarrow (m + 30)(m - 10) = 0$$
$$\Rightarrow m = -30 \text{ or } 10$$

Analyse   The standard method of solving a quadratic equation by factorisation is applied.

m cannot be -30 and so
$m = 10$.
Mike is 10 and Ann is 30.

Interpret/validate   The two mathematical solutions yield only one 'real' solution. This solution is then stated in everday language.

You will have plenty of opportunity to use your modelling skills in your work in mechanics or statistics.

After working through section 4.3 you should be able to recognise and apply the following stages in the modelling process:

set up model: define the real problem, decide which variables are relevant, decide what relationships can be assumed;

analyse: solve the mathematical problem;

interpret: interpret the solution in real terms;

validate: compare the solution with reality, modify your model as necessary.

4 Problem solving

.4 Mathematical articles

4.4.1 Introduction

The purpose of this section is to help you both to *read* and to *write* mathematics. It contains some pure and some 'real' case studies. These provide models for writing mathematics and give an idea of what is expected when you write up your own investigations.

In reading the best mathematical writing a considerable effort of self-discipline is needed to keep going through to the end. (The same applies to the worst writing, but for different reasons!) In a good article, ideas will arise which suggest investigations not followed in the text and you may find it difficult to keep your mind on the job in hand. You can comfort yourself with the thought that side-lines can always be followed up later. Mathematical articles cannot be read as you would read a novel; the information content is usually very dense and you should take time to check calculations, verify assertions made and *understand thoroughly* the definitions and the argument as it develops.

The two case studies below are interspersed with questions of the kind you should be asking yourself when you read a piece of mathematics. The questions should help you to develop your understanding and to check that the writer's argument is correct.

▷ **Case Studies**
1 – The Platonic solids (page 321)
2 – The gravity model in geography (page 325)

Case studies 1 and 2 include questions interspersing the text at various stages. In the remaining case studies the exposition will be uninterrupted, all questions being set at the end. To help to bridge the gap between the two styles, here is an exercise based upon the beginning of an article published in *Mathematical Spectrum* (volume 19, number 1 (1986/87)).

4.4 **Exercise 1**

Read the following article carefully and carry out the necessary thinking and writing at all the points indicated by numbered asterisks.

On doodles and 4-regular graphs

J. C. Turner, *University of Waikato*

The next time you are doodling on a piece of paper, let your pen come back to its starting point and then consider what kind of mathematical figure you have drawn.

If you have always let your pen trace a smooth continuous curve, and whenever you have met a previous point on the curve you have crossed directly over the old curve, it is probable that you have drawn what graph-theorists call a 4-regular graph: figure 1 is an example.[1] In this case n, the number of crossing points = 9, m, the number of edges (an edge is a curve joining two adjacent crossing points) = 18 and r, the number of regions (one is shown shaded, 34589) = 11, including the region of the plane exterior to the graph.[2] Such diagrams are called *4-regular graphs* because every crossing point (these are usually called *vertices*, or *nodes*) has four edges adjoined to it.

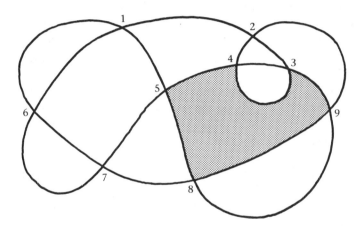

You might like to think what you would have to do whilst doodling if the result were not to be a 4-regular graph,[3] and conversely, whether there are 4-regular graphs which are not doodles![4] You might like to think of how many *small* regions (ones with few edges) you have managed to draw in your doodle.

Let us say a region is a *k-gon* if it is bounded by k edges. Then the smallest region possible is a 1-gon or loop; then a 2-gon; then a 3-gon; and so on. In the doodle shown in figure 1 there are four 2-gons and three 3-gons. There are also two 4-gons, one 5-gon, and the outer-region 6-gon.[5]

The purpose of this article is to discuss the possibility of bounds on the frequencies of small regions in 4-regular graphs. Simple questions to ask are:

(i) Can one draw a doodle without a 2-gon?

(ii) Can one draw a doodle without a 3-gon?

(iii) Can one draw a doodle without either a 2-gon or a 3-gon?

▷ **Further Case Studies**

After working through section 4.4 you should:

1 have developed a strategy for reading mathematical articles with understanding;

2 appreciate the need for a clear and orderly style when presenting a mathematical argument.

The Platonic solids

For $n = 3, 4, 5, \ldots$ there is precisely one shape of polygon with n equal sides and n equal angles. We say that there are infinitely many **regular polygons**.

1 What do you understand by the term 'regular polygon'?
What is meant by 'infinitely many' regular polygons?

A regular polygon is a two-dimensional shape. The analogous three-dimensional shape is a solid whose faces are congruent regular polygons with the same number of these polygons meeting at each vertex (or corner) of the solid.

Such solids were considered in Plato's *Timaeus* and became known as the Platonic solids.

2 Name a three-dimensional shape which fits the description of a Platonic solid.

Given that there are infinitely many regular polygons, you might expect there to be infinitely many Platonic solids. We shall investigate whether or not this is the case.

To try to classify the Platonic solids systematically, we can start with solids with the 'simplest' possible faces: equilateral triangles.

Case 1 – Equilateral triangular faces
To form a corner, at least three faces meet at any vertex. For triangular faces, at most five such faces meet at a vertex because if the angles at a vertex totalled $360°$ or more, then the faces could not form a corner.

3 Explain fully why six triangular faces cannot meet at a vertex.

We need to consider the cases of three, four or five faces meeting at each vertex. As an example, let us examine the second possibility.

Four faces meet at each vertex
It is easy to form the required solid by taping together equilateral triangles, four at each vertex. The shape obtained is known as the **regular octahedron** and has eight faces.

CASE STUDY 1

From a model of an octahedron we can verify the figures in the following table:

Number of faces	F	8
Number of vertices	V	6
Number of edges	E	12

4 What are the values of F, V and E for a cube?

The mathematician Euler found that the equation $F + V = E + 2$ is true for all polyhedra.

5 Find $F + V - E$ for: (a) the octahedron (b) the cube.

Remarkably, we could have used Euler's formula to obtain the number of faces, vertices and edges of the octahedron without ever making the model!

We are looking for a shape formed by F triangular faces.

 , , ... ,

These have $3F$ sides and $3F$ corners. When they are taped together, each edge of the solid is formed from a pair of these sides and so

$$E = \frac{3F}{2}$$

Each vertex of the solid is formed from four corners and so

$$V = \frac{3F}{4}$$

Substituting these results into Euler's formula, we obtain

$$F + \frac{3F}{4} = \frac{3F}{2} + 2$$

$$\Rightarrow \quad 4F + 3F = 6F + 8$$

$$\Rightarrow \quad F = 8$$

Then $E = 12$ and $V = 6$, as required.

This kind of analysis can be very helpful in showing precisely what possibilities there are for particular solids. By a similar analysis, we can show that the only Platonic solids with three or five triangular faces at a vertex are the **tetrahedron** and the **icosahedron**.

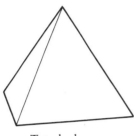

Tetrahedron

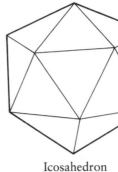

Icosahedron

6 Use Euler's formula to show that a Platonic solid with three triangular faces at each vertex must have precisely four faces.

Case 2 – Square faces
In this case three faces must meet at each vertex.

7 Explain the assertion above. Explain also why $E + \dfrac{4F}{2}$ and $V = \dfrac{4F}{3}$.

Substituting $E = \dfrac{4F}{2}$ and $V = \dfrac{4F}{3}$ into Euler's formula gives

$$F + \frac{4F}{3} = \frac{4F}{2} + 2$$

from which we obtain $F = 6$, $V = 8$ and $E = 12$. So the solid *must* be a cube.

Case 3 – Faces with five or more edges
Three hexagons or four pentagons at a vertex would give an angle of 360° or greater – impossible for a three-dimensional solid. So the only remaining case is that of three regular pentagons meeting at each vertex, because $3 \times 108° < 360°$.

8 What is the significance of the 108° mentioned above?

A similar analysis to that carried out in cases 1 and 2 shows that a Platonic solid with pentagonal faces must have $F = 12$, $V = 20$, $E = 30$.

CASE STUDY 1

There is one such solid.

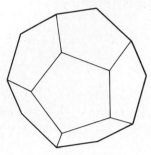

Dodecahedron

9 Obtain the given values of F, V and E.

It is interesting that there should be infinitely many two-dimensional regular shapes yet only five regular three-dimensional shapes, the five Platonic solids: tetrahedron, octahedron, icosahedron, cube and dodecahedron. Mathematicians have shown that there are six regular four-dimensional 'solids' and, curiously, only three in any space of more than four dimensions – the n-dimensional cube, tetrahedron and octahedron.

The gravity model in geography

Newton's law of universal gravitation states that two bodies with masses m_1 and m_2 attract each other with a force

$$\frac{Gm_1m_2}{d^2}$$

where d is the distance between the centres of mass of the bodies and G is constant. This equation has been used successfully in modelling planetary motion, by Newton and others.

The term 'gravity model' is applied in geography in a looser way. Some authors use it of any model where the intensity of an interaction between places decreases with distance. The interaction could be one of trade or transportation or migration, for instance. Others insist upon a stricter analogy with Newton's model in which, if the two places had measures of attractiveness W_1 and W_2 and were separated by a distance d, then if T were some measure of the intensity of interaction between the places,

$$T = \frac{kW_1W_2}{d^\beta}$$

where k is a constant and β a positive number.

1 What value does β have in Newton's model of gravitation?

Telephone calls
Start with an example using a model closely resembling Newton's. The populations and distances separating towns are given below.

Town	Population (in thousands)	Distances (km) from Sheffield	Derby
Sheffield	537	–	52
Derby	216	52	–
Nottingham	271	50	20

Suppose that the number of telephone calls made in a given time between town A and town B can be found using the equation

$$T_{AB} = \frac{kP_AP_B}{d_{AB}^2}$$

where k is a constant, P_A and P_B are the populations of towns A and B respectively and d_{AB} is the distance between them.

Using this model, the number of telephone calls between Sheffield and Derby is

$$T_{\text{SD}} = \frac{k \times 537 \times 216}{52^2} = 43k$$

If the model were to be used to predict numbers of calls between towns, it would first be tested with known data. This would enable the 'calibration' of the model, in which the value of k would be found. At the same time, a check would be made to find whether the inverse square model was most appropriate or whether some other exponent should be substituted for 2 in the formula for the number of telephone calls.

2 (a) Use the model to find T_{DN} and T_{SN}.
  (b) Which pair of the towns of Sheffield, Derby and Nottingham has the most telephone calls between them according to the model?

Two competing shopping centres
If, in a rural area, there is a good network of roads and two towns satisfy the shopping needs of the scattered community, then the application of a simple gravity model may be considered.

Suppose towns A and B have populations P_A and P_B respectively. An individual lives at C which is distance d_A km from A and d_B km from B, as shown in the diagram.

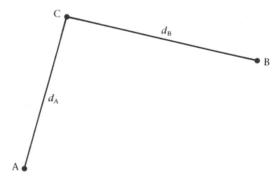

The gravity model suggests that the attractiveness of A to the individual is of the form

$$\frac{kP_A}{d_A^2}$$

3 What is the attractiveness of B to the individual?

Now you can introduce the idea of an **area of influence**. If A is more attractive than B, then the individual is in A's area of influence, and vice versa.

First you should investigate this idea in a simple theoretical case. Suppose that A and B have populations of 40 000 and 10 000 respectively. Then for a point P, the attractiveness of A is $\dfrac{40\,000\,k}{AP^2}$ and that of B is $\dfrac{10\,000\,k}{BP^2}$.

If A and B are equally attractive then

$$\frac{40\,000\,k}{AP^2} = \frac{10\,000\,k}{BP^2}$$

$$AP^2 = 4BP^2$$

$$AP = 2BP$$

If P_1 divides AB in the ratio 2 : 1, then P_1 will be on the locus of points where A and B are equally attractive. Similarly, the point P_2 dividing AB externally in the ratio 2 : 1 will be on this locus.

If AB $= 3a$ then it is not difficult to verify that

$$AP_2 = 6a, \qquad AP_1 = 2a, \qquad P_1P_2 = 4a$$

Now let AB be the x-axis and take as origin O the midpoint of P_1P_2.

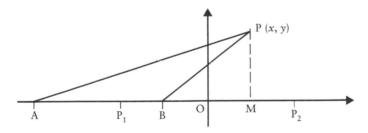

Let P (x, y) be any point on the locus of equal attractions. You know that

$$AP = 2BP$$

$$\Rightarrow \quad AP^2 = 4BP^2$$

From the diagram,

$$AM^2 + PM^2 = 4(BM^2 + PM^2)$$

$$(x + AO)^2 + y^2 = 4(x + BO)^2 + 4y^2$$

$$(x + 4a)^2 + y^2 = 4(x + a)^2 + 4y^2$$

$$3x^2 + 3y^2 = 12a^2$$

$$x^2 + y^2 = 4a^2$$

This last equation will be recognised as that of the circle with P_1P_2 as diameter. All points inside the circle are in B's area of influence. Points outside the circle are in A's area of influence.

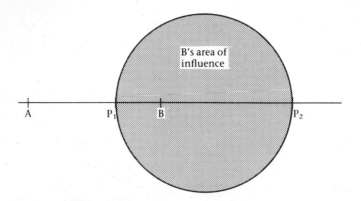

You can now apply the theory to an actual case.

The map on the next page shows the area around Wisbech and King's Lynn, whose populations are respectively 17 000 and 30 000. You may assume that they are the only shopping attractions in the area.

To find the areas of shopping influence of Wisbech and King's Lynn, consider someone for whom they are equally attractive, who lives distance d_W from Wisbech and distance d_L from King's Lynn.

$$\frac{k \times 17\,000}{d_W^2} = \frac{k \times 30\,000}{d_L^2}$$

So $\qquad 17\,000\,d_L^2 = 30\,000\,d_W^2$

You can take square roots to obtain $130d_L = 173d_W$.

People for whom this equation holds live on a circle whose centre lies somewhere along the line through Wisbech and King's Lynn. Two points on the circle's circumference, X and Y, are marked on the diagram below.

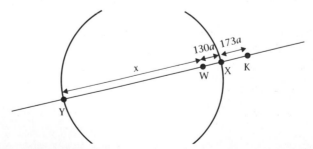

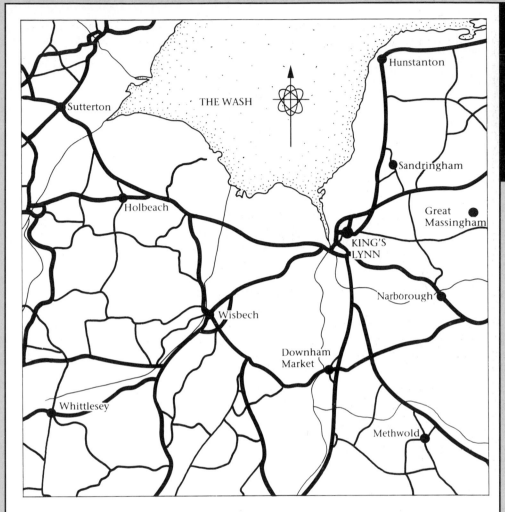

If the distance from Wisbech to King's Lynn is 13 miles, then in mile units $a = 0.043$ and the point X is 5.6 miles from Wisbech and 7.4 miles from King's Lynn.

4 Explain the calculation that leads to $a = 0.043$.

To locate the point Y, find the distance x as follows:

$$\frac{x + 13}{x} = \frac{173}{130}$$

$$43x = 130 \times 13$$

$$x = 39.3$$

Therefore the point Y is 39.3 miles beyond Wisbech and the diameter of the circle is 44.9 miles.

5 (a) Explain the statement
$$\frac{x + 13}{x} = \frac{173}{130}$$

(b) Shrewsbury and Welshpool are 19 miles apart and have populations of 56 000 and 7000 respectively. Using the same gravity model, write down expressions for the attractiveness of the two towns to an individual who lives distance d_S from Shrewsbury and d_W from Welshpool.

(c) Using the method outlined above, carry out the necessary calculations and describe as fully as possible Welshpool's area of influence.

(d) In areas of the USA, it is easy to travel long distances by car. What difference would this make to the value of β taken in the model?

The game of Hex

The game of Hex was invented in 1942 by Piet Hein at Niels Bohr's Institute for Theoretical Physics in Copenhagen. *Blockbusters*, a popular television quiz, used a variation of this game.

The original game, for two players, is played on a diamond-shaped board made up of hexagons. One player has a set of white counters, the other a set of black counters. The players, White and Black, alternately place one of their counters on any vacant hexagon. The object of the game is for White to try to complete a chain of white counters between the two edges marked 'White', while Black tries to form a chain of black counters joining the 'Black' edges. The game ends as soon as one player completes such an unbroken chain.

Here is a diagram showing a game won by Black on a 4 × 4 board.

The game went as follows:

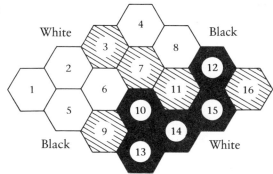

White	Black
3	10
7	15
11	14
16	12
9	13

Black wins because of the chain 13–14–15–12.

In this game, Black's first two moves, at 10 and 15, illustrate a useful tactic when playing Hex.

Result 1
Black cannot be prevented from connecting 10 and 15 because if White plays on 11 Black can play on 14, whereas if White plays on 14 Black can play on 11. Therefore, Black can always complete the chain 10–11/14–15.

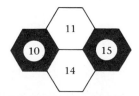

When playing the game, it is also helpful to know another type of connecting result.

Result 2
Black, to play, cannot prevent White connecting her counter on 1 to the White edge. For example, if Black plays on 2 or 4, White can simply play on 3 and then form the chain 1–3–6/7.

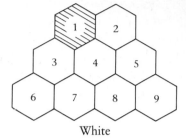

White

On small boards, the first player to move has such a strong advantage that she should always win. For example, White to play first on a 4 × 4 board will win easily, especially if she knows the following result, which is easy to prove with the help of result 2.

Result 3
An opening play by White on 4, 7, 10 or 13 wins. Any other opening play loses.

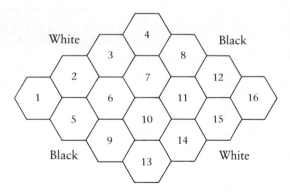

On larger boards it is much more difficult to make such a full analysis of the game and in practice an 11 × 11 board is used for serious games.

Questions
1 For result 2, show how White can connect 1 to the white edge when Black's initial move is 3, 6 or 7.

2 After the sample game of the article, White claimed that her third move, 11, was the losing one. She believed that she could have won the game by playing another move instead. Sketch the position immediately *before* her third move, and prove or disprove her claim.

3 For result 3, prove that White can force a win by playing at either 7 or 10.

Archimedes and π

π may be defined as the ratio of the circumference of a circle to its diameter.

$$\pi = \frac{\text{circumference}}{\text{diameter}}$$

The aim is to estimate the value of π by finding sequences of converging upper and lower bounds for the circumference of a circle of radius 1 unit. This method was used by the Greek mathematician Archimedes.

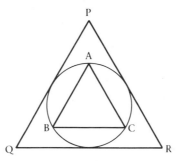

In the diagram, $\begin{array}{c}\text{perimeter of}\\\text{triangle ABC}\end{array} < \begin{array}{c}\text{circumference}\\\text{of the circle}\end{array} < \begin{array}{c}\text{perimeter of}\\\text{triangle PQR}\end{array}$

The two triangles are equilateral. The circle has radius 1 unit, so its circumference is 2π units. Let O be the centre of the circle.

As AC is a chord of the circle, the line OD bisects it at right angles and so

$$DC = \cos 30° = \frac{\sqrt{3}}{2}$$

The perimeter of the triangle ABC is then $3\sqrt{3}$.

For triangle PQR, the sides PQ, QR and PR form tangents to the circle and so, for example, line OS bisects PR at right angles.

Then $SR = \dfrac{1}{\tan 30°} = \sqrt{3}$ and the perimeter of triangle PQR is $6\sqrt{3}$.

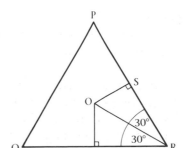

So the first upper and lower bounds for π are given by $\dfrac{3\sqrt{3}}{2} < \pi < 3\sqrt{3}$.

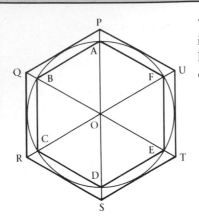

The figure shows a regular hexagon ABCDEF, **inscribed** within the circle, and a regular hexagon PQRSTU, **circumscribed** around the circle.

You require the lengths of the perimeters of both these hexagons.

Since the circle has radius 1, you know that both OM and AB are 1 unit long, so the perimeter of the *inscribed* hexagon is 6.

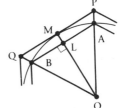

The circumscribed hexagon is an enlargement of the inscribed hexagon by scale factor $\dfrac{\text{OM}}{\text{OL}}$. By Pythagoras' theorem,

$$\text{OL} = \sqrt{\left(1 - \left(\frac{1}{2}\right)^2\right)} = \frac{\sqrt{3}}{2}$$ and so the scale factor of the enlargement is $\dfrac{2}{\sqrt{3}}$.

It follows that the perimeter of the circumscribed hexagon is $\dfrac{12}{\sqrt{3}}$ or $4\sqrt{3}$, and so $3 < \pi < 2\sqrt{3}$.

To bring the upper and lower bounds for π still closer together you need to consider polygons with more than 6 sides.

A polygon with n sides is called an 'n-gon'. You can demonstrate that it is possible to calculate the length of the side of a regular $2n$-gon inscribed in the circle from the length of the side of the regular inscribed n-gon.

You can use an enlargement argument, similar to that for the hexagon case above, to find the perimeters of the circumscribing n-gon and $2n$-gon, so you can extend your sequences of converging upper and lower bounds for π.

Let x_n be the length of the side of a regular inscribed n-gon,

I_n be the perimeter of a regular inscribed n-gon, $I_n = nx_n$,

C_n be the perimeter of a regular circumscribed n-gon.

An enlargement argument, similar to that used in the hexagon case, gives

$$C_n = \frac{I_n}{\sqrt{\left(1 - \frac{x_n^2}{4}\right)}}$$

You can obtain a regular inscribed $2n$-gon from the regular inscribed n-gon by drawing the line of symmetry of each triangle OAB, OBC, and so on, to obtain triangles OAM, OMB, OBN, ONC, and so on, as shown in the diagram below.

Now

$$AM^2 = AL^2 + LM^2 \quad \text{(Pythagoras' theorem)}$$

$$= \left(\frac{x_n}{2}\right)^2 + (1 - OL)^2$$

But $OL^2 = OA^2 - AL^2 = 1 - \left(\frac{x_n}{2}\right)^2$

So $AM^2 = \left(\frac{x_n}{2}\right)^2 + \left[1 - \sqrt{\left(1 - \left(\frac{x_n}{2}\right)^2\right)}\right]^2$

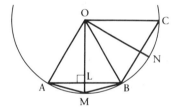

That is $x_{2n} = \sqrt{\left(\frac{x_n^2}{4} + \left[1 - \sqrt{\left(1 - \frac{x_n^2}{4}\right)}\right]^2\right)}$

These equations make it possible to find successive approximations for π as shown in the table.

n	x_n	I_n	C_n	Inequality
3	$\sqrt{3}$	$3\sqrt{3}$	$6\sqrt{3}$	$\dfrac{3\sqrt{3}}{2} < \pi < 3\sqrt{3}$
6	1	6	$4\sqrt{3}$	$3 < \pi < 2\sqrt{3}$
12				
24				

You may like to continue the table and so find π to any desired accuracy.

Questions

1 Explain what is meant by 'converging upper and lower bounds'.

2 Give a detailed explanation of why (in the diagrams on page 333)

    (a) $DC = \cos 30°$ (b) $SR = \dfrac{1}{\tan 30°}$.

3 Show how the two results from question 2 lead to the inequality

$$\frac{3\sqrt{3}}{2} < \pi < 3\sqrt{3}$$

4 Explain the meaning of the terms (a) inscribed, (b) circumscribed.

5 Justify the statement 'you know both OM and AB are 1 unit long, so the perimeter of the inscribed hexagon is 6'.

6 (a) Give the details of the calculations leading to the value of $4\sqrt{3}$ for the perimeter of the circumscribed hexagon.

  (b) Show how this results in the inequality $3 < \pi < 2\sqrt{3}$.

7 Give the details of the argument that

$$C_n = \frac{I_n}{\sqrt{\left(1 - \dfrac{x_n^2}{4}\right)}}$$

8 (a) Write down the formula for x_{12} in terms of x_6.

  (b) Hence find x_{12}.

9 Showing all details of the working, complete the row of the table for $n = 12$.

10 Explain how continuing the table would lead to a value of π of any desired accuracy, provided that sufficiently accurate computational equipment is used.

5 Mathematical methods

.1 The power of Pythagoras

5.1.1 Pythagoras and right-angled triangles

The great mathematician Pythagoras is best remembered for stating a relationship (now known as Pythagoras' theorem, although it was certainly not his only theorem) connecting the lengths of the sides of right-angled triangles.

Pythagoras' theorem states that, in a right-angled triangle with sides a, b and h as shown,

$$h^2 = a^2 + b^2$$

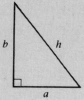

Little is known for certain about the Greek mathematician Pythagoras. Born on the island of Samos, just off the coast of Asia Minor, around 570 BC, he travelled much throughout his life, notably in Egypt, Asia Minor and Italy. He eventually established a community of scholars at Croton, a Greek settlement in what is now southern Italy. They formed a select brotherhood sharing philosophical and political ideals as well as their study of mathematics, and lived under a strict code of discipline – temperance, purity and obedience were their watchwords. They were a secret society, and the pentagram was used as a sign of recognition. Although women were forbidden by law from attending public meetings, many went to Pythagoras' lectures, and a few were even admitted to the inner circle. The Pythagoreans believed that mathematics was the key to the world. Everything was assigned a number. For example, 1 represented reason, 2 man, 3 woman, 4 justice and 5 marriage (the union of 2 and 3).

The sign of the Pythagoreans

Pythagoras' influence continued after his death and his followers developed a custom of assigning all work to 'the Master' (Pythagoras). This has made it very difficult to know how much of the work assigned to him was his own, and how much his students.

It is believed that the theorem for which Pythagoras is best remembered genuinely is his own work. It can be stated as

The square on the hypotenuse of a right-angled triangle is equal to the sum of the squares on the other two sides.

Pythagoras' theorem has countless practical applications.

Pythagoras and his students searched for sets of whole numbers which satisfied the relationship $a^2 + b^2 = c^2$. The smallest such values are 3, 4 and 5, since $9 + 16 = 25$, i.e. $3^2 + 4^2 = 5^2$.

Sets of numbers like this are known as Pythagorean triples. Since they satisfy the relationship, any triangle with these measurements must be right-angled. This fact is still used for marking out sportsfields: a rope marked in the correct proportions and arranged in a triangle will form a right-angle.

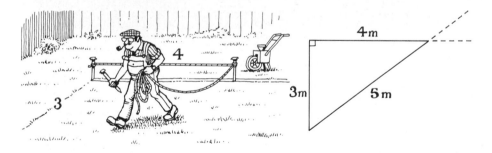

Since any triangle with these proportions must be right-angled, it follows that $(6, 8, 10)$, $(9, 12, 15)$ and $(12, 16, 20)$ must also be Pythagorean triples.

The Pythagoreans could see that the hypotenuse of an isosceles right-angled triangle with two equals sides of length 1 unit would not be a whole number.

Using $b^2 = a^2 + b^2$, the hypotenuse must be $\sqrt{2}$.

You will find this triangle useful for remembering the values of the circular functions at 45°.

$$\sin 45° = \frac{1}{\sqrt{2}} \qquad \cos 45° = \frac{1}{\sqrt{2}} \qquad \tan 45° = 1$$

Similarly, if an equilateral triangle is divided along a line of symmetry, two right-angled triangles are formed. Using half of an equilateral triangle of side 2 units, the values of $\sin 30°$, $\cos 30°$, $\tan 30°$ and $\sin 60°$, $\cos 60°$, $\tan 60°$ can all be obtained in exact form.

By Pythagoras' theorem $BD^2 = 4 - 1 = 3$

i.e. $BD = \sqrt{3}$

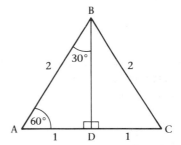

You can then read off the required trigonometric ratios, for example,

$$\sin 30° = \frac{1}{2}, \quad \cos 30° = \frac{\sqrt{3}}{2}$$

It is very useful to know the following trigonometric ratios.

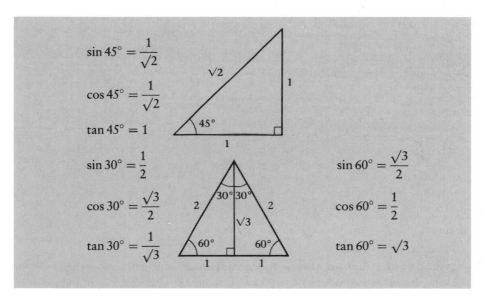

Pythagoras' theorem can easily be extended into three dimensions.

Example 1

(a) A frame is to be constructed from thirteen metal rods. Twelve of the rods are welded together to form a cuboid. The thirteenth is fitted as a crosspiece between opposite corners, thus increasing the rigidity of the structure.

If the cuboid is made from rods measuring 18 cm, 24 cm and 11 cm, what is the length of the crosspiece?

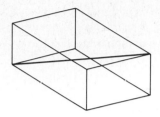

(b) The frames are made to a variety of sizes. If the rods used to form the cuboid measure x cm, y cm, and z cm, find an expression for the length of the crosspiece.

Solution

(a)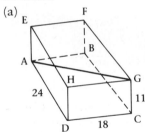

The diagonal AG is the hypotenuse of the right-angled triangle AGC

i.e. $AG^2 = AC^2 + CG^2$

AC is the hypotenuse of the right-angled triangle ADC

i.e. $AC^2 = AD^2 + CD^2$

$$\Rightarrow AC = 30$$

and $AG = \sqrt{(900 + 121)} = 31.95 \text{ cm}$

(b) Generalising this result, if $AD = x$, $CD = y$, $CG = z$

$$\text{then } AC^2 = x^2 + y^2$$

$$\text{so } AG^2 = AC^2 + CG^2$$

$$= (x^2 + y^2) + z^2$$

$$= x^2 + y^2 + z^2$$

$$\Rightarrow AG = \sqrt{(x^2 + y^2 + z^2)}$$

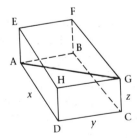

If d is the long diagonal of a cuboid of dimensions a, b and c, then

$$d^2 = a^2 + b^2 + c^2$$

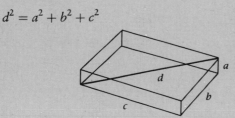

5.1 Exercise 1

1 Use Pythagoras' theorem for right-angled triangles to find the hypotenuse of

(a) (b)

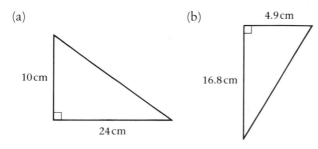

2 Two pigeons fly off Nelson's Column. The first flies 3.7 km due east and lands on the Tower of London. The other flies 0.9 km due south and lands on Westminster Abbey. How far apart are Westminster Abbey and the Tower of London?

3 A ramp is to be built to allow wheelchairs and pushchairs to enter a hotel more easily. The height of the step is 10 cm. The planks to be used are 0.7 m long. How much space will be needed in front of the step?

4 A flag-pole is supported half-way up by four guy ropes, each of length 12 m. The ropes are tethered at the four corners of a rectangle measuring 5 m by 8 m. How tall is the flag-pole?

5 Find eight Pythagorean triples which use only numbers less than 30. Group them to show which triples represent triangles with the same proportions.

5.1.2 The equation of a circle

Pythagoras' theorem can be used to find the equation of a circle. The necessary ideas are developed in the following questions.

 .1A

1 (a) Use Pythagoras' theorem to find the distance of the point $(3, 3)$ from the origin.

   (b) Use Pythagoras' theorem to find the distance of the point $(4, 6)$ from the point $(1, 2)$.

A circle is made up of all the points that are a fixed distance from its centre. The distance from the centre is the radius r of the circle.

2 (a) Use Pythagoras' theorem to decide which of the following points lie on a circle with centre $(0, 0)$, radius 5.

   $(4, 3),\quad (2.5, 2.5),\quad (-3, 4),\quad (-5, 0),\quad (1, -4.5)$

   (b) Write down an equation connecting x and y which is satisfied by all points (x, y) which lie on this circle.

   (c)* Use a graph plotter to draw the graph of this equation.

* Note that for some graph plotters, you may need to rearrange the equation to give y in terms of x. This form of the equation will involve a square root, so the graph will be drawn in two sections, one part using the positive square root, and one using the negative square root.

3 (a) Use Pythagoras' theorem to decide which of the following points lie on a circle with centre $(2, 5)$, radius 25.

   $(27, 5),\quad (17, 25),\quad (-5, 29),\quad (-22, -2),\quad (-18, -10)$

   (b) Write down an equation connecting x and y which is satisfied by all points (x, y) which lie on this circle.

   (c) Use a graph plotter to draw the graph of this equation.

4 Use Pythagoras' theorem to prove that the equation of a circle

   (a) centre $(0, 0)$ and radius r is $\quad x^2 + y^2 = r^2$

   (b) centre (a, b) and radius r is $\quad (x - a)^2 + (y - b)^2 = r^2$

The equation of a circle of radius r about the point (a, b) is

$$(x - a)^2 + (y - b)^2 = r^2$$

When the circle has its centre at the origin, $a = b = 0$, so the equation becomes

$$x^2 + y^2 = r^2$$

This can be rewritten as

$$y = \pm\sqrt{(r^2 - x^2)}$$

Example 2

Find the equation of the circle radius 4, centre $(2, 3)$. Does the point $(5, 5)$ lie inside or outside the circle?

Solution

The equation of the circle is
$(x - 2)^2 + (y - 3)^2 = 16$.

The distance between the points $(2, 3)$ and $(5, 5)$ is $\sqrt{(3^2 + 2^2)} = \sqrt{13}$.

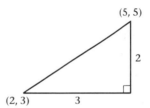

Since $\sqrt{13}$ is less than the radius of the circle, $(5, 5)$ must lie inside the circle.

Example 3

Find the radius and coordinates of the centre of the circle having equation

$$x^2 - 2x + y^2 + 4y + 1 = 0$$

Solution

You need to write the equation in the form $(x - a)^2 + (y - b)^2 = r^2$. The method of completing the square is used to do this.

$(x - 1)^2 - 1 + y^2 + 4y + 1 = 0$ Complete the square on the x terms...

$(x - 1)^2 + (y + 2)^2 - 4 = 0$ ...and on the y terms

$(x - 1)^2 + (y + 2)^2 = 4$

The circle has radius 2 and centre $(1, -2)$.

Again, we can easily extend these ideas into three dimensions and obtain the equation for a sphere.

.1B

1 A point in space can be represented by the use of three-dimensional coordinates (x, y, z). Write down the length of OP if P is:

(a) $(4, 5, 6)$

(b) $(3, 0, 4)$

(c) $(-3, 0, 4)$

(d) $(-2, -1, 3)$

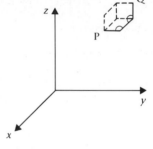

2 If P is the point $(3, 4, 5)$ and Q is $(6, 6, 9)$, write down the difference between their:

(a) x-coordinates,

(b) y-coordinates,

(c) z-coordinates.

Hence find the distance PQ.

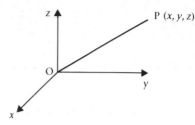

3 Find the distance PQ in each of the following cases.

(a) P (5, 1, 9)   Q (8, 2, 3)

(b) P (−1, 3, 0)   Q (−5, −8, 1)

(c) P (x, y, z) Q (a, b, c)

4 (a) P is a point on a sphere of radius r, centre O, with coordinates (x, y, z). Write down the length OP in terms of x, y and z and hence write down the equation of a sphere (i.e. find a relationship between x, y, z and r).

(b) Generalise the method of part (a) to write down the equation of a sphere of radius r whose centre is at the point with coordinates (a, b, c).

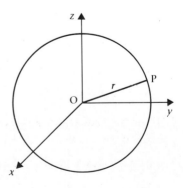

The equation of a sphere centre (a, b, c) and radius r is

$$(x - a)^2 + (y - b)^2 + (z - c)^2 = r^2$$

A sphere of radius r centred at the origin has equation

$$x^2 + y^2 + z^2 = r^2$$

5.1 Exercise 2

1 Find the equations of the following circles with centre the origin:

   (a) radius 15 units   (b) diameter 8 units

   (c) circumference 10 units   (d) passing through the point $(12, 16)$

2 Find the equations of the following circles:

   (a) radius 3 units, centre $(1, 1)$

   (b) diameter 16 units, centre $(-4, 6)$

3 A lighthouse has a grid reference $(20, 85)$ on a map, where each unit represents one nautical mile. The light is powerful enough to be seen from up to 18 nautical miles away. Write an equation involving E, the easterly map reference, and N, the northerly map reference, to show the boundary beyond which ships cannot see the lighthouse.

   How might this equation be misleading?

4 Find the equation of the sphere, centre $(2, 3, 1)$, radius 4 units.

5 Do the following points lie inside or outside the figures given by the equations?

   (a) $(3, 2)$; $(x - 1)^2 + (y - 4)^2 = 9$

   (b) $(4, -1)$; $(x + 1)^2 + (y - 2)^2 = 30$

   (c) $(-1, 3, 5)$; $(x - 1)^2 + (y + 1)^2 + (z - 3)^2 = 24$

   (d) $(-1, 3, 5)$; $(x - 1)^2 + (y + 1)^2 + (z - 3)^2 = 25$

6 Find the radius and the coordinates of the centre for the circles having equation:

   (a) $x^2 - 4x + y^2 - 2y + 1 = 0$

   (b) $x^2 - 2x + y^2 - 8 = 0$

   (c) $4x^2 - 4x + 4y^2 + 2y + 1 = 0$

7E Two aerial fireworks are timed to go off at the same time. Relative to an observer on the ground, their centres are at $(120, 150, 30)$ and $(160, 180, 40)$. The radius of the first firework extends to 20 units, that of the second to 30 units. Assuming that both fireworks make a spherical pattern in the sky, will the patterns intersect?

8E Find the centre, radius and equation of the circle passing through the points $(6, 9)$, $(13, -8)$ and $(-4, -15)$.

[Hint: You could let the equation be $(x - a)^2 + (y - b)^2 = r^2$, or plot the points and consider a geometric approach.]

9E Find the possible equations of circles, radius 10 units, which pass through the points $(10, 9)$ and $(8, -5)$. Which of these equations describes a circle which also passes through the point $(-6, -3)$?

5.1.3 Trigonometric identities

Points on a circle of unit radius, centre the origin, have coordinates given by $(\cos \theta, \sin \theta)$ where θ is the angle measured anticlockwise from the x-axis.

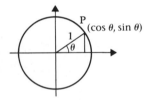

The diagram can be used to illustrate two useful identities.

By Pythagoras' theorem,

$$x^2 + y^2 = 1, \quad \text{where } (x, y) \text{ are the coordinates of P on the circle.}$$

Since $x = \cos \theta$ and $y = \sin \theta$, then $\cos^2 \theta + \sin^2 \theta = 1$

Also, as $\tan \theta = \dfrac{y}{x}$, then $\tan \theta = \dfrac{\sin \theta}{\cos \theta}$

Both of these results are true for any value of θ. They are trigonometric **identities**.

Example 4

In the triangle shown above, if $\sin \theta = \frac{1}{3}$, find: (a) $\cos \theta$ (b) $\tan \theta$

Solution

(a) Since $\cos^2 \theta = 1 - \sin^2 \theta$, $\cos \theta = \sqrt{\left(1 - \dfrac{1}{9}\right)} = \dfrac{2\sqrt{2}}{3}$

(b) Using $\tan \theta = \dfrac{\sin \theta}{\cos \theta}$, $\tan \theta = \dfrac{1}{3} \div \dfrac{2\sqrt{2}}{3} = \dfrac{1}{2\sqrt{2}}$

$$\tan \theta = \frac{\sin \theta}{\cos \theta}; \qquad \sin^2 \theta + \cos^2 \theta = 1$$

You can make use of the identities above to solve some trigonometric equations.

Example 5
Solve the equation $2 \sin^2 x = 3 \cos x$ for $0 \le x \le 2\pi$.

Solution
$2 \sin^2 x = 3 \cos x$

$\Rightarrow 2(1 - \cos^2 x) = 3 \cos x$ replace $\sin^2 x$ with $1 - \cos^2 x$

$\Rightarrow 2 - 2 \cos^2 x = 3 \cos x$

$\Rightarrow 2 \cos^2 x + 3 \cos x - 2 = 0$ rearrange and note that this is a quadratic equation of the form $2c^2 + 3c - 2 = 0$ with $c = \cos x$

$\Rightarrow (2 \cos x - 1)(\cos x + 2) = 0$ factorising to give $(2c - 1)(c + 2) = 0$

$\Rightarrow \cos x = \frac{1}{2}$ or $\cos x = -2$ $\cos x = -2$ gives no solutions

$\Rightarrow x = \dfrac{\pi}{3}$ or $\dfrac{5\pi}{3}$ in the range $0 \le x \le 2\pi$

The solutions can be illustrated by sketch graphs.

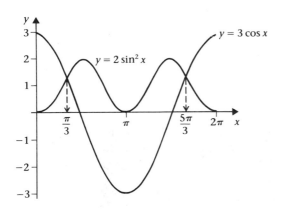

$x = \dfrac{\pi}{3}$ and $\dfrac{5\pi}{3}$ are sensible solutions to the equation $2 \sin^2 x = 3 \cos x$.

Example 6

Solve the equation $3 \sin \theta = 4 \cos \theta$ for $0° \leq \theta \leq 360°$.

Solution

As $\cos \theta = 0$ is not a possible solution, you can divide through by $\cos \theta$.

$$\frac{3 \sin \theta}{\cos \theta} = 4 \qquad \text{(dividing both sides by } \cos \theta)$$

$$\Rightarrow 3 \tan \theta = 4 \qquad \left(\text{using } \frac{\sin \theta}{\cos \theta} = \tan \theta \right)$$

$$\Rightarrow \quad \tan \theta = \tfrac{4}{3} = 1.33$$

$$\Rightarrow \qquad \theta = 53.1° \quad \text{or} \quad 233.1°$$

5.1 Exercise 3

1 (a) By replacing $\sin^2 x$ by $1 - \cos^2 x$, show that the equation
$1 + \cos x = 3 \sin^2 x$ is equivalent to $3 \cos^2 x + \cos x - 2 = 0$.

 (b) By writing $c = \cos x$, factorise the left-hand side of this equation.

 (c) Solve the equation to find all values of x between $0°$ and $360°$.

2 Solve the following equations for $0° \leq \theta \leq 360°$.

 (a) $3 \sin \theta = 2 \cos \theta$ (b) $0.5 \sin \theta = 0.8 \cos \theta$

 (c) $5 \sin 2\theta = 7 \cos 2\theta$

3 Solve the following equations for $0 \leq \theta \leq 2\pi$.

 (a) $2 \cos^2 \theta = \cos \theta + 1$ (b) $\sin \theta - \sqrt{3} \cos \theta = 0$

 (c) $8 \sin^2 \theta = 7 - 2 \cos \theta$

4 Solve the following equations for $0 \leq x \leq 2\pi$:

 (a) $\sin^2 x = 0.25$ (b) $\cos^2 x - \sin^2 x = 1$

 (c) $\cos^2 x - 4 \sin^2 x = 0$ (d) $3 \cos^2 x = 2 + 2 \sin x$

5E A cyclist, C, cycles around a circular track, centre O and
of radius 100 m. A photographer is at P, 30 m from the
edge of the track.

 (a) If angle $COP = \theta$ show that

$$PC^2 = (100 \sin \theta)^2 + (130 - 100 \cos \theta)^2$$

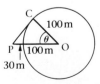

 (b) Hence show that $PC = \sqrt{(26\,900 - 26\,000 \cos \theta)}$.

 (c) If the photographer has a lens which can focus on objects at between
30 m and 70 m, for what range of values of θ is he able to take
photographs of the cyclist?

6E Find y as a function of x, given that

$$x = 3\cos\theta, \qquad y = 2\sin\theta$$

5.1.4 $r\sin(\theta + \alpha)$

In the last section you saw how to solve equations of the form $a\sin\theta = b\cos\theta$. This section looks at equations of the form $a\sin\theta + b\cos\theta = c$.

Two men are trying to carry a wardrobe through a doorway which is too low to allow them to carry it upright. The wardrobe is 2.5 metres high and 1.5 metres wide and the doorway is 2 metres high. If the men tip the wardrobe, as shown in the diagram, they will be able to carry it through the doorway.

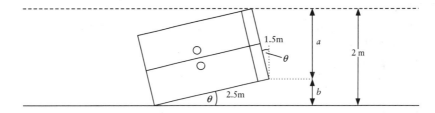

From the diagram, $\quad a = 1.5\cos\theta$

$$b = 2.5\sin\theta$$

If the wardrobe is to pass through the doorway, $a + b \le 2$

$$\Rightarrow 1.5\cos\theta + 2.5\sin\theta \le 2$$

You do not yet know how to solve the equation $2.5\sin\theta + 1.5\cos\theta = 2$ using analytic methods. In the questions which follow you will look at alternative ways of writing this equation in order to solve it.

5 .1c

The graphs of $1.5 \cos \theta$ and $2.5 \sin \theta$ are illustrated. The function $1.5 \cos \theta + 2.5 \sin \theta$ is the sum of the two separate functions.

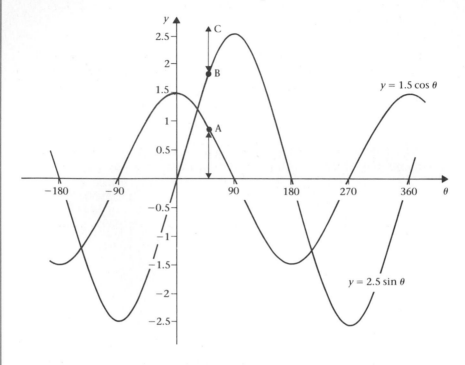

1 (a) In order to find the sum of two graphs, you may use the method of 'pointwise addition'. The value of the graph at A is added to the value at B in order to give the value at C. By adding pointwise the two graphs shown above, obtain a sketch of the graph of

$$y = 2.5 \sin \theta + 1.5 \cos \theta \quad \text{for } -180° \leq \theta \leq 360°$$

(b) Check your sketch using a graph plotter, and write down an approximate solution to the equation.

$$2.5 \sin \theta + 1.5 \cos \theta = 2 \quad \text{between } 0° \text{ and } 90°$$

(c) The wardrobe on page 349 can be rotated through any angle between 0° and 90°.

(i) What is the greatest height of the top corner above the ground, and for what value of θ is this height achieved?

(ii) Through what range of angles can the wardrobe be tipped so that it fits through the door?

2 (a) Use a graph plotter to examine the graph of $y = 3 \sin \theta + 4 \cos \theta$.

    (b) The resulting graph should be of the form $y = r \sin (\theta + \alpha)$. Find the values of r and α from your graph.

    (c) Repeat parts (a) and (b) for one or two more graphs of the form $y = a \sin \theta + b \cos \theta$.

3 The first two questions suggest that the graph of $y = a \sin \theta + b \cos \theta$ is identical to a graph of the form $y = r \sin (\theta + \alpha)$. The diagram shows how the two expressions are connected.

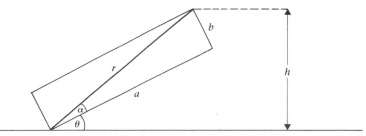

    (a) Explain why

        (i) $h = a \sin \theta + b \cos \theta$

       (ii) $h = r \sin (\theta + \alpha)$

    (b) Express r and α in terms of a and b.

4 (a) Use the result in question 3 to express $4 \sin \theta + 7 \cos \theta$ in the form $r \sin (\theta + \alpha)$.

    (b) Verify your answer using a graph plotter.

The expression $a \sin \theta + b \cos \theta$ is equivalent to the expression $r \sin (\theta + \alpha)$ where r and α can be found from the triangle

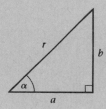

$$r = \sqrt{(a^2 + b^2)} \quad \text{and} \quad \alpha = \tan^{-1} \frac{b}{a}$$

$r \sin (\theta + \alpha)$ is a sine wave, amplitude r, phase-shifted by α in the negative x-direction.

Example 7

Solve the equation

$$6 \sin \theta + 9 \cos \theta = 7$$

for values of θ in the range $0° \leq \theta \leq 360°$.

Solution

$6 \sin \theta + 9 \cos \theta$ is equivalent to the expression $r \sin (\theta + \alpha)$, where r and α are found from the triangle shown below.

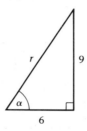

$$r = \sqrt{(6^2 + 9^2)} = 10.82 \quad \text{and} \quad \alpha = \tan^{-1} \tfrac{9}{6} = 56.31°$$

So,

$$6 \sin \theta + 9 \cos \theta = 10.82 \sin (\theta + 56.31)$$

$$\Rightarrow 10.82 \sin (\theta + 56.31) = 7$$

$$\Rightarrow \qquad \sin (\theta + 56.31) = 0.6472$$

Solving the equation $\sin x = 0.6472$, where $x = \theta + 56.31$, gives $x = 40.33°$.

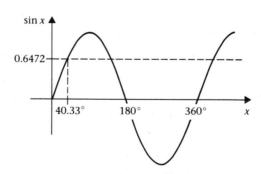

From the sketch graph, you can see that the solutions are

$$x = 40.33°, 139.67°, 400.33°, 499.67°, \text{and so on}$$

Since $x = \theta + 56.31$,

$$\theta = -16.0°, 83.4°, 344.0°, 443.4°, \text{and so on}$$

The solutions in the range $0° \leq \theta \leq 360°$ are

$$\theta = 83.4°, 344.0° \quad \text{correct to 1 decimal place}$$

5.1 Exercise 4

1 (a) Express $3 \sin \theta + 2 \cos \theta$ in the form $r \sin (\theta + \alpha)$.

(b) Solve the equation $3 \sin \theta + 2 \cos \theta = 3$ for $0° \leq \theta \leq 90°$.

2 (a) Explain why the maximum value of $5 \sin \theta + 12 \cos \theta$ is 13.

(b) Solve the equation $5 \sin \theta + 12 \cos \theta = 9$ for $0° \leq \theta \leq 360°$.

3 Any point on the ellipse has coordinates of the form $(4 \cos \theta, 3 \sin \theta)$.

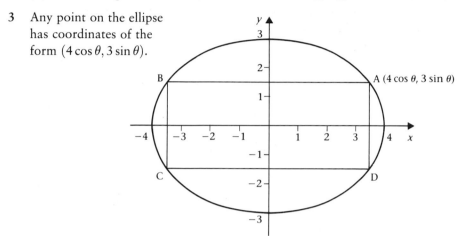

(a) In terms of θ what are the lengths of:

(i) AD   (ii) AB   (iii) the perimeter of the rectangle ABCD?

(b) If the rectangle ABCD has a perimeter of 14 units, explain why $3 \sin \theta + 4 \cos \theta = 3.5$.

(c) Solve the equation $3 \sin \theta + 4 \cos \theta = 3.5$, and hence find the lengths of sides of the rectangle whose perimeter is 14.

(d) What is the largest possible perimeter, and for what value of θ does it occur?

4E The octopus ride is a common feature of fun-fairs. There are various designs: the one illustrated moves in a combination of horizontal circles.

The diagram below shows the position after an arm has moved through an angle of $\theta°$.

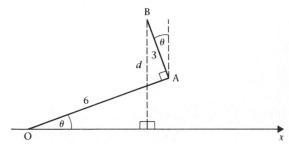

To simplify matters, assume that the arm rotates about O, but that the chairs (at B, etc.) do not rotate about A.

(a) Explain why the chair at B will move in a circle, and find the centre and radius of this circle.

(b) Calculate, in terms of θ, the distance, d, of B from the x-axis.

(c) Write the expression for d in the form $r\sin(\theta + a)$.

(d) For what values of θ is the chair at B farthest from the x-axis?

▶ 5.1 **Tasksheet E1 – Extending the method (page 559)**

5.1.5 Addition formulas

In section 5.1.4 you considered the use of the expression $r\sin(\theta + \alpha)$. Here we are concerned with general formulas for the sine and cosine of the sums of angles. Consider a rotated rectangle with a diagonal of length 1 unit.

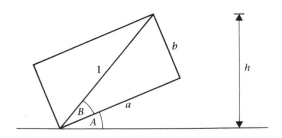

We can obtain a formula for $\sin (A + B)$ as follows.

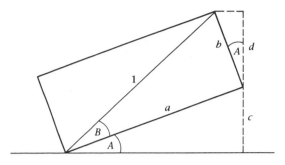

$$c + d = 1 \sin (A + B)$$

also, $\qquad c + d = a \sin A + b \cos A$

$$\Rightarrow \sin (A + B) = a \sin A + b \cos A$$

Then $\qquad a = \cos B, \quad b = \sin B$

$$\Rightarrow \sin (A + B) = \sin A \cos B + \cos A \sin B$$

Similarly, for the cosine of angle $(A + B)$:

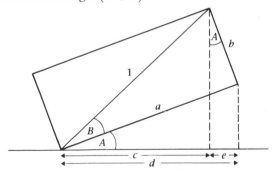

From the diagram, $c = d - e$

$$d = a \cos A, \quad e = b \sin A$$

$$c = 1 \cos (A + B)$$

$$\Rightarrow \cos (A + B) = a \cos A - b \sin A$$

$$\Rightarrow \cos (A + B) = \cos A \cos B - \sin A \sin B$$

If we let $B = A$ in each of the expressions we obtain important results known as the **double angle formulas.**

$$\sin (A + B) = \sin A \cos B + \cos A \sin B$$

Let $B = A$; then

$$\sin 2A = \sin A \cos A + \cos A \sin A = 2 \sin A \cos A$$

Similarly,

$$\cos(A + B) = \cos A \cos B - \sin A \sin B$$

Let $B = A$:

$$\cos 2A = \cos^2 A - \sin^2 A$$

or, using $\sin^2 A + \cos^2 A = 1$, so that $\sin^2 A = 1 - \cos^2 A$, we obtain

$$\cos 2A = 2\cos^2 A - 1$$

Other formulas for $\sin(A - B)$ and $\cos(A - B)$ can be obtained from the formulas for $\sin(A + B)$ and $\cos(A + B)$ simply by replacing B by $-B$. You should familiarise yourself with the following identities, which are known as the **addition formulas,** together with the **double angle formulas** for $\sin 2A$ and $\cos 2A$ which are derived from them.

Addition formulas

$$\sin(A + B) = \sin A \cos B + \cos A \sin B$$
$$\sin(A - B) = \sin A \cos B - \cos A \sin B$$
$$\cos(A + B) = \cos A \cos B - \sin A \sin B$$
$$\cos(A - B) = \cos A \cos B + \sin A \sin B$$

Double angle formulas

$$\sin 2A = 2 \sin A \cos A$$
$$\cos 2A = \cos^2 A - \sin^2 A$$
$$= 2\cos^2 A - 1$$
$$= 1 - 2\sin^2 A$$

Example 8

Show that $\sin\left(x + \dfrac{\pi}{6}\right) = \dfrac{1}{2}(\sqrt{3}\sin x + \cos x)$.

Solution

$$\sin\left(x + \frac{\pi}{6}\right) = \sin x \cos \frac{\pi}{6} + \cos x \sin \frac{\pi}{6}$$

$$= \frac{\sqrt{3}}{2}\sin x + \frac{1}{2}\cos x \quad \left(\cos \frac{\pi}{6} = \frac{\sqrt{3}}{2} \quad \text{and} \quad \sin \frac{\pi}{6} = \frac{1}{2}\right)$$

$$= \frac{1}{2}(\sqrt{3}\sin x + \cos x)$$

5.1 Exercise 5

1   (a) Use the formula for $\sin(A+B)$ to show that
$$\sin(x+60°) = \frac{1}{2}\sin x + \frac{\sqrt{3}}{2}\cos x$$

   (b) Check this result using a graph plotter.

2   (a) Use an addition formula to simplify $\sin(x+\pi)$.

   (b) Explain your result graphically. (Note that x is in radians here.)

3   (a) Show that $\cos(A+B) + \cos(A-B) = 2\cos A\cos B$.

   (b) Simplify $\cos(A-B) - \cos(A+B)$.

4   (a) By writing $\sin 75°$ as $\sin(45° + 30°)$, show that $\sin 75° = \dfrac{\sqrt{3}+1}{2\sqrt{2}}$.

   (b) Use the method of part (a) to express $\sin 15°$ in surd form (i.e. using square roots).

5   If A and B are acute angles with $\sin A = \frac{4}{5}$ and $\cos B = \frac{12}{13}$, find $\sin(A+B)$ without using a calculator. [The Pythagorean triangles with sides 3, 4, 5 and 5, 12, 13 may be useful in finding $\cos A$ and $\sin B$.]

6   Solve the following equations for x, where $0° \leq x \leq 360°$.

   (a) $\cos 2x = 7\cos x + 3$

   (b) $4\cos^3 x + 2\cos x = 5\sin 2x$

7E Show that $\tan\left(x + \dfrac{\pi}{4}\right) = \dfrac{1 + \tan x}{1 - \tan x}$.

8E (a) By writing $\sin 3x = \sin(2x + x)$ show that $\sin 3x = 3\sin x - 4\sin^3 x$.

   (b) Express $\cos 3x$ in terms of $\cos x$. Verify your answer by plotting appropriate graphs.

9E Show that $\tan 2x = \dfrac{2\tan x}{1 - \tan^2 x}$.

10E Solve $\sin 3x = \sin^2 x$ for x, where $0° \leq x \leq 360°$.

11E (a) Show by a numerical method that
$$\lim_{h \to 0}\left(\frac{\sin h}{h}\right) = 1 \text{ and } \lim_{h \to 0}\left(\frac{\cos h - 1}{h}\right) = 0.$$

   (b) By expanding and factorising the expression $\sin(x+h) - \sin x$, show from first principals that $\dfrac{d}{dx}(\sin x) = \cos x$.

   (c) Show that $\dfrac{d}{dx}(\cos x) = -\sin x$.

5.1.6 Solution of non-right-angled triangles: the cosine rule

To 'solve a triangle' means to find all the angles and lengths of sides in the triangle. It is easy to do this for right-angled triangles. In the rest of this section, methods for other triangles will be considered.

 .1D

A triangle with sides a, b, c and angles A, B, C can be divided into two right-angled triangles:

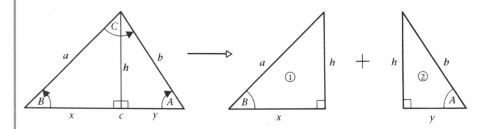

From triangle ①, Pythagoras' theorem gives

$$a^2 = h^2 + x^2$$

1 From triangle ②, express both h and y in terms of b and angle A.

2 Explain why $x = c - y$. Using this and the previous result, express x in terms of b, c and angle A.

3 Replace h and x in $a^2 = h^2 + x^2$ by the expressions found for h and x in terms of b, c and A.

4 Simplify the expression for a^2 found in question 3 by multiplying out the brackets and using the fact that $\cos^2 A + \sin^2 A = 1$.

The result is known as the **cosine rule** for triangles.

5 How does the cosine rule relate to Pythagoras' theorem for right-angled triangles?

6 By treating side b as the base of the triangle and using properties of symmetry, find a similar expression for:

(a) c^2 (b) b^2

7 So far, you have only considered acute-angled triangles. Modify the diagram and extend the proof to obtuse-angled triangles.

The cosine rule for a triangle with sides a, b, c and angles A, B, C:

$$a^2 = b^2 + c^2 - 2bc \cos A$$

$$b^2 = a^2 + c^2 - 2ac \cos B$$

$$c^2 = a^2 + b^2 - 2ab \cos C$$

The cosine rule applies to both acute- and obtuse-angled triangles.

Example 9

The hands of a clock are 10 cm and 7 cm long. Calculate the distance between their tips at 2 o'clock.

Solution

The angle between the hands is $60°$. Using the cosine rule with the triangle labelled as shown:

$$a^2 = 10^2 + 7^2 - 2 \times 10 \times 7 \times \cos 60°$$

$$= 100 + 49 - 70$$

$$= 79$$

$$a = \sqrt{79} = 8.9 \text{ cm} \quad \text{(to 1 decimal place)}$$

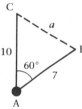

5.1 Exercise 6

1   Triangle ABC is such that AB = 4 cm, AC = 8 cm and angle $A = 43°$. Calculate the length of BC.

2   (a)   For triangle ABC, with sides BC = a, AC = b, AB = c, express $\cos A$ in terms of a, b, c.

(b)   A triangle has sides 4 cm, 5 cm, 7 cm. Calculate its angles.

3   The hands of a clock have lengths 10 cm and 7 cm. Calculate the distance between the tips of the hands at:

(a) 4:30   (b) 8:00   (c) 6:00

4   ABC is a triangle in which BC = 8, CA = 6, AB = 7, and M is the midpoint of BC. Suppose that angle AMC = θ. Write down by the cosine rule expressions for AB^2 and AC^2 in terms of $\cos \theta$ and add the results. Hence calculate the length of AM.

5   A is 2.1 km due north of B; C is 3.7 km from B on a bearing $136°$. Find the distance from C to A.

5.1.7 Solution of non-right-angled triangles: the sine rule

 .1E

The area of a triangle can be found using area $= \frac{1}{2} \times$ base $\times$ height.

Complete the following:

1 In the triangle with sides a, b, c and angles A, B, C as shown, the height h_1
can be expressed as

$$h_1 = \underline{\quad} \sin A$$

Thus the area of the triangle is

$$\frac{1}{2}bh_1 = \underline{\quad\quad\quad}$$

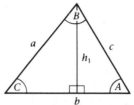

Since triangles are normally described using lengths of sides and angles, the
formula area $= \frac{1}{2}$ base $\times$ height cannot be applied directly. The new formula
gives the area in terms of the lengths of two sides and the angles between
them, i.e.

$$\text{Area} = \frac{1}{2}bc \sin A$$

$$= \frac{1}{2} \times \text{product of two sides} \times \text{sine of included angle}$$

2 Treating a as the base, the height h_2 of the triangle can be expressed as

$$h_2 = b \sin \underline{\quad}$$

Thus the area of the triangle is $\frac{1}{2}ah_2 = \underline{\quad\quad\quad}$

3 Use these two expressions for the area of the triangle to form an equation.
Simplify it and write it in the form $\dfrac{a}{\sin A} = \underline{\quad\quad\quad}$

4 Treating side c as the base, find an expression for the height of the triangle
in terms of a and B, and hence find an expression for the area of the
triangle.

5 Use the expression obtained in question 4 with each of the previous
expressions to obtain two more equations simplified to the form

$$\frac{b}{\sin B} = \underline{\quad\quad\quad} \qquad \frac{c}{\sin C} = \underline{\quad\quad\quad}$$

6 Find the area of triangle ABC such that $AC = 7\,\text{cm}$, $BC = 4\,\text{cm}$ and angle
$C = 30°$.

The sine rule for a triangle with sides a, b, c and angles A, B, C:

$$\frac{a}{\sin A} = \frac{b}{\sin B} = \frac{c}{\sin C}$$

The area of the triangle is $\frac{1}{2} ab \sin C$

Example 10

In a triangle with sides $a = 7$, $b = 12$ and angle $A = 23°$, angle A is opposite side a and angle B is opposite side b. Find angle B.

Solution

The first step in solving this triangle is to calculate the value of

$$\frac{a}{\sin A} = \frac{7}{\sin 23} = 17.915$$

Using the sine rule, $\dfrac{b}{\sin B} = 17.915$

and since $b = 12$, $\quad \dfrac{12}{\sin B} = 17.915$

Rearranging this equation gives

$$\sin B = \frac{12}{17.915} = 0.670 \Rightarrow B = 42.1° \quad \text{(to 1 decimal place)}$$

However, a sketch of the triangle shows **two** possible positions for B, corresponding to the two solutions.

This is sometimes called the 'ambiguous case' of the sine rule.

There are many angles which have sine equal to 0.670. Two of these angles are in the range $0° < \theta < 180°$.

From the graph, θ could be either $42.1°$ or $180° - 42.1° = 137.9°$.

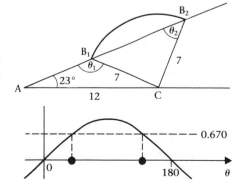

When solving triangles:

- always draw a diagram as a rough check on possible solutions;

- remember, there are simpler methods of solving *right-angled* triangles – there is no need to use the sine or cosine rule!

5.1 **Exercise 7**

Remember that to 'solve a triangle' means to find *all* the unknown sides and angles.

1 Use the sine rule to solve these triangles:

(a)   (b)

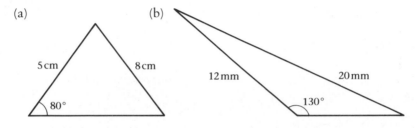

2 Use the cosine rule and then the sine rule to solve these triangles:

(a)   (b)

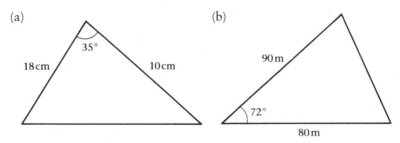

3 Find the areas of the two triangles in question 2.

4 Solve these triangles:

(a)   (b)

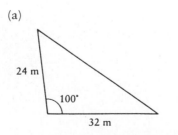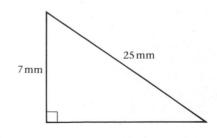

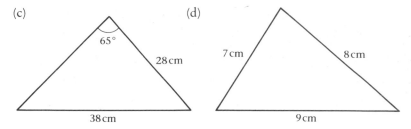

(c) 65° 28 cm 38 cm

(d) 7 cm 8 cm 9 cm

5   A plane flies north-east with an airspeed of $400 \, \text{km h}^{-1}$. If the wind is
blowing at a steady speed of $50 \, \text{km h}^{-1}$ from the west, calculate the distance
covered over the ground in one hour, and the direction in which the plane
has travelled.

After working through section 5.1, you should:

1 be able to apply Pythagoras' theorem in two and three dimensions;

2 be able to find the equation of a circle or sphere, given its centre and
radius;

3 know, and be able to use for simplification, the trigonometric identities
$$\tan \theta = \frac{\sin \theta}{\cos \theta}$$
$$\sin^2 \theta + \cos^2 \theta = 1$$

4 be able to find a single trigonometric function which is equivalent to
$a \sin \theta + b \cos \theta$;

5 be able to solve equations of the form $a \sin \theta + b \cos \theta = c$;

6 know and be able to use the addition formulas for $\sin (A \pm B)$ and
$\cos (A \pm B)$;

7 know and be able to use the double angle formulas for $\sin 2A$ and
$\cos 2A$;

8 be able to solve triangles using Pythagoras' theorem, the cosine rule and
the sine rule as appropriate;

9 know that the area of a triangle is $\frac{1}{2} ab \sin C$.

5 Mathematical methods

.2 Vector geometry

5.2.1 Vector and position vectors

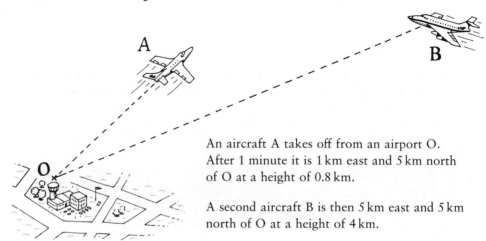

An aircraft A takes off from an airport O. After 1 minute it is 1 km east and 5 km north of O at a height of 0.8 km.

A second aircraft B is then 5 km east and 5 km north of O at a height of 4 km.

A situation of this kind, concerning the relative position of two aircraft and how this may change with time, is handled most conveniently using the notation and mathematics of vectors. Many problems in mathematics, and in the application of mathematics, are best handled using vectors – you may have already done vector work in mechanics, for example. In this section we extend this work to consider the vector equations of lines and planes.

Taking the vector $\begin{bmatrix} a \\ b \\ c \end{bmatrix}$ to represent a position a km east and b km north of O, at a height of c km, aircraft A has position vector $\overrightarrow{OA} = \begin{bmatrix} 1 \\ 5 \\ 0.8 \end{bmatrix}$ and B has position vector $\overrightarrow{OB} = \begin{bmatrix} 5 \\ 5 \\ 4 \end{bmatrix}$.

$\overrightarrow{OA}$ and $\overrightarrow{OB}$ are the position vectors from the point O of the points A and B respectively.

They are given in **column vector** form above. The position vector $\overrightarrow{OA}$ of a point is often denoted by $\underset{\sim}{a}$ or **a**.

A **vector diagram** shows the relationship between the vectors.

$$\overrightarrow{OA} + \overrightarrow{AB} = \overrightarrow{OB}$$

or $\quad \overrightarrow{AB} = \overrightarrow{OB} - \overrightarrow{OA}$

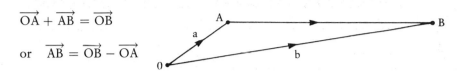

The vector $\overrightarrow{AB}$ gives the displacement from A to B, that is the distance and the direction of a movement *from A to B*.

 .2A

1 Using squared paper, draw the position vectors from the origin $(0, 0)$ for each of the two points A and B and find the vector $\overrightarrow{AB}$ in each case.

(a) $\mathbf{a} = \begin{bmatrix} 3 \\ 2 \end{bmatrix}; \quad \mathbf{b} = \begin{bmatrix} -1 \\ 2 \end{bmatrix}$ \qquad (b) $\mathbf{a} = \begin{bmatrix} 5 \\ -2 \end{bmatrix}; \quad \mathbf{b} = \begin{bmatrix} 5 \\ 4 \end{bmatrix}$

2 If $\mathbf{p} = \overrightarrow{OP}$ and $\mathbf{q} = \overrightarrow{OQ}$, write down $\overrightarrow{PQ}$ in terms of $\mathbf{p}$ and $\mathbf{q}$.

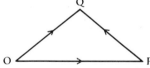

3 It is not always necessary to use a square grid for vectors.
Vectors **a** and **b** are as shown on this isometric grid.

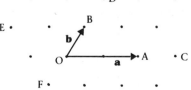

(a) Write down the position vectors of C, D, E and F in terms of **a** and **b**.

(b) Find the vectors $\overrightarrow{AB}, \overrightarrow{CD}, \overrightarrow{DE}, \overrightarrow{EF}$ and $\overrightarrow{FC}$ in terms of **a** and **b**.

(c) Check that $\overrightarrow{CD} + \overrightarrow{DE} + \overrightarrow{EF} + \overrightarrow{FC} = \mathbf{0}$. Why is this so?

(d) Compare $\overrightarrow{AD}$ and $\overrightarrow{EF}$. Explain what you notice.

4 On squared paper plot the points (x, y) whose position vectors are given by the following vector equations. Take $0, \pm 1, \pm 2$ and ± 3 as values of the parameter t.

(a) $\begin{bmatrix} x \\ y \end{bmatrix} = t \begin{bmatrix} 2 \\ 3 \end{bmatrix}$

(b) $\begin{bmatrix} x \\ y \end{bmatrix} = \begin{bmatrix} 3 \\ -1 \end{bmatrix} + t \begin{bmatrix} 2 \\ 3 \end{bmatrix}$

(c) $\begin{bmatrix} x \\ y \end{bmatrix} = \begin{bmatrix} 2 \\ 4 \end{bmatrix} + t \begin{bmatrix} 2 \\ 3 \end{bmatrix}$

What do you notice about each set of points?

What is the significance of the vector $\begin{bmatrix} 2 \\ 3 \end{bmatrix}$?

5 On squared paper draw the triangle OAB where A and B have position vectors $\begin{bmatrix} 12 \\ 0 \end{bmatrix}$ and $\begin{bmatrix} 0 \\ 6 \end{bmatrix}$.

Taking 0, 1, 2 and 3 as the values of each of the parameters s, t and u in turn, draw the lines whose vector equations are:

(a) $\begin{bmatrix} x \\ y \end{bmatrix} = \begin{bmatrix} 0 \\ 6 \end{bmatrix} + s \begin{bmatrix} 2 \\ -2 \end{bmatrix}$

(b) $\begin{bmatrix} x \\ y \end{bmatrix} = \begin{bmatrix} 6 \\ 3 \end{bmatrix} + t \begin{bmatrix} -2 \\ -1 \end{bmatrix}$

(c) $\begin{bmatrix} x \\ y \end{bmatrix} = \begin{bmatrix} 12 \\ 0 \end{bmatrix} + u \begin{bmatrix} -4 \\ 1 \end{bmatrix}$

What do you notice about the three lines? Where is their point of intersection?

6 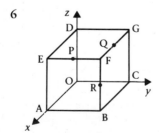 OABCDEFG is a cube with edges of length 6 and axes as shown. P, Q, R are the midpoints of the edges EF, FG and FB.

(a) Find the position vectors of the points P, Q and R.

(b) Demonstrate that $\overrightarrow{PQ} + \overrightarrow{QR} + \overrightarrow{RP} = 0$.

7E The vector equation $\begin{bmatrix} x \\ y \end{bmatrix} = \begin{bmatrix} 3 \\ -1 \end{bmatrix} + t \begin{bmatrix} 2 \\ 3 \end{bmatrix}$ in question 4 can be written in terms of its components as:

$$x = 3 + 2t \qquad ①$$

$$y = -1 + 3t \qquad ②$$

(a) Express t in terms of x from equation ①.

(b) Substitute this for t in equation ② to find the Cartesian equation of the line in the form $y = mx + c$.

(c) What is the gradient of the line? How is this related to the vector $\begin{bmatrix} 2 \\ 3 \end{bmatrix}$?

8E Find Cartesian equations for the lines:

(a) $\begin{bmatrix} x \\ y \end{bmatrix} = \begin{bmatrix} 3 \\ -2 \end{bmatrix} + s \begin{bmatrix} -2 \\ 1 \end{bmatrix}$ (b) $\begin{bmatrix} x \\ y \end{bmatrix} = \begin{bmatrix} 1 \\ -1 \end{bmatrix} + t \begin{bmatrix} 2 \\ -1 \end{bmatrix}$

A point may be described in terms of its **coordinates** (x, y) or in terms of its **position vector** $\begin{bmatrix} x \\ y \end{bmatrix}$, which describes a translation from the origin to the point.

For two points P and Q, with position vectors **p** and **q**, the vector describing a translation from P to Q is given by $\overrightarrow{PQ} = \mathbf{q} - \mathbf{p}$.

The **vector equation** of a line through the point with position vector $\begin{bmatrix} a_1 \\ a_2 \end{bmatrix}$ and in the direction $\begin{bmatrix} b_1 \\ b_2 \end{bmatrix}$ is:

$$\begin{bmatrix} x \\ y \end{bmatrix} = \begin{bmatrix} a_1 \\ a_2 \end{bmatrix} + t \begin{bmatrix} b_1 \\ b_2 \end{bmatrix}, \text{ where } t \text{ is a parameter}$$

Position vector of *any* point on the line

Position of a *particular* point on the line

This vector is the *direction* of the line

Example 1

Find a vector equation of the line joining the points A $(2, 3)$ and B $(5, 4)$.

Solution

The position vector of a point on the line is $\begin{bmatrix} 2 \\ 3 \end{bmatrix}$ and the direction of the line is given by the vector $\overrightarrow{AB} = \begin{bmatrix} 3 \\ 1 \end{bmatrix}$. Thus the equation of the line AB is

$$\begin{bmatrix} x \\ y \end{bmatrix} = \begin{bmatrix} 2 \\ 3 \end{bmatrix} + t \begin{bmatrix} 3 \\ 1 \end{bmatrix}$$

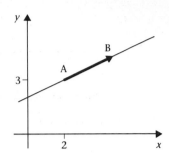

Note that this answer is not unique.

5.2 Exercise 1

1 Find vector equations for:

(a) the line joining the points $(4, 1)$ and $(7, 7)$,

(b) the line joining the points $(2, 1)$ and $(-1, 5)$,

(c) the line through the point $(5, 1)$ parallel to the vector $\begin{bmatrix} -2 \\ 4 \end{bmatrix}$,

(d) the line $y = x$,

(e) the y-axis.

2 The position vectors of four points P, Q, R and S are

$$\begin{bmatrix} 3 \\ 1 \end{bmatrix}, \begin{bmatrix} 5 \\ -2 \end{bmatrix}, \begin{bmatrix} 2 \\ -4 \end{bmatrix} \text{ and } \begin{bmatrix} 0 \\ -1 \end{bmatrix}.$$

(a) Find the vectors $\overrightarrow{PQ}$ and $\overrightarrow{SR}$.
What does this tell you about the quadrilateral PQRS?

(b) What can you say about the vectors $\overrightarrow{PS}$ and $\overrightarrow{QR}$?

3 OABCDE is a triangular prism with

$$\overrightarrow{OA} = \begin{bmatrix} 6 \\ 0 \\ 0 \end{bmatrix}, \quad \overrightarrow{OB} = \begin{bmatrix} 0 \\ 8 \\ 0 \end{bmatrix}, \quad \overrightarrow{OC} = \begin{bmatrix} 0 \\ 0 \\ 10 \end{bmatrix}$$

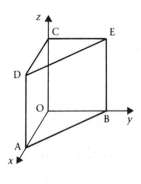

(a) (i) Find the position vectors of D and E.

(ii) Find the vectors $\overrightarrow{AB}, \overrightarrow{AD}, \overrightarrow{AC}, \overrightarrow{AE}$ and $\overrightarrow{DE}$.

(b) M is the midpoint of AB and N is the midpoint of DE.

(i) Find the position vectors of M and N.

(ii) Find the vectors $\overrightarrow{AN}$ and $\overrightarrow{ME}$.

(iii) Explain what you notice about the results.

4

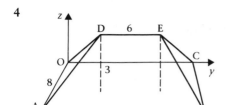

OABCDE is the roof of a house. OABC is a rectangle with OA of length 8 m and OC of length 10 m. The ridge DE of length 6 m is positioned symmetrically, 3 m above the rectangle.

(a) With axes as shown, find the position vectors of A, B, C, D and E.

(b) Find the vectors $\overrightarrow{AD}$, $\overrightarrow{OD}$, $\overrightarrow{BE}$ and $\overrightarrow{CE}$, representing the slant edges of the roof.

(c) What is the length of a slant edge?

5.2.2 Equations of lines

The ideas of section 5.2.1 can easily be extended to three dimensions.

Consider the motion of the two aircraft described.

The position of aircraft A, t minutes after take-off, is given by the equation

$$\begin{bmatrix} x \\ y \\ z \end{bmatrix} = t \begin{bmatrix} 1 \\ 5 \\ 0.8 \end{bmatrix}$$

The position of aircraft B at the same time, t minutes, is given by the vector equation

$$\begin{bmatrix} x \\ y \\ z \end{bmatrix} = \begin{bmatrix} 5 \\ 0 \\ 4 \end{bmatrix} + t \begin{bmatrix} 0 \\ 5 \\ 0 \end{bmatrix}$$

Aircraft B is flying in the direction of the vector $\begin{bmatrix} 0 \\ 5 \\ 0 \end{bmatrix}$.

The position vector of each aircraft after 2 minutes is

$$\overrightarrow{OA} = \begin{bmatrix} 2 \\ 10 \\ 1.6 \end{bmatrix} \quad \text{and} \quad \overrightarrow{OB} = \begin{bmatrix} 5 \\ 10 \\ 4 \end{bmatrix}$$

The displacement vector $\overrightarrow{AB}$ at this moment is given by $\overrightarrow{OB} - \overrightarrow{OA}$

$$\text{i.e.} \quad \overrightarrow{AB} = \begin{bmatrix} 3 \\ 0 \\ 2.4 \end{bmatrix}$$

Notice that when $t = 4$ the aircraft have the same position vectors – a collision occurs!

Each aircraft is moving in a straight line. The following examples examine in more detail the vector equation of a line.

 .2B

Questions 1 to 6 refer to the cuboid CFGEOADB with OA = 4, OB = 6 and OC = 3.

$$\overrightarrow{OA} = \begin{bmatrix} 4 \\ 0 \\ 0 \end{bmatrix},$$

$$\overrightarrow{OB} = \begin{bmatrix} 0 \\ 6 \\ 0 \end{bmatrix},$$

$$\overrightarrow{OC} = \begin{bmatrix} 0 \\ 0 \\ 3 \end{bmatrix}$$

1 Find the position vectors of the points D, E, F and G.

2 Points are given by the vector equation

$$\begin{bmatrix} x \\ y \\ z \end{bmatrix} = \lambda \begin{bmatrix} 4 \\ 6 \\ 0 \end{bmatrix}, \quad \text{where } \lambda \text{ is a parameter.}$$

   (a) Which points correspond to $\lambda = 0$ and $\lambda = 1$?

   (b) On a large copy of the diagram, mark points corresponding to $\lambda = \frac{1}{4}, \frac{1}{2}$ and $\frac{3}{4}$. What do you notice about them?

   (c) What can you say about the positions of the points where $\lambda = 2$ and $\lambda = -1$?

3 $\begin{bmatrix} x \\ y \\ z \end{bmatrix} = \lambda \begin{bmatrix} 4 \\ 6 \\ 0 \end{bmatrix}$ is the **vector equation** of the line OD.

Identify the lines whose vector equations are:

(a) $\begin{bmatrix} x \\ y \\ z \end{bmatrix} = \lambda \begin{bmatrix} 0 \\ 0 \\ 3 \end{bmatrix}$

(b) $\begin{bmatrix} x \\ y \\ z \end{bmatrix} = \lambda \begin{bmatrix} 0 \\ 6 \\ 3 \end{bmatrix}$

Give vector equations for the lines:

(c) OB   (d) OF   (e) OG

4 Which points correspond to $\lambda = 0$ and $\lambda = 1$ on the line with vector equation

$$\begin{bmatrix} x \\ y \\ z \end{bmatrix} = \begin{bmatrix} 0 \\ 0 \\ 3 \end{bmatrix} + \lambda \begin{bmatrix} 4 \\ 6 \\ 0 \end{bmatrix} ?$$

On your copy of the diagram, mark points corresponding to $\lambda = \frac{1}{4}, \frac{1}{2}$ and $\frac{3}{4}$. Where would be the points corresponding to $\lambda = 2$ and $\lambda = -1$?

5 Identify the lines whose vector equations are:

(a) $\begin{bmatrix} x \\ y \\ z \end{bmatrix} = \begin{bmatrix} 0 \\ 6 \\ 0 \end{bmatrix} + \lambda \begin{bmatrix} 0 \\ 0 \\ 3 \end{bmatrix}$

(b) $\begin{bmatrix} x \\ y \\ z \end{bmatrix} = \begin{bmatrix} 4 \\ 0 \\ 3 \end{bmatrix} + \lambda \begin{bmatrix} -4 \\ 6 \\ 0 \end{bmatrix}$

What is the significance of the vectors $\begin{bmatrix} 0 \\ 0 \\ 3 \end{bmatrix}$ in (a) and $\begin{bmatrix} -4 \\ 6 \\ 0 \end{bmatrix}$ in (b)?

6 Give vector equations for the lines:

(a) AD   (b) AG   (c) AE

7 (a) On squared paper, draw the straight lines whose vector equations are given below by plotting points, taking $0, \pm1, \pm2$ as the values of the parameters λ and μ.

$$\begin{bmatrix} x \\ y \end{bmatrix} = \begin{bmatrix} 1 \\ 0 \end{bmatrix} + \lambda \begin{bmatrix} 1 \\ 1 \end{bmatrix}; \qquad \begin{bmatrix} x \\ y \end{bmatrix} = \begin{bmatrix} 1 \\ 3 \end{bmatrix} + \mu \begin{bmatrix} 2 \\ -1 \end{bmatrix}$$

(b) Where do the lines intersect?

(c) What are the values of λ and μ at this point?

(d) By equating components, write down the two simultaneous equations given by

$$\begin{bmatrix} 1 \\ 0 \end{bmatrix} + \lambda \begin{bmatrix} 1 \\ 1 \end{bmatrix} = \begin{bmatrix} 1 \\ 3 \end{bmatrix} + \mu \begin{bmatrix} 2 \\ -1 \end{bmatrix}$$

(e) Solve the simultaneous equations and confirm your values of λ and μ.

8 Use simultaneous equations to find the intersection of

$$\begin{bmatrix} x \\ y \end{bmatrix} = \begin{bmatrix} 2 \\ 2 \end{bmatrix} + \lambda \begin{bmatrix} 1 \\ 2 \end{bmatrix} \quad \text{and} \quad \begin{bmatrix} x \\ y \end{bmatrix} = \begin{bmatrix} 1 \\ 3 \end{bmatrix} + \mu \begin{bmatrix} 2 \\ -1 \end{bmatrix}$$

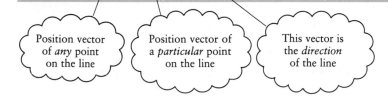

The vector equation of a line through a point with position vector

$$\mathbf{a} = \begin{bmatrix} a_1 \\ a_2 \\ a_3 \end{bmatrix} \text{ and in the direction } \mathbf{b} = \begin{bmatrix} b_1 \\ b_2 \\ b_3 \end{bmatrix} \text{ is:}$$

$$\begin{bmatrix} x \\ y \\ z \end{bmatrix} = \begin{bmatrix} a_1 \\ a_2 \\ a_3 \end{bmatrix} + \lambda \begin{bmatrix} b_1 \\ b_2 \\ b_3 \end{bmatrix} \qquad \text{or } \mathbf{r} = \mathbf{a} + \lambda\mathbf{b}, \text{ where } \mathbf{r} \text{ is a general point on the line and } \lambda \text{ is a parameter.}$$

Position vector of *any* point on the line

Position vector of a *particular* point on the line

This vector is the *direction* of the line

Example 2

Find the point of intersection of the lines with equations

$$\begin{bmatrix} x \\ y \end{bmatrix} = \begin{bmatrix} -3 \\ 5 \end{bmatrix} + \lambda \begin{bmatrix} 2 \\ 1 \end{bmatrix} \quad \text{and} \quad \begin{bmatrix} x \\ y \end{bmatrix} = \begin{bmatrix} 4 \\ 1 \end{bmatrix} + \mu \begin{bmatrix} 1 \\ -2 \end{bmatrix}$$

Note that it is necessary to have *different* parameters, λ and μ, for the two lines as it would otherwise be impossible to generate points independently.

Solution

At the point of intersection the two position vectors will be equal.

$$-3 + 2\lambda = 4 + \mu$$

and $\quad 5 + \lambda = 1 - 2\mu$

or, $\qquad 2\lambda - \mu = 7$

$$\lambda + 2\mu = -4$$

Solving these two equations for λ and μ gives $\lambda = 2$, $\mu = -3$ and the position vector of the point of intersection as $\begin{bmatrix} -3 \\ 5 \end{bmatrix} + \begin{bmatrix} 4 \\ 2 \end{bmatrix} = \begin{bmatrix} 1 \\ 7 \end{bmatrix}$.

The method of example 2 can easily be extended to lines in three dimensions. The x- and y-coordinates can still be equated to find λ and μ. Then, when these values of λ and μ are substituted into the z-coordinates, two possibilities exist:

 (i) the coordinates are equal and so the lines meet;

(ii) the coordinates are unequal and so the lines do not meet.

In two dimensions, the lines in case (ii) would be parallel. In three dimensions there is a further possibility, because a pair of distinct lines may have no point in common and yet *not* be parallel. In this case they are called **skew lines**.

Example 3

Show that the lines $\mathbf{r} = \begin{bmatrix} 2 \\ 3 \\ 5 \end{bmatrix} + t \begin{bmatrix} 4 \\ -1 \\ 3 \end{bmatrix}$ and $\mathbf{r} = \begin{bmatrix} 4 \\ 7 \\ 2 \end{bmatrix} + s \begin{bmatrix} 2 \\ -2 \\ 3 \end{bmatrix}$ meet and find the point of intersection.

Solution

If the point (x, y, z) lies on both lines then

$$\begin{bmatrix} x \\ y \\ z \end{bmatrix} = \begin{bmatrix} 2 \\ 3 \\ 5 \end{bmatrix} + t \begin{bmatrix} 4 \\ -1 \\ 3 \end{bmatrix} = \begin{bmatrix} 4 \\ 7 \\ 2 \end{bmatrix} + s \begin{bmatrix} 2 \\ -2 \\ 3 \end{bmatrix}$$

for suitable values of s and t, which must satisfy the three equations

$$2 + 4t = 4 + 2s$$

$$3 - t = 7 - 2s$$

$$5 + 3t = 2 + 3s$$

Adding the first two of these equations gives

$$5 + 3t = 11 \quad \Rightarrow \quad t = 2 \quad \text{and} \quad s = 3$$

The third equation is also satisfied by $t = 2$, $s = 3$, which means that there *is* a point common to the two lines. Substituting $t = 2$ in the equation of the first line gives the coordinates of the point, $(10, 1, 11)$.

Example 4

Show that the lines $\mathbf{r} = \begin{bmatrix} 2 \\ 3 \\ 6 \end{bmatrix} + t \begin{bmatrix} 4 \\ -1 \\ 5 \end{bmatrix}$ and $\mathbf{r} = \begin{bmatrix} 4 \\ 7 \\ 8 \end{bmatrix} + s \begin{bmatrix} 2 \\ -2 \\ 1 \end{bmatrix}$ are skew lines.

Solution

Following the method of example 3 to find a point of intersection gives the equations

$$2 + 4t = 4 + 2s$$

$$3 - t = 7 - 2s$$

$$6 + 5t = 8 + s$$

As before, the first two equations are satisfied simultaneously by $t = 2$ and $s = 3$. But these values do not satisfy the third equation so there is no point common to the two lines. The lines are not parallel, since the directions of

$\begin{bmatrix} 4 \\ -1 \\ 5 \end{bmatrix}$ and $\begin{bmatrix} 2 \\ -2 \\ 1 \end{bmatrix}$ are different. The lines are therefore skew.

In three dimensions, lines which do not intersect and are not parallel are called skew lines.

5.2 Exercise 2

1

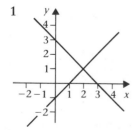

Write down vector equations for the two lines shown in the diagram.

Calculate the point of intersection of the two lines.

2 OABCDEFG is a cuboid with edges OA, OC and OD of lengths 4, 5 and 3 respectively.

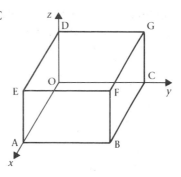

Which lines have the following vector equations?

(a) $\begin{bmatrix} x \\ y \\ z \end{bmatrix} = \lambda \begin{bmatrix} 0 \\ 5 \\ 3 \end{bmatrix}$

(b) $\begin{bmatrix} x \\ y \\ z \end{bmatrix} = \begin{bmatrix} 4 \\ 0 \\ 3 \end{bmatrix} + \lambda \begin{bmatrix} -4 \\ 5 \\ 0 \end{bmatrix}$

(c) $\begin{bmatrix} x \\ y \\ z \end{bmatrix} = \begin{bmatrix} 0 \\ 5 \\ 0 \end{bmatrix} + \lambda \begin{bmatrix} 4 \\ -5 \\ 3 \end{bmatrix}$

(d) $\begin{bmatrix} x \\ y \\ z \end{bmatrix} = \begin{bmatrix} 4 \\ 5 \\ 0 \end{bmatrix} + \lambda \begin{bmatrix} -4 \\ -5 \\ 3 \end{bmatrix}$

3 For the cuboid of question 2, find vector equations for the lines:

(a) AB   (b) AC   (c) AF   (d) AG

4 Two slant edges of a square-based pyramid, with its base on the xy plane, have equations:

$$\begin{bmatrix} x \\ y \\ z \end{bmatrix} = \begin{bmatrix} 4 \\ 3 \\ 0 \end{bmatrix} + \lambda \begin{bmatrix} -1 \\ -1 \\ 1 \end{bmatrix} \quad \text{and} \quad \begin{bmatrix} x \\ y \\ z \end{bmatrix} = \begin{bmatrix} 4 \\ -3 \\ 0 \end{bmatrix} + \mu \begin{bmatrix} -1 \\ 1 \\ 1 \end{bmatrix}$$

Find values of λ and μ such that the y and z components are equal.

Check that these values both give the same value for the x-coordinate. Hence write down the position vector of the vertex of the pyramid.

5 Find whether the following pairs of lines meet. If they meet, find the coordinates of the common point; if they do not, find whether they are parallel or skew lines.

(a) $\mathbf{r} = \begin{bmatrix} 2 \\ 3 \\ 5 \end{bmatrix} + t \begin{bmatrix} 1 \\ 0 \\ 2 \end{bmatrix}$, $\quad \mathbf{r} = \begin{bmatrix} 5 \\ 0 \\ 4 \end{bmatrix} + s \begin{bmatrix} 0 \\ 3 \\ 7 \end{bmatrix}$

(b) $\mathbf{r} = \begin{bmatrix} 4 \\ 5 \\ 2 \end{bmatrix} + \lambda \begin{bmatrix} 1 \\ 2 \\ 3 \end{bmatrix}$, $\quad \mathbf{r} = \begin{bmatrix} 1 \\ -3 \\ 4 \end{bmatrix} + \mu \begin{bmatrix} 2 \\ 4 \\ 6 \end{bmatrix}$

(c) $\mathbf{r} = \begin{bmatrix} 2 \\ 1 \\ 3 \end{bmatrix} + s \begin{bmatrix} 4 \\ 2 \\ -5 \end{bmatrix}$, $\quad \mathbf{r} = \begin{bmatrix} -3 \\ 6 \\ -8 \end{bmatrix} + t \begin{bmatrix} 3 \\ -1 \\ 2 \end{bmatrix}$

(d) $\mathbf{r} = \begin{bmatrix} 4 \\ 3 \\ 1 \end{bmatrix} + \lambda \begin{bmatrix} 5 \\ -2 \\ 4 \end{bmatrix}$, $\quad \mathbf{r} = \begin{bmatrix} 2 \\ 1 \\ 6 \end{bmatrix} + \mu \begin{bmatrix} 3 \\ 1 \\ 2 \end{bmatrix}$

6 Prove that the two lines with equations

$$\mathbf{r} = \begin{bmatrix} 0 \\ 2 \\ -3 \end{bmatrix} + s \begin{bmatrix} 6 \\ -1 \\ -1 \end{bmatrix} \quad \text{and} \quad \mathbf{r} = \begin{bmatrix} -4 \\ 6 \\ -4 \end{bmatrix} + t \begin{bmatrix} 2 \\ 1 \\ -1 \end{bmatrix}$$

have a common point.

5.2.3 Scalar products

You are familiar with the idea of adding and subtracting vectors. Here we consider one way in which a meaning can be given to multiplication of vectors. This problem is closely related to finding the angle between two vectors.

Consider vectors **a** and **b** as shown.

$$\mathbf{a} = \begin{bmatrix} 3 \\ 1 \end{bmatrix} \quad \mathbf{b} = \begin{bmatrix} 2 \\ 3 \end{bmatrix}$$

How could you find the angle, θ, between the two vectors?

One way would be to use the cosine rule on triangle OAB. The lengths OA and OB can be found using Pythagoras' theorem and since $\overrightarrow{AB} = \overrightarrow{OB} - \overrightarrow{OA}$ its length can also be found.

$$OA = \sqrt{(3^2 + 1^2)} = \sqrt{10} \qquad OB = \sqrt{(2^2 + 3^2)} = \sqrt{13}$$

$$\overrightarrow{AB} = \mathbf{b} - \mathbf{a} = \begin{bmatrix} -1 \\ 2 \end{bmatrix} \qquad AB = \sqrt{(1^2 + 2^2)} = \sqrt{5}$$

So, by the cosine rule $AB^2 = OA^2 + OB^2 - 2\,OA\,OB\cos\theta$

$$\Rightarrow \qquad 5 = 10 + 13 - 2\sqrt{10}\sqrt{13}\cos\theta$$

$$\Rightarrow \cos\theta = \frac{9}{\sqrt{130}} = 0.7894 \Rightarrow \theta = 37.9°$$

The aim of the following questions is to develop a more convenient method of finding the angle between two vectors.

 .2c

1

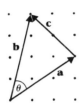

For the triangle illustrated above, $\mathbf{a} = \begin{bmatrix} 3 \\ 2 \end{bmatrix}$ and $\mathbf{b} = \begin{bmatrix} 1 \\ 4 \end{bmatrix}$.

(a) Find the magnitudes (or lengths) of vectors $\mathbf{a}$ and $\mathbf{b}$.

(b) Write vector $\mathbf{c}$ in terms of $\mathbf{a}$ and $\mathbf{b}$ and then express it as a column vector. Find the magnitude of vector $\mathbf{c}$.

(c) Use the cosine rule with your values of a, b and c (the magnitudes of $\mathbf{a}$, $\mathbf{b}$ and $\mathbf{c}$) to calculate $\cos\theta$ and find the angle θ.

> The magnitude or length of the vector $\mathbf{c}$ is denoted by $|\mathbf{c}|$ or simply c. Similarly the magnitude of vector $\overrightarrow{AB}$ is $|AB|$ or AB.

2 For any triangle, $\mathbf{a} = \begin{bmatrix} a_1 \\ a_2 \end{bmatrix}$ and $\mathbf{b} = \begin{bmatrix} b_1 \\ b_2 \end{bmatrix}$.

(a) Explain why $a^2 = a_1^2 + a_2^2$ and write down a similar expression for b^2.

(b) As before, $\mathbf{c} = \mathbf{b} - \mathbf{a} = \begin{bmatrix} b_1 - a_1 \\ b_2 - a_2 \end{bmatrix}$. Since the magnitude of $\mathbf{c}$ is c, you can write

$$c^2 = (b_1 - a_1)^2 + (b_2 - a_2)^2$$

By multiplying out the brackets and using the results of (a), show that

$$c^2 = a^2 + b^2 - 2(a_1 b_1 + a_2 b_2)$$

(c) By comparing with the cosine rule, explain why

$$a_1 b_1 + a_2 b_2 = ab \cos \theta$$

3 Use the result in 2(c) to calculate θ in question 1.

The **scalar product** of two vectors $\mathbf{a} = \begin{bmatrix} a_1 \\ a_2 \end{bmatrix}$ and $\mathbf{b} = \begin{bmatrix} b_1 \\ b_2 \end{bmatrix}$ is defined as

$a_1 b_1 + a_2 b_2$ or $ab \cos \theta$ where a and b are the **magnitudes** of the two vectors and θ is the angle between them.

The word **scalar** is used to emphasise that the product is not a vector quantity. In fact, a second product, known as a vector product, exists but is beyond the scope of this book.

The scalar product is written as $\begin{bmatrix} a_1 \\ a_2 \end{bmatrix} \cdot \begin{bmatrix} b_1 \\ b_2 \end{bmatrix}$ or as $\mathbf{a} \cdot \mathbf{b}$ which is pronounced 'a dot b'. For obvious reasons some writers refer to it as the 'dot product'.

The angle between two vectors can be found by using

$$\cos \theta = \frac{\mathbf{a} \cdot \mathbf{b}}{ab}, \quad \text{where } \mathbf{a} \cdot \mathbf{b} = a_1 b_1 + a_2 b_2$$

Consider the following three situations.

(i) 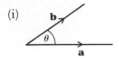 (ii) 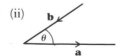 (iii)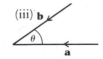

Applying the scalar product definition in each case:

(i) $\mathbf{a} \cdot \mathbf{b} = |a|\,|b|\cos\theta$

(ii) $\mathbf{b}$ is in the opposite direction so $\mathbf{a} \cdot \mathbf{b}$ is
$|a|\,|b|\cos(180 - \theta) = -|a|\,|b|\cos\theta$

(iii) Both $\mathbf{a}$ and $\mathbf{b}$ are pointing towards the origin
so $\mathbf{a} \cdot \mathbf{b} = |a|\,|b|\cos\theta$

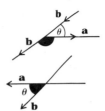

In three dimensions, if the two vectors are $\mathbf{a} = \begin{bmatrix} a_1 \\ a_2 \\ a_3 \end{bmatrix}$ and $\mathbf{b} = \begin{bmatrix} b_1 \\ b_2 \\ b_3 \end{bmatrix}$,

the definition extends naturally to $a_1b_1 + a_2b_2 + a_3b_3$ or $ab\cos\theta$, where, in order to find a, the length of $\mathbf{a}$, it is now necessary to use the three-dimensional form of Pythagoras' theorem.

Example 5

Find the angle between the vectors $\begin{bmatrix} 5 \\ 2 \\ -3 \end{bmatrix}$ and $\begin{bmatrix} 2 \\ 4 \\ 1 \end{bmatrix}$.

Solution

$$\mathbf{a} \cdot \mathbf{b} = 5 \times 2 + 2 \times 4 + (-3) \times 1 = 15$$

$$a = \sqrt{(25 + 4 + 9)} = \sqrt{38} \qquad b = \sqrt{(4 + 16 + 1)} = \sqrt{21}$$

$$\text{So } \cos\theta = \frac{15}{\sqrt{38}\sqrt{21}} \Rightarrow \theta = 57.9°$$

5.2 Exercise 3

1 Find the angles between:

(a) $\begin{bmatrix} 5 \\ 2 \end{bmatrix}$ and $\begin{bmatrix} 3 \\ 2 \end{bmatrix}$ (b) $\begin{bmatrix} 5 \\ 2 \end{bmatrix}$ and $\begin{bmatrix} -3 \\ 2 \end{bmatrix}$

2 In triangle ABC, $A = (3, 2)$, $B = (-1, 3)$, $C = (1, 7)$.

(a) Find vectors $\overrightarrow{AB}$ and $\overrightarrow{AC}$.

(b) Explain why, to calculate angle A, you should find $\overrightarrow{AB} \cdot \overrightarrow{AC}$ and not $\overrightarrow{AB} \cdot \overrightarrow{CA}$. Hence calculate angle A.

3 Find the angles between:

(a) $\begin{bmatrix} 12 \\ 1 \\ -12 \end{bmatrix}$ and $\begin{bmatrix} 8 \\ 4 \\ 1 \end{bmatrix}$ (b) $\begin{bmatrix} 4 \\ -1 \\ -8 \end{bmatrix}$ and $\begin{bmatrix} 7 \\ 4 \\ -4 \end{bmatrix}$

4   In triangle PQR, $P = (5, -3, 1)$, $Q = (-2, 1, 5)$, $R = (9, 5, 0)$.
Find the angles of the triangle.

5   If $A = (2, 5, 2)$, $B = (3, 11, -3)$, $C = (7, 12, -1)$, $D = (6, 6, 4)$,
show that ABCD is a parallelogram and find its sides and angles.

6E Use the scalar product method to find the angle made by a longest diagonal
of a cube with:

(a) an edge of the cube,   (b) a face diagonal,

(c) another longest diagonal.

5.2.4 Properties of the scalar product

The usefulness of the scalar product extends beyond providing a convenient
method for finding the angle between vectors. Some of its properties are explored
further in the following questions and applied later to three-dimensional
geometry. Many of the properties of the scalar product are similar to those of
ordinary algebra. Here we examine the similarities and differences.

 .2D

Consider the vectors:

$$a = \begin{bmatrix} 3 \\ 4 \end{bmatrix} \quad b = \begin{bmatrix} 5 \\ 5 \end{bmatrix} \quad c = \begin{bmatrix} 2 \\ 6 \end{bmatrix} \quad d = \begin{bmatrix} 4 \\ -3 \end{bmatrix} \quad e = \begin{bmatrix} -8 \\ 6 \end{bmatrix}$$

1 (a) Draw a diagram showing these five vectors.

(b) Which pairs of vectors are parallel and which are perpendicular?

2 (a) Calculate the magnitude of each vector.

(b) Calculate the scalar products: $a \cdot a$, $b \cdot b$, $c \cdot c$, $d \cdot d$, $e \cdot e$.

(c) What do you notice?

3 (a) Calculate $a \cdot b$ and $b \cdot a$.

(b) Calculate $a \cdot c$ and $c \cdot a$.

(c) What do you notice? Explain why this occurs.

4 (a) Calculate $a \cdot b + a \cdot c$.

(b) Calulate $a \cdot (b + c)$.

(c) What do you notice?

5   (a) Calculate the scalar products $\mathbf{a} \cdot \mathbf{b}$, $\mathbf{a} \cdot \mathbf{d}$, $\mathbf{a} \cdot \mathbf{e}$.

(b) What can you say about two vectors which are perpendicular?

(c) Find a vector which is perpendicular to $\mathbf{b}$.

(d) Does it follow that, if two vectors have scalar product zero, then they are perpendicular?

6E $A'A$ is the diameter of a circle centre O and P is any point on the circumference.

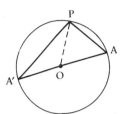

(a) With $\mathbf{a} = \overrightarrow{OA}$ and $\mathbf{p} = \overrightarrow{OP}$, express $\overrightarrow{OA'}$, $\overrightarrow{AP}$ and $\overrightarrow{A'P}$ in terms of $\mathbf{a}$ and $\mathbf{p}$.

(b) Calculate $\overrightarrow{AP} \cdot \overrightarrow{A'P}$.

(c) What is the geometrical significance of the value of this scalar product?

For the scalar product:

$$\mathbf{a} \cdot \mathbf{b} = \mathbf{b} \cdot \mathbf{a}$$

$$\mathbf{a} \cdot (\mathbf{b} + \mathbf{c}) = \mathbf{a} \cdot \mathbf{b} + \mathbf{a} \cdot \mathbf{c}$$

$$\mathbf{a} \cdot \mathbf{b} = 0 \Rightarrow \mathbf{a} \text{ is perpendicular to } \mathbf{b} \text{ or } \mathbf{a} = 0 \text{ or } \mathbf{b} = 0$$

$$\mathbf{a} \cdot \mathbf{a} = |\mathbf{a}|^2 = a^2$$

5.2 Exercise 4

1 $\mathbf{a} = \begin{bmatrix} 3 \\ 2 \end{bmatrix}$ $\mathbf{b} = \begin{bmatrix} 5 \\ 3 \end{bmatrix}$ $\mathbf{c} = \begin{bmatrix} -2 \\ 3 \end{bmatrix}$

(a) Calculate the magnitudes of $\mathbf{a}$, $\mathbf{b}$, and $\mathbf{c}$.

(b) Calculate the scalar products $\mathbf{a} \cdot \mathbf{b}$, $\mathbf{b} \cdot \mathbf{c}$, $\mathbf{c} \cdot \mathbf{a}$.

(c) Which pairs of vectors are perpendicular?

(d) Find a vector which is perpendicular to $\mathbf{b}$.

2 $\mathbf{a} = \begin{bmatrix} 2 \\ 2 \\ 1 \end{bmatrix}$ $\mathbf{b} = \begin{bmatrix} 1 \\ 0 \\ -2 \end{bmatrix}$ $\mathbf{c} = \begin{bmatrix} 4 \\ -5 \\ 2 \end{bmatrix}$

(a) Calculate the scalar products $\mathbf{a} \cdot \mathbf{b}$, $\mathbf{b} \cdot \mathbf{c}$, $\mathbf{c} \cdot \mathbf{a}$.

(b) Which pairs of vectors are perpendicular?

3 $\mathbf{a} = \begin{bmatrix} 10 \\ 0 \end{bmatrix}$ $\mathbf{b} = \begin{bmatrix} -6 \\ 8 \end{bmatrix}$

(a) Find the position vector $\mathbf{c}$ of the midpoint of AB.

(b) Find the vector $\mathbf{d} = \overrightarrow{BA}$.

(c) Calculate the scalar product $\mathbf{c} \cdot \mathbf{d}$.

(d) Draw a diagram of the triangle OAB with the point C included. What can you deduce from the value of the scalar product $\mathbf{c} \cdot \mathbf{d}$?

4E OAB is a triangle with the altitudes from A and B intersecting at H as shown.

[The **altitude** of a triangle is the perpendicular from a vertex to the opposite side.]

$\overrightarrow{OA}$, $\overrightarrow{OB}$ and $\overrightarrow{OH}$ are denoted by $\mathbf{a}$, $\mathbf{b}$ and $\mathbf{h}$.

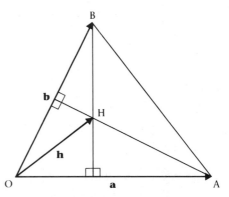

(a) Why is $\mathbf{a} \cdot (\mathbf{b} - \mathbf{h}) = 0$?

(b) Write down a similar equation involving $\mathbf{a} - \mathbf{h}$.

(c) By subtracting the two equations, show that $(\mathbf{a} - \mathbf{b}) \cdot \mathbf{h} = 0$.

(d) Explain how this proves that the altitudes of a triangle are concurrent. (**Concurrent** lines all pass through a single point.)

5E (a)

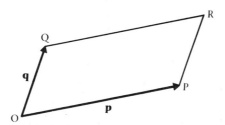

OPRQ is a parallelogram.
Write down the vectors $\overrightarrow{OR}$ and $\overrightarrow{QP}$ in terms of $\mathbf{p}$ and $\mathbf{q}$.

(b) Explain why $(\mathbf{p} + \mathbf{q}) \cdot (\mathbf{p} - \mathbf{q}) = p^2 - q^2$.

(c) If $\overrightarrow{OR} \cdot \overrightarrow{QP} = 0$ what can you say about

(i) the lines OR and QP,   (ii) the sides of the parallelogram?

5.2.5 Vector equations of planes

In three dimensions, as well as the equations of lines, a description of planes can be important. In describing crystals, for example, you might be interested in the various faces and the way they are related. Suppose A, B and C are three points with position vectors

$$\begin{bmatrix} 3 \\ 0 \\ 0 \end{bmatrix}, \quad \begin{bmatrix} 0 \\ 5 \\ 0 \end{bmatrix} \quad \text{and} \quad \begin{bmatrix} 0 \\ 0 \\ 4 \end{bmatrix} \text{ respectively.}$$

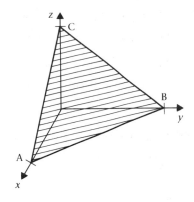

Example 6

(a) What are the vectors $\overrightarrow{AB}$ and $\overrightarrow{AC}$?

(b) Where are the points with the following position vectors?

(i) $\overrightarrow{OA} + \frac{1}{2}\overrightarrow{AB} + \frac{1}{2}\overrightarrow{AC}$

(ii) $\overrightarrow{OA} + \frac{1}{4}\overrightarrow{AB} + \frac{1}{4}\overrightarrow{AC}$

(iii) $\overrightarrow{OA} + 2\overrightarrow{AB} - \overrightarrow{AC}$

(iv) $\overrightarrow{OA} + \lambda\overrightarrow{AB} + \mu\overrightarrow{AC}$

(c) Can *every* point in the plane ABC be found from a suitable choice of λ and μ in (b)(iv)?

Solution

(a) $\overrightarrow{AB} = \mathbf{b} - \mathbf{a} = \begin{bmatrix} -3 \\ 5 \\ 0 \end{bmatrix}$ $\qquad \overrightarrow{AC} = \mathbf{c} - \mathbf{a} = \begin{bmatrix} -3 \\ 0 \\ 4 \end{bmatrix}$

(b) (i) M, the midpoint of BC.

(ii) D, the midpoint of AM.

(iii) $\overrightarrow{OA} + 2\overrightarrow{AB} - \overrightarrow{AC}$ is the point F in the plane ABC, where $\overrightarrow{AE} = 2\overrightarrow{AB}$ and $\overrightarrow{EF} = \overrightarrow{AC}$.

(iv) $\overrightarrow{OA} + \lambda\overrightarrow{AB} + \mu\overrightarrow{AC}$ is a general point in the plane ABC.

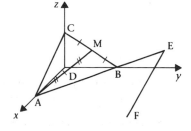

(c) Every point in the plane ABC can be reached by the vector $\overrightarrow{OA}$ together with some combination of vectors $\overrightarrow{AB}$ and $\overrightarrow{AC}$.

.2E

1

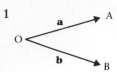

Points A and B have position vectors **a** and **b** relative to an origin O as shown.

Copy the diagram and mark on it the points having the following position vectors:

(a) $\overrightarrow{OC} = 2\mathbf{a}$ (b) $\overrightarrow{OD} = \frac{1}{2}\mathbf{b}$

(c) $\overrightarrow{OE} = 2\mathbf{a} + \mathbf{b}$ (d) $\overrightarrow{OF} = 2\mathbf{a} - \frac{1}{2}\mathbf{b}$

(e) $\overrightarrow{OG} = 3\mathbf{a} + 2\mathbf{b}$ (f) $\overrightarrow{OH} = \frac{1}{2}\mathbf{a} + \frac{2}{3}\mathbf{b}$

2 .

H × . × D . G ×

. . **b** × I .

. **a** → A . C ×

. . . . .

E × F × . . .

A and B are described by the position vectors **a** and **b** as shown. Express the position vectors of the points C, D, E, F, G, H, I in terms of vectors **a** and **b**.

Questions 1 and 2 illustrate that it is possible for position vectors of all points in the plane OAB to be expressed in the form $\lambda\mathbf{a} + \mu\mathbf{b}$ for some values of λ and μ. The remaining questions illustrate how this technique may be used to find the equation of any plane, not necessarily through O.

The diagram shows a cube with sides of length 6 cm. The origin is at O. The following questions all refer to this cube.

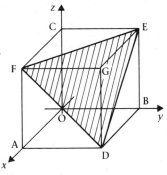

3 Consider the plane DEF. Find the vectors $\overrightarrow{DE}$ and $\overrightarrow{DF}$.

Explain why the position vector of any point in the plane DEF can be written as

$$\begin{bmatrix} x \\ y \\ z \end{bmatrix} = \begin{bmatrix} 6 \\ 6 \\ 0 \end{bmatrix} + \lambda \begin{bmatrix} -6 \\ 0 \\ 6 \end{bmatrix} + \mu \begin{bmatrix} 0 \\ -6 \\ 6 \end{bmatrix}$$

This equation is known as the **vector equation of the plane**.

4 State the points with the following values of λ and μ and find the coordinates of each point.

(a) $\lambda = 0, \quad \mu = 0$ (b) $\lambda = 1, \quad \mu = 0$ (c) $\lambda = 0, \quad \mu = 1$

(d) $\lambda = \frac{1}{2}, \quad \mu = \frac{1}{2}$ (e) $\lambda = \frac{1}{3}, \quad \mu = \frac{1}{3}$

5 Consider the equilateral triangle ABC.

What are the direction vectors $\overrightarrow{CB}$ and $\overrightarrow{CA}$?

Using $\overrightarrow{OC}$ as the position vector write down the vector equation of the plane ABC.

What do you notice about the planes ABC and DEF?

6 Repeat question 4 for the plane ABC.

7 (a) Suggest a possible vector equation for a plane parallel to ABC which passes through the origin.

(b) Likewise suggest an equation for a parallel plane through G.

8 If H is the midpoint of the line CF, find a vector equation for the plane DEH.

The vector equation of a plane through a point with position vector $\begin{bmatrix} a_1 \\ a_2 \\ a_3 \end{bmatrix}$

where the vectors $\begin{bmatrix} b_1 \\ b_2 \\ b_3 \end{bmatrix}$ and $\begin{bmatrix} c_1 \\ c_2 \\ c_3 \end{bmatrix}$ are parallel to the plane is:

$$\begin{bmatrix} x \\ y \\ z \end{bmatrix} = \begin{bmatrix} a_1 \\ a_2 \\ a_3 \end{bmatrix} + \lambda \begin{bmatrix} b_1 \\ b_2 \\ b_3 \end{bmatrix} + \mu \begin{bmatrix} c_1 \\ c_2 \\ c_3 \end{bmatrix}, \text{ where } \lambda \text{ and } \mu \text{ are parameters.}$$

Position vector of *any* point on the plane

Position vector of a *particular* point on the plane

Vectors *parallel* to the plane, but not parallel to each other

Example 7

Find the vector equation of the plane through the point $(2, 5, -6)$, parallel to the

vector $\begin{bmatrix} 4 \\ 1 \\ 3 \end{bmatrix}$ and to the z-axis.

Solution

Since the z-axis is parallel to the vector $\begin{bmatrix} 0 \\ 0 \\ 1 \end{bmatrix}$, the vector equation of the plane is

$$\begin{bmatrix} x \\ y \\ z \end{bmatrix} = \begin{bmatrix} 2 \\ 5 \\ -6 \end{bmatrix} + \lambda \begin{bmatrix} 4 \\ 1 \\ 3 \end{bmatrix} + \mu \begin{bmatrix} 0 \\ 0 \\ 1 \end{bmatrix}$$

5.2 **Exercise 5**

1 Find a vector equation for the plane through the three points
   A $(2, 3, 1)$, B $(-1, 2, 4)$ and C $(-4, 1, 5)$.

2 A plane cuts the x-, y- and z-axes at $x = 2$, $y = -1$ and $z = 3$. Find a vector
   equation for the plane.

3 OABCD is a regular square-based pyramid with
   base edges of length 4 and height 3.

   (a) What is the position vector of the vertex D?

   (b) Find vector equations for the faces OAD and
        BCD.

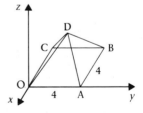

4 Explain why it is not possible to find the vector equation of the plane through
   the three points A $(2, 3, 1)$, B $(-1, 2, 4)$ and C $(-4, 1, 7)$.

5.2.6 Cartesian equations of planes

Section 5.2.5 showed you how to write the equation of a plane in vector form.
Here we consider what the equation of a plane will look like in Cartesian form,
and the relationship between the two alternative forms of the equation.

Consider the Cartesian equation $x + y + z = 4$. The point $(1, 3, 0)$ satisfies this
equation. Other obvious points which satisfy the equation are, for example,

$(4, 0, 0)$, $(0, 4, 0)$, $(0, 0, 4)$, $(3, 1, 0)$, $(2, 2, 0)$ and so on. Clearly, there are infinitely many such points. If these points are plotted, the following diagram is obtained.

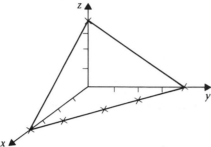

This suggests that $x + y + z = 4$ represents a plane.

 .2F

1 The vector equation of the plane DEF is:

$$\begin{bmatrix} x \\ y \\ z \end{bmatrix} = \begin{bmatrix} 6 \\ 6 \\ 0 \end{bmatrix} + \lambda \begin{bmatrix} -6 \\ 0 \\ 6 \end{bmatrix} + \mu \begin{bmatrix} 0 \\ -6 \\ 6 \end{bmatrix}$$

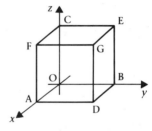

Considering the components separately, you can write the x components as

$x = 6 - 6\lambda$

Write down the corresponding equations for the y and z components.

Add the three equations together and simplify. The result should involve x, y and z only and not λ and μ.

This equation is known as the **Cartesian equation** of the plane.

2 (a) What is the Cartesian equation of the plane ABC? Check your suggestion by working from the vector equation as in question 1.

In 5.2E you found that this was $\begin{bmatrix} x \\ y \\ z \end{bmatrix} = \begin{bmatrix} 0 \\ 0 \\ 6 \end{bmatrix} + \lambda \begin{bmatrix} 0 \\ 6 \\ -6 \end{bmatrix} + \mu \begin{bmatrix} 6 \\ 0 \\ -6 \end{bmatrix}$.

(b) In 5.2E, the vector equations of the planes through O and G parallel to ABC and DEF were found to be

$$\begin{bmatrix} x \\ y \\ z \end{bmatrix} = \lambda \begin{bmatrix} 0 \\ 6 \\ -6 \end{bmatrix} + \mu \begin{bmatrix} 6 \\ 0 \\ -6 \end{bmatrix} \quad \text{and}$$

$$\begin{bmatrix} x \\ y \\ z \end{bmatrix} = \begin{bmatrix} 6 \\ 6 \\ 6 \end{bmatrix} + \lambda \begin{bmatrix} 0 \\ 6 \\ -6 \end{bmatrix} + \mu \begin{bmatrix} 6 \\ 0 \\ -6 \end{bmatrix}$$

respectively. What are the Cartesian equations of these planes?

3 The vector equation of the plane DEH, where H is the midpoint of CF, is

$$\begin{bmatrix} x \\ y \\ z \end{bmatrix} = \begin{bmatrix} 6 \\ 6 \\ 0 \end{bmatrix} + \lambda \begin{bmatrix} -6 \\ 0 \\ 6 \end{bmatrix} + \mu \begin{bmatrix} -3 \\ -6 \\ 6 \end{bmatrix}$$

Write down equations for the x, y and z components.

By eliminating λ from the first and third equations and then eliminating μ, find the Cartesian equation of the plane DEH.

4 A plane has vector equation $\begin{bmatrix} x \\ y \\ z \end{bmatrix} = \begin{bmatrix} 5 \\ 2 \\ 4 \end{bmatrix} + \lambda \begin{bmatrix} -3 \\ 0 \\ -6 \end{bmatrix} + \mu \begin{bmatrix} 2 \\ 3 \\ 1 \end{bmatrix}$.

Find the Cartesian equation of the plane.

5 The Cartesian equation of the plane DEF is $x + y + z = 12$.

Using scalar product notation, this could be written as $\begin{bmatrix} 1 \\ 1 \\ 1 \end{bmatrix} \cdot \begin{bmatrix} x \\ y \\ z \end{bmatrix} = 12$.

To investigate the significance of the vector $\begin{bmatrix} 1 \\ 1 \\ 1 \end{bmatrix}$, first note that it is in the same direction as $\overrightarrow{OG}$, which is $\begin{bmatrix} 6 \\ 6 \\ 6 \end{bmatrix}$.

How is this vector $\begin{bmatrix} 1 \\ 1 \\ 1 \end{bmatrix}$ related to the plane DEF?

Calculate the scalar products of $\begin{bmatrix} 1 \\ 1 \\ 1 \end{bmatrix}$ with $\overrightarrow{DE}$ and $\overrightarrow{DF}$. What do the results tell you?

By eliminating λ and μ, the Cartesian equation of the plane
$px + qy + rz = s$ may be obtained from the vector equation of the plane

$$\begin{bmatrix} x \\ y \\ z \end{bmatrix} = \begin{bmatrix} a_1 \\ a_2 \\ a_3 \end{bmatrix} + \lambda \begin{bmatrix} b_1 \\ b_2 \\ b_3 \end{bmatrix} + \mu \begin{bmatrix} c_1 \\ c_2 \\ c_3 \end{bmatrix}$$

Using these ideas, the equation $x + y + z = 12$ can be written, using scalar product notation, as

$$\begin{bmatrix} 1 \\ 1 \\ 1 \end{bmatrix} \cdot \begin{bmatrix} x \\ y \\ z \end{bmatrix} = 12$$

You saw in 5.2F that the vector $\begin{bmatrix} 1 \\ 1 \\ 1 \end{bmatrix}$ is at right angles to the plane. This vector

is known as the **normal vector** to the plane and is usually written **n**. The result suggests that $\mathbf{n} \cdot \mathbf{r} = k$, a constant, for any point **r** in the plane.

Since a plane is two-dimensional it is not possible to choose a single direction in which to measure the gradient. However, since the plane has a unique direction to which it is perpendicular, it is possible to specify its orientation using the normal vector.

The vector equation of any plane can be written in the form

$$\mathbf{r} = \mathbf{a} + \lambda \mathbf{b} + \mu \mathbf{c}$$

where **r** is a general point on the plane, **a** is a particular point on the plane and **b** and **c** are two vectors parallel to the plane.

Choosing a vector **n**, which is perpendicular to the plane, as normal vector and considering the scalar product $\mathbf{n} \cdot \mathbf{r}$, you obtain

$$\mathbf{n} \cdot \mathbf{r} = \mathbf{n} \cdot \mathbf{a} + \lambda \mathbf{n} \cdot \mathbf{b} + \mu \mathbf{n} \cdot \mathbf{c}$$

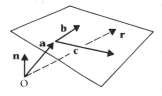

Since the vector **n** is perpendicular to the plane, the dot products $\mathbf{n} \cdot \mathbf{b}$ and $\mathbf{n} \cdot \mathbf{c}$ will be zero. The product $\mathbf{n} \cdot \mathbf{a}$ will be a constant because **a** is a fixed point in the plane, so $\mathbf{n} \cdot \mathbf{a}$ is the product of two fixed vectors.

The equation therefore reduces to

$$\mathbf{n} \cdot \mathbf{r} = \mathbf{n} \cdot \mathbf{a} \quad \text{or} \quad \mathbf{n} \cdot \mathbf{r} = d \quad \text{where } d \text{ is a constant}$$

In the case of $ax + by + cz = d$,

$$\mathbf{n} = \begin{bmatrix} a \\ b \\ c \end{bmatrix} \qquad \mathbf{r} = \begin{bmatrix} x \\ y \\ z \end{bmatrix}$$

The equation of a plane can be written as $\mathbf{n} \cdot \mathbf{r} = \mathbf{n} \cdot \mathbf{a}$, where $\mathbf{n}$ is a normal vector and $\mathbf{a}$ is the position vector of a point on the plane.

The normal vector to the plane $ax + by + cz = d$ is $\begin{bmatrix} a \\ b \\ c \end{bmatrix}$.

Example 8

A plane through a point with position vector $\begin{bmatrix} 2 \\ 1 \\ 3 \end{bmatrix}$ has normal vector $\begin{bmatrix} 3 \\ -1 \\ 4 \end{bmatrix}$. Find the Cartesian equation of the plane.

Solution

Using $\mathbf{n} \cdot \mathbf{r} = \mathbf{n} \cdot \mathbf{a}$, $\qquad \begin{bmatrix} 3 \\ -1 \\ 4 \end{bmatrix} \cdot \begin{bmatrix} x \\ y \\ z \end{bmatrix} = \begin{bmatrix} 3 \\ -1 \\ 4 \end{bmatrix} \cdot \begin{bmatrix} 2 \\ 1 \\ 3 \end{bmatrix}$

$\Rightarrow 3x - y + 4z = 17$

5.2 Exercise 6

1 Find the Cartesian equations of the following:

(a) a plane through the origin with normal vector $\begin{bmatrix} 2 \\ -3 \\ 1 \end{bmatrix}$;

(b) a plane through the point $(3, 1, -2)$ parallel to the plane of part (a);

(c) a plane through the point $(3, 1, -2)$ with normal vector $\begin{bmatrix} 5 \\ -2 \\ 0 \end{bmatrix}$.

2 OABCDEFG is a unit cube with x-, y- and z-axes as shown.

For each of the following planes, use inspection to write down a normal vector and give the Cartesian equation of the plane.

(a) ACGE   (b) OBFD   (c) ADC

(d) EGB   (e) OABC

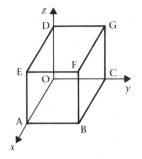

3 A, B and C are 2, 3 and 4 units from the origin along the x-, y- and z-axes.

(a) What is the position vector of C?

(b) Write down the vectors $\overrightarrow{CA}$ and $\overrightarrow{CB}$.

(c) What is the vector equation of the plane ABC?

(d) Write down equations for x, y and z in terms of the parameters λ and μ.

(e) Eliminate λ and μ to find the Cartesian equation of the plane ABC.

(f) What is the normal vector to the plane ABC?

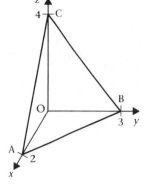

4E A regular octahedron ABCDEF is placed with its vertices on the x-, y- and z-axes, each at one unit from the origin.

(a) Find the Cartesian equations of the planes AEB and DCF.

(b) What do you notice about these two planes?

(c) Find the Cartesian equations of the planes ECB and FAD.

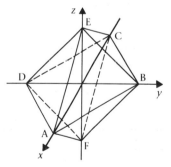

▶ 5.2 **Tasksheet E1 – Intersections (page 561)**

5.2.7 Finding angles

When describing a polyhedron or a crystal, it is often useful to know the angle between adjacent faces, the **dihedral** angle.

It is conventional to consider the angle between two planes to be the angle formed by the two perpendiculars to the line of intersection of the plane.

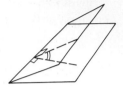

Since it is the *normals* that specify the direction between the planes, the angle between the planes can be found from the angle between the two normals.

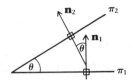

Example 9
Find the angle between:

(a) the planes $3x + y - 2z = 4$ and $2x - y + 5z = 1$

(b) the plane $3x + y - 2z = 4$ and the line $\begin{bmatrix} x \\ y \\ z \end{bmatrix} = \begin{bmatrix} 1 \\ 2 \\ 3 \end{bmatrix} + \lambda \begin{bmatrix} -1 \\ 3 \\ -5 \end{bmatrix}$

Solution

(a)
$$\mathbf{n}_1 = \begin{bmatrix} 3 \\ 1 \\ -2 \end{bmatrix} \qquad \mathbf{n}_2 = \begin{bmatrix} 2 \\ -1 \\ 5 \end{bmatrix}$$

$$\mathbf{n}_1 \cdot \mathbf{n}_2 = 6 - 1 - 10 = -5$$

$$|n_1| = \sqrt{(9 + 1 + 4)} = \sqrt{14}$$

$$|n_2| = \sqrt{(4 + 1 + 25)} = \sqrt{30}$$

$$\mathbf{n}_1 \cdot \mathbf{n}_2 = |n_1| |n_2| \cos \theta \Rightarrow -5 = \sqrt{14}\sqrt{30} \cos \theta$$

$$\Rightarrow \quad \theta = 104°$$

The acute angle between the planes is $76°$.

(b) The direction of the line is given by the vector $\mathbf{b} = \begin{bmatrix} -1 \\ 3 \\ -5 \end{bmatrix}$.

Thus the angle between the line and the normal $\mathbf{n} = \begin{bmatrix} 3 \\ 1 \\ -2 \end{bmatrix}$

is given by $\mathbf{b} \cdot \mathbf{n} = |b|\,|n|\cos\theta$

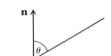

$\Rightarrow \qquad 10 = \sqrt{35}\sqrt{14}\cos\theta$

$\Rightarrow \qquad \theta = 63.1°$

Thus the angle between the line and the plane is
$90° - 63.1° = 26.9°$

5.2 Exercise 7

1 Use the result $\cos\theta = \dfrac{\mathbf{a} \cdot \mathbf{b}}{ab}$ for the angle between two vectors to calculate the angle between the normal vectors for each pair of planes. What is the angle between the planes in each case?

(a) $x + y + z = 5;$ $\qquad 2x + 3y + z = 4$

(b) $x - 3y - 2z = 1;$ $\qquad 5x + 2z = -5$

(c) $x - 2z = 4;$ $\qquad y + 3z = 6$

2 Find the angles between these pairs of lines.

(a) $\begin{bmatrix} x \\ y \end{bmatrix} = \begin{bmatrix} -1 \\ 5 \end{bmatrix} + \lambda \begin{bmatrix} 2 \\ 1 \end{bmatrix};$ $\qquad \begin{bmatrix} x \\ y \end{bmatrix} = \begin{bmatrix} 2 \\ 0 \end{bmatrix} + \mu \begin{bmatrix} -1 \\ 1 \end{bmatrix}$

(b) $\begin{bmatrix} x \\ y \\ z \end{bmatrix} = \begin{bmatrix} 1 \\ 2 \\ 3 \end{bmatrix} + \lambda \begin{bmatrix} -1 \\ 0 \\ 3 \end{bmatrix};$ $\qquad \begin{bmatrix} x \\ y \\ z \end{bmatrix} = \begin{bmatrix} 0 \\ 1 \\ 1 \end{bmatrix} + \mu \begin{bmatrix} -2 \\ 3 \\ 4 \end{bmatrix}$

3 Calculate the angle between the line

$$\begin{bmatrix} x \\ y \\ z \end{bmatrix} = \begin{bmatrix} 1 \\ -2 \\ 1 \end{bmatrix} + \lambda \begin{bmatrix} 2 \\ 1 \\ 1 \end{bmatrix}$$

and the normal vector to the plane $2x + 3y - z = 6$.
What is the angle between the line and the plane?

4 The equations of the faces AEB and ECB of the regular octahedron in question 4E of exercise 6 are

$$x + y + z = 1 \quad \text{and} \quad -x + y + z = 1$$

Calculate the angle between the planes.
What is the dihedral angle of a regular octahedron?

5E OABC is a tetrahedron where O is the origin and A, B, C are the points $(1, 1, 0)$, $(0, 1, 1)$ and $(1, 0, 1)$.

(a) Draw a diagram to show the tetrahedron.

(b) Calculate the lengths of the six edges to show that the tetrahedron is regular.

(c) Find the Cartesian equations of the faces OAB and OAC and calculate the angle between them. What is the dihedral angle of a regular tetrahedron?

(d) Write down the vector equations of the edges BC and OA and find the angle between them. What can be said about opposite pairs of edges of a regular tetrahedron?

(e) Calculate the angle between the edge BC and the face OAC and use the result to calculate the height of the tetrahedron, taking OAC as base.

After working through section 5.2 you should:

1 be able to use vectors in three dimensions;

2 be familiar with vector equations of lines in two and three dimensions;

3 understand the scalar product and know its main properties;

4 be familiar with vector equations and Cartesian equations of planes, and understand the significance of normal vectors;

5 be able to calculate angles in three-dimensional situations involving lines and/or planes.

5 Mathematical methods

.3 Binomials

5.3.1 Binomial expansions

Algebraic expressions which have two terms, for example $a + b$, $2x - 3y$ and $p^2 + 2p$, are known as **binomials**. In the same way, an expression like $a + b + c$, with three terms, is referred to as **trinomial**.

If you expand the brackets for $(a + b)(a + b)$, you obtain the identity

$$(a + b)^2 = a^2 + 2ab + b^2$$

 .3A

1 Expand $(a + b)(a^2 + 2ab + b^2)$ to show that

$$(a + b)^3 = a^3 + 3a^2b + 3ab^2 + b^3$$

2 Find a similar expansion for $(a + b)^4$.

If you include the obvious results that $(a + b)^0 = 1$ and $(a + b)^1 = a + b$ and also include the (usually unnecessary) coefficient of 1, you can tabulate your results as follows.

$$
\begin{array}{llllllll}
(a + b)^0 = & & & & 1 & & & \\
(a + b)^1 = & & & 1a & + & 1b & & \\
(a + b)^2 = & & 1a^2 & + & 2ab & + & 1b^2 & \\
(a + b)^3 = 1a^3 & + & 3a^2b & + & 3ab^2 & + & 1b^3 &
\end{array}
$$

3 (a) Can you spot the pattern produced by the coefficients of the various terms?

   (b) Check whether your answer for $(a + b)^4$ fits the pattern.

   (c) Assuming the pattern continues, write down what you would expect for the expansion of $(a + b)^5$.

   [The answer should have six terms, involving a^5, a^4b, a^3b^2, a^2b^3, ab^4 and b^5.]

You should have spotted that the coefficients of the various terms are the binomial coefficients you may already have met in Pascal's triangle. The pattern continues for *all* positive integer powers of $a + b$.

4E Find $(a + 2b)^4$.

> The binomial expression $(a + b)^n$ can be expanded using the nth line of Pascal's triangle.

To expand $(a + b)^4$, use Pascal's triangle:

$$
\begin{array}{ccccccccc}
 & & & & 1 & & & & \\
 & & & 1 & & 1 & & & \\
 & & 1 & & 2 & & 1 & & \\
 & 1 & & 3 & & 3 & & 1 & \\
1 & & 4 & & 6 & & 4 & & 1 \\
\end{array}
$$

$$\bullet \quad \bullet \quad \bullet \quad \bullet \quad \bullet \quad \bullet \quad \bullet$$

$$(a + b)^4 = a^4 + 4a^3b + 6a^2b^2 + 4ab^3 + b^4$$

The coefficients of a particular power of $a + b$ are formed by adding pairs of coefficients of the previous power, just as in Pascal's triangle. This is illustrated below.

$$(a + b)(1a^3 + 3a^2b + 3ab^2 + 1b^3) = a^4 + 3a^3b \boxed{+3} a^2b^2 + \quad ab^3 +$$
$$a^3b \boxed{+3} a^2b^2 + 3ab^3 + b^4$$

$$\Rightarrow (a + b)^4 = \quad \cdots \boxed{+6} a^2b^2 \cdots$$

The result for $(a + b)^n$ can be extended to any binomial expression.

Example 1
Expand $(2x - 3y)^3$.

Solution

$$((2x) + (-3y))^3 = 1(2x)^3 + 3(2x)^2(-3y) + 3(2x)(-3y)^2 + 1(-3y)^3$$
$$= 8x^3 - 36x^2y + 54xy^2 - 27y^3$$

5.3 Exercise 1

1 Expand:

  (a) $(a + b)^6$ (b) $(p - q)^5$ (c) $(3x + y)^4$ (d) $(1 + z)^6$

2 (a) Expand $(a + b)^3$ and $(a - b)^3$.

  (b) Show that $(a + b)^3 + (a - b)^3 = 2a(a^2 + 3b^2)$.

  (c) Find a corresponding result for $(a + b)^3 - (a - b)^3$.

3E (a) By putting $p = a + b$ and $q = a - b$ in question 2(b), find the factors of $p^3 + q^3$.

  (b) Hence, or otherwise, factorise $p^3 - q^3$.

4E By writing 11 as $10 + 1$, explain the pattern of powers of 11.

5.3.2 Binomial coefficients

If a binomial expansion such as $(a + b)^3$ is expanded to give $1a^3 + 3a^2b + 3ab^2 + 1b^3$, then the coefficients are referred to as **binomial coefficients**. (For example, the binomial coefficient of a^2b is 3.)

The notation $\begin{pmatrix} n \\ r \end{pmatrix}$ is used for binomial coefficients, where n and r are the rows and columns of Pascal's triangle as indicated below.

				r		
n	0	1	2	3	4	5
0	1					
1	1	1				
2	1	2	1			
3	1	3	3	1		
4	1	4	6	4	1	
5	1	5	10	10	5	1

So, for example, $\begin{pmatrix} 5 \\ 0 \end{pmatrix} = 1$, $\begin{pmatrix} 5 \\ 3 \end{pmatrix} = 10$ and so on.

It is also useful to notice the symmetry of the table, so, for example, $\begin{pmatrix} 8 \\ 3 \end{pmatrix} = \begin{pmatrix} 8 \\ 5 \end{pmatrix}$, $\begin{pmatrix} 10 \\ 2 \end{pmatrix} = \begin{pmatrix} 10 \\ 8 \end{pmatrix}$ and so on.

It is sensible to link n to the power of the binomial expansion as follows.

$$1$$

line number 1 $(a + b)^1$ 1 1

line number 2 $(a + b)^2$ 1 2 1

line number 3 $(a + b)^3$ 1 3 3 1

line number 4 $(a + b)^4$ 1 4 6 4 1

The top line therefore corresponds to $n = 0$.

Similarly, the first term in each row corresponds to the coefficient of $a^n b^0$ and is therefore the term corresponding to $r = 0$.

It is easy enough to write down the first few lines of Pascal's triangle. However, if you want the 20th line it is a hard task to write down the preceding 19 lines! The following questions develop a general formula for the binomial coefficients.

.3B

You can always write down the first two terms of any line of Pascal's triangle. The 10th line certainly starts 1   10, but it is not immediately obvious how to write down the next term unless you already know the 9th line.

1 The 4th line is 1   4   6   4   1. Each number is related to the previous number as shown below.

How are the multipliers 4 and $\frac{3}{2}$ related to the multipliers $\frac{2}{3}$ and $\frac{1}{4}$?

2 (a) Find multipliers in a similar form for the 5th line of Pascal's triangle. (Express the multipliers with denominators $1, 2, 3, 4$ and 5.)

  (b) What patterns do you notice?

3 (a) Use the pattern you have found to generate the 6th line.

  (b) Check that your result is correct by using the 5th line to generate the 6th line in the usual way.

4 Use the pattern of multipliers to generate the 10th line of Pascal's triangle.

5E Add up the terms you have generated in question 4. How does the sum act as a check that the terms are correct?

6 Find the first four terms of the 80th line of Pascal's triangle.

The next step is to consider how any individual binomial coefficient can be found independently of any others.

Consider how the method of multipliers is used to generate the 12th line.

$$\times \frac{12}{1} \qquad \times \frac{11}{2} \qquad \times \frac{10}{3} \qquad \times \frac{9}{4}$$

$$1 \longrightarrow \frac{12}{1} \longrightarrow \frac{12 \times 11}{1 \times 2} \longrightarrow \frac{12 \times 11 \times 10}{1 \times 2 \times 3} \longrightarrow \frac{12 \times 11 \times 10 \times 9}{1 \times 2 \times 3 \times 4} \qquad \text{etc.}$$

$$= 12 \qquad\qquad = 66 \qquad\qquad = 220 \qquad\qquad = 495$$

Using $\dbinom{n}{r}$ notation, $\dbinom{12}{1} = \dfrac{12}{1}$, $\dbinom{12}{2} = \dfrac{12 \times 11}{1 \times 2}$,

$$\dbinom{12}{3} = \dfrac{12 \times 11 \times 10}{1 \times 2 \times 3}, \ \dots$$

7 In a similar way, write down $\begin{pmatrix} 12 \\ 5 \end{pmatrix}$.

Results such as these can be simplified using **factorials**. For example $4 \times 3 \times 2 \times 1$ is written 4!, which is read as '4 factorial'. Most calculators have keys labelled $x!$

8 (a) By writing out the factorials and cancelling, explain why
$$\frac{12!}{7!} = 12 \times 11 \times 10 \times 9 \times 8$$

(b) Show that $\begin{pmatrix} 12 \\ 5 \end{pmatrix} = \frac{12!}{5!\,7!}$.

(c) Use your calculator to evaluate $\begin{pmatrix} 12 \\ 5 \end{pmatrix}$.

9 Use factorial notation to explain why $\begin{pmatrix} 12 \\ 4 \end{pmatrix} = \begin{pmatrix} 12 \\ 8 \end{pmatrix}$.

10 Evaluate: (a) $\begin{pmatrix} 12 \\ 9 \end{pmatrix}$ (b) $\begin{pmatrix} 12 \\ 7 \end{pmatrix}$ (c) $\begin{pmatrix} 12 \\ 11 \end{pmatrix}$.

11 Suggest a formula, using factorial notation, for $\begin{pmatrix} n \\ r \end{pmatrix}$ in terms of n and r.

12 (a) What are the values of $\begin{pmatrix} 12 \\ 0 \end{pmatrix}$ and $\begin{pmatrix} 12 \\ 12 \end{pmatrix}$?

(b) How are these expressed in factorial notation, assuming that 0! has a meaning?

(c) How should 0! be defined?

The notation $n!$ (called n factorial) is used to denote
$$n(n-1)(n-2) \times \cdots \times 2 \times 1$$

0! is defined to be equal to 1.

The binomial coefficients are then $\begin{pmatrix} n \\ r \end{pmatrix} = \frac{n!}{r!(n-r)!}$

For example,
$$\begin{pmatrix} 7 \\ 2 \end{pmatrix} = \frac{7!}{2!\,5!} = \frac{7 \times 6 \times 5 \times 4 \times 3 \times 2 \times 1}{2 \times 1 \times 5 \times 4 \times 3 \times 2 \times 1} = \frac{7 \times 6}{2 \times 1} = 21$$

Binomial coefficients may be found directly using some scientific calculators.

The binomial expansion can now be summarised in terms of binomial coefficients. The result is known as the **binomial theorem**.

For n a positive integer,

$$(a + b)^n = \binom{n}{0}a^n b^0 + \binom{n}{1}a^{n-1}b^1 + \binom{n}{2}a^{n-2}b^2 + \cdots$$

$$+ \binom{n}{r}a^{n-r}b^r + \cdots + \binom{n}{n}a^0 b^n$$

where

$$\binom{n}{r} = \frac{n!}{r!(n-r)!}$$

The series is valid for all values of a and b.

5.3 **Exercise 2**

1 Evaluate: (a) $\binom{8}{3}$ (b) $\binom{5}{2}$ (c) $\binom{9}{6}$ (d) $\binom{100}{98}$

2 Expand $(a + b)^7$ using the binomial theorem.

3 Find the first four terms of the expansions of:

(a) $(a - b)^8$ (b) $(2a - 3b)^{10}$ (c) $\left(x^2 - \dfrac{1}{x^2}\right)^6$

4 If $\binom{15}{4} = \binom{15}{a}$ find a.

5 Evaluate: (a) $\dfrac{100!}{80!} \times \dfrac{78!}{99!}$ (b) $\binom{80}{20} \div \binom{80}{19}$

6E (a) Show that $\binom{10}{4} = \binom{9}{3} + \binom{9}{4}$.

(b) Generalise the result in (a) and prove your result.

5.3.3 Binomial series

When the binomial theorem is applied to the function $(1+x)^n$, the resulting series is particularly useful and important. Sir Isaac Newton saw that this result could be extended to powers other than positive integers. The binomial series was Newton's first major discovery, which he published in 1676 in a letter to the Royal Society.

We can use the binomial theorem to obtain the expansion of $(1+x)^n$ as follows.

$$(1+x)^n = 1^n + \binom{n}{1}1^{n-1}x + \binom{n}{2}1^{n-2}x^2 + \binom{n}{3}1^{n-3}x^3 + \cdots + x^n$$

$$= 1 + \frac{n!}{1!(n-1)!}x + \frac{n!}{2!(n-2)!}x^2 + \frac{n!}{3!(n-3)!}x^3 + \cdots + x^n$$

$$= 1 + nx + \frac{n(n-1)}{2!}x^2 + \frac{n(n-1)(n-2)}{3!}x^3 + \cdots + x^n$$

There are $n+1$ terms in the expansion.

A number of possibilities arise which you should now explore. Can you use the binomial theorem when the value of n is not an integer (for example, $(1+x)^{\frac{1}{2}}$) or when n is negative (for example, $(1+x)^{-2}$)?

 .3c

1   $(1+x)^3 = 1 + 3x + 3x^2 + x^3$

(a) Use a graph plotter to plot the graph of the function $(1+x)^3$.

(b) Plot the function $1 + 3x$, taken from the first two terms of the expansion. What do you notice about the line that is produced?

(c) Calculate the values of $1 + 3x$ and $(1+x)^3$ for x from 0.05 to 0.25 at intervals of 0.05. What do you notice about the results?

$1 + 3x$ is a *linear* approximation to $(1+x)^3$ and you will notice from your graphs and your numerical calculations that the approximation is good for small values of x.

2   (a) Compare the graphs of the functions $(1+x)^3$ and $1 + 3x + 3x^2$.

(b) Calculate values of $1 + 3x + 3x^2$ for the same values of x as before and compare them with the values obtained for $(1+x)^3$ and $1 + 3x$.

$1 + 3x + 3x^2$ is a *quadratic* approximation to $(1+x)^3$. This is a better approximation than $1 + 3x$ for small values of x.

3 (a) Find a quadratic approximation to $(1+x)^8$.

   (b) Use a graph plotter to compare the graph of your quadratic approximation with that of $y = (1+x)^8$.

The binomial expansion of $(1+x)^n$ can be written in the form

$$(1+x)^n = 1 + nx + \frac{n(n-1)}{2!}x^2 + \frac{n(n-1)(n-2)}{3!}x^3 + \cdots$$

4 (a) By putting $n = -1$ in the series above, show that a possible quadratic approximation to $(1+x)^{-1}$ is $1 - x + x^2$.

   (b) Use a graph plotter to compare the graphs of $y = (1+x)^{-1}$ and $1 - x + x^2$ using a domain of $-2 < x < 2$ (and $-5 < y < 5$).

   For what range of values of x is the comparison a good one?

5 (a) By putting $n = \frac{1}{2}$ into the binomial expansion, show that a possible quadratic approximation to $\sqrt{(1+x)}$ is $1 + \frac{1}{2}x - \frac{1}{8}x^2$.

   (b) Use a graph plotter to compare the graphs of $\sqrt{(1+x)}$ and $1 + \frac{1}{2}x - \frac{1}{8}x^2$. For what range of values of x is the comparison a good one?

6 Use the binomial series to show that $1 + \frac{1}{2}x - \frac{1}{8}x^2 + \frac{1}{16}x^3$ is a possible cubic approximation to $\sqrt{(1+x)}$. Check your result using a graph plotter.

Questions 4 to 6 suggest that the following is true for *all* values of n, provided x is small.

$$(1+x)^n = 1 + nx + \frac{n(n-1)x^2}{2!} + \frac{n(n-1)(n-2)x^3}{3!} + \cdots$$

The result is known as the **binomial series**.

7E Further evidence to support the use of the binomial series may be found by summing a geometric series.

   (a) Find the sum to infinity of $1 - x + x^2 - x^3 + \cdots$

   (b) Expand $(1+x)^{-1}$ from the binomial series. How does your answer relate to the sum in (a)?

8E Work out $(1 + \frac{1}{2}x - \frac{1}{8}x^2)^2$ and comment on your answer.

You have seen that the binomial expansion appears to generalise to values of n which are rational and/or negative, though with the restriction that the result only works for $-1 < x < 1$.

The following result, although *not proven here*, is always true.

Binomial series   For $-1 < x < 1$ and *any* value of n,
$$(1 + x)^n = 1 + nx + \frac{n(n-1)}{2!}x^2 + \frac{n(n-1)(n-2)}{3!}x^3 + \cdots$$

Example 2

Show that $\sqrt[3]{(1 - 2x)} = 1 - \frac{2}{3}x - \frac{4}{9}x^2 - \frac{40}{81}x^3 + \cdots$

Solution

$$(1 - 2x)^{\frac{1}{3}} = 1 + \frac{1}{3}(-2x) + \frac{(\frac{1}{3})(-\frac{2}{3})}{2!}(-2x)^2 + \frac{(\frac{1}{3})(-\frac{2}{3})(-\frac{5}{3})}{3!}(-2x)^3 + \cdots$$

$$= 1 - \frac{2}{3}x - \frac{4}{9}x^2 - \frac{40}{81}x^3 + \cdots$$

The result is valid for $-1 < -2x < 1$

$$\Rightarrow \quad -\tfrac{1}{2} < -x < \tfrac{1}{2}$$

$$\Rightarrow \quad -\tfrac{1}{2} < x < \tfrac{1}{2}$$

Example 3

Show that, for small values of x, $\dfrac{1}{(1+x)^2} \approx 1 - 2x$

Solution

$$\frac{1}{(1+x)^2} = (1 + x)^{-2} = 1 + (-2)x + \frac{(-2)(-3)}{2!}x^2 + \cdots$$

$$\approx 1 - 2x \quad \text{(where } x^2 \text{ and higher powers of } x \text{ are ignored)}$$

5.3 Exercise 3

1   Use the formula for the binomial series to expand the following as far as the term in x^3.

(a) $(1 + x)^{\frac{1}{3}}$ (b) $(1 + x)^{-3}$

2. Use the laws of indices to write the following in the form $(1 + x)^n$. (There is no need to expand the functions.)

   (a) $\sqrt{(1 + x)}$ (b) $\dfrac{1}{(1 + x)^3}$ (c) $\sqrt[5]{(1 + x)}$ (d) $\dfrac{1}{\sqrt[3]{(1 + x)}}$

3. Expand the following as far as the term in x^3.

   (a) $\dfrac{1}{(1 + x)^4}$ (b) $\sqrt{(1 - 2x)}$ (c) $\dfrac{1}{\sqrt{(1 + x^2)}}$

4. (a) Show that $\sqrt{(9 - 18x)} = 3\sqrt{(1 - 2x)}$.

   (b) Hence show that $\sqrt{(9 - 18x)} \approx 3 - 3x - \dfrac{3}{2}x^2 - \dfrac{3}{2}x^3 - \dfrac{15}{8}x^4$, for $-\dfrac{1}{2} < x < \dfrac{1}{2}$.

5. Find the first three terms of the series expansion of:

   (a) $\dfrac{1}{\sqrt{(4 + 4x)}}$ (b) $\dfrac{1}{(3 + 3x)^2}$

6. The binomial expansion for $\sqrt{(1 + x)} = 1 + \dfrac{x}{2} - \dfrac{x^2}{8} + \dfrac{x^3}{16} \cdots$

   (a) Why would it be incorrect to conclude that

   $$\sqrt{50} = \sqrt{(1 + 49)} = 1 + \frac{49}{2} - \frac{49^2}{8} + \frac{49^3}{16} \cdots ?$$

   (b) Show that $\sqrt{50} = 7\sqrt{\left(1 + \dfrac{1}{49}\right)}$ and hence find an approximate value for $\sqrt{50}$ using the binomial expansion for $\sqrt{(1 + x)}$.

7E Einstein's theory of relativity predicts that if a stick of length l moves with velocity v in the direction of its length it will shrink by a factor $\left(1 - \dfrac{v^2}{c^2}\right)^{\frac{1}{2}}$ where c is the speed of light.

   (a) Show that for low speeds this factor is approximately $1 - \dfrac{v^2}{2c^2}$.

   (b) Hence show that if $v = \dfrac{c}{3}$, the stick shrinks to approximately 94% of its original length.

5.3.4 Error and relative error

Much of science and engineering is dependent on measurement. Since all measurement is subject to error, it is important to understand how to deal with these errors when making calculations. You may have met some of these ideas before – the following example will serve as a reminder. Later, you will see how the binomial theorem can extend your understanding of the theory of errors.

The accuracy of a measurement depends on the instrument used for measuring. For example, using a ruler you might measure the length of a line to be between 43 and 44 mm. This can be written as 43.5 ± 0.5 mm.

Example 4

The measurements of the length and width of a rectangle are as shown.

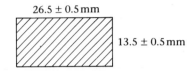

26.5 ± 0.5 mm

13.5 ± 0.5 mm

(a) What are the greatest and least possible values for

    (i) the perimeter   (ii) the area?

(b) (i) Express the perimeter of the rectangle in the form $p \pm e$.

    (ii) Express the area in the form $a \pm e$.

Solution

(a)   (i) Minimum perimeter $= 2(26 + 13) = 78$ mm

         Maximum perimeter $= 2(27 + 14) = 82$ mm

   (ii) Minimum area $= 26 \times 13 = 338$ mm^2

         Maximum area $= 27 \times 14 = 378$ mm^2

(b)   (i) Perimeter $= 80 \pm 2$ mm

   (ii) Area $= 358 \pm 20$ mm^2

Note that the perimeter is found by adding four numbers, each with an 'error' of 0.5 mm. The error in the perimeter is then found to be $4 \times 0.5 = 2$ mm.

However, multiplying numbers with errors is not as straightforward. This is investigated later, where the idea of **relative error** is introduced.

Expressing a result in the form $a \pm e$ is a way of stating that the result lies between $a - e$ and $a + e$. The 'error', e, measures the largest possible difference between the actual value and the number a.

Example 5

An isosceles triangle has perimeter 72 ± 1.5 mm and base 18 ± 0.5 mm.

Express a in the form $a \pm e$.

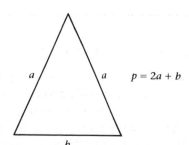

a a $p = 2a + b$

b

Solution

$$2a = p - b$$

Maximum value of $2a = 72 + 1.5 - (18 - 0.5) = 54 + 2 \, \text{mm}$

Maximum value of $a = \frac{1}{2}(54 + 2) = 27 + 1 \, \text{mm}$

Minimum value of $2a = 72 - 1.5 - (18 + 0.5) = 54 - 2 \, \text{mm}$

Minimum value of $a = \frac{1}{2}(54 - 2) = 27 - 1 \, \text{mm}$

$$a = 27 \pm 1 \, \text{mm}$$

In example 5, the error in $p - b$ was found by *adding* the errors in p and b. The error in a was then found by *halving* the error in $2a$.

These are particular cases of the following general result.

> If measurements are added or subtracted, then the errors add.
> $$(a \pm e) + (b \pm f) = (a + b) \pm (e + f)$$
> $$(a \pm e) - (b \pm f) = (a - b) \pm (e + f)$$
>
> If a measurement is multiplied by a precise number then the error is also multiplied by that number.
> $$k(a \pm e) = ka \pm ke$$

We now investigate the effect of multiplying and dividing measurements.

 .3D

1 A rectangle has area $350 \pm 10 \, \text{mm}^2$ and base $14 \pm 0.5 \, \text{mm}$. Find the greatest and least possible values for the height h. Hence express h in the form $a \pm e$.

When measurements are multiplied or divided, the connection between their errors and the error in the resultant is by no means obvious. However, the binomial series can be used to show that simple connections are possible when the original measurements are in the form $1 \pm e$.

2 (a) Use the binomial series to show that, for small r,
$$(1 + r)^2 \approx 1 + 2r$$
$$\frac{1}{1 + r} \approx 1 - r$$

   (b) The length of the side of a square is $1 \pm 0.05 \, \text{m}$. Use the results of part (a) to find approximate bounds for

   (i) the area of the square,

   (ii) the reciprocal of the length of the side.

More generally, any two numbers of the form $1 \pm e$ can be multiplied or divided easily as is shown in question 3.

3 (a) Show that $(1 \pm r)(1 \pm s) \approx [1 \pm (r + s)]$ if rs is small enough to be ignored.

(b) By expressing $\dfrac{1 \pm r}{1 \pm s}$ as $(1 \pm r)(1 \pm s)^{-1}$, show that

$$\frac{1 \pm r}{1 \pm s} \approx 1 \pm (r + s)$$

4 Express the area in question 1 as $350(1 \pm \frac{1}{35})$ and the base length as $14(1 \pm \frac{1}{28})$. The height, h, is therefore $\dfrac{350}{14} \times \dfrac{(1 \pm \frac{1}{35})}{(1 \pm \frac{1}{28})}$.

Use the result from question 3 to write the height, h mm, in the form $h \pm e$. How does this compare with your answer to question 1?

A measurement, $a \pm e$, can be written as $a(1 \pm r)$.

The quantity $r = \dfrac{e}{a}$ is called the **relative error**.

Unlike absolute errors, relative errors combine in a straightforward way when measurements are multiplied or divided.

If measurements are multiplied or divided and if the relative errors are small, then you can add the relative errors to obtain the approximate relative error of the result.

$$a(1 \pm r) \times b(1 \pm s) \approx ab[1 \pm (r + s)]$$

$$\frac{a(1 \pm r)}{b(1 \pm s)} \approx \frac{a}{b}[1 \pm (r + s)]$$

Example 6

A piece of wire, length l cm, is bent to form three sides of a rectangle.

$l = 2a + b$

If $l = 20 \pm 0.4$ cm and $b = 8 \pm 0.2$ cm, calculate:

(a) the value of a (b) the area of the rectangle

Solution

(a) $2a = l - b$

$\quad 2a = (20 \pm 0.4) - (8 \pm 0.2) = 12 \pm 0.6$

$\quad a = 6 \pm 0.3 \,\text{cm}$

(b) $ab = (6 \pm 0.3)(8 \pm 0.2)$

$\quad\quad = 6(1 \pm 0.05) \times 8(1 \pm 0.025)$

$\quad\quad \approx 48(1 \pm 0.075)$

$\quad\quad \approx 48 \pm 3.6 \,\text{cm}^2$

5.3 Exercise 4

1 (a) Calculate the area of the rectangle in example 6 (to 1 decimal place) if the wire is bent so that $b = 19 \pm 0.2 \,\text{cm}$.

(b) Use the idea of relative error to explain why the calculation is so inaccurate.

2 Calculate the height of the trapezium shown below if the area is $125 \pm 2.5 \,\text{cm}^2$.

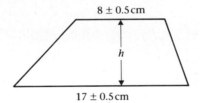

$8 \pm 0.5 \,\text{cm}$

h

$17 \pm 0.5 \,\text{cm}$

3 In a mechanics practical, a ball (travelling at a constant speed) is measured as travelling 50 cm in 1.32 seconds. Calculate its speed if the student can measure distance to the nearest centimetre and time to ± 0.1 second. (Give your answer in cm s^{-1} to 1 decimal place.)

After working through section 5.3 you should:

1 be able to use Pascal's triangle to find $(a + b)^n$ for small integral values of n;

2 know that $n! = n \times (n - 1) \times \cdots \times 2 \times 1$;

3 understand and be able to use the notation for binomial coefficients
$$\binom{n}{r} = \frac{n!}{r!(n - r)!};$$

4 be able to expand $(a + b)^n$ using the binomial theorem;

5 know how to use the binomial series and be aware of its limitations;

6 be able to calculate errors and relative errors when measurements are combined in various ways.

5 Mathematical methods

Miscellaneous exercise 5

1 Use the sine and cosine rules to find the remaining sides and angles of triangles PQR and XYZ, given that

(a) PQ = 6.1 cm, QR = 7.4 cm, angle QPR = 43°

(b) XY = 19 km, XZ = 33 km, angle YXZ = 27°

2 If the angle α is obtuse and $\cos 2\alpha = \frac{1}{8}$, calculate $\cos \alpha$ without using a calculator.

3 If $\sin \theta = \cos 2\theta$ show that $2s^2 + s - 1 = 0$ where $s = \sin \theta$. Solve the equation for $0 \le \theta \le 2\pi$.

4 If $2 \sin^2 \phi = 5 \cos \phi - 1$, deduce a quadratic equation for $\cos \phi$ and find all solutions in the domain $0° \le \phi \le 360°$.

5 (a) Without using a calculator show that $\sin 15° = \dfrac{\sqrt{3} - 1}{2\sqrt{2}}$.

(b) Use a double-angle formula to show that $\cos 22\frac{1}{2}° = \frac{1}{2}\sqrt{(2 + \sqrt{2})}$.

6 Find the vector equation of the straight line

(a) through the origin and the point $(3, 2, -1)$,

(b) through $(6, 1, 3)$ parallel to the straight line in part (a).

7 Write down a vector equation

(a) of the line AB

(b) of the plane ABC

where A is $(1, 2, 3)$, B is $(4, -5, 6)$ and C is $(7, 8, -9)$.

Does the point $(12, -8, -6)$ lie in the plane ABC?

8 Find the equations of the planes through the given points and parallel to the given planes.

(a) $2x - 3y - z = 3$, $(1, 0, 1)$ (b) $4x - y = 6$, $(5, 1, -2)$

9 Find the angle between the lines

   (a) $3x + y = 2$ and $4x - 3y = 1$

   (b) $5x + 12y + 3 = 0$ and $12x + 5y = 11$

10 Find the angle between the planes

   (a) $3x + 6y - 2z = 3$ and $8x - 4y + z = 1$

   (b) $2x + 3y - z = 0$ and $x - y - z = 4$

11 Use the binomial theorem to find approximations in the form of cubic polynomials to the following functions for small values of h:

   (a) $\dfrac{1}{(1+h)^3}$ (b) $\sqrt[3]{(1+h)}$ (c) $\sqrt{(1-h)}$

12 (a) Writing $\sqrt{(4+h)}$ as $2\sqrt{(1+\frac{1}{4}h)}$, use the binomial theorem to find a cubic polynomial which approximates to $\sqrt{(4+h)}$ for small h.

   (b) Evaluate $\sqrt{4.2}$ to three decimal places.

   (c) Writing $\sqrt{15}$ as $\sqrt{(16-1)} = 4\sqrt{(1-\frac{1}{16})}$ and using the binomial theorem, find $\sqrt{15}$ to three decimal places.

13 Simplify:

   (a) $\cos\left(\frac{1}{2}\pi + \theta\right)$, $\sin(\pi - \theta)$, $\cos(\theta + \pi)$ (b) $\dfrac{\sin^3 \theta}{1 - \cos^2 \theta}$

   (c) $\sin 3\theta \cos \theta + \cos 3\theta \sin \theta$ (d) $\dfrac{\tan 2\theta - \tan \theta}{1 + \tan 2\theta \tan \theta}$

14 (a) Sketch the curves $y = \tan x$ and $y = 2 \sin 2x$ on the same diagram for $-\frac{1}{2}\pi \le x \le \frac{1}{2}\pi$.

   (b) Show that at the points where they meet, apart from the origin, $\cos^2 x = \frac{1}{4}$, and determine the coordinates of these points of intersection.

6 Calculus methods 1

.1 The chain rule

6.1.1 Functions of functions

You already know how to differentiate polynomial functions such as $x^3 + 2x^2 - 3$ and other simple functions such as $\sin x$ and e^x. Here we extend these methods to more complicated functions. We consider **composite functions**, which you can think of as functions of other functions. Previously you have used function notation to represent such relationships.

Example 1
If $f(x) = 3x + 7$ and $g(x) = x^3$, find $fg(x)$ and $gf(x)$.

Solution

$$fg(x) = f(x^3)$$
$$= 3x^3 + 7$$
$$gf(x) = g(3x + 7)$$
$$= (3x + 7)^3$$

We now examine the rates of change of composite functions. Initially, only linear relationships will be considered.

 .1A

A rod with initial temperature $50\,°C$ is being heated so that its temperature increases by $2\,°C$ per minute. What is C, the temperature in degrees celsius, after t minutes?

To convert from degrees celsius to degrees fahrenheit, multiply by 1.8 and add on 32. Express F, the temperature in degrees fahrenheit after t minutes, in terms of C and then in terms of t.

What are $\dfrac{dF}{dt}$, $\dfrac{dF}{dC}$ and $\dfrac{dC}{dt}$? Can you find a connection between these rates of change? Think of other examples which involve two linear functions and see if there is a similar relationship.

If z is a function of y and y is a function of x, then the relationship

$$\frac{dz}{dx} = \frac{dz}{dy} \times \frac{dy}{dx}$$

is easy to prove for linear functions such as $z = my + c$ and $y = nx + d$.

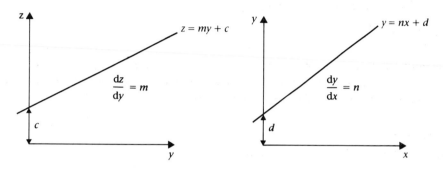

Then
$$z = m(nx + d) + c$$

$$\Rightarrow \quad z = mnx + md + c$$

$$\Rightarrow \frac{dz}{dx} = mn$$

and so
$$\frac{dz}{dx} = \frac{dz}{dy} \times \frac{dy}{dx}$$

This relationship is called the **chain rule**.

If z is a linear function of y and y is a linear function of x, then to find $\dfrac{dz}{dx}$ it is not in fact necessary to first express z in terms of x. This would be an especially useful result if the chain rule were true for non-linear functions as well. It may very well extend to non-linear functions; as you saw earlier, if you zoom in at any chosen point on a **locally straight** function, then it will look increasingly like a linear function. You might, therefore, expect the chain rule to be true for any locally straight functions.

For example, $y = \sin x^3$ is a composite of the locally straight functions $y = \sin u$ and $u = x^3$.

If the chain rule does work for non-linear functions then

$$\frac{dy}{dx} = \frac{dy}{du} \times \frac{du}{dx} \quad \text{where} \quad \frac{dy}{du} = \cos u \quad \text{and} \quad \frac{du}{dx} = 3x^2$$

$$\Rightarrow \frac{dy}{dx} = (\cos u) \times (3x^2)$$

$$= (\cos x^3) \times (3x^2)$$

$$= 3x^2 \cos x^3$$

The example above shows that if the chain rule works, then

$$f(x) = \sin x^3 \Rightarrow f'(x) = 3x^2 \cos x^3$$

You can check this for any particular value of x by using a numerical method for differentiating the function and comparing it with the above formula for the derivative. Alternatively, you could use a graphical calculator or a computer to numerically differentiate the function for several different values of x and then plot the $(x, f'(x))$ points as a graph. You can then superimpose $y = 3x^2 \cos x^3$ and check that the graphs are the same.

 6 .1B

1 Assume that the chain rule holds for any locally straight functions and use it to find $\dfrac{dy}{dx}$ if:

(a) $y = u^3$ and $u = \sin x$ (i.e. $y = \sin^3 x$)

(b) $y = e^u$ and $u = x^2$

(c) $y = u^2$ and $u = e^x$

2 Check the answers you have obtained for question 1 by a numerical method. (When you check (a), note that x is in radians, of course.)

Example 2
Water being poured into a paddling pool spreads at such a rate that the area in square metres covered after t minutes is $S = (5 + 4t)^2$.

(a) Find the rate at which the area is increasing after 2 minutes by multiplying out $(5 + 4t)^2$ and differentiating with respect to t.

(b) Alternatively, let $R = 5 + 4t$ so that $S = R^2$. Find $\dfrac{dS}{dt}$ by considering $\dfrac{dS}{dR} \times \dfrac{dR}{dt}$. Check that your results agree.

Solution

(a) $S = 25 + 40t + 16t^2$

$$\Rightarrow \frac{dS}{dt} = 40 + 32t$$

When $t = 2$, $\dfrac{dS}{dt} = 104$

(b) $\dfrac{dS}{dR} = 2R$, $\dfrac{dR}{dt} = 4$

$$\Rightarrow \frac{dS}{dt} = \frac{dS}{dR} \times \frac{dR}{dt} = 2R \times 4 = 8R = 8(5 + 4t) = 40 + 32t$$

When $t = 2$, $R = 13$ and so $\dfrac{dS}{dt} = 104$.

Example 3

Find $\dfrac{dy}{dx}$ when:

(a) $y = e^{(x^2+1)}$ (b) $y = \ln(3x^2 + 1)$

Solution

(a) $y = e^{(x^2+1)}$ is a composite function of the two locally straight functions
$y = e^u$ and $u = x^2 + 1$. Using the chain rule,

$$\frac{dy}{dx} = \frac{dy}{du} \times \frac{du}{dx}$$

$$= e^u \times 2x$$

$$\Rightarrow \frac{dy}{dx} = 2x\, e^{x^2+1}$$

(b) $y = \ln(3x^2 + 1)$

Let $y = \ln u$ where $u = 3x^2 + 1$

$$\frac{dy}{dx} = \frac{dy}{du} \times \frac{du}{dx}$$

$$= \frac{1}{u} \times 6x$$

$$\Rightarrow \frac{dy}{dx} = \frac{6x}{3x^2 + 1}$$

Expressions such as $(x^2 + 3x)^4$ and $\sin(x^2)$ can be differentiated rapidly once the stages of their composition have been recognised.

For example, to differentiate $(x^2 + 3x)^4$, let $y = u^4$, where $u = x^2 + 3x$.

Then $\dfrac{dy}{dx} = \dfrac{dy}{du} \times \dfrac{du}{dx}$.

The derivative is therefore

$$4(x^2 + 3x)^3 \times (\text{derivative of } x^2 + 3x) = 4(2x + 3)(x^2 + 3x)^3$$

To differentiate $\sin(x^2)$, let $y = \sin u$, where $u = x^2$.

The derivative is therefore

$$\cos(x^2) \times (\text{derivative of } x^2) = 2x \cos(x^2)$$

6.1 Exercise 1

1 Find $\dfrac{dy}{dx}$ for each of the following by (a) using the chain rule and (b) multiplying out the brackets.

  (i) $y = (x + 1)^2$ (ii) $y = (2x - 1)^2$ (iii) $y = (x^2 - 2)^2$

  Show that your answers agree in each case.

2 Find $\dfrac{dy}{dx}$ for each of the following. You do not need to multiply out the brackets in your answers.

  (a) $y = (x^2 + 3)^4$ (b) $y = (5 + 2x)^5$
  (c) $y = (2x^2 - 3x)^3$ (d) $y = (x^3 - 3x^2)^4$

3 Differentiate each of the following. Hence find the gradient of each graph at the point $(0, 1)$.

  (a) $y = \cos x^2$ (b) $y = \sin 2x + 1$ (c) $y = e^{3x}$

4 Differentiate: (a) $\cos x^3$ (b) $\sin^3 x$ (c) $2\cos^4 x$

5 You have already discovered by numerical methods that the derivative of $\sin 2x$ appears to be $2 \cos 2x$.

  It is possible to obtain this result using the chain rule and making a substitution for $2x$.

  If $u = 2x$, then $y = \sin u$. Write down $\dfrac{dy}{du}$ and $\dfrac{du}{dx}$ and so find $\dfrac{dy}{dx}$.

6 Use the chain rule to show that the derivative of $\cos 3x$ is $-3 \sin 3x$.

7 Use the chain rule to obtain an expression for the derivative of $\sin ax$, where a is any constant.

8 Differentiate:

(a) e^{3x} (b) $\sin^2 x$ (c) e^{x^2} (d) $3\cos 2x$ (e) $2(x^2 + 1)^3$

9 A balloon is inflated at a rate of $200\,\text{cm}^3$ per second.

After t seconds, when the balloon has radius $r\,\text{cm}$ and volume $V\,\text{cm}^3$, the following formulas apply.

$$V = 200t \quad \text{and} \quad V = \tfrac{4}{3}\pi r^3$$

(a) Write down $\dfrac{dV}{dt}$ and $\dfrac{dV}{dr}$.

(b) By the chain rule, $\dfrac{dV}{dt} = \dfrac{dV}{dr} \times \dfrac{dr}{dt}$.

Use this to work out an expression for $\dfrac{dr}{dt}$ and so find the rate at which the radius is changing when $t = 1$.

10 When a hot-air balloon is being inflated, the balloonist finds that a good rule of thumb is that after t minutes the radius, r metres, is given by $r = 3 + 0.04t^2$. The balloon can be assumed to be roughly spherical.

(a) Work out expressions for $\dfrac{dr}{dt}$ and for $\dfrac{dV}{dr}$.

(b) Combine these two expressions to find $\dfrac{dV}{dt}$.

(c) How fast is the volume increasing after 2 minutes?

11 An ice cube is melting, and at time t hours it has the form of a cube of side $x\,\text{cm}$ and volume $V\,\text{cm}^3$.

(a) Find $\dfrac{dV}{dx}$ in terms of x.

(b) If $x = 4 - 0.5t$, write down $\dfrac{dx}{dt}$ and so find $\dfrac{dV}{dt}$.

(c) At what rate is the volume changing when $t = 2$?

12 Differentiate: (a) $\sin^2 2x$ (b) $3\cos^2 4x$ (c) $e^{\cos x}$

6.1.2 Applications to integration

The derivative of $\sin 2x$ is $2 \cos 2x$. It follows that

$$\int 2 \cos 2x \, dx = \sin 2x + c$$

and

$$\int \cos 2x \, dx = \tfrac{1}{2} \sin 2x + c$$

Being able to differentiate using the chain rule greatly increases the number of functions you are able to integrate. You need to know what type of integral function you are looking for.

Example 4

Find $\displaystyle\int_0^1 (2x - 1)^4 \, dx$.

Solution

First, try differentiating $(2x - 1)^5$.

$$y = (2x - 1)^5 \Rightarrow \frac{dy}{dx} = 5(2x - 1)^4 \times 2 = 10(2x - 1)^4$$

$$\text{So} \int_0^1 10(2x - 1)^4 \, dx = \Big[(2x - 1)^5 \Big]_0^1$$

$$\Rightarrow \int_0^1 (2x - 1)^4 \, dx = \frac{1}{10} \Big[(2x - 1)^5 \Big]_0^1$$

$$= \frac{1}{10} [1^5 - (-1)^5] = 0.2$$

6.1 Exercise 2

1 Write down the integrals of:

   (a) $\cos 3x$ (b) $\sin \tfrac{1}{2} x$ (c) $2 \sin 5x$ (d) e^{2x}

2 Find:

   (a) $\displaystyle\int_1^2 e^{0.5x} \, dx$ (b) $\displaystyle\int_{-1}^0 \sin 2x \, dx$

   (c) $\displaystyle\int_0^2 3 \cos \tfrac{1}{2} x \, dx$ (d) $\displaystyle\int_0^1 (2x + 3)^2 \, dx$

3   Work out the coordinates of the points A, B and C and then evaluate the shaded areas.

(a)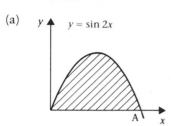

(b)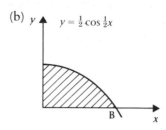

(c)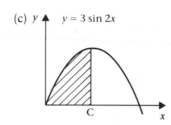

4E If $y = \sin x^2$, $\dfrac{dy}{dx} = 2x \cos x^2$.

Use a numerical method to check if $\displaystyle\int_1^2 \cos x^2 \, dx = \left[\dfrac{1}{2x} \sin x^2\right]_1^2$.

Try to explain what you find.

5E Some of these functions can be integrated by the methods of this section. Integrate as many of them as possible.

(a) $\cos\frac{1}{2}x$ (b) $e^{2.5x}$ (c) $(x^2 - 3)^3$

(d) $(5x + 3)^4$ (e) $\sin 5x$ (f) $\sin x^3$

6E Since $\dfrac{d}{dx}(\sin x^2) = 2x \cos x^2$, $\displaystyle\int x \cos x^2 \, dx = \frac{1}{2}\sin x^2 + c$

Find the following integrals.

(a) $\displaystyle\int x \sin x^2 \, dx$ (b) $\displaystyle\int x^2 e^{x^3} \, dx$ (c) $\displaystyle\int 2x(2x^2 + 1)^4 \, dx$

7E Use the identity $\cos 2x = 1 - 2\sin^2 x$ to find $\displaystyle\int_0^1 \sin^2 x \, dx$.

6.1.3 Small increments

One application of calculus is the calculation of small changes in one variable which are brought about by small changes in a related variable. For example, suppose the radius of a balloon is increased by 1%; by what percentage is the volume of the balloon increased?

Suppose that $y = f(x)$ and x is subjected to a small change δx, that is, it increases from x to $x + \delta x$. This will cause a change in y, from y to $y + \delta y$. You need to calculate the change, δy, in y brought about by the small change in x, as illustrated in the graph.

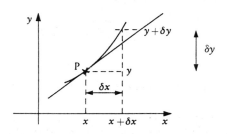

The gradient of the curve at P is $\dfrac{dy}{dx}$, but is also approximately equal to $\dfrac{\delta y}{\delta x}$ (for small changes).

$$\frac{\delta y}{\delta x} \approx \frac{dy}{dx}$$

or

$$\delta y \approx \left(\frac{dy}{dx}\right)\delta x$$

Example 5
A sphere of radius 5 cm increases its radius by 0.1 cm as a result of heating. Calculate the change in the surface area and the volume of the sphere.

Solution
Let A be the surface area and V the volume of the sphere.

$$A = 4\pi r^2$$

$$\frac{dA}{dr} = 8\pi r$$

When $r = 5$ cm, $\dfrac{dA}{dr} = 40\pi$

So, $\qquad \delta A \approx \left(\dfrac{dA}{dr}\right)\delta r = 40\pi \times 0.1$

$$= 4\pi$$

The area increases by about 4π cm^2.

Similarly,

$$V = \tfrac{4}{3}\pi r^3$$

$$\frac{dV}{dr} = 4\pi r^2$$

When $r = 5\,\mathrm{cm}$, $\dfrac{dV}{dr} = 100\pi$

So, $\qquad \delta V \approx \left(\dfrac{dV}{dr}\right)\delta r = 100\pi \times 0.1$

$$= 10\pi$$

The volume increases by about $10\pi\,\mathrm{cm}^3$.

Example 6

It is suspected that there is an error of 1% in the measurement of the sides of a cube. Calculate the percentage error in the calculated values of the surface area and the volume of the cube.

Solution

Suppose the cube has side x, area A and volume V.

$$A = 6x^2 \quad \text{and} \quad \frac{\delta x}{x} = 0.01 \qquad \text{(i.e. a 1\% error in } x\text{)}$$

$$\frac{dA}{dx} = 12x, \quad \text{so} \quad \delta A \approx \left(\frac{dA}{dx}\right)\delta x = 12x\,\delta x$$

Dividing by A $(= x^2)$,

$$\frac{\delta A}{A} \approx 12x\frac{\delta x}{6x^2} = 2\frac{\delta x}{x}$$

$$= 2 \times 0.01$$

$$= 0.02 \qquad \text{(i.e. 2\%)}$$

There is a 2% error in the area.

$$V = x^3$$

$$\frac{dV}{dx} = 3x^2 \quad \text{and} \quad \delta V \approx 3x^2\delta x$$

$$\frac{\delta V}{V} \approx 3x^2\frac{\delta x}{x^3} = 3\frac{\delta x}{x}$$

$$= 3 \times 0.01$$

$$= 0.03$$

There is a 3% error in the calculated volume.

This confirms the result in section 5.3 that an $r\%$ error in x leads to an approximate error of $nr\%$ in x^n.

6.1 Exercise 3

1 A cylinder has a height of 10 cm and a base radius of 6 cm.

(a) If the radius increases by 0.1 cm, calculate the change in the volume of the cylinder. (The height remains fixed.)

(b) If the radius remains fixed but the height increases by 0.2 cm, calculate the change in the volume.

2 The time T taken for a planet to revolve around the Sun is related to the mean distance, r, of the planet from the Sun by the formula

$$T = kr^{\frac{3}{2}}$$

If the Earth's orbit changed so that its mean distance from the Sun were to be increased by 2%, calculate how much longer the year would become.

3 A gravel heap is in the shape of a cone with its radius roughly equal to its height.

(a) The height of the heap is 10 m. If 0.5 m^3 of gravel is added to the heap, calculate the increase in height of the cone.

(b) If gravel is being added to the cone at a rate of 8 m^3 h^{-1}, find the rate at which the height of the gravel heap is increasing.

4 The radius of a spherical balloon is decreased by 1.5%. Calculate the percentage reduction in its volume.

5 Each week a factory produces N thousand topsy-turvies. The cost of production is reckoned to be £1000C, where $C = (N^2 + 5)^{\frac{1}{3}}$. At a certain time, $N = 2$ and N is increasing at the rate 0.1 per week.

(a) Calculate $\dfrac{\mathrm{d}C}{\mathrm{d}N}$. What does this represent?

(b) At what rate (in £ per week) is the weekly cost of production rising?

6.1.4 Inverse functions and x^n

You know how to differentiate x^2 but not the inverse of this function, $\sqrt{x}$. The chain rule enables you to find the derivative in such cases, using the fact that

$$\frac{\mathrm{d}x}{\mathrm{d}y} \times \frac{\mathrm{d}y}{\mathrm{d}x} = 1$$

This can be shown easily as follows.

For the locally straight curve shown, $\dfrac{dy}{dx} = \dfrac{b}{a}$ at P. The graph of the inverse function is a reflection of the graph of $y = f(x)$ in the line $y = x$. Its gradient at the equivalent point in P will be $\dfrac{dx}{dy}$. Since, in the reflection, the x- and y-coordinates are interchanged,

$$\frac{dx}{dy} = \frac{a}{b}$$

Hence, $\dfrac{dx}{dy} \times \dfrac{dy}{dx} = \dfrac{a}{b} \times \dfrac{b}{a} = 1$

This result may be written as

$$\frac{dx}{dy} = 1 \div \frac{dy}{dx}$$

y = f(x)

b

P

a

Example 7
Find the derivative of $y = \sqrt{x}$.

Solution

$$x = y^2$$

$$\Rightarrow \frac{dx}{dy} = 2y \quad \Rightarrow \quad \frac{dy}{dx} = \frac{1}{2y} = \frac{1}{2\sqrt{x}} \quad \text{or} \quad \frac{dy}{dx} = \frac{1}{2} x^{-\frac{1}{2}}$$

You already know that if n is a positive integer, then

$$y = x^n \Rightarrow \frac{dy}{dx} = nx^{n-1}$$

The working above shows that the rule is also applicable when $n = \frac{1}{2}$. In fact the result is generally true.

If $y = x^n$, then $\dfrac{dy}{dx} = nx^{n-1}$ for all values of n.

6.1 Exercise 4

1 (a) Show that the derivative of $\dfrac{1}{x^2}$ is $-\dfrac{2}{x^3}$.

(b) Find the derivative of $(1 + x)\sqrt{x}$.

2 Differentiate:

(a) $\sqrt[3]{x}$ (i.e. $x^{\frac{1}{3}}$) (b) $\dfrac{1}{x}$ (c) x^{-3} (d) $\dfrac{1}{x^2} + \sqrt{x}$

3 Find the derivative of $\sqrt[n]{x}$ (i.e. $x^{\frac{1}{n}}$) with respect to x.

4 If $y = \ln x$, then $x = e^y$.

Write down $\dfrac{dx}{dy}$ and use this to find $\dfrac{dy}{dx}$. Hence explain why the derivative of $\ln x$ is $\dfrac{1}{x}$.

5 Use the chain rule to find the derivative of $\ln 2x$. (Start by putting $u = 2x$.)

6 (a) Work out the derivatives of $\ln 3x$ and $\ln 5x$.

(b) What is the derivative of $\ln ax$, where a is any constant?

(c) Use the laws of logarithms to explain the result above.

7 (a) Integrate $\dfrac{1}{2x}$.

(b) What is the integral of $\dfrac{1}{ax}$ with respect to x, where a is any constant?

8E If $y = \sqrt[3]{x}$ then $x = y^3$. Find $\dfrac{dx}{dy}$ and hence find $\dfrac{dy}{dx}$.

Check that your answer agrees with that for question 2(a).

9E If $y = \sin^{-1} x$, then $x = \sin y$.

(a) Write down $\dfrac{dx}{dy}$ and $\dfrac{dy}{dx}$.

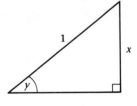

(b) Express the third side of the triangle illustrated in terms of x. Hence explain why the derivative of $\sin^{-1} x$ is $\dfrac{1}{\sqrt{(1 - x^2)}}$ for $-1 < x < 1$.

(c) By a similar method, find the derivative of $\cos^{-1} x$.

After working through section 6.1 you should:

1 know how to use the chain rule to solve problems involving rates of change;

2 be able to differentiate functions of functions such as $(3x^2 + 5)^3$ and $\sin^2 x$;

3 be aware that the relationship

$$\frac{\mathrm{d}}{\mathrm{d}x}(x^n) = nx^{n-1}$$

appears to hold even for non-integer values of n;

4 know how to differentiate inverse functions using the fact that

$$\frac{\mathrm{d}x}{\mathrm{d}y} = 1 \div \frac{\mathrm{d}y}{\mathrm{d}x}$$

6 Calculus methods 1

.2 Parametric form

6.2.1 Curves which vary with time

Consider the computer simulation of a game, where you need to describe the position of a ball on the computer screen. The x- and y-coordinates, giving the position of the ball, will vary with time t. The screen can be thought of as a Cartesian (x, y) plane, with the origin at the bottom left-hand corner of the screen. Suppose that the position of the ball at some time, t, is given by the equations

$$x = 2t \quad \text{and} \quad y = t$$

These equations are called **parametric equations**, and the time, t, which determines the x- and y-coordinates, is called the **parameter**.

You can plot the position of the ball at various times.

Time t	0	1	2	3	4	5
x	0	2	4	6	8	10
y	0	1	2	3	4	5

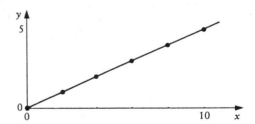

The equation of the path of the ball across the screen is $y = \frac{1}{2}x$. This may be obtained by eliminating the parameter t from the two parametric equations.

$$x = 2t \quad \text{①}$$
$$y = t \quad \text{②}$$

From ①, $\quad t = \frac{1}{2}x$

and so $\quad y = t$

$\Rightarrow \quad y = \frac{1}{2}x$

Most graph-plotting calculators will allow you to enter equations in parametric form and to plot their graphs. However, you do need some practice at drawing such graphs for yourself, and this is considered in the following examples. Later on we shall consider differentiation when relationships are expressed in parametric form.

To plot a parametric curve, it is *sometimes* sufficient to 'plot some suitable points and join the dots', as in the following example.

Example 1

Plot the curve given by the parametric equations

$$x = 3t, \quad y = t^2 \qquad \text{for } 0 \leq t \leq 3$$

Solution

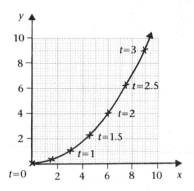

t	0	0.5	1	1.5	2	2.5	3
x	0	1.5	3	4.5	6	7.5	9
y	0	0.25	1	2.25	4	6.25	9

In this example, the (x, y) graph appears to be parabolic. You could confirm this by finding y as a function of x. This is done by eliminating the parameter t as follows.

$$x = 3t, \quad y = t^2$$
$$x^2 = 9t^2$$
$$x^2 = 9y \quad \text{or} \quad y = \frac{x^2}{9}$$

(y is a quadratic function of x. The graph is a parabola.)

This idea of eliminating the parameter to form the Cartesian equation is considered again in section 6.2.2.

6.2 Exercise 1

1 (a) For the curve given by the parametric equations

$$x = 20t, \quad y = 90 - 5t^2$$

Complete the following table of values and plot the points on an (x, y) graph.

t	0	1	2	3	4	5
x						
y						

(b) On the same graph, plot the points which would arise if t were to take the values $-1, -2, -3, -4$ and -5. You should not need to recalculate the values – look for symmetry with your answers to part (a).

(c) What is the general shape of the curve?

2 By choosing suitable values of t and drawing up a table, plot the following parametric curves using any properties of symmetry or general shape to obtain the complete sketch.

(a) $x = 2t^2$, $y = 4t^3$ (b) $x = 2t$, $y = \dfrac{2}{t}$

Check your results using a graph plotter.

6.2.2 Circles and ellipses

Pythagoras' theorem can be used to show that the equation of a circle of radius r centred on the origin is

$$x^2 + y^2 = r^2 \qquad \text{①}$$

Introducing θ, the angle between OP and the x-axis, gives a different view of the problem and leads to alternative *parametric* equations for the circle.

Consider a circle of radius 3.

You know that $x^2 + y^2 = 9$ is the Cartesian equation.

Using trigonometry in triangle OAP gives the parametric equations

$$x = 3\cos\theta, \quad y = 3\sin\theta$$

You can eliminate θ from these equations to show that they give the correct Cartesian equation for this circle as follows.

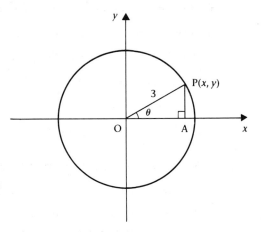

$$x^2 = (3\cos\theta)^2 = 9\cos^2\theta \quad \text{and} \quad y^2 = 9\sin^2\theta$$

$$x^2 + y^2 = 9\cos^2\theta + 9\sin^2\theta$$

$$= 9(\cos^2\theta + \sin^2\theta)$$

$$x^2 + y^2 = 9 \qquad (\text{as } \cos^2\theta + \sin^2\theta = 1)$$

The following questions develop the parametric form of the equation of an ellipse.

6 .2A

1 Suppose a circle of radius 3 is stretched by a factor of 2 in the x direction, so that the point P is transformed to P′ and the circle becomes an ellipse.

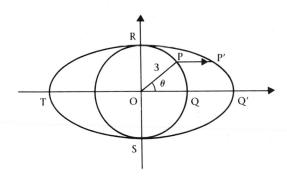

TQ′ is the **major axis** of the ellipse. SR is the **minor axis**.

(a) Write down the coordinates of P in terms of θ.

(b) Write down the y-coordinate of P′ in terms of θ.

(c) Write down the x-coordinate of P′ in terms of θ.

(d) Write down the parametric equations of the ellipse.

(e) Write down the coordinates of R, Q and Q′.

(f) Write down the area of:

   (i) the circle,   (ii) the ellipse.

2 (a) Sketch, on the same diagram, the curves:

   (i) $x = 4\cos\theta$, $y = 4\sin\theta$ (ii) $x = 5\cos\theta$, $y = 4\sin\theta$

(b) The ellipse in (ii) can be obtained from the circle in (i) by means of a one-way stretch. What is the scale factor for this transformation?

(c) What is the area of:

   (i) the circle,   (ii) the ellipse?

3 Sketch the graphs of the following curves, indicating the lengths of the major and minor axes.

(a) $x = 5\cos\theta$, $y = 6\sin\theta$ (b) $x = 2\cos\theta$, $y = \sin\theta$

(c) $x = a\cos\theta$, $y = b\sin\theta$

4 (a) Complete the following argument which leads to the Cartesian equation of an ellipse.

$$x = a\cos\theta, \quad y = b\sin\theta$$

$$\Rightarrow \cos\theta = ? \qquad \sin\theta = ?$$

So, since $\cos^2\theta + \sin^2\theta = ?$, it follows that

$$\left(\frac{?}{?}\right)^2 + \left(\frac{?}{?}\right)^2 = 1$$

or $\quad \dfrac{x^2}{?^2} + \dfrac{y^2}{?^2} = 1$

(b) Sketch the ellipse $\dfrac{x^2}{4} + \dfrac{y^2}{9} = 1$.

5 Consider the ellipse $\dfrac{x^2}{a^2} + \dfrac{y^2}{b^2} = 1$.

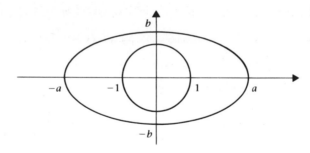

(a) This ellipse can be obtained from the circle $x^2 + y^2 = 1$ by means of a two-way stretch. What are the scale factors of this in the x and y directions?

(b) Write down the area of the circle $x^2 + y^2 = 1$. Hence write down the area of the ellipse.

For the **circle**, the Cartesian equation is

$$x^2 + y^2 = r^2$$

the parametric equations are

$$x = r\cos\theta, \quad y = r\sin\theta$$

and the area is πr^2.

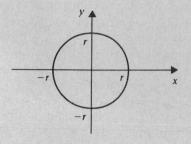

For the **ellipse**, the Cartesian equation is

$$\frac{x^2}{a^2} + \frac{y^2}{b^2} = 1$$

the parametric equations are

$$x = a\cos\theta, \quad y = b\sin\theta$$

and the area is πab.

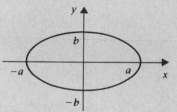

The major axis of the ellipse is of length $2a$ and its minor axis is of length $2b$.

6.2 Exercise 2

1 Copy and complete the following table.

Ellipse	Cartesian equation	Parametric equations	Area
A	$\dfrac{x^2}{9} + \dfrac{y^2}{16} = 1$		
B		$x = 3\cos\theta, \quad y = 5\sin\theta$	
C	$\dfrac{x^2}{0.25} + \dfrac{y^2}{0.16} = 1$		

2 Rewrite $9x^2 + 4y^2 = 36$ in the form $\dfrac{x^2}{a^2} + \dfrac{y^2}{b^2} = 1$. Hence write down the parametric equations and the area of this ellipse.

3 Repeat question 2 for the ellipse with equation $4x^2 + 25y^2 = 100$.

▶ 6.2 **Tasksheet E1 – Drawing parametric curves (page 562)**

6.2.3 Conversion

You have seen how to convert the parametric equations

$$x = a \cos \theta, \quad y = b \sin \theta$$

into the Cartesian equation

$$\frac{x^2}{a^2} + \frac{y^2}{b^2} = 1$$

by using the trigonometric identity $\cos^2 \theta + \sin^2 \theta = 1$.

We now introduce two other trigonometric identities which are sometimes encountered in work on parametric equations.

 .2B

You know that

$$\sin \theta = \frac{b}{c}$$

$$\cos \theta = \frac{a}{c}$$

$$\tan \theta = \frac{b}{a}$$

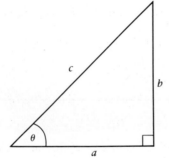

There are three other trigonometric ratios which are sometimes used. They are **secant** (usually abbreviated to sec), **cosecant** (cosec) and **cotangent** (cot).

In the triangle above,

$$\sec \theta \text{ is } \frac{c}{a}, \qquad \text{cosec } \theta \text{ is } \frac{c}{b}, \qquad \cot \theta \text{ is } \frac{a}{b}$$

1 Show that:

(a) $\sec \theta = \dfrac{1}{\cos \theta}$ (b) $\text{cosec } \theta = \dfrac{1}{\sin \theta}$

(c) $\cot \theta = \dfrac{1}{\tan \theta}$ (d) $\cot \theta = \dfrac{\cos \theta}{\sin \theta}$

2 The diagram shows the graph of $\cos\theta$ for $0 \le \theta \le 2\pi$ and part of the graph of $\sec\theta = \dfrac{1}{\cos\theta}$.

Copy the diagram and complete the graph of $\sec\theta$.

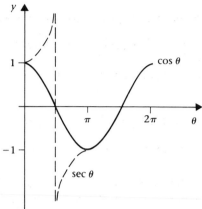

3 (a) Sketch on one diagram the graphs of $\sin\theta$ and $\operatorname{cosec}\theta$.

(b) Sketch on one diagram the graphs of $\tan\theta$ and $\cot\theta$.

4 You know that, for any value of θ,

$$\sin^2\theta + \cos^2\theta = 1 \qquad ①$$

(a) By dividing each term of equation ① by $\cos^2\theta$, show that

$$\tan^2\theta + 1 = \sec^2\theta \qquad ②$$

(b) By dividing each term of equation ① by $\sin^2\theta$, show that

$$1 + \cot^2\theta = \operatorname{cosec}^2\theta \qquad ③$$

If $x = 2\sec\theta$ and $y = 3\tan\theta$, identity ② above can be used to write x in terms of y.

$$\sec\theta = \frac{x}{2} \quad \text{and} \quad \tan\theta = \frac{y}{3}$$

Substituting in ②,

$$\left(\frac{y}{3}\right)^2 + 1 = \left(\frac{x}{2}\right)^2$$

$$\Rightarrow \frac{y^2}{9} + 1 = \frac{x^2}{4}$$

$$\Rightarrow 4y^2 + 36 = 9x^2$$

5 Use identity ③ to convert the parametric equations

$$x = \cot\theta \quad \text{and} \quad 2y = \operatorname{cosec}\theta$$

into the Cartesian equation.

$$\sec\theta = \frac{1}{\cos\theta}, \quad \operatorname{cosec}\theta = \frac{1}{\sin\theta}, \quad \cot\theta = \frac{1}{\tan\theta}$$

For any value of θ,

$$\cos^2\theta + \sin^2\theta = 1$$

$$1 + \tan^2\theta = \sec^2\theta$$

$$\cot^2\theta + 1 = \operatorname{cosec}^2\theta$$

You have used trigonometric identities to remove parameters from pairs of simultaneous equations. In general, conversion from parametric to Cartesian form involves the removal of a parameter using simultaneous equation techniques. While these may involve indirect elimination using trigonometric identities, simpler direct methods are often used. This is illustrated in example 2.

Example 2

Find the Cartesian equation of the curve given by the parametric equations

$$x = 20t \qquad \text{①}$$

$$y = 90 - 5t^2 \qquad \text{②}$$

Solution

Using equation ① to find t, $\qquad t = \dfrac{x}{20}$

Substituting for t in ②, $\qquad y = 90 - 5\left(\dfrac{x}{20}\right)^2 = 90 - \dfrac{x^2}{80}$

6.2 **Exercise 3**

1 Find the Cartesian equations of:

(a) $x = 2 + 3t, \quad y = 4 - 5t$ $\qquad$ (b) $x = 3t, \quad y = 5 - \dfrac{6}{t}$

(c) $x = 4t, \quad y = 10t - 5t^2$ $\qquad$ (d) $x = 2t - 1, \quad y = 4 - 2t$

2 Use appropriate trigonometric identities to find the Cartesian equations of:

(a) $2x = \sec\theta, \quad \dfrac{y}{3} = \tan\theta$ $\qquad$ (b) $x = 4\sin t, \quad y = 3\cos t$

(c) $x = \operatorname{cosec}\theta, \quad y = \dfrac{1}{2}\cot\theta$ $\qquad$ (d) $\dfrac{x}{3} = \sec\theta, \quad y = \tan\theta + 1$

3E (a) Obtain the Cartesian equation for the parametric equations

$$x = 1 + \sqrt{t}, \quad y = 4 + \sqrt{t}$$

(b) The curve given by the Cartesian equation is not quite the same as the curve given by the parametric equations. Why not?

4E For the curve given by

$$y = (x - 2)^2 + 4$$

suggest two different possible sets of parametric equations.

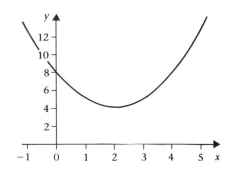

6.2.4 Differentiating parametric equations

You have used the chain rule to find rates of change in cases where there were two equations involving three variables.

For example, if $y = \sin \theta$ and $\theta = 3x^2 + 2$, then

$$\frac{dy}{dx} = \frac{dy}{d\theta} \times \frac{d\theta}{dx}$$

$$= \cos \theta \times 6x$$

$$= 6x \cos \theta$$

$$= 6x \cos (3x^2 + 2)$$

Parametric equations can also give two equations with three variables. For example, a circle with centre the origin and radius 3 units has parametric equations

$$x = 3 \cos \theta, \quad y = 3 \sin \theta$$

You can find $\dfrac{dy}{dx}$ using the chain rule.

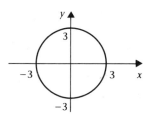

$$\frac{dy}{dx} = \frac{dy}{d\theta} \times \frac{d\theta}{dx}$$

From the parametric equations, you can write down $\dfrac{dy}{d\theta}$ and $\dfrac{dx}{d\theta}$, but not $\dfrac{d\theta}{dx}$. However, you should remember that $\dfrac{d\theta}{dx} = 1 \div \dfrac{dx}{d\theta}$.

This means that the chain rule can be rewritten as $\dfrac{dy}{dx} = \dfrac{dy}{d\theta} \div \dfrac{dx}{d\theta}$

Using this result for the circle $x = 3 \cos \theta$, $y = 3 \sin \theta$,

$$\frac{dy}{d\theta} = 3 \cos \theta \quad \text{and} \quad \frac{dx}{d\theta} = -3 \sin \theta$$

Then $\dfrac{dy}{dx} = \dfrac{dy}{d\theta} \div \dfrac{dx}{d\theta} = -\dfrac{3 \cos \theta}{3 \sin \theta} = -3 \cot \theta$

Example 3

For the curve defined parametrically by $x = 10t$, $y = 5t^2$, find $\dfrac{dy}{dx}$ and the equation of the tangent to the (x, y) graph at $t = 3$.

Solution

Differentiating, $\dfrac{dx}{dt} = 10$ and $\dfrac{dy}{dt} = 10t$

$$\frac{dy}{dx} = \frac{dy}{dt} \div \frac{dx}{dt} = \frac{10t}{10} = t$$

When $t = 3$, $\dfrac{dy}{dx} = 3$, $x = 30$ and $y = 45$.

The equation of the tangent is $\dfrac{y - 45}{x - 30} = 3$ or $y = 3x - 45$.

The process of differentiating expressions given in parametric form is known as **parametric differentiation**. It may have occurred to you that you could have found some of the gradients by first converting the parametric equations to Cartesian equations. This may occasionally be an easy method. For example, if

$$x = 2t + 3, \quad y = 6t + 9$$

you may spot at once that $y = 3x$, so $\dfrac{dy}{dx} = 3$.

Generally, however, parametric differentiation will be quicker.

Example 4

A curve is defined by $x = 2t + 1$, $y = t^2$.

(a) Use parametric differentiation to find the gradient at the point $(5, 4)$.

(b) Find y in terms of x and so write down $\dfrac{dy}{dx}$ and find the gradient at the point $(5, 4)$.

Solution

(a) $\dfrac{dy}{dt} = 2t$ and $\dfrac{dx}{dt} = 2$, so $\dfrac{dy}{dx} = \dfrac{2t}{2} = t$

When $x = 5$ and $y = 4$, $t = 2$, so the gradient is 2.

(b) Since $x = 2t + 1$, $t = \dfrac{(x - 1)}{2}$

So $y = \dfrac{(x - 1)^2}{4}$ and $\dfrac{dy}{dx} = \dfrac{2(x - 1)}{4} = \dfrac{(x - 1)}{2}$

When $x = 5$ the gradient is $\dfrac{4}{2} = 2$.

Even with this simple conversion, it is clear that parametric differentiation leads to a quicker solution, and there are many cases where the conversion to Cartesian equations is difficult or impossible.

6.2 **Exercise 4**

1   A curve has parametric equations $x = t$, $y = \dfrac{1}{t}$. Write down $\dfrac{dx}{dt}$ and $\dfrac{dy}{dt}$ and hence find $\dfrac{dy}{dx}$. Calculate the gradient of the curve at $t = 2$.

2   A curve has parametric equations $x = 3\cos\theta$, $y = 4\sin\theta$.
    Work out the Cartesian coordinates and gradient at the point where $\theta = \frac{1}{2}\pi$.

3   For the curve defined by $x = 4u$, $y = u^2$, find $\dfrac{dy}{dx}$ and the equation of the tangent to the curve at the point where $u = 2$.

4   Find the equation of the tangent to the curve $x = u^2$, $y = 2u^3$ at the point where $u = 1$.

5   For the curve $x = 2v$, $y = v^3 - 3v$

    (a) work out $\dfrac{dy}{dx}$;

    (b) write down the two values of v for which $\dfrac{dy}{dx} = 0$;

    (c) write down the x- and y-coordinates of the turning points on the curve.

6   Given that $x = 3s$ and $y = s^2$, find $\dfrac{dy}{dx}$, first by parametric differentiation and then by conversion to a Cartesian equation.

    Check that both methods give the same value for the gradient of the curve at $s = 1$.

7   For each part of this question, find $\dfrac{dy}{dx}$ by the method of your choice.
    (a) $x = (t + 2)^2$, $y = t^3 - 3$
    (b) $x = 2t^2$, $y = 6t^2 - 4$
    (c) $x = 2\cos\theta - \sin\theta$, $y = 3\sin\theta$
    (d) $x = \sin 2\theta$, $y = \sin 3\theta$

8   A curve has parametric equations $x = t^2 + 4$ and $y = 2t^3 + 4t$.

    (a) Find $\dfrac{dy}{dx}$ in terms of t and show that $\left(\dfrac{dy}{dx}\right)^2 \geq 24$.

    (b) Sketch the curve.

9E Find the equation of the tangent to the curve $x = \theta - \cos\theta$, $y = \sin\theta$ at the point where $\theta = \frac{1}{4}\pi$. Write down the coordinates of the points A and B at which this tangent cuts the x- and y-axes respectively and hence find the area of the triangle OAB.

6.2.5 Velocity vectors

The ideas encountered in this section so far may be usefully employed in describing the motion of a body. We have used parametric equations to describe the position of a body at various times; here we use the method to obtain the velocity vector.

Consider an ice hockey puck, moving across the surface of the ice with constant velocity. Its position at half-second intervals is given (in terms of its position vector at that time) in the table.

Time, t seconds	0	0.5	1	1.5	2
Position vector, metres (from origin in corner of pitch)	$\begin{bmatrix} 0 \\ 6 \end{bmatrix}$	$\begin{bmatrix} 6 \\ 10.5 \end{bmatrix}$	$\begin{bmatrix} 12 \\ 15 \end{bmatrix}$	$\begin{bmatrix} 18 \\ 19.5 \end{bmatrix}$	$\begin{bmatrix} 24 \\ 24 \end{bmatrix}$

The graph shows the motion of the puck and the arrow indicates its direction.

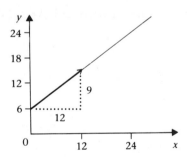

Starting from $x = 0$, the puck moves 12 m in the x direction every second. At time t it will have moved $12t$ m in the x direction (i.e. $x = 12t$). Similarly, starting from $y = 6$ on the y-axis, it moves 9 m every second in the y direction (i.e. $y = 6 + 9t$).

So the velocity of the puck is $\begin{bmatrix} 12 \\ 9 \end{bmatrix}$ m s^{-1} and its speed is the magnitude of this vector, which is given by $\sqrt{(12^2 + 9^2)} = 15$ m s^{-1}.

The parametric equations for the position of the puck are

$$x = 12t, \quad y = 6 + 9t \quad \text{or} \quad \mathbf{r} = \begin{bmatrix} 12t \\ 6 + 9t \end{bmatrix}$$

By differentiating, you can obtain the rates of change of the position of the puck along the x- and the y-axes, and hence obtain the velocity vector.

$$x = 12t, \quad y = 6 + 9t$$

Differentiating, $\quad \dfrac{dx}{dt} = 12 \quad$ is the rate at which the x-coordinate is increasing, a constant 12 m s^{-1} (the speed at which it is going *across* the pitch)

and $\quad \dfrac{dy}{dt} = 9 \quad$ is the rate at which the y-coordinate is increasing, a constant 9 m s^{-1} (the speed at which it is going *up* the pitch).

Notice that these are the components of the velocity vector in the directions of the x- and y-axes. That is,

$$\text{if} \quad \mathbf{r} = \begin{bmatrix} x \\ y \end{bmatrix} \quad \text{then} \quad \mathbf{v} = \begin{bmatrix} \dfrac{dx}{dt} \\ \dfrac{dy}{dt} \end{bmatrix} = \begin{bmatrix} \dot{x} \\ \dot{y} \end{bmatrix}$$

The notation $\dot{x}$ indicates differentiation with respect to time.

The gradient of the velocity vector is $\dfrac{\dot{y}}{\dot{x}}$, as illustrated on the diagram. This may also be obtained using the chain rule.

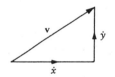

$$\frac{dy}{dt} = \frac{dy}{dx} \times \frac{dx}{dt} \quad \Rightarrow \quad \frac{dy}{dx} = \frac{dy}{dt} \div \frac{dx}{dt} = \frac{\dot{y}}{\dot{x}}$$

While the example considered above is one of motion in a straight line, the results are also true for non-linear motion.

If a moving particle has position vector $\mathbf{r} = \begin{bmatrix} x \\ y \end{bmatrix}$, then its velocity is given by $\mathbf{v} = \begin{bmatrix} \dot{x} \\ \dot{y} \end{bmatrix}$. The gradient of the velocity vector is

$$\frac{dy}{dx} = \frac{\dot{y}}{\dot{x}}$$

Example 5

A particle moves so that its position vector is given by

$$\mathbf{r} = \begin{bmatrix} 2t + 2 \\ t^2 + 2t \end{bmatrix}$$

Plot the positions of the particle over the first three seconds and sketch its path. Calculate the velocity of the particle and mark the velocity vectors on the graph at $t = 0$ and $t = 2$.

Solution

t	0	1	2	3
$\mathbf{r}$	$\begin{bmatrix} 2 \\ 0 \end{bmatrix}$	$\begin{bmatrix} 4 \\ 3 \end{bmatrix}$	$\begin{bmatrix} 6 \\ 8 \end{bmatrix}$	$\begin{bmatrix} 8 \\ 15 \end{bmatrix}$

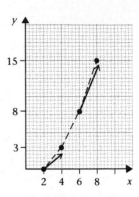

Differentiating, $\quad \mathbf{v} = \begin{bmatrix} \dot{x} \\ \dot{y} \end{bmatrix} = \begin{bmatrix} 2 \\ 2t + 2 \end{bmatrix}$

When $t = 0$, $\quad \mathbf{v} = \begin{bmatrix} 2 \\ 2 \end{bmatrix}$. When $t = 2$, $\quad \mathbf{v} = \begin{bmatrix} 2 \\ 6 \end{bmatrix}$.

Notice that the velocity vectors are in the direction of the tangent to the curve. The lengths of the arrows indicate their magnitudes.

6.2 Exercise 5

1 For the position vector $\mathbf{r} = \begin{bmatrix} t^2 \\ 3t \end{bmatrix}$, find the coordinates of the points when $t = 0, 1, 2$ and 3, and sketch the path. Differentiate to find the velocities when $t = 0, 1, 2$ and 3, and calculate their magnitudes. Mark each velocity on the curve using an arrow of appropriate length and direction.

2 The displacement in centimetres from the origin of a particle after t seconds is given by

$$\mathbf{r} = \begin{bmatrix} 2 + t^2 \\ 3t - t^2 \end{bmatrix}$$

(a) Find the velocity after t seconds.

(b) Calculate its initial speed and direction (i.e. when $t = 0$).

(c) Find at what time it is travelling in the direction $\begin{bmatrix} 1 \\ 1 \end{bmatrix}$.

(d) When is it travelling parallel to the x-axis?

3 A particle moves along a straight line $y = 3x + 1$ with a constant speed of $\sqrt{10}$ units. What is the velocity vector?

If the particle starts at $(0, 1)$ write down the position vector at time t.

After working through section 6.2 you should:

1 understand the word 'parameter' and recognise equations expressed in parametric form;

2 recognise the Cartesian and parametric forms of circles and ellipses;

3 be able to express equations written parametrically in Cartesian form and vice versa;

4 be able to plot or sketch a curve given in parametric form;

5 know that:

$$\operatorname{cosec} \theta = \frac{1}{\sin \theta} \qquad \sec \theta = \frac{1}{\cos \theta} \qquad \cot \theta = \frac{1}{\tan \theta}$$

and know the identities

$$1 + \tan^2 \theta = \sec^2 \theta$$

$$1 + \cot^2 \theta = \operatorname{cosec}^2 \theta$$

6 be able to find the gradient of a curve expressed in parametric form;

7 be able to find the equation of a tangent to a curve expressed in parametric form;

8 be able to find the velocity vector of a particle whose position vector is given in terms of t (time).

6 Calculus methods 1

.3 Further differentiation techniques

6.3.1 The product rule

It is always possible to estimate numerically the gradient at any point of a locally straight curve and you also know how to work out the gradients of many such curves algebraically.

You know how to deal with functions of functions (like $\sin x^2$) by using the chain rule.

You also know that, to differentiate compound functions which have been obtained by addition or subtraction (like $x^2 - \sin x$), you merely add or subtract the separate derivatives.

It is unfortunate that derivatives of products (like $x \sin x$) cannot be dealt with by multiplying the separate derivatives.

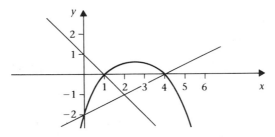

The diagram shows the graphs of the two linear functions $y = 1 - x$ and $y = \frac{1}{2}x - 2$, together with the graph of their product, $y = (1 - x)(\frac{1}{2}x - 2)$. It is clear that the two linear graphs have gradients -1 and $\frac{1}{2}$ respectively for any value of x. However, the gradient of the product graph is changing and so cannot have the value $-1 \times \frac{1}{2} = -\frac{1}{2}$ for every value of x.

You could, of course, differentiate the product function by first multiplying out the brackets, but this method will be lengthy for functions like $(2 + 3x)^2(3 - 2x)^3$ and it is not possible to 'multiply out' a product like $x \sin x$. It would therefore be very useful to find a formula for the derivative of a product.

Example 1

Let $y = uv$, where $u = ax + b$ and $v = cx + d$.

Work out $\dfrac{dy}{dx}$ and show that it is equal to $u\dfrac{dv}{dx} + v\dfrac{du}{dx}$.

Solution

$$y = (ax + b)(cx + d) = acx^2 + adx + bcx + bd$$

$$\frac{dy}{dx} = 2acx + ad + bc$$

$$u\frac{dv}{dx} + v\frac{du}{dx} = (ax + b)c + (cx + d)a = 2acx + ad + bc$$

So, for a function $y = uv$, where u and v are linear functions of x,

$$\frac{dy}{dx} = v\frac{du}{dx} + u\frac{dv}{dx}$$

This rule is called the **product rule**. It would be of limited use if it could only be used for products of linear functions. Here, we consider its use for other functions.

Any function which is differentiable has a graph which is locally straight. Since the product rule can be proved to be true for products of linear functions, you would expect the rule to be true for *any* two differentiable functions.

The following questions provide some evidence that the product rule works for any two differentiable functions.

 .3A

1

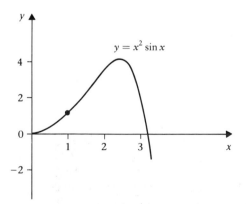

$y = x^2 \sin x$

(a) Use the product rule to find the gradient of $y = x^2 \sin x$ at $x = 1$ and check that your answer seems reasonable in view of the shape of the graph of $y = x^2 \sin x$.

(b) Use a numerical method to evaluate the gradient of $y = x^2 \sin x$ at $x = 1$ and check that it agrees with your answer to (a).

2 (a) Use the product rule to obtain the equation of the gradient graph for $y = uv$ where $u = \cos\frac{1}{2}x$ and $v = 4x - \frac{1}{2}x^2$.

   (b) Use a program for numerical gradients to check your answer to (a).

3 Repeat question 2 for any two functions you choose.

4 (a) x^5 can be written as $x^3 \times x^2$.

   Use the product rule with $u = x^3$ and $v = x^2$ and check that you do obtain the derivative of x^5.

   (b) Write x^8 as a product in at least two different ways. In each case, differentiate using the product rule and check that you obtain $8x^7$.

   (c) $x^{a+b} = x^a \times x^b$

   Differentiate $x^a \times x^b$ using the product rule. Do you obtain the expected answer?

You have seen some evidence for the following result.

The product rule holds for general functions u and v.

$$\frac{d}{dx}(uv) = u\frac{dv}{dx} + v\frac{du}{dx}$$

6.3 Exercise 1

1 Use the product rule to work out the derivatives of:

   (a) $e^x \sin x$ (b) $x^2 e^x$ (c) $x^3 \cos x$

2 Work out the gradients of:

   (a) the tangent to $y = x^3 e^x$ at $x = 2$

   (b) the tangent to $y = 2x^2 e^x$ at $x = 1$

3 Use the product rule to differentiate $x \sin x$ and hence work out the equation of the tangent at $x = 1.5$ on the graph of $y = x \sin x$. (Work to 2 s.f.)

4   A rectangle on a computer screen has width w, height h and area A.
    w and h are programmed to be functions of time, t.

   (a) (i) If $w = t^2$ and $h = \sin t$, use the product rule to find $\dfrac{dA}{dt}$ and so work

       out the rate at which the area of the rectangle is increasing when
       $t = 1$.

   (ii) What is happening to the area when $t = 2.5$?

   (b) (i) If $w = \sin t$ and $h = \cos t$, how fast is the area increasing when
       $t = 0.5$?

   (ii) At what value of t does the area of this rectangle first stop increasing?

5   Find the equation of the tangent to the graph of $y = 0.25x\,e^x$ at the point
    where $x = 1$. (Work to 2 d.p.)

6   Differentiate $x\,e^x$ and so work out the coordinates of the turning point on the
    graph of $y = x\,e^x$.

7   (a) Differentiate $x^2\,e^x$ and explain how this shows that the graph of $y = x^2\,e^x$
       must have a stationary point at $(0,0)$.

   (b) How do you know that there is only one other stationary point on the
       graph? Work out the coordinates of this stationary point.

8   (a) Let $y = uv$, where $u = x$ and $v = \dfrac{1}{x}$.

       It follows that $y = x \times \dfrac{1}{x} = 1$ and $\dfrac{dy}{dx} = 0$.

       But $\dfrac{dy}{dx} = v\dfrac{du}{dx} + u\dfrac{dv}{dx}$.

       Use the above to find $\dfrac{dv}{dx}$. Hence show that the derivative of $\dfrac{1}{x}$ is $-\dfrac{1}{x^2}$.

   (b) Show that the answer $\dfrac{dv}{dx} = -\dfrac{1}{x^2}$ agrees with the one obtained by using
       the nx^{n-1} rule.

9E Show that there is a stationary point on the curve $y = x\sin x$ when
    $x + \tan x = 0$. Show graphically that $x + \tan x = 0$ has three solutions in the
    region $-3 \le x \le 3$.

    One of these three solutions should be obvious. Use any method you wish to
    find the other two solutions and so work out the coordinates of the
    stationary points of $y = x\sin x$ in the region $-3 \le x \le 3$.

6.3.2 Product rule and chain rule

It is very important to be clear when you need to use the chain rule and when you need to use the product rule.

$e^x \sin x$ means $e^x \times \sin x$, so two simple functions are being multiplied together and the product rule is needed.

$e^{\sin x}$ is a composite function $fg(x)$ where $g(x) = \sin x$ and $f(x) = e^x$, so the chain rule is needed.

It is sometimes necessary to use both rules.

Example 2

Find $\dfrac{dy}{dx}$ where $y = e^{2x} \sin 0.5x$.

Solution
$y = uv$, where

$$u = e^{2x} \quad \text{and} \quad v = \sin 0.5x$$

By the chain rule, $\quad \dfrac{du}{dx} = 2e^{2x} \quad$ and $\quad \dfrac{dv}{dx} = 0.5 \cos 0.5x$

By the product rule, $\quad \dfrac{dy}{dx} = v\dfrac{du}{dx} + u\dfrac{dv}{dx}$

So $\dfrac{dy}{dx} = \sin 0.5x \times 2e^{2x} + e^{2x} \times 0.5 \cos 0.5x$

Or $\dfrac{dy}{dx} = e^{2x}(2 \sin 0.5x + 0.5 \cos 0.5x)$

6.3 **Exercise 2**

1 Differentiate these products, using both the chain rule and the product rule. Set out your working as in example 2.

(a) $2e^{3x} \sin 2x$ (b) $e^{2x} \cos 3x$ (c) $e^{x^2} \sin 4x$

2 Use the product rule or the chain rule or both in order to differentiate the following functions.

(a) $\ln(x^2 + 1)$ (b) $x \ln x$ (c) $x \sin^2 x$

(d) $x \sin x^2$ (e) $(x + \sin x)^2$ (f) $e^x \cos x + x \sin x$

(g) $(2x + 3)^{-1}$ (h) $x^2 e^{3x}$

3 Work out the gradient of each of these graphs at $x = 2$.

(a)

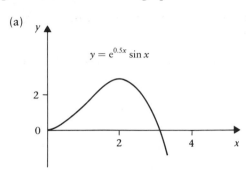

$y = e^{0.5x} \sin x$

(b)

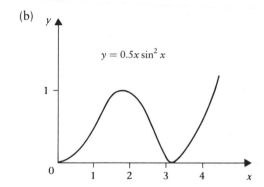

$y = 0.5x \sin^2 x$

4 The tip of a tuning fork moves so that its distance in centimetres from a central position is given by

$$s = 0.4 \sin 512\pi t, \quad \text{where } t \text{ is the time in seconds}$$

(a) What are the displacement and the velocity of the tip of the tuning fork after 1 second?

(b) How many vibrations per second does the fork make?

5 Differentiate $\dfrac{x+2}{x+1}$ by writing the function as $(x+2)(x+1)^{-1}$.

6.3.3 Differentiating quotients

When tackling exercise 2, you probably found the derivative of $\dfrac{(x+2)}{(x+1)}$ to be

$$(x+1)^{-1} + -1(x+1)^{-2}(x+2)$$

You may have rearranged the answer as $\dfrac{1}{x+1} - \dfrac{x+2}{(x+1)^2}.$

This is still not a very neat answer, and it can be simplified further.

$$\frac{(x+1)-(x+2)}{(x+1)^2} = \frac{-1}{(x+1)^2}$$

It is possible to differentiate any quotient by rewriting the function with negative indices and using the product rule, but the process of writing the answer in a neat form is tedious. It is therefore worthwhile to try to find a formula for the derivative of a quotient.

Suppose $y = \dfrac{u}{v}$ where both u and v are functions of x.

Start by writing y as a product and use the product rule.

$$y = uv^{-1}$$

$$\Rightarrow \frac{dy}{dx} = v^{-1}\frac{du}{dx} + u\frac{d(v^{-1})}{dx}$$

$\dfrac{d(v^{-1})}{dx}$ may be evaluated using the chain rule.

$$\frac{d(v^{-1})}{dx} = \frac{d(v^{-1})}{dv} \times \frac{dv}{dx}$$

$$= -\frac{1}{v^2}\frac{dv}{dx}$$

$$\Rightarrow \frac{dy}{dx} = \frac{1}{v}\frac{du}{dx} - \frac{u}{v^2}\frac{dv}{dx}$$

$$\frac{dy}{dx} = \frac{v\dfrac{du}{dx} - u\dfrac{dv}{dx}}{v^2}$$

This result is known as the **quotient rule**.

The quotient rule

If $y = \dfrac{u}{v}$, where u and v are functions of x,

then $\dfrac{dy}{dx} = \dfrac{v\dfrac{du}{dx} - u\dfrac{dv}{dx}}{v^2}$.

Example 3

(a) Use the quotient rule to differentiate $\dfrac{x^2}{(2x+3)}$.

(b) Show that the function has a local maximum at $x = -3$.

Solution

(a) $y = \dfrac{u}{v}$, where $u = x^2$ and $v = 2x + 3$

$$\frac{dy}{dx} = \frac{v\dfrac{du}{dx} - u\dfrac{dv}{dx}}{v^2} = \frac{2x(2x+3) - 2x^2}{(2x+3)^2} = \frac{2x^2 + 6x}{(2x+3)^2} = \frac{2x(x+3)}{(2x+3)^2}$$

(b) At stationary points, $\dfrac{dy}{dx} = 0$

$$x(x+3) = 0$$

$$\Rightarrow x = 0 \quad \text{or} \quad x = -3$$

There are stationary points at $(0,0)$ and $(-3,-3)$.

Examine the nature of the stationary point at $x = -3$.

When x is just less than -3 (say -3.1), $\dfrac{dy}{dx}$ is positive.

When x is just greater than -3 (say -2.9), $\dfrac{dy}{dx}$ is negative.

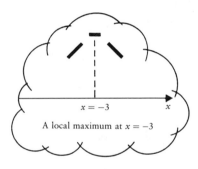

A local maximum at $x = -3$

$\Rightarrow (-3,-3)$ is a local maximum.

6.3 Exercise 3

1 Differentiate: (a) $\dfrac{\sin x}{x}$ (b) $\dfrac{x}{e^x}$ (c) $\dfrac{e^x}{\sin x}$ (d) $\dfrac{e^{3x}}{\sin 2x}$

2 Work out the gradients of:

(a) $y = \dfrac{\sin x}{e^x}$ at $x = -1$ (b) $y = \dfrac{e^{2x}}{x^2}$ at $x = 0.8$

Use a graph plotter to check that your answers look reasonable.

3 You can differentiate $\dfrac{1}{(2x+3)} = (2x+3)^{-1}$ by using either the quotient rule or the chain rule. Work out the derivative using each method in turn. Which method do you prefer?

4 (a) The graph of $y = \dfrac{x}{1 + x^2}$ has a local minimum and a local maximum.

Work out the coordinates of these points, showing clearly how you know which is the maximum and which is the minimum.

(b) Repeat (a) for $y = \dfrac{x^2}{x + 4}$.

5 Use the quotient rule to differentiate $\tan x = \dfrac{\sin x}{\cos x}$.

6 Work out the derivative of $\cot x$ by writing:

(a) $\cot x = \dfrac{\cos x}{\sin x}$ (b) $\cot x = \dfrac{1}{\tan x}$

(c) Check that your answers to parts (a) and (b) are consistent by writing each one in as simple a form as you can.

7E The first part of an alternative proof of the quotient rule, assuming that the product rule is true, is given below. Try to complete the proof.

$$y = \frac{u}{v} \quad \text{where } u \text{ and } v \text{ are functions of } x$$

Then $u = vy$

By the product rule, $\dfrac{du}{dx} = \ldots$

6.3.4 Implicit differentiation

You know how to differentiate functions of functions, sums, differences, products and quotients of functions.

However, all the functions which you have been asked to differentiate have been stated **explicitly**, i.e. as $y = f(x)$.

However, functions are sometimes stated **implicitly**. For example, the equation of the circle, centre $(0, 0)$ and radius 3 units, is usually given in the implicit form

$$x^2 + y^2 = 9$$

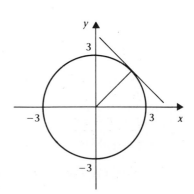

You can find $\dfrac{dy}{dx}$ from this implicit equation by finding the derivative of both sides of the equation, with respect to x.

$$\frac{d}{dx}(x^2) + \frac{d}{dx}(y^2) = \frac{d}{dx}(9)$$

The only difficulty here is with $\dfrac{d}{dx}(y^2)$, and this can be overcome by using the chain rule.

$$\frac{d}{dx}(y^2) = \frac{d}{dy}(y^2) \times \frac{dy}{dx}$$

$$\frac{d}{dx}(y^2) = 2y\frac{dy}{dx}$$

If $\qquad x^2 + y^2 = 9$

Then $\quad 2x + 2y\dfrac{dy}{dx} = 0 \qquad$ (differentiate throughout with respect to x)

$$\Rightarrow \frac{dy}{dx} = \frac{-x}{y}$$

The process used here is called **implicit differentiation**.

Example 4

The point $(1, 2)$ lies on the graph of $x^3 + 3y^2 - 4x + y = 11$.

(a) What is the gradient of the tangent at the point $(1, 2)$?

(b) Work out the equation of this tangent.

Solution

(a) $\dfrac{d}{dx}(x^3) + \dfrac{d}{dx}(3y^2) - \dfrac{d}{dx}(4x) + \dfrac{d}{dx}(y) = \dfrac{d}{dx}(11)$

$$3x^2 + 6y\frac{dy}{dx} - 4 + \frac{dy}{dx} = 0$$

$$\frac{dy}{dx}(6y + 1) + 3x^2 - 4 = 0$$

$$\frac{dy}{dx}(6y + 1) = 4 - 3x^2$$

$$\frac{dy}{dx} = \frac{4 - 3x^2}{6y + 1}$$

When $x = 1$ and $y = 2$, $\quad \dfrac{dy}{dx} = \dfrac{1}{13}$.

The tangent at $(1, 2)$ has gradient $\dfrac{1}{13}$.

(b) The equation of the tangent is

$$\frac{(y-2)}{(x-1)} = \frac{1}{13}$$

$$13(y-2) = x-1$$

or $\quad 13y - x = 25$

6.3 Exercise 4

1 Use implicit differentiation to find $\dfrac{dy}{dx}$ when:

(a) $2y^2 - 3y + 4x^2 = 2$ (b) $x^3 + \frac{1}{2}y^2 - 7x + 3y = 3$

2 The graph of $9x^2 + 4y^2 = 45$ is as shown.

(a) Use implicit differentiation to find $\dfrac{dy}{dx}$.

(b) Work out the y-coordinates of the two points where $x = 1$ and calculate the gradients at these points.
(Check that your results look reasonable.)

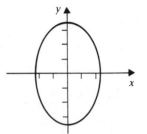

3 The circle with centre $(-3, 1)$ and radius 5 units has equation

$$(x+3)^2 + (y-1)^2 = 25$$

i.e. $\quad x^2 + 6x + y^2 - 2y = 15$

(a) Work out an expression for $\dfrac{dy}{dx}$ and use it to find the equation of the tangent to the circle at the point $(1, 4)$.

(b) The point $(1, -2)$ lies on the circumference of the circle. Work out the gradient of the tangent at this point and the gradient of the radius of the circle to this point. Check that your results are in agreement with the property of circles that a tangent is always perpendicular to the radius at that point.

(c) Repeat (b) for any other point on the circumference of the circle.

4 You have seen that the circle $x^2 + y^2 = 9$ can be written in parametric form as

$$x = 3\cos\theta, \qquad y = 3\sin\theta$$

Parametric differentiation gives the result

$$\frac{dy}{dx} = -\frac{\cos\theta}{\sin\theta}$$

Explain why this result is equivalent to the result $\dfrac{dy}{dx} = -\dfrac{x}{y}$. Also explain why the results show that the angle between tangent and radius must always be a right angle.

5 In section 3.4 you obtained the following results by numerical methods.

$$\frac{d}{dx}(2^x) = 0.693 \times 2^x$$

$$\frac{d}{dx}(3^x) = 1.10 \times 3^x$$

You can now obtain these results using implicit differentiation and the fact that

$$y = 2^x$$
$$\Rightarrow \ln y = \ln 2^x$$
$$\Rightarrow \ln y = x \ln 2$$

(a) Explain why $\dfrac{d}{dx}(\ln y) = \dfrac{1}{y}\dfrac{dy}{dx}$ and hence find $\dfrac{dy}{dx}$ (i.e. the derivative of 2^x). Show that your answer agrees with the numerical result.

(b) Work out the derivative of 3^x using implicit differentiation.

(c) What is the derivative of a^x, where a is any constant?

6.3.5 Implicit differentiation and the product rule

The equation considered in the previous section,

$$x^2 + y^2 = 9$$

could have been rewritten as

$$y = \pm\sqrt{(9 - x^2)}$$

and differentiated in the usual way. However, implicit differentiation is much easier. In some cases, just rewriting an equation in the form $y = f(x)$ is itself very difficult or even impossible.

Example 5

Find $\dfrac{dy}{dx}$ when $y^2 + xy + x^2 = 8$.

Solution
Consider the xy term first.

Let $z = xy$ and use the product rule with $u = x$ and $v = y$.

Then $\dfrac{du}{dx} = 1$ and $\dfrac{dv}{dx} = \dfrac{dy}{dx}$

$$\dfrac{dz}{dx} = v\dfrac{du}{dx} + u\dfrac{dv}{dx}$$

$$= y \times 1 + x \times \dfrac{dy}{dx}$$

$$= y + x\dfrac{dy}{dx}$$

Now differentiate each term of the original expression.

$$y^2 + \qquad xy \qquad + x^2 = 8$$

$$\Rightarrow 2y\dfrac{dy}{dx} + \left(y + x\dfrac{dy}{dx}\right) + 2x = 0$$

Then $(2y + x)\dfrac{dy}{dx} + y + 2x = 0$

$$\Rightarrow \dfrac{dy}{dx}(2y + x) = -(y + 2x)$$

$$\Rightarrow \dfrac{dy}{dx} \qquad = \dfrac{-(y + 2x)}{(2y + x)}$$

6.3 **Exercise 5**

1 Work out $\dfrac{dy}{dx}$ for:

(a) $2x^2 + 3xy - 4y + y^2 = 5$ (b) $y^2 - 2xy + 3x - x^2 = 1$

(c) $x^2 + 4y^2 - 4x + 8y = 28$ (d) $y^3 + x^3 + xy^2 = 4$

2 For $xy = 12$,

(a) differentiate implicitly to find $\dfrac{dy}{dx}$;

(b) express y as an explicit function of x and differentiate to find $\dfrac{dy}{dx}$;

(c) show that your answers to (a) and (b) are the same.

3 For $x^2y + x^3 = 4$,

(a) use implicit differentiation to find $\dfrac{dy}{dx}$ and so show that $(-2, 3)$ is a stationary point on the curve;

(b) rewrite the equation as a function of y and use the quotient rule to find $\dfrac{dy}{dx}$. Show that this also indicates a stationary point $x = -2$.

4 (a) Find $\dfrac{dy}{dx}$ if $3xy - 2x^2 = 8$ and so show that the graph of $3xy - 2x^2 = 8$ has stationary points at $(2, 2\frac{2}{3})$ and $(-2, -2\frac{2}{3})$.

 (b) Rewrite $3xy - 2x^2 = 8$ in the form $y = f(x)$ and use the quotient rule to check the coordinates of the stationary points.

 (c) Do you prefer implicit differentiation or rearrangement and use of the quotient rule for checking the coordinates of stationary points? Which would you use if you had to *find* the coordinates of stationary points?

▶ **6.3 Tasksheet S1 – Differentiation practice (page 539)**

After working through section 6.3 you should:

1 know how to differentiate products and quotients using the two rules:

   • Product rule:
   $$\frac{d}{dx}(uv) = v\frac{du}{dx} + u\frac{dv}{dx}$$

   • Quotient rule:
   $$\frac{d}{dx}\left(\frac{u}{v}\right) = \frac{v\dfrac{du}{dx} - u\dfrac{dv}{dx}}{v^2}$$

2 understand the importance of approaching differentiation systematically and recognise when to use the chain rule and when to use the product rule;

3 know how to use implicit differentiation and be aware that this will involve the use of the chain rule and sometimes also the product rule.

6 Calculus methods 1

Miscellaneous exercise 6

1 Use the chain rule to differentiate the following; then check your answers by applying an addition formula to y and differentiating each term separately:

(a) $y = \cos(3x + 2)$ (b) $y = \cos(4x - 1)$ (c) $y = \sin(5x - 11)$

2 Differentiate: (a) $\sin^2 x$ (b) $\sin(x^2)$ (c) $\cos^3 x$ (d) $\cos^2(3x)$

3 Use the chain rule to differentiate:

(a) $(3x + 5)^2$ (b) $\sin 4x$ (c) $6x^{\frac{1}{2}}$

(d) $\sqrt{(2x - 7)}$ (e) $4\cos(2x - 7)$ (f) $3(x^2 - 5)^{-\frac{1}{2}}$

(g) $\cos^2 x$ (h) $\cos^2 5x$ (i) $\sqrt{(x^2 - 3x)}$

(j) $x + \sqrt{(x^2 + 1)}$ (k) $\dfrac{1}{(3x + 4)^3}$

4 The radius of a spherical balloon is $2\,\text{m}$ and its volume is increasing at a rate of $0.1\,\text{m}^2\,\text{min}^{-1}$. At what rate are

(a) the radius,   (b) the surface area increasing?

5 At a certain moment each edge of a block of ice measures $10\,\text{cm}$ and the surface area is decreasing at $20\,\text{cm}^2\,\text{h}^{-1}$. At what rates are

(a) the length of an edge,   (b) the volume changing?

(Assume that the ice remains cubical in shape.)

6 Sketch the graph of $y = x + \dfrac{2}{2x + 1}$ and determine the coordinates of the maximum and minimum points.

7 A circular cylinder of radius $r\,\text{cm}$, height $h\,\text{cm}$ and constant volume $100\,\text{cm}^3$ is being rolled in a machine to reduce the radius. Write down a formula for h in terms of r.

(a) At a certain moment $r = 2$. If the height is increasing at $0.2\,\text{cm}\,\text{min}^{-1}$, at what rate is the radius being reduced?

(b) Under the same conditions, at what rate is the total surface area changing?

8 Find the equation of the tangent to the ellipse $3x^2 + 4y^2 = 12$ at the point $(-1, 1\frac{1}{2})$.

9 Differentiate both sides of the equation $x^2 + y^2 = 4x + 6y + 3$ with respect to x, and hence express $\dfrac{dy}{dx}$ in terms of x and y.

10 A particle moves along a straight line so that its distance from a fixed point A on the line is x metres after t seconds where $x = t^2(t-3)^2$. When is it at rest? What is its acceleration when $t = 3$?

11 The position vector of a particle at time t is $\begin{pmatrix} a \sin^3 t \\ a \cos^3 t \end{pmatrix}$. Find the velocity vector at time t, and hence the position and velocity when $t = 0$.

12 A cone is to be made from a sector of a circular piece of card, radius 30 cm. Obtain an expression for the volume of the cone in terms of θ where the angle at the vertex of the cone is 2θ. What is the maximum value of this volume?

13 Find $\dfrac{dy}{dx}$ in terms of x and y if:

(a) $6x^2 + 5y^2 = 7$ (b) $x^2(y+1) = 4$ (c) $3x = \cos y$

14 Find the gradient of the hyperbola $x^2 - y^2 + y = 1$ at $(1, 1)$.

15 Use the product and quotient rules to differentiate:

(a) $3x^2(2x-1)$ (b) $2x \cos x$ (c) $x(x+5)^3$

(d) $\dfrac{3x+2}{4x-1}$ (e) $\dfrac{\cos 3x}{x}$ (f) $(2x+1)\sin 3x$

(g) $x^2 \tan 2x$ (h) $\sin 3x \cos 4x$ (i) $\sin^2 x \cos x$

16 Differentiate:

(a) $\cot 3x$ (b) $\dfrac{\sin x}{1 + \cos x}$ (c) $\sin x \cos x$ (d) $1 + \tan^2 x$

17 (a) Given that $y = \dfrac{\cos x}{1 - \sin x}$, find $\dfrac{dy}{dx}$ and verify that $\cos x \dfrac{dy}{dx} = y$.

(b) Show that $\dfrac{\cos x}{1 - \sin x} = \sec x + \tan x$ and hence verify your answer to (a).

18 Differentiate $\cot x$ by treating it as $\dfrac{\cos x}{\sin x}$. Also show that the derivative of $\sec x$ is $\sec x \tan x$, and find the derivative of $\operatorname{cosec} x$ in a similar form.

7 Calculus methods 2

.1 Integration techniques

7.1.1 Volumes of revolution

Consider the section of pipe illustrated here.
The curved surface is bounded by the function
$y = x^2$ and the dimensions are as shown.

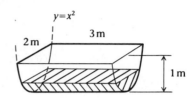

The problem is to calibrate a stick – called a
dipstick – which indicates the volume of
liquid in the container.

One way to solve this is to consider the liquid as a number of thin horizontal
slabs, each of thickness δh.

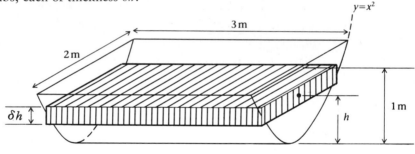

The width of a slab at distance h
from the bottom will be $2\sqrt{h}, \dots$

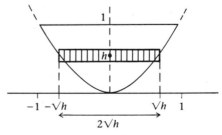

the horizontal cross-sectional area
will be $6\sqrt{h}, \dots$

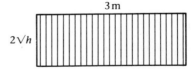

and the volume of the slab will
therefore be $6\sqrt{h}\,\delta h$.

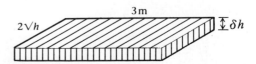

The total volume of the container will be the sum of the volumes of the thin slabs.

$$\sum 6\sqrt{h}\, \delta h$$

In the limit as $\delta h \to 0$, the exact volume is

$$V = \int_0^1 6\sqrt{h}\, dh \qquad \text{NB } \sqrt{h} = h^{0.5}$$

$$= \left[4h^{1.5} \right]_0^1$$

$$= 4\,\text{m}^3 \quad (\text{or } 4000 \text{ litres})$$

The (h, V) graph for the container is as shown.

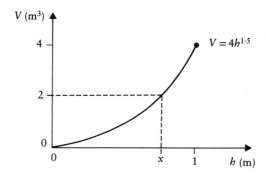

The container is half full at a height x as shown on the graph.

$$V = 4h^{1.5} = 2$$

$$\Rightarrow h^{\frac{3}{2}} = \left(\tfrac{1}{2} \right)$$

$$h = \left(\tfrac{1}{2} \right)^{\frac{2}{3}} \approx 0.63$$

$$\approx 63\,\text{cm}$$

.1A

1 At what depth will the container be:

(a) a quarter full,   (b) three-quarters full?

Another container is shown below.

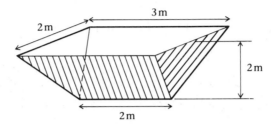

2 Explain why a thin slab at height h will have the dimensions shown below.

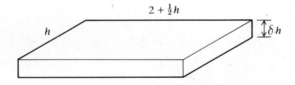

3 Calculate the volume of the container and sketch the (h, V) graph.

4 For what value of h is the container half full?

5 The depth of liquid in the container increases from 1.1 m to 1.4 m. What is the increase in volume?

This technique, often used to calculate the volume of a solid, is to imagine the solid as a large number of thin slabs. If the horizontal cross-sectional area can be expressed as a function of the vertical height, then the volume of the solid can be calculated.

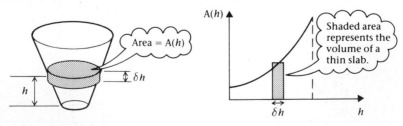

If $A(h)$ is the cross-sectional area of a solid at height h then the volume is given by

$$V = \int A(h)\, dh$$

Example 1
A container and a horizontal cross-section are shown below.

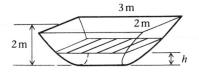

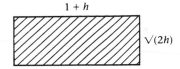

The depth of liquid increases from $h = 0.6$ m to $h = 1.2$ m. Calculate the increase in volume.

Solution
The horizontal cross-sectional area at depth h is

$(1 + h)\sqrt{(2h)} = \sqrt{2}(h^{0.5} + h^{1.5})\, \text{m}^2$.

$$\int_{0.6}^{1.2} (1 + h)\sqrt{(2h)}\, dh = \sqrt{2} \int_{0.6}^{1.2} (h^{0.5} + h^{1.5})\, dh$$

$$= \sqrt{2} \left[\tfrac{2}{3} h^{1.5} + \tfrac{2}{5} h^{2.5} \right]_{0.6}^{1.2}$$

$$= 1.536\, \text{m}^3 \quad (\text{or } 1536 \text{ litres})$$

You can apply these ideas when finding the volumes of shapes which are formed by rotating areas. For example, a solid with the same shape as a wine glass can be produced by spinning the area between the graph of $y = x^2$, the line $y = 4$ and the y-axis about the y-axis.

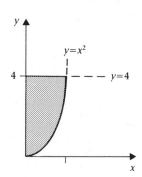

The horizontal cross-sectional areas you would use to calculate the volume of the glass are particularly simple, as they are all circles. Solids formed in such a way are called **solids of revolution**.

.1B

1 The graph of $y = x^2$ for $0 \leq x \leq 2$ is rotated about the x-axis.

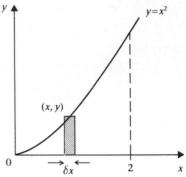

(a) Explain why the volume obtained by rotating the shaded strip is approximately $\pi y^2 \, \delta x$.

(b) If you consider the area as being made up of a large number of thin strips of this kind, the volume is

$$\int_0^2 \pi y^2 \, dx$$

To be able to integrate this you must write y^2 in terms of x. What will this give?

(c) Evaluate the volume.

2 Work out the volumes obtained by rotating each of these shaded areas about the x-axis.

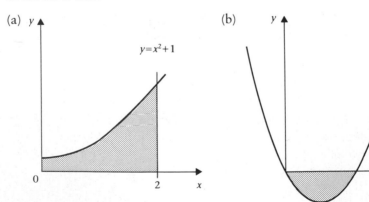

3 Work out the volume obtained by rotating $y = x^2$ for $0 \le y \le 4$ about the *y-axis*.

Work as in question 1 by first writing down the volume obtained by rotating the shaded strip about the y-axis.

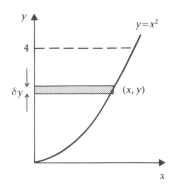

4 Work out the volume obtained by rotating the area bounded by the curve $y = \dfrac{1}{x}$, the y-axis and the lines $y = 1$ and $y = 2$ about the y-axis. (First draw a sketch to show the area being rotated.)

5 The two shaded areas shown on the graph are equal.

Would you expect the volume generated by rotating area A about the x-axis to be the same as that obtained by rotating B about the y-axis?

Justify your answer.

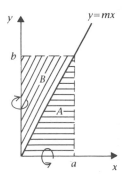

If the area between $y = f(x)$ and the x-axis for $a < x < b$ is rotated about the x-axis, then the solid formed will have volume:

$$V = \pi \int_a^b y^2 \, dx$$

Similarly, if the area between $y = f(x)$ and the y-axis for $c < y < d$ is rotated about the y-axis, then the solid formed will have volume

$$V = \pi \int_c^d x^2 \, dy$$

Example 2

The shaded area shown is part of a circle with centre at the origin and radius r.

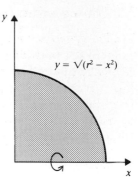

Rotate this area about the x-axis and hence prove that the volume of a sphere is given by the formula:

$$V = \tfrac{4}{3}\pi r^3$$

Solution

The solid generated will be a hemisphere and its volume is

$$V = \pi \int_0^r y^2 \, dx$$

But $y^2 = r^2 - x^2$

$$\Rightarrow V = \int_0^r r^2 - x^2 \, dx$$

$$= \pi \left[r^2 x - \tfrac{1}{3} x^3 \right]_0^r$$

$$= \tfrac{2}{3} \pi r^3$$

The volume of a sphere is twice the volume of a hemisphere and so the formula is proved.

7.1 Exercise 1

1 Find the volume formed when the area between the curve $y = x^2$, the x-axis and the lines at $x = 1$ and $x = 2$ is rotated about the x-axis.

2 The region between the curve $y = 2 - x^2$ and the x- and y-axes is rotated about:

(a) the y-axis,   (b) the x-axis.

Find the volumes of the solids formed.

3 Calculate the volumes formed by rotating about the x-axis the areas bounded by:

(a) the lines $y = x$, $x = 1$, $x = 2$ and the x-axis

(b) $y = x$ and $y = x^2$

(c) $y = x - x^2$ and $y = 0$

4 Find the points of intersection of the curve $y = x(4 - x)$ and the line $y = 2x$. Find the volume generated when the area enclosed between the curve and the line is rotated through 2π radians about the x-axis.

7.1.2 Integration by inspection

You have now used integration to find areas and volumes. You also know that to integrate a function you only need to find a function whose derivative is the original function. Unfortunately, this is far from simple in practice, as many functions *cannot* be integrated algebraically. Definite integrals can always be evaluated numerically, but having an algebraic solution is often more convenient and may even be essential in obtaining a complete solution to a problem. When integrating, it is important to know how to choose the best method.

Example 3

Find $\int (\sin 3x - x^2)\, dx$.

> **Solution**
> Always try to integrate by inspection first, since this is likely to give the answer more quickly.
>
> $$\int (\sin 3x - x^2)\, dx = -\tfrac{1}{3}\cos 3x - \tfrac{1}{3}x^3 + c$$

Example 4

Find $\int (x^5 - 3x^2)(4x^3 - 3)\, dx$.

> **Solution**
> In some cases it is necessary to multiply out brackets first.
>
> $$\int (x^5 - 3x^2)(4x^3 - 3)\, dx = \int (4x^8 - 15x^5 + 9x^2)\, dx$$
> $$= \tfrac{4}{9}x^9 - \tfrac{15}{6}x^6 + 3x^3 + c$$

To integrate a function by inspection, you must first think of a function which is likely to differentiate to the original function. You then compare the derived function with the function you want and make any small adjustment as necessary.

Example 5

Find $\int x\,e^{3x^2}\, dx$.

> **Solution**
> Differentiating the function e^{3x^2} seems to be a sensible starting point.
>
> $$\frac{d}{dx}(e^{3x^2}) = 6x\,e^{3x^2} \Rightarrow \frac{d}{dx}(\tfrac{1}{6} e^{3x^2}) = x\,e^{3x^2}$$
> $$\Rightarrow \int x\,e^{3x^2}\, dx = \tfrac{1}{6} e^{3x^2} + c$$

.1c

What functions might you try to differentiate to solve the following integrals? Find the integrals where possible.

(a) $\int x \cos x^2 \, dx$ (b) $\int x \cos 2x \, dx$

(c) $\int \cos 2x \, dx$ (d) $\int \cos x^2 \, dx$

The questions above illustrate the difficulty of integration compared with differentiation. In (a) and (b) the function being integrated is the product of two functions. (a) looks more complicated, but proves to be an easy 'backward' chain rule, while (b) requires the product rule and some very clear thinking. (c) and (d) both look straightforward, but (d) cannot be integrated algebraically.

7.1 Exercise 2

1 Find: (a) $\int \cos 3x \, dx$ (b) $\int (x+2)(x-2) \, dx$

(c) $\int e^{5x} \, dx$ (d) $\int \frac{1}{x} \, dx$

2 Write down the derivatives of:
   (a) $\sin x^3$ (b) $\cos 2x^2$ (c) $(x^2 - 3)^3$

3 Use your answers to question 2 to write down the integrals of:
   (a) $x^2 \cos x^3$ (b) $x \sin 2x^2$ (c) $x(x^2 - 3)^2$

4 The nose-cone of a rocket is obtained by rotating the area between the graph of $y = 3(1 - x^2)$ and the axes about the y-axis.
   (a) Draw a sketch showing the area being rotated.
   (b) Calculate the volume of the nose-cone.

5 (a) Sketch the parabolas $y^2 = 4x$ and $y^2 = 5x - 4$ on the same axes and find their points of intersection.
   (b) A bowl is made by rotating the area enclosed by the curves about the x-axis. Find the volume of the material used to make the bowl.

7.1.3 Integrating trigonometric functions

You have seen that not all functions can be integrated algebraically. However, many functions which may look impossible to integrate *can* be integrated if they are first rewritten. The trigonometric identities developed in Chapter 5 are particularly useful.

Example 6

Find $\int \cos^2 x \, dx$

Solution

The identity $2\cos^2 x - 1 = \cos 2x$ can be written as $\cos^2 x = \frac{1}{2} + \frac{1}{2}\cos 2x$

$$\Rightarrow \int \cos^2 x \, dx = \int \left(\frac{1}{2} + \frac{1}{2}\cos 2x \right) dx$$

$$= \frac{1}{2}x + \frac{1}{4}\sin 2x + c$$

The following identities are the **addition formulas**, developed in section 5.1.5.

$$\sin (A + B) = \sin A \cos B + \cos A \sin B \qquad ①$$

$$\sin (A - B) = \sin A \cos B - \cos A \sin B \qquad ②$$

$$\cos (A + B) = \cos A \cos B - \sin A \sin B \qquad ③$$

$$\cos (A - B) = \cos A \cos B + \sin A \sin B \qquad ④$$

These may be used to prove other useful results. For example,

$$\sin \left(\frac{\pi}{2} - \theta \right) = \sin \left(\frac{\pi}{2} \right) \cos \theta - \cos \left(\frac{\pi}{2} \right) \sin \theta \qquad \text{(from ①)}$$

$$= \cos \theta$$

$$\Rightarrow \sin \left(\frac{\pi}{2} - \theta \right) = \cos \theta$$

It may also be demonstrated easily that

$$\cos \left(\frac{\pi}{2} - \theta \right) = \sin \theta$$

$$\sec \left(\frac{\pi}{2} - \theta \right) = \operatorname{cosec} \theta$$

$$\tan \left(\frac{\pi}{2} - \theta \right) = \cot \theta$$

You should ensure that you are able to prove each of the results above.

You may have wondered about the significance of the prefix 'co' in the names of trigonometric functions. It comes from **complementary** angles, which are angles whose sum is $90°$ (or $\frac{1}{2}\pi$ radians).

The diagram shows that, when θ is acute,

$$\cos \theta = \sin \left(\tfrac{1}{2}\pi - \theta\right)$$

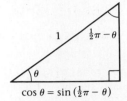

The cosine of an angle is the sine of the complementary angle.

$$\cos \theta = \sin \left(\tfrac{1}{2}\pi - \theta\right)$$

The addition formulas may also be used to prove the **sum and difference formulas.**

$$2 \cos A \cos B = \cos (A + B) + \cos (A - B)$$

$$2 \sin A \sin B = - \cos (A + B) + \cos (A - B)$$

$$2 \sin A \cos B = \sin (A + B) + \sin (A - B)$$

For example, using formulas ③ and ④ on page 467 and adding them, you obtain

$$
\begin{array}{ll}
\cos (A + B) = \cos A \cos B - \sin A \sin B & \text{③} \\
\cos (A - B) = \cos A \cos B + \sin A \sin B & \text{④} \\
\hline
\cos (A + B) + \cos (A - B) = 2 \cos A \cos B & \text{③ + ④}
\end{array}
\ +
$$

 .1D

1 Adapt the method used above to prove the remaining two sum and difference formulas.

2 Use the sum and difference formulas to prove that:

(a) $2 \cos^2 x = 1 + \cos 2x$

(b) $2 \sin^2 x = 1 - \cos 2x$

(c) $2 \sin x \cos x = \sin 2x$

All of these results, especially the **double angle** results proved in 7.1D, are useful in integration.

Example 7

Find $\displaystyle\int \sin 5x \cos 2x \, dx$

Solution

Using the identity $2 \sin A \cos B = \sin (A + B) + \sin (A - B)$,

$$\int \sin 5x \cos 2x \, dx = \int \left(\tfrac{1}{2} \sin 7x + \tfrac{1}{2} \sin 3x\right) dx$$

$$= -\tfrac{1}{14} \cos 7x - \tfrac{1}{6} \cos 3x + c$$

7.1 Exercise 3

1 Find (a) $\int \sin x \cos x \, dx$ (b) $\int \sin 3x \cos 3x \, dx$

2 Find (a) $\int \cos 5x \cos x \, dx$ (b) $\int \sin 3x \sin 7x \, dx$

3 Find $\int_0^{\frac{1}{4}\pi} \cos^2 x \, dx$

4 Calculate the volume generated by rotating the shaded area about the x-axis.

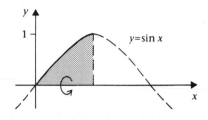

7.1.4 Integration by parts

You know that not all functions can be integrated using algebraic techniques and that those that can are not always straightforward. The first technique you should try when searching for an algebraic solution is 'trial and improvement' or 'inspection'. Think of a function which looks as though it might differentiate to the function you need to integrate, then differentiate it and make adjustments as necessary (for example, multiply or divide by a constant). We now develop some standard techniques which often prove useful when 'trial and improvement' fails.

The formula for the product rule for differentiation can be rearranged into a form which is helpful when integrating certain functions.

$$\frac{d}{dx}(uv) = v\frac{du}{dx} + u\frac{dv}{dx} \Rightarrow uv = \int v\frac{du}{dx}dx + \int u\frac{dv}{dx}dx$$

$$\Rightarrow \int u\frac{dv}{dx}dx = uv - \int v\frac{du}{dx}dx$$

This is called the formula for **integration by parts**. It provides an efficient method for integrating some products of functions.

Example 8

Find $\int x \cos 2x \, dx$

Solution

Let $u = x$, so $\dfrac{du}{dx} = 1$.

Let $\dfrac{dv}{dx} = \cos 2x$, so $v = \frac{1}{2}\sin 2x$.

$$\int x \cos 2x \, dx = \frac{1}{2}x \sin 2x - \int \frac{1}{2}\sin 2x \, dx$$

$$= \frac{1}{2}x \sin 2x + \frac{1}{4}\cos 2x + c$$

Integration by parts: $\quad \displaystyle\int u \frac{dv}{dx} dx = uv - \int v \frac{du}{dx} dx$

Integration by parts is only applicable to functions written as the *product* of two functions. When using the formula, always start by deciding which part of the product should be u and which should be $\dfrac{dv}{dx}$. Then write down $\dfrac{du}{dx}$ and v. Only when you have the functions u, v, $\dfrac{du}{dx}$ and $\dfrac{dv}{dx}$ clearly written down can you be reasonably sure of substituting correctly into the formula.

For instance, in example 8, if you had chosen to let $u = \cos 2x$ and $\dfrac{dv}{dx} = x$, then you would obtain

$$u = \cos 2x \Rightarrow \frac{du}{dx} = -2 \sin 2x \quad \text{and} \quad \frac{dv}{dx} = x \Rightarrow v = \frac{1}{2}x^2$$

$$\Rightarrow \int x \cos 2x \, dx = \frac{1}{2}x^2 \cos 2x + \int x^2 \sin 2x \, dx$$

This rearrangement of the integral does not make it simpler to evaluate. If you make the wrong choice as to which part of the product should be u and which should be $\dfrac{dv}{dx}$, then you will generally find that the integral has become more, rather than less, complicated. Experience will enable you to spot which part of the product to integrate and which to differentiate.

Integration by parts will *not always* prove successful for functions written as the product of two functions. Experience will help you decide when this method will work. The method works for all the functions in the next exercise.

7.1 Exercise 4

1 Find: (a) $\int x\,e^x\,dx$ (b) $\int x\,e^{3x}\,dx$ (c) $\int x\,e^{ax}\,dx$

2 Find: (a) $\int x\cos x\,dx$ (b) $\int x\cos 3x\,dx$ (c) $\int x\cos ax\,dx$

3 Use integration by parts twice to evaluate:

(a) $\int x^2\,e^x\,dx$ (b) $\int x^2\sin x\,dx$

4 Work out each of these definite integrals. Sketch diagrams to show the areas you have found and check that your answers seem reasonable.

(a) $\displaystyle\int_{-1}^{0} x\sin 2x\,dx$ (b) $\displaystyle\int_{-3}^{0} 2x\,e^{0.5x}\,dx$

▶ **7.1 Tasksheet E1 – By parts (page 563)**

7.1.5 Integration by substitution

Another useful technique of integration can be obtained from the chain rule for differentiation.

To find $\dfrac{dy}{dx}$ if $y = \sin(3x^2 + 5)$, let $u = 3x^2 + 5$ and $y = \sin u$.

$$\Rightarrow \frac{dy}{dx} = \frac{dy}{du} \times \frac{du}{dx} = \cos u \times 6x = 6x\cos(3x^2 + 5)$$

In the chain rule, the variable u is substituted for the original variable x and then x is substituted back at the end of the answer. The same technique can be used for integrating certain types of function. Changing the variable of the integral can be done using the chain rule.

$$\frac{dy}{du} = \frac{dy}{dx} \times \frac{dx}{du} \Rightarrow y = \int \frac{dy}{dx} \times \frac{dx}{du}\,du \quad \text{but } y = \int \frac{dy}{dx}\,dx$$

> The variable of the integral can be changed from x to u by replacing 'dx' by '$\dfrac{dx}{du}\,du$'.

Example 9

Find $y = \int x \cos(3x^2 + 5)\, dx$

Solution

Let $u = 3x^2 + 5 \Rightarrow \dfrac{du}{dx} = 6x$ This gives $\dfrac{dx}{du} = \dfrac{1}{6x}$.

$\Rightarrow y = \int x \cos(3x^2 + 5)\dfrac{1}{6x}\, du$ Replacing dx by $\dfrac{dx}{du}\, du$.

$\Rightarrow y = \frac{1}{6}\int \cos(3x^2 + 5)\, du$ This cannot be solved as it stands. You must express the integral entirely in terms of the new variable u.

$\Rightarrow y = \frac{1}{6}\int \cos u\, du$ and so $y = \frac{1}{6}\sin u + c = \frac{1}{6}\sin(3x^2 + 5) + c$

You may have been able to solve the integral in this example by inspection. While using substitution is not wrong in such a case, it is unnecessarily complicated. Substitution only works for some functions and even then it is sometimes no more than a rather slow method for finding integrals which can be found by inspection. However, there are many cases where it considerably simplifies the integral. Some of these cases are considered on tasksheet E2.

▶ 7.1 **Tasksheet E2 – Integrating the circle (page 564)**

It is important to choose the right substitution when using this method of integration. All the integrals in the exercise below lend themselves to integration by substitution, although you may feel that some of them could be done by inspection. Remember that whatever substitution you make, your final solution must be in terms of the original variable.

7.1 **Exercise 5**

1 Evaluate the following integrals by using the suggested substitution.

(a) $\int (x+3)^5\, dx$ (let $u = x + 3$)   (b) $\int x(2x-5)^6\, dx$ (let $u = 2x - 5$)

(c) $\int x^2(x-2)^7\, dx$ (let $u = x - 2$)   (d) $\int x(x^2-4)^8\, dx$ (let $u = x^2 - 4$)

(e) $\int x^2\sqrt{(x^3-2)}\, dx$ (let $u = x^3 - 2$)

2 Integrate the following functions using the suggested substitutions.

    (a) $\sin^2 x \cos x$ (let $u = \sin x$)   (b) $\cos^2 x \sin x$ (let $u = \cos x$)

3 Integrate the following functions using a suitable substitution.

    (a) $x^2 \sqrt{(x^3 + 3)}$ (b) $x(x - 3)^5$ (c) $x\sqrt{(x - 2)}$

    (d) $\cos x \sin^3 x$ (e) $\cos^5 x \sin x$ (f) $\dfrac{x}{(x + 2)^3}$

7.1.6 The reciprocal function

You know that

$$\frac{d}{dx}(\ln x) = \frac{1}{x}$$

and that

$$\int_a^b \frac{1}{x}\,dx = \left[\ln x\right]_a^b = \ln b - \ln a$$

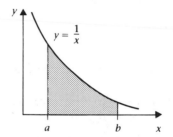

Negative values of x, however, present a problem as the function $\ln x$ is defined only for $x > 0$.

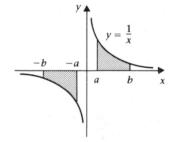

It is possible to get around this as follows, using the symmetry of the graph of $\dfrac{1}{x}$.

$$\int_{-b}^{-a} \frac{1}{x}\,dx = -\int_a^b \frac{1}{x}\,dx = -\left[\ln x\right]_a^b = \ln a - \ln b$$

This can be rewritten in a more conventional form using the modulus function, $|x|$.

$$\int_{-b}^{-a} \frac{1}{x}\,dx = \ln a - \ln b$$

$$= \ln|-a| - \ln|-b|$$

$$= \left[\ln|x|\right]_{-b}^{-a}$$

where the symbol $|x|$ denotes the absolute (or positive) value of x. For example, $|-3.5| = |3.5| = 3.5$.

You should be aware of integrals whose limits extend across the discontinuity of the $\dfrac{1}{x}$ function. For example, it is not possible to evaluate $\displaystyle\int_{-a}^{a}\frac{1}{x}\,dx$ or $\displaystyle\int_{0}^{2}\frac{1}{x-1}\,dx$. A sketch of the graph will usually reveal any problems.

$\displaystyle\int_{0}^{2}\frac{1}{x-1}\,dx$ cannot be evaluated.

The function must be continuous over the range of the integration.

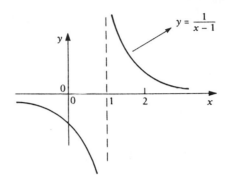

Care must be exercised; however, this forms the basis of a very useful integration technique.

Any integral of the form $\displaystyle\int\frac{f'(x)}{f(x)}\,dx$ can be integrated algebraically, as follows.

Let $u = f(x)$. Then $\dfrac{du}{dx} = f'(x)$ and $\dfrac{dx}{du} = \dfrac{1}{f'(x)}$.

The variable of the integral can be changed from x to u by replacing dx by $\dfrac{dx}{du}\,du$. So

$$\int\frac{f'(x)}{f(x)}\,dx = \int\frac{f'(x)}{f(x)}\times\frac{1}{f'(x)}\,du = \int\frac{1}{f(x)}\,du = \int\frac{1}{u}\,du$$

$$= \ln|u| + c$$

$$= \ln|f(x)| + c$$

If the graph of $f(x)$ is continuous (between a and b) then:

$$\int\frac{f'(x)}{f(x)}\,dx = \ln|f(x)| + c \quad\text{or}\quad \int_{a}^{b}\frac{f'(x)}{f(x)}\,dx = \Big[\ln|f(x)|\Big]_{a}^{b}$$

where $|f(x)|$ denotes the absolute value of $f(x)$.

Example 10

Find: (a) $\displaystyle\int \frac{3}{2x-5}\,dx$ (b) $\displaystyle\int \frac{x}{1+x^2}\,dx$ (c) $\displaystyle\int \tan x \, dx$

Solution

(a) $\displaystyle\int \frac{3}{2x-5}\,dx = \frac{3}{2}\int \frac{2}{2x-5}\,dx = \frac{3}{2}\ln|2x-5| + c$

(b) $\displaystyle\int \frac{x}{1+x^2}\,dx = \frac{1}{2}\int \frac{2x}{1+x^2}\,dx = \frac{1}{2}\ln|x^2+1| + c$

(c) $\displaystyle\int \tan x \, dx = \int \frac{\sin x}{\cos x}\,dx = -\int \frac{(-\sin x)}{\cos x}\,dx = -\ln|\cos x| + c$

7.1 Exercise 6

1 Find: (a) $\displaystyle\int \frac{3}{x-2}\,dx$ (b) $\displaystyle\int \frac{6}{2x+7}\,dx$ (c) $\displaystyle\int \frac{1}{3x-1}\,dx$

2 Evaluate: (a) $\displaystyle\int_1^2 \frac{2}{3x-2}\,dx$ (b) $\displaystyle\int_{-2}^{-1} \frac{2}{3x-2}\,dx$

3 Explain why you cannot evaluate $\displaystyle\int_1^4 \frac{3}{x-2}\,dx$.

4 Show that:

(a) $\displaystyle\int \tan x \, dx = \ln|\sec x| + c$ (b) $\displaystyle\int \cot x \, dx = \ln|\sin x| + c$

5 Find: (a) $\displaystyle\int \frac{x^2}{4-x^3}\,dx$ (b) $\displaystyle\int \frac{2x}{3+x^2}\,dx$

6E Find: (a) $\displaystyle\int \frac{x+1}{1+x^2}\,dx$ (b) $\displaystyle\int \frac{2x-1}{1+x^2}\,dx$ (c) $\displaystyle\int \frac{1}{x\ln x}\,dx$ (d) $\displaystyle\int \frac{\sin x}{1+\cos x}\,dx$

(For (a) and (b) you will need to use the substitution $\tan u = x$ with the identity $1 + \tan^2 u = \sec^2 u$.)

7.1.7 Partial fractions

Example 11

(a) Show that $\dfrac{5}{(x-3)(x+2)} = \dfrac{1}{x-3} - \dfrac{1}{x+2}.$

(b) Hence evaluate $\displaystyle\int_1^2 \dfrac{5}{(x-3)(x+2)}\,dx.$

Solution

(a) $\dfrac{1}{x-3} - \dfrac{1}{x+2} = \dfrac{(x+2)}{(x-3)(x+2)} - \dfrac{(x-3)}{(x-3)(x+2)}$

$$= \dfrac{(x+2)-(x-3)}{(x-3)(x+2)}$$

$$= \dfrac{5}{(x-3)(x+2)}$$

(b) $\displaystyle\int_1^2 \left(\dfrac{1}{x-3} - \dfrac{1}{x+2}\right)dx = \Big[\ln|x-3| - \ln|x+2|\Big]_1^2$

$$= \ln(1) - \ln(4) - \ln(2) + \ln(3)$$

$$= \ln\left(\tfrac{3}{8}\right) = -0.981 \qquad \text{(to 3 s.f.)}$$

Example 11 illustrates an important technique for integrating certain polynomial fractions – splitting a single polynomial fraction into simpler fractions which can then be integrated. This process is known as splitting or **resolving** the fraction into **partial fractions**.

Example 12

Express $\dfrac{3x+1}{x+2}$ in the form $A + \dfrac{B}{x+2}$ and hence find $\displaystyle\int \dfrac{3x+1}{x+2}\,dx.$

Solution

$$\dfrac{3x+1}{x+2} = \dfrac{3x+6-5}{x+2} = \dfrac{3x+6}{x+2} - \dfrac{5}{x+2} = 3 - \dfrac{5}{x+2}$$

Hence $\displaystyle\int \dfrac{3x+1}{x+2}\,dx = \int\left(3 - \dfrac{5}{x+2}\right)dx$

$$= 3x - 5\ln|x+2| + c$$

Example 13

Express $\dfrac{3x-8}{(x+6)(2x-1)}$ in the form $\dfrac{A}{x+6} + \dfrac{B}{2x-1}.$

Hence find $\displaystyle\int \dfrac{3x-8}{(x+6)(2x-1)}\,dx.$

Solution

$$\frac{A}{x+6} + \frac{B}{2x-1} = \frac{A(2x-1) + B(x+6)}{(x+6)(2x-1)}$$

If $\quad \dfrac{A(2x-1) + B(x+6)}{(x+6)(2x-1)} = \dfrac{3x-8}{(x+6)(2x-1)}$

then $\quad A(2x-1) + B(x+6) = 3x-8 \qquad \textcircled{1}$

Putting $x = \frac{1}{2}$ in $\textcircled{1}$ to eliminate A gives

$$6\tfrac{1}{2}B = -6\tfrac{1}{2} \Rightarrow B = -1$$

Putting $x = -6$ in $\textcircled{1}$ to eliminate B gives

$$-13A = -26 \Rightarrow A = 2$$

Thus

$$\int \frac{3x-8}{(x+6)(2x-1)}\,\mathrm{d}x = \int \left(\frac{2}{x+6} - \frac{1}{2x-1} \right) \mathrm{d}x$$

$$= 2\ln|x+6| - \tfrac{1}{2}\ln|2x-1| + c$$

The following example illustrates how to deal with the situation where the denominator consists of a repeated linear factor.

 7 .1E

1 By trying to find A and B so that $\dfrac{5+x}{(x-2)(x+1)^2} = \dfrac{A}{x-2} + \dfrac{B}{(x+1)^2}$, explain why it is not possible to do so.

2 Show that by using $\dfrac{Bx+C}{(x+1)^2}$ instead of $\dfrac{B}{(x+1)^2}$ you can obtain a possible set of partial fractions.

3 Complete the process by finding A, D and E such that

$$\frac{5+x}{(x-2)(x+1)^2} = \frac{A}{x-2} + \frac{D}{x+1} + \frac{E}{(x+1)^2} \qquad (1)$$

Hence show that

$$\frac{5+x}{(x-2)(x+1)^2} = \frac{7}{9(x-2)} - \frac{7x+19}{9(x+1)^2} \qquad (2)$$

You now have two equivalent sets of partial fractions. You may find (2) simpler to calculate, although (1) is easier to integrate.

When resolving a fraction into partial fractions,

- each linear factor in the denominator has a partial fraction of the form
$$\frac{A}{(ax+b)}$$

- each repeated linear factor $\left[\text{such as } \dfrac{1}{(ax+b)^2}\right]$ has partial fractions of

the form $\dfrac{A}{(ax+b)} + \dfrac{B}{(ax+b)^2} = \dfrac{Cx+D}{(ax+b)^2}$

Example 14

Express $\dfrac{3x^2 - x}{x^2 - 1}$ in partial fractions and hence find $\displaystyle\int \frac{3x^2 - x}{x^2 - 1}\,dx$.

Solution

This example illustrates an important preliminary to the partial fraction process. When the degree of the numerator is equal to or greater than that of the denominator, you will need to divide out until the degree of the numerator is less than that of the denominator:

$$
\begin{array}{r}
3 \\
x^2 - 1 \overline{\smash{\big)}\; 3x^2 - x} \\
\underline{3x^2 - 3} \\
3 - x
\end{array}
$$

So $\dfrac{3x^2 - x}{x^2 - 1} = 3 + \dfrac{(3 - x)}{x^2 - 1}$

Then $\dfrac{3 - x}{x^2 - 1} = \dfrac{A}{x - 1} + \dfrac{B}{x + 1} = \dfrac{A(x + 1) + B(x - 1)}{(x - 1)(x + 1)}$

$\Rightarrow \qquad 3 - x = A(x + 1) + B(x - 1)$

Put $x = 1$ to give $A = 1$, and $x = -1$ to give $B = -2$. So finally

$$\frac{3x^2 - x}{x^2 - 1} = 3 + \left(\frac{1}{x - 1} + \frac{-2}{x + 1}\right)$$

$$= 3 + \frac{1}{x - 1} - \frac{2}{x + 1}$$

and $\displaystyle\int \frac{3x^2 - x}{x^2 - 1}\,dx = \int \left(3 + \frac{1}{x - 1} - \frac{2}{x + 1}\right)dx$

$$= 3x + \ln|x - 1| - 2\ln|x + 1| + c$$

7.1 Exercise 7

1 Split into partial fractions:

(a) $\dfrac{x}{(x+2)(x+3)}$ (b) $\dfrac{3}{(2x+1)(x+1)}$ (c) $\dfrac{x+7}{2x^2+3x-2}$

(d) $\dfrac{7x-12}{(x-1)(x-2)}$ (e) $\dfrac{5x+4}{(2x+1)(3x+2)}$ (f) $\dfrac{x-1}{x(x+1)}$

2 (a) Express $\dfrac{5x+1}{x^2-x-12}$ in the form $\dfrac{A}{x+3}+\dfrac{B}{x-4}$.

(b) Hence find $\displaystyle\int \dfrac{5x+1}{x^2-x-12}\,dx$.

3 Rewrite $\dfrac{x^2+8x+9}{x^2+3x+2}$ in the form $A+\dfrac{px+q}{x^2+3x+2}$

and then in the form $A+\dfrac{B}{x+1}+\dfrac{C}{x+2}$.

Hence evaluate $\displaystyle\int_0^1 \dfrac{x^2+8x+9}{x^2+3x+2}\,dx$.

4 By first resolving into partial fractions, find:

(a) $\displaystyle\int \dfrac{x+1}{(x-1)(x-2)}\,dx$ (b) $\displaystyle\int \dfrac{1}{x^2-4}\,dx$ (c) $\displaystyle\int \dfrac{x+1}{x^2+5x+6}\,dx$

5 (a) Express $\dfrac{8x-72}{(x+1)(x-3)^2}$ in the form $\dfrac{A}{x+1}+\dfrac{B}{x-3}+\dfrac{C}{(x-3)^2}$.

(b) Express $\dfrac{1}{(x+1)(x-1)^2}$ in partial fractions and hence find

$\displaystyle\int \dfrac{dx}{(x+1)(x-1)^2}$.

(c) Evaluate $\displaystyle\int_2^3 \dfrac{x}{(x+1)(x-1)^2}\,dx$.

6 Resolve into partial fractions:

(a) $\dfrac{x^2}{x^2-9}$ (b) $\dfrac{3x^2}{x^2-5x+4}$

After working through section 7.1 you should:

1 know how to use integration to calculate a volume by

- integrating a cross-sectional area with respect to height,

$$V = \int A(h)\, dh;$$

- rotating an area about the x-axis, $V = \pi \int y^2\, dx;$

- rotating an area about the y-axis, $V = \pi \int x^2\, dy;$

2 know how to integrate a function by inspection;

3 know how to use trigonometric identities to rewrite an expression so that it can be integrated by inspection;

4 understand how to use the technique of integration by parts;

5 know how integration by parts and the product rule for differentiation are related;

6 understand how to use the technique of substitution for integration;

7 know how integration by substitution and the chain rule for differentiation are related;

8 understand why it is necessary to use the absolute value of the function in the result

$$\int \frac{f'(x)}{f(x)}\, dx = \ln |f(x)| + c$$

9 know how to split a polynomial fraction into partial fractions so that the function can be integrated.

7 Calculus methods 2

.2 Polynomial approximations

7.2.1 Taylor's first approximation

You can determine the value of a function such as $\sin x$ or e^x for whatever value of x you choose, merely by pressing the appropriate button on a calculator. You may, however, have wondered how the calculator computes these values. When a computer evaluates a function such as $\sin x$, it does so by evaluating a polynomial approximation to the function. This chapter will look at how you can obtain and make use of polynomial approximations in order to solve equations and handle complicated functions.

The simplest polynomial approximation to a function is linear. You will recall that a differentiable function always appears to be locally straight under sufficient magnification and it is because of this that the first approximation of a function at a point is taken to be the tangent to the graph of the function at that point.

Such an approximation is known as **Taylor's first approximation**, after the English mathematician, Brook Taylor (1685–1731).

For example,

$$y = x$$

is Taylor's first approximation to

$$y = \sin x \quad \text{near the origin.}$$

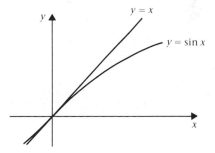

With x in radians, $\dfrac{\mathrm{d}}{\mathrm{d}x}(\sin x) = \cos x$.

When $x = 0$ (at the origin) the gradient of $\sin x$ is 1 ($\cos 0 = 1$).

The equation of the tangent to $\sin x$ at $(0,0)$ is therefore $y = x$.

This linear approximation is only valid near $(0,0)$. To illustrate this, the values of x and $\sin x$ are tabulated below.

x	1	0.5	0.2	0.1	0.01
$\sin x$	0.84	0.479	0.199	0.0998	0.009 999 8

If you plot the graphs of $y = x$ and $y = \sin x$ on the same axes on a graph plotter, you can see the 'error'.

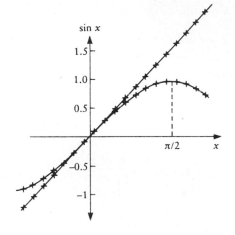

The percentage error is given by

$$100\left(\frac{x - \sin x}{\sin x}\right).$$

The error function can also be plotted on a graph plotter.

What constitutes a reasonable approximation is open to discussion. The approximation is good for $-0.5 < x < 0.5$ if an error of no more than 5% is considered reasonable.

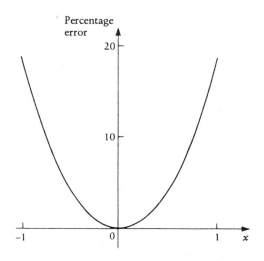

Taylor's first approximation is often used as a 'rule of thumb'. For example, you will sometimes find it useful to say that '$\sin x = x$ when x is small', although $\sin x$ is actually equal to x only when $x = 0$.

You should confirm for yourself that similar linear approximations for $\cos x$ and $\tan x$ at $x = 0$ are $\cos x \approx 1$ and $\tan x \approx x$.

For small x,

$$\sin x \approx x \qquad \cos x \approx 1 \qquad \tan x \approx x$$

where x is measured in radians.

It is possible to find a Taylor approximation at a point other than the origin. The process simply involves finding the equation of the tangent at the given point.

Example 1

Find Taylor's first approximation to the function $y = \sin x$ when $x = \frac{1}{6}\pi$.

Solution

The point P on $y = \sin x$ has coordinates $(\frac{1}{6}\pi, \frac{1}{2})$, i.e. $(0.52, 0.5)$.

Since $\dfrac{dy}{dx} = \cos x$, the gradient of the graph at P is $\cos\frac{1}{6}\pi = 0.87$.

The equation of the tangent at P is given by

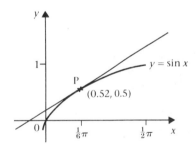

$$\frac{y - 0.5}{x - 0.52} = 0.87$$

$$\Rightarrow \quad y - 0.5 = 0.87(x - 0.52)$$

$$\Rightarrow \qquad y = 0.87x + 0.05$$

which is Taylor's first approximation.

7.2 **Exercise 1**

1 Find Taylor's first approximations to the following functions at the points given. Check your answers using a graph plotter.

(a) $y = x^3 + 5x - 2$ at $(2, 16)$ (b) $y = e^x$ at $(0, 1)$ (c) $y = \ln x$ at $(1, 0)$

(d) $y = x^4 - x^2$ at $(2, 12)$ (e) $y = x^2 + \ln x$ at $(1, 1)$

2 (a) Find Taylor's first approximation to $y = \cos x$ at $x = \frac{1}{2}\pi$.

(b) Use your approximation to estimate $\cos 1.5$ to 6 decimal places.

(c) What is the percentage error in your estimate?

7.2.2 The Newton–Raphson method

Taking a tangent as an approximation to a function has an extremely useful application. The contemporary and colleague of Isaac Newton, Joseph Raphson (1648–1715) realised that it was possible to use a tangent approximation to a curve in order to solve virtually *any* equation quickly and rapidly using an iterative approach.

Up to now you have used iterative methods for solving equations. While in some cases they can be quick and easy to use, in other cases they are slow and unreliable. The Newton–Raphson method, although using a more complex formula, is usually both fast and reliable.

All iterative methods require a first approximation to a root, which will normally be obtained by doing a quick sketch of the graph. The method can be illustrated by looking at a specific problem, such as solving $x^2 - 3\sin x = 0$.

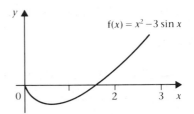

From the graph, it can be seen that $x = 2$ is a reasonable first approximation to the root. At $x = 2$, $f(2) = 4 - 3\sin 2 = 1.27$ and, since $f'(x) = 2x - 3\cos x$, the gradient of the tangent is $f'(2) = 4 - 3\cos 2 = 5.25$.

Using the method of section 7.2.1, Taylor's first approximation is $y = 5.25x - 9.23$.

By enlarging the region around the root it can be seen that a better approximation can be found where the tangent at $x = 2$ cuts the x-axis, i.e. where $5.25x - 9.23 = 0$. This gives $x = 1.758$.

This method will generalise to give a formula for the improved approximation.

Suppose the equation to be solved is $f(x) = 0$ and the root you are tying to find is α.

If $x = a$ is the first guess and the tangent at $x = a$ crosses the x-axis at $x = b$, then $x = b$ will be closer to the actual solution α than was $x = a$.

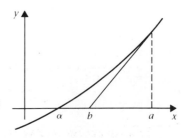

You can find the value of b as follows.

Since $f'(a)$ is the gradient of the graph at $x = a$,

$$\frac{f(a)}{a - b} = f'(a)$$

$$\Rightarrow \quad \frac{f(a)}{f'(a)} = a - b$$

$$\Rightarrow \quad b = a - \frac{f(a)}{f'(a)}$$

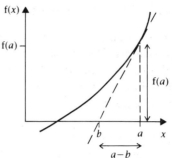

You can now use this 'improved guess' as the starting value in the process and hence obtain a value for x which is even closer to the root. So if you repeat the process several times you can get closer and closer to the solution of $f(x) = 0$.

 .2A

You have seen that, if $x = a$ is an approximation to the solution of $f(x) = 0$, then $b = a - \dfrac{f(a)}{f'(a)}$ appears to be a better approximation.

1 The equation $x^2 - 3 \sin x = 0$ has a solution near $x = 2$.

  (a) If $f(x) = x^2 - 3 \sin x$, write down $f'(x)$.

  (b) Use the formula, $b = a - \dfrac{f(a)}{f'(a)}$ with $a = 2$, to obtain a better approximation to the root.

  (c) Taking your improved approximation in (b) as your new value for a, find a new approximation.

  (d) Continue this process until you have an estimate of the root which is accurate to 6 decimal places.

2

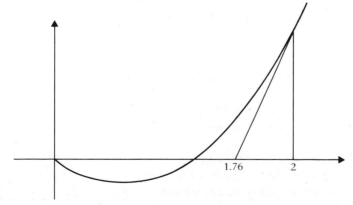

The diagram shows how the second approximation, 1.76, is obtained geometrically from the first approximation, $a = 2$. Copy the diagram and show how the third and fourth approximations can be constructed.

The Newton–Raphson process generates an iterative sequence, $x_1, x_2, x_3, x_4, \ldots, x_n$, and the equation

$$b = a - \frac{f(a)}{f'(a)}$$

can be written as

$$x_{n+1} = x_n - \frac{f(x_n)}{f'(x_n)}$$

3 (a) Sketch the graph of $f(x) = x^2 - 6 + 6e^{-x}$.

   (b) Find a suitable first approximation x_1 to the positive root of the equation

   $$x^2 - 6 + 6e^{-x} = 0$$

   (c) Write down $f'(x)$ and hence give the Newton–Raphson formula.

   (d) Use the Newton–Raphson formula to find the root correct to 4 decimal places.

Although the Newton–Raphson process is generally efficient, it can give rise to problems. The next example illustrates one such problem.

4

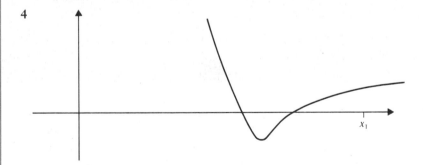

   Copy the diagram and use the method of question 2 to show how to construct the approximations x_2, x_3, from the starting value of x_1 given. Why is Newton–Raphson not appropriate in this case?

5E (a) Use a computer or calculator with function $f(x) = 30 - 15x - 2x^2 + x^3$ and $x_1 = 5$ to solve the equation $30 - 15x - 2x^2 + x^3 = 0$.

   (b) Do other starting values work? Can you find any that do not? What happens if $x_1 = 3, 3.1, 2.8, 2.9$?

(c) What range of starting values converges to the root $x = 2$?

(d) What happens when: (i) $x_1 = -0.68$ (ii) $x_1 = -0.69$?

(e) Change the function and solve $5 \cos x - x = 0$ with starting values

(i) $x_1 = -1$ (ii) $x_1 = -0.5$ (iii) $x_1 = -7$ (iv) $x_1 = -6.5$

Comment on your results.

(f) Change the function to $2\sqrt{x} - 1 = 0$. Can you find a suitable starting point?

6E Try to solve $\sin x - \frac{1}{50} \sin (100x) = 0$, with starting values $x = 1, 2$ or 3. Zoom in on the curve and explain what is happening.

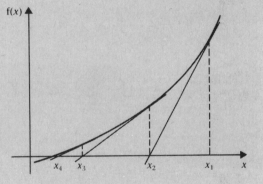

The Newton–Raphson method gives a sequence of numbers $x_1, x_2, x_3, \ldots$, which converges to a zero of a function $f(x)$. For a starting value x_1

$$x_2 = x_1 - \frac{f(x_1)}{f'(x_1)}$$

$$x_3 = x_2 - \frac{f(x_2)}{f'(x_2)}$$

$\ldots$

The general iterative formula is

$$x_{n+1} = x_n - \frac{f(x_n)}{f'(x_n)}$$

Providing the first estimate, x_1, is 'good', the method will usually converge to a zero of the function very quickly. A good first estimate is one such that the graph is locally straight at all points between the zero and the estimate, and has no turning points. If the initial estimate is itself near a turning point, the Newton–Raphson method will usually take you further from the zero, and becomes unpredictable.

In practice, not all equations are of the form

$$f(x) = 0$$

Sometimes an equation will take the form

$$h(x) = g(x)$$

Such an equation can always be rearranged into the form

$$h(x) - g(x) = 0$$

and so the problem becomes one of finding the zero of the function $h(x) - g(x)$.

Example 2
Solve $\sin 2x = x^2$.

Solution
(Note that you *must* work in radians here.)

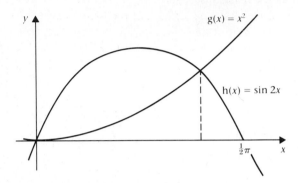

This equation cannot be solved algebraically, so a numerical method must be used.

The sketch shows that there are two solutions.

$x = 0$ is one solution, and the other is somewhere between $x = 0$ and $x = \frac{1}{2}\pi$.

This suggests a possible value of $x_1 = 1$.

The equation can be expressed in the form $f(x) = 0$ by writing

$$x^2 - \sin 2x = 0$$

Then $f(x) = x^2 - \sin 2x$ and $f'(x) = 2x - 2\cos 2x$

Hence the iteration formula will be

$$x_{n+1} = x_n - \frac{x_n^2 - \sin 2x_n}{2x_n - 2\cos 2x_n}.$$

Taking $x_1 = 1$, then $x_2 = 0.967\,976$, $x_3 = 0.966\,878$, $x_4 = 0.966\,877$ and $x_5 = 0.966\,877$. Since x_4 and x_5 agree to 6 decimal places, you can conclude that $x = 0.966\,877$ to 6 decimal places.

The Newton–Raphson method is usually extremely efficient. You will often find that if x_1 is accurate to 1 decimal place, then x_2 is accurate to 2 decimal places, x_3 to 4 decimal places, x_4 to 8 decimal places and x_5 to 16 decimal places!

7.2 Exercise 2

1 Solve $x = \cos x$ correct to 6 decimal places. How can you be sure there is only one root to this equation?

2 Use the Newton–Raphson method to find the three roots of $x^3 = 3x - 1$ to 6 decimal places.

3 Find the positive solution of $e^{2x} = 3\cos x$ correct to 6 decimal places.

4 A circular disc, centre O, is divided by a straight cut AB so that the smaller area ACB is $\frac{1}{10}$ the area of the whole circle.

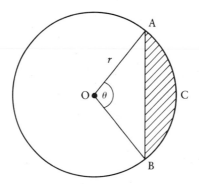

Show that, if angle AOB $= \theta$ radians, then $\theta - \frac{1}{5}\pi = \sin\theta$.

Solve the equation and find θ correct to 3 decimal places.

5 Two circles of radius r intersect as shown. The angle subtended by the common chord at the centre of each circle is 2θ.

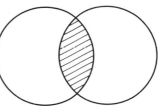

(a) Find an expression for the shaded area in terms of r and θ.

(b) If the shaded area is equal to $\frac{1}{4}$ of the area of one of the two circles, show that $8\theta - 4\sin 2\theta = \pi$ and hence find θ to 4 decimal places.

6 Two savers each have a regular income to invest. Tom invests in a savings account and calculates that after t years his savings will be worth £5000($e^{0.1t} - 1$). Jerry invests in life assurance and he estimates that after t years his savings will be worth £700$t(1 + 0.06t)$.

(a) Who has more savings:

  (i) in the short term;   (ii) in the long term?

(b) After how long will Tom's and Jerry's savings be equal? (Give your answer in years and months.)

7.2.3 Maclaurin's series

To calculate the equation of a linear function, you need to know either two points on the graph or one point and the gradient of the graph at that point. You need two pieces of information to define a linear graph. It seems logical to assume that you need three pieces of information to define a quadratic graph, and this is indeed the case.

If, for example, you know that the graph passes through three points, $(-2, 14)$, $(0, 30)$ and $(3, 24)$, and if you let the equation of the graph be $f(x) = a + bx + cx^2$, you can find three simultaneous equations in the three unknowns a, b and c.

If, on the other hand, you know that the graph passes through two specified points and if you also know the gradient of the graph at one of the points, again you have three pieces of information and can therefore deduce the equation of the graph.

These are two ways in which a set of three conditions can define a quadratic function. An alternative set of three conditions is the values of y and its first and second derivatives, $\dfrac{dy}{dx}$ and $\dfrac{d^2y}{dx^2}$, at a single point.

Two pieces of information are never sufficient. For example, there are infinitely many different quadratic functions, $f(x) = a + bx + cx^2$, which pass through the point $(0, 10)$ with gradient 4.

Since $f(0) = 10$, $\quad a + b \times 0 + c \times 0^2 = 10 \Rightarrow a = 10$

$$f'(x) = b + 2cx$$

and since $f'(0) = 4$,

$$b + 2c \times 0 = 4 \Rightarrow b = 4.$$

So $f(x) = 10 + 4x + cx^2$ satisfies the given conditions. Since any value of c will do, there are infinitely many quadratics which satisfy the stated conditions.

If you plot your equations on a graph plotter, they all pass through the same point $(0, 10)$ and they all have the same gradient (4) at that point. However, you will notice that some of the graphs are more *curved* than others. In fact, it is the rate at which the gradient is increasing or decreasing which is different for each of them. The rate at which a gradient is increasing or decreasing is easily calculated. You simply find the gradient of the gradient graph. In other words, differentiate the function twice.

The symbol $f''(x)$ is used when the function is differentiated twice, $f^{(3)}(x)$ is used when the function is differentiated three times, $f^{(4)}(x)$ when the function is differentiated four times, and so on.

For example,

$$f(x) = a + bx + cx^2$$

$$\Rightarrow f'(x) = b + 2cx$$

$$\Rightarrow f''(x) = 2c$$

The Leibnitz notation for $f^{(n)}(x)$ is $\dfrac{d^n y}{dx^n}$ $\left(\text{i.e. } f''(x) = \dfrac{d}{dx}\left(\dfrac{dy}{dx}\right) = \dfrac{d^2 y}{dx^2}\right).$

Example 3
Find the quadratic approximation to $f(x) = \cos x$ at $x = 0$.

Solution
Suppose $\quad f(x) = \cos x \approx a + bx + cx^2, \qquad f(0) = 1 \Rightarrow a = 1$

Then $\quad f'(x) = -\sin x \approx b + 2cx, \qquad f'(0) = 0 \Rightarrow b = 0$

$\quad\quad\quad f''(x) = -\cos x \approx 2c, \qquad f''(0) = -1 \Rightarrow c = -\tfrac{1}{2}$

The quadratic approximation to $\cos x$ at $x = 0$ is

$$\cos x \approx 1 - \tfrac{1}{2}x^2$$

Taylor's first approximation to a function at a point is a linear function which passes through the point with the same gradient as the function. A better approximation to a function can be found by using a quadratic graph. For example, the graph of $p(x) = 1 - \tfrac{1}{2}x^2$ is a good approximation to $f(x) = \cos x$,

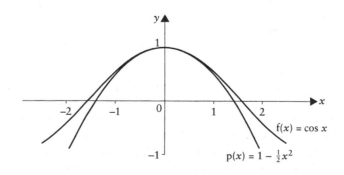

while $p(x) = 1 + x + \frac{1}{2}x^2$ is a good approximation to $f(x) = e^x$.

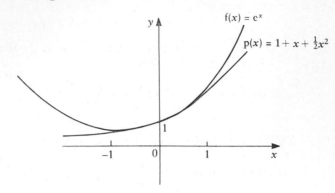

Comparing the properties of the function $f(x) = \cos x$ with its approximating quadratic $p(x) = 1 - \frac{1}{2}x^2$ gives:

- $f(0) = 1$, $p(0) = 1$
  i.e. they are equal at $x = 0$.

- $f'(x) = -\sin x \Rightarrow f'(0) = 0$, $p'(x) = -x \Rightarrow p'(0) = 0$
  i.e. their gradients are equal at $x = 0$.

- $f''(x) = -\cos x \Rightarrow f''(0) = -1$, $p''(x) = -1 \Rightarrow p''(0) = -1$
  i.e. their second derivatives are equal at $x = 0$.

Thus a quadratic approximation to $\cos x$ at $x = 0$ is a quadratic which passes through $(0, 1)$ and has the same gradient and second derivative as $\cos x$.

The cubic approximation will be a function which passes through the point and has the same gradient, the same second derivative and the same third derivative as the function.

Higher order polynomial approximations are possible if the function being approximated can be differentiated repeatedly at a point. You would, for example, have to differentiate a function five times at a point to calculate the fifth degree approximation.

This idea is developed in the questions which follow.

 .2B

You have seen that when you approximate to a function $f(x)$ using the quadratic $p(x) = a + bx + cx^2$, you have to solve

$$f(0) = a \qquad f'(0) = b \qquad f''(0) = 2c$$

To extend this method to general polynomials, you have to solve more equations of this form.

1 If $p(x) = a + bx + cx^2 + dx^3$ and $p(0) = 12$, $p'(0) = 11$, $p''(0) = 10$ and
   $p^{(3)}(0) = 6$, find a, b, c and d.

2 If $p(x) = a + bx + cx^2 + dx^3$ express a, b, c and d in terms of $p(0)$, $p'(0)$,
   $p''(0)$ and $p^{(3)}(0)$ and hence show that

   $$p(x) = p(0) + p'(0)x + p''(0)\frac{x^2}{2} + p^{(3)}(0)\frac{x^3}{6}$$

3 Explain why, if $p(x)$ is a polynomial of degree four, then

   $$p(x) = p(0) + p'(0)x + p''(0)\frac{x^2}{2!} + p^{(3)}(0)\frac{x^3}{3!} + p^{(4)}(0)\frac{x^4}{4!}$$

4 (a) In a similar way, if $p(x)$ is a polynomial of degree five write down $p(x)$
        in terms of its derivatives at $x = 0$.

   (b) Generalise this result to a polynomial of degree n.

5 If $f(x) = e^{2x}$, find $f(0)$, $f'(0)$, $f''(0)$, $f^{(3)}(0)$, $f^{(4)}(0)$.

   Hence explain why $1 + 2x + 2x^2 + \dfrac{4x^3}{3} + \dfrac{2x^4}{3}$ is a good approximation

   to e^{2x} for values of x near $x = 0$.

   Plot both of these functions on a graph plotter and suggest a range of
   x-values for which the approximation is good.

If a function $f(x)$ can be differentiated n times at $x = 0$, then a polynomial of
degree n which has the same derivatives as the function will be a good
approximation to the function for values of x near zero.

The result developed in 7.2B above was published by Colin Maclaurin
(1698–1746). Maclaurin was a Professor of Mathematics at Aberdeen by the age
of nineteen and a Fellow of the Royal Society at twenty-one. In 1742 he
published his book *Treatise on Fluxions*, which included a description of the
'Maclaurin series'. He took part in opposing the march of the Young Pretender
when the Jacobites attacked Edinburgh in 1745 and when the city fell he fled to
York, where he died. Despite its name, Maclaurin's series was first used by
James Stirling.

> **Maclaurin's series**
> If $f(x)$ can be differentiated n times at $x = 0$, then the approximation
>
> $$f(x) = f(0) + f'(0)x + \frac{f''(0)x^2}{2!} + \frac{f^{(3)}(0)x^3}{3!} + \frac{f^{(4)}(0)x^4}{4!} + \cdots$$
> $$+ \frac{f^{(n)}(0)x^n}{n!}$$
>
> will be good for values of x close to $x = 0$.

Example 4

(a) Find the Maclaurin's series for $\sin x$.

(b) Use the series found in (a) to find the series for $\sin(x^2)$.

Solution

(a) If $f(x) = \sin x$ then $f(0) = 0$

$f'(x) = \cos x \quad \Rightarrow \quad f'(0) = 1$

$f''(x) = -\sin x \Rightarrow \quad f''(0) = 0$

$f^{(3)}(x) = -\cos x \Rightarrow f^{(3)}(0) = -1$

$f^{(4)}(x) = \sin x \quad \Rightarrow \quad f^{(4)}(0) = 0$

$f^{(5)}(x) = \cos x \quad \Rightarrow \quad f^{(5)}(0) = 1 \qquad$ and the cycle repeats itself.

Thus, using the values for $f(0)$, $f'(0)$, $f''(0), \ldots$, Maclaurin's series will be

$$f(0) + f'(0)x + \frac{f''(0)x^2}{2!} + \frac{f^{(3)}(0)x^3}{3!} + \frac{f^{(4)}(0)x^4}{4!} + \cdots + \frac{f^{(7)}(0)x^7}{7!} + \cdots$$

$$= 0 + 1x + \frac{0x^2}{2!} - \frac{1x^3}{3!} + \frac{0x^4}{4!} + \frac{1x^5}{5!} + \frac{0x^6}{6!} - \frac{1x^7}{7!} + \cdots$$

$$\Rightarrow \sin x = x - \frac{x^3}{3!} + \frac{x^5}{5!} - \frac{x^7}{7!} + \frac{x^9}{9!} - \cdots$$

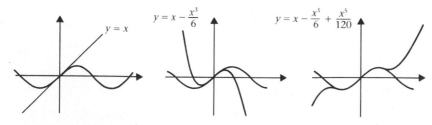

(b) You can use the series

$$\sin x = x - \frac{x^3}{3!} + \frac{x^5}{5!} - \frac{x^7}{7!} + \cdots$$

to find the series for $\sin x^2$ by replacing x by x^2.

Thus $\sin(x^2) = x^2 - \frac{(x^2)^3}{3!} + \frac{(x^2)^5}{5!} - \frac{(x^2)^7}{7!} + \cdots$

$$= x^2 - \frac{x^6}{3!} + \frac{x^{10}}{5!} - \frac{x^{14}}{7!}$$

 .2c

1 (a) Show that $\cos x = 1 - \frac{x^2}{2!} + \frac{x^4}{4!} - \frac{x^6}{6!} + \cdots$

(b) Find the Maclaurin's series for e^x.

For the following questions you will need to use the results given below.

$$\frac{d}{dx}(\ln(1+x)) = \frac{1}{1+x}$$

$$\frac{d}{dx}((1+x)^n) = n(1+x)^{n-1}$$

For example,

$$\frac{d}{dx}\left(\frac{1}{(1+x)^2}\right) = \frac{d}{dx}((1+x)^{-2}) = -2(1+x)^{-3}$$

2 (a) If $f(x) = \ln x$, explain what happens if you attempt to evaluate $f(0)$.

(b) Explain why it is not possible to find a Maclaurin's series for $\ln x$.

For the reason given in question 2, $\ln x$ does not have a series expansion. The series for $\ln(1+x)$ is found instead.

3 (a) If $f(x) = \ln(1+x)$, write down $f'(x)$.

(b) By writing $\frac{1}{1+x}$ as $(1+x)^{-1}$, write down $f''(x)$.

(c) Show that $f^{(3)}(x) = 2(1+x)^{-3}$ and find $f^{(4)}(x)$ and $f^{(5)}(x)$.

(d) Find $f(0)$, $f'(0)$, $f''(0)$, $f^{(3)}(0)$, $f^{(4)}(0)$ and $f^{(5)}(0)$.

(e) Show that the Maclaurin's series for $\ln(1+x)$ is

$$x - \frac{x^2}{2} + \frac{x^3}{3} - \frac{x^4}{4} + \frac{x^5}{5} \cdots$$

4E (a) If $f(x) = (1 + x)^n$, write down $f'(x)$.

(b) Write down $f''(x)$ and show that $f^{(3)}(x) = n(n-1)(n-2)(1+x)^{n-3}$.

(c) Use the results from parts (a) and (b) to show that the first four terms of $(1+x)^n$ are

$$1 + nx + \frac{n(n-1)}{2!}x^2 + \frac{n(n-1)(n-2)}{3!}x^3$$

Not all series are valid for all values of x. For example, although

$$\frac{1}{1+x} = 1 - x + x^2 - x^3 + x^4 \ldots$$

for values of x between -1 and 1, when x is put equal to 2 the result

$$\frac{1}{1+2} = 1 - 2 + 4 - 8 + 16 \ldots$$

is clearly untrue!

The following standard results are important.

$$\sin x = x - \frac{x^3}{3!} + \frac{x^5}{5!} - \frac{x^7}{7!} + \cdots \qquad (\text{all } x)$$

$$\cos x = 1 - \frac{x^2}{2!} + \frac{x^4}{4!} - \frac{x^6}{6!} + \cdots \qquad (\text{all } x)$$

$$e^x = 1 + x + \frac{x^2}{2!} + \frac{x^3}{3!} + \frac{x^4}{4!} + \cdots \qquad (\text{all } x)$$

$$\ln(1 + x) = x - \frac{x^2}{2} + \frac{x^3}{3} - \frac{x^4}{4} + \cdots \qquad (-1 < x \leq 1)$$

$$(1+x)^n = 1 + nx + \frac{n(n-1)}{2!}x^2 + \frac{n(n-1)(n-2)}{3!}x^3 + \cdots$$

$$(-1 < x < 1)$$

7.2 Exercise 3

1 Find the first five terms of the Maclaurin's series for $e^{\frac{1}{2}x}$

(a) by differentiation and evaluation of $f(0)$, $f'(0)$, $\ldots$

(b) by substituting into the series $e^x = 1 + x + \frac{x^2}{2!} + \frac{x^3}{3!} + \cdots$

2 (a) Use your calculator to find $\cos 0.5$.

(b) How many terms of the cosine series are needed to give an answer that is accurate to ± 0.001?

(c) How many terms of the cosine series are needed to give $\cos 1.0$ to an accuracy of ± 0.001?

3 Write down the nth term of the series for each of the functions:

(a) e^x (b) $\cos x$ (c) e^{x^2}

4 (a) Find the Maclaurin's series for $\ln(1 - x)$.

(b) Use the result $1 - x^2 = (1 - x)(1 + x)$, together with a property of logs, to find the series for $\ln(1 - x^2)$.

5 (a) Show that $e^{-x} \approx 1 - x$.

(b) Use your result in (a) to show that $\sqrt{(1 - e^{-x})} \approx \sqrt{x}$.

(c) What is the percentage error in using $\sqrt{x}$ as an approximation to $\sqrt{(1 - e^{-x})}$ when $x = 0.1$?

After working through section 7.2 you should:

1 be able to find Taylor's first approximation to a function;

2 know the Newton–Raphson method for solving equations;

3 be able to find second and higher derivatives and be familiar with the notations

$$f'(x), \quad f''(x), \quad f^{(3)}(x), \quad f^{(4)}(x), \quad \ldots, \quad f^{(n)}(x)$$

and

$$\frac{d^2y}{dx^2}, \quad \frac{d^3y}{dx^3}, \quad \ldots, \quad \frac{d^ny}{dx^2}$$

4 be able to use a Maclaurin's series to find a polynomial approximation to a function;

5 know the Maclaurin's series of particular functions such as $\sin x$, $\cos x$, e^x, $\ln(1 + x)$ and $(1 + x)^n$ and know the range of x for which these series are valid.

7 Calculus methods 2

.3 Differential equations

7.3.1 Introduction

Many situations where mathematics is used to model the real world lead to the formulation of differential equations. Any equation involving a derivative, such as $\dfrac{dy}{dx}$ or $\dfrac{ds}{dt}$ is called a **differential equation**.

For example, the cooling of an object which is hotter than its surroundings is described by Newton's law of cooling, which states that

The rate of cooling at any instant is directly proportional to the difference in temperature between the object and its surroundings.

Using calculus notation, this may be expressed as

$$\frac{dy}{dt} = -ky$$

where y is the difference in temperature between the object and its surroundings. $\dfrac{dy}{dt}$ is the rate at which the temperature difference is changing with respect to time. The constant of proportionality is k and the negative sign indicates that the object is cooling. The equation expressing Newton's law is therefore a differential equation.

Because of the frequency with which differential equations occur and their importance both within mathematics and in its areas of application, the understanding and solution of differential equations is a substantial element in any course in mathematics. In this section we consider some of the situations which give rise to these equations, and consider ways to solve them.

Finding a solution to a differential equation means expressing the relationship between the variables in a form which does not contain any derivatives. In the case of the equation for Newton's law,

$$\frac{dy}{dt} = -ky$$

it means expressing y as a function of t. We shall return to this particular equation as the necessary methods to solve it are developed.

Some differential equations can be solved algebraically by inspection. For example, if you know that $\dfrac{dy}{dx} = x^2$, then integrating the function gives $y = \frac{1}{3}x^3 + c$.

There is a family of solution curves which all satisfy the differential equation.

If, for example, you know that the graph passes through the point $(3, 1)$, then you can specify the **particular solution** as $y = \frac{1}{3}x^3 - 8$.

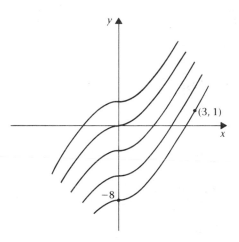

Example 1

Find the solution to the following differential equation, for which $y = 1$ when $x = 0$.

$$\frac{dy}{dx} = 3x + 2$$

Solution

The equation may be solved directly by integration with respect to the variable x.

$$y = \int (3x + 2)\, dx$$

$$\Rightarrow y = \frac{3x^2}{2} + 2x + c$$

$$y = 1 \quad \text{when } x = 0 \quad \Rightarrow \quad c = 1$$

So $\quad y = \dfrac{3x^2}{2} + 2x + 1 \quad$ is the particular solution required.

Notice that in this case the solution involves integration once only, and that this yields a single constant of integration. In the solution of differential equations, the constants of integration are a most important part of the solution process, and *must not be overlooked*.

Many differential equations can be solved *only* by numerical methods, and we consider some methods for doing this later in this section. Equally, there are a number of techniques for the solution of particular types of differential equation which do *not* require numerical methods. Example 2, together with exercise 1 which follows, will give you some practice with differential equations which can be solved by 'simple' algebraic methods.

Example 2

For the differential equation $\dfrac{dy}{dx} = 2x + \sin x$, find the value of y when $x = 2$ for the particular solution through $(3, 4)$.

Solution

$$y = \int (2x + \sin x)\, dx$$

$$\Rightarrow y = x^2 - \cos x + c, \quad \text{but } y = 4 \text{ when } x = 3$$

$$\Rightarrow 4 = 3^2 - \cos 3 + c$$

$$\Rightarrow 4 = 9 + 0.99 + c$$

$$\Rightarrow c = -5.99 \quad \text{(to 2 d.p.)}$$

$$\Rightarrow y = x^2 - \cos x - 5.99 \text{ and so when } x = 2, \quad y = -1.57 \quad \text{(to 2 d.p.)}$$

7.3 Exercise 1

1 Solve the following differential equations and in each case make a sketch showing some particular solutions.

(a) $\dfrac{dy}{dx} = e^x$ (b) $\dfrac{dy}{dx} = \cos 2x$ (c) $x^2 \dfrac{dy}{dx} + 1 = 0$

2 For each of the differential equations given below, find y when $x = 3$ for the particular solutions which pass through the point $(1, 0)$.

(a) $\dfrac{dy}{dx} = 4x^3$ (b) $\dfrac{dy}{dx} = 3x^2 - 2x + 2$

(c) $\dfrac{dy}{dx} = \dfrac{1}{x^3}$ (d) $\dfrac{dy}{dx} = 2e^{2x}$

3 A can of water is heated at a rate which decreases steadily with time. The temperature $y\,°C$ after t minutes satisfies the differential equation

$$\frac{dy}{dt} = 8 - \frac{4t}{3}$$

(a) Find y when $t = 4$ if $y = 32$ initially.

(b) Do you think the model will still be valid at time $t = 10$?

4E For each of the differential equations given below, find y when $x = 2$ for the particular solutions which pass through the origin.

(a) $\dfrac{dy}{dx} = \sin(3x + 2)$ (b) $\dfrac{dy}{dx} = x^2 e^{x^3}$ (c) $\dfrac{dy}{dx} = x \cos(x^2 + 1)$

7.3.2 Direction diagrams

From Newton's law of cooling, you know that the rate at which a cup of coffee cools is proportional to the number of degrees, y, that it is above room temperature.

For example, the differential equation $\dfrac{dy}{dt} = -0.2y$ expresses this in symbols, for a particular cup for which the constant of proportionality is 0.2. The negative sign indicates that the coffee is cooling rather than heating up.

The equation $\dfrac{dy}{dt} = -0.2y$ also determines the shape of the (t, y) graph.

At any point, the gradient is -0.2 times the value of the y-coordinate of the point. For example, at any point with y-coordinate 40, the gradient is -8. This gives the direction of the graph at such points. You can show this with small line-segments of gradient -8.

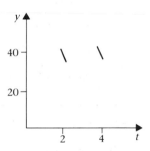

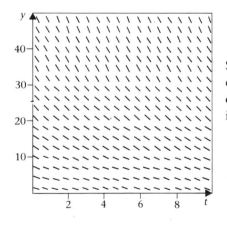

Similarly, you can calculate the direction at every point. This is shown in this **direction diagram** for some regularly spaced points in the first quadrant.

By looking at the direction diagram, it is clear that the graph is not a single curve but is a whole family of curves. There is a different cooling curve for each different starting temperature the cup could have.

The direction diagram can also be extended into the other three quadrants.

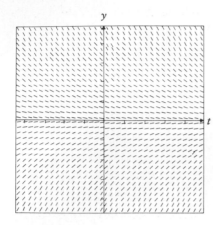

The second quadrant represents cooling curves before the (arbitrarily chosen) time $t = 0$.

In the third and fourth quadrants, the temperature difference, $y\,°C$, is negative and this difference gets smaller with time. These curves represent objects heating up, for example iced drinks.

This is a direction diagram for the differential equation

$$\frac{dy}{dx} = \frac{1}{1 + x^4}$$

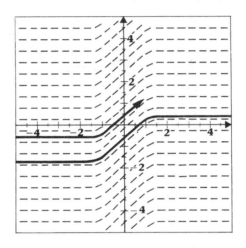

Each segment represents part of a solution through its centre. When sketching a solution curve it is important to try to imagine what the path of the solution might be as it follows its own path in the same general direction as the nearby line-segments. A curve which follows the direction of the line-segments is sketched on the direction diagram.

In the case above, the gradient is dependent only on x, so the line-segments in a *vertical* column (with fixed value of x) are all parallel.

The family of solutions for

$$\frac{dy}{dx} = y$$

are parallel in a *horizontal* direction.

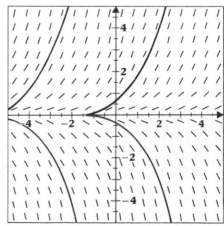

The following questions are designed to give some insight into how the direction diagram is calculated and how it can be used for hand-sketching of solutions.

 .3A

1 Sketch by hand a direction diagram for

$$\frac{dy}{dx} = x$$

(Use ranges $x = -5$ to 5, $y = -5$ to 5.) Sketch a solution through $(0, 1)$.

2 Sketch the direction diagram for $\frac{dy}{dx} = -y$. What happens to solutions which start with y *negative* as x increases?

3 One of the following pictures is the direction diagram for $\frac{dy}{dx} = x - y$; the other is the direction diagram for $\frac{dy}{dx} = x + y$. Which is which? In the case of $\frac{dy}{dx} = x - y$, sketch a few solution curves and suggest what happens to y as x increases.

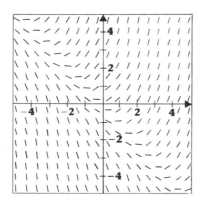 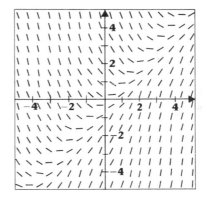

You should observe that:

(a) a differential equation has a family of solutions;

(b) there is a single solution through each starting point, found by following the direction given by the differential equation.

7.3 **Exercise 2**

1 With $-5 \leq x \leq 5$, $-4 \leq y \leq 4$, sketch those solutions to the differential equation $\dfrac{dy}{dx} = -\dfrac{x}{2y}$ which pass through the following points:

(a) $(0, 1)$ (b) $(0, 2)$

Describe the family of curves.

2 With $-4 \leq x \leq 4$, $0 \leq y \leq 6$, sketch solutions to the differential equation $\dfrac{dy}{dx} = -\dfrac{xy}{5}$ which pass through the following points:

(a) $(0, 1)$ (b) $(0, 2)$

Describe the family of curves.

3 Wilhelm's law states that, in a chemical reaction, the rate of change of mass is proportional to the mass, m, of the reacting substance present at any instant.

Explain briefly how this leads to the differential equation $\dfrac{dm}{dt} = -km$ where k is a constant.

Consider the case $\dfrac{dm}{dt} = -0.5m$.

With $0 \leq t \leq 5$, $0 \leq m \leq 10$, sketch the solution which passes through the point $(0, 8)$.

Explain the significance of the value 8, and investigate other curves in the family of solutions.

7.3.3 Numerical methods

Numerical methods for solving differential equations depend upon approximating the solution curve with a series of straight line-segments.

If (x, y) is a point on a graph, then the point $(x + \delta x, y + \delta y)$ is on the tangent. For a locally straight graph, and for small δx, the point $(x + \delta x, y + \delta y)$ is close to the graph.

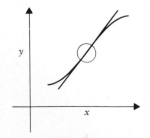
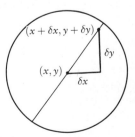

An approximate numerical solution can therefore be obtained by fixing a small numerical value for δx, then calculating a point farther along the curve as $(x + \delta x, y + \delta y)$ and taking this as a new starting point. Consider a particular situation for the simple differential equation $\dfrac{dy}{dx} = 2x$ and starting from the point $(1, 4)$.

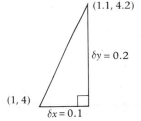

At $(1, 4)$ the gradient is 2, so a step along of $\delta x = 0.1$ will give a step up of $\delta y = 0.2$. The move along the tangent is from $(1, 4)$ to $(1.1, 4.2)$.

The gradient at $(1.1, 4.2)$ is $2 \times 1.1 = 2.2$.

Since $\delta x = 0.1$, then $\delta y = 0.22$ $\left(\delta y = \dfrac{dy}{dx} \times \delta x \right)$

So the next point will be $\quad x + \delta x = 1.2$

$$y + \delta y = 4.42$$

It may help to set the calculation out in a table, working down column by column.

	x	y	$\dfrac{dy}{dx}$	δx	δy	$x + \delta x$	$y + \delta y$
First step	1	4	2	0.1	0.2	1.1	4.2
Second step	1.1	4.2	2.2	0.1	0.22	1.2	4.42
⋮	⋮	⋮	⋮	⋮	⋮	⋮	⋮

Much numerical work of this sort is ideal for working with a spreadsheet or calculator. The next few steps in the solution are set out in the spreadsheet on the following page.

x	y	dy/dx	δx	δy	$x + \delta x$	$y + \delta y$
1	4	2	0.1	0.2	1.1	4.2
1.1	4.2	2.2	0.1	0.22	1.2	4.42
1.2	4.42	2.4	0.1	0.24	1.3	4.66
1.3	4.66	2.6	0.1	0.26	1.4	4.92
1.4	4.92	2.8	0.1	0.28	1.5	5.2
1.5	5.2	3	0.1	0.3	1.6	5.5
1.6	5.5	3.2	0.1	0.32	1.7	5.82
1.7	5.82	3.4	0.1	0.34	1.8	6.16
1.8	6.16	3.6	0.1	0.36	1.9	6.52

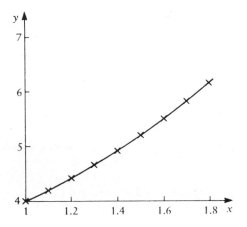

In this example, the actual solution curve is $y = x^2 + 3$.

So $y = 4.21$ when $x = 1.1$, whereas $y = 4.2$ is obtained by moving along the tangent instead of the curve.

The accuracy of the step-by-step method could be improved by using smaller step sizes for δx.

Example 3

For the differential equation

$$\frac{dy}{dx} = \frac{y}{1 + x^4}$$

find the value of y when $x = 2$ for the particular solution through $(1, 6)$.

Solution

The table below shows the start of the calculation, using five steps of $\delta x = 0.2$ and working to 3 significant figures.

x	y	$\dfrac{dy}{dx}$	δx	δy	$x + \delta x$	$y + \delta y$
1	6	3	0.2	0.6	1.2	6.6
1.2	6.6	2.15	0.2	0.43	1.4	7.03
1.4	7.03	1.45	0.2	0.29	1.6	7.32
1.6	7.32	0.97	0.2	0.19	1.8	7.51
1.8	7.51	0.65	0.2	0.13	2.0	7.64
2.0	7.64					

The step-by-step calculations are straightforward with a calculator but it is more efficient to use a program or spreadsheet as shown opposite.

7.3 Exercise 3

1 (a) What is the equation of the solution curve for $\dfrac{dy}{dx} = \cos x$ which passes through $(0, 0)$?

(b) Calculate the numerical solution of the differential equation $\dfrac{dy}{dx} = \cos x$ starting at $x = 0$, $y = 0$ with step 0.1. Record the values of x and y for $x = 0, 0.5, 1$ and so on, giving y values to 1 decimal place. How accurate is the numerical solution for different values of x?

2 (a) What is the equation of the solution curve for $\dfrac{dy}{dx} = 4x^3$ which passes through $(1, 0)$? Find the value of y when $x = 2$.

(b) Use a numerical method, with a step size of 0.2, to find the value of y when $x = 2$.

3 (a) What is the equation of the solution curve for $\dfrac{dy}{dx} = \sin 2x$ which passes through $(0, -0.5)$?

(b) Using a step size of 0.1, find the percentage error in the numerical solution for y at $x = 1$.

4 (a) $\dfrac{dy}{dx} = 2x \Rightarrow y = x^2 + c$

For $\dfrac{dy}{dx} = 2x$, what is the particular solution curve through $(1, 2)$?

Plot this solution curve on graph paper for $-1 \le x \le 3$.

(b) Calculate a numerical solution of $\dfrac{dy}{dx} = 2x$ starting at $x = 1$, $y = 2$.

Using steps of size 0.2, record the values from $x = 1$ to 3 and round off the y values to 1 decimal place. Record also the values from $x = 1$ to -1. Plot the numerical solutions for $-1 \le x \le 3$ on the same diagram as your graph of the solution curve and comment on the accuracy of the numerical method.

(c) Repeat part (b) with step size 0.1. Comment on the improvement in accuracy obtained with the smaller step value.

5E For equations where you can find a solution curve by integration, it is possible to write a program to check the accuracy of the numerical method for different-sized steps. The program could either print out both the numerical solution and the correct value of y as obtained by integration, or it could plot the numerical solutions and then superimpose the correct graph over them. Use one of these methods to investigate the accuracy of numerical solutions for $\dfrac{dy}{dx} = e^x$ for different step values, starting at $x = 0$, $y = 1$.

6E Write a table of values for a numerical solution to

$$\frac{dy}{dx} = \frac{1}{1 + x^2}$$

starting at $x = 0$, $y = 0$, with step $\delta x = 0.1$, from $x = 0$ to $x = 4$. Record selected values of x and y sufficiently accurately to plot a graph.

Also write a table of selected values starting at $x = 0$, $y = 0$, with step $\delta x = -0.1$ and sketch the graph for the solution through $x = 0$, $y = 0$ from $x = -4$ to $+4$.

Does the graph have a shape you recognise? If not, reflect it in the line $y = x$ to consider x as a function of y. Suggest a possible relationship between x and y and check a few values to see if your graph is (approximately) in agreement with your suggestion.

Write a brief report on what you find.

7.3.4 Growth and decay

The differential equation $\dfrac{dy}{dx} = y$ generates a family of solution curves which look like the graphs of growth functions.

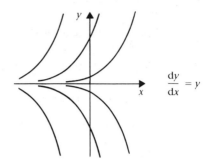

$$\frac{dy}{dx} = y$$

The equation $\dfrac{dy}{dx} = y$ cannot be solved by algebraic integration as it stands. However, a simple rearrangement is helpful.

$$\frac{dy}{dx} = y \Rightarrow \frac{dx}{dy} = \frac{1}{y}$$

$$\Rightarrow x = \int \frac{1}{y} \, dy$$

$$\Rightarrow x = \ln|y| + c$$

$$\Rightarrow x + k = \ln|y| \qquad (k = -c)$$

$$\Rightarrow y = \pm e^{x+k}$$

$$\Rightarrow y = \pm e^{k} e^{x}$$

$$\Rightarrow y = A e^{x} \qquad (A = \pm e^{k})$$

The solution curves are indeed the graphs of growth functions.

The solution may be generalised easily to solve $\dfrac{dy}{dx} = \lambda y$ as follows.

$$\frac{dy}{dx} = \lambda y \Rightarrow \frac{dx}{dy} = \frac{1}{\lambda y}$$

$$\Rightarrow x = \frac{1}{\lambda} \int \frac{1}{y} \, dy$$

$$\Rightarrow \lambda x = \ln|y| + c$$

$$\Rightarrow \lambda x + k = \ln|y| \qquad (k = -c)$$

$$\Rightarrow y = \pm e^{\lambda x + k}$$

$$\Rightarrow y = \pm e^{k} e^{\lambda x}$$

$$\Rightarrow y = A e^{\lambda x} \qquad (A = \pm e^{k})$$

Differential equations of the form $\dfrac{dy}{dx} = \lambda y$ generate families of solution curves which are the graphs of growth functions.

$$\frac{dy}{dx} = \lambda y \Rightarrow y = A e^{\lambda x}$$

Example 4

Earlier in the chapter, you considered the differential equation $\dfrac{dm}{dt} = -0.5m$, where m kg was the mass of a reacting chemical present t hours after the start of the reaction. Initially there was 8 kg of the substance. Find the mass of the substance after 1 hour.

Solution

$$\frac{dm}{dt} = -0.5m \Rightarrow m = A e^{-0.5t}$$

When $t = 0$, $m = 8 \Rightarrow A = 8$

Then $m = 8 e^{-0.5t}$ and, after 1 hour,

$$m = 8 e^{-0.5} \approx 4.85$$

After 1 hour there is approximately 4.85 kg of the substance remaining.

Example 5

A murder victim was discovered by the police at 6:00 a.m. The body temperature of the victim was measured and found to be 25 °C. A doctor arrived on the scene of the crime 30 minutes later and measured the body temperature again. It was found to be 22 °C. The temperature of the room had remained constant at 15 °C. The doctor, knowing normal body temperature to be 37 °C, was able to estimate the time of death of the victim. What would be your estimate for the time of death?

Solution

Assume Newton's law of cooling:

The rate of cooling at any instant is directly proportional to the difference in temperature between the object and its surroundings.

t hours after 6 a.m., let the body temperature be y °C above the temperature of the surroundings.

$$\frac{dy}{dt} = \lambda y \Rightarrow y = A e^{\lambda t}$$

When $t = 0$ and $y = 10$,

$$10 = A e^{0} \Rightarrow A = 10$$

When $t = 0.5$ and $y = 7$,

$$7 = 10\,e^{0.5\lambda} \Rightarrow 0.5\lambda = \ln 0.7$$

$$\Rightarrow \lambda = -0.713 \quad \text{(to 3 s.f.)}$$

So $y = 10\,e^{0.713t}$

You can find the time, t, when the temperature was 22 degrees above room temperature.

$$y = 22 \Rightarrow 22 = 10\,e^{-0.713t}$$

$$\Rightarrow \ln 2.2 = -0.713t$$

$$\Rightarrow t = -1.106$$

1.106 hours is 1 hour 6 minutes. The time of death was about 1 hour 6 minutes before 6:00 a.m., or 4:54 a.m.

7.3 Exercise 4

1 Find the equation of the solution curve of

$$\frac{dy}{dx} = -y$$

which passes through the point $(0, 2)$.

2 The mass, m kg, of a substance satisfies the differential equation

$$\frac{dm}{dt} = -0.1$$

where t is the time in hours after the start of a chemical reaction.

(a) Initially there was 2 kg of the substance. Find a formula for m in terms of t.

(b) Hence calculate the time taken for the mass of the substance to be halved.

3 Boiling water is left in a room and cools to $90\,°C$ in 5 minutes. If the room temperature is $20\,°C$, how long will the water take to cool to $60\,°C$?

4 A colony of insects initially has a population of 100 and is growing at the rate of 50 insects per day. If the rate of growth at any time is proportional to the population size at that time, how many insects will there be after 10 days?

5 A radioactive substance decays at a rate proportional to its mass. When the mass of a sample of the substance is 0.020 g it is decaying at a rate of 0.001 g per day. There are m grams left after t days.

(a) Formulate a differential equation connecting m and t.

(b) How long does the sample take to decay to 0.010 g?

▶ 7.3 **Tasksheet E1 – Carbon dating (page 566)**

7.3.5 Formulating differential equations

You have studied some of the numerical and analytical methods for solving differential equations. The geometrical picture of the family of solution curves is also valuable. In particular, it indicates the effect of different initial conditions.

The relative advantages and disadvantages of solving a differential equation by inspection or by a step-by-step method can be summarised as follows:

> Solving a differential equation by inspection has the advantage that precise solutions are obtained.
>
> The power of a step-by-step method is that it can be applied to calculate a solution however complicated the gradient function may be.

To be able to apply either of these methods you must be able to formulate the differential equation correctly. This section considers a few examples of formulation.

Example 6
High on the moors, perched on a rocky crag, lies a most curious boulder. It has fascinated the locals and tourists alike for years, for it is almost perfectly spherical in shape. Over the years it has gradually been eroded by the action of the winds, but it has retained its basic shape. In fact, according to the locals, it now has half the diameter it had 100 years ago. 'Be gone in another 100 years' they say. Are they right?

Solution
Set up a model
The locals will be right only if there is a linear relationship between the radius of the boulder and time. To decide if this is the case you need to make some assumptions about the rate of erosion and decide upon the variables and units to be used.

Volume of boulder	V cm^3
Radius of boulder	r cm
Time from 100 years ago	t years

It is reasonable to assume that the rate of erosion is proportional to the surface area, $A = 4\pi r^2$. Since the rate of erosion is $-\dfrac{dV}{dt}$, the important differential equation is

$$-\frac{dV}{dt} = kA \qquad \text{i.e. } \frac{dV}{dt} = -4k\pi r^2$$

Analyse the problem

Since $V = \dfrac{4}{3}\pi r^3$,

$$\frac{dV}{dt} = \frac{4}{3}\pi \times 3r^2 \frac{dr}{dt} \qquad \text{by the chain rule}$$

$$= 4\pi r^2 \frac{dr}{dt}$$

So $4\pi r^2 \dfrac{dr}{dt} = -4k\pi r^2$

$$\Rightarrow \frac{dr}{dt} = -k$$

Interpret/validate

The radius decreases at a constant rate and so the boulder *will* be gone in another 100 years. You cannot validate this conclusion directly although you could find out known facts about erosion rates. In fact, it is unlikely that the boulder will retain its shape as it is eroded.

Example 7

A child makes his way to school at a speed which is proportional to the distance he still has to cover. He leaves home, 2 km from school, running at $10\,\text{km h}^{-1}$. How long will it be before he has gone nine-tenths of the way?

Solution

Let x km be the distance from *home* that he has travelled at time t hours. At that instant he will be $(2 - x)$ km from school.

First record the initial conditions.

$$x = 0 \quad \text{and} \quad \frac{dx}{dt} = 10 \qquad \text{when } t = 0$$

Next, write down the differential equation which translates into symbols the statement 'the rate of change of distance from home equals a constant multiplied by the distance from school'.

$$\frac{dx}{dt} = k(2 - x)$$

Then use the second initial condition to find the constant k. Substitution into the differential equation gives

$$10 = 2k \Rightarrow k = 5$$

and the differential equation becomes

$$\frac{dx}{dt} = 5(2 - x)$$

or

$$\frac{dt}{dx} = \frac{1}{5(2 - x)} \qquad \left(\text{using } \frac{dx}{dt} = 1 \div \left(\frac{dt}{dx}\right)\right)$$

The general solution of this equation is

$$t = -\tfrac{1}{5}\ln|2 - x| + c \qquad \text{(check this carefully)}$$

Using the first initial condition, you can find the particular solution which fits the problem. $x = 0$ when $t = 0$ gives

$$0 = -\tfrac{1}{5}\ln 2 + c$$

$$\Rightarrow c = \tfrac{1}{5}\ln 2$$

$$\Rightarrow t = \tfrac{1}{5}\left[\ln 2 - \ln|2 - x|\right] = \tfrac{1}{5}\ln\left|\frac{2}{2 - x}\right|$$

When the child has travelled nine-tenths of the way, $x = 1.8$ and

$$t = \tfrac{1}{5}\left[\ln 2 - \ln 0.2\right]$$

$$= \tfrac{1}{5}\ln 10$$

$$\approx 0.46$$

So the child has gone nine-tenths of the way about 28 minutes after he leaves home.

Although the model we have been using is plausible enough for the earlier part of the journey, it is inappropriate for the whole journey to school. Why?

7.3 **Exercise 5**

1 The volume of a large spherical snowball decreases as it melts at a rate proportional to its surface area at any instant.

(a) Express this statement in symbols.

(b) Given that a snowball of radius $30\,\text{cm}$ takes 10 days to melt, find an expression for the radius r in terms of the time t.

(c) After how many days will:

(i) the radius be halved, (ii) the volume be halved?

2 In a lake, about 2000 newly hatched fish survive each year. However, about 10% of the fish in the lake die each year as the result of disease, predators or old age. These observations lead to the hypothesis that

$$\frac{dy}{dt} = \alpha + \beta y \qquad \text{where } y \text{ is the number of fish present.}$$

(a) Explain why $\beta = -0.1$ and state the value of α.

(b) In what units are y and $\frac{dy}{dt}$ measured?

(c) The lake had a stable population of 20 000 fish before a careless discharge of chemicals killed 5000 fish. Estimate how long it will take for the population to reach 19 000.

(d) Write down the differential equation which will apply if 12% of the fish die each year and 2500 newly hatched fish survive.

3E A full tea urn contains a hundred cupfuls.

Nine cups are filled from the urn in the first minute. The rate of flow is believed to be proportional to the square root of the height of the liquid in the urn.

Explain the relationship in symbols, stating their units and meaning.

How long does it take to fill four dozen cups?

[This question can be tackled either analytically or numerically. Use whichever method you prefer.]

7.3.6 Separating the variables

With the differential equations that we have so far solved by algebraic means, it has always been possible to do so with a single direct integration. Many other differential equations may be rearranged so that they are in a form suitable for direct integration. We examine here one important procedure for doing this for certain forms of differential equation.

Consider the problem of finding the general solution to the equation $\frac{dy}{dx} = xy$.

The solution requires one integration with respect to the variable x. However, on the right-hand-side this leads to the integral

$$\int xy \, dx$$

Since y is a function of x which is not known (that would be the solution we are trying to find!) then it is not possible to evaluate this integral.

However, we may proceed as follows

$$\text{If } \frac{dy}{dx} = xy, \quad \text{then } \frac{1}{y}\frac{dy}{dx} = x$$

Integrating with respect to x,

$$\int \left(\frac{1}{y}\frac{dy}{dx}\right) dx = \int x \, dx$$

$$\int \frac{1}{y} \, dy = \int x \, dx$$

$$\ln|y| = \frac{x^2}{2} + c$$

$$y = \pm e^{x^2/2 + c} = \pm e^c \, e^{x^2/2}$$

$$\text{or} \quad y = A \, e^{x^2/2} \qquad \text{(where } A \text{ is a constant)}$$

The technique illustrated above depends on your being able to 'separate' the two variables (here x and y) so that one side of the equation consists of a function of x alone, and the other side has a product of dy/dx and a function of y.

In other words, you must have an equation which can be rearranged in the form

$$f(y) \frac{dy}{dx} = g(x) \qquad \qquad \text{①}$$

Then, integrating with respect to x, you obtain

$$\int f(y) \frac{dy}{dx} \, dx = \int g(x) \, dx \qquad \text{②}$$

or

$$\int f(y) \, dy = \int g(x) \, dx \qquad \text{③}$$

Provided the two integrations can be performed, the differential equation has then been solved. The method is called **separating the variables**.

In practice ② is usually omitted and you can proceed directly from ① to ③. However, you should bear in mind that it is integrating *both* sides of ① with respect to x which leads to ③, in which one integral is with respect to x and the other with respect to y.

Example 8

Find the solution to the differential equation $\dfrac{dy}{dx} = x(y+1)$, given that $y = 2$ when $x = 0$.

Solution

$$\frac{dy}{dx} = x(y+1) \Rightarrow \frac{1}{y+1}\frac{dy}{dx} = x$$

Integrating with respect to x,

$$\int \frac{1}{y+1}\frac{dy}{dx}\,dx = \int x\,dx$$

$$\int \frac{1}{y+1}\,dy = \int x\,dx$$

$$\ln|y+1| = \frac{x^2}{2} + c$$

When $x = 0$, $y = 2 \Rightarrow \ln 3 = c$

So, $\ln|y+1| - \ln 3 = \frac{x^2}{2}$

$$\ln\left|\frac{y+1}{3}\right| = \frac{x^2}{2}$$

$$\frac{y+1}{3} = e^{x^2/2} \qquad \text{(l.h.s. must be positive)}$$

$$\Rightarrow y = 3\,e^{x^2/2} - 1$$

If a differential equation can be written in the form $g(y)\dfrac{dy}{dx} = f(x)$, then the solution can be obtained from

$$\int g(y)\,dy = \int f(x)\,dx$$

This procedure is known as the **separation of variables**.

7.3 Exercise 6

1 Find the general solution to the following differential equations.

(a) $\dfrac{dy}{dx} = xy$ (b) $\dfrac{dp}{dt} = \dfrac{t}{p}$ (c) $\dfrac{dm}{dt} = 2m$

(d) $\dfrac{dy}{dx} = \dfrac{e^x}{y}$ (e) $\dfrac{dy}{dx} = \dfrac{y+1}{x+1}$

2 Find the solution to the differential equation

$$\frac{dy}{dx} = 3 - 2y$$

for which $y = 0$ when $x = 0$.

3 The rate of increase of the population of a colony of insects t days after the beginning of an experiment is proportional to the population P at that time. If the colony initially contains 100 insects and at that time is growing at a rate of 50 insects per day, find how many there are after ten days.

4 A radioactive substance decays at a rate proportional to its mass. When the mass of a sample is 0.020 g, the decay rate is 0.001 g per day.

(a) t days later the mass is m g. Write down a differential equation and solve it to give m in terms of t for these initial conditions.

(b) How long does the sample take to decay to 0.010 g?

(c) How long does it take to decay from 0.012 g to 0.003 g?

(d) What is the rate of decay after 10 days?

5 Bacteria in a tank of water increase at a rate proportional to the number present. Water is drained out of the tank, initially containing 100 litres, at a steady rate of 2 litres per hour. Show that if N is the number of bacteria present at time t hours after the time at which the draining starts, then

$$\frac{dN}{dt} = kN - \frac{2N}{100 - 2t}$$

If $k = 0.7$ and, at $t = 0$, $N = N_0$, find in terms of N_0 the number of bacteria after 24 hours.

After working through section 7.3, you should:

1 be able to interpret and formulate differential equations;

2 know how to find the differential equation associated with a given family of curves;

3 be able to draw and interpret direction diagrams;

4 be able to calculate approximate solutions by a step-by-step method;

5 know how to obtain solutions by inspection when appropriate;

6 have developed an appreciation of the mathematical modelling implicit in the formulation and solution of differential equations;

7 have a deeper understanding of rates of change;

8 be able to solve differential equations by separating variables when appropriate;

9 know how to use initial conditions to obtain a particular solution to a differential equation.

7 Calculus methods 2

Miscellaneous exercise 7

1 Calculate the volume of the cone formed by rotating the area between $y = \frac{1}{2}x$, the line $x = 4$ and the x-axis, about the x-axis.

2 Find the volumes of the solids formed when the following areas are rotated about the x-axis:

(a) $y = \sin x$ for $0 \le x \le \pi$ (b) $y = 2e^{-x}$ for $-1 \le x \le 1$

(c) $y = \dfrac{2}{\sqrt{x}}$ for $1 \le x \le 4$

3 Find the values of:

(a) $\displaystyle\int_0^{\frac{1}{4}\pi} (\tan^2 x + 1)\, dx$ (b) $\displaystyle\int_0^{\frac{1}{4}\pi} \tan^2 x\, dx$

4 Try to integrate the following, using your experience of chain-rule differentiation. Alternatively, use a substitution.

(a) $\displaystyle\int 2x(1 - x^2)^3\, dx$ (b) $\displaystyle\int \frac{x}{(x^2 + 4)^2}\, dx$ (c) $\displaystyle\int x^2 \sqrt{(1 - x^3)}\, dx$

(d) $\displaystyle\int \frac{x^3}{\sqrt{(1 - x^4)}}\, dx$ (e) $\displaystyle\int \sin^5 x \cos x\, dx$ (f) $\displaystyle\int \frac{\sin x}{\cos^2 x}\, dx$

5 Using the suggested substitutions, integrate the following:

(a) $\displaystyle\int_1^3 x(x - 1)^4\, dx$, $u = x - 1$ (b) $\displaystyle\int_0^2 2x\sqrt{(1 + x)}\, dx$, $u = 1 + x$

(c) $\displaystyle\int_0^4 (1 + x)\sqrt{(3x + 1)}\, dx$, $u = 3x + 1$ (d) $\displaystyle\int_0^2 \frac{1 - x}{(1 + x)^4}\, dx$, $u = 1 + x$

6 Evaluate:

(a) $\displaystyle\int x^2 \sin x\, dx$ (b) $\displaystyle\int x^3 \cos x\, dx$ (c) $\displaystyle\int x \sin^2 x\, dx$

(For (c) use the formula for $\cos 2x$.)

7 Evaluate: (a) $\displaystyle\int_0^{\frac{1}{2}\pi} x\sin x\,dx$ (b) $\displaystyle\int_0^{\pi} x\sin\tfrac{1}{2}x\,dx$

8 (a) Find A and B when $\dfrac{3x+1}{(x-2)(x+5)} = \dfrac{A}{x-2} + \dfrac{B}{x+5}$

(b) Find A, B and C when $\dfrac{4x+2}{x(x-1)(x+2)} = \dfrac{A}{x} + \dfrac{B}{x-1} + \dfrac{C}{x+2}$

9 Use the method of partial fractions to find:

(a) $\displaystyle\int \dfrac{9x+1}{(x-3)(x+1)}\,dx$ (b) $\displaystyle\int \dfrac{8}{x^2-16}\,dx$

(c) $\displaystyle\int \dfrac{1}{x^2+3x-4}\,dx$ (d) $\displaystyle\int \dfrac{x^3+5x^2-3x+3}{(x-2)(x+3)^2}\,dx$

10 Use the Newton–Raphson method to find to 3 s.f. the greatest and least roots of $x^3 - 3x + 1 = 0$.

11 Make an estimate of the root of $x - \cos x = 0$, and improve it by a single application of the Newton–Raphson formula.

12 Draw a graph to show the approximate locations of the roots of $x^3 - 5x + 3 = 0$. Use the Newton–Raphson method to find the largest root correct to 4 s.f.

13 Using the series expansion for e^x or otherwise, obtain the power series expansion, as far as the term containing x^3, for

(a) e^{-x} (b) e^{2x} (c) $\ln(1+2x)$

14 Use the Maclaurin Series to find cubic approximations to the following:

(a) $(1+x)^{\frac{1}{2}}$ (b) $\dfrac{1}{(1+x)}$ (c) $\dfrac{1}{(2+x)}$

15 Find, as far as the term in x^4, Maclaurin Series for

(a) $\tan x$ (b) $\sec x$ (c) $e^x \sin x$

16 Using the chain rule, find $\dfrac{dy}{dx}$ when

(a) $y = \sin(x^2+1)$ (b) $y = \cos(1-2x)$ (c) $y = e^{x^2+1}$

(d) $y = e^{\sin x}$ (e) $y = e^{(\sin x + \cos x)}$

17 The size S of a population at time t satisfies the differential equation $\dfrac{\mathrm{d}S}{\mathrm{d}t} = kS$ where k is a constant.

Find S as a function of t.

The population was 32 000 in the year 1900 and had increased to 48 000 by 1970. Estimate what its size will be (correct to the nearest 1000) in the year 2000.

18 Solve the following differential equations; in each example, use the information given to find y as a function of x.

(a) $\dfrac{\mathrm{d}y}{\mathrm{d}x} = y$ and $y = 10$ when $x = 0$

(b) $\dfrac{\mathrm{d}y}{\mathrm{d}x} = -xy$ and $y = 2$ when $x = 1$

(c) $\dfrac{\mathrm{d}y}{\mathrm{d}x} = -y^2$ and $y = 1$ when $x = \frac{1}{2}$

The equation of a straight line

1 (a) Use a graph plotter to sketch the graph of $y = 2x + c$ where
$c = -2, -1, 0, 1, 2$.

(b) Describe the effect of varying c.

2 (a) Use a graph plotter to sketch the graph of $y = mx + 3$ where
$m = -2, -1, 0, 1, 2$.

(b) Describe the effect of varying m.

A gradient of 1 in 5, i.e. a rise of 1 unit for every 5 horizontal units travelled, is
described mathematically as a gradient of $\frac{1}{5}$ or 0.2.

> The gradient of a line measures how steeply it rises. Gradient is measured as
>
> $$\frac{\text{vertical } \textbf{increase}}{\text{horizontal } \textbf{increase}}$$
>
> Notice that if y decreases, then the 'vertical increase' will be negative.

Example
Find the gradient of the line AB.

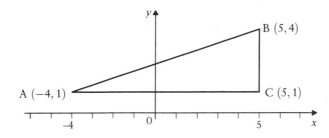

Solution
The gradient is $\dfrac{\text{BC}}{\text{AC}} = \dfrac{3}{9} = \dfrac{1}{3}$

3 Plot the points A $(1, 2)$ and B $(3, 10)$ and calculate the gradient of the line AB.

4 Find the gradient of the line AB for:

(a) A $(-1, 2)$, B $(2, 11)$ (b) A $(3, 1)$, B $(-1, 9)$ (c) A $(4, 1)$, B $(1, 1)$

5

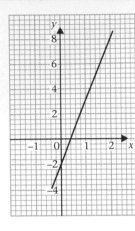

(a) Find the gradient of the line.

(b) Where does the line cross the y-axis?

(c) The equation of the line is $y = 2x + 1$. Show that the points $(0, 1)$ and $(2, 5)$ satisfy this equation.

(d) How can you relate the equation $y = 2x + 1$ to your answers to (a) and (b)?

6 (a) Find the gradient of the line.

(b) Where does the line cross the y-axis?

(c) The equation of the line is $y = -3x - 1$. Choose two points, and show that their coordinates satisfy this equation.

(d) How can you relate the equation $y = -3x - 1$ to your answers to (a) and (b)?

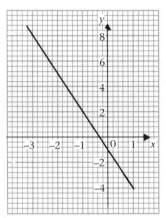

7 Find the equations of the lines.

(a)

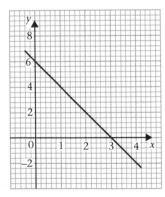

(b)

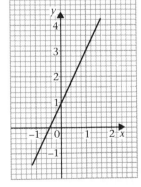

> Any equation in the form $y = mx + c$ represents a straight line.
>
> Its gradient is m and its intercept on the y-axis is c.

8 There are many alternative ways of writing $y = mx + c$. Find the gradients and y-intercepts of the following straight lines.

(a) $y = 9 - 4x$ 　　　　(b) $2y = 6x + 3$ 　　　　(c) $2y - 4x = 5$

(d) $3x + 5y + 10 = 0$ 　　(e) $y - 3 = 5(x - 2)$ 　　(f) $y = \dfrac{x}{3} - \dfrac{5}{4}$

(g) $\dfrac{x}{4} + \dfrac{y}{5} = 1$

You can use the form $y = mx + c$ to find the equation of a straight line which passes through *any* two given points.

Example

Find the equation of the straight line which passes through the points $(2, 5)$ and $(5, 11)$.

Solution

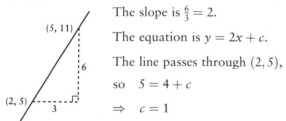

The slope is $\frac{6}{3} = 2$.

The equation is $y = 2x + c$.

The line passes through $(2, 5)$,

so　$5 = 4 + c$

$\Rightarrow \quad c = 1$

The line has equation $y = 2x + 1$.

9 Find the equation of the straight lines through

(a) $(5, 4)$ and $(10, 19)$ 　　　(b) $(-3, -2)$ and $(-1, 2)$

Multiplying brackets

You have met expressions like $3(x + 2)$ before.

$3(x + 2)$ means '3 lots of $(x + 2)$' or '3 lots of x' *plus* '3 lots of 2'.

i.e. $3(x + 2) = 3x + 6$

1 Multiply out:

    (a) $5(x + 3)$ (b) $2(x - 4)$ (c) $8(2x + 5)$

    (d) $-2(x + 6)$ (e) $-4(x - 7)$ (f) $6(x - 2y)$

Complicated expressions can sometimes be simplified by multiplication of any brackets, for example,

$$6x(x - 1) - 2(2x - 3) = 6x^2 - 6x - 4x + 6$$
$$= 6x^2 - 10x + 6$$

2 Multiply out and gather together like terms for:

    (a) $3 + 2(x + 3)$ (b) $3(x - 4)$ (c) $a + 5(8 - a)$

    (d) $t - 4(1 - t)$ (e) $p - 1 + 2(3p - 8)$ (f) $5 - 6(5x - 9)$

    (g) $y - 9(y - 2)$ (h) $4x - x(2 - x)$ (i) $2 - 3x(1 + 2x)$

You have seen how to multiply out expressions of the form $2x(x + 1)$. You can now consider expressions like $(x + 2)(x + 4)$.

$(x + 2)(x + 4)$ means 'x lots of $(x + 4)$' *plus* '2 lots of $(x + 4)$'.

So: $(x + 2)(x + 4)$ becomes $x(x + 4) + 2(x + 4)$
and the problem has been reduced to the earlier form with which you are familiar.

3 Multiply out:

    (a) $(x + 2)(x + 4)$ (b) $(x - 3)(x + 1)$ (c) $(x + 4)(x - 1)$

    (d) $(x - 5)(x - 2)$ (e) $(x + 5)(x - 7)$ (f) $(x + 8)(x + 2)$

    (g) $(x - 2)(x - 9)$ (h) $(x - 4)(x + 7)$

Expressions of the form $(x + 2)^2$ are called **perfect squares**. $(x + 2)^2$ means $(x + 2)(x + 2)$ and can be multiplied out in the standard way.

4 (a) Multiply out:
   (i) $(x + 3)^2$ (ii) $(x + 7)^2$ (iii) $(x - 9)^2$ (iv) $(x - 6)^2$

   (b) If $(x + p)^2 = x^2 + bx + c$, express:
   (i) b in terms of p (ii) c in terms of p

1.1 TASKSHEET S3

Further factorisation

1 (a) Write in the form $x^2 + bx + c$:

(i) $(x+2)(x+3)$ (ii) $(x-2)(x-3)$

(iii) $(x+4)(x+5)$ (iv) $(x-4)(x-5)$

(b) How is the constant term c related to the numbers in the brackets?

(c) How is the coefficient b related to the numbers in the brackets?

When you multiply the brackets $(x+4)(x+7)$, you find

> the coefficient of x by *adding* 4 to 7,
>
> the constant term by *multiplying* 4 by 7.

$$(x+4)(x+7) = x^2 + (4+7)x + 4 \times 7$$

$$= x^2 + 11x + 28$$

When you factorise $x^2 + 11x + 28$ you have to do the opposite and find two numbers

(a) whose product is $+28$ and   (b) whose sum is $+11$.

Since 28 has a limited set of factors, i.e. $(\pm 28, \pm 1)$, $(\pm 14, \pm 2)$, $(\pm 7, \pm 4)$, it is not hard to see that the numbers must be 7 and 4.

2 Factorise:

(a) $x^2 + 9x + 14$ (b) $x^2 + 13x + 40$ (c) $x^2 - 9x + 14$

(d) $x^2 + 12x + 36$ (e) $x^2 - 7x - 8$ (f) $x^2 + 3x - 28$

(g) $x^2 - 8x + 12$ (h) $x^2 - 5x - 36$ (i) $x^2 - 2x - 48$

(j) $x^2 + 2x - 24$

You should be familiar with the following important special cases.

- If the constant term is missing, x will be a factor, for example

$$x^2 + 6x = x(x+6)$$

- If the expression has the form $x^2 - a^2$, then it factorises into $(x-a)(x+a)$, for example

$$x^2 - 16 = x^2 - 4^2 = (x-4)(x+4)$$

- Expressions of the form $x^2 + a^2$ will not factorise.

3 Factorise where possible:

(a) $x^2 + 2x$

(b) $x^2 - 9$

(c) $x^2 - 8x$

(d) $x^2 + 25$

(e) $x^2 + 25x$

(f) $x^2 - 25$

(g) $x^2 + 1$

(h) $x^2 - 1$

(i) $x^2 - x$

(j) $6x^2 + 5x + 1$

(k) $2x^2 + 7x + 6$

(l) $4x^2 - 1$

(m) $9x^2 - 4$

Review of equations

You have already met several types of algebraic equation. This tasksheet reviews methods of solving such equations and gives you an opportunity for further practice.

Linear equations

Example

Solve $6x + 14 = 2x - 6$.

> **Solution**
>
> $$6x = 2x - 20 \quad \text{(subtracting 14 from both sides)}$$
> $$\Rightarrow 4x = -20 \quad \text{(subtracting } 2x \text{ from both sides)}$$
> $$\Rightarrow \quad x = -5 \quad \text{(dividing both sides by 4)}$$

1 Solve:

(a) $5x + 30 = 0$ (b) $4x + 3 = 2x$ (c) $5x + 2 = 3x - 7$

(d) $4(x - 3) = 6x$ (e) $3(2x + 5) = 3(x + 2)$ (f) $x + 4 = 3 - 2x$

Quadratic equations

Example

Solve the equation $x^2 + 6x - 7 = 0$.

> **Solution**
>
> $$x^2 + 6x - 7 = 0 \quad \text{(Try to factorise first.)}$$
> $$\Rightarrow (x - 1)(x + 7) = 0$$
> $$\Rightarrow \text{either} \quad x - 1 = 0 \quad \text{or} \quad x + 7 = 0$$
> $$\Rightarrow x = 1 \quad \text{or} \quad x = -7$$

2 Solve:

(a) $(x - 3)(x + 5) = 0$ (b) $x(x - 2) = 0$ (c) $x^2 + 3x - 18 = 0$

(d) $x^2 - 3x - 10 = 0$ (e) $x^2 - 4x = 0$ (f) $x^2 - 6x + 9 = 0$

Other methods

Some equations can be solved by inspection, though care sometimes needs to be taken not to miss solutions – for example, $x^2 = 9$ clearly has $x = 3$ as a solution, but it also has the solution $x = -3$.

Other equations may need some rearrangement before solving.

Example

Solve the equation

$$x = \frac{6}{x+1}$$

Solution $\quad x(x+1) = 6 \quad$ (multiplying throughout by $x+1$)

$$x^2 + x = 6 \quad \text{(expanding)}$$

$$x^2 + x - 6 = 0$$

$$(x-3)(x+2) = 0 \quad \text{(factorising the quadratic)}$$

$$\Rightarrow x = 3 \quad \text{or} \quad x = -2$$

3 Solve:

(a) $x^2 = 49$ 　　　　(b) $x^2 - 9 = 0$ 　　(c) $x = \dfrac{9}{x}$

(d) $x^2 + 2x = 35$ 　　(e) $x^2 = 5x$ 　　　(f) $x - \dfrac{1}{x} = 0$

(g) $\dfrac{2}{x} = x + 1$ 　　(h) $\dfrac{x}{x+6} = \dfrac{1}{x}$ 　(i) $\dfrac{1}{x} + \dfrac{1}{2} = \dfrac{x}{2}$

Simultaneous equations may be solved by a variety of methods; the method shown here is substitution from one equation into the other.

Example

Solve the simultaneous equations $2x + y = 13$ and $3x - 2y = 9$.

Solution $\qquad\qquad\qquad y = 13 - 2x \quad$ (from the first equation)

$$\Rightarrow 3x - 2(13 - 2x) = 9 \qquad \text{(substitute into the second)}$$

$$7x - 26 = 9$$

$$x = 5$$

$$\therefore \qquad\qquad y = 13 - 2x = 5$$

So $x = 5$, $y = 3$.

4 Solve the simultaneous equations:

(a) 　$x + y = 8$ 　　(b) $2x + 3y = 17$ 　(c) $2y + 3x = 4$
　　$3x - 2y = 19$ 　　　$2x - y = 5$ 　　　　$y - 2x = 9$

Working in surd form

1 The diagram shows a spiral of triangles based
around an initial right angled triangle.

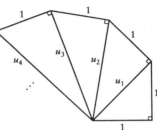

Find the lengths of the hypotenuses labelled u_1, u_2 and u_3 in the diagram.

It is best in this example to work in *exact* form, where you observe the lengths
to be $\sqrt{2}$, $\sqrt{3}$ and $\sqrt{4}$. This suggests that the next might be $\sqrt{5}$, which it is, and
that the nth length u_n will be $\sqrt{n}$.

This pattern would never be apparent if you worked in approximate form,
where the first few lengths would be

$$1.414, \quad 1.732, \quad 2, \quad 2.236, \quad 2.449, \quad \ldots$$

Numerical expressions which contain one or more irrational roots of numbers,
such as $3 + \sqrt{5}$, are known as **surds**. Familiarity with the methods of working
with surds often means that patterns can be easily spotted, and that numbers
containing irrational parts can be written and dealt with in *exact form*.

2 Evaluate, leaving your answers in exact form

(a) $(3 + \sqrt{5})^2$ (b) $(2 - \sqrt{13})^2$ (c) $(3 - 2\sqrt{5})^2$

(d) $(3 - \sqrt{2})^3$ (e) $(\sqrt{3} - \sqrt{2})^2$ (f) $(5\sqrt{3} - 3\sqrt{5})^2$

3 A circle has an area of $50\,\text{cm}^2$. Show that the radius is $5\sqrt{\dfrac{2}{\pi}}$ cm and the
circumference is $10\sqrt{(2\pi)}$ cm.

4 Solve, leaving your solutions in simplified surd form:

(a) $x^2 + 5x + 1 = 0$ (b) $x^2 - 3x - 9 = 0$ (c) $3x^2 + 7x - 3 = 0$

It can easily be shown, by squaring each expression, that

$$\sqrt{ab} = \sqrt{a}\sqrt{b} \qquad \text{and} \qquad \sqrt{\dfrac{a}{b}} = \dfrac{\sqrt{a}}{\sqrt{b}}$$

These results are useful when simplifying surds.

5 Express each of the following in terms of the simplest possible surds.

(a) $\sqrt{8}$ (b) $\sqrt{60}$ (c) $\sqrt{32}$ (d) $\dfrac{\sqrt{512}}{\sqrt{63}}$

6 (a) Show that if a and b are rational (i.e. contain no surds), so is $(a + \sqrt{b})(a - \sqrt{b})$.

(b) Evaluate: (i) $(2 + \sqrt{3})(2 - \sqrt{3})$
                 (ii) $(1 - 2\sqrt{5})(1 + 2\sqrt{5})$
                 (iii) $(-2 - \sqrt{3})(-2 + \sqrt{3})$

The results obtained in question 6 help in dealing with fractions which contain surds. It is usual to simplify them so that the denominator of the fraction does *not* contain any surds – it is rational. Such a process, illustrated in the following example, is known as **rationalisation** (of the fraction).

Example
Rationalise the denominator of $\dfrac{2\sqrt{2} - \sqrt{3}}{\sqrt{2} + \sqrt{3}}$.

Solution

$$\frac{2\sqrt{2} - \sqrt{3}}{\sqrt{2} + \sqrt{3}} \times \frac{\sqrt{2} - \sqrt{3}}{\sqrt{2} - \sqrt{3}} = \frac{4 - 2\sqrt{2}\sqrt{3} - \sqrt{3}\sqrt{2} + 3}{2 - 3}$$

$$= 3\sqrt{6} - 7$$

7 Rationalise the denominators of the following.

(a) $\dfrac{1}{1 + \sqrt{3}}$ (b) $\dfrac{1 + \sqrt{2}}{1 - \sqrt{3}}$ (c) $\dfrac{\sqrt{2} + \sqrt{3}}{\sqrt{5}}$

(d) $\dfrac{\sqrt{5} + 4}{\sqrt{2} + 1}$ (e) $\dfrac{2}{\sqrt{2} + \sqrt{5}}$

8 Write down the *exact* values, using surd form as necessary, for the sine, cosine and tangent of $30°$, $45°$ and $60°$.

Hence express in surd form, and rationalise, the following expressions:

(a) $\dfrac{1}{1 + \sin 45°}$ (b) $\dfrac{1}{\sin 60° - \cos 45°}$

(c) $\dfrac{1 + \sin 60°}{1 - \sin 60°}$ (d) $(1 + \tan 30°)^2$

Expanding brackets

When multiplying out more than two brackets, a well-organised, methodical and careful approach is important if careless mistakes are to be avoided.

With three sets of brackets

$$(x - 1)(x + 3)(x - 4)$$

$= (x - 1)(x^2 - x - 12)$ Expand brackets in pairs only.

$= x(x^2 - x - 12) - (x^2 - x - 12)$ This may be omitted, but errors with signs are common and this is when they usually occur.

$= x^3 - x^2 - 12x - x^2 + x + 12$

$= x^3 - 2x^2 - 11x + 12$ Gather together like terms.

1 Expand:

(a) $(x - 1)(x^2 + x + 1)$ (b) $(x - 2)(x^2 + 2x + 4)$

(c) $(x + 1)(x^2 - x + 1)$ (d) $(x + 2)(x^2 - 2x + 4)$

2 Expand:

(a) $(x + 1)(x + 2)(x - 4)$ (b) $(x - 2)(x - 3)(x - 4)$

(c) $(x - 1)(x + 1)(x + 5)$ (d) $(x - 1)^2(x + 3)$

With more than three sets of brackets

$$(x + 1)(x - 2)(x - 3)(x + 2)$$

$= (x + 1)(x^2 - 4)(x - 3)$

$= (x + 1)(x^3 - 3x^2 - 4x + 12)$

$= x^4 - 3x^3 - 4x^2 + 12x$
$\quad + x^3 - 3x^2 - 4x + 12$

$= x^4 - 2x^3 - 7x^2 + 8x + 12$

The pairs of brackets may be expanded in any order. Your experience might help you to speed up the process by choosing a convenient pair.

Careful setting out makes any simplification easy.

3 Expand:

(a) $(x + 1)(x - 1)(x + 2)(x - 2)$ (b) $(x + 2)^2(x - 2)^2$

(c) $(x - 1)(x + 3)^3$ (d) $(x + 1)(x - 2)(x + 3)(x - 4)$

Functions of functions

1 The functions f and g given by $f(x) = x^2$ and $g(x) = 3x + 1$ can be described by the following flow charts.

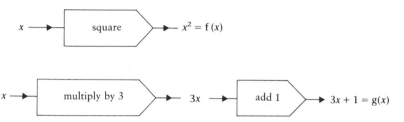

(a) (i) What is f(4)? (ii) What is g(16)?

(b) If the output from $f(x)$ is used as input to $g(x)$, you can write $g(f(x))$. What is $g(f(4))$?

(c) Write down: (i) $g(f(2))$ (ii) $g(f(-3))$ (iii) $f(g(-2))$

(d) Draw a flow chart to describe the composite function $gf(x)$ and hence find a formula for $gf(x)$.

(e) Check whether your formula is correct by substituting a few numbers in $gf(x)$ and in your formula.

(f) Now find a formula for $fg(x)$.

2 (a) Use the ideas above to find $gf(x)$ and $fg(x)$ for:

(i) $f(x) = \dfrac{1}{x}$, $g(x) = x - 3$ (ii) $f(x) = 2x$, $g(x) = \sqrt{x}$

(iii) $f(x) = x + 5$, $g(x) = x - 9$ (iv) $f(x) = 10 - x$, $g(x) = 10 - x$

(v) $f(x) = \dfrac{1}{x}$, $g(x) = \dfrac{1}{x}$

(b) Comment on the cases where $fg(x) = gf(x)$.

3 Each of the expressions below is of the form $fg(x)$ where $f(x) = 1 - x^2$. What is $g(x)$ in each case?

(a) $1 - (x + 2)^2$ (b) $1 - x^4$ (c) $1 - \dfrac{1}{x^2}$ (d) $1 - x$

4 Each of the expressions below is of the form $fg(x)$ where $g(x) = x^3$. What is $f(x)$ in each case?

(a) $x^3 + 8$ (b) x^6 (c) $3x^3 + 1$ (d) $\dfrac{12}{x^3}$ (e) x (f) $4x^3 - x^6$

Rearranging formulas

1 Complete the steps to make x the subject of the formula $y = 5(x - 7)^2$.

$$y = 5(x - 7)^2$$

$$\_\,\_\,\_ = (x - 7)^2 \qquad \text{divide both sides by 5}$$

$$\_\,\_\,\_ = (x - 7) \qquad \text{find the square root of each side}$$

$$\_\,\_\,\_ = x \qquad \text{add 7 to both sides}$$

2 Make x the subject of the formula:

(a) $y = 3x^2 - 7$ (b) $y = \dfrac{(2x + 1)^2}{9}$ (c) $y = 3\sqrt{x} - 1$

3 Complete the steps to find x in terms of y if $y = \dfrac{3}{x} - 4$

$$y = \frac{3}{x} - 4$$

$$\_\,\_\,\_ = 3 - 4x \qquad \text{multiply both sides by } x$$

$$\_\,\_\,\_ = 3 \qquad \text{add } 4x \text{ to both sides to collect terms in } x \text{ together}$$

$$(\_\,\_\,\_)x = 3 \qquad \text{factorise the left-hand side}$$

$$x = \frac{3}{\_\,\_\,\_}$$

4 Make x the subject of the formula:

(a) $y = 2 - \dfrac{1}{x}$ (b) $y = \dfrac{3}{x^2}$ (c) $y = 5 + \dfrac{1}{2\sqrt{x}}$

(d) $y = \dfrac{2}{x + 1}$ (e) $y = \dfrac{4}{2x + 1}$ (f) $y = \dfrac{7}{1 - 2x}$

(g) $y = (1 + x)^2$ (h) $y = (1 - 2x)^2$ (i) $y = 1 - \left(\dfrac{x}{2}\right)^2$

Solving equations

This tasksheet is designed to emphasise and give extra practice in the methodology needed to solve equations involving sine and cosine functions.

1 To solve the equation $4 \cos x° = 3$:

   (a) Write down the value of $\cos x°$.

   (b) Use your calculator to give one solution for x.

   (c) Sketch the graph of $y = \cos x°$.

   (d)   (i) Mark on the graph the solution from the calculator.

   (ii) Mark on the graph the other solution between 0 and 360.

   (iii) Write down the value of this other solution.

2 Find all the solutions between 0 and 360 for the following equations, illustrating your answers with sketch graphs.

   (a) $\cos x° = 0.56$ (b) $\sin x° = -0.23$ (c) $\cos x° = -0.5$

3 Find all the solutions between -180 and 180 for these equations, illustrating your answers with sketch graphs.

   (a) $\sin x° = 0.65$ (b) $\cos x° = -0.38$ (c) $\sin x° = -0.47$

4 Find all the solutions between 0 and 360 for the following equations.

   (a) $3 \sin x° = 2$ (b) $5 \cos x° + 2 = 0$ (c) $2 \cos x° + 5 = 0$

5 Copy and complete the solution of $5 \sin (3t + 40)° = 4$.

$$5 \sin (3t + 40)° = 4 \Rightarrow \sin (3t + 40)° = \ldots$$

This is equivalent to $\sin x° = \ldots$, where $x = 3t + 40$

From the calculator, $x = \ldots$

So (using a sketch of the graph of $\sin x°$) six possible solutions are

$$x = \ldots, \quad \ldots, \quad \ldots, \quad \ldots, \quad \ldots, \quad \ldots$$
$$\Rightarrow 3t + 40 = \ldots, \quad \ldots, \quad \ldots, \quad \ldots, \quad \ldots, \quad \ldots$$
$$\Rightarrow \qquad t = \ldots, \quad \ldots, \quad \ldots, \quad \ldots, \quad \ldots, \quad \ldots$$

6 Solve these equations for values of t between 0 and 360.

   (a) $\sin 2t° = 0.7$ (b) $2 \cos 3t° = 1$ (c) $3 \cos (0.5t + 20)° = 2$

Laws of indices

1 Express the following as single powers of 2.

(a) $2^5 \times 2^7$ (b) $2^{10} \div 2^7$ (c) $2^5 \div 2^4$ (d) $2^3 \div 2$

(e) $2^4 \div 2^4$ (f) $(2^3)^2$ (g) $(2^2)^3$ (h) $(2^4)^4$

2 Simplify the following.

(a) $y^5 \times y^7$ (b) $b^{10} \div b^7$ (c) $c^5 \div c^4$ (d) $x^3 \div x$

(e) $y^4 \div y^4$ (f) $(a^3)^2$ (g) $(a^2)^3$ (h) $(b^4)^4$

3 Evaluate:

(a) 2^{-5} (b) 5^{-1} (c) 4^{-2} (d) $2^{-3} \times 2^{-1}$

(e) $5^2 \times 5^{-4}$ (f) $8^0 \times 8^{-2}$ (g) $2^{-3} \div 2^{-4}$ (h) $3^{-4} \div 3$

4 Simplify:

(a) $x^{-3} \times x^4$ (b) $a^3 \div a^5$ (c) $b^2 \times b^{-2}$ (d) $(d^{-2})^3$

(e) $x^{-5} \div x^5$ (f) $(y^3)^{-1}$ (g) $(a^5)^0$ (h) $x^3 \times x^{-2} \times x$

5 Evaluate:

(a) $8^{\frac{1}{3}}$ (b) $16^{-\frac{1}{4}}$ (c) $27^{\frac{2}{3}}$ (d) 3^{-2}

(e) $16^{\frac{3}{4}}$ (f) $1000^{-\frac{1}{3}}$ (g) 25^0 (h) $100^{\frac{3}{2}}$

(i) $\left(\frac{1}{4}\right)^{-2}$ (j) $1^{\frac{3}{5}}$ (k) $\left(\frac{1}{2}\right)^{-3}$ (l) 0.1^{-4}

(m) $81^{\frac{3}{4}}$ (n) $125^{-\frac{2}{3}}$ (o) $1\,000\,000^{\frac{1}{3}}$ (p) $0.01^{-\frac{3}{2}}$

Differentiation practice

Work through this tasksheet if you feel that you need more practice at differentiation techniques and choosing which technique to use. You will need to use the chain rule, product rule and quotient rule, as well as parametric and implicit differentiation.

Find $\dfrac{dy}{dx}$ when:

1 $y = \sin^2 x$

2 $y = 3\cos 4x$

3 $y = \dfrac{1}{x^2}$

4 $y = \dfrac{1}{2x + 5}$

5 $x = t^2; \quad y = 3(2t + 1)$

6 $y = e^{2x} \sin \frac{1}{2}x$

7 $y = (2x^2 - 3)^3$

8 $y = \ln 4x$

9 $x^2 y = 36$

10 $x = 4\cos\theta; \quad y = 3\sin\theta$

11 $y = x(2x - 3)^4$

12 $y = x^4(2x - 3)$

13 $x = \sin 2\theta; \quad y = 2\cos 3\theta$

14 $x^2 + y^2 = 25$

15 $y = \sqrt{(5x)}$

16 $x = \dfrac{1}{t}; \quad y = t^3$

17 $x^2 + 3xy + 2y^2 = 8$

18 $y = \dfrac{\sin x}{\cos 2x}$

19 $e^{3x}y = x^2$

20 $x^2 + y = 12$

Using sigma

When manipulating series, sigma notation can be a very powerful and useful notation. To exploit it to the full you need to become confident in its use.

1 For the series $u_1 + u_2 + u_3 + \cdots + u_n$

   (a) Write down an expression for the sum of the series in sigma notation.

   (b) Write down a simple series and investigate the effect on the sum of the series when each term of the series is multiplied by the same constant.

   (c) Show that $\displaystyle\sum_{i=1}^{n} au_i = a\left(\sum_{i=1}^{n} u_i\right)$ for any constant a.

2 (a) Investigate how the sum of a series changes when you add a constant to each term of the series.

   (b) Show that $\displaystyle\sum_{i=1}^{n} (u_i + b) = \left(\sum_{i=1}^{n} u_i\right) + nb$

   (c) Show that $\displaystyle\sum_{i=1}^{n} (au_i + b) = a\left(\sum_{i=1}^{n} u_i\right) + nb$

For any constants a and b,

$$\sum_{i=1}^{n} (au_i + b) = a\left(\sum_{i=1}^{n} u_i\right) + nb$$

Example

Evaluate $\displaystyle\sum_{i=1}^{n} (4i + 2)$.

Solution

$$\sum_{i=1}^{n} (4i + 2) = 4\left(\sum_{i=1}^{n} i\right) + 2n$$

$$\sum_{i=1}^{n} i = \frac{n(n+1)}{2} \qquad \text{using the formula for the sum of an arithmetic series}$$

So $\displaystyle\sum_{i=1}^{n} (4i + 2) = \frac{4n(n+1)}{2} + 2n = 2n^2 + 4n$

3 Find: (a) $\displaystyle\sum_{i=1}^{n} (2i - 3)$ (b) $\displaystyle\sum_{i=1}^{n} (5i + 1)$

4 Generalise the result of question 2 by showing that

$$\sum_{i=1}^{n} (u_i + v_i) = \left(\sum_{i=1}^{n} u_i \right) + \left(\sum_{i=1}^{n} v_i \right)$$

5 (a) Write down the result of subtracting $1^3 + 2^3 + \cdots + n^3$ from $2^3 + 3^3 + \cdots + (n+1)^3$.

(b) Hence show that

$$\sum_{i=1}^{n} (i+1)^3 - \sum_{i=1}^{n} i^3 = (n+1)^3 - 1$$

(c) Simplify $(i+1)^3 - i^3$ and show that

$$\sum_{i=1}^{n} (i+1)^3 - \sum_{i=1}^{n} i^3 = 3\sum_{i=1}^{n} i^2 + 3\sum_{i=1}^{n} i + n$$

(d) Hence obtain the formula

$$\sum_{i=1}^{n} i^2 = \frac{n}{6}(n+1)(2n+1)$$

6 Use the result you have obtained in question 5 to find the sum of the first 99 squares.

7 Use the method of question 4 and the result from question 5 to find:

(a) $\displaystyle\sum_{i=1}^{n} (2i^2 - 6i + 4)$ (b) $1^2 + 3^2 + 5^2 + 7^2 + \cdots + (2n-1)^2$

You should now be familiar with the following results.

- $1 + 2 + 3 + \cdots + n = \displaystyle\sum_{i=1}^{n} i = \frac{n}{2}(n+1)$

- $1^2 + 2^2 + 3^2 + \cdots + n^2 = \displaystyle\sum_{i=1}^{n} i^2 = \frac{n}{6}(n+1)(2n+1)$

- $\displaystyle\sum_{i=1}^{n} (au_i + bv_i) = a\sum_{i=1}^{n} u_i + b\sum_{i=1}^{n} v_i$

Zeno's paradox

In a paradox, two different, seemingly sound arguments lead to contradictory conclusions. The Greek, Zeno of Elia (c. 450 BC), expounded a famous set of paradoxes on the subject of motion. The following is an illustration of one of them.

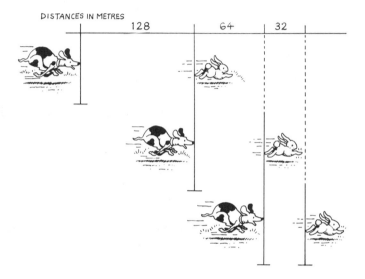

DISTANCES IN METRES

The dog chasing the rabbit is running at $8\,\mathrm{m\,s}^{-1}$ and the rabbit at $4\,\mathrm{m\,s}^{-1}$. Both are running in a straight line. When the dog first spotted the rabbit the distance between them was 128 m.

Now consider Zeno's argument.

1 (a) When the dog has run 128 m the rabbit will have moved away. How far will it have moved?

(b) When the dog has run the next 64 m, the rabbit will have moved away again. How far will it have moved?

(c) When the dog has run the next 32 m, the rabbit will have moved away again. How far will it have moved?

Each time the dog arrives at a position previously occupied by the rabbit it will have moved away. Thus the rabbit will always be in front of the dog and it will never be caught.

2 The distance in metres travelled by the dog in the first five intervals is

$$128 + 64 + 32 + 16 + 8$$

(a) Work out the sum for the first n intervals.

(b) What is the value of the sum for an infinite number of intervals?

3 The distance in metres travelled by the rabbit in the first five intervals is

$$64 + 32 + 16 + 8 + 4$$

(a) Work out the sum for the first n intervals.

(b) What is the value of the sum for an infinite number of intervals?

It appears to take an infinite number of steps for the dog to catch the rabbit.

4 (a) How far will the dog run in 40 seconds?

(b) How far will the rabbit run in 40 seconds?

(c) After 40 seconds, which animal will be in the lead?

5 From your answer to question 4 it is clear that the dog *will* catch the rabbit. Can you explain the fallacy in the arguments which led to the conclusions stated after questions 1 and 3?

Other entertaining paradoxes are outlined in the book *Riddles in Mathematics* by Eugene P. Northrop (Penguin).

Regular pentagons and the Fibonacci sequence

1 Why is the interior angle of a regular pentagon 108°?

If you have ever tried to draw a regular pentagon of given edge length, you will have found that it is difficult to get an accurate diagram if you use a method that involves measuring the interior angles of 108° with a protractor.

A better method would involve measuring lengths only, using compasses to construct the diagram. To do this you need to know the length of the diagonals of a regular pentagon. The procedure for drawing the pentagon is then as shown below, where the edge length is 1 and the diagonal length is denoted by the Greek letter ϕ ('phi').

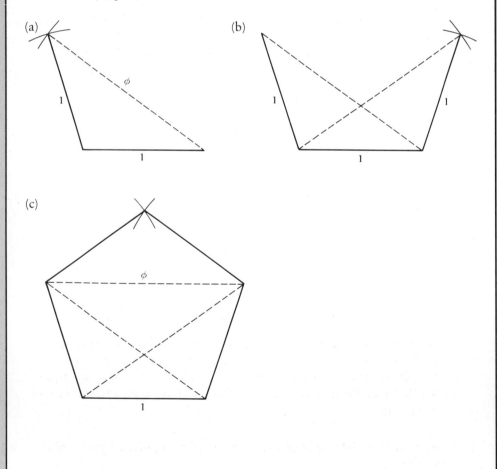

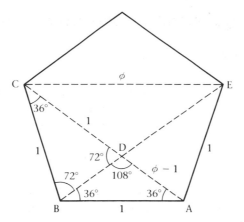

ϕ can be calculated using the fact that triangle CDE is an enlargement of triangle ABD with ϕ as the scale factor. Since it is a diagonal, $AC = \phi$. Also $CD = 1$, so $AD = \phi - 1$. By comparing the sides AD and CD in triangles ABD and CDE, it then follows that

$$\phi(\phi - 1) = 1 \qquad \text{①}$$

2 Explain the values for the angles in triangle ABC.

3 Explain why $CD = 1$ and $\phi(\phi - 1) = 1$.

Rearranging ① gives:

$$\phi^2 - \phi - 1 = 0$$
$$(\phi - \tfrac{1}{2})^2 - \tfrac{5}{4} = 0$$
$$\phi = \tfrac{1}{2}(1 + \sqrt{5}) \quad \text{or} \quad \phi = \tfrac{1}{2}(1 - \sqrt{5})$$
$$\phi \approx 1.618 \quad \text{or} \quad \phi \approx -0.618 \quad \text{(to 3 decimal places)}$$

As far as the diagonal of the regular pentagon is concerned, the negative root is meaningless, so the diagonal length is 1.618, or, perhaps more usefully, the diagonal length is the edge length multiplied by 1.618. You now have a simpler means of calculating the diagonal for a given edge and then drawing an accurate regular pentagon.

4 Using a suitable diagonal length, draw accurately a regular pentagon with 5 cm edges.

The story does not end at this point, because regular pentagons can be enlarged by extending pairs of sides and joining the five points of intersection, as illustrated below.

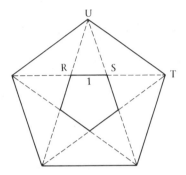

Two of the outer triangles making up the shape above are shown below.

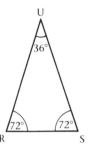
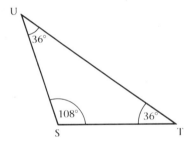

These triangles are similar to those used on page 545 and so

$$SU = \phi \times RS = \phi \qquad UT = \phi \times SU = \phi^2$$

5 Explain why $SU = \phi$ and $UT = \phi^2$.

The edge length of the larger pentagon is ϕ^2. Moreover, the diagonal of the larger pentagon must be ϕ^3. So you can see the striking fact that the sequence of lengths

$$\text{edge, diagonal, edge, diagonal, ...}$$

for a succession of regular pentagons, formed by extending the sides, takes the form of a simple geometric sequence

$$1, \quad \phi, \quad \phi^2, \quad \phi^3, ...$$

6 Why is a diagonal of the larger pentagon given by ϕ^3?

Previously, the value of ϕ has been calculated as $\frac{1}{2}(1 + \sqrt{5})$. It is interesting to examine the sequence of powers of ϕ expressed in surd form.

$$\phi = \tfrac{1}{2}(1 + \sqrt{5}) \qquad \phi^4 = \tfrac{1}{2}(7 + 3\sqrt{5})$$

$$\phi^2 = \tfrac{1}{2}(3 + \sqrt{5}) \qquad \phi^5 = \tfrac{1}{2}(11 + 5\sqrt{5})$$

$$\phi^3 = \tfrac{1}{2}(4 + 2\sqrt{5}) \qquad \phi^6 = \tfrac{1}{2}(18 + 8\sqrt{5})$$

ϕ^2 may be calculated from $\phi = \frac{1}{2}(1 + \sqrt{5})$ by multiplying out brackets and simplifying as follows.

$$\phi^2 = \tfrac{1}{2}(1 + \sqrt{5}) \times \tfrac{1}{2}(1 + \sqrt{5})$$

$$\phi^2 = \tfrac{1}{4}(1 + \sqrt{5} + \sqrt{5} + 5)$$

$$\phi^2 = \tfrac{1}{4}(6 + 2\sqrt{5})$$

$$\phi^2 = \tfrac{1}{2}(3 + \sqrt{5})$$

However, it is easier to observe that $\phi^2 = \phi + 1$.

So

$$\phi^2 = \tfrac{1}{2}(1 + \sqrt{5}) + 1$$
$$= \tfrac{1}{2}(3 + \sqrt{5})$$

Similarly, $\phi^3 = \phi^2 + \phi$, $\phi^4 = \phi^3 + \phi^2$, and so on.

7   Check the values for ϕ^3 up to ϕ^6 in the same way, and calculate ϕ^7 and ϕ^8.

Two important sequences are known as the **Lucas sequence**

$$1, \quad 3, \quad 4, \quad 7, \quad 11, \quad 18, \quad \ldots$$

and the **Fibonacci sequence**

$$1, \quad 1, \quad 2, \quad 3, \quad 5, \quad 8, \quad \ldots$$

In both sequences, successive terms are found by adding the two previous terms.

We next consider how you can find formulas for the general terms of these two sequences.

When ϕ was calculated there was a second root, $\frac{1}{2}(1 - \sqrt{5})$, which will now be referred to as ψ ('psi'). This generates a sequence similar to that for ϕ. The two sequences are placed alongside each other for comparison.

$$\phi = \tfrac{1}{2}(1 + \sqrt{5}) \qquad \psi = \tfrac{1}{2}(1 - \sqrt{5})$$
$$\phi^2 = \tfrac{1}{2}(3 + \sqrt{5}) \qquad \psi^2 = \tfrac{1}{2}(3 - \sqrt{5})$$
$$\phi^3 = \tfrac{1}{2}(4 + 2\sqrt{5}) \qquad \psi^3 = \tfrac{1}{2}(4 - 2\sqrt{5})$$
$$\phi^4 = \tfrac{1}{2}(7 + 3\sqrt{5}) \qquad \psi^4 = \tfrac{1}{2}(7 - 3\sqrt{5})$$
$$\phi^5 = \tfrac{1}{2}(11 + 5\sqrt{5}) \qquad \psi^5 = \tfrac{1}{2}(11 - 5\sqrt{5})$$
$$\phi^6 = \tfrac{1}{2}(18 + 8\sqrt{5}) \qquad \psi^6 = \tfrac{1}{2}(18 - 8\sqrt{5})$$

If you add corresponding members of the two sequences you obtain the Lucas sequence. The Fibonacci sequence is obtained by subtracting corresponding members and then dividing by $\sqrt{5}$.

$$\phi + \psi = 1 \qquad \phi - \psi = \sqrt{5}$$
$$\phi^2 + \psi^2 = 3 \qquad \phi^2 - \psi^2 = \sqrt{5}$$
$$\phi^3 + \psi^3 = 4 \qquad \phi^3 - \psi^3 = 2\sqrt{5}$$
$$\phi^4 + \psi^4 = 7 \qquad \phi^4 - \psi^4 = 3\sqrt{5}$$
$$\phi^5 + \psi^5 = 11 \qquad \phi^5 - \psi^5 = 5\sqrt{5}$$
$$\phi^6 + \psi^6 = 18 \qquad \phi^6 - \psi^6 = 8\sqrt{5}$$

You now have formulas for the general or nth terms, L_n and F_n, of the Lucas and Fibonacci sequences:

$$L_n = \phi^n + \psi^n = \left[\tfrac{1}{2}(1 + \sqrt{5})\right]^n + \left[\tfrac{1}{2}(1 - \sqrt{5})\right]^n$$

$$F_n = \frac{1}{\sqrt{5}}(\phi^n - \psi^n) = \frac{1}{\sqrt{5}}\left[(\tfrac{1}{2}(1 + \sqrt{5}))^n - (\tfrac{1}{2}(1 - \sqrt{5}))^n\right]$$

8   Verify that $\phi^7 + \psi^7$ and $\dfrac{1}{\sqrt{5}}(\phi^7 - \psi^7)$ give the seventh terms of the Lucas and Fibonacci sequences and verify the eighth terms in the same way.

9   Use a calculator or computer to tabulate ϕ^n, ψ^n, L_n and F_n for a range of values of n. In particular observe the behaviour of ψ^n.

It is instructive to look at the four sequences ϕ^n, ψ^n, L_n and F_n numerically, using a calculator or a spreadsheet program on a computer. In particular, it will be noted that the terms of ψ^n rapidly become small because ψ is numerically less than 1. The first terms in the formulas for L_n and F_n give approximations to the sequences, which improve in accuracy as n gets larger.

The approximations are

$$L_n \approx \left(\tfrac{1}{2}(1 + \sqrt{5})\right)^n$$

$$F_n \approx \frac{1}{\sqrt{5}}\left(\tfrac{1}{2}(1 + \sqrt{5})\right)^n$$

10 Calculate the ratios of successive pairs of terms in each sequence. In other words, calculate

$$\frac{L_n}{L_{n-1}} \quad \text{and} \quad \frac{F_n}{F_{n-1}}$$

What do you notice and how can this be explained in relation to the approximations of L_n and F_n?

The Greeks derived ϕ from the **golden rectangle**, which was thought to display particularly pleasing proportions, and is, for example, the shape used for the frontage of the Parthenon in Athens. ϕ is known as the **golden ratio**, the ratio of the sides of a golden rectangle. A golden rectangle is such that when a square of the same width is removed the remaining rectangle is also golden, as shown below.

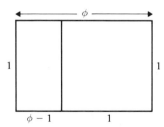

Since the length of the golden rectangle is the width multiplied by ϕ, it follows that

$$\phi(\phi - 1) = 1$$

$$\phi^2 - \phi - 1 = 0$$

which is precisely the equation derived earlier in relation to the diagonal length of a regular pentagon.

These two sources of the golden ratio – the regular pentagon and the golden rectangle – are brought together very nicely in the regular icosahedron.

The regular icosahedron is a polyhedron with twenty faces in the form of equilateral triangles. If three golden rectangles are fitted together so that they are mutually perpendicular, their twelve vertices form the vertices of a regular icosahedron.

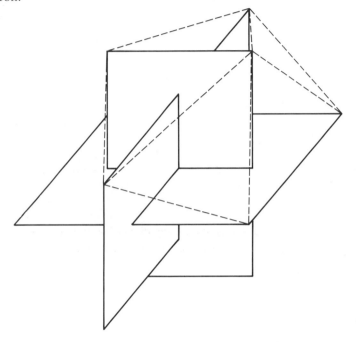

In this icosahedron, five equilateral triangles meet at a vertex. Such a set of triangles forms a pyramid with a regular pentagon as its base. One of these pentagonal pyramids is shown by the dotted lines above. Note that the edges of the icosahedron are the same length as the shorter edges of the golden rectangles and that the one diagonal of the regular pentagon that is shown is the longer edge of one of the golden rectangles. So the icosahedron provides a link between regular pentagons and golden rectangles.

Tangents and normals

A line with gradient $-\frac{1}{2}$ makes a right angle with a line with gradient 2.

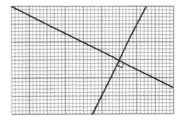

Each line is said to be **normal** to the other.

1 If a line is drawn with a gradient g, what can you say about the gradient of a line which is normal to it?

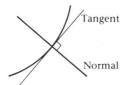

A line is said to be a normal to a curve at a given point if it is normal to the tangent at that point.

2 The graph of $y = \frac{1}{3}x^3$ has tangents drawn at $x = 1$ and at $x = -1$. These two tangents and the normals to the tangents form a rectangle.

(a) Sketch the graph with the tangents and normals shown.

(b) Find the equations of the two tangents.

(c) Find the equations of the two normals.

(d) Use your answers to (b) and (c) to find the coordinates of all four corners of the rectangle.

(e) What is the area of the rectangle?

3 Tangents and normals drawn on the graph of $y = x^2$ form a square as shown.

(a) Find the coordinates of the four corners of the square.

(b) Show that the area of the square is $\frac{1}{2}$.

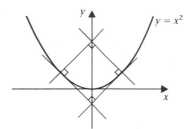

4

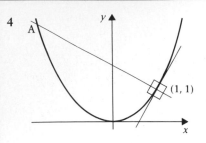

The normal to the graph of $y = x^2$ at $(1, 1)$ cuts the graph at A as shown.

Find A.

Optimisation problems

1 A mathematical ornament consists of a cone inside a sphere of radius 5 cm, such that the top and the perimeter of the base of the cone touch the sphere. Design the ornament so that the cone has maximum volume.

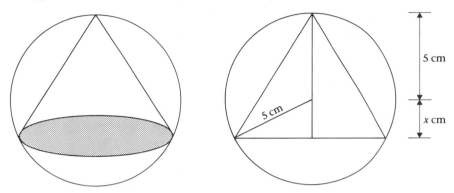

To use calculus to solve this design problem, you must first express the volume, V cm^3, of the cone in terms of another quantity which can then be varied to maximise V. The depth of the base of the cone below the centre of the sphere, x cm, seems a suitable quantity for this purpose.

(a) Why can x be neither greater than 5 nor less than -5?

(b) Without doing any calculations, write down what you think happens to the volume of the cone as x gradually changes from -5 to 5.

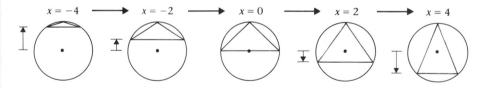

(c) Draw a rough sketch of the (x, V) graph which more or less fits your answer to part (b). Mark the value of x which you think will result in the greatest volume.

(d) The volume of a cone is $\frac{1}{3}\pi r^2 h$ where h is the height of the cone and r is the radius of its base. Calculate the volume of the cone for the value of x which you think gives the greatest volume.

(e) Suppose you choose as your variable not x, but y, where y cm is the height of the base of the cone above the lowest point of the sphere as shown in the diagram.

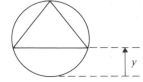

Again without doing any calculations, sketch what you think the graph (y, V) will look like.

(f) Whether you choose x or y is unimportant, except that the mathematics involved may be easier for one rather than the other.

Express V in terms of x, sketch the graph of V against x and use calculus to find the maximum value of V.

(g) Now express V in terms of y and again use calculus to find the maximum value of V.

Check that this results in exactly the same shape for the ornament.

(h) You could also have expressed V in terms of θ, where θ is the angle shown in the diagram.

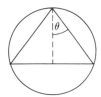

Without doing any calculations, sketch what you think the (θ, V) graph looks like.

Express V in terms of θ, use a graph plotter to plot the graph and determine the value of θ which maximises the volume. Check that this results in the same shape as before.

2   A bicycle manufacturer has designed a new model and has the problem of fixing the price in such a way that profits are maximised. After an initial cost of £50 000 to set up the production line, it will cost £85 in labour, raw materials and components to produce each bike. Market research suggests that the firm can hope to sell 5000 bikes if the price is fixed at £100, but they can only expect to sell 1000 if the price is £200 per bike. They assume the relationship between price and demand is linear between these two extremes.

How many bikes would you advise the company to manufacture and at what price should they be sold?

Traffic

Car B is being driven at a speed of 45 m.p.h. ($20\,\text{m s}^{-1}$). Car A can accelerate from 0 to $20\,\text{m s}^{-1}$ in 10 seconds in such a way that its speed after t seconds is given by the formula:

$$\text{speed} = \frac{t(20 - t)}{5}$$

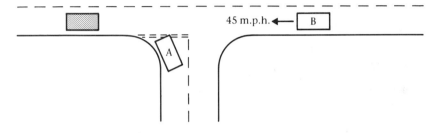

The (time, speed) graphs for the two cars are sketched below.

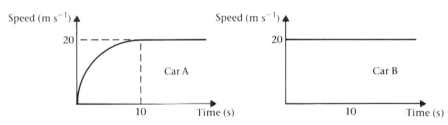

State clearly the assumptions you make when answering each of the following questions.

1 Evaluate the integral

$$\int_0^{10} \frac{t(20 - t)}{5}\, dt$$

and explain what information it gives you about the motion of car A.

2 What is the least distance B can be from A at the start of the manoeuvre if B is to avoid slowing down?

3 If 1200 cars per hour use the road, is A likely to find a gap of sufficient length?

Derivative of $\sin^2 x$

1 (a) Sketch the graph of $y = \sin^2 x$.

   (b) By sketching the gradient graph of $y = \sin^2 x$, suggest an appropriate expression for the derivative of $\sin^2 x$.

2 (a) $\sin^2 x$ may be written as $a \cos bx + c$. What are the values of a, b, c?

   (b) Use your results in (a) to write down the derivative of $\sin^2 x$. Compare your answer with that found in question 1.

3 Find the derivative of $\cos^2 x$, checking your answer.

4 (a) Find the derivative of $\sin^2 x + \cos^2 x$.

   (b) Sketch the graph of $y = \sin^2 x + \cos^2 x$.

   (c) Explain the result in (a), using your graph.

Another way to find the derivative of $\sin^2 x$ uses an important identity, which can be developed as follows. Consider the triangle OAB shown.
AD is perpendicular to OB.

   Let OA $= 1$

   Then OD $= \cos 2x$ (in triangle OAD)

Angle DAB $= 90° -$ angle ABD $= x$

   AC $= \sin x \Rightarrow$ AB $= 2 \sin x$

   DB $= (2 \sin x) \sin x = 2(\sin x)^2 = 2 \sin^2 x$

   Since OB $= 1$, then OD $= 1 - $ DB $= 1 - 2 \sin^2 x$

      But OD $= \cos 2x$

   So $\cos 2x = 1 - 2 \sin^2 x$

Although this result is proven here for acute angles, it is in fact true for *all* angles x. (This will be proven in a later chapter.)

5 Use this result to show that $\dfrac{\mathrm{d}}{\mathrm{d}x}(\sin^2 x) = \sin 2x$.

6 Using also the result $\sin^2 x + \cos^2 x = 1$, show that $\dfrac{\mathrm{d}}{\mathrm{d}x}(\cos^2 x) = -\sin 2x$.

Prime number formulas

Many quadratic formulas generate long strings of prime numbers. The formula $n^2 - n + 41$ is a much quoted example.

First conjecture $n^2 - n + 41$ is always prime.

This is not true; for example when $n = 41$, $n^2 - n + 41 = 41^2$, which is not prime.

After trying many other expressions you might make a totally different type of conjecture.

Second conjecture   No quadratic expression in n is prime for all integral values of n.

1 Write down various quadratic expressions in n, for example

$$n^2 + 7n + 5, \quad n^2 - 1, \quad 3n^2 + 2$$

Can you always find a value of n for which the expression is not prime?

It is likely that the more quadratic expressions you try, the more you will become convinced of the truth of the second conjecture. But, as you know, it is not sufficient simply to try lots of examples – you may miss the one example which turns out to be a counter-example!

This is the exciting phase of the solution of a mathematical problem where all sorts of ideas must be tried out as you search for either a convincing proof or a counter-example. Two attempts at proof are given below.

First attempted proof
The general quadratic is of the form $an^2 + bn + c$.

Putting $n = c$ gives $ac^2 + bc + c = c(ac + b + 1)$, which is not prime because it is divisible by both $ac + b + 1$ and c. Therefore no quadratic expression in n can be prime for all integral values of n.

2 Check over the 'proof' above carefully. Which particular cases spoil the 'proof'?

Second attempted proof ('by contradiction')
Suppose $an^2 + bn + c$ to be prime for all integers n. In particular, for $n = 1$, $a + b + c$ must be a prime. Let $a + b + c = p$.

For $n = 1 + p$,

$$an^2 + bn + c = a(p + 1)^2 + b(p + 1) + c$$
$$= ap^2 + 2ap + bp + a + b + c$$
$$= ap^2 + 2ap + bp + p$$

$an^2 + bn + c$ is therefore $(ap + 2a + b + 1)p$.

3 Find a similar expression for $an^2 + bn + c$ when $n = 1 + 2p$.

$an^2 + bn + c$ is divisible by p when $n = 1$, $n = 1 + p$ and $n = 1 + 2p$. If it is prime for each of these values then $an^2 + bn + c$ must equal p itself and we would have three points on a quadratic graph as shown.

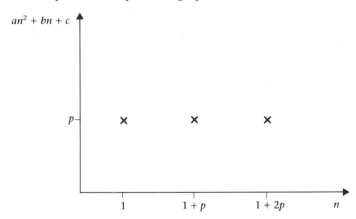

This is not possible for a quadratic.

So $an^2 + bn + c$ is *not* prime for at least one of these three values.

There may be some points on which you are still not convinced. If so, first try to fill in the necessary details yourself and then discuss the unclear points with fellow students and your teacher. Do not be convinced too easily!

Extending the method

The method of section 5.1.4, although useful, has only been developed for the expression $a \sin \theta + b \cos \theta$ on the assumption that a and b are positive. In this tasksheet, other possibilities are considered.

1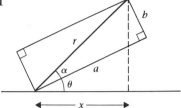

(a) Use the diagram to find an expression for x

    (i) in terms of r, θ and α,

    (ii) in terms of a, b and θ.

(b) Use your result from (a) to obtain an alternative expression for $a \cos \theta - b \sin \theta$.

2

By expressing y in two different ways, explain why

$$a \sin \theta - b \cos \theta = r \sin (\theta - \alpha)$$

3 Using the diagram of question 2, explain why

$$a \cos \theta + b \sin \theta = r \cos (\theta - \alpha)$$

The expression you have just found is an alternative to the expression used in section 5.1.4 where you wrote $a \sin \theta + b \cos \theta = r \sin (\theta + \alpha)$.

4 (a) Express $7 \sin \theta + 4 \cos \theta$ in the form $r_1 \sin (\theta + \alpha_1)$.

(b) Express $4 \cos \theta + 7 \sin \theta$ in the form $r_2 \cos (\theta - \alpha_2)$.

(c) By plotting the two graphs show that these give the same result.

(d) What is the relationship between α_1 and α_2?

$$a \sin \theta + b \cos \theta = r \sin (\theta + \alpha)$$
$$a \sin \theta - b \cos \theta = r \sin (\theta - \alpha)$$
$$a \cos \theta + b \sin \theta = r \cos (\theta - \alpha)$$
$$a \cos \theta - b \sin \theta = r \cos (\theta + \alpha)$$

where $r = \sqrt{(a^2 + b^2)}$ and $\alpha = \tan^{-1}\dfrac{b}{a}$

5 Express each of the following as a phase-shifted sine or cosine wave.

(a) $7 \cos \theta + 24 \sin \theta$ (b) $12 \sin \theta + 5 \cos \theta$

(c) $9 \sin \theta - 40 \cos \theta$ (d) $4 \sin \theta + 2 \cos \theta$

It is not necessary for α to be acute, although practically it is much easier to work with if it is. The next question demonstrates alternative forms.

6 This graph may be regarded either as a sine graph or as a cosine graph, phase-shifted either to the right or to the left.

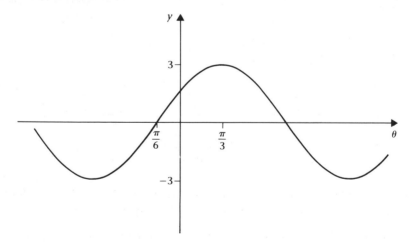

Express the graph in the form:

(a) $r \sin (\theta + \alpha)$ (b) $r \cos (\theta - \alpha)$

(c) $r \sin (\theta - \alpha)$ (d) $r \cos (\theta + \alpha)$

Intersections

1 Three points have coordinates:

A $(2, 2, 2)$;   B $(-1, 1, 6)$;   C $(0, 2, 5)$

(a) Find the vector equation of the plane ABC in the form:

(i) $\mathbf{r} = \overrightarrow{OC} + \lambda \overrightarrow{CA} + \mu \overrightarrow{CB}$

(ii) $\mathbf{r} = \overrightarrow{OA} + \lambda \overrightarrow{AB} + \mu \overrightarrow{AC}$

(b) Show that both vector equations give the same Cartesian equation:

$3x - y + 2z = 8$

2 Find two points which both lie on the line of intersection of the planes $3x - y + 2z = 8$ and $x - 2y + z = 1$. Hence find a vector in the direction of the line of intersection and write down the vector equation of this line.

3 By substituting for x, y and z in the equation of the plane, find the value of the parameter t at the point of intersection of the line with vector equation

$$\begin{bmatrix} x \\ y \\ z \end{bmatrix} = \begin{bmatrix} 0 \\ 2 \\ 5 \end{bmatrix} + t \begin{bmatrix} 3 \\ -1 \\ -5 \end{bmatrix}$$

and the plane with Cartesian equation $2x + 3y + z = 7$.

Hence, write down the coordinates of the point of intersection.

4 Find the point of intersection of the three planes
$x - 2y + z = 9$, $x + y + 2z = 8$ and $x - 3y + 3z = 2$.

5 What happens if you try to find the point of intersection of the three planes
$x - 2y + z = 1$, $3x - y + 2z = 8$ and $4x - 3y + 3z = 5$?

In question 2, you found the direction vector of the line of intersection of the first two of these planes. In the same way, find the direction vectors of the lines of intersection of the other two pairs of planes.

How does this explain what has happened?

How are the planes related geometrically?

How is your result modified if the third equation is $4x - 3y + 3z = 9$?

Drawing parametric curves

1 (a) For the curve given by the parametric equations $x = \cos^3 \theta$ and $y = \sin^3 \theta$, complete the table and sketch the branch of the curve which is formed.

θ	0	$\frac{1}{6}\pi$	$\frac{1}{4}\pi$	$\frac{1}{3}\pi$	$\frac{1}{2}\pi$
x					
y					

(b) How are the values of x and y for $\frac{1}{2}\pi < \theta \le \pi$ related to the values in the table? Use these relationships to sketch the part of the curve $\frac{1}{2}\pi < \theta \le \pi$.

(c) Use symmetry properties to complete the sketch of the curve.

(d) Check your curve using a graph plotter.

2 Sketch the curve given by
$$x = \theta - \sin \theta, \quad y = 1 - \cos \theta$$

3 It is often possible to sketch a curve without plotting a large number of points. Consider, for example, the curve given by
$$x = \frac{1+t}{2-t}, \quad y = \frac{2+t}{4-t}$$

(a) Write down where the curve cuts the axes.

As $t \to 2$ from above, $2 - t$ is a small negative quantity, so $x \to -\infty$.

As $t \to 2$, $y \to 2$, so $y = 2$ is an asymptote.

(b) Explain what happens as $t \to 2$ from below (i.e. through values smaller than 2).

(c) Write down any further asymptotes.

(d) Write down any *obvious* points.

(e) Sketch the curve. (Do *not* plot!)

4 Use the method developed so far to sketch the curve
$$x = \frac{2t}{1-t}, \quad y = \frac{t^2}{1-t}$$

In particular you should find any asymptotes and examine what happens as $t \to \pm\infty$.

By parts

1 To find $\int e^x \cos x \, dx$ you could start as follows.

Let $u = e^x$ and $\dfrac{dv}{dx} = \cos x$

So $\int e^x \cos x \, dx = e^x \sin x - \int e^x \sin x \, dx$

If $I = \int e^x \cos x \, dx$, then

$$I = e^x \sin x - \int e^x \sin x \, dx$$

Using integration by parts again, you should find that I appears on the right-hand side. Show how this enables you to find I.

2 Find $\int e^x \cos x \, dx$ by first putting $u = \cos x$ and $\dfrac{dv}{dx} = e^x$.

Discuss whether the choice of u and $\dfrac{dv}{dx}$ makes any difference to integrating this product.

3 Integrate each of these functions:

   (a) $e^x \sin x$ (b) $e^{2x} \cos x$ (c) $e^x \sin 2x$ (d) $e^{0.5x} \cos 2x$

4 (a) Use integration by parts to find $\int \sin x \cos x \, dx$.

   (b) You could integrate $\sin x \cos x$ by using the chain rule in reverse or by first using a trigonometric formula to rewrite $\sin x \cos x$ in a simpler form. Work out the integral by these methods and check that the answers are consistent with the one you obtained in part (a).

5 To find $\int \ln x \, dx$, write $\ln x = \ln x \times 1$ and integrate by parts, letting $u = \ln x$ and $\dfrac{dv}{dx} = 1$.

Evaluate $\displaystyle\int_2^3 \ln x \, dx$ and draw a sketch to show the area you have worked out.

Integrating the circle

1 Explain why $\int_0^1 \sqrt{(1 - x^2)} \, dx = \frac{1}{4}\pi$

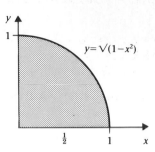

It is not so easy to evaluate $\int_0^{\frac{1}{2}} \sqrt{(1 - x^2)} \, dx$. This integral can, however, be integrated using the method of substitution.

2 (a) The obvious substitution to try would be $u = 1 - x^2$. What happens when you try this substitution?

   (b) Try the trigonometric substitution, $\sin \theta = x$, and show that

$$\int \sqrt{(1 - x^2)} \, dx = \int \cos^2 \theta \, d\theta$$

$$= \frac{1}{2}x\sqrt{(1 - x^2)} + \frac{1}{2}\sin^{-1} x + c$$

   (Hint: Use the identity $2\cos^2 \theta = 1 + \cos 2\theta$.)

   (c) Confirm that $\int_0^1 \sqrt{(1 - x^2)} \, dx = \frac{1}{4}\pi$ and evaluate $\int_0^{\frac{1}{2}} \sqrt{(1 - x^2)} \, dx$.

There is a more elegant way of evaluating a definite integral than using the method of substitution, and that is to substitute the limits at the same time as you substitute the function.

3 If $\sin \theta = x$, explain why $x = 0$ if $\theta = 0$ and why $x = \frac{1}{2}$ if $\theta = \frac{1}{6}\pi$.

Thus $\int_0^{\frac{1}{2}} \sqrt{(1 - x^2)} \, dx = \int_0^{\frac{1}{6}\pi} \cos^2 \theta \, d\theta$

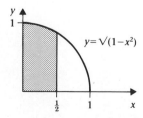
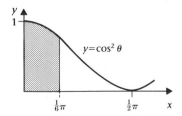

The two shaded areas are precisely equal.

4 Evaluate $\int_0^{\frac{1}{6}\pi} \cos^2\theta \, d\theta$ and confirm your answer to 2(c).

5 (a) Give a geometrical reason why the triangle OAB has area $= \frac{1}{8}\sqrt{3}$ and why the sector OBC has area $= \frac{1}{12}\pi$.

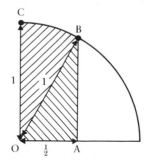

    (b) Do these results agree with the answer you found by integration?

6 Use the method of substitution to evaluate $\int_{1.5}^{3} \sqrt{(9-x^2)} \, dx$.

7 (a) Use the trigonometric substitution, $\tan u = x$, to evaluate $\int \dfrac{1}{1+x^2} \, dx$.

    (Hint: Use the identity $1 + \tan^2 u = \sec^2 u$.)

  (b) Find $\int \dfrac{1}{1+4x^2} \, dx$.

8 Use the trigonometric substitution $\sin u = x$ to evaluate

$$\int \frac{1}{\sqrt{(1-x^2)}} \, dx$$

9 Repeat question 8 but use the substitution $\cos v = x$.

10 Use a graph plotter to graph, on the same axes, the graphs of:

  (a) $y = \sin^{-1} x$ (b) $y = -\cos^{-1} x$

How do these graphs explain the apparent discrepancy in your answers to questions 8 and 9?

Carbon dating

Radioactive chemical elements
The isotopes (see below) of many of the chemical elements are radioactive. This means that the structures of their atoms are unstable and the atoms readily decay to form other stable elements, releasing radiation in the process. There are three main types of radiation: alpha particles, which are essentially helium nuclei; beta particles, which are very fast moving electrons; and gamma rays, which are electromagnetic radiation of very high intensity.

For example, uranium-238 is radioactive and decays to eventually become lead-207. (238 and 207 are the atomic weights of uranium and lead respectively.)

Half-life
The half-life of a radioactive isotope is the time it takes for half the radioactive atoms in a sample to decay. In other words, if a sample of radioactive substance contains N atoms at some particular time, then the time it takes for this to decay so that $\dfrac{N}{2}$ atoms remain is the half-life.

Isotopes
Isotopes are different atoms of the same element, in that the nuclei of the atoms are different. All nuclei of a certain element contain the same number of protons, thus defining the atomic number and the characteristic chemical properties, but isotopes contain different numbers of neutrons in the nuclei.

Half-lives vary from a fraction of a second to millions of years. Some examples are:

uranium-238	4.5×10^9 years	iodine-128	25 minutes
carbon-14	5730 years	lawrencium-257	8 seconds
radium-226	1600 years	polonium-214	1.64×10^{-4} seconds

Representation as a differential equation
The principles of radioactivity were discovered and developed at the beginning of the twentieth century by the New Zealand physicist Ernest Rutherford (1871–1937) while he was at McGill University in Canada. It was for his work in this field that he was awarded the Nobel Prize for chemistry in 1908.

Rutherford discovered that if at a particular time, t, a sample of radioactive substance contains N atoms of the radioactive element per unit mass of the substance, then the number of atoms decreases with time according to the differential equation

$$\frac{dN}{dt} = -kN$$

Radio carbon dating

One of the applications of this differential equation and its solution is found in archaeology. In a scientific paper published in 1949, the American chemist Professor Willard F. Libby first proposed a figure for the half-life of the radioactive isotope of carbon, carbon-14. He showed, further, how it could be used to date wooden artefacts and other remains containing carbon found on archaeological sites. This was a breakthrough of great significance for archaeology and, in 1961, Libby received the Nobel Prize for his work.

Libby first calculated the half-life of carbon-14 as 5568 years, but the accepted value is now about 5730 years. This is equivalent to about 1% of the carbon-14 atoms decaying every 83 years. Carbon-14 emits beta particles, becoming nitrogen in the process.

Carbon has three isotopes. Carbon-12 accounts for roughly 99% of carbon in the world and carbon-13 the other 1%. So the occurrence of carbon-14 is tiny, the ratio of carbon-14 to carbon-12 atoms being about $1:10^{12}$. It is the fact that it is possible to measure the radioactivity of carbon-14 that makes it possible to date ancient remains, whether they are of wood, flesh or bone. Carbon-14 in living organisms is radioactive, and its radioactivity level is measured at 6.68 pico-curies per gram (1 pico-curie is equivalent to 3.7×10^{10} disintegrations per second), but the loss is made up by natural processes and there is only a net decay after the carbon-containing organism dies.

Carbon-dating is usually accepted as a dating method valid up to about 40 000 years, when carbon-14 levels become too low to measure. Some error is inevitable, not least because radiation itself is a random process. Great care must be taken to avoid contamination of artefacts with fresh carbon when preparing to measure their radioactivity, otherwise gross errors could occur. However, the carbon dating method has been verified back to about 5000 BC using dendrochronology. Dendrochronology is the counting of tree rings, one new ring being formed in the trunk for each year of growth. This check is possible since some trees are incredibly old and yet still growing. For instance, the bristle-cone pines of California are over 4000 years old and still growing.

Solution of the differential equation

$$\frac{dN}{dt} = -kN \Rightarrow N = N_0\, e^{-kt}$$

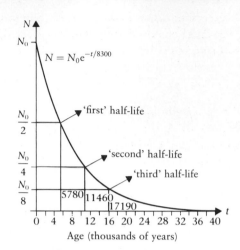

$$N = N_0 e^{-t/8300}$$

'first' half-life

'second' half-life

'third' half-life

Age (thousands of years)

where N_0 is the number of atoms of carbon-14 per unit mass in the substance at time $t = 0$.

1 Show that if the half-life of carbon-14 is 5730 years then

$$k \approx \frac{1}{8300}$$

If you know how many carbon-14 atoms there are per gram for a dead organism (for example, a piece of wood) then knowing how many there should have been when the organism was alive (i.e. a tree) would enable you to estimate the time that has elapsed since its death. It would be difficult to establish the number of carbon-14 atoms in one gram of substance. What can be measured with accuracy is the radioactivity level of any carbon-14 atoms present in a gram of substance.

Suppose $R(t)$ represents the measured radioactivity of carbon-14 at time t. Because radioactivity is proportional to the total number of carbon-14 atoms present it follows that

$$\frac{R(0)}{R(t)} = \frac{N_0\, e^0}{N_0\, e^{-t/8300}}$$

2 Explain how this equation can be rearranged to give

$$t = 8300 \ln\left(\frac{R(0)}{R(t)}\right)$$

How old is Pete Marsh?
Pete Marsh is a name popularly given to the remains of a man whose body was found in a bog in Lindow Moss in Cheshire. The man had apparently been murdered by garrotting before being thrown in the bog; but when did it happen? Readings of the carbon-14 radioactivity levels from the body were about 5.3 pico-curies per gram.

It is reasonable to assume that his radioactivity would have been 6.68 when he was alive and so the time that has elapsed since the death of Pete Marsh can be estimated by

$$t = 8300 \ln \left(\frac{6.68}{5.3} \right) = 1920 \text{ years}$$

This suggests that the murder took place nearly 2000 years before the body was discovered. Latest estimates from the Radiocarbon Unit at Oxford University suggest that Pete Marsh died between 2 BC and AD 119, at the time of the Roman occupation of Britain.

3 Historical records indicate that the Egyptian king, Sneferu, died some time between 2700 BC and 2550 BC. Radioactivity levels from carbon-containing artefacts in his tomb gave a reading of about 3.8 pico-curies per gram.

   Does this reading agree with the historical records?

4 For a long time, historians believed that the origins of agriculture were in the Near East around 4500 BC. Archaeological investigations at the ancient city of Jericho (in modern day Israel) found farming implements that gave a radiocarbon reading of 2.8 pico-curies per gram.

   Why did this lead to a storm in historical circles?

SOLUTIONS
1 FOUNDATIONS

1.1 Graphs

1.1.1 Introduction

1.1 A

1 (a)

Profit (£) per radio	0	1	2	3	4	5	6
Number of radios sold		60	50	40	30	20	10	0
Total profit (£) from sales		0	50	80	90	80	50	0

(b)

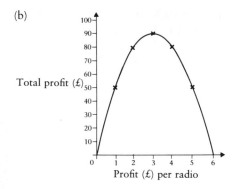

(c) The maximum total profit is £90, which is obtained with a profit per radio of £3.

2 (a) The expression $60 - 10x$ or $10(6 - x)$ can be established fairly easily.

(b) The table was completed by multiplying

'profit per radio' × 'number of radios sold'.

The answer given in part (a) leads to

$$x \times (60 - 10x) = x(60 - 10x)$$
$$= 60x - 10x^2$$

or any equivalent expression.

(c) The graph on page 1 shows the number of radios sold at a given profit per radio. If y stands for the number of radios sold, then (a) gives

$$y = 60 - 10x$$

This is the equation of the first graph.

The graph that you have drawn for 1(b) shows the total profit for a given profit per radio. If t stands for the total profit, then (b) gives

$$t = x(60 - 10x)$$

This is the equation of the second graph.

1.1 B

1 For each graph, you might consider:

- general impression of shape;
- whether or not it passes through the origin;
- steepness of the graph in different places;
- symmetries – reflection, rotation, translation;
- values of x for which the function is undefined;
- what happens when x is close to the undefined values;
- what happens when x is very large (positive or negative);
- whether or not there are any restrictions on the values of y;
- similarities to graphs of other functions;
- how the functions might be classified.

The list is not exhaustive, nor is it necessary for you to record all features at this stage.

2 The graphs are related by reflection in the x-axis.

3 You should notice that they are related by reflection in the line $y = x$. This is true for both pairs of graphs.

1.1.2 Linear graphs

1.1 C

	No. of days	Distance walked (miles)	Distance from Land's End (miles)
(a)	1	30	770
(b)	2	60	740
(c)	t	$30t$	$800 - 30t$

(d) In the first graph, s represents the distance, in miles, walked from John O'Groats, which is $30t$. Therefore, $s = 30t$ is the equation of the graph.

In the second graph, s represents the distance, in miles, from Land's End, which is $800 - 30t$. Therefore, $s = 800 - 30t$ is the equation of the graph..

1.1 Exercise 1

1 (a)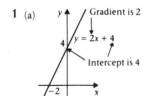

(b)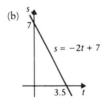

(c)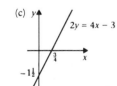

(d)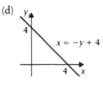

(e)

(f)

2 (a) $y = 2x + 2$ (b) $y = -2x + 4$

(c) $s = \frac{1}{2}t + 3$ or $2s = t + 6$

(d) $y = \frac{3}{2}x - 2$ or $2y = 3x - 4$

3 (a) $y = 2x + 3$ (b) $y = 2x + 2$

(c) $y = -x - 4$ (d) $3y = x + 5$

4 (a) no   (b) yes, gradient $-\frac{1}{2}$, intercept 2

(c) no   (d) no

(e) yes, gradient $-\frac{1}{2}$, intercept $\frac{5}{2}$

(f) yes, parallel to the y-axis

(g) yes, gradient 4, intercept 7

(h) yes, gradient $-\frac{3}{2}$, intercept 3

(i) no

An equation will *only* have a straight-line graph if it can be written in the form $y = mx + c$.

5 (a) $y - 4x + 7 = 0$ (b) $y - 3x + 1 = 0$

(c) $3y + 2x - 13 = 0$

1.1.3 Quadratic functions

1.1 D

You have seen that the graph of the quadratic function $y = ax^2 + bx + c$ may be obtained from the graph of $y = x^2$ through a series of scalings and translations. The questions on pages 7–8 explore the translations involved in obtaining the graph of $y = (x + p)^2 + q$ from that of $y = x^2$.

It should be apparent that the graph of $y = (x + p)^2 + q$ is a parabola with vertex at $(-p, q)$. It may be drawn by translating the graph of $y = x^2$ by $\begin{bmatrix} -p \\ q \end{bmatrix}$.

1 The graph of $y = x^2 + 3$ is that of $y = x^2$ translated upwards by 3 units.

2 Similarly, the graph of $y = x^2 + q$ is that of $y = x^2$ translated upwards by q units. This is not surprising since to get from $y = x^2$ to $y = x^2 + q$ you simply add q to the y-coordinates.

3 The graph of $y = (x + 4)^2$ is that of $y = x^2$ translated 4 units to the left.

4 Similarly, the graph of $y = (x + p)^2$ is that of $y = x^2$ translated p units to the left. Notice that the vertex occurs when $x = -p$, not at $x = p$.

5 (a) To obtain the graph of $y = (x + p)^2 + q$, the graph of $y = x^2$ is translated through p units to the left and q units upwards.

   (b) The vertex of the resulting parabola is at $(-p, q)$.

   (c) Its line of symmetry has equation $x = -p$.

6 (a) $y = x^2 + 3$ (b) $y = (x - 2)^2$

   (c) $y = x^2 - 4$ (d) $y = (x + 5)^2$

   (e) $y = (x - 2)^2 + 3$ (f) $y = -x^2 + 4$

   (g) $y = -(x - 3)^2$ (h) $y = -(x - 2)^2 + 4$

   (i) $y = (x + 2)^2 + 5$

7 The curves meet at $(-2, 0)$ and $(2, 0)$.

8 The curves meet at $(0, 11)$ and $(6, 11)$.

9E The vertex of $y = (x + 2)^2 + 3$ is at $(-2, 3)$. So $y = ax^2$ passes through $(-2, 3)$.

   Substituting in the equation gives
   $$3 = a(-2)^2$$
   $$\Rightarrow 3 = 4a$$
   $$\Rightarrow a = \tfrac{3}{4}$$

10E The curves must be parallel, so $a = c$ and $b \neq d$.

1.1.4 Completing the square

1.1 E

If you wish to sketch the graph of a quadratic function given in the conventional form $y = x^2 + bx + c$, then it is helpful to be able to rewrite it in the completed square form $y = (x + p)^2 + q$, so that the translation from $y = x^2$ is obvious. These questions develop an appropriate strategy.

1 (b) It can be seen from the graph that $y = x^2 + 2x$ has its vertex at $(-1, -1)$, so a translation of $\begin{bmatrix} -1 \\ -1 \end{bmatrix}$ maps $y = x^2$ onto $y = x^2 + 2x$.

   Hence $y = x^2 + 2x$ is equivalent to $y = (x + 1)^2 - 1$.

2 (ii) (a) $\begin{bmatrix} -5 \\ -25 \end{bmatrix}$ $x^2 + 10x = (x + 5)^2 - 25$

   (b) $\begin{bmatrix} 3 \\ -9 \end{bmatrix}$ $x^2 - 6x = (x - 3)^2 - 9$

   (c) $\begin{bmatrix} -3.5 \\ -12.25 \end{bmatrix}$ $x^2 + 7x = (x + 3.5)^2 - 12.2$

3 (a) $x^2 + 4x = (x + 2)^2 - 4$

   (b) $x^2 + 4x = (x + 2)^2 - 4$
   $$\Rightarrow x^2 + 4x + 9 = (x + 2)^2 - 4 + 9$$
   $$\Rightarrow x^2 + 4x + 9 = (x + 2)^2 + 5$$

4 (a) $x^2 + 14x + 2 = (x + 7)^2 - 49 + 2$
   $$= (x + 7)^2 - 47$$

   (b) $x^2 - 8x + 5 = (x - 4)^2 - 11$

   (c) $x^2 - 3x + 1 = (x - \tfrac{3}{2})^2 - \tfrac{5}{4}$

5 (a) $x^2 + bx = (x + \tfrac{1}{2}b)^2 - \tfrac{1}{4}b^2$
   $$\Rightarrow p = \tfrac{1}{2}b \text{ and } q = -\tfrac{1}{4}b^2$$

   (b) $x^2 + bx + c = (x + \tfrac{1}{2}b)^2 - \tfrac{1}{4}b^2 + c$
   $$\qquad\qquad \uparrow \qquad\qquad \uparrow$$
   Halve b Subtract $\tfrac{1}{4}b^2$ from c

6 (a) $(x - 1)^2$

   (b) $(x - 1)^2 \geq 0$ for all x.
   Hence $x^2 - 2x + 1 \geq 0$.

7 (a) $(x + 2)^2 - 6$

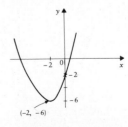

$(-2, -6)$

(b) $(x - \frac{5}{2})^2 - \frac{13}{4}$

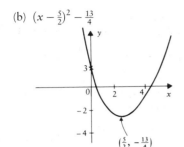

(c) $(x + 6)^2 - 41$

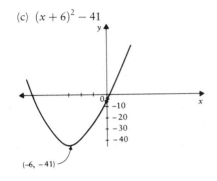

8E $2\left[(x + \frac{3}{2})^2 - \frac{27}{4}\right] = 0$

$$x = \frac{\pm\sqrt{27} - 3}{2}$$

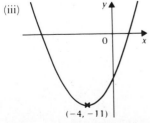

1.1 Exercise 2

1 (a) (i) $(x + 4)^2 - 11$

(ii) $x^2 + 8x + 16 - 11$
$= x^2 + 8x + 5$

(iii)

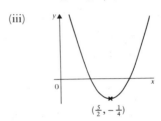

(b) (i) $(x - 2)^2 - 7$

(ii) $x^2 - 4x + 4 - 7$
$= x^2 - 4x - 3$

(iii)

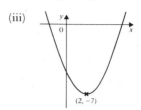

(c) (i) $(x - \frac{5}{2})^2 - \frac{1}{4}$

(ii) $x^2 - 5x + \frac{25}{4} - \frac{1}{4}$
$= x^2 - 5x + 6$

(iii)

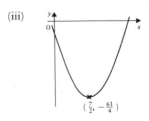

(d) (i) $(x - \frac{7}{2})^2 - \frac{61}{4}$

(ii) $x^2 - 7x + \frac{49}{4} - \frac{61}{4}$
$= x^2 - 7x - 3$

(iii)

2 (a) (i) $y = (x + 2)^2 + 3$ (ii) $y = (x - 2)^2 - 5$

(b) (i) $y = x^2 + 4x + 7$

(ii) $y = x^2 - 4x + 4 - 5$
$\Rightarrow y = x^2 - 4x - 1$

1.1.5 Zeros of quadratics

1.1 F

1 (a) The graph shows that 1 and 5 give the
points $x = -1$ and $x = -5$ where the

curve cuts the x-axis. The values are also the zeros of the function because

$$(x+1)(x+5) = 0$$

$$\Rightarrow x+1=0 \text{ or } x+5=0$$

$$\Rightarrow x=-1 \text{ or } x=-5$$

(b) When α and β are distinct real numbers, the graph will cross the x-axis at two points, irrespective of whether α and β are positive, negative or zero. If α and β are equal then the two crossing points coincide and the graph touches the x-axis. α and β give the points $x=-\alpha$ and $x=-\beta$ where the graph cuts the x-axis. The values $-\alpha$ and $-\beta$ are also the zeros of the function with that graph.

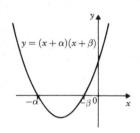

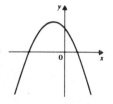

2

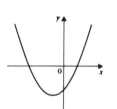

$y = -(x+\alpha)(x+\beta)$
is the reflection in the x-axis of
$y = (x+\alpha)(x+\beta)$

3 (a) $y = (x-1)(x-5)$

(b) $y = (x+3)(x-9)$

(c) $y = (x+10)(x+2)$ (d) $y = x(x-4)$

(e) $y = -(x-1)(x-5)$

(f) $y = -(x+2)(x-6)$

(g) $y = -(x-7)^2$ (h) $y = (x+2)^2$

(i) $y = -(x+5)(x-5)$

4 (a) $y = (x+2)(x-1)$

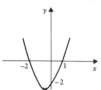

Vertex at $\left(-\frac{1}{2}, -\frac{9}{4}\right)$

(b) $y = (x-2)^2$ (c) $y = x^2 + 5x + 6$

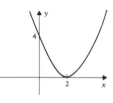

Vertex at $(2, 0)$

Vertex at $\left(-\frac{5}{2}, -\frac{1}{4}\right)$

(d) $y = -(x+1)^2$ (e) $y = x^2 - 4$
$= (x-2)(x+2)$

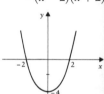

Vertex at $(-1, 0)$

Vertex at $(0, -4)$

1.1.6 Factorising quadratics

1.1 Exercise 3

1 (a) $(x+3)(x+4)$ (b) $(x-3)(x+1)$

(c) $(x-5)(x-2)$ (d) $(x+2)(x-2)$

(e) $x(x-7)$ (f) $(x-3)^2$

(g) $(x+1)(x+2)$ (h) $(x+2)^2$

(i) $(x+7)(x-7)$

2 (a)

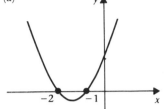

   (i) Zeros at -1 and -2

  (ii) $(x+1)(x+2)$

(b)

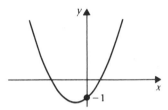

   (i) Zeros at roughly 0.6 and -1.6

  (ii) There are *no* factors of the form
     $ax+b$, a and b whole numbers.

(c)

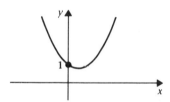

   (i) There are no zeros.

  (ii) Hence there are no factors.

3 (a) $0, \frac{2}{3}$ (b) $-10, 9$ (c) $-3, 0, 3$

  (d) $-2, -1, 0$

4 $2x^2 - 5x + 3$

  $x = 1, \quad x = \frac{3}{2}$

5 $2s, 6s$

6E $2\,m$

7E 30×40 or 20×60

8E 8 and 15

1.2 Sequences
1.2.1 Introduction – notation

1.2 A

1 (a) $u_1 = 2, \quad u_4 = 20$

  (b) $u_5 = 26, \quad u_5 = u_4 + 6$

  (c) $u_{i+1} = u_i + 6$

2 (a) $t_2 = 4 + 9 = 13, \quad t_3 = 13 + 9 = 22,$
     $t_4 = 31, \quad t_5 = 40$

  (b) $t_{20} = 4 + (19 \times 9) = 175$

1.2 B

1 (a) $u_1 = -5$
    Putting $i = 1$ gives
    $u_2 = u_1 + 2 = -5 + 2 = -3,$
    putting $i = 2$ gives
    $u_3 = u_2 + 2 = -3 + 2 = -1$ and so on.
    $u_1 = -5, \quad u_2 = -3, \quad u_3 = -1,$
    $u_4 = 1, \quad u_5 = 3$
    $u_{20} = -5 + (19 \times 2) = 33$

  (b) $u_1 = 15, \quad u_2 = 11, \quad u_3 = 7, \quad u_4 = 3,$
    $u_5 = -1$
    $u_{20} = 15 - (19 \times 4) = -61$

  (c) $u_1 = 2, \quad u_2 = 3 \times 2 = 6,$
    $u_3 = 3 \times 6 = 18, \quad u_4 = 3 \times 18 = 54,$
    $u_5 = 3 \times 54 = 162$
    $u_{20} = 3^{19} \times 2 \approx 2.3 \times 10^9$

    Note how *multiplying* by 3 gives a rapid
    increase in magnitude.

  (d) $u_1 = 3, \quad u_2 = \frac{1}{3}, \quad u_3 = 3,$
    $u_4 = \frac{1}{3}, \quad u_5 = 3, \quad u_{20} = \frac{1}{3}$

    The sequence oscillates.

2 (a) The sequence alternates in sign. The
    magnitude of each term is twice that of
    the previous term.
    With $u_1 = 3$ for example, the sequence is
    $3, -6, 12, -24, 48, -96, \ldots$

  (b) The sequence diverges rapidly unless
    $u_1 = -4.$
    If $u_1 < -4$ the sequence approaches
    negative infinity.

If $u_1 > -4$ the sequence approaches infinity.

(c) If $u_1 > 0$ the sequence approaches infinity. If $u_1 < 0$ the sequence approaches negative infinity.

(d) The sequence approaches zero.

(e) The sequence alternates between the values u_1 and u_2, for example $u_1 = 7$, $u_2 = \frac{2}{7}$, $u_3 = 7$, $u_4 = \frac{2}{7}, \ldots$

(f) The sequence increases. The difference between successive terms increases by 2 each time.

3E (a) If $u_1 = u_2 = 1$ the Fibonacci sequence
1, 1, 2, 3, 5, 8, 13, $\ldots$
is obtained. Otherwise, a similar sequence where each term is the sum of the two preceding terms is obtained.

(b) The sequence eventually converges to a value of -4 unless $u_1 = 2.5$.

4E The sequence always appears to settle into the cycle 4, 2, 1, 4, 2, 1, $\ldots$ This has never been proved and is known as Thwaite's conjecture.

1.2 Exercise 1

1 $u_1 = 4$, $u_2 = 8$, $u_3 = 16$, $u_4 = 32$, $u_5 = 64$. The sequence is diverging.

2 (a) $u_1 = 9$, $u_2 = 6$, $u_3 = 4$, $u_4 = \frac{8}{3}$; converging

(b) $u_1 = 2$, $u_2 = \frac{1}{4}$, $u_3 = 16$; diverging

(c) $u_1 = 1$, $u_2 = 5$, $u_3 = 1$, $u_4 = 5$; oscillating

3 $u_1 = 1$, $u_2 = 1\frac{1}{2}$, $u_3 = 1\frac{3}{4}$, $u_4 = 1\frac{7}{8}$, $u_5 = 1\frac{15}{16}$

The sequence is converging, approaching the limit of 2.

4 The sequence is
1, 2, 3, 5, 8, 13, 21, 34, $\ldots$
which diverges.

5 The sequence is
2, 6.75, 0.5926, 76.88, 0.0046, 1 294 319.3, $\ldots$

Odd terms approach zero, whilst the remaining terms become very large.

6 (a) $u_1 = 1$, $u_{i+1} = \frac{1}{2}u_i$

(b) $u_1 = 1$, $u_{i+1} = (-\frac{1}{2})u_i$

1.2.2 The general term

1.2 C

1 (a) $s_{50} = 300$ (b) $s_t = 6t$

(c) The inductive method requires every term in turn to be calculated, in this case a further forty-nine terms!

2 (a) Each term is 3 times the previous term, so

$$t_2 = 2 \times 3$$

$$t_3 = (2 \times 3) \times 3 = 2 \times 3^2$$

$$t_4 = (2 \times 3 \times 3) \times 3 = 2 \times 3^3$$

To obtain t_n, t_1 must be multiplied by 3 a total of $n - 1$ times. Therefore, $t_n = 2 \times 3^{n-1}$.

(b) $u_1 = (-1)^1 \frac{1}{1} = -1$, $u_2 = (-1)^2 \frac{1}{4} = \frac{1}{4}$, $u_3 = (-1)^3 \frac{1}{9} = -\frac{1}{9}$, $u_4 = (-1)^4 \frac{1}{16} = \frac{1}{16}$
and so on.

The $(-1)^i$ causes the sign to change for alternate terms.

1.2 Exercise 2

No. of triangles	1	2	3	4	5	10	20	100	i
No. of matchsticks	3	5	7	9	11	21	41	201	$2i + 1$

In this case the idea of adding on two matches each time helps you to find the first few terms of the sequence. In order to find the later terms you need to spot that the number of matches is found by doubling the number of triangles and adding 1.

2

Position in pattern	1	2	3	4	5	10	20	100	i
No. of dots									
(a)	1	4	7	10	13	28	58	298	$3i - 2$
(b)	4	8	12	16	20	40	80	400	$4i$
(c)	1	3	5	7	9	19	39	199	$2i - 1$
(d)	1	4	9	16	25	100	400	10 000	i^2
(e)	2	8	18	32	50	200	800	20 000	$2i^2$
(f)	3	8	15	24	35	120	440	10 200	$i(i + 2)$

3 (a) $i = 1$: $\quad u_1 = 3 \times 1 + 2 = 5$
$\quad i = 2$: $\quad u_2 = 3 \times 2 + 2 = 8$
$\quad u_3 = 3 \times 3 + 2 = 11$
$\quad u_4 = 3 \times 4 + 2 = 14$
$\quad u_5 = 3 \times 5 + 2 = 17$

(b) $u_1 = 5 \times 2^1 = 10$, $\quad u_2 = 5 \times 2^2 = 20$,
$\quad u_3 = 5 \times 2^3 = 40$, $\quad u_4 = 80$, $\quad u_5 = 160$

(c) $u_1 = 3 \times 1^2 = 3$, $\quad u_2 = 3 \times 2^2 = 12$,
$\quad u_3 = 27$, $\quad u_4 = 48$, $\quad u_5 = 75$

4 (a) (i) -1, $\quad 1$, $\quad -1$, $\quad 1$, $\quad -1$, $\quad \ldots$
(ii) 1, $\quad -1$, $\quad 1$, $\quad -1$, $\quad 1$, $\quad \ldots$
(iii) -1, $\quad 1$, $\quad -1$, $\quad 1$, $\quad -1$, $\quad \ldots$
(iv) -1, $\quad 2$, $\quad -4$, $\quad 8$, $\quad -16$, $\quad \ldots$

(b) (i) $u_i = 3 \times (-1)^{i+1}$ $\quad$ (ii) $u_i = 3 \times (-1)^i$

5

		Term			
	5	6	9	100	i
A	10	12	18	200	$2i$
B	14	17	26	299	$3i - 1$
C	32	64	512	2^{100}	2^i
D	96	192	1536	3×2^{100}	3×2^i
E	1	-1	1	-1	$(-1)^{i+1}$
F	-5	6	-9	100	$(-1)^i i$
G	5	-6	9	-100	$(-1)^{i+1} i$
H	10	-12	18	-200	$(-1)^{i+1} 2i$
I	$\dfrac{1}{6}$	$\dfrac{1}{7}$	$\dfrac{1}{10}$	$\dfrac{1}{101}$	$\dfrac{1}{i+1}$
J	25	-36	81	$-10\,000$	$(-1)^{i+1} i^2$

1.2.3 Arithmetic series

1.2 D

The numbers from 1 to 100 can be paired up into 50 pairs, each with a total of 101, as shown.

$$1 + 2 + 3 + \cdots + 99 + 100$$

The total is therefore $50 \times 101 = 5050$.

1.2 E

1 (a) (i) Each pair of terms adds up to 21, so the total is $10 \times 21 = 210$.

(ii) Note that, because there is an odd number of terms, not all terms pair up. However, the same result may be obtained by finding the average of the first and last terms and multiplying by the number of terms.

The average of the first and last terms is

$$\frac{(1 + 9)}{2} = 5$$

so the total is $9 \times 5 = 45$.

(iii) $\dfrac{(1 + 29)}{2} \times 29 = 435$

(b) There are many possible ways. One way is to find the average of the first and last terms and multiply by the number of terms. This works for series with either an even or an odd number of terms.

2 There are many ways of doing this. For example, subtracting 4 from each term gives 1, 2, $\ldots$, 101 with 101 terms.

3 (a) 50; 1275 $\quad$ (b) 81; 4050 $\quad$ (c) 101; 15 150

4 The same principle applies here as in question 1. You can find the average of the first and last terms, and then multiply by the number of terms.

(a) $\dfrac{16}{2} \times 8 = 64$ $\qquad$ (b) $\dfrac{104}{2} \times 33 = 1716$

(c) $\dfrac{267}{2} \times 26 = 3471$

5 (a) $1 + 2i$ (b) $2 + 4i$ (c) $17 - 5i$

6 (a) (i) 61   (ii) 495

  (b) (i) $4i + 1$ (ii) $i(2i + 3)$

7 (a) $a + 4d$ (b) $a + 49d$

  (c) $a + (n - 1)d$

  (d) $\dfrac{a + (a + 49d)}{2} \times 50 = 25(2a + 49d)$

1.2 Exercise 3

1 (a) 4060   (b) 7500

  (c) $10\,049\frac{1}{2}$ (d) 2356

2 (a) Last term $= 8 + 17 \times 2 = 42$;

  $$\text{sum} = \left(\dfrac{8 + 42}{2}\right) \times 18 = 450$$

  (b) Number of terms $= \dfrac{303 - 6}{9} + 1 = 34$;

  $$\text{sum} = \left(\dfrac{6 + 303}{2}\right) \times 34 = 5253$$

  (c) Common difference $= \dfrac{195 - 3}{24} = 8$;

  $$\text{sum} = \left(\dfrac{3 + 195}{2}\right) \times 25 = 2475$$

3 The volume under the bottom step is

  $$V = 50 \times \tfrac{1}{4} \times \tfrac{3}{4} \, \text{m}^3$$

  Successive steps up have volumes $2V, 3V, \ldots, 15V$.

  The total volume is therefore

  $$15 \times \dfrac{V + 15V}{2} = 120V = 1125 \, \text{m}^3$$

4 (a) $2n - 1$

  (b) 7   (This uses 49 bricks.)

  (c) $S = \tfrac{1}{2}n(2 + (n - 1)2)$

  $ = \tfrac{1}{2}n(2n)$

  $ = n^2$

5E (a) $4n - 2$

  (b) $S = \tfrac{1}{2}n(4 + (n - 1)4) = 2n^2$

  This is twice as many as in question 4.

6E (a) $\pounds(5 + 10 + \cdots + 90) = \pounds 855$

  (b) $\quad \tfrac{5}{2}n(n + 1) > 500$

  $\Rightarrow n(n + 1) > 200$

  $\Rightarrow n = 14$

7E $8.2 + 8.3 + \cdots = 22\,000$

  $\tfrac{1}{2}n(16.4 + (n - 1) \times 0.1) = 22\,000$

  $n(n + 163) = 440\,000$

  $n \approx 587$

1.2.4 Finance – APR

1.2 F

1 £1200 is repaid, which includes £400 interest. This is a rate of 50%.

2 The outstanding debt after 12 months is £0 (approximately!) and so the debt is fully repaid.

3 $\pounds 100 \times 1.016\,5^{12} = \pounds 121.699$

  The original £100 must be repaid together with interest of approximately 21.7%.

4 (a) 12.7%   (b) 26.8%   (c) 79.6%

5 Possibly the simplest algorithm is:

  divide rate by 100,
  add 1,
  raise to the power 12,
  subtract 1,
  multiply by 100.

6 The reversed algorithm is:

  divide APR by 100,
  add 1,
  find the 12th root,
  subtract 1,
  multiply by 100.

  The rate is 5.95%.

8 Monthly interest rate $= 7.93\%$ (7.930 83%);

  APR $= 149.9\%$

9 (a) $\frac{30}{100} \times 7292.86$

(b) $2187.86 + 36 \times 127.52 + 1786.75$

(c) 12 months and 52 weeks are assumed to be equivalent with $29.43 = \frac{12}{52} \times 127.52$

(d) $0.978\,874\,5\%$ (approximately!)

For normally structured financial facilities, companies have printed charts for APR. More unusually structured facilities like that for the car are often calculated using special financial calculators, with functions embodying the approved methods of calculating APR. The regulations and financial formulas relating to APR calculation are governed by the Consumer Credit Act 1974 and form a very detailed body of information with prescribed mathematical techniques.

1.2.5 Sigma notation

1.2 **G**

1 $£1000 \times 1.08^{10} = £2158.92$

2 $£1000 \times 1.08^{9} = £1999.00$

3 Continuing this pattern, the third investment will be worth $£1000 \times 1.08^{8}$ since it earns interest for eight years.

The final investment earns interest for one year and will be worth $£1000 \times 1.08^{1}$.

The total investment is therefore

$£(1000 \times 1.08^{1} + 1000 \times 1.08^{2} + \cdots + 1000 \times 1.08^{10})$

$= £1000(1.08 + 1.08^{2} + 1.08^{3} + \cdots + 1.08^{10})$

1.2 **Exercise 4**

1 (a) $1 + \frac{1}{2} + \frac{1}{3} + \frac{1}{4} + \frac{1}{5}$

(b) $9 + 16 + 25 + 36 + 49$

(c) $\frac{1}{2} + \frac{1}{6} + \frac{1}{12} + \frac{1}{20} + \frac{1}{30}$

(d) $11 - 13 + 15 - 17 + 19$

(e) $1 + 8 + 27 + 64 + 125 + 216$

(f) $1 + 8 + 27 + 64 + 125 + 216$

Note that (e) and (f) are different representations of the same sum.

2 (a) $\sum_{i=1}^{50} \sqrt{i}$ (b) $\sum_{i=1}^{50} (2i)^2$

(c) $\sum_{i=1}^{49} \frac{1}{2i+1}$ (d) $\sum_{i=1}^{19} (-1)^{i+1} i^3$

(e) $\sum_{i=1}^{99} \frac{i}{i+1}$

3 (a) $35 + 33 + \cdots + (-3)$

$$= 20 \times \frac{35 - 3}{2} \quad \text{(20 terms)}$$

$$= 320$$

(b) 400

4 (a) $\sum_{1}^{25} (15 + 5i)$ (b) $\sum_{1}^{10} 10\,000 \times \left(\frac{1}{10}\right)^i$

(c) $\sum_{0}^{14} 1.1^i$ (d) $\sum_{1}^{8} \frac{1}{i + (i+1)}$

(e) $\sum_{1}^{20} i \times 3^i$

5 (a) $1 \times 2 + 4 \times 3 + 9 \times 4 + 16 \times 5 + 25 \times 6 + 36 \times 7$

(b) $(-1)^0 \times 1 + (-1)^1 \times 2 + (-1)^2 \times 3 + (-1)^3 \times 4 + (-1)^4 \times 5$
(i.e. $1 - 2 + 3 - 4 + 5$)

(c) $1 + x + x^2 + x^3 + x^4 + x^5$

(d) $\frac{0}{1} + \frac{1}{2} + \frac{2}{3} + \frac{3}{4} + \frac{4}{5}$

(e) $f(x_1) + f(x_2) + f(x_3) + \cdots + f(x_6)$

1.2.6 Geometric series

1.2 **Exercise 5**

1 (a) $\dfrac{2(3^8 - 1)}{2} = 6560$ (b) $122\,070\,312$

(c) 1 743 392 200   (d) 15.984 375

(e) 5.328 125

2 (a) $1 + 3 + 9 + 27 + 81 = 121$

(b) $1 + 8 + 8^2 + \cdots + 8^9 = 153\,391\,689$
$\approx 1.53 \times 10^8$, which is a more practical expression.

(c) $2 + 2^2 + \cdots + 2^7 = 2\left(\dfrac{2^7 - 1}{2 - 1}\right) = 254$

(d) $\left(\dfrac{1}{2}\right)^3\left[1 + \dfrac{1}{2} + \cdots + \left(\dfrac{1}{2}\right)^5\right] = \dfrac{63}{256}$

(e) $\dfrac{1 - (-\frac{3}{4})^{20}}{1 - (-\frac{3}{4})} = 0.570$ (to 3 s.f.)

3 (a) He requested $1 + 2 + 4 + 8 + \cdots + 2^{63}$
$= \dfrac{2^{64} - 1}{2 - 1} \approx 1.84 \times 10^{19}$ grains!

(b) 3.7×10^{17} g or 3.7×10^{11} tonnes!

4 (a) The value increases by a factor of 1.01 per annum. After 2090 years it would be worth $1 \times 1.01^{2090} = 1\,075\,650\,555$p or approximately £10.8 million.

(b) Replacing 1.01 by 1.05 in (a) gives $£1.9 \times 10^{42}$.

5 $\dfrac{200 \times 1.05(1.05^{50} - 1)}{1.05 - 1} = £43\,963$
(to the nearest pound)

6 Taking the school leaver's salary as £8000, the total earnings over a 45-year period would be

$£8000(1 + 1.05 + 1.05^2 + \cdots + 1.05^{44})$

$= £8000\dfrac{(1.05^{45} - 1)}{1.05 - 1} = £1.28$ million

7 (a) $\dfrac{1000 \times 1.075(1.075^n - 1)}{1.075 - 1}$

(b) The conditions lead to the equation
$\dfrac{1000 \times 1.075(1.075^n - 1)}{1.075 - 1} = 2000n$
The conditions are met after 17 years.

1.2.7 Infinity

1.2 Exercise 6

1 (a) $\dfrac{\frac{9}{10}}{1 - \frac{1}{10}} = 1$ (b) $\dfrac{4}{1 + \frac{3}{4}} = \dfrac{16}{7}$

(c) The sum diverges   (d) $\dfrac{5}{1 - \frac{1}{2}} = 10$

2 (a) $\frac{3}{2}$ (b) $\frac{4}{3}$ (c) 1

3 (a) The sum is $\frac{1}{3}$

(b) If you consider the diagram to be made up from a sequence of nested L shapes,

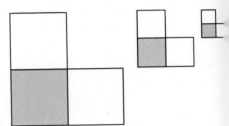

it can be seen that each L shape is made up of one shaded and two unshaded squares, i.e. $\frac{1}{3}$ of the diagram is shaded.

4 (a) 3   (b) 4   (c) $\frac{16}{3}$ (d) $3 \times \left(\frac{4}{3}\right)^n$

$\frac{4}{3} > 1$, therefore $\left(\frac{4}{3}\right)^n \to \infty$ as $n \to \infty$. This means $P_n \to \infty$ as $n \to \infty$.

The limiting curve is of infinite length, yet encloses a finite area!

5 The sum to n terms is

$\dfrac{2(1 - \left(\frac{2}{5}\right)^n)}{1 - \frac{2}{5}} = \dfrac{10}{3}\left(1 - \left(\frac{2}{5}\right)^n\right)$

The sum to infinity is $\frac{10}{3}$.

The difference, $\frac{10}{3}\left(\frac{2}{5}\right)^n$, is less than 0.01 when $n = 7$.

1.3 Functions and graphs

1.3.1 Function notation

1.3 Exercise 1

1 (a) 3 (b) 4 (c) 5 (d) 4

2 (a) $\dfrac{5}{9}$ (b) $\dfrac{5}{3}$ (c) 5 (d) 15 (e) $\dfrac{5}{3^x}$

3 (a) (i) 6 (ii) 0 (iii) 2 (iv) 0
(v) $n^2 + 3n + 2$

(b) (i) 6 (ii) 0 (iii) 2 (iv) 0
(v) $n^2 + 3n + 2$

(c) No, except that a different symbol is used for the variable.

4 (a) (i) $(x-2)^2$ (ii) $a^2 + 4a + 5$

(b) $x = 0$ (c) $x = 3$

5 (a) $\dfrac{x^2 + 2x + 1}{x + 1} = \dfrac{(x+1)^2}{x+1} = x + 1$

(b) (i) $4x^2 + 4x + 1$ (ii) x^2

1.3.2 Using function notation

1.3 A

1 (b) $f(x-2) + 5 = (x-2)^2 + 5$
$$= x^2 - 4x + 4 + 5$$
$$= x^2 - 4x + 9$$

(c)

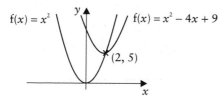

$f(x) = x^2$ $f(x) = x^2 - 4x + 9$

$(2, 5)$

The graph of $f(x-2) + 5$ is obtained from the graph of $f(x)$ by a translation of $\begin{bmatrix} 2 \\ 5 \end{bmatrix}$.

2 (a) (ii) $g(x-2) + 5 = (x-2)^3 + 5$
$$= x^3 - 6x^2 + 12x - 3$$

(b) (ii) $g(x-2) + 5 = 2^{x-2} + 5$

(c) (ii) $g(x-2) + 5 = \sqrt{(x-2)} + 5$

(iii) In each case, a translation of $\begin{bmatrix} 2 \\ 5 \end{bmatrix}$ will superimpose $g(x)$ onto $g(x-2) + 5$.

3

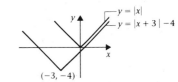

$y = |x|$
$y = |x + 3| - 4$
$(-3, -4)$

4 The graph of $f(x)$ is translated onto the graph of $f(x + a) + b$ by a translation of $\begin{bmatrix} -a \\ b \end{bmatrix}$, for any function f.

5E The effect of a is to translate the graph through $-a$ parallel to the x-axis.

The effect of b is to translate the graph through b parallel to the y-axis.

The graph of $\sin(x + a) + b$ will be identical to the graph of $\sin x$ if $b = 0$ and a is any multiple of 2π.

6E The effect of a is a stretch, parallel to the y-axis.

The effect of b is a stretch, parallel to the x-axis.

The effect of c is a translation, parallel to the x-axis.

The effect of d is a translation, parallel to the y-axis.

1.3.3 Defining functions

1.3 Exercise 2

1 (a) (i) $\dfrac{1}{2}$ (ii) 1 (iii) $\dfrac{1}{a+2}$ (iv) $\dfrac{1}{a}$
(v) $f(-2)$ is undefined.

(b) All values of x, except $x = -2$

(c)

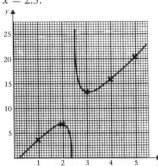

2 (a) (i) $\sqrt{2}$ (ii) 3 (iii) $\sqrt[4]{2}$ (iv) $\sqrt{\pi}$ (v) π

(b) $x \geq 0$

(c)

3 (a) All values of x, except $x = -5$

(b) $x > 3$; note that $x \neq 3$ because division by zero is undefined.

(c) All values of x

(d) All values of x, except $x = -2$

4 (a) (i) 5 (ii) 7 (iii) $\sqrt{2}$ (iv) π (v) 0

(b) $x \in \mathbb{R}$

(c) (i)   (ii)

(iii)

1.3.4 To plot or to sketch?

1.3 B

1 There is a temptation here just to join up the crosses with a smooth curve; this would produce an *incorrect* graph.

2 $y = -0.2$, $y = -40.04$, $y = -490.004$

These values show that y decreases very rapidly as x approaches 2.5 from below.

3 When $x = 2.5$, $2x - 5 = 0$ and $\dfrac{1}{2x - 5}$ is not defined.

At this point there is a **discontinuity** in the graph.

4 The graph plotter shows the discontinuity at $x = 2.5$.

Important features of the graph can be missed if you simply plot points. It is therefore necessary to be able to recognise these features of a graph from its equation.

1.3 C

1 (b) All the graphs pass through $(0, 0)$ and $(1, 1)$.

(c) $y = x^5$ increases most rapidly and $y = x^2$ least rapidly. The graphs for the higher powers of x become steeper more rapidly than those for the lower powers of x as x increases above 1 or decreases below -1.

(d) The graphs of the even powers of x have line symmetry in the y-axis, and the graphs of odd powers have rotational symmetry of order 2 about the origin.

2 (b) When x is a large positive or negative number the graphs of $y = x^2$ and $y = x^2 + 4x$ are **similar**, in that, although they are not very close to each other, they increase at a similar rate. The x^2 term is said to be **dominant**.

(c) When x is a small positive or negative number the graphs of $y = 4x$ and $y = x^2 + 4x$ are very close together; the x^2 term has very little effect and the $4x$ term is said to be **dominant**.

3 The graph of $y = x^3 - 4x^2$ is similar to that of $y = -4x^2$ for small values of x and is similar to that of $y = x^3$ for large values of x.

4 The graph of $y = x^3 + x^2 - 2x + 1$ is similar to that of $y = -2x + 1$ for small values of x and is similar to that of $y = x^3$ for large values of x.

5 The graph crosses the x-axis at $x = 0, -1$ and 3. These values are related to the factors of $3x + 2x^2 - x^3$, i.e. x, $(x + 1)$ and $(3 - x)$. They are the solutions of $x = 0$, $x + 1 = 0$ and $3 - x = 0$.

In the expansion of $x(x + 1)(3 - x)$ the term of highest degree is $-x^3$ and the term of lowest degree is $3x$. So the graph of $y = x(x + 1)(3 - x)$ is similar to the graph of $y = -x^3$ for large positive and negative values of x, and similar to the graph of $y = 3x$ for small positive and negative values of x near the origin.

6 (a) $-x^3$ (b) x^2

(c) $2x^2 - x^3$ (You might have thought of trying $x^2 - x^3$ first.)

1.3 **D**

1 The relevant terms from each bracket are multiplied.
$$f(0) = (-2)^2 \times 7 = 28 \quad \text{and}$$
$$x^2 \times (2x) = 2x^3$$

2 From the factorised form for $f(x)$, the graph can only cross (or touch) the x-axis at $-3\frac{1}{2}$ and 2.

1.3 **Exercise 3**

1 The zeros are at $-3, 2, \frac{7}{3}$. The dominant parts of the graph are indicated by the line segments. The dashes indicate the completed sketch.

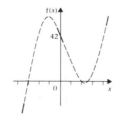

2 The zeros are at $-\frac{2}{5}, 1, 4$ and the graph is as illustrated here.

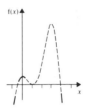

3 $x^3(x + 4)(x - 7) = x^5 - 3x^4 - 28x^3$
x^5 dominates for large x.
$-28x^3$ dominates for very small x.

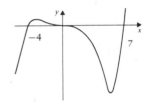

4 (a) The stone is level with the point of release when h is zero. This occurs when $t = 0$ or 2.4, and the relevant answer is 2.4 seconds.

(b) When $t = 4$ then $h = -32$. The point of release is 32 m above sea level and the height of the cliff will be a little less than this.

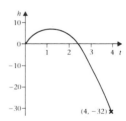

1.3.5 Rational functions

1.3 Exercise 4

1 (a)

(b)

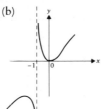

(c)

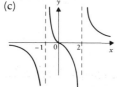

(d)

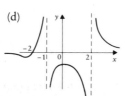

(e)

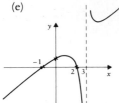

(f)

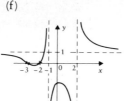

(g)

(h)

(i)

2 $v, u > 0$

$v, u > 2.5 \, \text{km h}^{-1}$

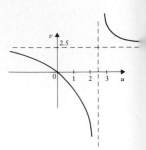

3 $R = \dfrac{R_1 R_2}{(R_1 + R_2)}$

For small R_1, $R \approx R_1$; for large R_1, $R \approx R_2$.

4 $h = \dfrac{A - 2\pi r^2}{2\pi r}$

$0 < r < \sqrt{\left(\dfrac{A}{2\pi}\right)}$

5 (a) $y = \dfrac{1}{(x-2)^2}$ (b) $y = \dfrac{-1}{(x-3)(x+1)}$

1.4 Expressions and equations
1.4.1 The language of algebra

1.4 Exercise 1

1 (a) $x = -3$ (b) $x = \pm 5$ (c) $x = -6, 1$

(d) $x = \pm 2$ (e) $x = 0$ (f) $x = 0, 4$

(g) $5, 4$ (h) $-1, \frac{1}{2}$ (i) $-2, 1$

2 (a) $1 + 2 + \cdots + n = 210$

$$\tfrac{1}{2}n(n+1) = 210$$

$$n^2 + n - 420 = 0$$

(b) $(n - 20)(n + 21) = 0$

$n = 20$ (positive root)

3 (a) The sum of three consecutive numbers is always 3 times the middle number.

(b) $n + (n + 1) + (n + 2) = 3n + 3 = 3(n + 1)$, giving the sum as 3 times the middle number $(n + 1)$ as expected.

4 (a) For example,
$$9^2 - 7^2 = 81 - 49 = 32 = 4 \times 8$$

(b) Any two consecutive odd numbers can be written algebraically as $2n - 1$, $2n + 1$. The difference between their squares is given by

$$(2n + 1)^2 - (2n - 1)^2$$

$$= 4n^2 + 4n + 1 - (4n^2 - 4n + 1)$$

$$= 4n^2 + 4n + 1 - 4n^2 + 4n - 1$$

$$= 8n$$

which is a multiple of 8.

5 The problem can be represented by the diagram.

By Pythagoras,

$$(18 - h)^2 = h^2 + 6^2$$

$$324 - 36h + h^2 = h^2 + 36$$

$$36h = 288$$

$$h = 8$$

The bamboo is divided into pieces of lengths 8 and 10 cubits.

6 Treating the area as one large square, it is $(a + b)^2$.

Treating the area as one small square (area c^2) and four triangles (each of area $\frac{1}{2}ab$), it is $c^2 + 4 \times \frac{1}{2}ab = c^2 + 2ab$.

Equating these two expressions for the area gives

$$(a + b)^2 = c^2 + 2ab$$

$$\Rightarrow \quad a^2 + b^2 + 2ab = c^2 + 2ab$$

$$\Rightarrow \quad a^2 + b^2 = c^2$$

Since a, b and c are the three sides of each of the right-angled triangles in the diagram, this proves Pythagoras' theorem.

1.4.2 Quadratic equations

1.4 A

1 $x^2 + 6x + 4 = 0 \Rightarrow (x + 3)^2 - 5 = 0$

$$\Rightarrow x + 3 = -\sqrt{5} \quad \text{or} \quad \sqrt{5}$$

$$\Rightarrow x \approx -5.24 \quad \text{or} \quad -0.76$$

2 (a) $x^2 + bx + \dfrac{b^2}{4} = \left(x + \dfrac{b}{2}\right)^2$

$$\Rightarrow x^2 + bx = \left(x + \dfrac{b}{2}\right)^2 - \dfrac{b^2}{4}$$

(b) $-c = -\dfrac{4c}{4}$

(c) The squares of both $\pm \dfrac{\sqrt{(b^2 - 4c)}}{2}$ are equal to $\dfrac{b^2 - 4c}{4}$.

3 (a) -5.24, -0.76 (b) 0.76, 5.24
   (c) -4.19, 1.19

1.4 Exercise 2

1 (i) $\dfrac{-5 \pm \sqrt{13}}{2} = -4.30$ or -0.70

(ii) $\dfrac{-6 \pm \sqrt{12}}{6} = -1.58$ or -0.42

(iii) $\dfrac{-4 \pm \sqrt{28}}{6} = -1.55$ or 0.22

(iv) $\dfrac{8 \pm \sqrt{84}}{10} = -0.12$ or 1.72

(v) $x = -3.24$ or 1.24

(vi) -0.84 or 0.24

2 (a) $(1.24, 7.73)$ or $(-0.64, 2.07)$

(b) $(5.56, -25.37)$ or $(1.44, -0.63)$

(c) $(1.19, 3.37)$ or $(-1.69, -2.37)$

3 (a) 0, 8 (b) -1, 4 (c) -1.62, 0.62

(d) $x = \pm 5$ (e) no solutions   (f) 5

5 (a) $x = 0, y = 0$; $x = 4, y = 4$

(b) $0, 1$; $2, 3$

(c) $16, 4$; $-1, -64$

6 The numbers are n and $n + 1$. Therefore $n(n + 1) = 10$, so

$$n = \frac{-1 \pm \sqrt{41}}{2}, \quad n + 1 = \frac{1 \pm \sqrt{41}}{2}$$

7 (a) (i) no solutions (ii) $x = 2$
(iii) 0.76, 5.24

(b) From left to right, the graphs are for (i), (iii), (ii).

(c) If $b^2 - 4ac < 0$, the equation has no solutions.

If $b^2 - 4ac = 0$, the equation has a single (repeated) solution.

If $b^2 - 4ac > 0$, the equation has two solutions.

1.4.3 Inequalities

1.4 Exercise 3

1 (a) $x < -2$ (b) $-5 < 5x \Rightarrow -1 < x$

(c) $2x - 6 < 8 \Rightarrow x < 7$

(d) $3x + 15 < 2x + 3 \Rightarrow x < -12$

(e) $x > -2$

2 The square of any number except 0 is positive. Therefore x may take any value except 2.

3 (a) $-3 \leq x \leq 1$ (b) $x < -4$ or $x > 2$

(c) $-2 < x < 2$

4 (a) $x < -5$ or $x > 2$

(b) $x \leq 2$ or $x \geq 3$

(c) $-2 \leq x \leq 2$ or $x \geq 5$

(d) $x \geq -2$

5 (a) $0 < x < 3$ (b) $0 \leq x \leq 1$

(c) $-2 < x < 5$

(d) $x < \dfrac{-1 - \sqrt{5}}{2}$ or $x > \dfrac{-1 + \sqrt{5}}{2}$

6 $\dfrac{n^2 + n}{2} > 1000 \Rightarrow n^2 + n - 2000 > 0$; $n = 45$

7E (a) $0 < x < 1$ (b) $x > 0$ or $x < -\frac{1}{3}$

(c) $-1 < x < 0$

(d) $-2 < x < -1$ or $x > 0$

(e) $x < -1$ or $x > 1$

1.4.4 Inventing new numbers: $\sqrt{-1}$

1.4 Exercise 4

1 (a) -9 (b) -49 (c) -16 (d) -144

(e) $2j$ (f) $-5 - 12j$

2 (a) $3j$ (b) $4j$ (c) $j\sqrt{12} = 2j\sqrt{3}$

(d) $2j\sqrt{5}$

3 (a) $14 + j$ (b) $-4 - 6j$ (c) 10

(d) $13 - 4j$ (e) $-9 - 20j$

4 (a) $3 + j$, $3 - j$ (b) $-1 \pm j\sqrt{8}$

(c) $-2 \pm 4j$ (d) $\frac{1}{2} \pm \frac{1}{2}j$

5 (a) $3 \pm \sqrt{3}$; 2   (b) no real roots

(c) $-3, -3$; 2 real roots (repeated roots)

6E (a) $(x - 3j)(x + 3j)$

(b) $(x - (-1 + 2j))(x - (-1 - 2j))$
$= (x + 1 - 2j)(x + 1 + 2j)$

(c) $(x - (3 + j\sqrt{2}))(x - (3 - j\sqrt{2}))$
$= (x - 3 - j\sqrt{2})(x - 3 + j\sqrt{2})$

7E For example,

$$(x^2 + 1)(x^2 + 1)$$
$$= x^4 + 2x^2 + 1$$

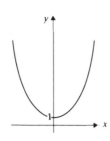

1.4.5 Polynomials

1.4 B

1 (a)   (i) −24   (ii) −30   (iii) −24
     (iv) 0   (v) 0   (vi) 6
     (vii) 0   (viii) −24

    (b) $x + 1$, $x + 3$, $x - 4$

    (c) $(x + 1)(x + 3)(x - 4)$

$$= (x^2 + 4x + 3)(x - 4)$$

$$= x^3 - 13x - 12$$

2 (a) $a = -2$. The value is chosen so that
       $x + 2 = 0$.

    (b) $P(-2) = 0$, therefore $x + 2$ is a factor of
       $P(x)$.

3 (a) $P(2) = (2 - 2)(2^2 - 2 - 2) = 0$

    (b) $P(a) = (a - a)Q(a) = 0 \times Q(a) = 0$

4 $(x - 3)(x - 1)(x + 1)$ since $P(3) = 0$,
    $P(1) = 0$, $P(-1) = 0$

1.4 Exercise 5

1 (a)
$$\require{enclose}\begin{array}{r} x^2 + x +7 \\ x+1 \enclose{longdiv}{x^3 + 2x^2 + 8x - 5} \end{array}$$

$$- \quad \underline{x^3 + x^2}$$
$$x^2 + 8x$$
$$- \quad \underline{x^2 + x}$$
$$7x - 5$$
$$- \quad \underline{7x + 7}$$
$$-12$$

quotient: $x^2 + x + 7$
remainder: −12

   (b)   quotient: $x^2 - 4x + 11$
       remainder: −27

   (c)
$$\begin{array}{r} 2x^2 + 2x - 3 \\ x-1 \enclose{longdiv}{2x^3 + 0x^2 - 5x + 3} \end{array}$$

$$- \quad \underline{2x^3 - 2x^2}$$
$$2x^2 - 5x$$
$$- \quad \underline{2x^2 - 2x}$$
$$-3x + 3$$
$$- \quad \underline{-3x + 3}$$
$$0$$

quotient: $2x^2 + 2x - 3$
remainder: 0   (so $x - 1$ is a factor)

   (d)   quotient: $2x^2 - \frac{1}{2}x + \frac{1}{4}$
       remainder: $-\frac{5}{4}$

   (e)
$$\begin{array}{r} x^2 + 2x - 3 \\ x^2-1 \enclose{longdiv}{x^4 + 2x^3 - 4x^2 - 2x + 1} \end{array}$$

$$- \quad \underline{x^4 + 0x^3 - x^2}$$
$$2x^3 - 3x^2 - 2x$$
$$- \quad \underline{2x^3 + 0x^2 - 2x}$$
$$-3x^2 + 0x + 1$$
$$- \quad \underline{-3x^2 + 0x + 3}$$
$$-2$$

quotient: $x^2 + 2x - 3$
remainder: −2

2 (a) $P(-3) = 0$ (b) $Q(x) = x^2 - 5x + 4$

3 (a) e.g. $P(-1) = 0 \Rightarrow x + 1$ is a factor

(b) $(x + 1)(x - 2)(x - 4)$ (c) $-1, 2, 4$

(d)

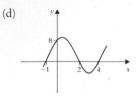

4 $1, -3$ (repeated root)

5 $(x + 2)(x^2 + 2x - 2) = 0$

$\Rightarrow x = -2, 0.73, -2.73$

6 (a) $(x + 2)(x^2 - 2x + 2) = 0$

$\Rightarrow x = -2$

(b)

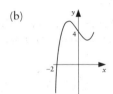

The quadratic equation $x^2 - 2x + 2 = 0$ has no real roots, hence the cubic equation has only one solution.

7 (a) Zeros are $-2, -1, 1$ and 3.

$P(x) = (x - 3)(x - 1)(x + 1)(x + 2)$

(b)

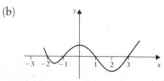

(c) $x < -2$ or $-1 < x < 1$ or $x > 3$

8 (a) (i) $x^3 - 8 = (x - 2)(x^2 + 2x + 4)$

(ii) $x^4 - 16 = (x^2 + 4)(x - 2)(x + 2)$

(b) (i)   (ii)

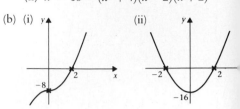

Each linear factor gives rise to a zero. Quadratic factors which cannot be factorised contribute no further zeros. Hence there will always be at least one real root. (Note that if we consider complex numbers then there will always be three roots – some of which may be repeated roots, of course.)

1.5 Numerical methods
1.5.1 The golden ratio

1.5 A

2 $1.61 < x < 1.62$

1.5.2 Locating roots

1.5 B

1 For $x^2 = x + 1$, draw the graphs $y = x^2$ and $y = x + 1$. The solutions are at the points of intersection of the two graphs.

For $x^2 - x - 1 = 0$, draw the graph of $y = x^2 - x - 1$. The solutions are the points where the graph cuts the x-axis.

2 *Either*

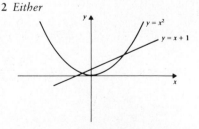

or

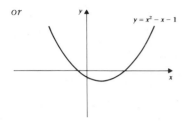

$y = x^2 - x - 1$

One root lies between -1 and 0. The second root lies between 1 and 2.

3 The roots are -0.618 and 1.618.

4 Without a graph plotter, $x^2 = x + 1$ gives two simple graphs to sketch, but care must be taken to ensure that *all* solutions are obtained. Note that approximate roots of *any* quadratic equation can be found by sketching $y = x^2$ and a straight line.

With $x^2 - x - 1 = 0$ it is simple to check that no solutions have been missed, but it is not so easy to sketch the graph without a graph plotter.

1.5 Exercise 1

1 (a) The interval $[3, 4]$

(b) $x = 1$ is one root; the other two lie in $[-1, 0]$ and $[-4, -3]$.

(c) $[1, 2]$ (d) $[-3, -2]$, $[2, 3]$

2 (a) 3.14 (b) -3.41, -0.59, 1.00

(c) 1.72 (d) -2.32, 2.32

1.5.3 Iterative formulas

1.5 Exercise 2

1 (a) $2x^2 = 5x - 1$

$$x^2 = \frac{5x - 1}{2}$$

$$x = \sqrt{\left(\frac{5x - 1}{2}\right)}$$

(b) $5x = 2x^2 + 1$

$$x = \frac{1 + 2x^2}{5}$$

(c) $2x^2 = 5x - 1$

$$2x = 5 - \frac{1}{x}$$

$$x = \frac{1}{2}\left(5 - \frac{1}{x}\right)$$

(d) $5x - 2x^2 = 1$

$$x(5 - 2x) = 1$$

$$x = \frac{1}{5 - 2x}$$

(e) Not possible

(f) $2x^2 - 4x - x + 1 = 0$

$$2x^2 - 4x + 1 = x$$

(g) Not possible   (h) Not possible

(i) $2x^2 = 5x - 1$

$$x^2 = 5x - 1 - x^2$$

$$x = \sqrt{(5x - 1 - x^2)}$$

(j) As is the case for several of the other formulas, it is easier to demonstrate correctness in reverse.

$$x - 2 = \sqrt{\left(\frac{7 - 3x}{2}\right)}$$

$$(x - 2)^2 = \frac{7 - 3x}{2}$$

$$x^2 - 4x + 4 = \frac{7 - 3x}{2}$$

$$2x^2 - 8x + 8 = 7 - 3x$$

$$2x^2 - 5x + 1 = 0$$

2 (a)   (i) $x^3 = 10 \Rightarrow x^2 = \frac{10}{x}$

$$\Rightarrow x = \sqrt{\left(\frac{10}{x}\right)}$$

(ii) $x_1 = 2$, $x_2 = 2.236\,067\,977$, $x = 2.154\,43$ to 5 decimal places

(b)   (i) $x^3 = 10 \Rightarrow x^4 = 10x$

$$\Rightarrow x^2 = \sqrt{(10x)}$$

$$\Rightarrow x = \sqrt{(\sqrt{(10x)})}$$

(ii) $x_1 = 2$, $x_2 = 2.114\,742\,527$, $x = 2.154\,43$ to 5 decimal places

In part (b) the convergence to the solution is much faster.

3 Using the iterative formula $x_{i+1} = \frac{1}{3}(2^{x_i})$

$x_1 = 3$

$x_2 = 2.\dot{6}$

$x = 0.4578$ to 4 decimal places

4 (a) $[3, 4]$

(b) $x^2 - 1 = 6\sqrt{x}$

$\Rightarrow x^2 = 6\sqrt{x} + 1$

$\Rightarrow x = \sqrt{(6\sqrt{x} + 1)}$

(c) With $x_1 = 3$, $x_2 = 3.375\,25$ and $x = 3.495\,358$ to 6 decimal places.

5 (b) $x^3 + 2x - 1 = 0$

$\Rightarrow 2x = 1 - x^3$

$\Rightarrow x = \frac{1}{2}(1 - x^3)$

(c) (i) $0.453\,40$ (ii) $0.453\,40$

(d) $x_1 = 2$ gives $x_2 = -3.5$, $x_3 = 21.9$, $x_4 = -5278$

The sequence diverges and $x_1 = 2$ is clearly an unsuitable starting value.

6 (b) (i) $x_1 = 0$ would give $\sqrt{\left(\dfrac{-1}{2}\right)}$, which cannot be found.

(ii) $x_1 = 1$ gives $2.280\,776$ after 27 iterations.

$x_1 = 2$ gives $2.280\,776$ after 24 iterations.

$x_1 = 10$ gives $2.280\,776$ after 30 iterations.

(c) $x_1 = 1$ gives $2.280\,776$ after 8 iterations.

$x_1 = 2$ gives $2.280\,776$ after 7 iterations.

$x_1 = 10$ gives $2.280\,776$ after 10 iterations.

(d) $x_1 = 1$ gives $0.219\,224$ after 11 iterations.

$x_1 = 2$ gives $0.219\,224$ after 14 iterations.

$x_1 = 3$ diverges.

(e) The iterations in (b) and (c) converge to the root in the interval $[2, 3]$ but not to the root in $[0, 1]$, even with a starting value of 1.

The convergence of (b) is very slow.

The iteration in (d) will converge to the root in $[0, 1]$ but not to the one in $[2, 3]$.

1.5.4E Convergence

1.5 C

1 (a) $\sqrt[3]{8} = 2$ so $\sqrt[3]{10} \approx 2.1$

(b) $x^3 = 10 \Rightarrow xx^2 = 10$, giving $x = \dfrac{10}{x^2}$

If $x_1 = 2.1$, $x_2 = 2.267\,57$,
$x_3 = 1.944\,81$, $x_4 = 2.6439$,
$x_5 = 1.430\,57$, $x_6 = 4.886\,33$,
$x_7 = 0.418\,83$, $x_8 = 57.0073$,
$x_9 = 0.003\,08$, $x_{10} = 1\,056\,139$.

Odd terms form a subsequence tending to zero, but even terms increase without limit. Other starting values will give a similar pattern. The sequence does not converge.

2 (b) (x_1, x_2) is the point on the graph of $y = \dfrac{10}{x^2}$ located by moving vertically from (x_1, x_1).

(x_2, x_2) is the point on the line $y = x$ located by moving horizontally from (x_1, x_2).

This method can be continued to generate further approximations. It can be described geometrically.

> Move vertically from the line to the curve, then move horizontally from the curve to the line. Repeat indefinitely.

3 The diagram illustrates that the sequence diverges *away* from the root.

4 (a)

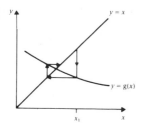

(b) The sequence converges.

5 (a)   **(b)**

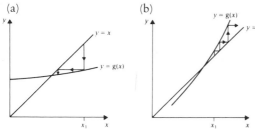

(a) converges to the root, whichever side of the root x_1 is on;

(b) diverges from the root, whichever side of the root x_1 is on.

6 A cobweb diagram is obtained if $g(x)$ is decreasing and a staircase diagram is obtained if $g(x)$ is increasing.

7 A rearrangement will converge to a root α if $g'(\alpha)$ lies between -1 and $+1$. In practice, since α is unknown, it is necessary to ensure that $g'(\alpha)$ lies between -1 and $+1$ on an interval which contains the root.

8 (a) $x^3 = 10 \Rightarrow x = \dfrac{10}{x^2}$

$$\Rightarrow 3x = 2x + \frac{10}{x^2}$$

$$\Rightarrow x = \frac{1}{3}\left(2x + \frac{10}{x^2}\right)$$

(b) If $\alpha = 2.1$ then $g'(\alpha)$ is approximately zero and so the sequence converges very rapidly. This particular kind of arrangement is very useful in finding roots of numbers.

Miscellaneous exercise 1

1 $y = 3x - 3$

2 $\left(-\frac{7}{5}, \frac{13}{5}\right)$

3 (a)   **(b)**

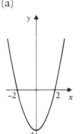 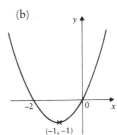

(c)   **(d)**

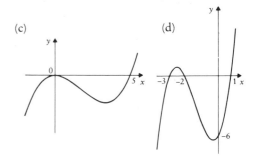

4 $A = 2\pi r^2 + \dfrac{1000}{r}, \quad r = 4.3$

5 (a) $y = (x - 1)^3$ **(b)** $y = x^3 + 2$

   (c) $y = (x - 2)^3 + 4$

6 (a) $y = 6x - x^2$ **(b)** $y = x^2 + 6x$

   (c) $y = x^2 - 7$

7 (a) 1660   **(b)** $100 + 190x$ **(c)** 765

   (d) $\frac{10}{9}$ **(e)** $\frac{64}{5}$

8 $S_n = \frac{23}{99}\left(1 - \left(\frac{1}{100}\right)^n\right), \quad \frac{23}{99}$

9 (a) 195   **(b)** 341   **(c)** $nr + \frac{3}{2}n(n + 1)$

   (d) $\dfrac{n(n - 1)}{2}$

10 (a) 100   **(b)** 0

11 (a) $(x+1)(x+4)$ (b) $x(x+3)$

(c) $(3x+4)(3x-1)$ (d) $(3x-2)(3x+2)$

(e) $(3x-4)(3x+1)$

12 (a) 2, 3   (b) $\frac{1}{2}$ (c) $0.5, -5$ (d) 2, 3.5

13 2 seconds

14 $(x-2)^2 - 2;$ 3.41,   0.586

15 (a) $x > 4$ or $x < -1$

(b) $1 < x < 3$

(c) $x < -3$ or $2 < x < 5$

(d) $x < 0$ or $0.59 < x < 8.41$

16 (a) -6 (b) 12   (c) 0

$A = (x+2)(x+1)(2x-3)$

$x = -2, -1, \frac{3}{2}$

17 5

18 (a) Yes   (b) No   (c) Yes

19 $(x+1)(x-2)(x-3);$

$x > 3$ or $-1 < x < 2$

20 $x = 5,$ $x = -1$ (a repeated root)

21 $(-1, -1)$ and $(3, 3)$

22 8, 15, 17

23 (a) 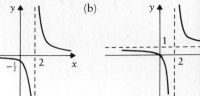 (b)

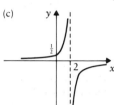 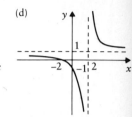

(c) 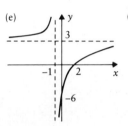 (d)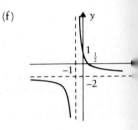

(e) (f)

2 INTRODUCTORY CALCULUS

2.1 Rates of change

2.1.1 Introduction

2.1 Exercise 1

1 (a) 3   (b) 3

2 (a) Difference in y-coordinates $= -6$; difference in x-coordinates $= 2$

(b) $\dfrac{dy}{dx} = \dfrac{-6}{2} = -3$

3 (a) -7 (b) 1   (c) -2 (d) $\frac{1}{2}$

4 (a) Difference in y-coordinates $= -2$; difference in x-coordinates $= 4$

(b) $\dfrac{dy}{dx} = \dfrac{-2}{4} = -\dfrac{1}{2}$

5 (a) $y = \dfrac{1}{2}x + 2 \Rightarrow \dfrac{dy}{dx} = \dfrac{1}{2}$

(b) $y = -x + 7 \Rightarrow \dfrac{dy}{dx} = -1$

(c) $-y = -x + 6 \Rightarrow y = x - 6 \Rightarrow \dfrac{dy}{dx} = 1$

(d) $2y = -x + 4 \Rightarrow y = -\dfrac{1}{2}x + 2 \Rightarrow \dfrac{dy}{dx} = -\dfrac{1}{2}$

6 (a) $C = 702 + 2.87n$

(b) $\dfrac{dC}{dn} = 2.87$. This represents the extra cost (change in cost) for each unit used.

7 (a) $\dfrac{ds}{dt} = -8$ (b) $\dfrac{dy}{dt} = 4$ (c) $\dfrac{dz}{dy} = -1$

(d) $\dfrac{dy}{dx} = 10$ (e) $y = 12 - 20x \Rightarrow \dfrac{dy}{dx} = -20$

8 (a) $\dfrac{dC}{dr} = 2\pi$. This is by how much the circumference increases when the radius increases by one unit.

(b) Using the result of (a), an extra $2 \times 2\pi = 4\pi$ metres would be needed (neglecting any deviation of the equator from a perfect circle).

(c) Surprisingly, this would still be 4π metres.

2.1.2 Linear functions

2.1 A

1 (a) $v = 20w + 16$ (b) $T = 35w + 46$

(c) $\dfrac{du}{dw} = 15$, $\dfrac{dv}{dw} = 20$, $\dfrac{dT}{dw} = 35$

For the first stage, $\dfrac{du}{dw}$ is the change in the time taken in minutes per kilogram of weight (that is, the extra number of minutes needed for an increase in weight of 1 kg).

$\dfrac{dv}{dw}$ and $\dfrac{dT}{dw}$ represent the corresponding changes for the second stage and the overall process.

(d) For each extra kilogram of weight, the total extra cooking time is the sum of the extra times needed for each of the two stages.

2 (a) $\dfrac{du}{dx} = 3$, $\dfrac{dv}{dx} = 2$

(b) (i) $y = (3x + 1) + (2x - 3) \Rightarrow y = 5x - 2$
(ii) $y = 2(3x + 1) + (2x - 3)$
$\Rightarrow y = 8x - 1$
(iii) $y = x + 4$
(iv) $y = 6x + 13$

(c) (i) $\dfrac{dy}{dx} = 5$ (ii) $\dfrac{dy}{dx} = 8$

(iii) $\dfrac{dy}{dx} = 1$ (iv) $\dfrac{dy}{dx} = 6$

(d) (i) $\dfrac{dy}{dx} = \dfrac{du}{dx} + \dfrac{dv}{dx}$ (ii) $\dfrac{dy}{dx} = 2\dfrac{du}{dx} + \dfrac{dv}{dx}$

(iii) $\dfrac{dy}{dx} = \dfrac{du}{dx} - \dfrac{dv}{dx}$ (iv) $\dfrac{dy}{dx} = 4\dfrac{du}{dx} - 3\dfrac{dv}{dx}$

(e) The rule should now be apparent. If $y = au + bv$, then

$$\frac{dy}{dx} = a\frac{du}{dx} + b\frac{dv}{dx}$$

(y is called a **linear combination** of u and v.)

3 (a) $u = 12 + 5t$

(b) $v = 9 + 6t$

(c) The first firm is cheaper for jobs lasting longer than 3 hours. The second firm is cheaper for jobs lasting less than 3 hours because of its smaller basic fee.

(d) $\frac{du}{dt} = 5$ and $\frac{dv}{dt} = 6$ are the two firms' respective extra charges in £ per hour worked.

(e) $c = 3u + 2v \Rightarrow \frac{dc}{dt} = 3\frac{du}{dt} + 2\frac{dv}{dt} = 27$

(f) Each extra hour that the job takes costs an extra £27.

2.1 Exercise 2

1 $\frac{dy}{dx} = 5$ (gradient)

So the line has equation $y = 5x + c$.
$(-1, 2)$ is a point on the line, so

$$2 = 5 \times -1 + c \Rightarrow c = 7$$

The equation is $y = 5x + 7$.

2 (a) $y = -2x + 8$ (b) $s = \frac{1}{2}t + 1$

(c) $p = \frac{2}{3}x + 3$

3 $\frac{dy}{dx} = \frac{6}{3} \Rightarrow \frac{dy}{dx} = 2$, $y = 2x + 3$

4 (a) (i) $C = 5 + 7t$ (ii) $\frac{dC}{dt} = 7$

(b) (i) $\frac{dC}{dt} = 6$ (ii) $C = 8 + 6t$

5

Test mark, T	25	26	49	50
Rescaled mark, R	0	4	96	100

(a) $\frac{dR}{dT} = 4$ (b) $R = 4T - 100$

6 (a) $P = 38 + \frac{10}{50}t$ or $P = 38 + 0.2t$

(b) $\frac{dP}{dt} = 0.2$. The population is increasing by 0.2 million each year.

(c) $P = 38 + 0.2 \times 98 = 57.6$ million
This may be reasonably close to the actual population. However, 1998 is outside the first half of the century so the simple linear model is being applied inappropriately. During the second half of the twentieth century the population growth has been more irregular.

7 (a) $\frac{du}{dx} = 2$, $\frac{dy}{dx} = -4$

(b)   (i) $2 + (-4) = -2$
    (ii) $2 - (-4) = 6$
    (iii) $3 \times 2 + (-4) = 2$
    (iv) $2 - 3 \times (-4) = 14$
    (v) $3 \times 2 + 2 \times (-4) = -2$
    (vi) $2 \times 2 - 3 \times (-4) = 16$

(c)   (i) $y = (4 + 2x) + (5 - 4x)$, so $y = 9 - 2x$
    (ii) $y = -1 + 6x$
    (iii) $y = 17 + 2x$
    (iv) $y = -11 + 14x$
    (v) $y = 22 - 2x$
    (vi) $y = -7 + 16x$

8 (a) $s = 15 + \frac{f - 200}{15}$, $\frac{ds}{df} = \frac{1}{15}$

The change in steaming time is $\frac{1}{15}$ minutes (4 seconds) for each extra gram of flour.

(b) $p = 25 + \frac{f - 200}{15}$, $\frac{dp}{df} = \frac{1}{15}$

The change in pressure time is $\frac{1}{15}$ minutes (4 seconds) for each extra gram of flour.

(c) $T = s + p \Rightarrow \frac{dT}{df} = \frac{ds}{df} + \frac{dp}{df}$

$$\frac{dT}{df} = \frac{2}{15}$$

The change in total cooling time is $\frac{2}{15}$ minutes (8 seconds) for each extra gram of flour.

2.2 Gradients of curves

2.2.1 Locally straight curves

2.2 A

1 With an increasing magnification, the curve looks more and more like a straight line. At $x = 4$ the graph looks more and more like a horizontal straight line.

2 You should expect to see the curve looking more and more like a horizontal straight line.

3 (a) $y = |x|$ is locally straight near all values of x, except $x = 0$.

   (b) $y = 100x^2$ is locally straight everywhere.

   (c) $y = \text{Int}(x)$ is locally straight near any value of x which is *not* an integer but has a discontinuity at each integer value.

   (d) $y = |x^2 - 4|$ is locally straight near all values of x, except $x = \pm 2$.

4E (a) $y = \frac{1}{5}\sin 3x$ has $\frac{1}{5}$ of the amplitude (y stretch; scale factor $\frac{1}{5}$) and oscillates three times as frequently (x stretch, scale factor $\frac{1}{3}$) as $y = \sin x$.

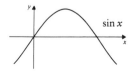

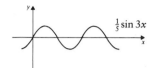

   (b) Both graphs look like the graph of $y = \sin x$ with 'wrinkles'. When magnified the wrinkles become more obvious.

   (c) $y = \sin x + \frac{1}{1000}\sin 1000x$ or any similar function.

2.2.2 Gradient graphs

2.2 **Exercise 1**

1 Any points where the tangent to the curve is horizontal correspond to a point where the gradient graph meets the x-axis.

(a)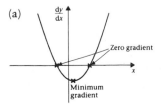

The gradient decreases to zero and becomes negative. The gradient then increases and becomes positive again.

(b)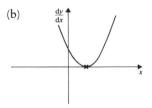

The gradient never becomes negative but there is just one point where it is zero.

(c)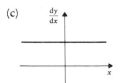

The gradient is constant for all x.

(d)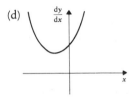

The gradient is always positive for all x. It decreases to a minimum gradient but never to zero (over the range shown).

(e)

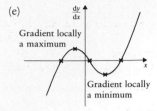

Gradient locally a maximum

Gradient locally a minimum

There are two points where the gradient is zero. (At one of them, the gradient is also locally a minimum.)

(f)

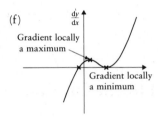

Gradient locally a maximum

Gradient locally a minimum

The three points where the gradient is zero correspond to stationary points on the original graph.

2 (a)

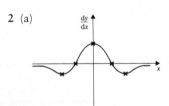

(b)

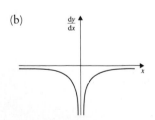

As x becomes numerically large, the gradients tend towards zero. As x tends to zero, the gradient reaches its maximum value in (a), whereas in (b) the gradient becomes very large and negative.

3 (a) (i)

(ii)

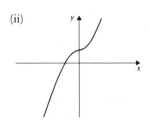

(b) There are infinitely many possible original graphs – formed by translating the above graphs parallel to the y-axis.

2.2.3 Obtaining a gradient

2.2 **B**

Your results for the gradients may vary slightly from the answers given.

1 (a) 1.5

(b)

x	-2	-1.5	-1	0	1	1.5	2
$\dfrac{dy}{dx}$	-2	-1.5	-1	0	1	1.5	2

(c)

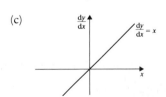

2	x	-4	-2	0	2	4	6	8
	(a) Gradient	12	8	4	0	-4	-8	-12
	(b) $4 - 2x$	12	8	4	0	-4	-8	-12

2.2 C

1 (c) You should find that, whatever points you chose, the gradient is the same as the x-coordinate value.

The equation is $\dfrac{dy}{dx} = x$.

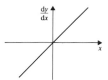

(d) The graphs are related by translations up or down. For any particular value of x the graphs will all have the same gradient.

(e) All the graphs have the same gradient

graph $\dfrac{dy}{dx} = x$.

2 (b)

The equation of the gradient graph is $\dfrac{dy}{dx} = 2x$.

(c) For any value of x, the value of y on the graph of $y = x^2$ is twice the value of y on the graph of $y = \frac{1}{2}x^2$. So for any change in value of x the corresponding change in the value of y will be twice as great.

(d) $\dfrac{dy}{dx} = 6x$

(e) $\dfrac{dy}{dx} = 2ax$. The gradient graph of any quadratic with equation $y = ax^2$ is a straight line through the origin.

3 The graph of $y = ax^2 + c$ is the translation of that of $y = ax^2$ by $\begin{bmatrix} 0 \\ c \end{bmatrix}$. It has the same gradient graph, with equation $\dfrac{dy}{dx} = 2ax$.

2.2 D

u	3.2	3.1	3.01	3.001
Estimate of gradient	6.2	6.1	6.01	6.001

The gradient is approaching 6.

The gradient of $y = x^2$ at $x = 3$ is 6.

2.2 Exercise 2

1 12   2 12   3 6   4 8   5 9

6 (a) 6   (b) 10   (c) 0   (d) −4

   (e) 30   (f) 7.2

2.2.4 Gradient functions

2.2 E

1 (a)

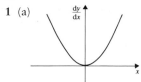

(b)

Value of x	0	1	−2	3
Gradient	0	3	12	27

(c) $\dfrac{dy}{dx} = 3x^2$

2 $\dfrac{dy}{dx} = 3ax^2$

4 $\dfrac{dy}{dx} = b + 2cx + 3dx^2$

For example,

$$y = 3 + 5x^2 + x^3 \Rightarrow \dfrac{dy}{dx} = 10x + 3x^2$$

5E You should have investigated the gradient functions of graphs such as, for example,

$$y = 3x^2 + 4x^3, \qquad y = 5x^3 - 3x^4$$

The general conclusion you should have reached is that, if a and b are constants,

$$y = ax^n + bx^m$$

$$\Rightarrow \frac{dy}{dx} = anx^{n-1} + bmx^{m-1}$$

The gradient of the sum is the sum of the gradients.

2.2 Exercise 3

1 (a) $\dfrac{dy}{dx} = 6x$ (b) $\dfrac{dv}{du} = 15u^2 - 4u$

(c) $\dfrac{dy}{dx} = -2x$ (d) $\dfrac{ds}{dt} = 4 - 2t$

2 (a) $\dfrac{dy}{dx} = 10x$

(b) (i) 10   (ii) 20   (iii) -10

3 (a) $\dfrac{dy}{dx} = -6x^2$

When $x = 0$, gradient $= 0$
When $x = 2$, gradient $= -24$

(b) $\dfrac{dy}{dx} = 5 - 2x$

When $x = 2$, gradient $= 1$
When $x = 4$, gradient $= -3$

4 (a) $\dfrac{dy}{dx} = 2 - 2x$

At $(2, 3)$, $\dfrac{dy}{dx} = 2 - 2 \times 2 = -2$

The tangent passes through $(2, 3)$ and has gradient -2. Its equation is therefore
$y - 3 = -2(x - 2)$, or $y = -2x + 7$.

(b) $y = 12x - 21$ (c) $y = -8x + 19$

5 $\dfrac{dy}{dx} = 1 + 4x$

When $x = 3$, $\dfrac{dy}{dx} = 13$ and $y = 21$

The equation of the tangent is
$y - 21 = 13(x - 3)$, or $y = 13x - 18$.

6 (a) $\dfrac{dy}{dx} = 1 - 3x^2$

At $(0, 5)$ the gradient is 1.
The equation of the tangent is
$y - 5 = x - 0$, or $y = x + 5$.

(b) $y = 5 - 3x$

(c) $y = 5$

2.2.5 Differentiation from first principles

2.2 F

1 (a) -2 (b) 3

2 (a) $\displaystyle\lim_{h \to 0} (h + 2) = 2$

(b) $\displaystyle\lim_{h \to 0} (5h - 2) = -2$

(c) $\displaystyle\lim_{h \to 0} (4h - h^2) = 0$

(d) $\displaystyle\lim_{h \to 2} (h + 2) = 4$

(e) $\displaystyle\lim_{h \to -3} \frac{2(h - 3)(h + 3)}{h + 3} = \lim_{h \to -3} 2(h - 3)$

$$= -12$$

2.2 Exercise 4

1 (a) $\displaystyle\lim_{h \to 0} \frac{3(1 + h)^2 - 3}{h} = \lim_{h \to 0} \frac{3 + 6h + 3h^2 - 3}{h}$

$$= \lim_{h \to 0} (6 + 3h) = 6$$

(b) $\dfrac{dy}{dx} = \displaystyle\lim_{h \to 0} \frac{3(x + h)^2 - 3x^2}{h}$

$$= \lim_{h \to 0} (6x + 3h) = 6x$$

2 $\displaystyle\lim_{h \to 0} \frac{[5(x + h)^2 + 3(x + h)] - [5x^2 + 3x]}{h}$

$$= 10x + 3$$

3 $\displaystyle\lim_{h \to 0} \frac{[4(x + h)^2 - 2(x + h) + 7] - [4x^2 - 2x + 7]}{h}$

$$= 8x - 2$$

4E $\dfrac{dy}{dt} = \lim_{h \to 0} \left[\dfrac{\dfrac{1}{2(t+h)+5} - \dfrac{1}{2t+5}}{h} \right]$

$\qquad = \lim_{h \to 0} \left[\dfrac{-2\not{h}}{\not{h}(2t+5)(2t+2h+5)} \right]$

$\qquad = \dfrac{-2}{(2t+5)^2}$

5E $\dfrac{dy}{dx} = \lim_{h \to 0} \left[\dfrac{(x+h)^3 - x^3}{h} \right]$

$\qquad = \lim_{h \to 0} \left[\dfrac{x^3 + 3hx^2 + 3h^2x + h^3 - x^3}{h} \right]$

$\qquad = \lim_{h \to 0} \left[\dfrac{3hx^2 + 3h^2x + h^3}{h} \right]$

$\qquad = \lim_{h \to 0} [3x^2 + 3hx + h^2] = 3x^2$

So $y = x^3 \Rightarrow \dfrac{dy}{dx} = 3x^2$

2.3 Optimisation
2.3.1 Graphs and gradient graphs

2.3 A

1 (a) For large positive and negative values of x, the graph has a shape similar to $y = x^3$.

When x is small, the graph has a shape similar to $y = x + 1$.

(b) The zeros of the $\left(x, \dfrac{dy}{dx} \right)$ graph correspond to the x-coordinates of the two stationary points.

The value of $\dfrac{dy}{dx}$ is negative between the two zeros, corresponding to the negative gradient of the graph between the two stationary points. Elsewhere the gradient is positive.

(c) The cubic graph has at most two stationary points.

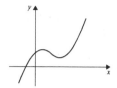

Consideration of the gradient graph confirms the general shape of the (x, y) graph. Final confirmation would come from calculating the positions of the two stationary points.

2 The local maxima and minima consist of the three points marked with dots.

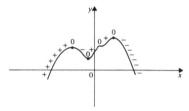

3 $\dfrac{dy}{dx}$ is negative at the given point, so the gradient of the graph is also negative, as shown.

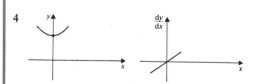

4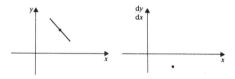

As x increases through $x = 0$, $\dfrac{dy}{dx}$ changes from negative to positive, actually becoming zero at $x = 0$.

Since the gradient of the graph is negative for $x < 0$ and positive for $x > 0$, there is a minimum on the graph at $x = 0$.

2.3 Exercise 1

1 $y = (x - 1)(x - 2)(x - 4)$

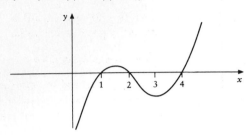

The coordinates of the stationary points could be determined precisely by using calculus. (Note that the stationary points are *not* at $x = 1.5$ and $x = 3$.)

2 (a)

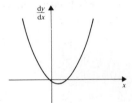

Zeros of the gradient graph correspond to stationary points on the (x, y) graph. The sign of $\dfrac{dy}{dx}$ corresponds to the sign of the gradient on the (x, y) graph.

(b)

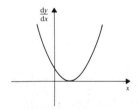

The stationary point on the (x, y) graph corresponds to the single zero on the gradient graph. $\dfrac{dy}{dx}$ is positive for all other values of x because the gradient of the (x, y) graph is positive everywhere except at the stationary point.

(c)

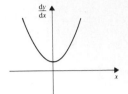

The gradient graph has no zeros because there are no stationary points on the (x, y) graph. $\dfrac{dy}{dx}$ is always positive, and so is the gradient of the (x, y) graph.

3

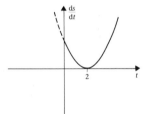

4 (a) $\dfrac{ds}{dt} = 3t^2 - 12t + 12 = 3(t - 2)^2$

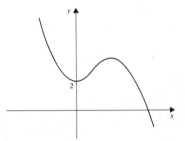

(b)

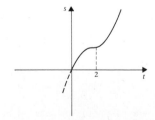

(c) The particle is initially moving with speed $\dfrac{ds}{dt} = 12$. It slows down until it comes to rest instantaneously when $t = 2$. It then speeds up again and increases in speed forever.

2.3.2 Quadratics and cubics

2.3 B

1 $\dfrac{dy}{dx} = 3x^2 - 12$

$\dfrac{dy}{dx} = 0$ when $x = \pm 2$

At $x = 2$, $y = 2^3 - (12 \times 2) + 2 = -14$
At $x = -2$, $y = (-2)^3 - (12 \times -2) + 2 = 18$

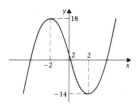

2 $\dfrac{du}{dx} = 6x + 6$

$\dfrac{du}{dx} = 0$ when $x = -1$

$u = 3 \times (-1)^2 + 6 \times (-1) + 5 = 2$

3 $\dfrac{dy}{dx} = 3x^2 + 6x + 5$. From the graph for

question 2 you can see that the least value of
$\dfrac{dy}{dx}$ is 2 and so the equation $\dfrac{dy}{dx} = 0$ has no
solutions.

The (x, y) graph therefore has *no* stationary
point and its gradient is minimum when
$x = -1$.

4 $a > 0$: $\dfrac{dy}{dx} = 0$ has no solutions, and so there
are no stationary points.

$a = 0$: gives the cubic $y = x^3$, with a
stationary point at the origin.

$a < 0$: $\dfrac{dy}{dx} = 0$ has two solutions,

$x = \pm\sqrt{(-\tfrac{1}{3}a)}$, and so there are two
stationary points.

2.3 Exercise 2

1 $\dfrac{dy}{dx} = 3x^2 - 12 = 3(x^2 - 4)$

The stationary points occur when $\dfrac{dy}{dx} = 0$, that
is when $x = 2$ or -2. The stationary points
are $(2, -11)$ and $(-2, 21)$.

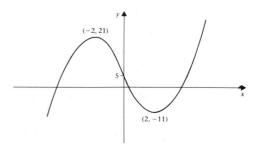

2 $\dfrac{dy}{dx} = 6x^2 - 18x + 12$

$= 6(x^2 - 3x + 2)$

$= 6(x - 1)(x - 2)$

$\dfrac{dy}{dx} = 0$ when $x = 1$ or $x = 2$. The stationary

points are $(1, -2)$ and $(2, -3)$.

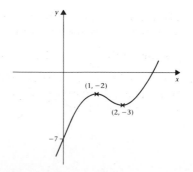

3 (a) (i) $y = 5x - x^2 = x(5 - x)$

$\dfrac{dy}{dx} = 0$ for $x = 2.5$

Maximum at $(2.5, 6.25)$

(ii)

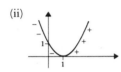

(b) (i) $y = (1 - x)^2 = 1 - 2x + x^2$

$\dfrac{dy}{dx} = 0$ for $x = 1$

Minimum at $(1, 0)$

(ii)

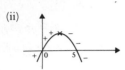

(c) (i) $y = x^3 - 3x^2 + 5$

$\dfrac{dy}{dx} = 0$ for $x = 0, x = 2$

Maximum at $(0, 5)$,
minimum at $(2, 1)$

(ii)

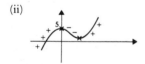

(d) (i) $y = 4x - x^2 - 4$

$\dfrac{dy}{dx} = 0$ for $x = 2$

Maximum at $(2, 0)$

(ii)

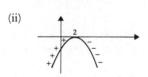

(e) (i) $y = 2x^3 - 9x^2 + 12$

$\dfrac{dy}{dx} = 0$ for $x = 0, x + 3$

Maximum at $(0, 12)$,
minimum at $(3, -15)$

(ii)

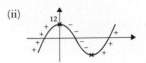

(f) (i) $y = x^4 - 8x^2 + 12$

$\dfrac{dy}{dx} = 0$ for $x = 0, x = \pm 2$

Maximum at $(0, 12)$,
minima at $(2, -4)$ and $(-2, -4)$

(ii)

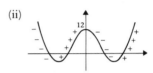

4 (a) $+6, +3, 0$

The quadratic has reflection symmetry
and so B's x-coordinate is $\dfrac{+6 + 0}{2}$.

(b) $+6, +4, 0$. The cubic does *not* have
reflection symmetry.

2.3.3 Maxima and minima

2.3 C

1 5000 people per square kilometre. (Note:
putting $r = 0$ is an idealisation; there has to be
a small radius for there to be space in which
people may live.)

2 Not valid for $r < 0$ or $r > 2.15$ since $P < 0$ is
meaningless.

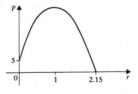

3 $\dfrac{dP}{dr} = 30 - 30r = 30(1 - r)$

r	0.5	1	2
$\dfrac{dP}{dr}$	15	0	-30

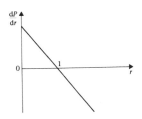

4 The population density rises to a maximum of 20 000 people per square kilometre at a distance of 1 km from the city centre.

The population density then decreases as you go farther out from the centre.

The $\left(r, \dfrac{dP}{dr}\right)$ graph shows that the maximum value of P corresponds to the value of r where $\dfrac{dP}{dr} = 0$.

For $r < 1$, the population density increases with r.

For $r > 1$, it decreases with r.

2.3 Exercise 3

1 $F = 25 + v - 0.012v^2, \quad 30 \leq v \leq 80$

(The inequality for v suggests that the car is in top gear.)

(a) $\dfrac{dF}{dv} = 1 - 0.024v$

v	35	60
F	45.3	41.8
$\dfrac{dF}{dv}$	0.16	-0.44

At the higher speed, the number of miles per gallon is lower.

At 35 m.p.h., the number of miles per gallon *increases* with increasing speed. At 60 m.p.h. it *decreases*.

(b) $\dfrac{dF}{dv} = 0$ when $v = 41.7$. The most economical speed is 41.7 m.p.h.

2 $n = 30 - 2P, \quad R = 30P - 2P^2$

(a) $\dfrac{dR}{dP} = 30 - 4P$ gives the rate at which revenue from the items changes with their price. The best selling price is £7.50.

At this price, $\dfrac{dR}{dP} = 0$.

(b) When $P = 5, \dfrac{dR}{dP} = 10$.

When $P = 10, \dfrac{dR}{dP} = -10$.

(c) $\dfrac{dR}{dP} = 30 - 4P$ must be positive and so $P < 7.50$.

3 If h is the variable height of the gutter, then the cross-sectional area A is given by

$A = (20 - 2h)h = 20h - 2h^2$

$\dfrac{dA}{dh} = 20 - 4h$

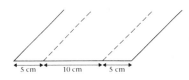

The area is maximised when $h = 5$.

4 (a) $P = 500 + 100t$

$\dfrac{dP}{dt} = 100$

This represents the rate at which the population is increasing each year.

(b) $P = 100(5 + t - 0.25t^2)$

$$\frac{dP}{dt} = 100 - 50t$$

$t = 1, \dfrac{dP}{dt} = 50; \quad t = 2, \dfrac{dP}{dt} = 0;$

$t = 3, \dfrac{dP}{dt} = -50$

The population stopped increasing after 2 years, and then it decreased.

The maximum population occurred when $t = 2$ and was

$$100(5 + 2 - 0.25 \times 2^2) = 600$$

The population decreased to zero and so the estate was abandoned.

5 If integers only are permitted, the minimum is 7 when the numbers are 2 and 5.

If all positive numbers are permitted, the minimum is approximately 6.3, when both numbers are just less than 3.2.

If negative numbers are permitted, there is no limit to the minimum value that the sum takes.

2.3.4 Graphical optimisation

2.3 D

Two possible ways of expressing the cross-sectional area in terms of a variable are given below, but several others are possible.

$A = (2 + \cos\theta)\sin\theta$

$A = (2 + \sqrt{(1 - h^2)})h$

Whichever way is chosen should lead to a maximum value for A when the shape is as shown.

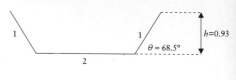

2.3 Exercise 4

1 (a) The length of the net is
$$w + l + w + l = 100.$$
$$2l + 2w = 100$$
$$l + w = 50$$
$$l = 50 - w$$

(b) The width of the net is
$$\tfrac{1}{2}w + h + \tfrac{1}{2}w = 40.$$
$$h + w = 40$$
$$h = 40 - w$$

(c) $V = whl$
$$V = w(40 - w)(50 - w)$$

(d) The maximum volume (of approximately 13 130 cm³) occurs when $w \approx 14.7$. The dimensions are then approximately 14.7 cm by 35.3 cm by 25.3 cm.

2 (a) The dimensions of the box are
$$\text{length} = 6 - 2x, \quad \text{width} = 4 - 2x,$$
$$\text{height} = x$$
so the volume is
$$V = (4 - 2x)(6 - 2x)x$$

(b) V is maximum when $x \approx 0.8$. The approximate dimensions are 0.8 cm by 2.4 cm by 4.4 cm.

3 The maximum volume is given by a cube of side 18.4 cm.
$$V = 6270 \text{ cm}^3$$

4 Maximum velocity = 17 m min⁻¹
Maximum acceleration = 6.75 m min⁻²

2.4 Numerical integration

2.4.1 Areas under graphs

2.4 A

1 (a) km   (b) miles   (c) cm^3 (d) g

2 $\frac{1}{60}$th of a revolution

2.4 B

1,3 The area under the graph represents the distance travelled in the 60 seconds.

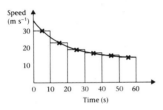

2 $10 \times (29.9 + 23.1 + \cdots + 15.0) =$
$10 \times 119.9 \approx 1200\,\text{m}$

4 The area under the 'steps' is close to the area under the curve of the graph.

5 The 'step' area is an *under*-estimate because of the way the graph curves ('concave upwards').

2.4 C

1,2

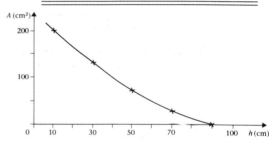

3 $10 \times \left\{ \dfrac{35 + 26}{2} + \dfrac{26 + 20.9}{2} + \cdots \right.$

$\left. + \dfrac{15.3 + 14.7}{2} \right\} \approx 1210\,\text{m}$

4 This is an *over*-estimate. Because of the way the graph curves, the six straight-line segments are all *above* it.

2.4 Exercise 1

1 Cross-sectional area $\approx 42.6\,\text{m}^2$

2 (a) Assuming that the cross-section is always circular, you can first calculate the cross-sectional area, A, from the circumference, C, by the formula

$$A = \frac{C^2}{4\pi}$$

Height, h (cm)	10	30	50	70	90
Area, A (cm^2)	198.9	127.3	71.6	31.8	8.0

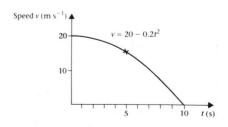

(b) Area under graph

$\approx 20[198.9 + 127.3 + 71.6 + 31.8 + 8.0]$

≈ 8750

This area represents the volume of the stalagmite in cm^3.

3 The train comes to rest when $t = 10$.

Speed v (m s^{-1})

$v = 20 - 0.2t^2$

By the trapezium rule, the area under the graph from $t = 0$ to $t = 10$ is approximately

$\frac{1}{2} \times 2 \times (20 + 19.2) + \frac{1}{2} \times 2 \times (19.2 + 16.8)$

$\qquad + \frac{1}{2} \times 2 \times (16.8 + 12.8)$

$\qquad + \frac{1}{2} \times 2 \times (12.8 + 7.2)$

$\qquad + \frac{1}{2} \times 2 \times (7.2 + 0) = 132$

The distance travelled is about 132 m.

2.4.2 Integration

2.4 Exercise 2

1 The integral represents the area under the graph of $y = x$ between $x = 0$ and $x = 3$.

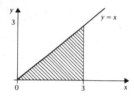

This is the area of a triangle (shaded), $\frac{1}{2} \times 3 \times 3 = 4.5$.

Thus $\int_0^3 x \, dx = 4.5$

2 (a) $3 \times \frac{5}{2} = 7.5$ (area of trapezium)

  (b) 10   (area of rectangle)

  (c) $3 \times \frac{1}{2}(5 + 11) = 24$ (area of trapezium)

3 (a) $10t \text{ m s}^{-1}$ (assuming it is dropped from rest)

  (b) $\int_0^5 10t \, dt$

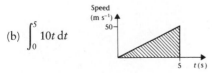

  (c) Area of triangle shaded, $\frac{5}{2} \times 50 = 125 \text{ m}$

4 $\sqrt{(10 - 1.5^2)} + \sqrt{(10 - 2.5^2)} = 4.72$

2.4.3 Numerical methods

2.4 D

1 (a) $h = \dfrac{b - a}{n}$

  (b) $x_1 = a + \dfrac{h}{2}$

  (c) x is increased by h each time.

2 Area $= \frac{1}{2}h(y_0 + y_1) + \frac{1}{2}h(y_1 + y_2) + \cdots$

$\qquad + \frac{1}{2}h(y_{n-1} + y_n)$

$\quad = \frac{1}{2}h(y_0 + 2y_1 + 2y_2 + \cdots + 2y_{n-1} + y_n)$

So

$$\int_a^b f(x) \, dx \approx \tfrac{1}{2}h(y_0 + 2y_1 + \cdots + 2y_{n-1} + y_n)$$

2.4 Exercise 3

1 (a) Too small
  (b) Neither – exactly the same
  (c) Neither clearly too large nor too small
  (d) Too large

2 (a) Too large   (b) Exact
  (c) Not clear   (d) Too small

3 Type A: Shaded area $\approx 6\frac{2}{3} \text{ cm}^2$
          Volume $\approx 6\frac{2}{3} \times 80 \approx 533 \text{ cm}^3$

  Type B: Shaded area $\approx 4\frac{2}{3} \text{ cm}^2$
          Volume $\approx 4\frac{2}{3} \times 15 = 70 \text{ cm}^3$

  Total needed $\approx (533 \times 12\,000) + (70 \times 8000) \text{ cm}^3$

$\qquad\qquad\qquad \approx 6.96 \times 10^6 \text{ cm}^3$

$\qquad\qquad\qquad \approx 6.96 \text{ m}^3$

  Adding 5% gives $6.96 \times 1.05 = 7.3 \text{ m}^3$.

4

x	0.1	0.3	0.5	0.7	0.9
y	0.9901	0.9174	0.8000	0.6711	0.5525

Area ≈ 0.786 (to 3 s.f.)

2.4.4 'Negative' areas

2.4 Exercise 4

1 (a) From 5 p.m. until 9 a.m. The increase is about 70 mg.

(b) The 'negative' area between $t = 9$ and $t = 17$ is also about 70. So the amount dissolved stays roughly constant.

2 (a) $y = x^2 - x - 2 = (x+1)(x-2)$

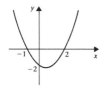

(b) (i) $26\frac{2}{3}$ (ii) $22\frac{1}{2}$ (iii) $-4\frac{1}{2}$ (iv) $8\frac{2}{3}$

(c) $4\frac{1}{2}$

3 (a) At $t = 2$ the net flow into the tank is zero. So this is the moment when the water level is highest (it stops rising and begins to fall).

(b) Area represents change in volume of water in the tank during the appropriate time interval. 'Positive' area represents increase in volume and 'negative' area represents decrease in volume.

(c) (i) About 10.6. This represents a net increase of 10.6 litres during the first 2 minutes.
   (ii) About -5.0. This represents a net decrease from $t = 2$ to $t = 5$.
   (iii) About 5.6. This represents a net increase from $t = 0$ to $t = 5$.

(d) 60.6, 55.6 litres. About 24.5 minutes.

4 $\displaystyle\int_0^5 x\,dx = 12.5$

The mid-ordinate estimates should be approximately

$\displaystyle\int_4^5 (x^2 - 4x)\,dx \approx 2.3$

So $\displaystyle\int_0^4 (x^2 - 4x)\,dx \approx -10.6$

Shaded area $\approx (12.5 - 2.3) + 10.6$

≈ 21 square units

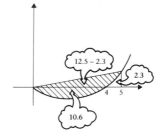

5 $\displaystyle\int_0^5 (x+5)\,dx = \left(\frac{5+10}{2}\right) \times 5 = 37.5$

$\displaystyle\int_0^5 (x^2 - 4x + 5)\,dx \approx 16.7$

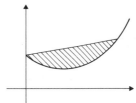

Shaded area $\approx 37.5 - 16.7$

≈ 21 square units

This confirms the value obtained in question 4.

2.5 Algebraic integration

2.5 **A**

1 $u = 1$

$A(u) = \frac{1}{3}$

2 (a) $\displaystyle\int_2^4 x^2\,dx = A(4) - A(2)$

$\displaystyle = \int_0^4 x^2\,dx - \int_0^2 x^2\,dx$

$= 21\frac{1}{3} - 2\frac{2}{3}$

$= 18\frac{2}{3}$

(b) $\displaystyle\int_1^3 x^2\,dx = A(3) - A(1)$

$= 9 - \frac{1}{3}$

$= 8\frac{2}{3}$

3 (b) (i)

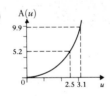

$\displaystyle\int_{2.5}^{3.1} x^2\,dx = A(3.1) - A(2.5)$

$\approx 9.9 - 5.2 = 4.7$

(ii)

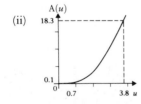

$\displaystyle\int_{0.7}^{3.8} x^2\,dx = A(3.8) - A(0.7)$

$\approx 18.3 - 0.1 = 18.2$

(c) $A = \dfrac{u^3}{3}$

2.5 **B**

1 (a)

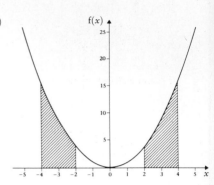

(b) $\displaystyle\int_2^4 x^2\,dx$ and $\displaystyle\int_{-4}^{-2} x^2\,dx$ are the areas of the regions shaded above. By symmetry these are equal.

(c) $\displaystyle\int_2^4 x^2\,dx = \left[\tfrac{1}{3}x^3\right]_2^4 = 18\frac{2}{3}$. Similarly,

$\displaystyle\int_{-4}^{-2} x^2\,dx = 18\frac{2}{3}$.

2 (a) (i) $\displaystyle\int_{-3}^{-1.5} x^2\,dx = \left[\tfrac{1}{3}x^3\right]_{-3}^{-1.5} = 7.875$

(ii) 2.25   (iii) 7.875   (iv) 10.125

(b) $\displaystyle\int_{-3}^{-1.5} x^2\,dx = \int_{1.5}^{3} x^2\,dx$

$\displaystyle\int_{-1.5}^{1.5} x^2\,dx + \int_{1.5}^{3} x^2\,dx = \int_{-1.5}^{3} x^2\,dx$

3 (a) Shaded area $= \frac{1}{2} \times u \times 2u = u^2$

(b) $\displaystyle\int_0^u 2x\,dx = \left[x^2\right]_0^u = u^2$

4 (a)

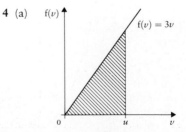

(b) Shaded area $= \frac{1}{2} \times u \times 3u = \frac{3}{2}u^2$

5 (i) (a)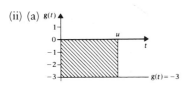

(b) Shaded area = $2u$

(ii) (a)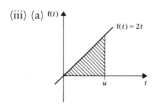

(b) Shaded area = $-3u$

(iii) (a)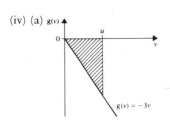

(b) Shaded area = u^2

(iv) (a)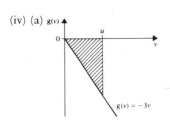

(b) Shaded area = $-\frac{3}{2}u^2$

6 (a) $A(x) = mx$ (b) $A(x) = \frac{1}{2}mx^2$

2.5.2 Integrals of polynomials

2.5 C

1 (a), (b)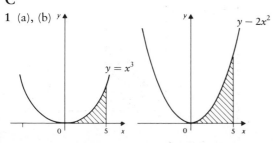

(c) The graph of $y = 2x^2$ is obtained by a one-way stretch $\times 2$ from the y-axis. Areas are therefore increased by a factor of 2.

(d) $\displaystyle\int_a^b kx^2\,dx = k\int_a^b x^2\,dx$

2 (a)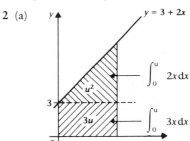

(b)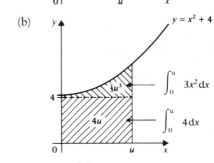

3, 4 $f(x) = ax^2 + bx + c$

$\Rightarrow A(x) = \dfrac{ax^3}{3} + \dfrac{bx^2}{2} + cx$

5, 6 $f(x) = ax^3 + bx^2 + cx + d$

$\Rightarrow A(x) = \dfrac{ax^4}{4} + \dfrac{bx^3}{3} + \dfrac{cx^2}{2} + dx$

2.5 Exercise 1

1 (a) $\displaystyle\int_2^4 (3x^2 - 5)\,dx$ (b) $\left[x^3 - 5x\right]_2^4 = 46$

2 (a) $\displaystyle\int_{-2}^1 (t^3 + 2t^2 - 3)\,dt = \left[\tfrac{1}{4}t^4 + \tfrac{2}{3}t^3 - 3t\right]_{-2}^1$

$= -6\tfrac{3}{4}$

(b)

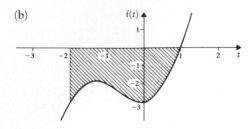

Between $t = -2$ and $t = 1$, the graph lies completely below the t-axis and hence the shaded area is negative.

3 (a)

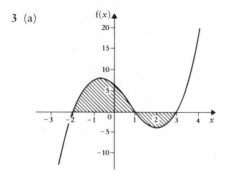

(b) $\int_{-2}^{1} (x^3 - 2x^2 - 5x + 6)\, dx = \frac{63}{4}$

$\int_{1}^{3} (x^3 - 2x^2 - 5x + 6)\, dx = -\frac{16}{3}$

The total area is $\frac{63}{4} + \frac{16}{3} = \frac{253}{12} \approx 21.08$.

4 (a) 30 m (b) $t = 2.5$ seconds (when $v = 0$)
  (c) 31.25 m

5 (a) $-\frac{1}{4}$ (b) 0 (c) $-2\frac{1}{3}$ (d) $\frac{1}{3}$
  (e) $1\frac{3}{4}$ (f) $3\frac{5}{6}$

6 Area $= 13\frac{1}{6}$

7 $a = 1$ and 4

8 $21\frac{1}{3}$ metres

2.5.3 Numerical or algebraic integration

2.5 D

1 $\int_{0}^{3} 4(t - 5)^2\, dt = 4 \int_{0}^{3} (t^2 - 10t + 25)\, dt$

$$= 4\left[\tfrac{1}{3}t^3 - 5t^2 + 25t \right]_{0}^{3}$$

$$= 156 \,(\text{kg})$$

2 (a) Average productivity is $\dfrac{156}{3\frac{1}{2}}$ kg per hour
  $= 44.6$ kg per hour.

  (b) $\int_{0}^{1.5} 4(t - 5)^2\, dt = 4\left[\tfrac{1}{3}t^3 - 5t^2 + 25t \right]_{0}^{1.5}$
    $= 109.5$

  This is the number of kilograms produced in 2 hours, so the average productivity is 54.75 kg per hour.

  (c) $\int_{0}^{\frac{2}{3}} 4(t - 5)^2\, dt = 58.17$ kg produced in
    1 hour 10 minutes.

  Average productivity is 49.86 kg per hour.

3 If the catalyst is changed after t hours, the output in kg per hour is:

$$\frac{4(\tfrac{1}{3}t^3 - 5t^2 + 25t)}{t + 0.5}$$

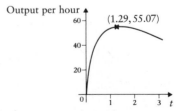

Using a graph plotter you can see that maximum output per hour is achieved when the catalyst is renewed after approximately 1.29 hours (1 hour 17 minutes), giving average productivity of 55.07 kg per hour.

4E In a $3\frac{1}{2}$ hour production cycle 156 kg is produced.

Profit in £s is

$$(156 \times 3) - (50 \times 3\tfrac{1}{2}) - 150 = £143$$

(a) Profit per kg sold $= £143 \div 156 = £0.92$

(b) Profit per hour $= 143 \div 3\frac{1}{2} = £40.86$

5E Profit per kg is a maximum £0.94 when $t = 2.53$, i.e. the catalyst is changed after 2 hours 32 minutes.

Profit per hour is a maximum £47.13 when $t = 2.155$, i.e. the catalyst is changed after 2 hours 9 minutes.

The company should maximise profit per hour to achieve maximum profit per annum.

2.5.4 The fundamental theorem of calculus

2.5 E

1 (a)

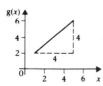
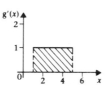

Area $= 4$

(b)

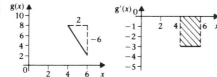

Area $= -6$

(c)

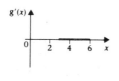

Area $= 0$

The difference in the y-coordinates of the end points equals the area under the gradient graph.

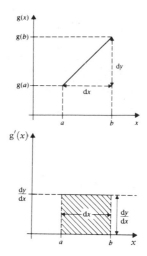

Area of shaded rectangle

$$= \frac{\text{difference in } y}{\text{difference in } x} \times \text{difference in } x$$

$$= \text{difference in } y = g(b) - g(a)$$

2

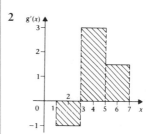

$g(7) = 10$ and $g(1) = 3$, so $g(7) - g(1) = 7$

The result $\displaystyle\int_{1}^{7} g'(x)\,dx = g(7) - g(1)$ is always true.

3 $\displaystyle\int_{a}^{b} g'(x)\,dx = g(b) - g(a)$ for any function g

whose graph consists of a series of **connected** line segments.

4E

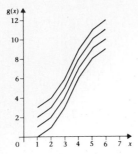

(a) Any of the graphs shown should give the $(x, g'(x))$ graph shown on page 168.

(b) Each graph is a simple translation (up or down) of one of the other graphs. There is an infinite number of such graphs, all sharing the same gradient graph.

(c) From the graph on page 168 you can see that $\int_1^6 g'(x)\,dx = 9$

$\int_1^6 g'(x)\,dx = g(6) - g(1)$ for any *correct* $(x, g(x))$ graph.

2.5 Exercise 2

1 (a) (i) 4   (ii) 0

(b)

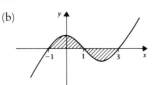

The graph has rotational symmetry about $(1, 0)$. The areas shaded are equal.

2 $\left[x^3 - 5x^2 + 7 \right]_1^2 = -8$

3 (a) $10x + 3$ (b) $6t^2$

Note that $h(t) = 6t^2$ for *any* integral function of the type $2t^3 + c$ where c is constant.

4 (a) (i) The graphs intersect where $x^2 = 8 - x^2 \Rightarrow x = 2$ (since $x > 0$). The graph of $y = 8 - x^2$ intersects the x-axis where $x^2 = 8 \Rightarrow x = \sqrt{8}$. The integrals arise from splitting the areas as shown.

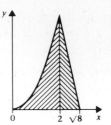

(ii) $A = \left[\tfrac{1}{3}x^3 \right]_0^2 + \left[8x - \tfrac{1}{3}x^3 \right]_2^{\sqrt{8}} \approx 4.42$

(b) (i) The graphs intersect at $(0, 0)$ and $(1, 1)$. The shaded area is

$$\tfrac{1}{2} \times 1 \times 1 - \int_0^1 x^2\,dx = \tfrac{1}{2} - \tfrac{1}{3} = \tfrac{1}{6}$$

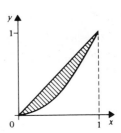

(ii) Area $A + B = 6 \times 4 = 24$
Area $C = 2 \times 2 = 4$

$$\text{Area } B + C = \int_2^4 \tfrac{1}{2}x^2\,dx = 9\tfrac{1}{3}$$

So area $A = 24 + 4 - 9\tfrac{1}{3} = 18\tfrac{2}{3}$
Required area $= 37\tfrac{1}{3}$

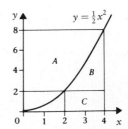

(iii) The graphs $y = 3x^2 - 12$ and $y = 12 - 3x^2$ both intersect the x-axis at $x = \pm 2$.

By symmetry, the shaded area is twice the area enclosed by the curve $y = 12 - 3x^2$ and the x-axis from $x = -2$ to $x = 2$.

$$\text{Shaded area} = 2\int_{-2}^{2}(12 - 3x^2)\,dx$$

$$= 2\left[12x - x^3\right]_{-2}^{2} = 64$$

5 $\text{Shaded area} = \int_{0}^{c}x^2\,dx = \left[\tfrac{1}{3}x^3\right]_{0}^{c} = \tfrac{1}{3}c^3 = 6$

$$\Rightarrow c^3 = 18$$

$$\Rightarrow c = \sqrt[3]{18} \approx 2.62$$

6E $\left[x^3 - x^2\right]_{0}^{a} = 0$

$$\Rightarrow a^3 - a^2 = 0$$

$\Rightarrow a = 0$ (which does not apply here)

or $a = 1$

2.5.5 The indefinite integral

2.5 F

They each differentiate to $2x + 5$.

$\int(2x + 5)\,dx = x^2 + 5x + k$. When evaluating the integral between $x = 1$ and $x = 2$, the constant k will 'cancel out':

$$\int_{1}^{2}(2x + 5)\,dx = \left[x^2 + 5x + k\right]_{1}^{2}$$

$$= (14 + k) - (6 + k)$$

$$= 8$$

Hence any of the functions *could* have been used.

2.5 Exercise 3

1 (a) $\tfrac{1}{4}x^4 - x + c$

(b) $\int_{1}^{3}(x + 1)(x - 2)\,dx$

$$= \int_{1}^{3}(x^2 - x - 2)\,dx$$

$$= \left[\tfrac{1}{3}x^3 - \tfrac{1}{2}x^2 - 2x\right]_{1}^{3} = \tfrac{2}{3}$$

2 (a) $y = \tfrac{1}{2}x^2 - 4x + c$

(b) $y = x^3 + \tfrac{1}{2}x^2 + c$

(c) $y = \tfrac{1}{3}x^3 + \tfrac{1}{2}x^2 + x + c$

(d) $(x + 1)(x - 2) = x^2 - x - 2$

$$\Rightarrow y = \tfrac{1}{3}x^3 - \tfrac{1}{2}x^2 - 2x + c$$

3 (a) $y = x^3 + 2x^2 + 2$

(b) $y = \tfrac{1}{3}x^3 + \tfrac{1}{2}x^2 + x + 3$

4 (a) $x^3 - x^2 + 5x$

(b) $(2t + 1)(t - 4) = 2t^2 - 7t - 4$

$$k(t) = \tfrac{2}{3}t^3 - \tfrac{7}{2}t^2 - 4t$$

5 $P = 0.2t + c$

58 million

6 (a) $s = \int 4t\,dt = 2t^2 + c$

c is the value of s when $t = 0$, i.e. the distance of the sphere from the top of the ramp when it is released.

(b) $s = 2t^2 + 0.5$

The ramp is 2.5 m in length.

(c) $t = 0.87$ seconds (to 2 d.p.)

Miscellaneous exercise 2

1 (a) $2x$ (b) $8x^3 + 3$ (c) $-12x^2$

    (d) 6 (e) $10x - 1$ (f) $1 - 5x^4$

2 (a) 5 (b) -16 (c) -13

3 (a) $y = -2x + 3$ (b) $y = 12x - 8$

    (c) $y = -1$

4 (a) $(\frac{1}{2}, 3\frac{1}{2})$ (b) $(1\frac{1}{2}, 7\frac{1}{2})$ (c) $(0, 3)$

5 $(3, 11)$

6 $(2, 4)$

7 $y = 4x - 4$, $y = -2x - 1$

8 $y = 3x - 3$, $y = 12x - 17$, $(\frac{14}{9}, \frac{15}{9})$

9 (a) $v = 3t^2 - 6t$ (b) $t = 0$ or 2

    (c) Backwards, $2\,\text{s}$

10 (a) $30\,\text{m s}^{-1}$ (b) $t = 3$

     (c) $45\,\text{m}$

11 (a) $20\,\text{m s}^{-1}$ (b) $125\,\text{m}$ (c) $15.625\,\text{s}$

12 (a) $30\,\text{m}$ (b) $1, \;\; 7$

13 (a) $(2, -1)$ (b) $(\frac{1}{2}, 4\frac{1}{4})$

     (c) $(2, 2)$ (d) $(4, 48)$

14 $v = \dfrac{ds}{dt} = \frac{3}{4}t^2 - \frac{3}{2}t; \quad t = 0, 2$

15 (a) $(2, -1)$ (minimum)

     (b) $(0, 0)$, $(\frac{3}{2}, -1\frac{11}{16})$ (minimum)

     (c) $(3, -8)$ (minimum), $(-1, 2\frac{2}{3})$ (maximum)

16 $x = 4\frac{1}{2}$, $y = 3$

17 (a) 0 and $8\,\text{s}$ (b) 2 and $6\,\text{s}$

     (c) $48\,\text{m s}^{-1}$

18 (a) (i) $83\frac{7}{8}$ (ii) 84

     (b) (i) $27\frac{3}{16}$ (ii) $27\frac{3}{4}$

19 (a) $4\frac{1}{2}$ (b) $57\frac{1}{6}$ (c) 108

20 $20\frac{5}{6}$

21 (a) 0.693 (b) 1.57 (c) 1.26

22 $39, 39$

     $x^2 + 2x + 1$ is obtained from $x^2 + 1$ by a

     translation $\begin{bmatrix} -1 \\ 0 \end{bmatrix}$

23 (a) $\frac{1}{4}x^4 + 2x^3 + k$ (b) $\frac{1}{4}x^4 + \frac{1}{2}x^2 + k$

     (c) $\frac{1}{3}ax^3 + \frac{1}{2}bx^2 + cx + k$

24 $x = 2.5t^2 - t^3 + 2$;

     x is greatest when $t = 1\frac{2}{3}$, v when $t = \frac{5}{6}$.

25 (a) The volume of water flowing between 12 noon and 4 p.m.

     (b) $2340\,\text{m}^3$

26 (a) 4 (b) 21 (c) 3.75

27 (a) $\frac{15}{4}t^4$ (b) $2t + 8$

28 (a) $b = 4$ (b) $b = 6$ (c) $b = 0.354$

3 FUNCTIONS

3.1 Algebra of functions

3.1.1 Composition of functions

3.1 Exercise 1

1 (a) (i) $2x^3 + 3$ (ii) $(2x + 3)^3$

  (b) (i) $\dfrac{2}{x} + 1$ (ii) $\dfrac{1}{2x + 1}$

  (c) (i) $3(5 - x) + 2 = 17 - 3x$
    (ii) $5 - (3x + 2) = 3 - 3x$

  (d) (i) $1 - (1 - 2x)^2 = 4x - 4x^2$
    (ii) $1 - 2(1 - x^2) = 2x^2 - 1$

2 (a) $ct(x) = 9 + 0.4 \times (1.034x) = 9 + 0.4136x$

  (b) The cost in pounds of x cubic feet of gas.

3 There are alternative answers for all of the following questions.

  (a) $f(x) = \dfrac{1}{x}$, $g(x) = x + 2$

  (b) $f(x) = x + 2$, $g(x) = \dfrac{1}{x}$

  (c) $f(x) = \dfrac{1}{x}$, $g(x) = 2x + 3$

  (d) $f(x) = 2x - 1$, $g(x) = \sqrt{x}$

  (e) $f(x) = \dfrac{1}{x} + 3$, $g(x) = x^2$

  (f) $f(x) = x^4$, $g(x) = 2x + 1$

  (g) $f(x) = x^2 - 4x - 3$, $g(x) = x^4$

4 (a) $x + 4$ (b) x^4 (c) $4x - 9$
  (d) x (e) $\sin(\sin x)$ (f) x

5 (a) $f(g(f(x))) = f(g(x - 3))$
    $= f((x - 3)^2) = (x - 3)^2 - 3$

  (b) (i) $fg(x)$ (ii) $gfg(x)$ (iii) $f^2(x)$
    (iv) $fg^3(x)$ (v) $f^2g^2f(x)$

6 (a) $qs(x)$ (b) $sq(x)$ (c) $s^2(x)$

7 (a) $fg(x) = (x + 3)^2$, $gf(x) = x^2 + 3$, $x = -1$

  (b) $fg(x) = x - 3$, $gf(x) = x - 3$,
  all values of x

(c) $fg(x) = 6x + 1$, $gf(x) = 6x - 2$,
  no values of x

(d) $fg(x) = \dfrac{1}{x^3}$, $gf(x) = \dfrac{1}{x^3}$,   all values of x

(e) $fg(x) = x + 2$, $gf(x) = x + 1$,
  no values of x

(f) $fg(x) = \sqrt{(x - 1)}$, $gf(x) = \sqrt{(x)} - 1$,
  $x = 1$

8

	e	f	g	h
e	e	f	g	h
f	f	e	h	g
g	g	h	e	f
h	h	g	f	e

3.1.2 Range and domain

3.1 A

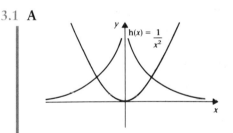

Domain $\{x \in \mathbb{R} : x \neq 0\}$

Range $\{y \in \mathbb{R} : y > 0\}$

3.1.3 Inverse functions

3.1 B

1 (a) f^{-1} reverses the effect of f and so
    $f^{-1}(f(x)) = x$.

  (b) If $f(x) = y$, then $f^{-1}(y) = x$. Any point in the domain of f is therefore in the range of f^{-1} and vice versa.

(c)

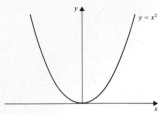

(d) If a function is many-to-one (as is $y = x^2$ in (c)), then the inverse is not a function because it is one-to-many.

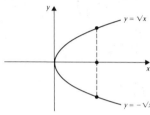

2 (a)

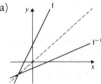

$$f^{-1}(x) = \tfrac{1}{3}(x - 5)$$

Domain of f = $\{x \in \mathbb{R}\}$

(b)

$$g^{-1}(x) = \sqrt{(x + 7)}$$

Domain of g = $\{x \in \mathbb{R} : x \geq 0\}$

(c)

$$h^{-1}(x) = \sqrt{x + 7}$$

Domain of h = $\{x \in \mathbb{R} : x \geq 7\}$

(d)

$$r^{-1}(x) = (x - 6)^2$$

Domain of r = $\{x \in \mathbb{R} : x \geq 0\}$

3 Reflection in $y = x$ (resulting in interchange of x and y in the equation)

4 (a) $y = \pm\sqrt{(x + 3)} - 5$ (b) $y = \tfrac{1}{2}(\tfrac{1}{3}x + 1)$

5 (a) (i) The reciprocal sequence alternates between two values, except when $x_1 = 0$ (x_2 undefined) or $x_1 = \pm 1$ (constant sequence).

  (ii) The 'change sign' sequence behaves similarly; it is constant for $x_1 = 0$.

  (b) Both functions are self-inverse and hence $f^2(x) = x$ in each case.

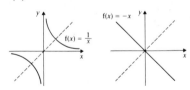

The graphs of both functions reflect in the line $y = x$ onto themselves.

6 (a) $\dfrac{1 - x}{2x}$ (b) $12 - x$ (c) $\dfrac{1}{x + 1}$

  (d) $\sqrt{\left(\dfrac{8}{x}\right)} - 1$ (e) $\sqrt{(1 - x^2)}$

  (f) $\sqrt{(4 - x)} + 2$

  (b) and (e) are self-inverse and have $y = x$ as a line of symmetry.

3.1.4 Rearranging formulas

3.1 Exercise 2

1 (a) $x = \frac{1}{5}(2y + 3)$ (b) $x = \frac{4}{3}y + 5$

(c) $x = 5 \pm \sqrt{(y - 4)}$ (d) $x = 3 + \dfrac{1}{y}$

2 (a) $f^{-1}(x) = \frac{1}{5}(2x + 3)$;
f has domain and range $\{x \in \mathbb{R}\}$

(b) $f^{-1}(x) = \frac{4}{3}x + 5$;
f has domain and range $\{x \in \mathbb{R}\}$

(c) $f^{-1}(x) = 5 + \sqrt{(x - 4)}$;
f has domain $x \geq 5$, and range $y \geq 4$
or $f^{-1}(x) = 5 - \sqrt{(x - 4)}$;
f has domain $x \leq 5$, and range $y \geq 4$

(d) $f^{-1}(x) = 3 + \dfrac{1}{x}$;
f has domain $x \neq 3$, and range $y \neq 0$

3 (a) $a = \dfrac{2y}{900 - y}$

(b) Since a and y are both positive, the
denominator $(900 - y)$ must be positive.

4 (a) $x = \dfrac{1 + y}{1 - y}$ (b) $x = \dfrac{2 - 3y}{1 + y}$

5 The image will be $y = f^{-1}(x) = \dfrac{x}{1 - 2x}$

6 $f^{-1}(x) = -\sqrt{\left(\dfrac{x - 1}{x + 1}\right)}$ $(x < -1)$

3.1.5 Parameters and functions

3.1 Exercise 3

1 (a) $W = \dfrac{p - b}{a}$ or $\dfrac{1}{a}(p - b)$

(b) $r = \dfrac{C}{2\pi}$

(c) $l = \dfrac{2s}{n} - a$ (d) $r = 1 - \dfrac{a}{s}$ or $\dfrac{s - a}{s}$

(e) $x = \dfrac{yR}{y - R}$ $\left(\text{since } \dfrac{1}{x} = \dfrac{1}{R} - \dfrac{1}{y} = \dfrac{y - R}{yR}\right)$

2 (a) (i) 75 feet (ii) 175 feet (iii) 315 feet

(b) $v = \sqrt{[20(d + 5)]} - 10$ (c) 61.4 m.p.h.

3 $\alpha = 1.7 \times 10^{-5}$

4 $c = \sqrt{\left(\dfrac{E}{m}\right)}$

5 $v = \sqrt{\left(\dfrac{2E + mu^2}{m}\right)}$ $\left[\text{or } v = \sqrt{\left(\dfrac{2E}{m} + u^2\right)}\right]$

6 $T = 2\pi\sqrt{\left(\dfrac{l}{g}\right)}$

$\Rightarrow \dfrac{T}{2\pi} = \sqrt{\left(\dfrac{l}{g}\right)}$

$\Rightarrow \dfrac{T^2}{4\pi^2} = \dfrac{l}{g}$

$\Rightarrow \dfrac{T^2 g}{4\pi^2} = l$

$l = \dfrac{2^2 \times 9.81}{4\pi^2} = 0.9940$

7 (a) Area of cylindrical surface $= 2\pi rh$
Area of ends $= 2\pi r^2$
Total surface area $= 2\pi rh + 2\pi r^2$
$S = 2\pi r(h + r)$

(b) $h = \dfrac{S}{2\pi r} - r$

8 (a) $r = \sqrt{\left(\dfrac{3V}{\pi h}\right)}$ (b) $r = \dfrac{100I}{Pn}$

9 (a) $I = \dfrac{nE}{R + nr} \Rightarrow I(R + nr) = nE$

$\Rightarrow IR = nE - nrI$

$\Rightarrow R = \dfrac{n(E - rI)}{I}$

(b) $E = \frac{1}{2}mv^2 \Rightarrow 2E = mv^2$

$\Rightarrow \dfrac{2E}{m} = v^2$

$\Rightarrow v = \sqrt{\left(\dfrac{2E}{m}\right)}$

3.1.6 Functions and transformations of graphs

3.1 C

1 Graphs b, c and e can be mapped onto each other. Graphs a and d can be mapped onto each other.

2 (a) The translation through $\begin{bmatrix} 5\frac{1}{2} \\ -2\frac{3}{4} \end{bmatrix}$

(b) The translation through $\begin{bmatrix} 7 \\ -2 \end{bmatrix}$

(c) The translation through $\begin{bmatrix} 11 \\ 0 \end{bmatrix}$

3 b can be mapped onto e by a reflection in the y-axis.

3.1 D

1 (a) $f(x) = x^4$, $f(x) + 2 = x^4 + 2$,
$f(x + 3) = (x + 3)^4$

(b) The three graphs are congruent and the transformations needed are:

(i) translation $\begin{bmatrix} 0 \\ 2 \end{bmatrix}$

(ii) translation $\begin{bmatrix} -3 \\ 0 \end{bmatrix}$

2 $g(x) = \dfrac{1}{x}$, $g(x + 4) = \dfrac{1}{x + 4}$,

$g(x + 4) + 3 = \dfrac{1}{x + 4} + 3$

The three graphs are congruent and the transformations needed are:

(i) translation $\begin{bmatrix} -4 \\ 0 \end{bmatrix}$

(ii) translation $\begin{bmatrix} -4 \\ 3 \end{bmatrix}$

3 In questions 1 and 2 you saw that replacing 'x' by '$x - 5$' resulted in a translation of 5 parallel to the x-axis; and that adding 2 to the function was equivalent to a translation of 2 parallel to the y-axis.

So it is reasonable to suggest that the image of $y = \dfrac{3}{x^2}$ under a translation $\begin{bmatrix} 5 \\ 2 \end{bmatrix}$ is

$$y = \frac{3}{(x - 5)^2} + 2$$

4 $y = (x + 2)^2 - 1$, a translation by $\begin{bmatrix} -2 \\ -1 \end{bmatrix}$

3.1 Exercise 4

1

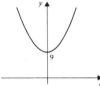

$y = x^2$ translated through $\begin{bmatrix} 0 \\ 9 \end{bmatrix}$

2

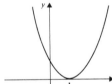

$y = x^2$ translated through $\begin{bmatrix} 1 \\ 0 \end{bmatrix}$

3 $y = \dfrac{3}{x}$ translated through $\begin{bmatrix} -\frac{1}{2} \\ 0 \end{bmatrix}$

4 $y = x^3$ translated through $\begin{bmatrix} 0 \\ -2 \end{bmatrix}$

5

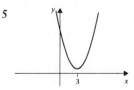

$y = 5x^2$ translated through $\begin{bmatrix} 3 \\ 6 \end{bmatrix}$

6

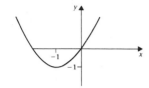

$y = x^2 + 2x = (x + 1)^2 - 1$

i.e. $y = x^2$ translated through $\begin{bmatrix} -1 \\ -1 \end{bmatrix}$

3.1.7 Combining transformations of graphs

3.1 E

1 (a) $f(x) = x^2 - x, \quad f(-x) = x^2 + x,$
$-f(x) = -x^2 + x$

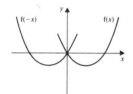

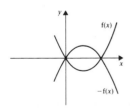

(b) (i) reflection in y-axis
(ii) reflection in x-axis

(c) Yes
(i) If (a, b) is a point on the graph of $y = f(x)$, then $(-a, b)$ will be a point on the graph of $y = f(-x)$.
(ii) Similarly, if (a, b) is on the graph of $y = f(x)$, then $(a, -b)$ is on the graph of $y = -f(x)$.

2 (a) The equation of the reflected graph will be $y = -f(x) = -x^4 + 2x^3$.

(b) The equation of the reflected graph will be $y = f(-x) = x^4 + 2x^3$.

3 (a) $f(-x) = 3x^2 - x^4$

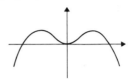

The graphs of $f(x)$ and $f(-x)$ coincide, since $(-x)^2 = x^2$ and $(-x)^4 = x^4$.

(b) $f(-x) = -x^3 + 5x = -f(x)$

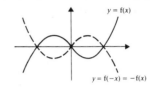

Here $f(-x) = -f(x)$, since $(-x)^3 = -x^3$ and $5(-x) = -5x$.

4 (a) Even   (b) odd   (c) neither

5 (a) Even   (b) neither   (c) neither
(d) odd   (e) odd   (f) even

6 (a) After the first reflection,
$$y = -f(x) = -x^2 - 3x + 2 = g(x)$$
After the second reflection,
$$y = g(-x) = -x^2 + 3x + 2$$

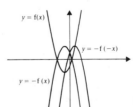

(b) A single equivalent transformation is a $180°$ rotation about the origin.

7 The equation of the curve obtained by reflection is
$$y = f(-x) = 2x^2 + \frac{1}{x} = g(x)$$

The equation of the curve obtained after translation is

$$y = g(x - 4) + 3$$

$$= 2(x - 4)^2 + \frac{1}{x - 4} + 3$$

3.1 Exercise 5

1 (a) $y = (x - 4)^2$ (b) $y = \dfrac{1}{(x - 3)^2}$

(c) $y = -2 - |x|$ (d) $y = 3 - 2(x - 4)^2$

(e) $y = (x + 3)^3 + 2$

(f) $y = (x + 3 - 4)\sqrt{(x + 3)} + 1$
$= (x - 1)\sqrt{(x + 3)} + 1$

2 (a) $y = \dfrac{-1}{x + 6} - 7$ (b) $y = 3x + 7$

(c) $y = 3 - \dfrac{1}{(x - 2)^2}$

3.2 Circular functions

3.2.1 Rotation

3.2 Exercise 1

1 (a) $\sin 50° = 0.77$

(b) e.g. $130°, 410°, 490°, 790°, -230°, -310°$

2 (a) $\cos 163° = -0.96$

(b) $-197°, -163°, 197°, 523°, 557°$

3 (a) $\sin 339° = -0.36$

(b) $201°, 561°, 699°, -21°, -159°$

3.2.2 Transformations

3.2 A

1 $y = \sin \theta°$ maps onto $y = a \sin \theta°$ by a stretch of factor a in the y-direction.

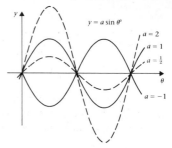

2 (a) $y = \sin \theta°$ maps onto $y = \sin b\theta°$ by a stretch of factor $\dfrac{1}{b}$ in the θ-direction.

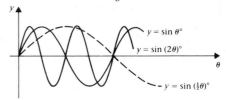

(b) The period of $\sin b\theta°$ is $\left(\dfrac{360}{b}\right)°$.

3

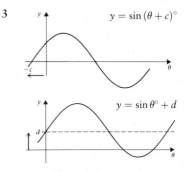

$y = \sin (\theta + c)°$ is obtained by a translation of $-c$ in the θ-direction. $-c$ is known as the **phase shift**.

$y = \sin \theta° + d$ is obtained by a translation of d in the y-direction.

$y = \sin (\theta + c)° + d$ is obtained by a translation of $\begin{bmatrix} -c \\ d \end{bmatrix}$.

4 (a) As in question 2, $y = \cos b\theta°$ has period $\dfrac{360}{b}$.

(b) $y = \cos\theta°$ is mapped onto $y = \cos(b\theta + c)°$ by a stretch of $\dfrac{1}{b}$ followed by a translation in the θ-direction.

Thus $y = \cos(b\theta + c)°$ has period $\dfrac{360}{b}$,

and phase shift $-\dfrac{c}{b}$.

NB   This is not surprising, since the maximum value of $\cos(b\theta + c)°$ is 1, which occurs when $b\theta + c = 0$,

i.e. $\theta = -\dfrac{c}{b}$.

5 One combination is $a = 2$, $b = 3$, $c = 30$

6 $y = \cos\theta°$ is mapped onto $y = a\cos(b\theta + c)° + d$ by stretches of a and $\dfrac{1}{b}$ in the y- and θ-directions followed by a translation $\begin{bmatrix} -c/b \\ d \end{bmatrix}$. Note that the stretches have been done before the translation.

3.2 **Exercise 2**

1 In each case there are alternative correct answers.

(a) $y = 2\cos\theta°$ (b) $y = -3\sin\theta°$

(c) $y = 10\cos\theta°$ (d) $y = 4\cos\theta° + 4$

(e) $y = \sin\theta° + 2$ (f) $y = 3\sin 2\theta°$

(g) $y = 2\cos 6\theta° + 1$

(h) $y = 4\sin(3\theta + 30)° + 3$

2

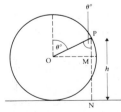

$PN = PM + MN$

So $h = 0.2 + 0.2\cos\theta°$

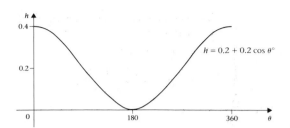

$h = 0.2 + 0.2\cos\theta°$

3 (a) A one-way stretch of scale factor $\frac{1}{3}$ parallel to the x-axis, followed by a translation $\begin{bmatrix} -20 \\ 0 \end{bmatrix}$ and then a one-way stretch of scale factor 2 parallel to the y-axis.

(b) (i) $(180°, 0) \to (60°, 0) \to (40°, 0)$
$\to (40°, 0)$

(ii) $(90°, 1) \to (30°, 1) \to (10°, 1)$
$\to (10°, 2)$

3.2.3 Modelling periodic behaviour

3.2 **B**

1 $\theta = 6t$

2

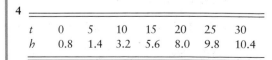

$h = 5.6 - 4.8\cos\theta°$ $h = 5.6 - 4.8\cos 6t°$

3

θ	0	30	60	90	120	150	180
h	0.8	1.4	3.2	5.6	8.0	9.8	10.4

4

t	0	5	10	15	20	25	30
h	0.8	1.4	3.2	5.6	8.0	9.8	10.4

3.2 Exercise 3

1 (a) (i)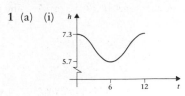

(ii) $h = 0.8 \cos 30t° + 6.5$

(b) $h = 0.65 \cos 30t° + 4.25$

2 From your first graph you will see that the points from April to October, inclusive, do not conform because of the British Summer Time adjustment. To make the data easier to graph you might proceed as follows:

- subtract 1 hour from sunset times in BST,
- change from hours and minutes to hours written in decimal form,
- count days from 12 December (when sunset is earliest).

This should give the table shown below, where t is the number of days after 12 December and s is the sunset hour.

t	20	48	76	103	131	159	187
s	16.05	16.75	17.60	18.40	19.18	19.92	20.35

t	215	243	261	299	327	355
s	20.17	19.45	18.43	17.37	16.43	15.90

The graph of s against t is an approximate sine or cosine curve, having amplitude about 2.28 (hours). A possible equation is

$$s = 18.11 - 2.28 \cos \left(\frac{360t°}{365} \right)$$

3 $l = 12 + 2.5 \cos 360t°$

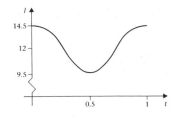

4E (a) $E = \sin \left(\frac{360t}{28} \right)°$

$I = \sin \left(\frac{360t}{33} \right)°$

(c) Critical days occur every 11.5, 14 and 16.5 days respectively for the three cycles.

(d) All these cycles are critical about once every $7\frac{1}{4}$ years.

3.2.4 Inverse trigonometric functions

3.2 C

1 (a) $x = 23.6$

(b)

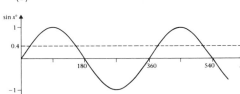

From the graph the other solutions are:
$180 - 23.6 = 156.4$, $360 + 23.6 = 383.6$,
$540 - 23.6 = 516.4$

(c) $3600 + 23.6 = 3623.6$,
$3600 + 156.4 = 3756.4$

(d) $360n + 23.6$, $360n + 156.4$

(e) Yes. For example, if $n = -1$, the solutions $23.6 - 360$ and $156.4 - 360$ are generated. The graph has period 360 in both positive and negative directions.

2 (a) $p = 30$

(b) $540 - 30$, $720 + 30$

(c) $180 \times 20 + 30 = 3600 + 30$,
$180 \times 21 - 30 = 3780 - 30$

(d) $180n + 30$ if n is even, $180n - 30$ if n is odd.
Using the $(-1)^n$ notation,
$x = 180n + (-1)^n 30$.

3 (a) The principal value is 44.4
   The general solution is $180n + (-1)^n 44.4$

(b) The principal value is -44.4
   The general solution is $180n - (-1)^n 44.4$

(c) The principal value is 45.6
   Other solutions are $360 - 45.6$, $360 + 45.6$, $720 + 45.6$, $720 - 45.6$, etc.
   The general solution is $360n \pm 45.6$

3.2 Exercise 4

1 (a) $11.5°$ (b) $25.8°$ (c) $-21.1°$

   (d) $137.7°$ (e) $90°$ (f) $180°$

2 (a) $17.5, 162.5, 377.5, 522.5, -197.5, -342.5$

   (b) $36.9, 323.1, 396.9, 683.1, -36.9, -323.1$

   (c) $107.5, 252.5, 467.5, 612.5, -107.5, -252.5$

   (d) $-30, -150, 210, 330, 570, 690$

   (e) $-180, 180, 540$

   (f) $19.5, 160.5, 379.5, 520.5, -199.5, -340.5$

3 (a) $\sin x° = 0.2$
   Calculator value for $x = 11.5$ (to 3 s.f.)
   Solutions are $90 \pm 78.5 \pm 360n$.

(b) Calculator value for $x = 143$ (to 3 s.f.)
   General solution $x = \pm 143 \pm 360n$

Other forms are possible in both (a) and (b).

3.2.5 Solving equations

3.2 D

1 If $h = 6$,

$$6 = 2.5 \sin 30t + 5 \Rightarrow \sin 30t = 0.4$$

Using a calculator, $\sin x° = 0.4 \Rightarrow x = 23.58$ and, using the symmetry of the sine graph, $x = 156.42$ is also a solution. So

$$30t = 23.58 \text{ or } 156.42$$
$$\Rightarrow \quad t = 0.786 \text{ hours or } 5.214 \text{ hours}$$

The height is 6 m at 0047 hours and 0513 hours.

You could find subsequent times by extending the range of values of x beyond 360. The next two are

$$x = 383.58 \text{ and } 516.42$$
$$\Rightarrow 30t = 383.58 \text{ and } 516.42$$
$$\Rightarrow \quad t = 12.786 \text{ and } 17.214$$

giving, as expected, 1247 and 1747.

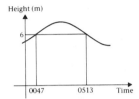

2 From the graph, the depth is greater than 6 m between 0047 and 0513, i.e. for 4 hours 26 min, twice each day.

3.2 Exercise 5

1 (a) $8 \sin 10t° = 5 \Rightarrow \sin 10t° = 0.625$
   $\Rightarrow \sin x° = 0.625$ where $x = 10t$
   If $0 \leq t \leq 60$, then $0 \leq x \leq 600$
   $x = 38.7$ or 141.3 or 398.7 or 501.3
   $\Rightarrow t = 3.87, 14.13, 39.87$ or 50.13

(b) $7 \cos (t + 35)° = 4$. So, if $x = t + 35$,
   $\cos x° = 0.571$
   $\Rightarrow x = 55.2$ or 304.8
   $\Rightarrow t + 35 = 55.2$ (or 304.8)
   $\Rightarrow t = 20.2$, since remaining solutions are not in the required interval.

(c) $t = 31.2$ or 41.6

(d) $t = 51.6$

2 $5.6 - 4.8 \cos 6t° = 9 \Rightarrow \cos 6t° = \dfrac{-3.4}{4.8}$

$$\Rightarrow \quad t = 22.5, \quad 37.5$$

The chair is above 9 metres for $37.5 - 22.5 = 15$ seconds.

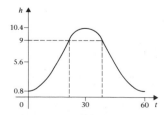

3 (a) $5 + 2.5 \sin 30t° = 6.7 \Rightarrow \sin 30t° = \dfrac{1.7}{2.5}$

$\Rightarrow t = 1.43, 4.57, 13.43, 16.57$

Times: 0126, 0434, 1326, 1634

(b) $5 + 2.5 \sin 30t° = 4.5 \Rightarrow \sin 30t° = \dfrac{-0.5}{2.5}$

$\Rightarrow t = 6.38, 11.62, 18.38, 23.62$

Times: 0623, 1137, 1823, 2337

4 (a) $2 + 1.5 \sin 500t° = 2.75 \Rightarrow \sin 500t° = 0.5$
$\Rightarrow t = 0.06, 0.3$
0.06 and 0.3 seconds from the start and
repeatedly every 0.72 seconds

(b) $2 + 1.5 \sin 500t° = 2 \Rightarrow \sin 500t° = 0$
$\Rightarrow t = 0, 0.36, 0.72, \ldots$
Every 0.36 seconds from the start

(c) $2 + 1.5 \sin 500t° = 3.5 \Rightarrow \sin 500t° = 1$
$\Rightarrow t = 0.18$
0.18 seconds from the start and every 0.72
seconds thereafter

3.2.6 $\tan \theta°$

3.2 E

1 (a) $5 \tan \theta°$ (b) the acute angle whose
tangent is 3; $\tan^{-1} 3 \approx 71.6°$

2 (a)   (b)

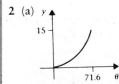

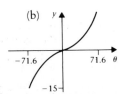

3 $\tan \theta° = \dfrac{a}{b}$

$\dfrac{\sin \theta°}{\cos \theta°} = \dfrac{a}{c} \div \dfrac{b}{c} = \dfrac{a}{b}$

4 All real numbers θ for which $\cos \theta° \neq 0$

5 $-90° < \tan^{-1} x < 90°$

3.2 Exercise 6

1 (a) $45°$ (b) $-80.5°$ (c) $0°$

2 (a)

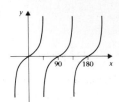

$y = \tan 2x°$

(b)

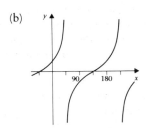

$y = \tan(x + 45)°$

3 (a) $x = 71.6$ or $180 + 71.6 = 251.6$

(b) $\tan(2x + 30)° = 0.8$
$\Rightarrow 2x + 30 = 38.7$ or 218.7 or 398.7
or 578.7
$\Rightarrow x = 4.4$ or 94.4 or 184.4 or 274.4

(c) $\tan x° = \pm 1$
$\tan x° = +1 \Rightarrow x = 45$ or 225
$\tan x° = -1 \Rightarrow x = 135$ or 315

(d) $4 \sin x° = 3 \cos x°$

$\Rightarrow \dfrac{4 \sin x°}{\cos x°} = 3$

$\Rightarrow \tan x° = \dfrac{3}{4}$

$\Rightarrow x = 36.9$ or 216.9

4 (a) $x = 71.6 \pm 180n$ $(n = 0, 1, 2, \ldots)$

(b) $2x + 30 = 38.7 \pm 180n$

$2x = 8.7 \pm 180n$

$x = 4.4 \pm 90n$ (to 2 s.f.)

$(n = 0, 1, 2, \ldots)$

3.3 Growth functions

3.3.1 Exponential growth

3.3 Exercise 1

1 Although the growth factors show slight variations, they are all 1.20 to 3 s.f. Allowing for the error introduced in rounding the profit figures, the profit is growing exponentially.

2 In each case the annual growth factor is 1.09. This means that the amount in the account at the end of the year is 109% of that at the beginning, so the increase or interest rate is 9%.

Since the growth factor is constant, the growth is exponential.

3

Age	Pocket money (£)	Growth factor
0	50	
1	60	1.2
2	70	1.17
3	80	1.14
4	90	1.13
5	100	1.11

Since the yearly growth factor is not constant, this is not exponential growth.

4 Notice that the time intervals are sometimes 4 years and sometimes 8 years.

Over the 4-year intervals, the growth factor is approximately 1.12 in each case.

Over the 8-year intervals, the growth factor is approximately 1.24 in each case.

Over two 4-year intervals the population would increase by a factor of 1.12 twice, giving an 8-year factor of $1.12 \times 1.12 \approx 1.25$.

The growth is therefore approximately exponential.

5 (a)

Time (s)	0	1	2	3	4	5
Charge (V)	9	8	7	6	5	4
Growth factor		0.89	0.88	0.86	0.83	0.80

Time (s)	6	7	8	9
Charge (V)	3	2	1	0
Growth factor	0.75	0.67	0.50	0

The decay is not exponential.

(b)

Time (s)	0	1	2	3	4	5
Charge (V)	9	6.75	5.063	3.797	2.848	2.136
Growth factor		0.75	0.75	0.75	0.75	0.75

The decay is exponential with growth factor 0.75.

3.3.2 Indices

3.3 A

1 (a) (i) $2^m 2^n = (\underbrace{2 \times 2 \times \cdots \times 2}_{m \text{ factors}})$

$\times (\underbrace{2 \times 2 \times \cdots \times 2}_{n \text{ factors}})$

$= (\underbrace{2 \times 2 \times \cdots \times 2}_{(m+n) \text{ factors}}) = 2^{m+n}$

(ii) A similar argument may be used, or the observation that, from (i),

$$2^{m-n} 2^n = 2^m$$

(b) $(2^m)^2 = 2^m \times 2^m = 2^{m+m} = 2^{2m}$
$(2^m)^3 = (2^m)^2 \times 2^m = 2^{2m+m} = 2^{3m}$
The nth term in this sequence of results is

$$(2^m)^n = 2^{mn}$$

2 $2^0 = 1$. Initially (when $t = 0$) the area of algae was 1 cm^2.

The result may be obtained in many ways from the rules found in part (a); for example,

$$2^0 = 2^{1-1} = 2^1 \div 2^1 = 1$$

3 (a) 0.5 cm, $2^{-1} = \dfrac{1}{2}$

(b) (i) $2^{-2} = \dfrac{1}{4}$ (ii) $2^{-3} = \dfrac{1}{8}$ (iii) $2^{-n} = \dfrac{1}{2^n}$

4 (a) $3^{-2} = \dfrac{1}{3^2} = \dfrac{1}{9}$ (b) $5^0 = 1$

(c) $10^{-6} = \dfrac{1}{10^6}$ (d) $a^0 = 1$ (e) $a^{-n} = \dfrac{1}{a^n}$

5 (a) $2^{-4} 2^{-3} = 2^{-7}$

(b) $2^{-4} = \dfrac{1}{16}$, $2^{-3} = \dfrac{1}{8}$

(c) $2^{-7} = \dfrac{1}{2^7} = \dfrac{1}{128} = \dfrac{1}{16} \times \dfrac{1}{8} = 2^{-4} \times 2^{-3}$

(d) (i) $2^{-3} \times 2^0 = \dfrac{1}{8} \times 1 = \dfrac{1}{8} = 2^{-3} = 2^{-3+0}$

(ii) $2^{-1} \times 2 = \dfrac{1}{2} \times 2 = 1 = 2^0 = 2^{-1+1}$

(iii) $2^{-4} \div 2^{-3} = \dfrac{1}{16} \div \dfrac{1}{8} = \dfrac{1}{2} = 2^{-1}$

$= 2^{-4-(-3)}$

(iv) $2 \div 2^{-3} = 2 \div \dfrac{1}{8} = 16 = 2^4 = 2^{1-(-3)}$

6 (a), (b), (d) and (e) are equal.

7 (a) $(2^{\frac{1}{2}})^2 = 2^{\frac{1}{2} \times 2}$ (or $2^{\frac{1}{2}+\frac{1}{2}}$) $= 2^1 = 2$

(b) Since $(\sqrt{2})^2 = 2$, $2^{\frac{1}{2}}$ is defined as $\sqrt{2}$

Since $(2^{\frac{1}{3}})^3 = 2$, $2^{\frac{1}{3}}$ is defined as $\sqrt[3]{2}$

Similarly, $2^{\frac{1}{n}} = \sqrt[n]{2}$ and $a^{\frac{1}{n}} = \sqrt[n]{a}$

8 (a) $9^{\frac{1}{2}} = \sqrt{9} = 3$

(b) $8^{\frac{1}{3}} = \sqrt[3]{8} = 2$

(c) $64^{\frac{1}{4}} = \sqrt[4]{64} = \sqrt{(\sqrt{64})} = \sqrt{8}$ (or $2\sqrt{2}$)

(d) $81^{0.5} = 9$

9 (a) $\left(4^{\frac{1}{q}}\right)^p = 4^{\frac{1}{q}} \times 4^{\frac{1}{q}} \times \cdots \times 4^{\frac{1}{q}}$ (p factors)

$= 4^{\frac{1}{q}+\frac{1}{q}+\cdots+\frac{1}{q}}$ (p terms)

$= 4^{\frac{p}{q}}$

$(4^p)^{\frac{1}{q}} = (4 \times 4 \times \ldots \times 4)^{\frac{1}{q}}$ (p factors)

$= 4^{\frac{1}{q}} \times 4^{\frac{1}{q}} \times \ldots \times 4^{\frac{1}{q}}$

$= 4^{\frac{p}{q}}$

(b) Similarly,

(i) $8^{\frac{2}{3}} = \left(8^{\frac{1}{3}}\right)^2 = 2^2 = 4$

(ii) $16^{\frac{3}{4}} = \left(16^{\frac{1}{4}}\right)^3 = 2^3 = 8$

10 You should investigate all the laws and include cases in which an index is negative and others in which an index is not a whole number or a simple fraction.

3.3 Exercise 2

1 (a) 2^5 (b) 2^{10} (c) 2^5 (d) 2^{15}

2 (a) x^5 (b) a^{10} (c) d^5 (d) b^{15}

3 (a) $\frac{1}{9}$ (b) $\frac{1}{1000}$ (c) 27 (d) 125

4 (a) y^{-2} (b) c^5 (c) $x^0 = 1$ (d) x^6

5 (a) 2 (b) $\frac{1}{5}$ (c) $\frac{1}{125}$

(d) 100 (e) 0.1

6 3.32

3.3.3 Growth factors

3.3 B

1 (a)

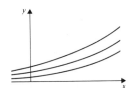

The family of graphs is as shown. The graph of the function cuts the y-axis where $y = K$.

(b) If $y = K \times a^x$, $y = K$ when $x = 0$

2 (a) $y = 1$ when $t = 0$ (b) $y = K$ when $t = 0$

3

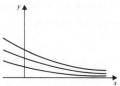

This time the graph shows exponential decay. The graph of $y = K \times (\frac{1}{2})^x$ is obtained by reflecting that of $y = K \times 2^x$ in the y-axis.

Again, K is the value of y when $x = 0$.

4 (a)
$y = 5 \times 3^t$

(b)
$y = 2 \times \left(\frac{1}{3}\right)^t$

(c)
$y = \frac{1}{2} \times 5^t$

(d)
$y = 2 \times \left(\frac{1}{5}\right)^t$

5 (a) $K = 1.5 \times 10^6$, i.e. the initial value.

(b) In 1700, $P = 6.1 \times 10^6 = Ka^{634}$, since
$t = 634$
i.e. $6.1 \times 10^6 = 1.5 \times 10^6 a^{634}$

$\Rightarrow a^{634} = \dfrac{6.1}{1.5}$

$\Rightarrow \quad a = \left(\dfrac{6.1}{1.5}\right)^{\frac{1}{634}} = 1.002\,22$

(c) In 1990, $t = 924$
$P = Ka^{924} = 1.5 \times 10^6 \times 1.002\,22^{924}$

$\qquad = 11.59 \times 10^6$

(d) The annual growth factor since 1700 has been considerably greater than 1.002 22, since the population of the United Kingdom is approximately 55 million.

3.3 Exercise 3

1 (a) There will be 14 400 bacteria after 2 hours.

(b) There will be 1 000 000 bacteria after 4–5 hours.

(c) Since the growth factor is constant, a growth function can be used.

Number of bacteria $= 400 \times 6^t$

2 (a) 1.08

(b) The value of the investment after n years is £4000×1.08^n. When the value is £5000,

$5000 = 4000 \times 1.08^n$

Dividing by 4000,

$1.25 = 1.08^n$

(c) $n \approx 2.899$. In practice, there would be £5000 at the end of the third year.

3 (a) The growth factor over the 10 days is
$\dfrac{2.48}{10} = 0.248$.

The daily growth factor is $(0.248)^{\frac{1}{10}} = 0.87$.

(b) $M = 10 \times 0.87^t$

(c)

t (days)	0	2	3	6	7	10
Mass (kg)	10	7.57	6.57	4.34	3.77	2.48
M	10	7.57	6.59	4.34	3.77	2.48

(d) After 3 weeks, when $t = 21$ the mass is 0.54 kg.

(e) Approximately 5 days

4 If $V = Ka^t$,

$V = 15$ when $t = 0 \Rightarrow K = 15$

Growth factor $a = \left(\frac{6}{15}\right)^{\frac{1}{12}} \approx 0.93$

$V = 15 \times \left(\frac{6}{15}\right)^{\frac{1}{12}t} \approx 15 \times 0.93^t$

3.3.4 Logarithms

3.3 C

1 (a) $2^6 = 64 \Rightarrow \log_2 64 = 6$

(b) $2^{-3} = \frac{1}{8} \Rightarrow \log_2 \frac{1}{8} = -3$

(c) $2^1 = 2 \Rightarrow \log_2 2 = 1$

(d) $2^{\frac{1}{2}} = \sqrt{2} \Rightarrow \log_2 \sqrt{2} = \frac{1}{2}$

2 (a) $3^2 = 9 \Rightarrow \log_3 9 = 2$ (b) 3

(c) -2 (d) 0 (e) -3

(f) $\frac{1}{4}$, since $\sqrt[4]{3} = 3^{\frac{1}{4}}$

(g) $\frac{1}{2}$, since $2 = 4^{\frac{1}{2}}$ (h) 1

(i) cannot be found since 3^x is always positive.

3 (a) $a^0 = 1 \Rightarrow \log_a 1 = 0$

(b) $a^1 = a \Rightarrow \log_a a = 1$

(c) $a^{-1} = \dfrac{1}{a} \Rightarrow \log_a \dfrac{1}{a} = -1$

(d) $\log_a a^2 = 2$

4 (a) $\log_{10} 10^{3.7} = 3.7$ (b) $10^{\log_{10} 3.7} = 3.7$

This is to be expected, since $\log_{10} x$ and 10^x are inverse functions. In each case 3.7 is operated on by the function and its inverse and so is its own image.

5 (a)   (i) $\log_2 8 = 3$ (ii) $\log_2 16 = 4$
      (iii) $\log_2 128 = 7$

(b) $8 \times 16 = 128$ becomes $2^3 \times 2^4 = 2^7$ so $a = 3, b = 4, c = 7$ and $a + b = c$.

(c) Since $a = \log_2 8, b = \log_2 16, c = \log_2 128$ it follows that $\log_2 8 + \log_2 16 = \log_2 128$.

6 As with question 5, $2 + 3 = 5$, but $2 = \log_3 9, 3 = \log_3 27$ and $5 = \log_3 243 = \log_3 (9 \times 27)$ so $\log_3 9 + \log_3 27 = \log_3 (9 \times 27)$.

7 (b)   (i) $\log_{10} 3 = 0.4771$
      (ii) $\log_{10} 5 = 0.6990$

(c) $\log_{10} 15 = \log_{10} (3 \times 5)$
$\phantom{(c) \log_{10} 15} = \log_{10} 3 + \log_{10} 5 = 0.4771 + 0.6990$
$\phantom{(c) \log_{10} 15} = 1.1761$

8 $\log_{10} 9 = 0.954, \quad \log_{10} 8 = 0.903,$
$\log_{10} 72 = 1.857 = 0.954 + 0.903$

9 $\log_a m + \log_a \dfrac{l}{m} = \log_a m \times \dfrac{l}{m} = \log_a l$

$\Rightarrow \log_a l - \log_a m = \log_a \dfrac{l}{m}$

10 $\log_{10} \dfrac{1}{2} = \log_{10} 1 - \log_{10} 2 = 0 - 0.3010$
$\phantom{10 \log_{10} \dfrac{1}{2}} = -0.3010$

$\log_{10} 1.5 = \log_{10} \dfrac{3}{2} = \log_{10} 3 - \log_{10} 2$
$\phantom{\log_{10} 1.5} = 0.4771 - 0.3010 = 0.1761$

$\log_{10} 2.5 = \log_{10} \dfrac{10}{4} = \log_{10} \dfrac{10}{2 \times 2}$
$\phantom{\log_{10} 2.5} = \log_{10} 10 - \log_{10} 2 - \log_{10} 2$
$\phantom{\log_{10} 2.5} = 1 - 2 \times 0.3010 = 0.398$

$\log_{10} 4 = 0.6020 \qquad \log_{10} 5 = 0.6990$

$\log_{10} 6 = 0.7781 \qquad \log_{10} 8 = 0.9030$

$\log_{10} 9 = 0.9542$

3.3 Exercise 4

1 (a) $\log_3 9 = 2$ (b) $\log_4 \left(\frac{1}{64}\right) = -3$

(c) $\log_{0.5} 4 = -2$ (d) $\log_{\frac{1}{8}} 2 = -\frac{1}{3}$

(e) $\log_{27} 9 = \frac{2}{3}$

2 (a) -2 (b) 3   (c) -1 (d) $-\frac{2}{3}$

3 (a) By the laws of logarithms,

$\log_3 9 + \log_3 27 - \log_3 81$

$= \log_3 \left(\dfrac{9 \times 27}{81}\right) = \log_3 3 = 1$

(b) $\log_5 15 - \log_5 3 = \log_5 \left(\dfrac{15}{3}\right) = \log_5 5 = 1$

(c) $2\log_7 \sqrt{7} = \log_7 \sqrt{7} + \log_7 \sqrt{7}$
$\phantom{(c) 2\log_7 \sqrt{7}} = \log_7 (\sqrt{7} \times \sqrt{7}) = \log_7 7 = 1$

4

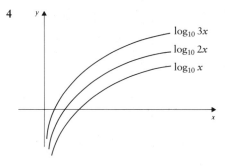

The graphs of $\log_{10} 2x$ and $\log_{10} 3x$ can be considered *either* as scalings of $\log_{10} x$ by factors of $\frac{1}{2}, \frac{1}{3}$ from the y-axis *or* as translations in the y direction.

By the laws of logs,

$\log_{10} 2x = \log_{10} 2 + \log_{10} x$

$\phantom{\log_{10} 2x} = \log_{10} x + 0.3010$

$\log_{10} 3x = \log_{10} 3 + \log_{10} x$

$\phantom{\log_{10} 3x} = \log_{10} x + 0.4771$

5 (a) $\log 1.05 = 0.0212, \quad \log 1.267 = 0.1028$

$\log (1.05 \times 1.267) = 0.0212 + 0.1028$

$\qquad\qquad\qquad\quad = 0.1240$

Using the table in reverse,

$\log 1.330 = 0.1240,$

so $1.05 \times 1.267 = 1.330$

(b) $\log_{10} 10.5 = \log_{10} (10 \times 1.05)$

$\qquad\qquad = \log_{10} 10 + \log_{10} 1.05$

$\qquad\qquad = 1 + 0.0212 = 1.0212$

$\log_{10} 1267 = \log_{10} (10^3 \times 1.267)$

$\qquad\qquad = 3 + 0.1028 = 3.1028$

$\log_{10} (10.5 \times 1267) = 1.0212 + 3.1028$

$\qquad\qquad\qquad\qquad = 4.1240$

Now, since $\log 1.330 = 0.1240$

$4.1240 = 4 + \log 1.330$

$\qquad\quad = \log 10^4 + \log 1.330 = \log 13\,300$

$10.5 \times 1267 \approx 13\,300$

6 $\log_5 5! = \log_5 (5 \times 4 \times 3 \times 2 \times 1)$

$\qquad\quad = \log_5 5 + \log_5 (4 \times 3 \times 2 \times 1)$

$\qquad\quad = \log_5 5 + \log_5 4!$

$\qquad\quad = 1 + 1.9746$

$\qquad\quad = 2.9746$

7 $\quad t = \log_2 1000$

$2^9 = 512, \quad 2^{10} = 1024 \qquad 9 < t < 10$

$t = 9.97$

3.3.5 The equation $a^x = b$

3.3 D

1 (a) (i) $\log_{10} 49 = 1.6902, \quad \log_{10} 7 = 0.8451,$
$\log_{10} 49 = 2 \log_{10} 7$

(ii) $\log_{10} 64 = 1.806, \quad \log_{10} 2 = 0.301,$
$\log_{10} 64 = 6 \times \log_{10} 2$

(iii) $\log_{10} 125 = 2.0969, \quad \log_{10} 5 = 0.6990,$
$\log_{10} 125 = 3 \times \log_{10} 5$

(b) The results above suggest that
$\log_{10} m^p = p \log_{10} m.$

2 (a) $\log_a m^2 = \log_a (m \times m)$

$\qquad\qquad = \log_a m + \log_a m = 2 \log_a m$

(b) For any positive index,

$\log_a m^p = \log_a \underbrace{m \times m \times \cdots \times m}_{p \text{ factors}}$

$\qquad\qquad = \underbrace{\log_a m + \log_a m + \cdots + \log_a m}_{p \text{ terms}}$

$\qquad\qquad = p \log_a m$

3 $\log 2^x = x \log 2$

If $2^x = 7$, then $\log 2^x = \log 7$

$\Rightarrow x \log 2 = 7$

$\Rightarrow x = \dfrac{\log 7}{\log 2} = 2.807$

4 (a) 1% interest represents a monthly growth factor of 1.01. After m months the amount in the account will be 1000×1.01^m. There will be £2000 in the account when $1000 \times 1.01^m = 2000$. Dividing by 1000,

$1.01^m = 2$

(b) $\qquad\qquad 1.01^m = 2$

$\log (1.01^m) = \log 2$

$m \log 1.01 = \log 2$

$m = \dfrac{\log 2}{\log 1.01} = 69.66$

The amount will be a little over £2000 (£2006.76) after 70 months.

5 $t = 4.98$

The half-life is 5.0 days.

3.3 Exercise 5

1 (a) $x = 5$ (b) $x = 2.5$ (c) $x = 2.67$

    (d) $x = 2.10$ (e) $x = 1.38$ (f) $x = 2.71$

2 (a) $2 \times 2 \times 2 \times 2 \times 2 = 32 \Rightarrow 2^5 = 32$

    (b) $9 \times 9 \times 3 = 243$
$$\Rightarrow 9^2 \times 9^{\frac{1}{2}} = 243 \Rightarrow 9^{2.5} = 243$$

    (c) $8 \times 8 \times 2 \times 2 = 256$
$$\Rightarrow \quad 8^2 \times 2^2 = 256$$
$$\Rightarrow 8^2 \times \left(8^{\frac{1}{3}}\right)^2 = 256$$
$$\Rightarrow \quad 8^2 \times 8^{\frac{2}{3}} = 256$$
$$\Rightarrow \quad 8^{2.67} = 256$$

3 (a) The number of bacteria after t hours is given by 250×3.7^t.

    (b) There will be 10 000 bacteria when
$$250 \times 3.7^t = 10\,000$$
$$\Rightarrow \quad 3.7^t = 40$$
$$\Rightarrow \quad t = 2.82$$
i.e. after 2 hours 49 minutes.

4 The time when there is $\frac{1}{5}$ of the original charge is given by the solution of
$$0.9^t = 0.2$$
i.e. $t = 15.28$ (seconds)

5 The equation used was $1.08^n = 1.25$.
$n = 2.90$ (years).

6 $1000 = 470 \times 1.029^t$
$$\Rightarrow 1.029^t = \frac{1000}{470} = 2.128$$
$$\Rightarrow \quad t = \frac{\log 2.128}{\log 1.029} = 26.4$$
i.e. the population will reach one thousand million in 2006.

7 They will be equal t years after 1980, where
$$t = \frac{\log 995 - \log 470}{\log 1.029 - \log 1.014} = 51$$

3.3.6 Using logarithms in experimental work

3.3 Exercise 6

1 3

2 $Q = 65 \times 0.35^t$

3 $P = 3.2\sqrt{L}$; 8.7 should be 7.8.
(There may be some variation in answers to questions 2 and 3, depending on the graphs drawn.)

4 13.2

3.4 The number e

3.4.1 e^x

3.4 **A**

1 (a)

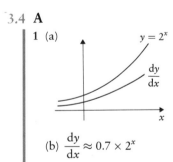

    (b) $\dfrac{dy}{dx} \approx 0.7 \times 2^x$

2 (a)

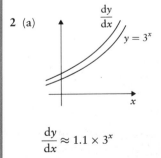

    $\dfrac{dy}{dx} \approx 1.1 \times 3^x$

(b)

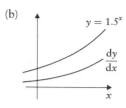

$$\frac{dy}{dx} \approx 0.4 \times 1.5^x$$

(c)

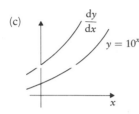

$$\frac{dy}{dx} \approx 2.3 \times 10^x$$

3

a	$\dfrac{d}{dx}(a^x)$
1.5	0.4×1.5^x
2	0.7×2^x
3	1.1×3^x
10	2.3×10^x

The value of a will lie somewhere between 2 and 3, probably around 2.7.

4 Since multiplication by k represents a scaling by a factor of k in the y-direction, the gradient will also be multiplied by k.

$$\frac{d}{dx}(ke^x) = ke^x$$

5 (a) The x-coordinate of Q is $x + 0.001$
$\Rightarrow$ the y-coordinate of Q is
$$2^{x+0.001} = 2^{0.001} \times 2^x.$$

(b) The gradient is

$$\frac{\text{change in } y}{\text{change in } x} = \frac{2^{0.001} \times 2^x - 2^x}{0.001}$$

(c) $$\frac{2^{0.001} \times 2^x - 2^x}{0.001} = \frac{(2^{0.001} - 1)2^x}{0.001}$$
$$\approx 0.693 \times 2^x$$

(d) You could zoom in even more so that the difference in x between P and Q is even less than 0.001. For example,

$$\frac{2^{0.00001} - 1}{0.00001} \times 2^x \approx 0.6931 \times 2^x$$

6 $$\frac{5^{0.00001} - 1}{0.00001} \times 5^x \approx 1.6094 \times 5^x$$

3.4 Exercise 1

1 (a) (i) 20.09　　(ii) 164.0　　(iii) 0.1353
　　(iv) 0.249　　(v) 1.649

(b) For many calculators it is 230.2 (to 4 s.f.) because $e^{230.3} > 10^{100}$.

2 (a)

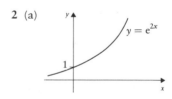

(b)

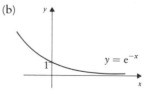

3

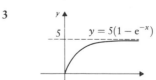

4 (a) (i) When $t = 0$, $y = 5$　　(ii) 0.677

(iii)

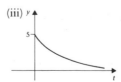

The graph exhibits exponential decay.

(b) Since $0.5 > 0.2$, it decays more rapidly.

5 $y = 4e^t \Rightarrow \dfrac{dy}{dt} = 4e^t = y$

The rate of growth is equal to the size of the colony. It is growing at a rate equal to its size, i.e. at 500 bacteria per hour.

6E $y = e^x$

$$\dfrac{dy}{dx} = \lim_{h \to 0} \left(\dfrac{e^{x+h} - e^x}{h} \right)$$

$$= \lim_{h \to 0} \left(\dfrac{e^x e^h - e^x}{h} \right)$$

$$= \lim_{h \to 0} \left(\dfrac{e^x (e^h - 1)}{h} \right)$$

$$= e^x \lim_{h \to 0} \left(\dfrac{e^h - 1}{h} \right)$$

$$= e^x$$

3.4.2 e^{ax}

3.4 B

1 (b) (i) $a = 1.46$ (ii) $a = 1.77$
 (iii) $a = 0.63$

2 (a) (i) $a > 0$

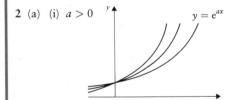

(ii) $a < 0$

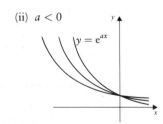

If $a = 0$, $y = e^0 = 1$. The graph is a straight line.

(b) If $a > b > 0$ then e^{ax} lies above e^{bx} for positive values of x and below e^{bx} for negative values.

3 (a) 1.61   (b) 2.08   (c) 0.69

4 (a) $\dfrac{d}{dx}(e^{0.69x}) = \dfrac{d}{dx}(2^x) = 0.69 \times 2^x$
$$= 0.69 \times e^{0.69x}$$

(b) As in (a), $\dfrac{d}{dx}(e^{5x}) = 5e^{5x}$

5 (a) e^{2q} (b) q

(c) It multiplies the gradient of the graph by $_\cdot$

(d) $2g$, from part (c)

(e) The gradient is e^x, which at R is e^{2q}. Therefore the gradient at Q is $2 \times e^{2q}$.

(f) $\dfrac{d}{dx}(e^{2x}) = 2 \times e^{2x}$

3.4 C

(a) $\displaystyle\int e^{ax}\, dx = \dfrac{1}{a} e^{ax} + \text{constant}$

(b) (i) $\dfrac{d}{dx}(f(ax)) = a\, g(ax)$

The graph of $f(ax)$ is mapped onto the graph of $f(x)$ by a one-way stretch, factor $\dfrac{1}{a}$, from the y-axis. This squashing transformation increases the gradient by a factor of a.

(ii) $\displaystyle\int g(ax)\, dx = \dfrac{1}{a} f(ax) + \text{constant}$

3.4 Exercise 2

1 (a) $4e^{4x}$ (b) $-2e^{-2x}$

(c) $\dfrac{d}{dx}(e^x)^5 = \dfrac{d}{dx}(e^{5x}) = 5e^{5x}$

(d) $\dfrac{d}{dx}\left(\dfrac{1}{e^{3x}}\right) = \dfrac{d}{dx}(e^{-3x}) = -3e^{-3x}$

(e) $20e^{4x}$ (f) $e^x - \dfrac{1}{e^x}$

(g) $\tfrac{1}{2}e^{\frac{1}{2}x}$ (h) $-45e^{-9x} = -\dfrac{45}{e^{9x}}$

2 (a) $\frac{1}{4}e^{4x}$ (b) $-\frac{1}{2}e^{-2x}$ (c) $\frac{1}{5}e^{5x}$

(d) $-\frac{1}{3}e^{-3x}$ (e) $\frac{5}{4}e^{4x}$ (f) $e^{x} - \frac{1}{e^{x}}$

(g) $2\sqrt{e^{x}}$ (h) $-\frac{5}{9e^{9x}}$

The constant of integration has been omitted in all cases.

3 (a) 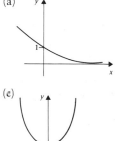   (b)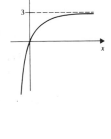

(c)

4 (a), (b)

t	0	2	4	6	8
x	10	7.8	6.1	4.7	3.7

(b) 3.7 becomes 13.7 mg.

(c)

t	0	2	4	6	8
x	13.7	10.7	8.3	6.5	5.0

(d)

t	0	2	4	6	8
x	15.0	11.7	9.1	7.1	5.5

t	0	2	4	6	8
x	15.5	12.1	9.4	7.3	5.7

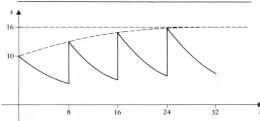

The maximum level of the drug in the body approaches 16 mg, which is approximately 1.6 times the administered dose. (In fact, you can show that it is $\dfrac{10e}{e-1} = 15.82$ mg.)

5

t	0	2	4	6	8
x	16	12.5	9.7	7.6	$5.9 \rightarrow 15.9$

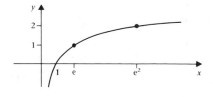

Thus, with a single booster dose, the required level is reached immediately and subsequent doses of 10 mg give a stable level of 16 mg.

3.4.3 The natural log

3.4 D

1 (a)   (i) $x = \ln 1 \Rightarrow e^{x} = 1 \Rightarrow x = 0$
     (ii) $\ln e = \ln e^{1} = 1$
     (iii) $\ln e^{2} = 2$
     (iv) $\ln \dfrac{1}{e} = \ln e^{-1} = -1$
     (v) $\ln \dfrac{1}{e^{5}} = \ln e^{-5} = -5$
     (vi) $\ln(-1) = x \Rightarrow e^{x} = -1$, which has no solution. That is, $\ln(-1)$ is not defined.

(b)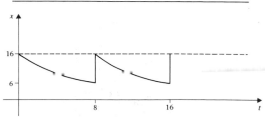

2 (a) $b = e^a$ (b) (b, a)

(c) From the triangle 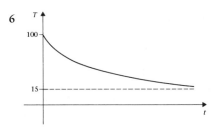, the gradient of

$y = e^x$ at P is $\dfrac{\beta}{\alpha}$. From the triangle

$\alpha\,\llcorner\!\!\!\!\!\diagup^{\beta}$, the gradient of $y = \ln x$ at Q is

$\dfrac{\alpha}{\beta}$. With x and y interchanged, the gradient at Q is the reciprocal of the gradient at P.

(d) Using a result in (c), the gradient is $\dfrac{1}{e^a}$.

(e) The gradient of $y = \ln x$ at Q is $\dfrac{1}{e^a} = \dfrac{1}{b}$.

The x-coordinate of Q is b and so

$$\dfrac{d}{dx}(\ln x) = \dfrac{1}{x}.$$

3.4 Exercise 3

1 (a) 1.25   (b) -1.05 (c) 1.95

2 (a) $\ln 3 + \ln 4 = \ln(3 \times 4) = \ln 12$

(b) $\ln 10 - \ln 2 = \ln \frac{10}{2} = \ln 5$

(c) $3 \ln 5 = \ln 5^3 = \ln 125$

(d) $\dfrac{\ln 20}{\ln 4} \neq \ln 5$ since this does not correspond to one of the laws of logs.

3 (a) $\ln x^3 = 3 \ln x$

(b) $\ln 4x = \ln 4 + \ln x$

(c) $\ln \frac{1}{3}x = \ln x - \ln 3$

4 (a) $\dfrac{4}{x}$

(b) $\dfrac{d}{dx}(\ln x^3) = \dfrac{d}{dx}(3 \ln x) = \dfrac{3}{x}$

(c) $\dfrac{d}{dx}(\ln 4x) = \dfrac{d}{dx}(\ln 4 + \ln x) = \dfrac{1}{x}$

5 90% represents 180 individuals.

$$180 = \dfrac{200}{1 + 199e^{-0.2t}}$$

$\Rightarrow 180(1 + 199e^{-0.2t}) = 200$

$\Rightarrow 199e^{-0.2t} = 0.1111$

$\Rightarrow \quad e^{-0.2t} = 5.58 \times 10^{-4}$

$\Rightarrow \quad -0.2t = \ln(5.58 \times 10^{-4})$

$\Rightarrow t = -\dfrac{1}{0.2}\ln(5.58 \times 10^{-4}) = 37.5$ days

6

$t = 9.8$ minutes

7 (a) $\quad \frac{1}{2}m_0 = m_0 e^{-5570K}$

$\Rightarrow \quad e^{-5570K} = \frac{1}{2}$

$\Rightarrow \quad -5570K = \ln\frac{1}{2}$

$\Rightarrow \quad K = \frac{-1}{5570}\ln\frac{1}{2} = 1.24 \times 10^{-4}$

(b) $\quad \frac{9}{10}m_0 = m_0 e^{-Kt}$

$\Rightarrow \quad 0.9 = e^{-Kt}$

$\Rightarrow t = -\dfrac{1}{1.24 \times 10^{-4}}\ln 0.9 = 847$ years

3.5 Radians
3.5.1 Rates of change

3.5 A

1 (a) (i)

θ	10	5	2	1	0.1
$\dfrac{\sin \theta°}{\theta}$	0.017 36	0.017 34	0.017 45	0.017 45	0.017 45

(ii) The sequence tends to a value of 0.017 45 rounded to five decimal places.

2 (a)

θ	10	5	2	1	0.1
(i) BC	0.1736	0.0872	0.0349	0.01745	0.001745
(ii) arc BA	0.1745	0.0873	0.0349	0.01745	0.001745

(b) The lengths of BC and arc BA become closer in value as θ gets smaller. Both tend to $0.01745 \times \theta$, the same limit as question 1.

3 Length BC $= \sin \theta°$

$$\text{Arc BA} = \frac{\theta}{360} \times 2\pi = \frac{\pi\theta}{180}$$

Since the lengths are approximately equal for small values of θ,

$$\sin \theta° \approx \frac{\pi\theta}{180} \Rightarrow \frac{\sin \theta°}{\theta} \approx \frac{\pi}{180}$$

4 $\dfrac{\pi}{180} = 0.01745$, rounded to five decimal places.

5 The gradient of $\sin \theta°$ at the origin is $\dfrac{\pi}{180}$.

6 $y = \sin \theta° \Rightarrow \dfrac{dy}{d\theta} = \dfrac{\pi}{180} \cos \theta°$

3.5 B

(a) Sketching the gradient graph of $y = \cos x°$ gives the graph of $\dfrac{dy}{dx} = -k \sin x°$.

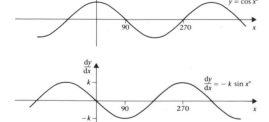

(b) Working in radians, you can make the maximum gradient (i.e. the value of k) equal to 1. So,

$$y = \cos x^c \Rightarrow \frac{dy}{dx} = -\sin x^c$$

So, if x is measured in radians,

$$\frac{d}{dx}(\cos x) = -\sin x$$

If x is in degrees, then

$$\frac{d}{dx}(\cos x°) = -\frac{\pi}{180} \sin x°$$

3.5.2 Radian measure

3.5 C

1 (a) 0.841   (b) 0.017   (c) 0.996

   (d) 0.284   (e) 1.000   (f) 0.014

2 (a) $\sin 30° = \sin (\frac{1}{6}\pi)^c = 0.5$

(b)

Radians	π	$\frac{1}{2}\pi$	$\frac{1}{3}\pi$	$\frac{1}{4}\pi$	$\frac{1}{6}\pi$	$\frac{3}{2}\pi$	2π
Degrees	180	90	60	45	30	270	360

(c) To convert $\theta°$ to radians, multiply by $\dfrac{\pi}{180}$.

(d) To convert θ^c to degrees, multiply by $\dfrac{180}{\pi}$.

3 (a) 1.047   (b) 0.866   (c) 0.018

4 $\sin 60° = 0.866$. In radian mode, this will probably give an error on a calculator. In fact, $\sin 60^c = -0.305$.

5 Plotting a graph of $y = \sin x$ with x in radians, using simple numerical values rather than multiples of π, helps to emphasise that multiples of π are not the only way to express angles measured in radians.

3.5 Exercise 1

1 (a) $\frac{1}{2}\pi$ (b) 2π (c) $\frac{1}{4}\pi$

   (d) $\frac{2}{3}\pi$ (e) $\frac{1}{3}\pi$ (f) 4π

   (g) $-\frac{1}{6}\pi$ (h) $\frac{3}{4}\pi$

2 (a) 45°   (b) 540°   (c) −180°

(d) 270°   (e) −360°

3 2π

4 (a) 2π   (b) 2   (c) $\dfrac{2\pi}{\omega}$

3.5.3 Area and arc lengths

3.5 Exercise 2

1 (a) $\frac{1}{2} \times 2^2 \times \frac{1}{4}\pi = \frac{1}{2}\pi$

(b) $2 \times \frac{1}{4}\pi = \frac{1}{2}\pi$ (c) $4 + \frac{1}{2}\pi$

2 The perimeter of CDE $= 3r$
Area CDE $= \frac{1}{2}r^2$
So $3r = \frac{1}{2}r^2$, giving $r = 6$ (since $r \neq 0$).

3 (a) 1600 m
(b) Area $= 160\,000\ \text{m}^2$
The largest crowd is 80 000.

4 (a) BC $= r\sin\theta$ (b) $\frac{1}{2}r^2\sin\theta$ (c) $\frac{1}{2}r^2\theta$

(d) Area of segment $=$ area of sector OAB

$\qquad\qquad\qquad$ − area of triangle OAB

$\qquad\qquad = \frac{1}{2}r^2\theta - \frac{1}{2}r^2\sin\theta$

$\qquad\qquad = \frac{1}{2}r^2(\theta - \sin\theta)$

5 $104.7\ \text{cm}^2$, $43.3\ \text{cm}^2$, $61.4\ \text{cm}^2$

3.5.4 More about derivatives

3.5 D

1

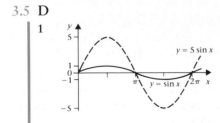

(a) $y = \sin x$ is mapped onto $y = 5\sin x$ by a stretch of factor 5 in the y-direction.

(b) The gradient is multiplied by a factor of 5.

(c) $y = 5\sin x \Rightarrow \dfrac{dy}{dx} = 5\cos x$

2

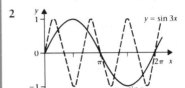

(a) $y = \sin x$ is mapped onto $y = \sin 3x$ by a stretch of factor $\frac{1}{3}$ in the x-direction.

(b) The gradient is multiplied by a factor of 3.

(c) $y = \sin 3x \Rightarrow \dfrac{dy}{dx} = 3\cos 3x$

3 $y = 5\sin 3x$ is obtained from $y = \sin x$ by applying both stretches from the previous questions.

$$y = 5\sin 3x \Rightarrow \dfrac{dy}{dx} = 15\cos 3x$$

4 (a) $-2\sin 2x$ (b) $20\cos 2x$

(c) $0.5\cos 0.5x$

5 (a)

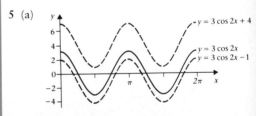

(b) These curves are mapped onto each other by translations in the y-direction.

The derivatives are all the same:

$$\dfrac{dy}{dx} = -6\sin 2x$$

6 (a)   (i) $y = a\sin x \;\Rightarrow\; \dfrac{dy}{dx} = a\cos x$

(ii) $y = \sin bx \;\Rightarrow\; \dfrac{dy}{dx} = b\cos bx$

(iii) $y = a\sin bx \Rightarrow \dfrac{dy}{dx} = ab\cos bx$

(b) $y = a\cos bx \Rightarrow \dfrac{dy}{dx} = -ab\sin bx$

3.5 Exercise 3

1 (a) $\frac{1}{2}\cos x$ (b) $-5\sin x$

   (c) $0.1\cos x$ (d) $4\cos 4x$

   (e) $-2\pi\sin 2\pi x$ (f) $0.2\cos 0.2x$

   (g) $-6\sin 2x$ (h) $3\pi\cos\frac{1}{2}\pi x$

   (i) $\cos\frac{1}{3}x$

2 (a) $\dfrac{dy}{dx} = -2\sin 2x$

   (b) $\displaystyle\int \sin 2x\ dx = -\frac{1}{2}\cos 2x$

   (c) Since the derivative of $\sin 3x$ is $3\cos 3x$,

$$\int \cos 3x\ dx = \tfrac{1}{3}\sin 3x.$$

3.5.5 Applications

3.5 Exercise 4

1 (a) $L = 12 + 2.5\cos 2\pi t \Rightarrow \dfrac{dI.}{dx} = -5\pi\sin 2\pi t$

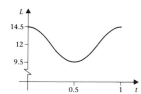

(b)

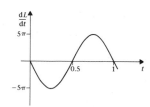

t		0	0.1	0.25	0.4	0.5
(i) Length (cm)		14.5	14.0	12	10.0	9.5
(ii) Velocity (cm s^{-1})		0	-9.2	-5π	-9.2	0

This represents the motion between the maximum and minimum positions. The velocity is momentarily zero at the extreme positions, and the speed is greatest at the midway position.

2 (a) $h = 0.8\cos\frac{1}{6}\pi t + 6.5 \Rightarrow \dfrac{dh}{dt} = -\frac{2}{15}\pi\sin\frac{1}{6}\pi t$

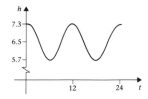

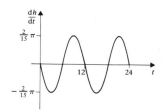

(b) $0.8\cos\frac{1}{6}\pi t + 6.5 = 6$
     $\Rightarrow \cos\frac{1}{6}\pi t = -0.625$
     $\Rightarrow t = 4.29, 7.71$ (0417 hours and 0743 hours)

When $t = 4.29$, $\dfrac{dh}{dt} = -0.33\ (\text{m h}^{-1})$;

when $t = 7.71$, $\dfrac{dh}{dt} = 0.33\ (\text{m h}^{-1})$

The rates of change are numerically the same but opposite in sign because in one case the tide is falling and in the other it is rising.

(c) The tide is falling most rapidly at $t = 3$.

$$\frac{dh}{dt} = -0.42\ (\text{m h}^{-1})$$

(d) Tidal current is greatest when the tide is rising or falling most rapidly and is least near high and low tides.

Depth of water and strength of tidal current are the two important factors in deciding when it is safe to enter or leave harbour.

3 (a) $\dfrac{dh}{dt} = 0.16\pi \sin\frac{1}{30}\pi t$

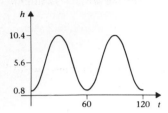

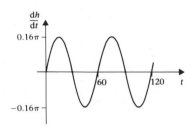

(b) $0.16\pi \sin\frac{1}{30}\pi t = -0.4$
$\Rightarrow t = 38.8, 51.2, 98.8, 111.2$

The speed is over $0.4\,\text{m s}^{-1}$ between
$t = 38.8$ and $t = 51.2$ and again between
$t = 98.8$ and $t = 111.2$. The chair descends
most rapidly at $t = 45$; speed $= 0.5\,\text{m s}^{-1}$.

4 (a) (i)

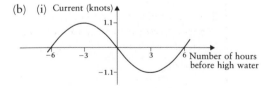

(ii) $h = 3.15 + 1.45\cos\frac{1}{6}\pi t$

(b) (i)

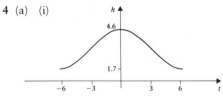

Since the period is 12 hours,
$$\omega = \tfrac{2}{12}\pi = \tfrac{1}{6}\pi$$

(ii) $c = -1.1\sin\frac{1}{6}\pi t$

(iii) Since current represents the rate at
which water is entering or leaving the
harbour, this is proportional to the
rate of change of the height of the tide.

(c) (i) $\dfrac{dh}{dt} = -0.76\sin\frac{1}{6}\pi t$

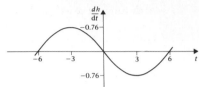

(ii) As indicated above, this is directly
proportional to the current,
demonstrating the direct relationship
between the speed of the current and
the rate of rise and fall of the tide.

3.6 Transformations
3.6.1 Graph sketching

3.6 **A**

1 (a) Replacing x with $x + k$ results in the
translation $\begin{bmatrix} -k \\ 0 \end{bmatrix}$.

   (i) $y = \frac{1}{2}(x + k)^2 - 4(x + k)$
  (ii) $y\sin(x + k)$
 (iii) $y = e^{x+k}$
 (iv) $y = \pm\sqrt{(1 - (x + k)^2)}$

(b) Replacing y with $y + k$ results in the
translation $\begin{bmatrix} 0 \\ -k \end{bmatrix}$.

   (i) $y + k = \frac{1}{2}x^2 - 4x$
     $\Rightarrow y = \frac{1}{2}x^2 - 4x - k$
  (ii) $y + k = \sin x \Rightarrow y = \sin x - k$
 (iii) $y + k = e^x \Rightarrow y = e^x - k$
 (iv) $y + k = \pm\sqrt{(1 - x^2)}$
     $\Rightarrow y = -k \pm \sqrt{(1 - x^2)}$

(c) Replacing x with kx results in a one-way
stretch from the y-axis with scale factor $\dfrac{1}{k}$.

   (i) $y = \frac{1}{2}(kx)^2 - 4kx$ (ii) $y = \sin kx$
 (iii) $y = e^{kx}$ (iv) $y = \pm\sqrt{(1 - (kx)^2)}$

(d) Replacing y with ky results in a one-way stretch from the x-axis with scale factor $\frac{1}{k}$.

$$ky = \frac{x^2}{2} + 4x \Rightarrow y = \frac{x^2}{2k} - \frac{4x}{k}$$

$$ky = \sin x \Rightarrow y = \frac{\sin x}{k}$$

$$ky = e^x \Rightarrow y = \frac{e^x}{k}$$

$$ky = \pm\sqrt{(1-x^2)} \Rightarrow y = \pm\frac{\sqrt{(1-x^2)}}{k}$$

2 (a) Replacing x with $-x$ reflects the graph in the y-axis.

(b) Replacing y with $-y$ reflects the graph in the x-axis.

(c) Interchanging x and y reflects the graph in the line $y = x$.

3 (a) (i) Translation $\begin{bmatrix} -1 \\ 0 \end{bmatrix}$

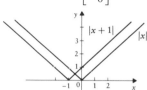

(ii) One-way stretch from y-axis of scale factor $\frac{1}{2}$, followed by a translation $\begin{bmatrix} -\frac{1}{2} \\ 0 \end{bmatrix}$

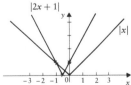

(iii) Translation $\begin{bmatrix} -1 \\ 0 \end{bmatrix}$ followed by a one-way stretch from the x-axis of scale factor 2

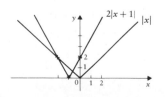

(b) The transformations are identical to those described in (a)(i), (ii) and (iii).

3.6 B

The equation would become $y = 2e^{3(x+1)}$ instead of $y = 2e^{3x+1}$.

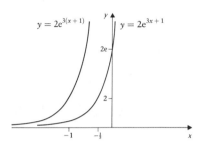

3.6.2 Stretching a circle

3.6 C

1 If you transform the unit circle, $x^2 + y^2 = 1$, with a stretch factor r from the y-axis and a stretch factor r from the x-axis then you obtain the circle with radius r shown in the diagram on page 275.

Replacing x with $\frac{x}{r}$ and y with $\frac{y}{r}$ in the equation $x^2 + y^2 = 1$ gives

$$\frac{x^2}{r^2} + \frac{y^2}{r^2} = 1 \Rightarrow x^2 + y^2 = r^2$$

2 Transforming the unit circle, $x^2 + y^2 = 1$, by a stretch factor a along the x-axis and by a stretch factor b along the y-axis gives

$$\frac{x^2}{a^2} + \frac{y^2}{b^2} = 1$$

3 Giving the circle in question 1 a translation $\begin{bmatrix} p \\ q \end{bmatrix}$ by replacing x with $x - p$ and y with $y - q$, you obtain

$$(x - p)^2 + (y - q)^2 = r^2$$

3.6 Exercise 1

1 The equation $y = \ln x$ can be transformed onto $y = \ln 3x$ by replacing x with $3x$. The graph of $y = \ln x$ can therefore be fitted to the graph of $y = \ln 3x$ by a one-way stretch from $x = 0$, factor $\frac{1}{3}$.

The equation $y = \ln 3$ can be rewritten

$$y = \ln 3x \Rightarrow y = \ln 3 + \ln x$$

$$\Rightarrow y - \ln 3 = \ln x$$

The equation $y = \ln x$ can be transformed onto $y = \ln 3x$ by replacing y with $y - \ln 3$. The graph of $y = \ln x$ can be fitted to the graph of $y = \ln 3x$ by a translation $\begin{bmatrix} 0 \\ \ln 3 \end{bmatrix}$.

2 (a) $y = 4x^2 \Rightarrow y = (2x)^2$

The graph of $y = x^2$ can be fitted to the graph of $y = 4x^2$ by a one-way stretch from $x = 0$, factor $\frac{1}{2}$.

(b) $y = 4x^2 \Rightarrow \frac{1}{4}y = x^2$

The graph of $y = x^2$ can be fitted to the graph of $y = 4x^2$ by a one-way stretch from $y = 0$, factor 4.

3 (a) A one-way stretch from $x = 0$, factor 2, followed by a translation $\begin{bmatrix} 2 \\ 0 \end{bmatrix}$.

Replace x with $\frac{1}{2}x$, then replace x with $x - 2$.

$$x^2 + y^2 = 1 \rightarrow (\tfrac{1}{2}x)^2 + y^2 = 1$$

$$\rightarrow [\tfrac{1}{2}(x - 2)]^2 + y^2 = 1$$

(b) A translation $\begin{bmatrix} 1 \\ 0 \end{bmatrix}$ followed by a one-way stretch from $x = 0$, factor 2.

Replace x with $x - 1$, then replace x with $\frac{1}{2}x$.

$$x^2 + y^2 = 1 \rightarrow (x - 1)^2 + y^2 = 1$$

$$\rightarrow (\tfrac{1}{2}x - 1)^2 + y^2 = 1$$

The two equations are equivalent. You are, however, less likely to make a mistake with the translation if you stretch the circle before you translate it.

Miscellaneous exercise 3

1 (a) (i) $\dfrac{3}{2 - x}$ (ii) $\dfrac{3}{4 - 3x}$ (b) $x = \frac{5}{6}$

2 $7, -17, -25, 5 - 6x, 13 - 6x, 4, -\frac{1}{3},$ $\frac{1}{6}(5 - x), \frac{1}{2}(7 - 3x), \frac{1}{3}(7 - 2x)$

3 (a) $\dfrac{x - 10}{7}$ (b) $\dfrac{6 - 3x}{8}$

   (c) $\dfrac{5x + 1}{4x - 1}$ $(x \neq \frac{1}{4})$

   (d) $\sqrt{(4 - x)}$ $(x \leq 4)$

4 (a) $y = \sqrt{(x - 2)}$, $(27, 5)$

   (b) $y = 5 + \sqrt{(x + 1)}$, $(24, 10)$

   (c) $y = \sqrt{(-x)}$, $(-25, 5)$

   (d) $y = -\sqrt{x}$, $(25, -5)$

   (e) $x = \sqrt{y}$, $(5, 25)$

5 $\dfrac{x - 12}{x(x + 3)(x + 4)}$

6 (b) e.g. $y = 3 \cos 4x°$

7 (a) $2 - 2 \sin 1^c$

8 (a) 1.62   (b) -2 (c) 5.76   (d) -2.31

9 (a) 3 a.m.   (b) 9.5 m and 1.5 m

   (c) The graph oscillates about $h = 5.5$ with period 12 h and amplitude 4.

   (d) $1.05 \, \text{m h}^{-1}$

10 (a) 90   (b) $45, 135$ (c) $18, 54, 90, 126, 162$

   (d) 120   (e) $40, 80, 160$

11 (a) 20 cm   (b) 10 cm   (c) 2 s

   (d) $y = 20 + 10 \cos 360t°$

   (e) $y = 20 + 10 \cos 120t°$

12 (a) 2, 360   (b) 3, 360   (c) 0.5, 180

   (d) 5, 1080   (e) 3, 540

(a)

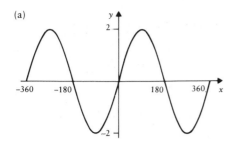

(b)

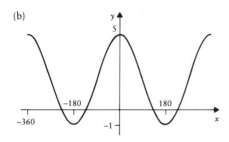

(c)

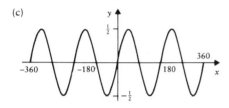

(d)

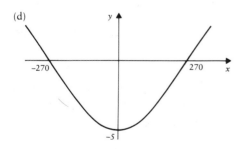

(e)

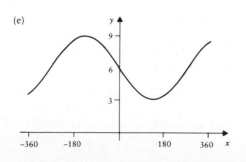

13 Many possible answers, for example

(a) $y = \sin 4x°$ (b) $y = \frac{5}{2}\sin\frac{1}{2}x°$

(c) $y = 3\sin 6x°$ (d) $y = \frac{1}{2}\sin\frac{1}{4}x°$

14 (a) 1.262   (b) 1.316   (c) 1.262

15 $P = 100 \times (0.98)^T$

(a) 38.4%   (b) 34.3 hours

16 $y = kx^p$;   plotting $\log y$ against $\log x$, the gradient gives p and k is given by 10^c where c is the intercept with the vertical axis.

17 $\theta = 83 \times (0.96)^T$

20 $A = 20.0$

21 (b) $m_0 = 10$

(c) (i) 14.92 g   (ii) 22.26 g

(d) (i) 49.2% increase   (ii) 49.2% increase

22 (a) 0.18 kg   (b) 3.47 h

(c) (i) 6.93 h   (ii) 10.4 h

(d) $\dfrac{dm}{dt} = -0.2m$

23 (b) $2\,\text{m s}^{-2}$ (c) $3\frac{2}{3}\,\text{m}$

24 (a) $x^{-2}y^2$

(b) (i) $\dfrac{3x + 2}{12x^2}$ (ii) $\dfrac{2}{(2 - x)(2 + x)}$

25 (a)

(b) $y = (x - 1)^2(2 - x)$

4 PROBLEM SOLVING

4.1 Mathematical enquiries

4.1.1 Introduction

4.1 A

1

	First organiser	Second organiser
(a) byes	5	2
(b) rounds	4	4
(c) matches	10	10

The type of notation used can be an important aid in solving the problem. The first organiser's method of running the tournament could be illustrated like this.

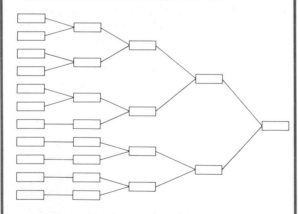

Are there any better ways of recording the investigation?

The number of matches played is always one less than the number of competitors. An amusingly brief proof of this can be given – everybody loses once except the winning finalist!

The number of byes is zero only if there are 2^n players.

For P players under the first system, the number of rounds is given by n where $2^{n-1} < P \le 2^n$. The number of byes is then $2^n - P$.

Under the second system there can be at most one bye per round. You could try to find a more precise rule.

2 Differences formed from numbers with an odd number of digits are divisible by 99. Differences from numbers with an even number of digits are divisible by 9.

By looking at particular examples such as

$$365 = (3 \times 100) + (6 \times 10) + 5$$

you can see the general result that a number *looking like ABC* actually has the value $100A + 10B + C$. So the difference between this number and the one with digits reversed is

$$100A + 10B + C - (100C + 10B + A)$$
$$= 99(A - C)$$

(You may have managed to give an explanation for these results without using algebra.)

One fruitful line of further investigation concerns using 'differencing' to form chains of numbers. All chains from non-repeating two-digit numbers end in the cycle:

For example, $63 - 36 = 27$, so $63 \to 27$, and so on.

What happens with three-digit numbers, four-digit numbers, ... ?

3

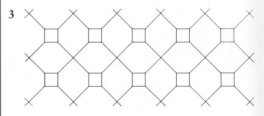

A tessellation originally was the result of covering an area with **tesserae**, the small square blocks used by the Romans to make mosaics. Nowadays, from the primary school onward, it is generally accepted as any covering or 'tiling' of a plane surface of indefinite extent by a regular pattern of one or more congruent non-overlapping shapes. For example:

(a) A parallelogram tessellation can be obtained from one for rectangles by a shear:

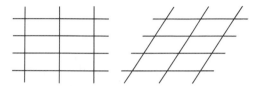

For extensions it might be more useful to think of the parallelograms forming strips which can then be fitted together easily.

(b) Perhaps the most obvious method is to fit copies of the triangle together in pairs to form parallelograms

but finding other patterns might be a profitable exercise.

(c) The 108° corners cannot be fitted together to form 360° and so regular pentagons cannot tessellate.

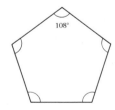

This idea might be used to establish the fact that only three regular shapes will tessellate on a plane surface – an equilateral triangle, a square and a regular hexagon.

Further extensions might include tackling questions such as the following:

Do all pentagons with one pair of parallel sides tessellate?

Are there any other pentagons which will tessellate?

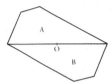

Quadrilateral B has been obtained from quadrilateral A by rotating it through 180° about O, the midpoint of a side. Repeated applications of this principle give a tessellation of quadrilaterals.

As an extension you could check that the method works for re-entrant quadrilaterals, such as

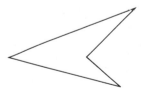

and explain *why* the method always works.

4.1 B

1 If $a = 0$ then x is the cube root of $-b$.

If $b = 0$ then

$$x^3 + ax = 0$$

$$\Rightarrow x(x^2 + a) = 0$$

$$\Rightarrow x = 0 \quad \text{or} \quad x^2 + a = 0$$

and further roots can be found only if $a < 0$.

2 The right-angled triangle might be a useful first example, since such a triangle is half a rectangle and since *any* triangle may be dissected into two right-angled triangles.

3 $x = 0$ (y is not defined)

x small and positive (y is large and positive)

x small and negative (y is large and negative)

x large (y is approximately equal to x)

4 Two such examples are:

(a) $a = 1, b = 2, c = 4, d = 3, e = 6, f = 7$

(b) $a = 1, b = 2, c = 4, d = 3, e = 6, f = 12$

Write out the equations with these coefficients to see why. You will also see that there is an infinity of possible answers.

4.1 C

1 (a) The numbers in the sequence are $25, 121, 361$ and these are all perfect squares ($5^2, 11^2, 19^2$).

Further terms give 29^2 and 41^2.

If the consecutive digits start at n, then the general term will be

$$[n(n + 1)(n + 2)(n + 3)] + 1$$

If you expand and factorise, looking for a perfect square, the expression becomes $(n^2 + 3n + 1)^2$. You should confirm this.

(b) $43\,681 = 209^2$. So, assuming that d is the greatest of a, b, c and d, $d = (n + 3)$ where

$$n^2 + 3n + 1 = 209$$

The numbers are 13, 14, 15 and 16.

2 The recurrence relation is

$$u_{n+2} = u_{n+1} + u_n$$

(a) 21, 34

(b) $8^2 = (13 \times 5) - 1$, $13^2 = (21 \times 8) + 1$, and so on.

(c) The 4th, 8th and 12th terms are 3, 21 and 144. They are all multiples of 3.

(d) The 5th, 10th and 15th terms are all multiples of 5. Generally, every nth term is divisible by u_n.

4.1 Exercise 1

1 (a) $\displaystyle\sum_{i=1}^{n}(2i - 1) = n^2$

(b) The sum of the first n odd numbers is n^2.

2 (a) Divisible by 3; divisible by 8.

(b) The sum of n consecutive odd numbers is divisible by n if n is odd, and by $2n$ if n is even.

3 $2, 5, 9, \frac{1}{2}n(n - 3)$

4 A polygon of given perimeter has greatest area if it is regular, i.e. all its angles are equal and all its sides are equal.

4.1.2 Organising your work

4.1 D

1 Labelling the points is a useful first step.

You would need to say which pairs of points are linked, for example A–B, A–C, and so on. You might also give distances and directions between points or, alternatively, you might give the approximate coordinates of each point.

2 RSLSSL

The route is shown in this grid.

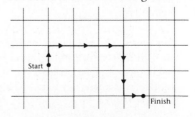

3 A simple pictorial notation might be ⊔ for an upright tumbler, and ⊓ for one which is upside down.

However, the explanation hinges on ideas of oddness and evenness (parity) and so a numerical notation is better.

Let 1 represent an upright tumbler and 0 one which is upside down. Start with a sum $1 + 0 + 1 = 2$, which is even. Because you change two at a time the sum will remain even, i.e. always be 0 or 2, and never 3 as required.

4.1 Exercise 2

1 (a) Acute, right, obtuse, straight, reflex, . . .

   (b) Scalene, isosceles, equilateral, right-angled, . . .

   (c) Prisms, shapes having one curved surface, shapes having a plane of symmetry, . . .

2 Using the notation for cells as shown:

1	2	3
4	5	6
7	8	9

first moves in cells 1, 3, 7 and 9 are essentially alike, as are those in cells 2, 4, 6 and 8. There are therefore three essentially different first moves.

3 Rectangles and rhombi

4 The possible cases are:

● a and b both even, then $a^2 + b^2$ is a multiple of 4;
● one odd, one even, then $a^2 + b^2 = 4k + 1$ (see below);
● a and b both odd, then $a^2 + b^2 = 4k + 2$.

If, for example,

$$a = (2m + 1) \text{ and } b = 2n, \text{ then}$$

$$a^2 + b^2 = 4m^2 + 4m + 1 + 4n^2$$

$$= 4(m^2 + m + n^2) + 1$$

$$= 4k + 1, \text{ say}$$

5 Is it shaded? Is it made up of straight lines (rectilinear)? Has it more than two lines of symmetry?

4.1.3 Tabulation

4.1 E

1 As an example, you might take

$$E(n) = n^2 - n + 2$$

Then $E(1) = 2$, $E(2) = 4$, $E(3) = 8$, and so on.

2 ⊤ 4 ⊤ 8 ⊤ 14 ⊤ 22
 2 ⊤ 4 ⊤ 6 ⊤ 8
  2   2   2

Whichever quadratic expression was chosen the second differences should be equal.

You may have realised that there was an unnecessary restriction in this question. a, b and c can be any numbers but, of course, it simplifies calculations if they are integers.

2 The third differences should be equal.

3
Sequence	−1		−6		3		68		255		654		1379 . . .

First differences   −5   9   65   187   399   725. . .

Second differences   14   56   122   212   326. . .

Third differences   42   66   90   114. . .

Fourth differences   24   24   24. . .

On the basis of the pattern established in questions 1 and 2, you should conjecture that the sequence was generated by a quartic expression.

4 (a) First differences are all 1.

   (b) Second differences are all 2.

   (c) Third differences are all 6.

   (d) Fourth differences are all 24 (see next page).

Sequence (n^4)	1	16	81	256	625	1296	2401...
First differences		15	65	175	369	671	1105...
Second differences			50	110	194	302	434...
Third differences				60	84	108	132...
Fourth differences					24	24	24...

5 From the answers to question 4, a generalisation is that n^k generates a sequence giving kth differences all $k!$ (and hence $(k + 1)$th differences all 0). So a polynomial with leading term n^5 would generate a sequence with fifth differences all $5! = 120$. The likely answer to the question is that the sequence was generated by a polynomial of fifth degree, leading term $\frac{1}{4}n^5$.

4.1 Exercise 3

1 n	3	4	5	6
$D(n)$	0	2	5	9

$D(n)$ is the number of diagonals of an n-gon.

A decagon has 35 diagonals.

2 Shape	No. of lines of symmetry	Order of rotational symmetry
Parallelogram	0	2
Rhombus	2	2
Rectangle	2	2
Kite	1	1
Square	4	4

3 n	1	2	3	4	5	6
$r(n)$	1	2	2	3	3	4
$s(n)$	1	2	3	5	8	13

$$r(n) = \begin{cases} \frac{1}{2}(n+1) & \text{if } n \text{ is odd} \\ \frac{1}{2}n + 1 & \text{if } n \text{ is even} \end{cases}$$

$$s(n) = s(n-1) + s(n-2) \quad \text{for } n \geq 3$$

with $s(1) = 1$, $s(2) = 2$

4.2 Proof

4.2.1 Introduction

4.2 **Exercise 1**

1 $x = -1$, $y = 0$ disproves the statement.

2 False. The three-dimensional Cartesian axes are a counter-example.

3 False. 21 is the first counter-example.

4 $t_1 = 1$, $t_2 = 2$, $t_3 = 3$, $t_4 = 4$, $t_5 = 29$. The value of t_5 is *not* 5 as might be expected if you considered only the first four terms.

4.2.2 Making a proof

4.2 **Exercise 2**

1 (a) $2n$ is $2 \times n$ and is therefore even because it is divisible by 2.

(b) $2n + 1$. This number is $2 \times n + 1$ and is therefore odd because it has a remainder of 1 when divided by 2.

(c) $(2n + 1) + (2n + 3) + (2n + 5) = 6n + 9$ $= 3 \times (2n + 3)$ is divisible by 3.

2 (a) $10b + a$

(b) $11a + 11b = 11 \times (a + b)$

(c) The rule does *not* work for three-digit numbers, for example $102 + 201 = 303$.

The rule *does* work for four-digit numbers.

$$(1000a + 100b + 10c + d)$$
$$+ (1000d + 100c + 10b + a)$$
$$= 1001a + 110b + 110c + 1001d$$
$$= 11 \times (91a + 10b + 10c + 91d)$$

3 (b) $(10a + b) \times 11 = 110a + 11b$
$$= 100a + 10a + 10b + b$$
$$= 100a + 10(a + b) + b$$

So 'ab' $\times 11 \;\; = \boxed{a}\boxed{a+b}\boxed{b}$

(c) For examples of this kind you have to 'carry' digits in the addition.
The method works, but you have to be more careful!

$11 \times 392 = 3 \; \boxed{12} \; \boxed{11} \; 2$
$$= 4 \; 2 \; \boxed{11} \; 2$$
$$= 4 \; 3 \; 1 \; 2$$

4 In the 5×13 'rectangle' a very thin parallelogram of area 1 is missing.

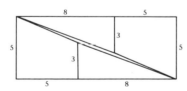

A 'similar triangles' argument shows this: $\frac{3}{8} \neq \frac{5}{13}$

5 (a) The numbers may in general be written as $(2a - 1)$ and $(2a + 1)$, with sum $4a$.

(b) The sum of the numbers may be written as

$$(2a + 1) + (2a + 3) + (2a + 5)$$
$$+ \cdots + (2a + 2n - 1)$$
$$= (2a + 2a + 2a + 2a + \cdots + 2a)$$
$$+ (1 + 3 + 5 + \cdots + 2n - 1)$$
$$= 2na + n^2$$
$$= n(2a + n)$$

This expression is divisible by n. For n even, it is divisible by $2n$.

6E There are a number of ways in which this proof can be made. The following is based on the classic method attributed to Euclid, which employs **contradiction**.

Suppose $\sqrt{2} = \dfrac{a}{b}$, where a and b have no common factors.

$$\sqrt{2} = \frac{a}{b} \Rightarrow 2b^2 = a^2$$
$$\Rightarrow a^2 \text{ is even} \quad (\text{has a factor a 2})$$
$$\Rightarrow a \text{ is even}$$

Let $\;\; a = 2m$
$$a^2 = 4m^2$$

Since $\;\; b^2 = \dfrac{a^2}{2}, \; b^2 = \dfrac{4m^2}{2} = 2m^2$
$$\Rightarrow b^2 \text{ is even}$$
$$\Rightarrow b \text{ is even}$$

If $\sqrt{2} = \dfrac{a}{b}$ then we have shown that *both* a and b are even and consequently have a common factor of 2.

This contradicts our original statement, so

$$\sqrt{2} \neq \frac{a}{b}$$

and so $\sqrt{2}$ is an irrational number.

4.2.3 Fermat and proof

4.2 **A**

1	n	1	2	3	4
	r_n	1	2	4	8

n is the number of points, and r_n is the corresponding number of regions.

Apparently the number of regions doubles every time a point is added, i.e.

$r_{n+1} = 2 \times r_n$, in which case

$r_n = 2^{n-1}$

2 $r_5 = 16$, which agrees with the conjecture. However, $r_6 = 31$, so the conjecture is false.

3 n	1	2	3	4	5	6	7
r_n	1	2	4	8	16	31	57

4 First differences 1   2   4   8   15   26
  Second differences 1   2   4   7   11
  Third differences   1   2   3   4
  Fourth differences   1   1   1

5 The formula for r_n is probably a quartic polynomial.

The polynomial

$$r_n = an^4 + bn^3 + cn^2 + dn + e$$

can be found by solving five equations (for the five unknown coefficients), obtained by substituting corresponding values of n and r_n. The first is

$$a + b + c + d + e = 1$$

and the second is

$$16a + 8b + 4c + 2d + e = 2$$

The study could be taken further, either as a class or by an individual student.

4.2 B

1 4; namely 1×1, 2×2, 3×3 and 4×4 squares.

2 There are

16   1×1 squares

9   2×2 squares

4   3×3 squares.

So the total is $1 + 4 + 9 + 16 = 30$.

3 Using a similar method of counting, the total number is

$$1 + 4 + 9 + \cdots + n^2 = \tfrac{1}{6}n(n + 1)(2n + 1)$$

4 There are 27 in all, including 16 of edge 1, 7 of edge 2 and 3 of edge 3.

5 (a) 13   (b) 48

6 Classifying into triangles pointing upwards ($\triangle$) and those pointing downwards ($\triangledown$) and

making separate counts for the two classes, you will find patterns occurring in which sequences of triangular numbers appear. For example in the $4 \times 4 \times 4$ grid there are

$$1 + 3 + 6 + 10 \text{ pointing upwards}$$

and

$$1 + 6 \text{ pointing downwards.}$$

For the $6 \times 6 \times 6$ grid, using the patterns found, there should be

$$1 + 3 + 6 + 10 + 15 + 21 \text{ upwards}$$

and

$$1 + 6 + 15 \text{ downwards,}$$

giving a total of 78 triangles.

4.4 Mathematical articles

4.4.1 Introduction

4.4 Exercise 1

*1 At this stage you should draw a few doodles such that your pen comes back to its starting point each time. For example:

When the author of the article makes definitions about such graphs you can then use your own drawings as illustrations.

At this point you would probably read on a few lines to check that the author is going to define the phrase '4-regular'.

*2 Each of the author's definitions and statements should be checked.

(a) Number of crossing points, $n = 9$.

(b) Number of edges, $m = 18$.

(c) Number of regions, $r = 11$.

(d) 34 589 defines the shaded region.

(e) There is a region exterior to the graph!

(a, b, c) For the doodles given in answer to question 1,

$$n = 1 \quad n = 7 \quad n = 4$$
$$m = 2 \quad m = 14 \quad m = 8$$
$$r = 3 \quad r = 9 \quad r = 6$$

(d, e) The region exterior to the graph of figure 1 is defined by 167 892.

*3 It could be argued that in the doodle

   the only crossing point has 2

edges adjoined to it. In fact, mathematicians would still count this figure-of-eight doodle as 4-regular. One simple way to prevent the doodle being 4-regular is to retrace the path at some point, for example,

*4 To answer this you must be clear about precisely what is allowable as a 'doodle'.

In fact, it is a result of graph theory that *any* connected 4-regular graph can be drawn without retracing your path or lifting your pen off the paper.

(A graph such as 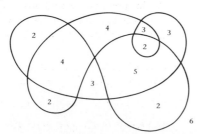

is 4-regular but **disconnected**.)

*5 The assertions should be checked on the doodle of figure 1. The values of k for the k-gons are shown below.

The Platonic solids

1 (a) A 'polygon' is a closed plane figure bounded by straight edges.

A 'regular polygon' is a polygon all of whose edges are equal and all of whose angles are equal.

(b) There is no limit to the number of different regular polygons that can be drawn.

   ...

2 As will be seen, there are actually five Platonic solids. In view of the picture in the text, the cube is the one most likely to be chosen to answer this question.

3 The triangular faces must all be equilateral triangles and so the angles at the vertex from the six faces would total precisely 360°. The six triangles would then each be part of a single flat hexagonal face and would not in fact be individual faces.

4 $F = 6, \quad V = 8, \quad E = 12$

5 (a) $F + V - E = 8 + 6 - 12 = 2$ (octahedron)

(b) $F + V - E = 6 + 8 - 12 = 2$ (cube)

6 The shape is formed by F triangular faces with a total of $3F$ sides and $3F$ corners. As before,

$$E = \frac{3F}{2}$$

Each vertex of the solid is at a corner of each of three faces and so

$$V = \frac{3F}{3}$$

Then

$$V + F = E + 2$$

$$\Rightarrow F + F = \frac{3F}{2} + 2$$

$$\Rightarrow \quad F = 4$$

Therefore

$$E = \frac{3F}{2} = 6, \quad V = F = 4$$

The solid is a tetrahedron.

7 As before, there must be at least three faces at each vertex. Four or more faces would contribute an angle count of at least $4 \times 90°$, in which case the faces would not form a corner. There are therefore precisely three faces at each vertex.

There are F square faces, having $4F$ sides and $4F$ corners. When joined together, each edge is formed from a pair of sides, so

$$E = \frac{4F}{2}$$

and each vertex is formed from three corners, so

$$V = \frac{4F}{3}$$

8 Each angle of a regular pentagon is $108°$.

9 $E = \dfrac{5F}{2}$ and $V = \dfrac{5F}{3}$

From Euler's formula,

$$F + \frac{5F}{3} = \frac{5F}{2} + 2$$

Multiplying both sides by 6,

$$6F + 10F = 15F + 12 \Rightarrow F = 12$$

Then $V = \dfrac{5F}{3} = 20$ and $E = \dfrac{5F}{2} = 30$

The gravity model in geography

The motivation for an inverse square model may be worth examining, especially if Newton's law is not familiar. You might compare the intensity of gravitational attraction with the intensity of light.

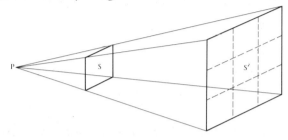

Think of a cine projector P illuminating in turn two screens S and S'. If S is three times as far from P as S then the area of light on S' is nine times that on S. But the same amount of light falls on both S and S'. So the intensity of light on S' is only $\frac{1}{9}$ of that on S. In fact, the intensity is inversely proportional to the square of the distance from P. (Replace 'cine projector' by 'candle' to give the analogy the right Newtonian flavour!)

1 $\beta = 2$

2 (a) $T_{DN} = \dfrac{k \times 216 \times 271}{20^2} \approx 146k, \qquad T_{SN} = \dfrac{k \times 537 \times 271}{50^2} \approx 58k$

   (b) Derby and Nottingham

3 $\dfrac{kP_B}{d_B^2}$

4 $WK = 130a + 173a = 303a$

   So in mile units,

$$303a = 13$$

$$a \approx 0.043$$

5 (a) Y divides WK externally in the ratio 130 : 173, i.e.

$$\frac{WY}{YK} = \frac{130}{173}$$

   Since $WY = x$ and $YK = (x + 13)$

$$\frac{x}{x + 13} = \frac{130}{173}$$

(b) Expressions for the attractiveness of Shrewsbury and Welshpool are respectively

$$\frac{56\,000\,k}{d_S^2} \quad \text{and} \quad \frac{7000\,k}{d_W^2}$$

(c) The expressions for attractiveness are equal when

$$7d_S^2 = 56d_W^2$$

$$d_S^2 = 8d_W^2$$

$$d_S \approx 2.83d_W$$

Welshpool's area of influence is the circle diameter XY where X, Y divide SW internally and externally in the ratio 2.83 : 1. In mile units,

$$SW = 19, \quad XW = \frac{1}{3.83} \times 19 = 4.96, \quad \frac{SY}{YW} = 2.83$$

so if YW = x,

$$\frac{x + 19}{x} = 2.83$$

$$x = \frac{19}{1.83} \approx 10.38$$

XY = 10.38 + 4.96 ≈ 15.3

Welshpool's area of influence is a circle of diameter 15.3 miles, centred at a point 2.7 miles from Welshpool on the side opposite Shrewsbury.

(d) The 'distance decay' would be less marked, making β smaller.

The value $\beta = 1$ is often used in US models.

The game of Hex

1 If Black plays at 7, White plays at 5, and connects 1–2/4–5–8/9.

If Black plays at 3 or 6, White plays at 4 and connects 1–4–7/8.

2 (a)

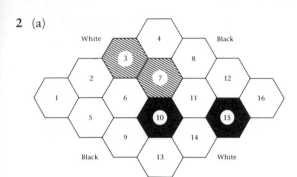

(b) The claim is false. Black connects 9/13–10–11/14–15–12/16.

3 *If White plays at 7*
White 7 can be connected to the top left edge by 7–3/4. It can be connected to the bottom right edge by Result 1. White therefore cannot be stopped from completing a winning chain.

If White plays at 10
The fact that White cannot be prevented from completing a winning chain follows from the result above by symmetry (rotate the board 180°).

Archimedes and π

1 An upper bound for the circumference is a value above which the circumference cannot possibly lie. Similarly, a lower bound is a value below which the circumference cannot possibly lie.

The actual value lies between the upper and lower bounds. The actual value is known with greater precision as the lower and upper bounds are brought closer together – precision improves as the bounds converge.

2 (a)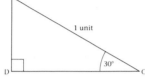

OC is a radius of the circle, so has length 1 unit.

$DC = OC\cos 30° = 1 \times \cos 30° = \cos 30°$

(b)

PR is a tangent to the circle, with point of contact at S. OS is a radius of the circle and so has length 1 unit.

$$SR = \frac{OS}{\tan 30°} = \frac{1}{\tan 30°}$$

3 Perimeter of $\triangle ABC = 6 \times DC = 6\cos 30° = 3\sqrt{3}$

Perimeter of $\triangle PQR = 6 \times SR = 6\cot 30° = 6\sqrt{3}$

Thus $3\sqrt{3} < \text{circumference} < 6\sqrt{3}$

or $3\sqrt{3} < 2\pi < 6\sqrt{3}$

or $\dfrac{3\sqrt{3}}{2} < \pi < 3\sqrt{3}$

4 (a) An inscribed figure is a figure that is totally within the circle but touches the circle at its vertices.

(b) A circumscribed figure is a figure that is totally outside the circle but such that its edges form tangents to the circle.

5 M is the point of contact of the tangent PQ with the circle, so OM is a radius and has length 1 unit. OA and OB are also radii so have length 1 unit. $\triangle OAB$ is equilateral since ABCDEF is a regular hexagon, i.e. OA = OB = AB. Hence AB has length 1 unit. The perimeter of ABCDEF is $6 \times AB = 6$ units.

6 (a) In $\triangle OLB$, $OB = 1$ unit, since it is a radius. $LB = \frac{1}{2}$ unit, since L is the mid-point of AB.

Angle $OLB = 90°$, so by Pythagoras' theorem,

$$OL = \sqrt{\left(1 - \left(\frac{1}{2}\right)^2\right)} = \frac{\sqrt{3}}{2}$$

So $OM = 1$ and $OL = \frac{\sqrt{3}}{2}$

The scale factor of the enlargement is $\dfrac{OM}{OL} = \dfrac{1}{\left(\frac{\sqrt{3}}{2}\right)} = \dfrac{2}{\sqrt{3}}$

Hence $PQ = \dfrac{2}{\sqrt{3}} \times AB = \dfrac{2}{\sqrt{3}}$

and the perimeter of $PQRSTU = 6 \times PQ = \dfrac{12}{\sqrt{3}} = \dfrac{4 \times 3}{\sqrt{3}} = 4\sqrt{3}$

(b) Perimeter of $ABCDEF <$ circumference $<$ perimeter of PQRSTU

$$6 < 2\pi < 4\sqrt{3}$$
$$3 < \pi < 2\sqrt{3}$$

7

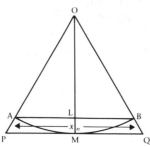

Let AB be a side of the regular inscribed n-gon so that

$$AB = x_n$$

Then $LB = \dfrac{x_n}{2}$, since L is the mid-point of AB.

OB has length 1 unit.

By Pythagoras' theorem in $\triangle OLB$,

$$OL = \sqrt{\left(1^2 - \left(\tfrac{1}{2}x_n\right)^2\right)} = \sqrt{\left(1^2 - \tfrac{1}{4}x_n^2\right)}$$

The scale factor of the enlargement is

$$\frac{OM}{OL} = \frac{1}{\sqrt{\left(1 - \tfrac{1}{4}x_n^2\right)}}$$

so $PQ = \dfrac{AB}{\sqrt{\left(1 - \tfrac{1}{4}x_n^2\right)}} = \dfrac{x_n}{\sqrt{\left(1 - \tfrac{1}{4}x_n^2\right)}}$

Multiplying by the number of sides n, in order to obtain the perimeter, gives

$$C_n = \frac{I_n}{\sqrt{\left(1 - \tfrac{1}{4}x_n^2\right)}}$$

8 (a) $x_{12} = \sqrt{(\frac{1}{4}x_6{}^2 + [1 - \sqrt{(1 - \frac{1}{4}x_6{}^2)}]^2)}$

(b) $x_6 = 1$ since x_6 is the length of the side of the inscribed hexagon.

$$x_{12} = \sqrt{(\frac{1}{4} + [1 - \sqrt{(1 - \frac{1}{4})}]^2)} \approx 0.518$$

9 $I_{12} = 12x_{12} = 12 \times 0.518 = 6.212$

$$C_{12} = \frac{I_{12}}{\sqrt{(1 - \frac{1}{4}x_{12}{}^2)}} = 6.658$$

n	x_n	I_n	C_n	Inequality
12	0.518	6.212	6.658	$3.106 < \pi < 3.329$

(All calculations are quoted to 3 decimal places, having been evaluated using $x_{12} = 0.517\,638$.)

10 As the number of sides of a regular n-gon increases, the n-gon becomes a closer and closer approximation to the circle itself. So the inscribed and circumscribed n-gons both have perimeters that approach the circumference of the circle, getting arbitrarily close as n increases without limit. By increasing n, increasingly accurate approximations to π are obtained. The difference between the approximation and π itself can be made arbitrarily small by taking a sufficiently large value of n.

5 MATHEMATICAL METHODS

5.1 The power of Pythagoras

5.1.1 Pythagoras and right-angled triangles

5.1 Exercise 1

1 Calling the hypotenuse x,

    (a) $x^2 = 10^2 + 24^2 = 676 \Rightarrow x = 26\,\text{cm}$
    [This is simply a scaled up 5, 12, 13 triangle.]

    (b) $x = 17.5\,\text{cm}$

2 Westminster Abbey and the Tower of London are 3.8 km apart.

3 The space needed in front of the step is 69 cm.

4 Height $= 22.1\,\text{m}$

5 By 'trial and error' you can find

    3 4 5   5 12 13 8 15 17   7 24 25 20 21 29
    6 8 10   10 24 26
    9 12 15
    12 16 20
    15 20 25

5.1.2 The equation of a circle

5.1 A

1 (a) $\sqrt{(3^2 + 3^2)} = \sqrt{18}$

    (b) $\sqrt{((4-1)^2 + (6-2)^2)} = \sqrt{25} = 5$

2 (a) If a point lies on the circle, its coordinates will satisfy the equation $x^2 + y^2 = 25$.

    Thus, since $4^2 + 3^2 = 25$, the point $(4, 3)$ lies on the circle.

Further points which lie on the circle are $(-3, 4)$ and $(-5, 0)$.

    (b) From the argument above, the equation of the circle is $x^2 + y^2 = 25$.

3 (a) If the point P lies on the circle, then $CQ^2 + PQ^2 = 25^2$.

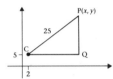

All the given points satisfy this equation.

    (b) Since $CQ = x - 2$ and $PQ = y - 5$, the equation of the circle is $(x - 2)^2 + (y - 5)^2 = 25^2$.

4 (b)

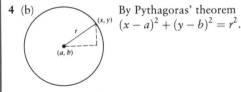

By Pythagoras' theorem $(x - a)^2 + (y - b)^2 = r^2$.

5.1 B

1 (a) If Q is the foot of the perpendicular from P to the x–y plane, then PQ has length 6.

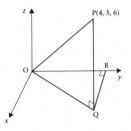

So, applying Pythagoras to triangle OPQ,

$$OP^2 = PQ^2 + OQ^2 = 6^2 + OQ^2$$

You can find OQ by applying Pythagoras to triangle ORQ.

$$OR = 5, RQ = 4 \Rightarrow OQ^2 = 5^2 + 4^2$$

Thus $OP^2 = 6^2 + 5^2 + 4^2 = 77$
$\Rightarrow OP \approx 8.77$

You can use a similar method to give:

(b) 5   (c) 5   (d) $\sqrt{14} \approx 3.74$

2 (a) 3   (b) 2   (c) 4

$$PQ^2 = 3^2 + 2^2 + 4^2 = 29$$
So $PQ = \sqrt{29} \approx 5.39$

3 (a) $PQ = \sqrt{46} \approx 6.78$

(b) $PQ = \sqrt{138} \approx 11.75$

(c) $PQ = \sqrt{[(x-a)^2 + (y-b)^2 + (z-c)^2]}$

4 (a) $OP = \sqrt{(x^2 + y^2 + z^2)}$
Since $OP = r$, the equation of the sphere is
$$\sqrt{(x^2 + y^2 + z^2)} = r$$
This is more usually written as
$$x^2 + y^2 + z^2 = r^2$$

(b) If the centre is at (a, b, c), the distance of a point on the sphere from (a, b, c) is
$$\sqrt{[(x-a)^2 + (y-b)^2 + (z-c)^2]}$$
Hence the equation is
$$\sqrt{[(x-a)^2 + (y-b)^2 + (z-c)^2]} = r$$
or $(x-a)^2 + (y-b)^2 + (z-c)^2 = r^2$

5.1 Exercise 2

1 Using $x^2 + y^2 = r^2$ the equations are:

(a) $x^2 + y^2 = 225$ (b) $x^2 + y^2 = 16$

(c) $x^2 + y^2 = 2.53$ since $2\pi r = 10$, so $r = 1.59$

(d) $x^2 + y^2 = 400$ since the radius is the distance of $(12, 16)$ from the origin

2 Using the formula $(x-a)^2 + (y-b)^2 = r^2$, the equations are:

(a) $(x-1)^2 + (y-1)^2 = 9$

(b) $(x+4)^2 + (y-6)^2 = 64$

3 By Pythagoras,
$$(E-20)^2 + (N-85)^2 = 18^2$$

The equation fails to take account of varying levels of visibility.

4 If (x, y, z) are the coordinates of a point on the sphere, the $(\text{distance})^2$ of this point from the centre $(2, 3, 1)$ is:
$$(x-2)^2 + (y-3)^2 + (z-1)^2$$
The equation of the sphere is therefore:
$$(x-2)^2 + (y-3)^2 + (z-1)^2 = 4^2 = 16$$

5 (a) The square of the distance from $(3, 2)$ to $(1, 4)$ is:
$$(3-1)^2 + (2-4)^2 = 8$$
Since $8 < 9$, the $(\text{radius})^2$, it follows that $(3, 2)$ lies inside the circle.

A similar argument works for (b), (c), (d).

(b) outside   (c) the point lies on the sphere

(d) inside

6 (a) radius 2 units,   centre $(2, 1)$

(b) radius 3 units,   centre $(1, 0)$

(c) radius $\frac{1}{2}$ unit,   centre $\left(\frac{1}{2}, -\frac{1}{4}\right)$

7E The distance between the centres is:
$$\sqrt{[(120-160)^2 + (150-180)^2 + (30-40)^2]}$$
$$= \sqrt{2600} \approx 51$$

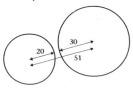

Since this is greater than the sum of the two radii, they do not intersect.

8E Suppose the equation is

$$(x - a)^2 + (y - b)^2 = r^2$$

Each point which lies on this circle will satisfy the equation.

$$(6 - a)^2 + (9 - b)^2 = r^2$$

$$(13 - a)^2 + (-8 - b)^2 = r^2$$

$$(-4 - a)^2 + (-15 - b)^2 = r^2$$

These simplify to

$$a^2 + b^2 - 12a - 18b + 117 = r^2 \quad ①$$

$$a^2 + b^2 - 26a + 16b + 233 = r^2 \quad ②$$

$$a^2 + b^2 + 8a + 30b + 241 = r^2 \quad ③$$

Eliminating r^2,

$$① - ② \Rightarrow 14a - 34b - 116 = 0$$

$$③ - ② \Rightarrow 34a + 14b + 8 = 0$$

giving $a = 1$, $b = -3$, $r = 13$

So the centre is $(1, -3)$, radius 13 and equation $(x - 1)^2 + (y + 3)^2 = 169$.

9E Suppose the equation is
$$(x - a)^2 + (y - b)^2 = 100.$$

Since it passes through $(10, 9)$ and $(8, -5)$ it follows that

$$(10 - a)^2 + (9 - b)^2 = 100$$

$$(8 - a)^2 + (-5 - b)^2 = 100$$

which become

$$a^2 + b^2 - 20a - 18b + 81 = 0 \quad ①$$

and

$$a^2 + b^2 - 16a + 10b - 11 = 0 \quad ②$$

Firstly, eliminate $a^2 + b^2$ by subtracting ① from ②

$$4a + 28b = 92$$

i.e. $\quad a = 23 - 7b$

Now substitute for a in ① to obtain a quadratic in b

$$(23 - 7b)^2 + b^2 - 20(23 - 7b) - 18b + 81 = 0$$

which reduces to $b^2 - 4b + 3 = 0$

Hence $b = 1$ or $b = 3$
If $b = 1$, $\quad a = 16$, and if $b = 3$, $\quad a = 2$

So the two equations are

$$(x - 16)^2 + (y - 1)^2 = 100$$

and $\quad (x - 2)^2 + (y - 3)^2 = 100$

$(-6, -3)$ lies on the second circle.

NB   You may have looked at the problem geometrically and spotted a 6, 8, 10 triangle pattern.

5.1.3 Trigonometric identities

5.1 Exercise 3

1 (a) $1 + \cos x = 3(1 - \cos^2 x)$

$$\Rightarrow 3\cos^2 x + \cos x - 2 = 0$$

(b) $(3c - 2)(c + 1)$

(c) $48.2°$, $\quad 180°$, $\quad 311.8°$

2 (a) $\tan \theta = \frac{2}{3}$, $\quad \theta = 33.7°, 213.7°$

(b) $\tan \theta = 1.6$, $\quad \theta = 58.0°, 238.0°$

(c) $\tan 2\theta = 1.4$, $\quad \theta = 27.2°, 117.2°, 207.2°,$
$\qquad\qquad\qquad\qquad 297.2°$

3 (a) 0, $\quad \dfrac{2\pi}{3}$, $\quad \dfrac{4\pi}{3}$, $\quad 2\pi$

(b) $\dfrac{\pi}{3}$, $\quad \dfrac{4\pi}{3}$

(c) $1.05 \left(= \dfrac{\pi}{3} \right)$, $1.82, 4.46, 5.24\left(= \dfrac{5\pi}{3} \right)$

4 (a) 0.52, $\quad 2.62$, $\quad 3.67$, $\quad 5.76$

(b) 0, $\quad \pi$, $\quad 2\pi$

(c) 0.46, $\quad 2.68$, $\quad 3.61$, $\quad 5.82$

(d) 0.34, $\quad 2.80$, $\quad 4.71$

5E (a) Let N be the foot of the perpendicular from C to OP.
Then $PC^2 = NC^2 + PN^2$,
where $NC = 100 \sin \theta$ and
$PN = 130 - 100 \cos \theta$.

(b) $PC^2 = 100^2 \sin^2 \theta + 100^2 \cos^2 \theta$
$\qquad - 2 \times 130 \times 100 \cos \theta + 130^2$
$\qquad = 26\,900 - 26\,000 \cos \theta$

(c) $-32.2° \le \theta \le 32.2°$

6E $4x^2 + 9y^2 = 36$ or $\left(\dfrac{x}{3}\right)^2 + \left(\dfrac{y}{2}\right)^2 = 1$

The curve is a stretched circle (i.e. an ellipse).

5.1.4 $r \sin(\theta + \alpha)$

5.1 C

1 (a)

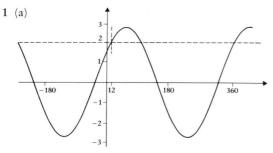

(b) The approximate solution is $10°$.
[The value predicted by theory is $12.4°$.]

(c) (i) The greatest height above ground is $2.9\,\text{m}$, which occurs at an angle of approximately $60°$ ($59°$ in theory).

   (ii) The wardrobe may be tipped at any angle between $0°$ and $12°$.

2 (a)

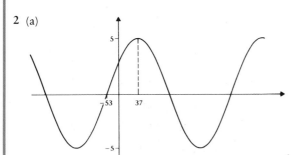

The graph is a phase-shifted sine wave.

(b) $y = 5 \sin(x + 53°)$ since the graph has amplitude 5 and is $y = 5 \sin x$ translated through $\begin{bmatrix} -53 \\ 0 \end{bmatrix}$.

3

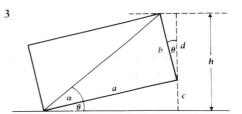

(a) (i) $h = c + d = a \sin \theta + b \cos \theta$

   (ii) $\dfrac{h}{r} = \sin(\theta + \alpha) \Rightarrow h = r \sin(\theta + \alpha)$

(b) $r^2 = a^2 + b^2$ and $\tan \alpha = \dfrac{b}{a}$

Thus, you can write $a \sin \theta + b \cos \theta$ in the form $r \sin(\theta + \alpha)$, where $r^2 = a^2 + b^2$ and $\tan \alpha = \dfrac{b}{a}$.

4 (a) $r = \sqrt{(4^2 + 7^2)} = 8.06$

$\tan \alpha = \dfrac{7}{4} \Rightarrow \alpha = 60.3°$

$\Rightarrow 4 \sin \theta + 7 \cos \theta = 8.06 \sin(\theta + 60.3°)$

5.1 Exercise 4

1 (a) $3 \sin \theta + 2 \cos \theta = r \sin(\theta + \alpha)$
   where $r = \sqrt{(3^2 + 2^2)} = 3.61$
   and $\tan \alpha = \tfrac{2}{3} \Rightarrow \alpha = 33.7°$

(b) $3.61 \sin(\theta + 33.7°) = 3$
$\Rightarrow \theta + 33.7° = 56.3°$ or $123.7°$
$\Rightarrow \qquad \theta = 22.6°$ or $90°$

2 (a) $5 \sin \theta + 12 \cos \theta$ is equivalent to $r \sin(\theta + \alpha)$ where r and α can be found from the triangle below.

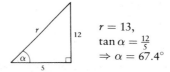

$r = 13$,
$\tan \alpha = \tfrac{12}{5}$
$\Rightarrow \alpha = 67.4°$

Since $5 \sin \theta + 12 \cos \theta = 13 \sin(\theta + 67.4°)$, the maximum value is 13, which occurs when $\theta + 67.4° = 90°$, i.e. at $\theta = 22.6°$.

(b)

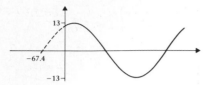

$13 \sin (\theta + 67.4°) = 9$

$\Rightarrow \quad \theta + 67.4° = 43.8°, 136.2°, 403.8°,$ etc.
$\Rightarrow \qquad \theta = 68.8°$ or $336.4°$

3 (a) (i) $AD = 6 \sin \theta$
(ii) $AB = 8 \cos \theta$
(iii) perimeter $= 12 \sin \theta + 16 \cos \theta$

(b) $12 \sin \theta + 16 \cos \theta = 14$
$\Rightarrow 3 \sin \theta + 4 \cos \theta = 3.5$

(c) $3 \sin \theta + 4 \cos \theta = 5 \sin (\theta + 53.1°)$
$\Rightarrow \theta = 82°$

The sides have length 5.9 and 1.1.

(d) Largest perimeter is 20, when $\theta = 36.9°$.

4E (a) B will move in a circle because OB
remains constant.
$OB = \sqrt{(6^2 + 3^2)} = \sqrt{45} = 6.71$ m

(b)

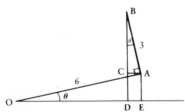

$d = CD + BC = AE + BC$
$= 6 \sin \theta + 3 \cos \theta$

(c)

$6 \sin \theta + 3 \cos \theta = r \sin (\theta + \alpha)$
where $r = \sqrt{(6^2 + 3^2)} = 6.71$ m
$\tan \alpha = \frac{3}{6} = \frac{1}{2} \Rightarrow \alpha = 26.6°$

(d) The maximum distance is 6.71 m, when
$\sin (\theta + 26.6°) = 1$, i.e. $\theta = 63.4°$.

5.1.5 Addition formulas

5.1 Exercise 5

1 (a) $\sin (x + 60°) = \sin x \cos 60° + \cos x \sin 60°$
$$= \frac{1}{2} \sin x + \frac{\sqrt{3}}{2} \cos x$$

2 (a) $\sin (x + \pi) = \sin x \cos \pi + \cos x \sin \pi$
$$= - \sin x$$

(b)

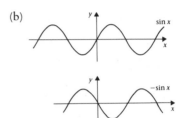

A translation of the sine graph by $-\pi$ in
the x-direction has the same effect as a
reflection in the x-axis.

3 (a) $\cos (A + B) + \cos (A - B)$
$$= \cos A \cos B - \sin A \sin B$$
$$+ \cos A \cos B + \sin A \sin B$$
$$= 2 \cos A \cos B$$

(b) $\cos (A - B) - \cos (A + B) = 2 \sin A \sin B$

4 (a) $\sin (45° + 30°)$
$$= \sin 45° \cos 30° + \cos 45° \sin 30°$$
$$= \frac{1}{\sqrt{2}} \times \frac{\sqrt{3}}{2} + \frac{1}{\sqrt{2}} \times \frac{1}{2}$$
$$= \frac{\sqrt{3} + 1}{2\sqrt{2}}$$

(b) $\sin 15° = \sin (45° - 30°) = \dfrac{\sqrt{3} - 1}{2\sqrt{2}}$

5 $\dfrac{63}{65}$

6 (a) $120°, 240°$

(b) $30°, 90°, 150°, 270°$

7E $\tan\left(x + \dfrac{\pi}{4}\right) = \dfrac{\sin\left(x + \dfrac{\pi}{4}\right)}{\cos\left(x + \dfrac{\pi}{4}\right)}$

$$= \dfrac{\dfrac{1}{\sqrt{2}}(\cos x + \sin x)}{\dfrac{1}{\sqrt{2}}(\cos x - \sin x)}$$

$$= \dfrac{\cos x + \sin x}{\cos x - \sin x}$$

Dividing the numerator and the denominator by $\cos x$,

$$\tan\left(x + \dfrac{\pi}{4}\right) = \dfrac{1 + \tan x}{1 - \tan x}$$

8E (a) $\sin 3x = \sin 2x \cos x + \cos 2x \sin x$

$$= (2 \sin x \cos x)\cos x$$
$$+ (1 - 2 \sin^2 x)\sin x$$
$$= 2 \sin x (1 - \sin^2 x)$$
$$+ \sin x - 2 \sin^3 x$$
$$= 3 \sin x - 4 \sin^3 x$$

(b) $\cos 3x = 4 \cos^3 x - 3 \cos x$

9E $\tan 2x = \dfrac{\sin 2x}{\cos 2x} = \dfrac{2 \sin x \cos x}{\cos^2 x - \sin^2 x}$

Dividing by $\cos^2 x$,

$$\dfrac{2 \tan x}{1 - \dfrac{\sin^2 x}{\cos^2 x}} = \dfrac{2 \tan x}{1 - \tan^2 x}$$

10E $0°,\ 48.6°,\ 131.4°,\ 180°,\ 270°,\ 360°$

5.1.6 Solution of non-right-angled triangles: the cosine rule

5.1 **D**

1 $h = b \sin A$
  $y = b \cos A$

2 $x = c - y$, because $x + y = c$
  $x = c - b \cos A$

3 $a^2 = h^2 + x^2$
  $= (b \sin A)^2 + (c - b \cos A)^2$

4 $a^2 = b^2 \sin^2 A + c^2 - 2bc \cos A + b^2 \cos^2 A$
  $= b^2 + c^2 - 2bc \cos A,$
  since $\cos^2 A + \sin^2 A = 1$
  $\Rightarrow a^2 = b^2 + c^2 - 2bc \cos A$

5 If $A = 90°$, $\cos A = 0$ and the cosine rule gives $a^2 = b^2 + c^2$, which is Pythagoras' theorem.

If $A < 90°$, then $a^2 < b^2 + c^2$, which corresponds with the result given by the cosine rule.

6 (a) $c^2 = a^2 + b^2 - 2ab \cos C$

(b) $b^2 = a^2 + c^2 - 2ac \cos B$

7

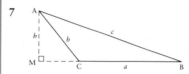

MB $= c \cos B$
MC $= c \cos B - a$
In triangle ACM,
$$b^2 = h^2 + (c \cos B - a)^2 \qquad ①$$
and in triangle ABM,
$$c^2 = h^2 + (c \cos B)^2 \qquad ②$$
Eliminating h^2 from ① and ② leads to the result.

5.1 **Exercise 6**

1 5.76 cm

2 (a) $\cos A = \dfrac{b^2 + c^2 - a^2}{2bc}$

(b) $34.0°,\quad 44.4°,\quad 101.5°$

3 (a) $a^2 = 10^2 + 7^2 - 2 \times 10 \times 7 \cos 45°$
    $a = 7.1$ cm

(b) $a^2 = 10^2 + 7^2 - 2 \times 10 \times 7 \cos 120°$
    $a = 14.8$ cm

(c) $a = 17$ cm

4 5.15

5 5.41 km

5.1.7 Solution of non-right-angled triangles: the sine rule

5.1 E

1 $h_1 = c \sin A$
$\frac{1}{2}bh_1 = \frac{1}{2}bc \sin A$

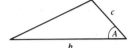

Note: This is a more useful expression for the area of a triangle than $\frac{1}{2}bh_1$, since it is given in terms of sides and angles.

Area of triangle $= \frac{1}{2}bc \sin A$

$\qquad = \frac{1}{2} \times$ product of two sides
$\qquad\qquad \times$ sine of included angle.

2 $h_2 = b \sin C$
Area $= \frac{1}{2}ab \sin C$

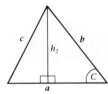

3 $\frac{1}{2}bc \sin A = \frac{1}{2}ab \sin C$
$\Rightarrow c \sin A = a \sin C$
$\Rightarrow \dfrac{a}{\sin A} = \dfrac{c}{\sin C}$

4 By symmetry, if c is the base, area $= \frac{1}{2}ac \sin B$

5 $\frac{1}{2}ac \sin B = \frac{1}{2}bc \sin A$
$\Rightarrow \dfrac{b}{\sin B} = \dfrac{a}{\sin A}, \quad \dfrac{c}{\sin C} = \dfrac{b}{\sin B}$

So, combining this result with that obtained in question 3 gives the sine rule:

$$\frac{a}{\sin A} = \frac{b}{\sin B} = \frac{c}{\sin C}$$

6 Area $= \frac{1}{2} \times 4 \times 7 \times \sin 30° = 7 \text{ cm}^2$

5.1 Exercise 7

1 (a) $\dfrac{8}{\sin 80°} = \dfrac{5}{\sin \theta}$

$\Rightarrow \sin \theta = \dfrac{5 \sin 80°}{8} = 0.6155,$

giving $\theta = 38°$

Thus the third angle is $62°$ and

$\dfrac{8}{\sin 80°} = \dfrac{x}{\sin 62°}$

giving $x = \dfrac{8 \sin 62°}{\sin 80°} = 7.17 \text{ cm}$

(b) $\theta = 27.4°$, the third angle is $22.6°$ and $x = 10.05 \text{ mm}$

2 (a) $x^2 = 18^2 + 10^2 - 2 \times 18 \times 10 \cos 35°$
$\Rightarrow x = 11.4 \text{ cm}$

$\dfrac{\sin \theta}{10} = \dfrac{\sin 35°}{11.4} \Rightarrow \theta = 30.2°$

(θ must be acute)
The remaining angles are $30.2°$ and $114.8°$

(b) $x = 100.3 \text{ m}$
The remaining angles are $49.3°$ and $58.7°$.

3 (a) 51.6 cm^2 **(b)** 3420 m^2 (to 3 s.f.)

4 (a) $43.2 \text{ m}, 33.2°$ and $46.8°$

(b) $24 \text{ mm}, 16.3°$ and $73.7°$

(c) $41.9°$ and $73.1°, 40.1 \text{ cm}$

(d) $48.2°, 58.4°, 73.4°$

5 $437 \text{ km}, 050°$

5.2 Vector geometry

5.2.1 Vectors and position vectors

5.2 A

1 (a) $\overrightarrow{AB} = \begin{bmatrix} -1 \\ 2 \end{bmatrix} - \begin{bmatrix} 3 \\ 2 \end{bmatrix} = \begin{bmatrix} -4 \\ 0 \end{bmatrix}$

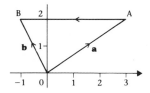

(b) $\overrightarrow{AB} = \begin{bmatrix} 5 \\ 4 \end{bmatrix} - \begin{bmatrix} 5 \\ -2 \end{bmatrix} = \begin{bmatrix} 0 \\ 6 \end{bmatrix}$

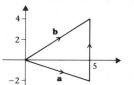

2 $\overrightarrow{PQ} = \overrightarrow{OQ} - \overrightarrow{OP} = \mathbf{q} - \mathbf{p}$

3 (a) $\mathbf{c} = \tfrac{3}{2}\mathbf{a}$
$\mathbf{d} = 2\mathbf{b}$
$\mathbf{e} = \mathbf{b} - \mathbf{a}$
$\mathbf{f} = -\mathbf{b}$

(b) $\overrightarrow{AB} = \mathbf{b} - \mathbf{a}$
$\overrightarrow{CD} = \mathbf{d} - \mathbf{c} = 2\mathbf{b} - \tfrac{3}{2}\mathbf{a}$
$\overrightarrow{DE} = \mathbf{e} - \mathbf{d} = (\mathbf{b} - \mathbf{a}) - 2\mathbf{b} = -\mathbf{a} - \mathbf{b}$
$\overrightarrow{EF} = \mathbf{f} - \mathbf{e} = -\mathbf{b} - (\mathbf{b} - \mathbf{a}) = \mathbf{a} - 2\mathbf{b}$
$\overrightarrow{FC} = \mathbf{c} - \mathbf{f} = \tfrac{3}{2}\mathbf{a} + \mathbf{b}$

(c) $\overrightarrow{CD} + \overrightarrow{DE} + \overrightarrow{EF} + \overrightarrow{FC}$
$= 2\mathbf{b} - \tfrac{3}{2}\mathbf{a} - \mathbf{a} - \mathbf{b} + \mathbf{a} - 2\mathbf{b} + \tfrac{3}{2}\mathbf{a} + \mathbf{b}$
$= 0$

The sum of the vectors is zero because the net displacement around the quadrilateral CDEFC is zero, i.e. the vectors have returned to their starting point.

(d) $\overrightarrow{AD} = 2\mathbf{b} - \mathbf{a} = -\overrightarrow{EF}$
$\overrightarrow{EF}$ is of the same magnitude as $\overrightarrow{AD}$ but in the opposite direction.

4 (a) Values of t generate the position vectors:

t	-3	-2	-1	0	1	2	3
$\begin{bmatrix} x \\ y \end{bmatrix}$	$\begin{bmatrix} -6 \\ -9 \end{bmatrix}$	$\begin{bmatrix} -4 \\ -6 \end{bmatrix}$	$\begin{bmatrix} -2 \\ -3 \end{bmatrix}$	$\begin{bmatrix} 0 \\ 0 \end{bmatrix}$	$\begin{bmatrix} 2 \\ 3 \end{bmatrix}$	$\begin{bmatrix} 4 \\ 6 \end{bmatrix}$	$\begin{bmatrix} 6 \\ 9 \end{bmatrix}$

giving the graph of the straight line.

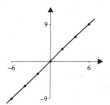

You can apply a similar method to (b) and (c) giving:

(b)

(c)

In each case the graph is a straight line.

The vector $\begin{bmatrix} 2 \\ 3 \end{bmatrix}$ gives the *direction* of the line.

5 The three lines join each vertex to the mid-point of the opposite side. [Such a line is called a **median**.]

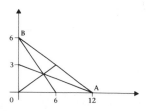

They intersect at the point $(4, 2)$.

6 (a) $\overrightarrow{OP} = \overrightarrow{OA} + \overrightarrow{AE} + \overrightarrow{EP}$ and $\overrightarrow{EP} = \frac{1}{2}\overrightarrow{EF}$

So $\overrightarrow{OP} = \begin{bmatrix} 6 \\ 0 \\ 0 \end{bmatrix} + \begin{bmatrix} 0 \\ 0 \\ 6 \end{bmatrix} + \begin{bmatrix} 0 \\ 3 \\ 0 \end{bmatrix} = \begin{bmatrix} 6 \\ 3 \\ 6 \end{bmatrix}$

Similarly $\overrightarrow{OQ} = \begin{bmatrix} 3 \\ 6 \\ 6 \end{bmatrix}$ and $\overrightarrow{OR} = \begin{bmatrix} 6 \\ 6 \\ 3 \end{bmatrix}$

(b) $\overrightarrow{PQ} = q - p = \begin{bmatrix} -3 \\ 3 \\ 0 \end{bmatrix}$

$\overrightarrow{QR} = \begin{bmatrix} 3 \\ 0 \\ -3 \end{bmatrix}$ $\overrightarrow{RP} = \begin{bmatrix} 0 \\ -3 \\ 3 \end{bmatrix}$

$\Rightarrow \overrightarrow{PQ} + \overrightarrow{QR} + \overrightarrow{RP}$

$= \begin{bmatrix} -3 \\ 3 \\ 0 \end{bmatrix} + \begin{bmatrix} 3 \\ 0 \\ -3 \end{bmatrix} + \begin{bmatrix} 0 \\ -3 \\ 3 \end{bmatrix} = \begin{bmatrix} 0 \\ 0 \\ 0 \end{bmatrix}$

7E (a) $t = \frac{1}{2}(x - 3)$

(b) $y = -1 + 3 \times \frac{1}{2}(x - 3) \Rightarrow y = \frac{3}{2}x - \frac{11}{2}$

(c) The gradient is $\frac{3}{2}$. The vector $\begin{bmatrix} 2 \\ 3 \end{bmatrix}$ has gradient $\frac{3}{2}$.

8E (a) $x = 3 - 2s$ **(b)** $x = 1 + 2t$

$y = -2 + s$ $y = -1 - t$

$\Rightarrow y = -\frac{1}{2}x - \frac{1}{2}$ $\Rightarrow y = -\frac{1}{2}x - \frac{1}{2}$

The two vector equations give the same straight line.

They have the same direction, $\begin{bmatrix} -2 \\ 1 \end{bmatrix}$ or $\begin{bmatrix} 2 \\ -1 \end{bmatrix}$, and appear to be different since different points on the line have been chosen.

5.2 Exercise 1

1 (a) The direction vector is

$$\begin{bmatrix} 7 \\ 7 \end{bmatrix} - \begin{bmatrix} 4 \\ 1 \end{bmatrix} = \begin{bmatrix} 3 \\ 6 \end{bmatrix},$$

so the line is $\begin{bmatrix} x \\ y \end{bmatrix} = \begin{bmatrix} 4 \\ 1 \end{bmatrix} + t\begin{bmatrix} 3 \\ 6 \end{bmatrix}$

(b) $\begin{bmatrix} x \\ y \end{bmatrix} = \begin{bmatrix} 2 \\ 1 \end{bmatrix} + t\begin{bmatrix} -3 \\ 4 \end{bmatrix}$

(c) $\begin{bmatrix} x \\ y \end{bmatrix} = \begin{bmatrix} 5 \\ 1 \end{bmatrix} + t\begin{bmatrix} -2 \\ 4 \end{bmatrix}$

(d) $\begin{bmatrix} x \\ y \end{bmatrix} = t\begin{bmatrix} 1 \\ 1 \end{bmatrix}$

(e) $\begin{bmatrix} x \\ y \end{bmatrix} = t\begin{bmatrix} 0 \\ 1 \end{bmatrix}$

2 (a) $\overrightarrow{PQ} = q - p = \begin{bmatrix} 5 \\ -2 \end{bmatrix} - \begin{bmatrix} 3 \\ 1 \end{bmatrix} = \begin{bmatrix} 2 \\ -3 \end{bmatrix}$

$\overrightarrow{SR} = r - s = \begin{bmatrix} 2 \\ -4 \end{bmatrix} - \begin{bmatrix} 0 \\ -1 \end{bmatrix} = \begin{bmatrix} 2 \\ -3 \end{bmatrix}$

Since $\overrightarrow{PQ} = \overrightarrow{SR}$ the vectors are of the same length and direction, i.e. PQ is parallel to SR and equal in length, so PQRS is a parallelogram.

(b) It follows that $\overrightarrow{PS}$ must also equal $\overrightarrow{QR}$.

3 (a) (i) $\overrightarrow{OD} = \begin{bmatrix} 6 \\ 0 \\ 10 \end{bmatrix}$ $\overrightarrow{OE} = \begin{bmatrix} 0 \\ 8 \\ 10 \end{bmatrix}$

(ii) $\overrightarrow{AB} = b - a = \begin{bmatrix} -6 \\ 8 \\ 0 \end{bmatrix}$

$\overrightarrow{AD} = \begin{bmatrix} 0 \\ 0 \\ 10 \end{bmatrix}$ $\overrightarrow{AC} = \begin{bmatrix} -6 \\ 0 \\ 10 \end{bmatrix}$

$\overrightarrow{AE} = \begin{bmatrix} -6 \\ 8 \\ 10 \end{bmatrix}$ $\overrightarrow{DE} = \begin{bmatrix} -6 \\ 8 \\ 0 \end{bmatrix}$

(b) (i) $\overrightarrow{OM} = \overrightarrow{OA} + \frac{1}{2}\overrightarrow{AB} = \begin{bmatrix} 3 \\ 4 \\ 0 \end{bmatrix}$

$\overrightarrow{ON} = \overrightarrow{OD} + \frac{1}{2}\overrightarrow{DE} = \begin{bmatrix} 3 \\ 4 \\ 10 \end{bmatrix}$

(ii) $\overrightarrow{AN} = \begin{bmatrix} -3 \\ 4 \\ 10 \end{bmatrix} \qquad \overrightarrow{ME} = \begin{bmatrix} -3 \\ 4 \\ 10 \end{bmatrix}$

(iii) $\overrightarrow{AN} = \overrightarrow{ME}$, which is to be expected since AN is parallel to ME and of equal length.

4 (a) $\mathbf{a} = \begin{bmatrix} 8 \\ 0 \\ 0 \end{bmatrix} \qquad \mathbf{b} = \begin{bmatrix} 8 \\ 10 \\ 0 \end{bmatrix} \qquad \mathbf{c} = \begin{bmatrix} 0 \\ 10 \\ 0 \end{bmatrix}$

$\mathbf{d} = \begin{bmatrix} 4 \\ 2 \\ 3 \end{bmatrix} \qquad \mathbf{e} = \begin{bmatrix} 4 \\ 8 \\ 3 \end{bmatrix}$

NB You can find **d** and **e** by viewing the roof from above:

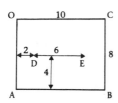

(b) $\overrightarrow{AD} = \mathbf{d} - \mathbf{a} = \begin{bmatrix} -4 \\ 2 \\ 3 \end{bmatrix} \qquad \overrightarrow{OD} = \begin{bmatrix} 4 \\ 2 \\ 3 \end{bmatrix}$

$\overrightarrow{BE} = \begin{bmatrix} -4 \\ -2 \\ 3 \end{bmatrix} \qquad \overrightarrow{CE} = \begin{bmatrix} 4 \\ -2 \\ 3 \end{bmatrix}$

(c) By Pythagoras, the length of $\overrightarrow{AD}$ is $\sqrt{(4^2 + 2^2 + 3^2)} = \sqrt{29} = 5.4\,\text{m}$

5.2.2 Equations of lines

5.2 **B**

1 $\mathbf{d} = \begin{bmatrix} 4 \\ 6 \\ 0 \end{bmatrix} \qquad \mathbf{e} = \begin{bmatrix} 0 \\ 6 \\ 3 \end{bmatrix}$

$\mathbf{f} = \begin{bmatrix} 4 \\ 0 \\ 3 \end{bmatrix} \qquad \mathbf{g} = \begin{bmatrix} 4 \\ 6 \\ 3 \end{bmatrix}$

2 (a) $\lambda = 0 \Rightarrow \begin{bmatrix} x \\ y \\ z \end{bmatrix} = \begin{bmatrix} 0 \\ 0 \\ 0 \end{bmatrix}$

$\lambda = 1 \Rightarrow \begin{bmatrix} x \\ y \\ z \end{bmatrix} = \begin{bmatrix} 4 \\ 6 \\ 0 \end{bmatrix}$

So $\lambda = 0$ gives O, $\lambda = 1$ gives D.

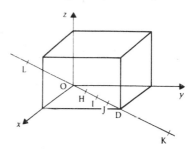

(b) H, I, J, K and L correspond to $\lambda = \frac{1}{4}, \frac{1}{2}, \frac{3}{4}$, 2 and -1 respectively. H, I and J are on the line between O and D.

(c) K and L are on the same line but outside OD.

3 (a) Since $\overrightarrow{OC} = \begin{bmatrix} 0 \\ 0 \\ 3 \end{bmatrix}$ the vector equation corresponds to the line OC.

(b) OE   (c) $\begin{bmatrix} x \\ y \\ z \end{bmatrix} = \lambda \begin{bmatrix} 0 \\ 6 \\ 0 \end{bmatrix}$

(d) $\begin{bmatrix} x \\ y \\ z \end{bmatrix} = \lambda \begin{bmatrix} 4 \\ 0 \\ 3 \end{bmatrix}$ (e) $\begin{bmatrix} x \\ y \\ z \end{bmatrix} = \lambda \begin{bmatrix} 4 \\ 6 \\ 3 \end{bmatrix}$

4 $\lambda = 0 \Rightarrow \begin{bmatrix} x \\ y \\ z \end{bmatrix} = \begin{bmatrix} 0 \\ 0 \\ 3 \end{bmatrix}$, i.e. point C

$\lambda = 1 \Rightarrow \begin{bmatrix} x \\ y \\ z \end{bmatrix} = \begin{bmatrix} 4 \\ 6 \\ 3 \end{bmatrix}$, point G

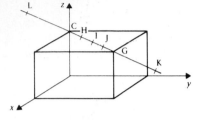

The points lie on the line CG.
H, I, J, K and L correspond to $\lambda = \frac{1}{4}, \frac{1}{2}, \frac{3}{4}, 2$ and -1 respectively.

5 (a) When $\lambda = 0$, $\begin{bmatrix} x \\ y \\ z \end{bmatrix} = \begin{bmatrix} 0 \\ 6 \\ 0 \end{bmatrix}$, i.e. point B.

When $\lambda = 1$, $\begin{bmatrix} x \\ y \\ z \end{bmatrix} = \begin{bmatrix} 0 \\ 6 \\ 3 \end{bmatrix}$, i.e. point E.

Hence the line is BE.

(b) $\lambda = 0$ gives F, $\lambda = 1$ gives E, so the line is FE. The two vectors each specify the *direction* of the line.

6 (a) The line AD passes through A and has

direction $\overrightarrow{AD} = \begin{bmatrix} 0 \\ 6 \\ 0 \end{bmatrix}$ so it has

equation $\begin{bmatrix} x \\ y \\ z \end{bmatrix} = \begin{bmatrix} 4 \\ 0 \\ 0 \end{bmatrix} + \lambda \begin{bmatrix} 0 \\ 6 \\ 0 \end{bmatrix}$.

(b) $\begin{bmatrix} x \\ y \\ z \end{bmatrix} = \begin{bmatrix} 4 \\ 0 \\ 0 \end{bmatrix} + \lambda \begin{bmatrix} 0 \\ 6 \\ 3 \end{bmatrix}$

(c) $\begin{bmatrix} x \\ y \\ z \end{bmatrix} = \begin{bmatrix} 4 \\ 0 \\ 0 \end{bmatrix} + \lambda \begin{bmatrix} -4 \\ 6 \\ 3 \end{bmatrix}$

NB These are *not* unique equations. For example, AE also passes through E and has

equation $\begin{bmatrix} x \\ y \\ z \end{bmatrix} = \begin{bmatrix} 0 \\ 6 \\ 3 \end{bmatrix} + \mu \begin{bmatrix} 4 \\ -6 \\ -3 \end{bmatrix}$. Thus the

point $(-4, 12, 6)$ is found either by starting from A and putting $\lambda = 2$, or by starting from E and putting $\mu = -1$.

7 (a)

λ	-2	-1	0	1	2
$\begin{bmatrix} x \\ y \end{bmatrix}$	$\begin{bmatrix} -1 \\ -2 \end{bmatrix}$	$\begin{bmatrix} 0 \\ -1 \end{bmatrix}$	$\begin{bmatrix} 1 \\ 0 \end{bmatrix}$	$\begin{bmatrix} 2 \\ 1 \end{bmatrix}$	$\begin{bmatrix} 3 \\ 2 \end{bmatrix}$

μ	-2	-1	0	1	2
$\begin{bmatrix} x \\ y \end{bmatrix}$	$\begin{bmatrix} -3 \\ 5 \end{bmatrix}$	$\begin{bmatrix} -1 \\ 4 \end{bmatrix}$	$\begin{bmatrix} 1 \\ 3 \end{bmatrix}$	$\begin{bmatrix} 3 \\ 2 \end{bmatrix}$	$\begin{bmatrix} 5 \\ 1 \end{bmatrix}$

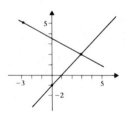

(b) The lines intersect at $(3, 2)$.

(c) $\lambda = 2$, $\mu = 1$ at the point of intersection.

(d) Since at the point of intersection both x- and y-coordinates are equal,

$$1 + \lambda = 1 + 2\mu \quad \text{and} \quad \lambda = 3 - \mu$$

(e) Solving these gives $\lambda = 2$, $\mu = 1$.

8 The intersection is at $(2\frac{1}{5}, 2\frac{2}{5})$.

5.2 Exercise 2

1 $\begin{bmatrix} x \\ y \end{bmatrix} = \begin{bmatrix} 3 \\ 0 \end{bmatrix} + \lambda \begin{bmatrix} -3 \\ 3 \end{bmatrix}$ and

$\begin{bmatrix} x \\ y \end{bmatrix} = \begin{bmatrix} 1 \\ 0 \end{bmatrix} + \mu \begin{bmatrix} 2 \\ 2 \end{bmatrix}$

$\Rightarrow 3 - 3\lambda = 1 + 2\mu$ and $3\lambda = 2\mu$
giving $\lambda = \frac{1}{3}$, $\mu = \frac{1}{2}$
and a point of intersection $(2, 1)$.

2 (a) OG

(b) $\lambda = 0$ gives $\begin{bmatrix} 4 \\ 0 \\ 3 \end{bmatrix}$;

$\lambda = 1$ gives $\begin{bmatrix} 0 \\ 5 \\ 3 \end{bmatrix}$ i.e. EG

(c) CE   (d) BD

3 Writing $\mathbf{r}$ for $\begin{bmatrix} x \\ y \\ z \end{bmatrix}$ gives:

(a) $\mathbf{r} = \overrightarrow{OA} + \lambda\,\overrightarrow{AB} = \begin{bmatrix} 4 \\ 0 \\ 0 \end{bmatrix} + \lambda \begin{bmatrix} 0 \\ 5 \\ 0 \end{bmatrix}$

(b) $\mathbf{r} = \overrightarrow{OA} + \lambda\,\overrightarrow{AC} = \begin{bmatrix} 4 \\ 0 \\ 0 \end{bmatrix} + \lambda \begin{bmatrix} -4 \\ 5 \\ 0 \end{bmatrix}$

(c) $\mathbf{r} = \overrightarrow{OA} + \lambda\,\overrightarrow{AF} = \begin{bmatrix} 4 \\ 0 \\ 0 \end{bmatrix} + \lambda \begin{bmatrix} 0 \\ 5 \\ 3 \end{bmatrix}$

(d) $\mathbf{r} = \overrightarrow{OA} + \lambda\,\overrightarrow{AG} = \begin{bmatrix} 4 \\ 0 \\ 0 \end{bmatrix} + \lambda \begin{bmatrix} -4 \\ 5 \\ 3 \end{bmatrix}$

4 When the y components are equal,
$3 - \lambda = -3 + \mu$, and when the z components
are equal, $\lambda = \mu$, i.e.
$\lambda = \mu = 3$
$\lambda = 3 \Rightarrow x = 4 - 3 = 1$
$\mu = 3 \Rightarrow x = 4 - 3 = 1$

Hence the vertex is at $(1, 0, 3)$.

5 (a) They meet at $(5, 3, 11)$.

(b) Parallel lines – no intersection.

(c) They meet at $(6, 3, -2)$.

(d) Skew lines – no intersection.

6 They meet at $(-9, 3.5, -1.5)$.

5.2.3 Scalar products

5.2 **C**

1 (a) The length of **a** is $\sqrt{13}$.
   The length of **b** is $\sqrt{17}$.

(b) $\mathbf{c} = \mathbf{b} - \mathbf{a} = \begin{bmatrix} -2 \\ 2 \end{bmatrix}$

   So the length of **c** is
   $\sqrt{((-2)^2 + 2^2)} = \sqrt{8} \approx 2.828$.

(c)
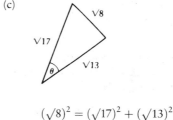

$(\sqrt{8})^2 = (\sqrt{17})^2 + (\sqrt{13})^2$
$\qquad\qquad - 2\sqrt{17}\sqrt{13}\cos\theta$

$\Rightarrow \cos\theta = \dfrac{11}{\sqrt{221}} \approx 0.7399$

$\Rightarrow \qquad \theta = 42.3°$

2 (a) As in question 1, by Pythagoras,
$$a = \sqrt{(a_1^2 + a_2^2)} \Rightarrow a^2 = a_1^2 + a_2^2$$
   Similarly $b^2 = b_1^2 + b_2^2$

(b) $c^2 = (b_1 - a_1)^2 + (b_2 - a_2)^2$
   $= b_1^2 - 2a_1 b_1 + a_1^2 + b_2^2 - 2a_2 b_2 + a_2^2$
   $= (a_1^2 + a_2^2) + (b_1^2 + b_2^2) - 2a_1 b_1 - 2a_2 b_2$
   $= a^2 + b^2 - 2(a_1 b_1 + a_2 b_2)$

(c) By the cosine rule,
$$c^2 = a^2 + b^2 - 2ab\cos\theta$$
   So $a_1 b_1 + a_2 b_2 = ab\cos\theta$, since the two
   expressions are otherwise identical.

3 $\mathbf{a} = \begin{bmatrix} 3 \\ 2 \end{bmatrix}$ $\mathbf{b} = \begin{bmatrix} -2 \\ 2 \end{bmatrix}$

$a_1 = 3, \quad a_2 = 2 \quad\quad b_1 = 1, \quad b_2 = 4$

$a = \sqrt{(9+4)} = \sqrt{13} \quad b = \sqrt{(1+16)} = \sqrt{17}$

$\Rightarrow 3 \times 1 + 2 \times 4 = \sqrt{13}\sqrt{17}\cos\theta$

$\Rightarrow \cos\theta = \dfrac{11}{\sqrt{221}} \approx 0.7399$

and $\theta = 42.3°$ as before.

5.2 Exercise 3

1 (a) Using $\cos\theta = \dfrac{\mathbf{a} \cdot \mathbf{b}}{ab}$ gives

$$\cos\theta = \frac{\begin{bmatrix} 5 \\ 2 \end{bmatrix} \cdot \begin{bmatrix} 3 \\ 2 \end{bmatrix}}{\sqrt{(25+4)}\sqrt{(9+4)}}$$

$$= \frac{5 \times 3 + 2 \times 2}{\sqrt{29}\sqrt{13}} = \frac{19}{\sqrt{377}}$$

$$\Rightarrow \theta = 11.9°$$

(b) $\theta = 124.5°$

2

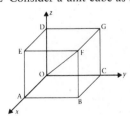

(a) $\overrightarrow{AB} = \mathbf{b} - \mathbf{a} = \begin{bmatrix} -1 \\ 3 \end{bmatrix} - \begin{bmatrix} 3 \\ 2 \end{bmatrix} = \begin{bmatrix} -4 \\ 1 \end{bmatrix}$

$\overrightarrow{AC} = \begin{bmatrix} -2 \\ 5 \end{bmatrix}$

(b) Both vectors must be pointing away from A.

$$\cos A = \frac{\overrightarrow{AB} \cdot \overrightarrow{AC}}{|AB|\,|AC|}$$

$$= \frac{8+5}{\sqrt{17}\sqrt{29}} = \frac{13}{\sqrt{493}}$$

$$\Rightarrow A = 54.2°$$

3 (a) $\theta = 54.9°$ (b) $\theta = 46.3°$

4 $\overrightarrow{PQ} = \begin{bmatrix} -7 \\ 4 \\ 4 \end{bmatrix}$ $\overrightarrow{PR} = \begin{bmatrix} 4 \\ 8 \\ -1 \end{bmatrix}$

$$\Rightarrow \cos P = \frac{-28 + 32 - 4}{\sqrt{(49+16+16)}\sqrt{(16+64+1)}} = 0$$

$$\Rightarrow P = 90°$$

$\overrightarrow{QP} = -\overrightarrow{PQ} = \begin{bmatrix} 7 \\ -4 \\ -4 \end{bmatrix}$ $\overrightarrow{QR} = \begin{bmatrix} 11 \\ 4 \\ -5 \end{bmatrix}$

$$\Rightarrow \cos Q = \frac{77 - 16 + 20}{\sqrt{(49+16+16)}\sqrt{(121+16+25)}}$$

$$= \frac{81}{9\sqrt{162}} = \frac{9}{\sqrt{2}\sqrt{81}} = \frac{1}{\sqrt{2}}$$

$$\Rightarrow Q = 45° \quad\text{and}\quad R = 180° - 90° - 45° = 45°$$

5 $\overrightarrow{AB} = \begin{bmatrix} 1 \\ 6 \\ -5 \end{bmatrix}$ $\overrightarrow{DC} = \begin{bmatrix} 1 \\ 6 \\ -5 \end{bmatrix}$

Since $\overrightarrow{AB} = \overrightarrow{DC}$, AB is parallel to DC and of equal length. Hence ABCD is a parallelogram.

$\overrightarrow{AD} = \begin{bmatrix} 4 \\ 1 \\ 2 \end{bmatrix}$

$|AB| = \sqrt{(1+36+25)} = \sqrt{62} = 7.87$
$|AD| = \sqrt{(16+1+4)} = \sqrt{21} = 4.58$

$$\cos A = \frac{\overrightarrow{AB} \cdot \overrightarrow{AD}}{|AB|\,|AD|} = \frac{4+6-10}{\sqrt{62}\sqrt{21}} = 0$$

$\Rightarrow A = 90°$ and the parallelogram is a rectangle.

6E Consider a unit cube as shown.

The longest diagonal is $\overrightarrow{OF} = \begin{bmatrix} 1 \\ 1 \\ 1 \end{bmatrix}$.

(a) You require DOF.

$$\cos \text{DOF} = \frac{\overrightarrow{OD} \cdot \overrightarrow{OF}}{|OD| \, |OF|}$$

$$= \frac{\begin{bmatrix} 0 \\ 0 \\ 1 \end{bmatrix} \cdot \begin{bmatrix} 1 \\ 1 \\ 1 \end{bmatrix}}{1 \times \sqrt{3}} = \frac{1}{\sqrt{3}}$$

$\Rightarrow$ angle DOF $= 54.7°$

(b) One face diagonal is OE.

$$\Rightarrow \cos \text{EOF} = \frac{\overrightarrow{OE} \cdot \overrightarrow{OF}}{|OE| \, |OF|}$$

$$= \frac{\begin{bmatrix} 1 \\ 0 \\ 1 \end{bmatrix} \cdot \begin{bmatrix} 1 \\ 1 \\ 1 \end{bmatrix}}{\sqrt{2}\sqrt{3}} = \frac{2}{\sqrt{6}}$$

$\Rightarrow$ angle EOF $= 35.3°$

(c) One other longest diagonal is CE, represented by

$$\begin{bmatrix} 1 \\ 0 \\ 1 \end{bmatrix} - \begin{bmatrix} 0 \\ 1 \\ 0 \end{bmatrix} = \begin{bmatrix} 1 \\ -1 \\ 1 \end{bmatrix}$$

If the angle between the diagonals is θ,

$$\cos \theta = \frac{\overrightarrow{CE} \cdot \overrightarrow{OF}}{|CE| \, |OF|}$$

$$= \frac{\begin{bmatrix} 1 \\ -1 \\ 1 \end{bmatrix} \cdot \begin{bmatrix} 1 \\ 1 \\ 1 \end{bmatrix}}{\sqrt{3}\sqrt{3}} = \frac{1}{3}$$

$\Rightarrow \theta = 70.5°$

5.2.4 Properties of the scalar product

5.2 D

1 (a)

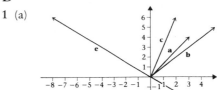

(b) **d** is parallel to **e**
a is perpendicular to **d** and **e**

2 (a) $|a| = 5$ $|b| = \sqrt{50}$ $|c| = \sqrt{40}$
$|d| = 5$ $|e| = 10$

(b) $\mathbf{a} \cdot \mathbf{a} = 25$ $\mathbf{b} \cdot \mathbf{b} = 50$ $\mathbf{c} \cdot \mathbf{c} = 40$
$\mathbf{d} \cdot \mathbf{d} = 25$ $\mathbf{e} \cdot \mathbf{e} = 100$

(c) $\mathbf{a} \cdot \mathbf{a} = |a|^2$
The scalar product of a vector with itself is equal to the square of its modulus.

3 (a) $\mathbf{a} \cdot \mathbf{b} = 35$ $\mathbf{b} \cdot \mathbf{a} = 35$

(b) $\mathbf{a} \cdot \mathbf{c} = 30$ $\mathbf{c} \cdot \mathbf{a} = 30$

(c) $\mathbf{a} \cdot \mathbf{b} = \mathbf{b} \cdot \mathbf{a}$ $\mathbf{a} \cdot \mathbf{c} = \mathbf{c} \cdot \mathbf{a}$
You can conclude that scalar multiplication is **commutative** as a consequence of the commutativity of ordinary multiplication.

4 (a) $\mathbf{a} \cdot \mathbf{b} + \mathbf{a} \cdot \mathbf{c} = 35 + 30 = 65$

(b) $\mathbf{a} \cdot (\mathbf{b} + \mathbf{c}) = \begin{bmatrix} 3 \\ 4 \end{bmatrix} \cdot \begin{bmatrix} 7 \\ 11 \end{bmatrix} = 21 + 44 = 65$

(c) So, the **distributive law** appears to hold, i.e. $\mathbf{a} \cdot \mathbf{b} + \mathbf{a} \cdot \mathbf{c} = \mathbf{a} \cdot (\mathbf{b} + \mathbf{c})$. In fact, it can be shown that the distributive law holds for all vectors **a**, **b**, **c**.

5 (a) $\mathbf{a} \cdot \mathbf{b} = 35$ $\mathbf{a} \cdot \mathbf{d} = 0$ $\mathbf{a} \cdot \mathbf{e} = 0$

(b) If the vectors are perpendicular then their scalar product is zero.

(c) $\begin{bmatrix} -5 \\ 5 \end{bmatrix}$ is perpendicular to **b**.

(d) Since $\mathbf{a} \cdot \mathbf{b} = ab \cos \theta$, $\mathbf{a} \cdot \mathbf{b} = 0 \Rightarrow a = 0$ or $b = 0$ or $\cos \theta = 0$. Thus *either* the vectors are perpendicular, *or* one of the vectors is the zero vector.

6E

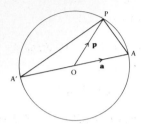

(a) $\overrightarrow{OA'} = -\overrightarrow{OA} = -\mathbf{a}$

$\overrightarrow{AP} = \mathbf{p} - \mathbf{a}$

$\overrightarrow{A'P} = \mathbf{p} - \mathbf{a}' = \mathbf{p} + \mathbf{a}$

(b) $\overrightarrow{AP} \cdot \overrightarrow{A'P} = (\mathbf{p} - \mathbf{a}) \cdot (\mathbf{p} + \mathbf{a})$
$= p^2 - a^2$
But, since $|p| = |a|$, $p^2 - a^2 = 0$

(c) $\overrightarrow{AP}$ is perpendicular to $\overrightarrow{A'P}$, i.e. the angle in a semi-circle is a right angle.

5.2 Exercise 4

1 (a) $|a| = \sqrt{13}$ $\quad |b| = \sqrt{34}$ $\quad |c| = \sqrt{13}$

(b) $\mathbf{a} \cdot \mathbf{b} = 21$ $\quad \mathbf{b} \cdot \mathbf{c} = -1$ $\quad \mathbf{c} \cdot \mathbf{a} = 0$

(c) $\mathbf{c}$ is perpendicular to $\mathbf{a}$.

(d) By inspection $\begin{bmatrix} 3 \\ -5 \end{bmatrix}$ is perpendicular to $\begin{bmatrix} 5 \\ 3 \end{bmatrix}$ $\left(\text{or any multiple of } \begin{bmatrix} 3 \\ -5 \end{bmatrix}\right)$.

2 (a) $\mathbf{a} \cdot \mathbf{b} = 0$ $\quad \mathbf{b} \cdot \mathbf{c} = 0$ $\quad \mathbf{c} \cdot \mathbf{a} = 0$

(b) All three sets of vectors are mutually perpendicular.

3 (a) $\mathbf{c} = \begin{bmatrix} 2 \\ 4 \end{bmatrix}$

(b) $\mathbf{d} = \mathbf{a} - \mathbf{b} = \begin{bmatrix} 16 \\ -8 \end{bmatrix}$

(c) $\mathbf{c} \cdot \mathbf{d} = 32 - 32 = 0$

(d) Since $\mathbf{c} \cdot \mathbf{d} = 0$, $\mathbf{c}$ is perpendicular to $\mathbf{d}$, i.e. OC is perpendicular to AB.

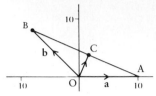

OC is called an **altitude** of the triangle.

4E (a) $\mathbf{b} - \mathbf{h}$ is the vector $\overrightarrow{HB}$ and since $\overrightarrow{HB}$ is perpendicular to $\overrightarrow{OA}$, $\mathbf{a} \cdot (\mathbf{b} - \mathbf{h}) = 0$

(b) $\overrightarrow{HA}$ is perpendicular to $\overrightarrow{OB}$ so $\mathbf{b} \cdot (\mathbf{a} - \mathbf{h}) = 0$

(c) $\mathbf{b} \cdot (\mathbf{a} - \mathbf{h}) - \mathbf{a} \cdot (\mathbf{b} - \mathbf{h}) = 0$
$\Rightarrow \mathbf{b} \cdot \mathbf{a} - \mathbf{b} \cdot \mathbf{h} - \mathbf{a} \cdot \mathbf{b} + \mathbf{a} \cdot \mathbf{h} = 0$
$\Rightarrow \mathbf{a} \cdot \mathbf{h} - \mathbf{b} \cdot \mathbf{h} = 0$ (since $\mathbf{b} \cdot \mathbf{a} = \mathbf{a} \cdot \mathbf{b}$)
$\Rightarrow (\mathbf{a} - \mathbf{b}) \cdot \mathbf{h} = 0$

(d) $\mathbf{a} - \mathbf{b}$ is the vector $\overrightarrow{BA}$ and this is perpendicular to $\overrightarrow{OH}$.
Thus $\overrightarrow{OH}$ is also an altitude of the triangle, i.e. in any triangle, the three altitudes are concurrent. (They intersect in a single point.)

5E (a) $\overrightarrow{OR} = \overrightarrow{OP} + \overrightarrow{PR} = \overrightarrow{OP} + \overrightarrow{OQ} = \mathbf{p} + \mathbf{q}$
$\overrightarrow{QP} = \mathbf{p} - \mathbf{q}$

(b) Using the result that $\mathbf{a} \cdot (\mathbf{b} + \mathbf{c}) = \mathbf{a} \cdot \mathbf{b} + \mathbf{a} \cdot \mathbf{c}$,
$(\mathbf{p} + \mathbf{q}) \cdot (\mathbf{p} - \mathbf{q})$
$= \mathbf{p} \cdot \mathbf{p} - \mathbf{p} \cdot \mathbf{q} + \mathbf{q} \cdot \mathbf{p} - \mathbf{q} \cdot \mathbf{q}$
$= p^2 - \mathbf{p} \cdot \mathbf{q} + \mathbf{q} \cdot \mathbf{p} - q^2$
(since $\mathbf{p} \cdot \mathbf{p} = p^2$ and $\mathbf{p} \cdot \mathbf{q} = \mathbf{q} \cdot \mathbf{p}$)

(c) (i) $\overrightarrow{OR} \cdot \overrightarrow{QP} = 0 \Rightarrow \overrightarrow{OR}$ is perpendicular to $\overrightarrow{QP}$.

(ii) If $\overrightarrow{OR} \cdot \overrightarrow{QP} = 0$
then $(\mathbf{p} + \mathbf{q}) \cdot (\mathbf{p} - \mathbf{q}) = 0$
i.e. $p^2 - q^2 = 0$
$\Rightarrow \mathbf{p} = \mathbf{q}$ and the parallelogram is a rhombus.

This proves the well-known result that the diagonals of a rhombus intersect at right angles.

5.2.5 Vector equations of planes

5.2 E

1

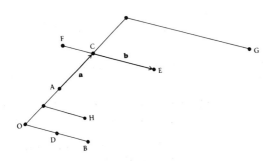

2
$c = 3a \qquad d = 2b \qquad e = -2b$
$f = -2b + a \qquad g = 2a + 2b$
$h = 2b - 2a \qquad i = \frac{1}{2}a + \frac{1}{2}b$

3
$$\overrightarrow{DE} = \begin{bmatrix} 0 \\ 6 \\ 6 \end{bmatrix} - \begin{bmatrix} 6 \\ 6 \\ 0 \end{bmatrix} = \begin{bmatrix} -6 \\ 0 \\ 6 \end{bmatrix}$$

$$\overrightarrow{DF} = \begin{bmatrix} 6 \\ 0 \\ 6 \end{bmatrix} - \begin{bmatrix} 6 \\ 6 \\ 0 \end{bmatrix} = \begin{bmatrix} 0 \\ -6 \\ 6 \end{bmatrix}$$

In order to reach any point in the plane DEF, it is necessary to go from O to D, followed by some combination of $\overrightarrow{DE}$ and $\overrightarrow{DF}$. Thus, if P is some point on the plane,

$$\overrightarrow{OP} = \overrightarrow{OD} + \overrightarrow{DP} = \overrightarrow{OD} + \lambda\overrightarrow{DE} + \mu\overrightarrow{DE}$$

for some λ and μ, i.e.

$$\begin{bmatrix} x \\ y \\ z \end{bmatrix} = \begin{bmatrix} 6 \\ 6 \\ 0 \end{bmatrix} + \lambda\begin{bmatrix} -6 \\ 0 \\ 6 \end{bmatrix} + \mu\begin{bmatrix} 0 \\ -6 \\ 6 \end{bmatrix}$$

4
The coordinates of each point are:

(a) (6, 6, 0) i.e. D   (b) (0, 6, 6) i.e. E

(c) (6, 0, 6) i.e. F   (d) (3, 3, 6)

(e) (4, 4, 4)

5
$$\overrightarrow{CB} = \begin{bmatrix} 0 \\ 6 \\ -6 \end{bmatrix} \qquad \overrightarrow{CA} = \begin{bmatrix} 6 \\ 0 \\ -6 \end{bmatrix}$$

ABC has equation
$$\begin{bmatrix} x \\ y \\ z \end{bmatrix} = \begin{bmatrix} 0 \\ 0 \\ 6 \end{bmatrix} + \lambda\begin{bmatrix} 0 \\ 6 \\ -6 \end{bmatrix} + \mu\begin{bmatrix} 6 \\ 0 \\ -6 \end{bmatrix}$$
The planes are parallel.

6
(a) (0, 0, 6) i.e. C   (b) (0, 6, 0) i.e. B

(c) (6, 0, 0) i.e. A

(d) (3, 3, 0)   (e) (2, 2, 2)

7
(a) If the plane is parallel to ABC then its direction will still be specified by vectors $\overrightarrow{CB}$ and $\overrightarrow{CA}$, but will pass through O instead of C.
The equation will therefore be:
$$\begin{bmatrix} x \\ y \\ z \end{bmatrix} = \begin{bmatrix} 0 \\ 0 \\ 0 \end{bmatrix} + \lambda\begin{bmatrix} 0 \\ 6 \\ -6 \end{bmatrix} + \mu\begin{bmatrix} 6 \\ 0 \\ -6 \end{bmatrix}$$

(b) Similarly the parallel plane through G will be:
$$\begin{bmatrix} x \\ y \\ z \end{bmatrix} = \begin{bmatrix} 6 \\ 6 \\ 6 \end{bmatrix} + \lambda\begin{bmatrix} 0 \\ 6 \\ -6 \end{bmatrix} + \mu\begin{bmatrix} 6 \\ 0 \\ -6 \end{bmatrix}$$

8
$\overrightarrow{OH}$ is $\begin{bmatrix} 3 \\ 0 \\ 6 \end{bmatrix}$ $\quad$ $\overrightarrow{HD}$ is $\begin{bmatrix} 3 \\ 6 \\ -6 \end{bmatrix}$ $\quad$ $\overrightarrow{HE}$ is $\begin{bmatrix} -3 \\ 6 \\ 0 \end{bmatrix}$

Plane DEH is
$$\begin{bmatrix} x \\ y \\ z \end{bmatrix} = \begin{bmatrix} 3 \\ 0 \\ 6 \end{bmatrix} + \lambda\begin{bmatrix} 3 \\ 6 \\ -6 \end{bmatrix} + \mu\begin{bmatrix} -3 \\ 6 \\ 0 \end{bmatrix}$$

5.2 Exercise 5

1
Taking A as a particular point on the plane,
$$\overrightarrow{AB} = \begin{bmatrix} -3 \\ -1 \\ 1 \end{bmatrix} \qquad \overrightarrow{AC} = \begin{bmatrix} -6 \\ -2 \\ 4 \end{bmatrix}$$

$$\begin{bmatrix} x \\ y \\ z \end{bmatrix} = \begin{bmatrix} 2 \\ 3 \\ 1 \end{bmatrix} + \lambda\begin{bmatrix} -3 \\ -1 \\ 3 \end{bmatrix} + \mu\begin{bmatrix} -6 \\ -2 \\ 4 \end{bmatrix}$$

2 The three points at which the plane cuts the axes are

$$A \begin{bmatrix} 2 \\ 0 \\ 0 \end{bmatrix}, \quad B \begin{bmatrix} 0 \\ -1 \\ 0 \end{bmatrix}, \quad C \begin{bmatrix} 0 \\ 0 \\ 3 \end{bmatrix}$$

$$\overrightarrow{AB} = \begin{bmatrix} -2 \\ -1 \\ 0 \end{bmatrix} \quad \overrightarrow{AC} = \begin{bmatrix} -2 \\ 0 \\ 3 \end{bmatrix}$$

so

$$\begin{bmatrix} x \\ y \\ z \end{bmatrix} = \begin{bmatrix} 2 \\ 0 \\ 0 \end{bmatrix} + \lambda \begin{bmatrix} -2 \\ -1 \\ 0 \end{bmatrix} + \mu \begin{bmatrix} -2 \\ 0 \\ 3 \end{bmatrix}$$

3 (a) $\overrightarrow{OD} = \begin{bmatrix} -2 \\ 2 \\ 3 \end{bmatrix}$

(b) Taking O as the particular point on OAD,

$$\begin{bmatrix} x \\ y \\ z \end{bmatrix} = \lambda \begin{bmatrix} -2 \\ 2 \\ 3 \end{bmatrix} + \mu \begin{bmatrix} 0 \\ 4 \\ 0 \end{bmatrix}$$

$$\overrightarrow{DC} = \begin{bmatrix} -2 \\ -2 \\ -3 \end{bmatrix} \quad \overrightarrow{DB} = \begin{bmatrix} -2 \\ 2 \\ -3 \end{bmatrix}$$

$$\begin{bmatrix} x \\ y \\ z \end{bmatrix} = \begin{bmatrix} -2 \\ 2 \\ 3 \end{bmatrix} + \lambda \begin{bmatrix} -2 \\ -2 \\ -3 \end{bmatrix} + \mu \begin{bmatrix} -2 \\ 2 \\ -3 \end{bmatrix}$$

for BCD.

4 $\overrightarrow{AB} = \begin{bmatrix} -3 \\ -1 \\ 3 \end{bmatrix} \quad \overrightarrow{AC} = \begin{bmatrix} -6 \\ -2 \\ 6 \end{bmatrix}$

i.e. $\overrightarrow{AC} = 2\overrightarrow{AB}$ and the three points are collinear.

5.2.6 Cartesian equations of planes

5.2 F

1 $x = 6 - 6\lambda$ ①
    $y = 6 \qquad - 6\mu$ ②
    $z = \qquad 6\lambda + 6\mu$ ③
    ① + ② + ③ $\Rightarrow x + y + z = 12$

2 (a) A is $(6, 0, 0)$, B is $(0, 6, 0)$, C is $(0, 0, 6)$, which suggests that $x + y + z = 6$.
    $x = \qquad 6\mu$ ①
    $y = \qquad 6\lambda$ ②
    $z = 6 - 6\lambda - 6\mu$ ③
    ① + ② + ③ $\Rightarrow x + y + z = 6$

(b) For the plane through O,
    $x = \qquad 6\mu$
    $y = \qquad 6\lambda$
    $z = \qquad - 6\lambda - 6\mu$
    $\Rightarrow x + y + z = 0$

For the plane through G,
    $x = 6 \qquad + 6\mu$
    $y = 6 + 6\lambda$
    $z = 6 - 6\lambda - 6\mu$
    $\Rightarrow x + y + z = 18$

3 $x = 6 - 6\lambda - 3\mu$ ①
    $y = 6 \qquad - 6\mu$ ②
    $z = \qquad 6\lambda + 6\mu$ ③
    ① + ③ $\Rightarrow x + z = 6 + 3\mu$ ④
Eliminating μ between equations ② and ④,
    ② + 2 × ④
    $\Rightarrow y + 2(x + z) = 6 - 6\mu + 2(6 + 3\mu)$
    $\Rightarrow 2x + y + 2z = 18$

4 Using the method of question 3,
    $x = 5 - 3\lambda + 2\mu$ ①
    $y = 2 \qquad + 3\mu$ ②
    $z = 4 - 6\lambda + \mu$ ③
    2 × ① − ③ $\Rightarrow 2x - z = 6 + 3\mu$ ④
    ④ − ② $\Rightarrow 2x - y - z = 4$

5 $\begin{bmatrix} 1 \\ 1 \\ 1 \end{bmatrix}$ is perpendicular to the plane DEF. It is called the **normal** to the plane.

$$\begin{bmatrix} 1 \\ 1 \\ 1 \end{bmatrix} \cdot \overrightarrow{DE} = \begin{bmatrix} 1 \\ 1 \\ 1 \end{bmatrix} \cdot \begin{bmatrix} -6 \\ 0 \\ 6 \end{bmatrix} = 0$$

$$\begin{bmatrix} 1 \\ 1 \\ 1 \end{bmatrix} \cdot \overrightarrow{DF} = \begin{bmatrix} 1 \\ 1 \\ 1 \end{bmatrix} \cdot \begin{bmatrix} 0 \\ -6 \\ 6 \end{bmatrix} = 0$$

So $\begin{bmatrix} 1 \\ 1 \\ 1 \end{bmatrix}$ is perpendicular to $\overrightarrow{DE}$ and $\overrightarrow{DF}$,

two vectors which lie in the plane.

5.2 Exercise 6

1 (a) $\mathbf{n} \cdot \mathbf{r} = \mathbf{n} \cdot \mathbf{a}$

$$\Rightarrow \begin{bmatrix} 2 \\ -3 \\ 1 \end{bmatrix} \cdot \begin{bmatrix} x \\ y \\ z \end{bmatrix} = \begin{bmatrix} 2 \\ -3 \\ 1 \end{bmatrix} \cdot \begin{bmatrix} 0 \\ 0 \\ 0 \end{bmatrix}$$

i.e. $2x - 3y + z = 0$

(b) $2x - 3y + z = 1$ (c) $5x - 2y = 13$

2 (a) $\mathbf{n} = \begin{bmatrix} 1 \\ 1 \\ 0 \end{bmatrix}$

$$\begin{bmatrix} 1 \\ 1 \\ 0 \end{bmatrix} \cdot \begin{bmatrix} x \\ y \\ z \end{bmatrix} = \begin{bmatrix} 1 \\ 1 \\ 0 \end{bmatrix} \cdot \begin{bmatrix} 1 \\ 0 \\ 0 \end{bmatrix}$$

i.e. $x + y = 1$

(b) $\mathbf{n} = \begin{bmatrix} -1 \\ 1 \\ 0 \end{bmatrix}$

$$\begin{bmatrix} -1 \\ 1 \\ 0 \end{bmatrix} \cdot \begin{bmatrix} x \\ y \\ z \end{bmatrix} = \begin{bmatrix} -1 \\ 1 \\ 0 \end{bmatrix} \cdot \begin{bmatrix} 0 \\ 0 \\ 0 \end{bmatrix}$$

i.e. $-x + y = 0$ or $y = x$
Although this looks like the equation of a line, it represents a plane, formed by the lines $y = x$ corresponding to various values of z.

(c) $\mathbf{n} = \begin{bmatrix} 1 \\ 1 \\ 1 \end{bmatrix}$, $x + y + z = 1$

(d) $\mathbf{n} = \begin{bmatrix} 1 \\ 1 \\ 1 \end{bmatrix}$, $x + y + z = 2$

(e) $\mathbf{n} = \begin{bmatrix} 0 \\ 0 \\ 1 \end{bmatrix}$, $z = 0$

3 (a) $\mathbf{c} = \begin{bmatrix} 0 \\ 0 \\ 4 \end{bmatrix}$

(b) $\overrightarrow{CA} = \begin{bmatrix} 2 \\ 0 \\ -4 \end{bmatrix}$ $\overrightarrow{CB} = \begin{bmatrix} 0 \\ 3 \\ -4 \end{bmatrix}$

(c) $\mathbf{r} = \begin{bmatrix} 0 \\ 0 \\ 4 \end{bmatrix} + \lambda \begin{bmatrix} 2 \\ 0 \\ -4 \end{bmatrix} + \mu \begin{bmatrix} 0 \\ 3 \\ -4 \end{bmatrix}$

(d) $x = 2\lambda$ ①
$y = 3\mu$ ②
$z = 4 - 4\lambda - 4\mu$ ③

(e) $6x + 4y + 3z = 12$

(f) $\mathbf{n} = \begin{bmatrix} 6 \\ 4 \\ 3 \end{bmatrix}$

4E The coordinates of the vertices are
A $(1, 0, 0)$,   B $(0, 1, 0)$,   C $(-1, 0, 0)$,
D $(0, -1, 0)$,   E $(0, 0, 1)$,   F$(0, 0, -1)$.

(a) The vector equation of AEB is:

$$\begin{bmatrix} x \\ y \\ z \end{bmatrix} = \begin{bmatrix} 1 \\ 0 \\ 0 \end{bmatrix} + \lambda \begin{bmatrix} -1 \\ 0 \\ 1 \end{bmatrix} + \mu \begin{bmatrix} -1 \\ 1 \\ 0 \end{bmatrix}$$

giving the Cartesian equation
$x + y + z = 1$
The vector equation of DCF is

$$\begin{bmatrix} x \\ y \\ z \end{bmatrix} = \begin{bmatrix} 0 \\ -1 \\ 0 \end{bmatrix} + \lambda \begin{bmatrix} -1 \\ 1 \\ 0 \end{bmatrix} + \mu \begin{bmatrix} 0 \\ 1 \\ -1 \end{bmatrix}$$

giving $x + y + z = -1$
[Or both planes may be found by inspection.]

(b) Since both have normal vector $\begin{bmatrix} 1 \\ 1 \\ 1 \end{bmatrix}$ the planes are parallel.

(c) ECB is $x - y - z = -1$
and FAD is $x - y - z = 1$

5.2.7 Finding angles

5.2 Exercise 7

1 (a) $n_1 = \begin{bmatrix} 1 \\ 1 \\ 1 \end{bmatrix}$ $n_2 = \begin{bmatrix} 2 \\ 3 \\ 1 \end{bmatrix}$

$$\cos\theta = \frac{2+3+1}{\sqrt{3}\sqrt{14}} = \frac{6}{\sqrt{42}}$$

$$\Rightarrow \theta = 22.2°$$

(b) $n_1 = \begin{bmatrix} 1 \\ -3 \\ -2 \end{bmatrix}$ $n_2 = \begin{bmatrix} 5 \\ 0 \\ 2 \end{bmatrix}$

$$\Rightarrow \theta = 87.2°$$

(c) $n_1 = \begin{bmatrix} 1 \\ 0 \\ -2 \end{bmatrix}$ $n_2 = \begin{bmatrix} 0 \\ 1 \\ 3 \end{bmatrix}$

$$\Rightarrow \theta = 148.1° \text{ or, taking the acute angle, } 31.9°$$

2 (a) The direction vectors for the two lines are
$\begin{bmatrix} 2 \\ 1 \end{bmatrix}$ and $\begin{bmatrix} -1 \\ 1 \end{bmatrix}$.
$\theta = 108.4°$ or $71.6°$

(b) Taking direction vectors $\begin{bmatrix} -1 \\ 0 \\ 3 \end{bmatrix}$ and
$\begin{bmatrix} -2 \\ 3 \\ 4 \end{bmatrix}$, $\theta = 34.7°$

3 $n = \begin{bmatrix} 2 \\ 3 \\ -1 \end{bmatrix}$ $\theta = 49.1°$

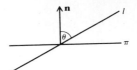

The required angle between the line and the plane is $90° - 49.1° = 40.9°$

4 $n = \begin{bmatrix} 1 \\ 1 \\ 1 \end{bmatrix}$ $n_1 = \begin{bmatrix} -1 \\ 1 \\ 1 \end{bmatrix}$

$$\cos\theta = \frac{-1+1+1}{\sqrt{3}\sqrt{3}} = \frac{1}{3} \Rightarrow \theta = 70.5°$$

However, the dihedral angle is obtuse in this case, so:

dihedral angle $= 180° - 70.5° = 109.5°$

5E (a)

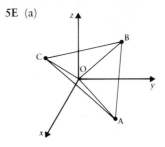

(b) $OA = \sqrt{2}$ $OB = \sqrt{2}$ $OC = \sqrt{2}$

$$\overrightarrow{AB} = \begin{bmatrix} -1 \\ 0 \\ 1 \end{bmatrix}$$

$$\Rightarrow |AB| = \sqrt{(1^2 + 0^2 + 1^2)} = \sqrt{2}$$

$$\overrightarrow{AC} = \begin{bmatrix} 0 \\ -1 \\ 1 \end{bmatrix} \Rightarrow |AC| = \sqrt{2}$$

$$\overrightarrow{BC} = \begin{bmatrix} 1 \\ -1 \\ 0 \end{bmatrix} \Rightarrow |BC| = \sqrt{2}$$

(c) OAB is $x - y + z = 0$ with normal

$$\begin{bmatrix} 1 \\ -1 \\ 1 \end{bmatrix}.$$

OAC is $x - y - z = 0$ with normal

$$\begin{bmatrix} 1 \\ -1 \\ -1 \end{bmatrix}.$$

$$\cos\theta = \frac{1+1-1}{\sqrt{3}\sqrt{3}} = \frac{1}{3}$$

$\Rightarrow \theta = 70.5°$
which is the (acute) dihedral angle of the tetrahedron.

(d) BC is $\mathbf{r} = \begin{bmatrix} 0 \\ 1 \\ 1 \end{bmatrix} + \lambda \begin{bmatrix} 1 \\ -1 \\ 0 \end{bmatrix}$

direction $\begin{bmatrix} 1 \\ -1 \\ 0 \end{bmatrix}$

OA is $\mathbf{r} = \mu \begin{bmatrix} 1 \\ 1 \\ 0 \end{bmatrix}$

$$\cos\theta = \frac{1-1+0}{\sqrt{2}\sqrt{2}} = 0 \Rightarrow \theta = 90°$$

i.e. opposite pairs of edges of a regular tetrahedron are perpendicular.

(e) The direction of BC is $\begin{bmatrix} 1 \\ -1 \\ 0 \end{bmatrix}$.

The normal to OAC is $\begin{bmatrix} 1 \\ -1 \\ -1 \end{bmatrix}$.

$$\Rightarrow \cos\theta = \frac{1+1}{\sqrt{2}\sqrt{3}} = \frac{2}{\sqrt{6}} \qquad \theta = 35.3°$$

Thus the angle between the edge and the face is
$90° - 35.3° = 54.7°$.
Hence the height h of the tetrahedron is
$BC\sin 54.7° = \sqrt{2}\sin 54.7° \approx 1.15$.

5.3 Binomials

5.3.1 Binomial expansions

5.3 A

1 $(a+b)^3 = (a+b)(a^2 + 2ab + b^2)$

$$= a^3 + 2a^2b + ab^2$$
$$ + a^2b + 2ab^2 + b^3$$
$$= a^3 + 3a^2b + 3ab^2 + b^3$$

2 $(a+b)^4 = (a+b)(a+b)^3$

$$= (a+b)(a^3 + 3a^2b + 3ab^2 + b^3)$$
$$= a^4 + 4a^3b + 6a^2b^2 + 4ab^3 + b^4$$

3 (a) The coefficients form the rows of Pascal's triangle.

(b) The next row is 1 4 6 4 1, as in the answer to question 2.

(c) $(a+b)^5 = a^5 + 5a^4b + 10a^3b^2 + 10a^2b^3$
$$+ 5ab^4 + b^5$$

4E $a^4 + 4a^3(2b) + 6a^2(2b)^2 + 4a(2b)^3 + (2b)^4$
$$= a^4 + 8a^3b + 24a^2b^2 + 32ab^3 + 16b^4$$

5.3 Exercise 1

1 (a) $(a+b)^6 = a^6 + 6a^5b + 15a^4b^2 + 20a^3b^3$
$$+ 15a^2b^4 + 6ab^5 + b^6$$

(b) $(p-q)^5 = p^5 - 5p^4q + 10p^3q^2 - 10p^2q^3$
$$+ 5pq^4 - q^5$$

(c) $(3x+y)^4 = (3x)^4 + 4(3x)^3y + 6(3x)^2y^2$
$$+ 4(3x)y^3 + y^4$$
$$= 81x^4 + 108x^3y + 54x^2y^2$$
$$+ 12xy^3 + y^4$$

(d) $(1+z)^6 = 1 + 6z + 15z^2 + 20z^3 + 15z^4$
$$+ 6z^5 + z^6$$

2 (a) $(a+b)^3 = a^3 + 3a^2b + 3ab^2 + b^3$
$(a-b)^3 = a^3 - 3a^2b + 3ab^2 - b^3$

(b) Adding the results in part (a),

$$(a+b)^3 + (a-b)^3 = 2a^3 + 6ab^2$$
$$= 2a(a^2 + 3b^2)$$

(c) Subtracting the results in part (a),

$$(a+b)^3 - (a-b)^3 = 6a^2b + 2b^3$$
$$= 2b(3a^2 + b^2)$$

3E (a) $p = a + b$ and $q = a - b$
$\Rightarrow a = \frac{1}{2}(p+q)$ and $b = \frac{1}{2}(p-q)$

Then

$$p^3 + q^3 = 2[\frac{1}{2}(p+q)]$$
$$\times [(\frac{1}{2}(p+q))^2 + 3(\frac{1}{2}(p-q))^2]$$
$$= (p+q)(p^2 - pq + q^2)$$

(b) $p^3 - q^3 = (p + (-q))$
$$\times (p^2 - p(-q) + (-q)^2)$$
$$= (p-q)(p^2 + pq + q^2)$$

4E Writing 11 as $10 + 1$,

$$11^2 = (10+1)^2 = 10^2 + 2 \times 10 + 1 = 121$$

$$11^3 = (10+1)^3$$
$$= 10^3 + 3 \times 10^2 \times 1 + 3 \times 10 \times 1^2 + 1^3$$
$$= 1331$$

$$11^4 = (10+1)^4$$
$$= 10^4 + 4 \times 10^3 \times 1 + 6 \times 10^2 \times 1^2$$
$$+ 4 \times 10 \times 1^3 + 1^4$$
$$= 14\,641$$

$11^5 = 15 \boxed{10} \boxed{10} 51 = 161\,051$
Pascal's triangle still applies, but you need to carry.

5.3.2 Binomial coefficients

5.3 B

1 The reciprocals of $\frac{4}{1}$ and $\frac{3}{2}$ are $\frac{1}{4}$ and $\frac{2}{3}$.

2 (a) The multipliers for the 5th line are:
$$\times \tfrac{5}{1} \quad \times \tfrac{4}{2} \quad \times \tfrac{3}{3} \quad \times \tfrac{2}{4} \quad \times \tfrac{1}{5}$$
$$1 \longrightarrow 5 \longrightarrow 10 \longrightarrow 10 \longrightarrow 5 \longrightarrow 1$$

(b) The sequence of multipliers is $\frac{5}{1}, \frac{4}{2}, \frac{3}{3}, \frac{2}{4}, \frac{1}{5}$, where the numerators decrease by 1 and the denominators increase by 1.

3 (a) The multipliers for the 6th line are:
$$\times \tfrac{6}{1} \quad \times \tfrac{5}{2} \quad \times \tfrac{4}{3} \quad \times \tfrac{3}{4} \quad \times \tfrac{2}{5} \quad \times \tfrac{1}{6}$$
$$1 \longrightarrow 6 \longrightarrow 15 \longrightarrow 20 \longrightarrow 15 \longrightarrow 6 \longrightarrow 1$$

(b) This agrees with the result from Pascal's triangle.

4 $\times \tfrac{10}{1} \quad \times \tfrac{9}{2} \quad \times \tfrac{8}{3} \quad \times \tfrac{7}{4} \quad \times \tfrac{6}{5} \quad \times \tfrac{5}{6} \quad \times \tfrac{4}{7} \quad \times \tfrac{3}{8} \quad \times \tfrac{2}{9}$
$$1 \longrightarrow 10 \longrightarrow 45 \longrightarrow 120 \longrightarrow 210 \longrightarrow 252 \longrightarrow 210 \longrightarrow 120 \longrightarrow 45 \longrightarrow$$

5E The sum is $1024 = 2^{10}$. The elements of the nth row of Pascal's triangle always sum to 2^n.

6 $\times \tfrac{80}{1} \quad \times \tfrac{79}{2} \quad \times \tfrac{78}{3}$
$$1 \longrightarrow 80 \longrightarrow 3160 \longrightarrow 82\,160$$

7 $\dbinom{12}{5} = \dfrac{12 \times 11 \times 10 \times 9 \times 8}{1 \times 2 \times 3 \times 4 \times 5}$

8 (a) $\dfrac{12!}{7!} = 12 \times 11 \times 10 \times 9 \times 8$

(b) $\dbinom{12}{5} = \dfrac{12 \times 11 \times 10 \times 9 \times 8}{1 \times 2 \times 3 \times 4 \times 5}$
$$= \dfrac{12 \times 11 \times 10 \times 9 \times 8}{5!}$$
$$= \dfrac{12!}{5!\,7!} \text{ from (a)}$$

(c) $\dbinom{12}{5} = 792$

9 $\dbinom{12}{4} = \dfrac{12!}{4!\,8!}$ and $\dbinom{12}{8} = \dfrac{12!}{8!\,4!}$

$\Rightarrow \dbinom{12}{8} = \dbinom{12}{4}$

10 (a) 220 (b) 792 (c) 12

11 $\dbinom{n}{r} = \dfrac{n!}{r!(n-r)!}$

12 (a) $\dbinom{12}{0} = \dbinom{12}{12} = 1$ (b) $\dfrac{12!}{0!\,12!} = 1$

(c) $0! = 1$

5.3 Exercise 2

1 (a) 56   (b) 10   (c) 84   (d) 4950

2 $(a+b)^7 = a^7 + 7a^6b + 21a^5b^2 + 35a^4b^3$
$\qquad + 35a^3b^4 + 21a^2b^5 + 7ab^6 + b^7$

3 (a) $(a-b)^8 = a^8 - 8a^7b + 28a^6b^2$
$\qquad - 56a^5b^3 + \cdots$

(b) $(2a - 3b)^{10} = (2a)^{10} - 10(2a)^9(3b)$
$\qquad + 45(2a)^8(3b)^2$
$\qquad - 120(2a)^7(3b)^3 + \cdots$
$\qquad = 1024a^{10} - 15\,360a^9b$
$\qquad + 103\,680a^8b^2$
$\qquad - 414\,720a^7b^3 + \cdots$

(c) $\left(x^2 - \dfrac{1}{x^2}\right)^6 = (x^2)^6 - 6(x^2)^5\left(\dfrac{1}{x^2}\right)$
$\qquad + 15(x^2)^4\left(\dfrac{1}{x^2}\right)^2$
$\qquad - 20(x^2)^3\left(\dfrac{1}{x^2}\right)^3 + \cdots$
$\qquad = x^{12} - 6x^8 + 15x^4 - 20 + \cdots$

4 $a = 11$ from the symmetry of the binomial coefficients.

5 (a) 0.0158   (b) 3.05

6E (a) $\dbinom{9}{3} = 84$, $\dbinom{9}{4} = 126$,

$\dbinom{10}{4} = 210 = \dbinom{9}{3} + \dbinom{9}{4}$

(b) $\dbinom{n+1}{r} = \dbinom{n}{r} + \dbinom{n}{r-1}$

$\dbinom{n}{r} = \dfrac{n!}{(n-r)!\,r!} = \dfrac{n!(n-r+1)}{(n-r+1)!\,r!}$

and $\dbinom{n}{r-1} = \dfrac{n!}{(n-r+1)!(r-1)!}$

$\qquad = \dfrac{n!\,r}{(n-r+1)!\,r!}$

So $\dbinom{n}{r} + \dbinom{n}{r-1} = \dfrac{n!(n-r+1) + n!\,r}{(n-r+1)!\,r!}$

$\qquad = \dfrac{(n+1)!}{(n+1-r)!\,r!}$

$\qquad = \dbinom{n+1}{r}$

5.3.3 Binomial series

5.3 C

1 (b) $y = 1 + 3x$ is the tangent of $y = (1+x)^3$ at $x = 0$, $y = 1$ and is a good approximation to the function near the origin.

(c)

x	0.05	0.1	0.15	0.2	0.25
$1 + 3x$	1.15	1.3	1.45	1.6	1.75
$(1+x)^3$	1.157 625	1.331	1.520 875	1.728	1.953 125

The results are close for small values of x but diverge as x increases.

2 (b)

x	0.05	0.1	0.15	0.2	0.25
$1 + 3x + 3x^2$	1.1575	1.33	1.5175	1.72	1.9375

$1 + 3x + 3x^2$ gives a better approximation than $1 + 3x$.

3 (a) $(1+x)^8 = 1 + 8x + 28x^2 + \cdots$ so $1 + 8x + 28x^2$ is a quadratic approximation to $(1+x)^8$.

(b) The approximation looks good for small positive and negative values of x. It is within about 10% of the correct value for $-0.1 < x < 0.17$.

4 (a) With $n = -1$, $1 + nx + \dfrac{n(n-1)}{2!}x^2$ becomes
$$1 + (-1)x + \dfrac{(-1)(-2)}{2!}x^2 = 1 - x + x^2$$

(b) For $-0.464 < x < 0.464$, the value of the quadratic is within 10% of the true value.

5 (a) $\sqrt{(1+x)} = (1+x)^{\frac{1}{2}}$

If $n = \frac{1}{2}$, the first three terms of the series are

$$1 + \frac{1}{2}x + \frac{(\frac{1}{2})(-\frac{1}{2})}{2!}x^2 = 1 + \frac{1}{2}x + \frac{(-\frac{1}{4})}{2}x^2$$

$$= 1 + \frac{1}{2}x - \frac{1}{8}x^2$$

(b) The value of $1 + \frac{1}{2}x - \frac{1}{8}x^2$ is within

10% of the value of $\sqrt{(1+x)}$ for $-0.7 < x < 1.7$.

6 The next term in the series is
$$\frac{n(n-1)(n-2)}{3!}x^3.$$

So, putting $n = \frac{1}{2}$ gives $\frac{\frac{1}{2}(-\frac{1}{2})(-\frac{3}{2})}{3!}x^3 =$

$\frac{\frac{3}{8}}{6}x^3 = \frac{3}{48}x^3 = \frac{1}{16}x^3$ and a sensible cubic

would be $1 + \frac{1}{2}x - \frac{1}{8}x^2 + \frac{1}{16}x^3$. This is a
better approximation than the quadratic, but
again is good only for small values of x.

7E (a) The series is a geometric series, common
ratio $-x$.

The sum is $\dfrac{1}{1-(-x)} = \dfrac{1}{1+x}$,

provided $-1 < x < 1$.

(b) Substituting $n = -1$ gives
$(1+x)^{-1} = 1 - x + x^2 - x^3 + \cdots$,

whose sum is known to be $\dfrac{1}{1+x}$ from (a).

If the binomial series is summed to infinity,
then the series is *equal* to $(1+x)^n$ for
$-1 < x < 1$ and is not merely an
approximation.

8E $1 + x - \dfrac{x^3}{8} + \dfrac{x^4}{64}$

Note that $1 + \frac{1}{2}x - \frac{1}{8}x^2 \approx \sqrt{(1+x)}$;
$(\sqrt{(1+x)})^2$ is of course $1 + x$.

5.3 Exercise 3

1 (a) $(1+x)^{\frac{1}{3}} = 1 + \frac{1}{3}x - \frac{1}{9}x^2 + \frac{5}{81}x^3 \cdots$

(b) $(1+x)^{-3} = 1 - 3x + 6x^2 - 10x^3 + \cdots$

2 (a) $(1+x)^{\frac{1}{2}}$ (b) $(1+x)^{-3}$

(c) $(1+x)^{\frac{1}{5}}$ (d) $(1+x)^{-\frac{1}{3}}$

3 (a) $1 - 4x + 10x^2 - 20x^3$

(b) $1 - x - \frac{1}{2}x^2 - \frac{1}{2}x^3$

(c) $1 - \frac{1}{2}x^2$

4 (a) $\sqrt{(9-18x)} = \sqrt{(9(1-2x))}$
$$= \sqrt{9}\sqrt{(1-2x)} = 3\sqrt{(1-2x)}$$

(b) $\sqrt{(9-18x)}$

$= 3(1-2x)^{\frac{1}{2}}$

$= 3\left(1 + \frac{1}{2}(-2x) + \frac{(\frac{1}{2})(-\frac{1}{2})}{2!}(-2x)^2\right.$

$+ \dfrac{(\frac{1}{2})(-\frac{1}{2})(-\frac{3}{2})}{3!}(-2x)^3$

$\left. + \dfrac{(\frac{1}{2})(-\frac{1}{2})(-\frac{3}{2})(-\frac{5}{2})}{4!}(-2x)^4 \cdots \right)$

$= 3 - 3x - \dfrac{3}{2}x^2 - \dfrac{3}{2}x^3 - \dfrac{15}{8}x^4 \cdots$

$-1 < 2x < 1 \Rightarrow -\dfrac{1}{2} < x < \dfrac{1}{2}$

5 (a) $\dfrac{1}{2}(1+x)^{-\frac{1}{2}} \approx \dfrac{1}{2} - \dfrac{1}{4}x + \dfrac{3}{16}x^2$

(b) $\dfrac{1}{9}(1+x)^{-2} \approx \dfrac{1}{9} - \dfrac{2}{9}x + 1\dfrac{1}{3}x^2$

6 (a) The binomial series is only valid for
$-1 < x < 1$.

(b) $7\sqrt{\left(1+\dfrac{1}{49}\right)} = \sqrt{\left(49\left(1+\dfrac{1}{49}\right)\right)} = \sqrt{50}$

$\sqrt{50} = 7\left(1 + \dfrac{1}{2}\left(\dfrac{1}{49}\right) - \dfrac{1}{8}\left(\dfrac{1}{49}\right)^2\right.$

$\left. + \dfrac{1}{16}\left(\dfrac{1}{49}\right)^3 \cdots \right) \approx 7.071\,068$

7E (a) $(1+x)^{\frac{1}{2}} \approx 1 + \dfrac{1}{2}x$

$$\Rightarrow \left(1 - \dfrac{v^2}{c^2}\right)^{\frac{1}{2}} \approx 1 + \dfrac{1}{2}\left(-\dfrac{v^2}{c^2}\right)$$

$$= 1 - \dfrac{v^2}{2c^2}$$

(b) $1 - \dfrac{1}{2}\left(\dfrac{1}{3}\right)^2 = \dfrac{17}{18} = 0.94$ (to 2 s.f.)

5.3.4 Error and relative error

5.3 D

1 $h = \dfrac{350 \pm 10}{14 \pm 0.5}$

$h_{\max} = \dfrac{360}{13.5} \approx 26.67 \text{ mm}$

$h_{\min} = \dfrac{340}{14.5} \approx 23.45 \text{ mm}$

$h = 25.06 \pm 1.61 \text{ mm}$

2 (a) $(1+r)^2 = 1 + 2r + r^2 \approx 1 + 2r$, if r^2 can be ignored.

$$\dfrac{1}{1+r} = (1+r)^{-1}$$

$$= 1 - r + r^2 - r^3 + \cdots$$

$$\approx 1 - r$$

(b) (i) $1 \pm 2 \times 0.05 = 1 \pm 0.1 \text{ m}^2$
(ii) $1 \pm 0.05 \text{ m}^{-1}$

3 (a) Maximum value:
$(1+r)(1+s) = 1 + r + s + rs$
$\qquad \approx 1 + (r+s)$
Minimum value:
$(1-r)(1-s) = 1 - r - s + rs$
$\qquad \approx 1 - (r+s)$

So $(1 \pm r)(1 \pm s) \approx 1 \pm (r+s)$

(b) Maximum value:

$$\dfrac{1+r}{1-s} \approx (1+r)(1+s) \approx 1 + (r+s)$$

Minimum value:

$$\dfrac{1-r}{1+s} \approx (1-r)(1-s) \approx 1 - (r+s)$$

So $\dfrac{1 \pm r}{1 \pm s} \approx 1 \pm (r+s)$

4 $h = \dfrac{350}{14} \times \dfrac{(1 \pm \frac{1}{35})}{(1 \pm \frac{1}{28})} \approx 25\left(1 \pm \left(\dfrac{1}{35} + \dfrac{1}{28}\right)\right)$

$$\approx 25\left(1 \pm \dfrac{9}{140}\right)$$

$$\approx 25 \pm 1.61 \text{ mm}$$

This compares well with the more accurate answer given in question 1.

5.3 Exercise 4

1 (a) $\qquad 2a = (20 \pm 0.4) - (19 \pm 0.2)$

$$= 1 \pm 0.6$$

$$\Rightarrow \quad a = 0.5 \pm 0.3$$

$$\Rightarrow \text{area} = (0.5 \pm 0.3)(19 \pm 0.2)$$

$$= 0.5(1 \pm 0.6) \times 19(1 \pm 0.01)$$

$$\approx 9.5(1 \pm 0.61)$$

$$\approx 9.5 \pm 5.8 \text{ cm}^2$$

(b) The calculation is inaccurate because the relative error of a is large.

2 $h = (125 \pm 2.5) \div \dfrac{(17 \pm 0.5 + 8 \pm 0.5)}{2}$

$$= (125 \pm 2.5) \div \dfrac{(25 \pm 1)}{2}$$

$$= 125(1 \pm 0.02) \div 12.5(1 \pm 0.04)$$

$$\approx 10(1 \pm 0.06)$$

$$\approx 10 \pm 0.6 \text{ cm}$$

3 Speed $= \dfrac{50 \pm 0.5}{1.32 \pm 0.1} \approx \dfrac{50(1 \pm 0.01)}{1.32(1 \pm 0.076)}$

$$\approx 37.9(1 \pm 0.086)$$

$$\approx 37.9 \pm 3.3 \text{ cm s}^{-1}$$

Miscellaneous exercise 5

1 (a) 10.6 cm, 102.8°, 34.2°

(b) 18.2 km, 124.8°, 28.2°

2 $\cos \alpha = -\frac{3}{4}$

3 $\theta = \dfrac{\pi}{6}, \dfrac{5\pi}{6}, \dfrac{3\pi}{2}$

4 $2\cos^2 \phi + 5\cos \phi - 3 = 0$

$\phi = 60°, 300°$

6 (a) $\mathbf{r} = t \begin{bmatrix} 3 \\ 2 \\ -1 \end{bmatrix}$ (b) $\mathbf{r} = \begin{bmatrix} 6 \\ 1 \\ 3 \end{bmatrix} + t \begin{bmatrix} 3 \\ 2 \\ -1 \end{bmatrix}$

7 (a) $\mathbf{r} = \begin{bmatrix} 1 \\ 2 \\ 3 \end{bmatrix} + \lambda \begin{bmatrix} 3 \\ -7 \\ 3 \end{bmatrix}$

(b) $\mathbf{r} = \begin{bmatrix} 1 \\ 2 \\ 3 \end{bmatrix} + \lambda \begin{bmatrix} 3 \\ -7 \\ 3 \end{bmatrix} + \mu \begin{bmatrix} 6 \\ 6 \\ -12 \end{bmatrix}$

No

8 (a) $2x - 3y - z = 1$ (b) $4x - y = 19$

9 (a) 55.3° (b) 44.8°

10 (a) 88.2° (or 91.8°) (b) 90°

11 (a) $1 - 3h + 6h^2 - 10h^3$

(b) $1 + \frac{1}{3}h - \frac{1}{9}h^2 + \frac{5}{81}h^3$

(c) $1 - \frac{1}{2}h - \frac{1}{8}h^2 - \frac{1}{16}h^3$

12 (a) $2 + \frac{1}{4}h - \frac{1}{64}h^2 + \frac{1}{512}h^3$

(b) Let $h = 0.2$ in the expansion.
$\sqrt{4.2} = 2.049$ (to 3 d.p.)

(c) 3.873

13 (a) $-\sin \theta$, $\sin \theta$, $-\cos \theta$

(b) $\sin \theta$ (c) $\sin 4\theta$ (d) $\tan \theta$

14 (a)

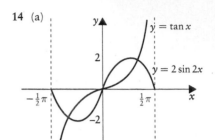

(b) $\left(-\frac{1}{3}\pi, -\sqrt{3}\right)$, $\left(\frac{1}{3}\pi, \sqrt{3}\right)$

6 CALCULUS METHODS 1

6.1 The chain rule

6.1.1 Functions of functions

6.1 A

$$C = 50 + 2t$$

$$F = 32 + 1.8C$$

$$\Rightarrow F = 32 + 1.8(50 + 2t)$$

$$F = 122 + 3.6t$$

$$\frac{dF}{dt} = 3.6, \quad \frac{dF}{dC} = 1.8, \quad \frac{dC}{dt} = 2$$

$$\frac{dF}{dt} = \frac{dF}{dC} \times \frac{dC}{dt}$$

For all your examples you should find that the rate of change of the composite function is the product of the other two rates of change.

6.1 B

1 (a) $\dfrac{dy}{du} = 3u^2$ and $\dfrac{du}{dx} = \cos x$

$$\Rightarrow \frac{dy}{dx} = \frac{dy}{du} \times \frac{du}{dx}$$

$$= 3u^2 \times \cos x$$

$$= 3(\sin x)^2 \times \cos x$$

$$= 3 \sin^2 x \cos x$$

(b) $y = e^{x^2}$

$$\frac{dy}{dx} = \frac{dy}{du} \times \frac{du}{dx}$$

$$= e^u \times 2x$$

$$= e^{x^2} \times 2x$$

$$= 2x e^{x^2}$$

(c) $y = (e^x)^2 = e^{2x}$

$$\frac{dy}{dx} = \frac{dy}{du} \times \frac{du}{dx}$$

$$= 2u \times e^x$$

$$= 2 e^x \times e^x$$

$$= 2 e^{2x}$$

2 The chain rule does in fact apply to any locally straight functions and you should have found that your results were confirmed by whatever numerical methods you tried.

6.1 Exercise 1

1 (a) (i) $2(x + 1)$ (ii) $4(2x - 1)$
    (iii) $4x(x^2 - 2)$

  (b) (i) $2x + 2$ (ii) $8x - 4$ (iii) $4x^3 - 8x$

2 (a) $8x(x^2 + 3)^3$ (b) $10(5 + 2x)^4$

  (c) $3(4x - 3)(2x^2 - 3x)^2$

  (d) $12x^7(x - 2)(x - 3)^3$

3 (a) $-2x \sin x^2$;   0   (b) $2 \cos 2x$;   2

  (c) $3 e^{3x}$;   3

4 (a) $-3x^2 \sin x^3$ (b) $3 \sin^2 x \cos x$

  (c) $-8 \cos^3 x \sin x$

5 $\dfrac{dy}{du} = \cos u, \qquad \dfrac{du}{dx} = 2$

   $\dfrac{dy}{dx} = 2 \cos u = 2 \cos 2x$

6 Let $u = 3x, \qquad y = \cos u$

   $\dfrac{dy}{dx} = 3 \times - \sin u = -3 \sin 3x$

7 Let $u = ax, \qquad y = \sin u$

   $\dfrac{dy}{dx} = a \cos u = a \cos ax$

8 (a) $3 e^{3x}$ (b) $2 \sin x \cos x$ (c) $2x e^{x^2}$

  (d) $-6 \sin 2x$ (e) $12x(x^2 + 1)^2$

9 (a) $\dfrac{dV}{dt} = 200$ $\qquad \dfrac{dV}{dr} = 4\pi r^2$

(b) $200 = 4\pi r^2 \dfrac{dr}{dt}$

$\dfrac{dr}{dt} = \dfrac{50}{\pi r^2}$

When $t = 1$, $\quad V = 200$

$\Rightarrow 200 = \dfrac{4}{3}\pi r^3$

$\Rightarrow \qquad r = 3.63$

$\Rightarrow \qquad \dfrac{dr}{dt} = \dfrac{50}{\pi \times 3.63^2}$

$\qquad \qquad = 1.21 \text{ cm s}^{-1}$ (to 2 d.p.)

10 (a) $r = 3 + 0.04t^2$ ① $\Rightarrow \dfrac{dr}{dt} = 0.08t$

Assuming the balloon is spherical,

$V = \dfrac{4}{3}\pi r^3 \Rightarrow \dfrac{dV}{dr} = 4\pi r^2$

(b) $\dfrac{dV}{dt} = \dfrac{dV}{dr} \times \dfrac{dr}{dt}$

$\dfrac{dV}{dt} = 4\pi r^2 \times 0.08t$

(c) When $t = 2$, $\quad r = 3.16$ from ①

$\Rightarrow \dfrac{dV}{dt} = 0.32\pi \times (3.16)^2 \times 2$

$\dfrac{dV}{dt} = 20.1 \text{ m}^3$ per minute (to 3 s.f.)

11 (a) $V = x^3$

$\dfrac{dV}{dx} = 3x^2$

(b) $\dfrac{dx}{dt} = -0.5$, $\qquad \dfrac{dV}{dt} = -1.5x^2$

$\dfrac{dV}{dt} = -1.5(4 - 0.5t)^2$

(c) When $t = 2$, $\dfrac{dV}{dt} = -13.5 \text{ cm}^3$ per hour

12 (a) $2 \times \sin 2x \times 2\cos 2x = 4\sin 2x \cos 2x$
$\qquad \qquad = 2\sin 4x$

(b) $-24\cos 4x \sin 4x = -12\sin 8x$

(c) $-\sin x \, e^{\cos x}$

6.1.2 Applications to integration

6.1 Exercise 2

1 (a) $\frac{1}{3}\sin 3x + c$

This is an indefinite integral and so the constant of integration must be included.

(b) $-2\cos\frac{1}{2}x + c$ $\qquad$ (c) $-\frac{2}{5}\cos 5x + c$

(d) $\frac{1}{2}e^{2x} + c$

2 (a) $\left[2\,e^{0.5x}\right]_1^2 = (2\,e) - (2\,e^{0.5}) = 2.14$
$\qquad \qquad \qquad \qquad \qquad$ (to 2 d.p.)

(b) $\left[-\frac{1}{2}\cos 2x\right]_{-1}^0 = (-\frac{1}{2}) - (-\frac{1}{2}\cos(-2))$
$\qquad \qquad \qquad = -0.71$ (to 2 d.p.)

Note: the angle is in radians.

(c) $\left[6\sin\dfrac{x}{2}\right]_0^2 = (6\sin 1) - (0) = 5.05$
$\qquad \qquad \qquad \qquad \qquad$ (to 2 d.p.)

(d) $\left[\frac{1}{6}(2x + 3)^3\right]_0^1 = (\frac{1}{6} \times 125) - (\frac{1}{6} \times 27)$
$\qquad \qquad \qquad \qquad = \frac{98}{6} = 16\frac{1}{3}$

3 (a) A is $\left(\dfrac{\pi}{2}, 0\right)$,

$\displaystyle\int_0^{\pi/2} \sin 2x \, dx = \left[-0.5\cos 2x\right]_0^{\pi/2} = 1$

(b) B is $(\pi, 0)$,

$\displaystyle\int_0^{\pi} \frac{1}{2}\cos\frac{1}{2}x \, dx = \left[\sin\frac{1}{2}x\right]_0^{\pi} = 1$

(c) C is $\left(\dfrac{\pi}{4}, 0\right)$,

$\displaystyle\int_0^{\pi/4} 3\sin 2x \, dx = \left[-1.5\cos 2x\right]_0^{\pi/4} = 1.5$

4E The result is *not* true.

$$\int_1^2 \cos x^2 \, dx = -0.44 \quad \text{(to 2 d.p.)}$$

by the trapezium rule

and $\left[\dfrac{1}{2x}\sin x^2\right]_1^2 = -0.61 \quad \text{(to 2 d.p.)}$

$$\dfrac{d}{dx}\left(\dfrac{1}{2x}\sin x^2\right) \neq \cos x^2$$

5E (a) $2\sin\frac{1}{2}x + c$　　(b) $\frac{2}{5}e^{2.5x} + c$

(c) Not possible by the methods of this chapter. The expression would have to be multiplied out before it could be integrated.

(d) $\frac{1}{25}(5x+3)^5 + c$　　(e) $-\frac{1}{5}\cos 5x + c$

(f) not possible

6E (a) $-\frac{1}{2}\cos x^2 + c$　　(b) $\frac{1}{3}e^{x^3} + c$

(c) $\frac{1}{10}(2x^2+1)^5 + c$

7E $= \displaystyle\int_0^1 \dfrac{1}{2}(1 - \cos 2x)\, dx$

$= \left[\dfrac{x}{2} - \dfrac{1}{4}\sin 2x\right]_0^1$

$= 0.27 \quad \text{(to 2 d.p.)}$

6.1.3 Small increments

6.1 Exercise 3

1 (a) $12\pi \, \text{cm}^3$　　(b) $7.2\pi \, \text{cm}^2$

2 It would increase by 3% (about 11 days).

3 (a) $0.16 \, \text{cm}$　　(b) $2.6 \, \text{cm h}^{-1}$

4 4.5%

5 (a) 0.308
This is the marginal cost in £1000 per 1000 articles.

(b) £31 per week

6.1.4 Inverse functions and x^n

6.1 Exercise 4

1 (a) $y = \dfrac{1}{x^2} = x^{-2} \Rightarrow \dfrac{dy}{dx} = -2x^{-3} = -\dfrac{2}{x^3}$

(b) An expression such as $(1+x)\sqrt{x}$ should be multiplied out before differentiation.

$$y = (1+x)\sqrt{x} = \sqrt{x} + x\sqrt{x} = x^{\frac{1}{2}} + x^{\frac{3}{2}}$$

Then $\dfrac{dy}{dx} = \dfrac{1}{2}x^{-\frac{1}{2}} + \dfrac{3}{2}x^{\frac{1}{2}} = \dfrac{1}{2\sqrt{x}} + \dfrac{3}{2}\sqrt{x}$

2 (a) $\frac{1}{3}x^{-\frac{2}{3}}$　　(b) $-x^{-2}$　　(c) $-3x^{-4}$

(d) $-2x^{-3} + \frac{1}{2}x^{-\frac{1}{2}}$

3 $y = x^{\frac{1}{n}} \Rightarrow \dfrac{dy}{dx} = \dfrac{1}{n}x^{\frac{1}{n}-1}$

4 $\dfrac{dx}{dy} = e^y = x$

Then $\dfrac{dy}{dx} = \dfrac{1}{dx/dy} = \dfrac{1}{x}$

5 Let $u = 2x \Rightarrow \dfrac{du}{dx} = 2$

$y = \ln u \Rightarrow \dfrac{dy}{du} = \dfrac{1}{u}$

$\dfrac{dy}{dx} = \dfrac{\cancel{2}}{\cancel{2}x} = \dfrac{1}{x}$

6 (a) $y = \ln 3x \Rightarrow \dfrac{dy}{dx} = \dfrac{1}{x}$

$y = \ln 5x \Rightarrow \dfrac{dy}{dx} = \dfrac{1}{x}$

(b) $y = \ln ax \Rightarrow \dfrac{dy}{dx} = \dfrac{1}{x}$

(c) $y = \ln ax$
$\Rightarrow y = \ln a + \ln x$
[because $\ln(A \times B) = \ln A + \ln B$]

$\Rightarrow \dfrac{dy}{dx} = 0 + \dfrac{1}{x}$

[$\ln a$ is a constant value and so has a zero derivative.]

7 (a) $\int \frac{1}{2x}\,dx = \frac{1}{2}\ln x + c$ (b) $\frac{1}{a}\ln x + c$

8E $\frac{dx}{dy} = 3y^2$

$\frac{dy}{dx} = \frac{1}{3y^2}$

$\frac{dy}{dx} = \frac{1}{3(\sqrt[3]{x})^2} = \frac{1}{3}x^{-\frac{2}{3}}$

9E (a) $\frac{dx}{dy} = \cos y \Rightarrow \frac{dy}{dx} = \frac{1}{\cos y}$

(b) The third side is $\sqrt{(1-x^2)}$.
Therefore $\cos y = \sqrt{(1-x^2)}$ and
$\frac{dy}{dx} = \frac{1}{\sqrt{(1-x^2)}}$

(c) For $y = \cos^{-1} x$, $\frac{dy}{dx} = \frac{-1}{\sqrt{(1-x^2)}}$

6.2 Parametric form
6.2.1 Curves which vary with time

6.2 Exercise 1

1 (a)

t	0	1	2	3	4	5
x	0	20	40	60	80	100
y	90	85	70	45	10	−35

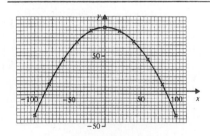

(b) Since $x = 20t$, negative values of t will simply give negative values of x and since $y = 90 - 5t^2$, the values of y will be unchanged. The result will be a graph that is symmetric about the y-axis.

(c) The curve is a parabola.

2 (a)

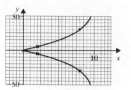

Note the symmetry in the x-axis. Note also that, since $x = 2t^2$, x will never be negative.

(b)

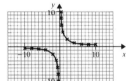

It is necessary to consider fractional values of t, for example $\frac{1}{2}, \frac{1}{3}, \frac{1}{4}$, in order to generate the arms of the hyperbola. Negative values of t result in a reflection in the origin.

6.2.2 Circles and ellipses

6.2 A

1 (a) $(3\cos\theta,\ 3\sin\theta)$

(b) $3\sin\theta$

(c) $6\cos\theta$

(d) $x = 6\cos\theta,\quad y = 3\sin\theta$

(e) $R(0,3),\quad Q(3,0),\quad Q'(6,0)$

(f) (i) 9π
(ii) Since the curve is stretched by a factor 2 in the x direction, the area of the ellipse is $2 \times 9\pi = 18\pi$.

2 (a)

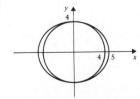

(b) The ellipse can be obtained from the circle by means of a one-way stretch, factor $\frac{5}{4}$ in the x direction.

(c) (i) 16π
(ii) 20π

3 (a) 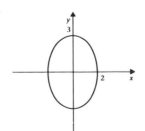 (b) (c)

$$x = 5\cos\theta \qquad x = 2\cos\theta \qquad x = a\cos\theta$$
$$y = 6\sin\theta \qquad y = \sin\theta \qquad y = b\sin\theta$$

4 (a) $\qquad x = a\cos\theta, \quad y = b\sin\theta$

$$\Rightarrow \cos\theta = \frac{x}{a}, \quad \sin\theta = \frac{y}{b}$$

So, since $\cos^2\theta + \sin^2\theta = 1$, it follows that

$$\left(\frac{x}{a}\right)^2 + \left(\frac{y}{b}\right)^2 = 1$$

or $\qquad \dfrac{x^2}{a^2} + \dfrac{y^2}{b^2} = 1,$

the Cartesian equation of the ellipse

(b) Comparing with $\dfrac{x^2}{a^2} + \dfrac{y^2}{b^2} = 1,$

$$a = 2, \quad b = 3$$

5 (a) The scale factors are:
a in the x direction,
b in the y direction.

(b) $\pi \times 1^2 = \pi$
Since the circle is stretched by a factor a, followed by b, the area of the ellipse is $\pi \times a \times b = \pi ab$.

6.2 **Exercise 2**

1

Ellipse	Cartesian equation	Parametric equations	Area
A	$\dfrac{x^2}{9} + \dfrac{y^2}{16} = 1$	$x = 3\cos\theta$ $y = 4\sin\theta$	12π
B	$\dfrac{x^2}{9} + \dfrac{y^2}{25} = 1$	$x = 3\cos\theta$ $y = 5\sin\theta$	15π
C	$\dfrac{x^2}{0.25} + \dfrac{y^2}{0.16} = 1$	$x = 0.5\cos\theta$ $y = 0.4\sin\theta$	0.2π

2 $\dfrac{x^2}{4} + \dfrac{y^2}{9} = 1$
$x = 2\cos\theta, \quad y = 3\sin\theta$
Area $= 6\pi$

3 $\dfrac{x^2}{25} + \dfrac{y^2}{4} = 1$
$x = 5\cos\theta, \quad y = 2\sin\theta$
Area $= 10\pi$

6.2.3 Conversion

6.2 **B**

1 (a) $\sec\theta = \dfrac{c}{a} \qquad \dfrac{1}{\cos\theta} = 1 \div \dfrac{a}{c} = \dfrac{c}{a}$

(b) $\operatorname{cosec}\theta = \dfrac{c}{b} \qquad \dfrac{1}{\sin\theta} = 1 \div \dfrac{b}{c} = \dfrac{c}{b}$

(c) $\cot\theta = \dfrac{a}{b} \qquad \dfrac{1}{\tan\theta} = 1 \div \dfrac{b}{a} = \dfrac{a}{b}$

(d) $\cot\theta = \dfrac{a}{b} \qquad \dfrac{\cos\theta}{\sin\theta} = \dfrac{a}{c} \div \dfrac{b}{c} = \dfrac{a}{b}$

2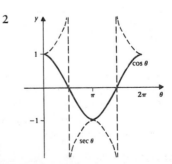

3 (a)

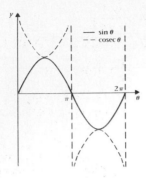

(b)

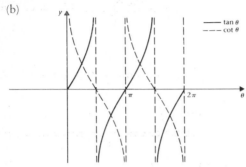

4 (a) $\dfrac{\sin^2\theta}{\cos^2\theta} + \dfrac{\cos^2\theta}{\cos^2\theta} = \dfrac{1}{\cos^2\theta}$

So, since $\dfrac{\sin\theta}{\cos\theta} = \tan\theta$ and $\dfrac{1}{\cos\theta} = \sec\theta$,

$\tan^2\theta + 1 = \sec^2\theta$

(b) $\dfrac{\sin^2\theta}{\sin^2\theta} + \dfrac{\cos^2\theta}{\sin^2\theta} = \dfrac{1}{\sin^2\theta}$

So, since $\dfrac{\cos\theta}{\sin\theta} = \cot\theta$ and $\dfrac{1}{\sin\theta} = \operatorname{cosec}\theta$,

$1 + \cot^2\theta = \operatorname{cosec}^2\theta$

5 $\cot\theta = x$ and $\operatorname{cosec}\theta = 2y$
So, using $1 + \cot^2\theta = \operatorname{cosec}^2\theta$,
$1 + x^2 = (2y)^2$ or $4y^2 - x^2 = 1$

6.2 Exercise 3

1 (a) $5x + 3y = 22$ (b) $y = 5 - \dfrac{18}{x}$

(c) $y = \dfrac{5x}{2} - \dfrac{5x^2}{16}$ (d) $x + y = 3$

2 (a) $4x^2 = 1 + \dfrac{y^2}{9}$ (b) $\dfrac{x^2}{16} + \dfrac{y^2}{9} = 1$

(c) $4y^2 + 1 = x^2$

(d) $1 + (y-1)^2 = \left(\dfrac{x}{3}\right)^3$

$\qquad y^2 - 2y + 2 = \dfrac{x^2}{9}$

3E (a) $y = 3 + x$

(b) Since $\sqrt{t} \geq 0$, it follows that $x \geq 1$, $y \geq 4$. Thus the parametric equations define a half-line.

4E $x = t + 2$, $y = t^2 + 4$;
$x = 2 \pm \sqrt{t}$, $y = t + 4$
Many others are possible.

6.2.4 Differentiating parametric equations

6.2 Exercise 4

1 $\dfrac{dy}{dx} = \dfrac{dy}{dt} \div \dfrac{dx}{dt}$

$\qquad = -\dfrac{1}{t^2} \div 1$

$\qquad = -\dfrac{1}{4}$ at $t = 2$

2 $\dfrac{dy}{dx} = \dfrac{4\cos\theta}{-3\sin\theta}$

At $\theta = \dfrac{\pi}{2}$,
$x = 0$, $\quad y = 4$, $\quad \dfrac{dy}{dx} = 0$

3 $\dfrac{dy}{dx} = \dfrac{u}{2}$, $\quad y = x - 4$

4 $y = 3x - 1$

5 (a) $\dfrac{3(v^2 - 1)}{2}$ (b) $v = \pm 1$

(c) $(2, -2)$ and $(-2, 2)$

6 $\dfrac{dy}{dx} = \dfrac{2s}{3}$

At $s = 1$ the gradient is $\frac{2}{3}$.

$$s = \frac{x}{3}, \quad \text{so } y = \left(\frac{x}{3}\right)^2 \quad \text{or} \quad \frac{x^2}{9}$$

$$\frac{dy}{dx} = \frac{2x}{9}$$

When $s = 1$, $x = 3$, so the gradient at $x = 3$ is $\frac{6}{9}$ or $\frac{2}{3}$.

7 (a) Parametric differentiation is the only sensible method.

$$\frac{dy}{dx} = \frac{3t^2}{2(t+2)}$$

(b) It is easy to spot that $y = 3x - 4$, so

$$\frac{dy}{dx} = 3.$$

(c) Parametric differentiation is the only sensible method.

$$\frac{dy}{dx} = \frac{-3\cos\theta}{(2\sin\theta + \cos\theta)}$$

(d) Parametric differentiation is the only method.

$$\frac{dy}{dx} = \frac{3\cos 3\theta}{2\cos 2\theta}$$

8 (a) $\dfrac{dy}{dx} = \dfrac{dy}{dt} \div \dfrac{dx}{dt}$

$$= \frac{6t^2 + 4}{2t}$$

$$= 3t + \frac{2}{t}$$

$$\Rightarrow \left(\frac{dy}{dx}\right)^2 = 9t^2 + 12 + \frac{4}{t^2}$$

$$= \left(3t - \frac{2}{t}\right)^2 + 24$$

Since $\left(3t - \dfrac{2}{t}\right)^2 \geq 0$ for all t, $\left(\dfrac{dy}{dx}\right)^2 \geq 24$

(b)

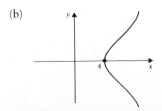

9E $\dfrac{dy}{dx} = \dfrac{\cos\theta}{1 + \sin\theta}$

At $\theta = \frac{1}{4}\pi$, $(x, y) \approx (0.0783, 0.707)$

and $\dfrac{dy}{dx} \approx 0.414$

$$y - 0.707 \approx 0.414(x - 0.0783)$$

$$y \approx 0.414x + 0.675$$

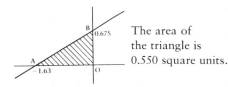

The area of the triangle is 0.550 square units.

6.2.5 Velocity vectors

6.2 **Exercise 5**

1

t	0	1	2	3
x	0	1	4	9
y	0	3	6	9
$\mathbf{v}$	$\begin{bmatrix}0\\3\end{bmatrix}$	$\begin{bmatrix}2\\3\end{bmatrix}$	$\begin{bmatrix}4\\3\end{bmatrix}$	$\begin{bmatrix}6\\3\end{bmatrix}$
v	3	$\sqrt{13}$	5	$\sqrt{45}$

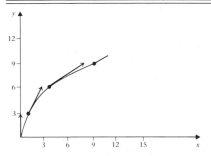

2 (a) $\mathbf{v} = \begin{bmatrix} 2t \\ 3 - 2t \end{bmatrix}$

(b) When $t = 0$, $\mathbf{v} = \begin{bmatrix} 0 \\ 3 \end{bmatrix}$. The speed is 3 cm s^{-1}, parallel to the y-axis.

(c) $\begin{bmatrix} 2t \\ 3 - 2t \end{bmatrix} = \lambda \begin{bmatrix} 1 \\ 1 \end{bmatrix}$

$\Rightarrow 2t = 3 - 2t \Rightarrow t = \frac{3}{4}$

(d) $t = \frac{3}{2}$

3 The line has gradient 3. It is parallel to the

vector $\begin{bmatrix} 1 \\ 3 \end{bmatrix}$, which has magnitude $\sqrt{10}$, so

$$\mathbf{v} = \begin{bmatrix} 1 \\ 3 \end{bmatrix} \quad \text{or} \quad \begin{bmatrix} -1 \\ -3 \end{bmatrix}$$

$$\mathbf{r} = \begin{bmatrix} 0 \\ 1 \end{bmatrix} + t \begin{bmatrix} 1 \\ 3 \end{bmatrix}$$

6.3 Further differentiation techniques
6.3.1 The product rule

6.3 A

1 (a) $\dfrac{dy}{dx} = 2x \sin x + x^2 \cos x$

$= 2.22$ at $x = 1$

2 (a) $\dfrac{dy}{dx} = -\frac{1}{2}\sin(\frac{1}{2}x) \times (4x - \frac{1}{2}x^2)$
$\quad\quad + \cos\left(\frac{1}{2}x\right) \times (4 - x)$

$= (\frac{1}{4}x^2 - 2x)\sin\left(\frac{1}{2}x\right) + (4 - x)\cos\left(\frac{1}{2}x\right)$

3 Whatever functions you choose, you should find that the product rule gives correct gradient functions.

4 (a) $\dfrac{d}{dx}(x^3 \times x^2) = 3x^2 \times x^2 + x^3 \times 2x$

$= 3x^4 + 2x^4$

$= 5x^4$ as expected.

(c) $\dfrac{d}{dx}(x^a \times x^b) = ax^{a-1} \times x^b + x^a \times bx^{b-1}$

$= ax^{a+b-1} + bx^{a+b-1}$

$= (a+b)x^{a+b-1}$ as expected.

6.3 Exercise 1

1 (a) $e^x(\sin x + \cos x)$ (b) $xe^x(2 + x)$

(c) $x^2(3\cos x - x\sin x)$

---

2 (a) 148   (b) 16.3

3 The gradient is 1.1.
The equation of the tangent is
$y = 1.1x - 0.16$.

4 (a) (i) $\dfrac{dA}{dt} = 2t\sin t + t^2\cos t$

At $t = 1$, the rate of change of area is 2.22.

(ii) When $t = 2.5$, $\dfrac{dA}{dt} = -2.01$, so the area is decreasing.

(b) (i) $A = \sin t \cos t$

$\dfrac{dA}{dt} = \cos^2 t - \sin^2 t$

When $t = 0.5$ the rate of increase of area is 0.540.

(ii) The area stops increasing when $\dfrac{dA}{dt} = 0$.

So $\cos^2 t = \sin^2 t$

$\tan^2 t = 1$

This first occurs when $\tan t = 1$.
$t = \frac{1}{4}\pi = 0.785$

5 The gradient at $x = 1$ is 1.36.
The equation of the tangent is
$y = 1.36x - 0.68$.

6 At the turning point $e^x(1 + x) = 0$, so $x = -1$.
So the coordinates of the turning point are $(-1, -0.37)$.

7 (a) At the stationary point, $e^x(2x + x^2) = 0$,
so $x = 0$ or -2.
When $x = 0$, $y = 0$, so $(0, 0)$ is a stationary point.

(b) e^x cannot equal 0, so the only stationary points are at $x = 0$ and $x = -2$.
The coordinates of the other stationary point are $(-2, 0.54)$.

8 (a) $0 = \dfrac{1}{x} + x\dfrac{dv}{dx}$

So $\dfrac{1}{x} = -x\dfrac{dv}{dx}$

or $\dfrac{dv}{dx} = -\dfrac{1}{x^2}$

9E $\dfrac{dy}{dx} = \sin x + x\cos x$, so at the stationary

point, $\sin x + x\cos x = 0$.
Dividing by $\cos x$ gives $\tan x + x = 0$.
One stationary point is $(0, 0)$.
The others are $(-2.03, 1.82)$ and $(2.03, 1.82)$
to 3 s.f.

6.3.2 Product rule and chain rule

6.3 Exercise 2

1 (a) $e^{3x}(6\sin 2x + 4\cos 2x)$

(b) $e^{2x}(2\cos 3x - 3\sin 3x)$

(c) $e^{x^2}(2x\sin 4x + 4\cos 4x)$

2 (a) $\dfrac{2x}{(x^2 + 1)}$ (b) $\ln x + 1$

(c) $\sin^2 x + 2x\sin x\cos x$

(d) $2x^2\cos x^2 + \sin x^2$

(e) $2(x + \sin x)(1 + \cos x)$

(f) $e^x(\cos x - \sin x) + \sin x + x\cos x$

(g) $-2(2x + 3)^{-2}$

(h) $2x\,e^{3x} + 3x^2\,e^{3x} = x\,e^{3x}(2 + 3x)$

3 (a) $\dfrac{dy}{dx} = e^{0.5x}(0.5\sin x + \cos x)$

The gradient at $x = 2$ is 0.105.

(b) The gradient at $x = 2$ is -0.343.

4 (a) Displacement $= 0$;

velocity $= \dfrac{ds}{dt}$

$= 0.4 \times 512\pi\cos(512\pi t)$

$= 643.4\,\text{cm s}^{-1}$ (when $t = 1$)

(b) $\dfrac{512\pi}{2\pi} = 256$

5 $(x + 1)^{-1} - (x + 2)(x + 1)^{-2}$

$= \dfrac{1}{(x + 1)} - \dfrac{(x + 2)}{(x + 1)^2}$

This is equal to $\dfrac{(x + 1) - (x + 2)}{(x + 1)^2}$

or $\dfrac{-1}{(x + 1)^2}$

$\left(\text{Note that } \dfrac{x + 2}{x + 1} = 1 + \dfrac{1}{x + 1}\right)$

6.3.3 Differentiating quotients

6.3 Exercise 3

1 (a) $\dfrac{x\cos x - \sin x}{x^2}$

(b) $\dfrac{e^x(1 - x)}{e^{2x}}$ or $\dfrac{1 - x}{e^x}$

(c) $\dfrac{e^x(\sin x - \cos x)}{\sin^2 x}$

(d) $\dfrac{e^{3x}(3\sin 2x - 2\cos 2x)}{\sin^2 2x}$

2 (a) $\dfrac{dy}{dx} = \dfrac{e^x\cos x - e^x\sin x}{e^{2x}}$

$= \dfrac{\cos x - \sin x}{e^x}$

At $x = -1$, the gradient is 3.76.

(b) $\dfrac{dy}{dx} = \dfrac{2x^2\,e^{2x} - 2x\,e^{2x}}{x^4} = \dfrac{2\,e^{2x}(x - 1)}{x^3}$

At $x = 0.8$, the gradient is -3.87.

3 The derivative obtained by using the quotient
rule is $\dfrac{-2}{(2x + 3)^2}$ and by using the chain rule it
is $-2(2x + 3)^{-2}$.
The two answers are equivalent.

4 (a) $\dfrac{dy}{dx} = \dfrac{(1 + x^2) - 2x^2}{(1 + x^2)^2} = \dfrac{1 - x^2}{(1 + x^2)^2}$

At the stationary points, $1 - x^2 = 0$ so
$x = \pm 1$.
When $x = -1$, $y = -0.5$;
when $x = 1$, $y = 0.5$

$x = -1.1 \Rightarrow \dfrac{dy}{dx} = -0.043$ and

$x = -0.9 \Rightarrow \dfrac{dy}{dx} = 0.058$,

so there is a local minimum at the point $(-1, -0.5)$.

$x = 0.9 \Rightarrow \dfrac{dy}{dx} = 0.058$ and

$x = 1.1 \Rightarrow \dfrac{dy}{dx} = -0.043$,

so there is a local maximum at the point $(1, 0.5)$.

(b) There is a local minimum at the point $(0, 0)$.
There is a local maximum at the point $(-8, -16)$.

5 $\dfrac{\cos^2 x + \sin^2 x}{\cos^2 x} = \dfrac{1}{\cos^2 x} = \sec^2 x$

6 (a) $\dfrac{-\sin^2 x - \cos^2 x}{\sin^2 x}$ (b) $\dfrac{0 - \sec^2 x}{\tan^2 x}$

(c) Both simplify to $\dfrac{-1}{\sin^2 x}$ or $-\csc^2 x$.

7E $\dfrac{du}{dx} = y\dfrac{dv}{dx} + v\dfrac{dy}{dx}$

$v\dfrac{dy}{dx} = \dfrac{du}{dx} - y\dfrac{dv}{dx}$

$= \dfrac{du}{dx} - \dfrac{u}{v}\dfrac{dv}{dx}$

$= \dfrac{v\dfrac{du}{dx} - u\dfrac{dv}{dx}}{v}$

So $\dfrac{dy}{dx} = \dfrac{v\dfrac{du}{dx} - u\dfrac{dv}{dx}}{v^2}$

6.3.4 Implicit differentiation

6.3 Exercise 4

1 (a) $4y\dfrac{dy}{dx} - 3\dfrac{dy}{dx} + 8x = 0$,

so $\dfrac{dy}{dx} = \dfrac{-8x}{(4y - 3)}$

(b) $3x^2 + y\dfrac{dy}{dx} - 7 + 3\dfrac{dy}{dx} = 0$,

so $\dfrac{dy}{dx} = \dfrac{(7 - 3x^2)}{(y + 3)}$

2 (a) $18x + 8y\dfrac{dy}{dx} = 0$,

so $\dfrac{dy}{dx} = \dfrac{-18x}{8y}$ or $\dfrac{-9x}{4y}$

(b) When $x = 1$, $y^2 = 9$, so $y = \pm 3$
At $(1, 3)$ the gradient is -0.75.
At $(1, -3)$ the gradient is 0.75.

3 (a) $\dfrac{dy}{dx} = \dfrac{-(2x + 6)}{(2y - 2)}$

At $(1, 4)$ the gradient is $-\frac{4}{3}$.
The equation of the tangent is
$3y + 4x = 16$.

(b) At $(1, -2)$ the gradient is $\frac{4}{3}$.
The radius joins $(1, -2)$ to $(-3, 1)$, so has
gradient $-\frac{3}{4}$.
Since this is the same as $-1 \div \frac{4}{3}$ the
tangent and radius are perpendicular.

(c) Other points on the circumference with
integral coordinates are:

$(0, 5), (0, -3), (-6, 5), (-7, 4), (-6, -3)$

and $(-7, -2)$

At all these points the gradient of the
curve should be equal to

$\dfrac{-1}{\text{gradient of radius}}$

4 Since $x = 3\cos\theta$
and $y = 3\sin\theta$,

$\dfrac{-x}{y} = \dfrac{-3\cos\theta}{3\sin\theta}$

So $\dfrac{-x}{y} = \dfrac{-\cos\theta}{\sin\theta}$

The radius joins $(0, 0)$ to (x, y), so has
gradient $\dfrac{y}{x}$. Hence $\dfrac{-1}{(\text{gradient of radius})}$ is equal
to the gradient of the tangent, so the radius
and tangent must be perpendicular.

5 (a) $\dfrac{d}{dx}(\ln y) = \dfrac{d}{dy}(\ln y)\dfrac{dy}{dx}$, by the chain rule

$\qquad = \dfrac{1}{y}\dfrac{dy}{dx}$

Now $\ln y = x\ln 2$

$\Rightarrow \dfrac{1}{y}\dfrac{dy}{dx} = \ln 2$

$\Rightarrow \dfrac{dy}{dx} = y\ln 2 = \ln 2 \times 2^x$

(b) $\dfrac{d}{dx}(3^x) = \ln 3 \times 3^x$

(c) $\dfrac{d}{dx}(a^x) = \ln a \times a^x$

6.3.5 Implicit differentiation and the product rule

6.3 Exercise 5

1 (a) $4x + 3y + 3x\dfrac{dy}{dx} - 4\dfrac{dy}{dx} + 2y\dfrac{dy}{dx} = 0$

$(3x - 4 + 2y)\dfrac{dy}{dx} = -(4x + 3y)$

$\dfrac{dy}{dx} = -\dfrac{4x + 3y}{3x + 2y - 4}$

(b) $\dfrac{dy}{dx} = \dfrac{2x + 2y - 3}{2y - 2x}$

(c) $\dfrac{2 - x}{4 + 4y}$

(d) $-\dfrac{3x^2 + y^2}{2xy + 3y^2}$

2 (a) $\dfrac{dy}{dx} = -\dfrac{y}{x}$

(b) $y = \dfrac{12}{x} \Rightarrow \dfrac{dy}{dx} = -\dfrac{12}{x^2}$

(c) Since $\dfrac{12}{x} = y$, $\dfrac{-12}{x^2} = -\dfrac{y}{x} = \dfrac{dy}{dx}$

3 (a) $2xy + x^2\dfrac{dy}{dx} + 3x^2 = 0$

$\dfrac{dy}{dx} = \dfrac{-(2xy + 3x^2)}{x^2}$

When $x = -2$ and $y = 3$, $\dfrac{dy}{dx} = 0$

So $(-2, 3)$ is a stationary point on the curve.

(b) By the quotient rule,

$\dfrac{dy}{dx} = \dfrac{x^2(-3x^2) - 2x(4 - x^3)}{x^4}$

When $x = -2$, $\dfrac{dy}{dx} = \dfrac{(-48 + 4(4 + 8))}{4}$
which is 0.

4 (a) $\dfrac{dy}{dx} = \dfrac{(4x - 3y)}{3x}$

When $x = 2$ and $y = 2\frac{2}{3}$, $\dfrac{dy}{dx} = 0$,

so $(2, 2\frac{2}{3})$ is a stationary point.

When $x = -2$ and $y = -2\frac{2}{3}$, $\dfrac{dy}{dx} = 0$,

so $(-2, -2\frac{2}{3})$ is a stationary point.

(b) $3xy - 2x^2 = 8$

$3xy = 8 + 2x^2$

$y = \dfrac{8 + 2x^2}{3x}$

$\dfrac{dy}{dx} = \dfrac{12x^2 - 3(8 + 2x^2)}{9x^2} = \dfrac{6x^2 - 24}{9x^2}$

At the stationary points, $6x^2 = 24$,
so $x = \pm 2$.

$x = 2 \Rightarrow y = 2\frac{2}{3}$; $x = -2 \Rightarrow y = -2\frac{2}{3}$,

so $(2, 2\frac{2}{3})$ and $(-2, -2\frac{2}{3})$ are stationary points.

(c) It is clear that implicit differentiation is quicker for checking stationary points, but it is not well designed for *finding* stationary points.

Miscellaneous exercise 6

1 (a) $-3\sin(3x+2)$ (b) $-4\sin(4x-1)$

    (c) $5\cos(5x-11)$

2 (a) $2\sin x\cos x = \sin 2x$ (b) $2x\cos(x^2)$

    (c) $-3\cos^2 x\sin x$

    (d) $-6\cos(3x)\sin(3x) = -3\sin(6x)$

3 (a) $6(3x+5)$ (b) $4\cos 4x$

    (c) $3x^{-\frac{1}{2}}$ (d) $(2x-7)^{-\frac{1}{2}}$

    (e) $-8\sin(2x-7)$ (f) $-3x(x^2-5)^{-\frac{3}{2}}$

    (g) $-2\sin x\cos x$ (h) $-10\sin 5x\cos 5x$

    (i) $\frac{1}{2}(2x-3)(x^2-3x)^{-\frac{1}{2}}$

    (j) $1+x(x^2+1)^{-\frac{1}{2}}$ (k) $-9(3x+4)^{-4}$

4 (a) $0.00199\,\text{m min}^{-1}$ (b) $0.1\,\text{m}^2\,\text{min}^{-1}$

5 (a) $-0.167\,\text{cm h}^{-1}$ (b) $-50\,\text{cm}^3\,\text{h}^{-1}$

6

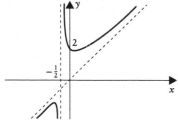

maximum at $(-1\frac{1}{2},-2\frac{1}{2})$

minimum at $(\frac{1}{2},1\frac{1}{2})$

7 $h=\dfrac{100}{\pi r^2}$

    (a) $-0.0251\,\text{cm min}^{-1}$

    (b) Increasing at $0.625\,\text{cm}^2\,\text{min}^{-1}$

8 $y=\frac{1}{2}x+2$

9 $\dfrac{dy}{dx}=\dfrac{2-x}{y-3}$

10 $t=0,\frac{3}{2},3;$ $18\,\text{m s}^{-2}$

11 $v=\begin{bmatrix} 3a\sin^2 t\cos t \\ -3a\cos^2 t\sin t \end{bmatrix}$

Initial position is $\begin{bmatrix} 0 \\ a \end{bmatrix}$ with velocity $\begin{bmatrix} 0 \\ 0 \end{bmatrix}$

12 $9000\pi\sin^2\theta\cos\theta;$ $10\,900\,\text{cm}^3$ (to 3 s.f.)

13 (a) $-\dfrac{6x}{5y}$ (b) $\dfrac{-2(1+y)}{x}$ (c) $\dfrac{-3}{\sin y}$

14 2

15 (a) $6x(3x-1)$ (b) $2\cos x-2x\sin x$

    (c) $(x+5)^2(4x+5)$ (d) $\dfrac{-11}{(4x-1)^2}$

    (e) $\dfrac{-3x\sin 3x-\cos 3x}{x^2}$

    (f) $2\sin 3x+3(2x+1)\cos 3x$

    (g) $2x\tan 2x+2x^2\sec^2 2x$

    (h) $3\cos 4x\cos 3x-4\sin 3x\sin 4x$

    (i) $2\cos^2 x\sin x-\sin^3 x$

16 (a) $-3\operatorname{cosec}^2(3x)$ (b) $\dfrac{1}{1+\cos x}$

    (c) $\cos^2 x-\sin^2 x$ (d) $2\tan x\sec^2 x$

17 (a) $\dfrac{dy}{dx}=\dfrac{1}{1-\sin x}$

18 $-\operatorname{cosec}^2 x;$ $-\operatorname{cosec} x\cot x$

7 CALCULUS METHODS 2

7.1 Integration techniques
7.1.1 Volumes of revolution

7.1 A

1 (a) $h \approx 40\,\text{cm}$ (b) $h \approx 83\,\text{cm}$

2 The width, w, of the slab increases uniformly from 0 to 2 as the height, h, increases from 0 to 2. So $w = h$.

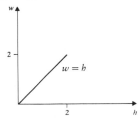

The length, l, of the slab increases uniformly from 2 to 3 as the height, h, increases from 0 to 2. So $l = 2 + \frac{1}{2}h$.

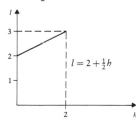

3 The volume of a slab at height h is $h\left(2 + \frac{1}{2}h\right)\delta h$. Hence, the volume of the container is

$$V = \int_0^2 h\left(2 + \tfrac{1}{2}h\right)\mathrm{d}h$$

$$= \int_0^2 \left(2h + \tfrac{1}{2}h^2\right)\mathrm{d}h$$

$$= \left[h^2 + \tfrac{1}{6}h^3\right]_0^2$$

$$= 5\tfrac{1}{3}\,\text{m}^3$$

4 The container is half full when $V = 2\frac{2}{3}$.

$$h^2 + \tfrac{1}{6}h^3 = 2\tfrac{2}{3} \Rightarrow h \approx 1.46\,\text{m}$$

The equation can be solved by decimal search or by plotting the graph and reading off the solution.

5 The increase in volume is

$$\left[h^2 + \tfrac{1}{6}h^3\right]_{1.1}^{1.4} = 0.9855\,\text{m}^3.$$

7.1 B

1 (a) If the rectangle of height y and width δx is rotated completely about the x-axis, it describes a cylinder of radius y and width δx and hence will have volume $\pi y^2\,\delta x$.

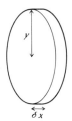

(b) If $y = x^2$, $y^2 = (x^2)^2 = x^4$

(c) Volume $= \displaystyle\int_0^2 \pi y^2\,\mathrm{d}x = \int_0^2 \pi x^4\,\mathrm{d}x$

$$= \left[\tfrac{1}{5}\pi x^5\right]_0^2 = \tfrac{1}{5}\pi 2^5 - \tfrac{1}{5}\pi 0^5 = \tfrac{32}{5}\pi$$

2 (a) Volume $= \displaystyle\int_0^2 \pi y^2\,\mathrm{d}x = \int_0^2 \pi(x^2 + 1)^2\,\mathrm{d}x$

$$= \int_0^2 \pi(x^4 + 2x^2 + 1)\,\mathrm{d}x$$

$$= \left[\pi\left(\tfrac{1}{5}x^5 + \tfrac{2}{3}x^3 + x\right)\right]_0^2 = 13\tfrac{11}{15}\pi$$

(b) The graph $y = x^2 - 2x$ cuts the x-axis where $x^2 - 2x = 0$
$\Rightarrow x(x - 2) = 0 \Rightarrow x = 0$ or $x = 2$

Volume $= \displaystyle\int_0^2 \pi y^2\,\mathrm{d}x$

$$= \int_0^2 \pi(x^4 - 4x^3 + 4x^2)\,\mathrm{d}x$$

$$= \left[\pi\left(\tfrac{1}{5}x^5 - x^4 + \tfrac{4}{3}x^3\right)\right]_0^2$$

$$= \tfrac{16}{15}\pi$$

3 When a rectangle, of length x and height δy, is rotated about the y-axis, it describes a cylinder of volume $\pi x^2 \delta y$. It follows that the volume of the solid obtained by rotating the area about the y-axis

$$= \int_0^4 \pi x^2 \, dy$$

$$= \int_0^4 \pi y \, dy = \left[\pi \tfrac{1}{2} y^2\right]_0^4 = 8\pi$$

4 $y = \dfrac{1}{x} \Rightarrow x = \dfrac{1}{y}$

Volume

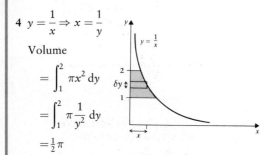

$$= \int_1^2 \pi x^2 \, dy$$

$$= \int_1^2 \pi \frac{1}{y^2} \, dy$$

$$= \tfrac{1}{2} \pi$$

5 Many people would expect the two volumes to be equal. It is easy to prove otherwise. Both volumes formed will be cones.

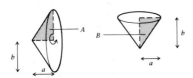

The volume of a cone is given by the formula $V = \tfrac{1}{3}\pi r^2 h$.

The two cones formed will have volumes $\tfrac{1}{3}\pi b^2 a$ for area A and $\tfrac{1}{3}\pi a^2 b$ for area B. These volumes will only be equal if $a = b$.

You could have calculated the volumes formed using integration. The volume formed by rotating area A about the x-axis is

$$\int_0^a \pi y^2 \, dx = \int_0^a \pi m^2 x^2 \, dx$$

$$= \left[\tfrac{1}{3}\pi m^2 x^3\right]_0^a$$

$$= \tfrac{1}{3}\pi m^2 a^3$$

$$= \tfrac{1}{3}\pi b^2 a \qquad \text{because } m^2 a^2 = b^2$$

This confirms the formula for the volume of a cone.

7.1 Exercise 1

1 $\tfrac{31}{5}\pi$

2 (a)

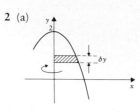

$$V = \pi \int_0^2 x^2 \, dy$$

$$= \pi \int_0^2 (2 - y) \, dy$$

$$= \pi \left[2y - \frac{y^2}{2}\right]_0^2$$

$$= 2\pi$$

(b) 9.48   (to 3 s.f.)

3 (a) $\tfrac{7}{3}\pi$

(b)

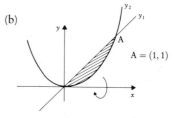

$A = (1, 1)$

$$V = \pi \int_0^1 y_1^2 \, dx - \pi \int_0^1 y_2^2 \, dx$$

$$= \pi \int_0^1 x^2 \, dx - \pi \int_0^1 x^4 \, dx$$

$$= \pi \left[\frac{x^3}{3}\right]_0^1 - \pi \left[\frac{x^5}{5}\right]_0^1 = \frac{2}{15}\pi$$

(c) $\dfrac{\pi}{30}$

4 $(0, 0)$ and $(2, 4)$

$$V = \tfrac{32}{5}\pi$$

7.1.2 Integration by inspection

7.1 C

(a) Differentiating the function $\sin x^2$ seems to be a sensible starting point.

$$\frac{d}{dx}(\sin x^2) = 2x \cos x^2$$

$$\text{using the chain rule}$$

so $\displaystyle\int x \cos x^2 \, dx = \tfrac{1}{2}\sin x^2 + c$

(b) Differentiating the function $x \sin 2x$ by the product rule,

$$\frac{d}{dx}(x \sin 2x) = 2x \cos 2x + \sin 2x$$

$$\Rightarrow \qquad x \sin 2x = 2 \int x \cos 2x \, dx$$

$$+ \int \sin 2x \, dx$$

$$\Rightarrow 2 \int x \cos 2x \, dx = x \sin 2x - \int \sin 2x \, dx$$

$$\Rightarrow 2 \int x \cos 2x \, dx = x \sin 2x + \tfrac{1}{2}\cos 2x + c$$

$$\Rightarrow \int x \cos 2x \, dx = \tfrac{1}{2}x \sin 2x + \tfrac{1}{4}\cos 2x + c$$

(c) Differentiating the function $\sin 2x$ by inspection,

$$\Rightarrow \frac{d}{dx}(\sin 2x) = 2 \cos 2x$$

so $\int \cos 2x \, dx = \tfrac{1}{2}\sin 2x + c$

(d) It is not possible to find an algebraic solution to $\int \cos x^2 \, dx$.

7.1 Exercise 2

1 (a) $\tfrac{1}{3}\sin 3x + c$

(b) $\int (x^2 - 4)\, dx = \tfrac{1}{3}x^3 - 4x + c$

(c) $\tfrac{1}{5}e^{5x} + c$ (d) $\ln|x| + c$

2 (a) $3x^2 \cos x^3$ (b) $-4x \sin 2x^2$

(c) $6x(x^2 - 3)^2$

3 (a) $\tfrac{1}{3}\sin x^3 + c$ (b) $-\tfrac{1}{4}\cos 2x^2 + c$

(c) $\tfrac{1}{6}(x^2 - 3)^3 + c$

4 (a)

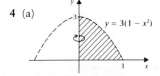

(b) $V = \pi \int_0^3 x^2 \, dy$

$$= \pi \int_0^3 1 - \tfrac{1}{3}y \, dy$$

$$= \pi \left[y - \tfrac{1}{6}y^2 \right]_0^3 = \tfrac{3}{2}\pi$$

5 (a)

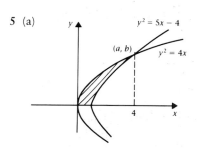

At the point of intersection,
$b^2 = 5a - 4, \quad b^2 = 4a$
$\Rightarrow 4a = 5a - 4$
$\Rightarrow \quad a = 4 \quad \text{and} \quad b = 4$

(b) $V_1 = \pi \int_0^4 y^2 \, dx$

$$= \pi \int_0^4 4x \, dx = 32\pi$$

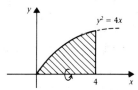

$$V_2 = \pi \int_{0.8}^4 y^2 \, dx$$

$$= \pi \int_{0.8}^4 (5x - 4)\, dx = 25.6\pi$$

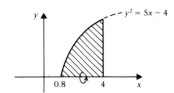

The volume of material is
$32\pi - 25.6\pi = 6.4\pi$ cubic units.

7.1.3 Integrating trigonometric functions

7.1 D

1
$$
\begin{array}{r}
- \cos(A+B) = -\cos A \cos B + \sin A \sin B \\
\cos(A-B) = \cos A \cos B + \sin A \sin B
\end{array} +
$$
$$
-\cos(A+B) + \cos(A-B) = 2\sin A \sin B
$$

$$
\begin{array}{r}
\sin(A+B) = \sin A \cos B + \cos A \sin B \\
\sin(A-B) = \sin A \cos B - \cos A \sin B
\end{array} +
$$
$$
\sin(A+B) + \sin(A-B) = 2\sin A \cos B
$$

2 (a) $2\cos A \cos B = \cos(A+B) + \cos(A-B)$
Let $A = B = x$
$\Rightarrow 2\cos^2 x = \cos 2x + \cos 0$
$\qquad = \cos 2x + 1$

(b) $2\sin A \sin B = -\cos(A+B) + \cos(A-B)$
Let $A = B = x$
$\Rightarrow 2\sin^2 x = -\cos 2x + \cos 0$
$\qquad = -\cos 2x + 1$

(c) $2\sin A \cos B = \sin(A+B) + \sin(A-B)$
Let $A = B = x$
$\Rightarrow 2\sin x \cos x = \sin 2x + \sin 0$
$\qquad = \sin 2x$

7.1 Exercise 3

1 (a) $\displaystyle\int \sin x \cos x \, dx = \int \tfrac{1}{2}\sin 2x \, dx$

$\qquad = -\tfrac{1}{4}\cos 2x + c$

(b) $\displaystyle\int \sin 3x \cos 3x \, dx = \int \tfrac{1}{2}\sin 6x \, dx$

$\qquad = -\tfrac{1}{12}\cos 6x + c$

2 (a) $\displaystyle\int \cos 5x \cos x \, dx = \int \left(\tfrac{1}{2}\cos 6x + \tfrac{1}{2}\cos 4x\right) dx$

$\qquad = \tfrac{1}{12}\sin 6x + \tfrac{1}{8}\sin 4x + c$

(b) $\displaystyle\int \sin 3x \sin 7x \, dx$

$\qquad = \displaystyle\int \left(-\tfrac{1}{2}\cos 10x + \tfrac{1}{2}\cos 4x\right) dx$

$\qquad = -\tfrac{1}{20}\sin 10x + \tfrac{1}{8}\sin 4x + c$

3 $\displaystyle\int_0^{\frac{1}{4}\pi} \cos^2 x \, dx = \int_0^{\frac{1}{4}\pi} \left(\tfrac{1}{2} + \tfrac{1}{2}\cos 2x\right) dx = \tfrac{1}{8}\pi + \tfrac{1}{4}$

4 $\displaystyle \pi \int_0^{\frac{1}{2}\pi} y^2 \, dx = \pi \int_0^{\frac{1}{2}\pi} \sin^2 x \, dx$

$\qquad = \tfrac{1}{2}\pi \displaystyle\int_0^{\frac{1}{2}\pi} (1 - \cos 2x) \, dx = \tfrac{1}{4}\pi^2$

7.1.4 Integration by parts

7.1 Exercise 4

1 (a) $x e^x - e^x + c$

(b) $\tfrac{1}{3}x e^{3x} - \tfrac{1}{9}e^{3x} + c$

(c) $\dfrac{1}{a}x e^{ax} - \dfrac{1}{a^2}e^{ax} + c$

2 (a) $x \sin x + \cos x + c$

(b) $\dfrac{x}{3}\sin 3x + \dfrac{1}{9}\cos 3x + c$

(c) $\dfrac{x}{a}\sin ax + \dfrac{1}{a^2}\cos ax + c$

3 (a) $\displaystyle\int x^2 e^x \, dx = x^2 e^x - \int 2x e^x \, dx$

$\qquad = x^2 e^x - 2x e^x + 2e^x + c$

(b) $\displaystyle\int x^2 \sin x \, dx = -x^2 \cos x + \int 2x \cos x \, dx$

$\qquad = -x^2 \cos x + 2x \sin x$
$\qquad \qquad + 2\cos x + c$

4 (a) Put $u = x \Rightarrow \dfrac{du}{dx} = 1$

and $\dfrac{dv}{dx} = \sin 2x \Rightarrow v = -\tfrac{1}{2}\cos 2x$

$\displaystyle\int_{-1}^0 x \sin 2x \, dx = \left[-\tfrac{1}{2}x \cos 2x\right]_{-1}^0$

$\qquad \qquad - \displaystyle\int_{-1}^0 1\left(-\tfrac{1}{2}\cos 2x\right) dx$

$\qquad \approx 0 + 0.208\,07 + \left[\tfrac{1}{4}\sin 2x\right]_{-1}^0 \approx 0.44$

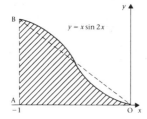

$y = x \sin 2x$

The area found is shaded in the diagram.
When $x = -1$, $x \sin 2x \approx 0.91$

The shaded area is close to that of triangle
$\text{AOB} \approx \frac{1}{2} \times 0.91 \times 1 = 0.455$, which
indicates that the answer is reasonable.

(b) Put $u = 2x \Rightarrow \dfrac{du}{dx} = 2$

and $\dfrac{dv}{dx} = e^{0.5x} \Rightarrow v = 2 e^{0.5x}$

$\displaystyle\int_{-3}^{0} 2x\, e^{0.5x}\, dx = [2x \times 2 e^{0.5x}]_{-3}^{0}$

$\displaystyle - \int_{-3}^{0} 2 \times 2\, e^{0.5x}\, dx$

$\approx 0 + 2.6776 - [8\, e^{0.5x}]_{-3}^{0}$

$\approx 2.6776 - 8 + 1.7850 \approx -3.54$

$y = 2xe^{0.5x}$ -1.47

The area found is shaded in the diagram.
The minimum value, -1.47, of $2x\, e^{0.5x}$ is
between $x = -3$ and $x = 0$.

An estimate of the integral is approximately
$-2\frac{1}{2} \times 1.47 \approx -3.67$ (negative because it is
below the x-axis), which indicates that the
answer is reasonable.

7.1.5 Integration by substitution

7.1 Exercise 5

1 (a) $u = x + 3 \Rightarrow \dfrac{du}{dx} = 1$

$\displaystyle\int u^5\, du = \frac{1}{6} u^6 + c$

$\qquad = \frac{1}{6}(x + 3)^6 + c$

(b) $u = 2x - 5 \Rightarrow \dfrac{du}{dx} = 2$

$\displaystyle\int \frac{1}{2}(u + 5)\, u^6\, \frac{1}{2}\, du = \frac{1}{4} \int (u^7 + 5u^6)\, du$

$\qquad = \frac{1}{32} u^8 + \frac{5}{28} u^7 + c$

$\qquad = \frac{1}{32}(2x - 5)^8 + \frac{5}{28}(2x - 5)^7 + c$

(c) $\displaystyle\int (u + 2)^2\, u^7\, du = \int (u^9 + 4u^8 + 4u^7)\, du$

$\qquad = \frac{1}{10}(x - 2)^{10} + \frac{4}{9}(x - 2)^9 + \frac{1}{2}(x - 2)^8 + c$

(d) $\frac{1}{18}(x^2 - 4)^9 + c$ (e) $\frac{2}{9}(x^3 - 2)^{\frac{3}{2}} + c$

2 (a) $\frac{1}{3}\sin^3 x + c$ (b) $-\frac{1}{3}\cos^3 x + c$

3 (a) Let $u = x^3 + 3 \Rightarrow \dfrac{du}{dx} = 3x^2$.

$\displaystyle\int x^2 \sqrt{(x^3 + 3)}\, dx = \int x^2 \sqrt{(x^3 + 3)}\, \frac{1}{3x^2}\, du$

$\qquad = \displaystyle\int \frac{1}{3} u^{\frac{1}{2}}\, du = \frac{2}{9}(x^3 + 3)^{\frac{3}{2}} + c$

(b) $\frac{1}{7}(x - 3)^7 + \frac{1}{2}(x - 3)^6 + c$

(c) Let $u = x - 2 \Rightarrow \dfrac{du}{dx} = 1$.

$\displaystyle\int x \sqrt{(x - 2)}\, dx = \frac{2}{5}(x - 2)^{\frac{5}{2}} + \frac{4}{3}(x - 2)^{\frac{3}{2}} + c$

(d) $\frac{1}{4}\sin^4 x + c$

(e) Let $u = \cos x \Rightarrow \dfrac{du}{dx} = -\sin x$.

$\displaystyle\int \cos^5 x \sin x\, dx = -\int u^5\, du$

$\qquad = -\frac{1}{6} u^6 + c$

$\qquad = -\frac{1}{6} \cos^6 x + c$

(f) Let $u = x + 2 \Rightarrow \dfrac{du}{dx} = 1$.

$$\int \frac{x}{(x+2)^3}\, dx = \frac{1}{(x+2)^2} - \frac{1}{(x+2)} + c$$

7.1.6 The reciprocal function

7.1 Exercise 6

1 (a) $3 \ln |x - 2| + c$ (b) $3 \ln |2x + 7| + c$

   (c) $\frac{1}{3} \ln |3x - 1| + c$

2 (a) $\frac{2}{3} \ln |4| - \frac{2}{3} \ln |1| = 0.9242$ (to 4 d.p.)

   (b) $\frac{2}{3} \ln |-5| - \frac{2}{3} \ln |-8| = -0.3133$
   (to 4 d.p.)

3 The function is not defined for $x = 2$.

4 (a) $\displaystyle\int \frac{\sin x}{\cos x}\, dx = -\ln |\cos x| + c$

   $\qquad\qquad\quad = \ln |\sec x| + c$

   (b) $\displaystyle\int \frac{\cos x}{\sin x}\, dx = \ln |\sin x| + c$

5 (a) $-\frac{1}{3} \ln |4 - x^3| + c$ (b) $\ln |3 + x^2| + c$

6E (a) $\frac{1}{2} \ln |1 + x^2| + \tan^{-1} x + c$

   (b) $\ln |1 + x^2| - \tan^{-1} x + c$

   (c) $\ln |\ln x| + c$

   (d) $-\ln |1 + \cos x| + c$

7.1.7 Partial fractions

7.1 E

1 The numerator of the partial fractions will contain an x^2 term which does not exist in the original fraction.

3 $A = \frac{7}{9}$, $D = -\frac{7}{9}$, $E = -\frac{4}{3}$.

7.1 Exercise 7

1 (a) $\dfrac{3}{x+3} - \dfrac{2}{x+2}$ (b) $\dfrac{6}{2x+1} - \dfrac{3}{x+1}$

   (c) $\dfrac{3}{2x-1} - \dfrac{1}{x+2}$ (d) $\dfrac{5}{x-1} + \dfrac{2}{x-2}$

   (e) $\dfrac{3}{2x+1} - \dfrac{2}{3x+2}$ (f) $\dfrac{2}{x+1} - \dfrac{1}{x}$

2 (a) $\dfrac{2}{x+3} + \dfrac{3}{x-4}$

   (b) $2 \ln |x+3| + 3 \ln |x-4| + c$

3 $\dfrac{x^2 + 3x + 2 + 5x + 7}{x^2 + 3x + 2} = 1 + \dfrac{5x+7}{x^2 + 3x + 2}$

   $\qquad\qquad\qquad\qquad = 1 + \dfrac{2}{x+1} + \dfrac{3}{x+2}$

   $\displaystyle\int_0^1 \left(1 + \frac{2}{x+1} + \frac{3}{x+2}\right) dx$

   $\qquad = \Big[x + 2\ln|x+1| + 3\ln|x+2|\Big]_0^1$

   $\qquad = 3.6027$ (to 4 d.p.)

4 (a) $\ln \left| \dfrac{(x-2)^3}{(x-1)^2} \right| + c$

   (b) $\frac{1}{4} \ln \left| \dfrac{x-2}{x+2} \right| + c$

   (c) $\ln \left| \dfrac{(x+3)^2}{x+2} \right| + c$

5 (a) $A = -5$, $B = 5$, $C = -12$

   (b) $\dfrac{1}{2(1-x)} + \frac{1}{4} \ln \left| \dfrac{x+1}{x-1} \right| + c$

   (c) $\frac{1}{4} \ln \left(\frac{3}{2} \right) + \frac{1}{4}$

6 (a) $1 + \dfrac{3}{2(x-3)} - \dfrac{3}{2(x+3)}$

   (b) $3 + \dfrac{1}{1-x} + \dfrac{16}{x-4}$

7.2 Polynomial approximations
7.2.1 Taylor's first approximation

7.2 Exercise 1

1 (a) $\dfrac{dy}{dx} = 3x^2 + 5$

The gradient at $x = 2$ is 17.

$\dfrac{y - 16}{x - 2} = 17$ gives $y = 17x - 18$.

(b) $y = x + 1$

(c) $y = x - 1$

(d) $y = 28x - 44$

(e) $y = 3x - 2$

2 (a) $y = -x + \frac{1}{2}\pi$

(b) 0.070 796

(c) 0.084%

7.2.2 The Newton–Raphson method

7.2 A

1 (a) $f'(x) = 2x - 3\cos x$

(b) $b = a - \dfrac{a^2 - 3\sin a}{2a - 3\cos a}$

If $a = 2$, $b = 2 - \dfrac{2^2 - 3\sin 2}{2 \times 2 - 3\cos 2} = 1.7576$
(Remember to work in radians.)

(c) If $a = 1.7576$, $b = 1.722\,891\,5$

(d) Now take $a = 1.722\,891\,5$
giving $b = 1.722\,125\,5$
then $a = 1.722\,125\,5$ and $b = 1.722\,125\,1$
and finally $a = 1.722\,125\,1$
gives $b = 1.722\,125\,1$

Thus, two successive values agree to 7 decimal places and you can conclude that the root is 1.722 125 (to 6 decimal places).

2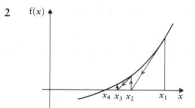

3 (a)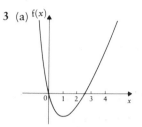

(b) From the graph, the root lies between 2 and 3.

Any value greater than 1 will work, for example $x_1 = 3$.

(c) $f'(x) = 2x - 6\,e^{-x}$

$x_{n+1} = x_n - \dfrac{x_n^2 - 6 + 6\,e^{-x_n}}{2x_n - 6\,e^{-x_n}}$

(d) $x_1 = 3$ $x_2 = 2.421\,406$ $x_3 = 2.329\,530$
$x_4 = 2.326\,890$ $x_5 = 2.326\,890$
$\Rightarrow x = 2.3269$ (to 4 decimal places)

4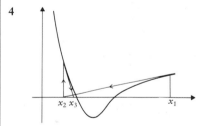

The Newton–Raphson process will not converge to the nearest root.

5E (a) $x = 3.8730$ to 4 decimal places

(b) All values greater than 2.87 will give the root 3.8730.

(c) Any start position between -0.67 and 2.87 will give the root $x = 2$.

(d) (i) $x_1 = -0.68$ gives the root 3.87.
(ii) $x_1 = -0.69$ gives the root -3.87.

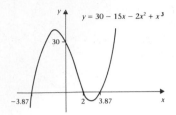

You cannot always predict to which root an iteration will converge. If the starting position is reasonably close to the root, you will usually home in on the root very quickly. However, if the iteration takes you near a turning point, then the method becomes very unpredictable. In this case, the method takes you near the turning point at $x = 3$.

(e)

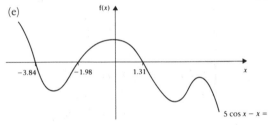

From an initial value of -1, the iteration quickly converges to the root -1.977. However, a starting value of -0.5 is near a turning point and the iteration converges to the root -3.837 and not -1.98, the nearest root. Starting values of -7 and -6.5 are some way from any of the roots, as well as being near turning points. In each case, the root which is eventually reached is difficult to predict and depends upon the accuracy of your calculator.

(f)

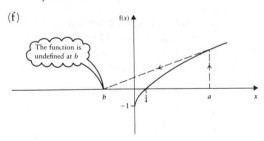

This is an equation which is easily solved by simple algebraic manipulation and you would not normally use the Newton–Raphson method to solve it. It does, however, illustrate how the method can fail to work even if the starting value is not near a turning point. In this case, a starting value must be chosen near the root $\frac{1}{4}$.

6E The graph looks like a standard sine curve, but when you zoom in you see that it has several small turning points very close to each other. To solve this equation you must have a starting point very close to the root you are trying to find.

7.2 **Exercise 2**

1 Using $x_{n+1} = x_n - \dfrac{x_n - \cos x_n}{1 + \sin x_n}$ with $x_1 = 1$,

then $x_2 = 0.750\,364\ldots$ and $x = 0.739\,085\ldots$ You can see that there is only one solution by plotting the graphs of $y = x$ and $y = \cos x$ on the same axes. They will only intersect at one point.

2 $x^3 = 3x - 1 \Rightarrow x \approx 1.532\,089,\ 0.347\,296$ or $-1.879\,385$

3 $x = 0.487\,404$

4 The area of sector OACB is $\frac{1}{2}\theta r^2$.
Triangle OAB is isosceles and has area
$r^2 \sin\frac{1}{2}\theta \cos\frac{1}{2}\theta = \frac{1}{2}r^2 \sin\theta$.

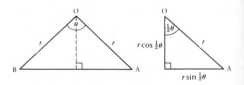

Hence the area of the segment is
$\frac{1}{2}\theta r^2 - \frac{1}{2}r^2 \sin\theta = \frac{1}{10}\pi r^2$
$\Rightarrow \theta - \frac{1}{5}\pi = \sin\theta$
$\theta = 1.627$ to 3 decimal places

5 (a) $2\theta r^2 - r^2 \sin 2\theta$

(b) $\theta = 0.8832$

6 (a) (i) Jerry

    (ii) Tom – exponential growth will always outperform quadratic growth eventually.

(b) 19.03 years, i.e. 19 years 0 months

7.2.3 Maclaurin's series

7.2 B

1 $p(0) \quad = 12 \Rightarrow a \quad = 12$
$p'(0) \quad = 11 \Rightarrow b \quad = 11$
$p''(0) \quad = 10 \Rightarrow 2c = 10$
$p^{(3)}(0) \quad = 6 \Rightarrow 6d = 6$

Hence $a = 12, \quad b = 11, \quad c = 5, \quad d = 1$

2 If $p(x) = a + bx + cx^2 + dx^3$
$p(0) \quad = a \quad \Rightarrow a = p(0)$
$p'(0) \quad = b \quad \Rightarrow b = p'(0)$
$p''(0) \quad = 2c \Rightarrow c = p'(0) \div 2$
$p^{(3)}(0) = 6d \Rightarrow d = p^{(3)}(0) \div 6$

Hence
$$p(x) = p(0) + p'(0)x + p''(0)\frac{x^2}{2} + p^{(3)}(0)\frac{x^3}{6}$$

3 If $p(x)$ is a polynomial of degree 4, then
$p(x) = a + bx + cx^2 + dx^3 + ex^4$
$\Rightarrow p'(x) \quad = b + 2cx + 3dx^2 + 4ex^3$
$p''(x) = \quad\quad 2c + 6dx + 12ex^2$
$p^{(3)}(x) = \quad\quad\quad\quad 6d + 24ex$
$p^{(4)}(x) = \quad\quad\quad\quad\quad 24e$

$\Rightarrow p(0) \quad = a$
$p'(0) \quad = b$
$p''(0) \quad = 2c$
$p^{(3)}(0) = 6d$
$p^{(4)}(0) = 24e$

But $24 = 4 \times 3 \times 2 \times 1$ is usually written as 4! (called 'factorial four').
So $e = p^{(4)}(0) \div 4!$
In a similar way, $d = p^{(3)}(0) \div 3!$ and $c = p''(0) \div 2!$

Hence
$$p(x) = p(0) + p'(0)x + p''(0)\frac{x^2}{2!} + p^{(3)}(0)\frac{x^3}{3!}$$
$$+ p^{(4)}(0)\frac{x^4}{4!}$$

4 (a) $p(x) = p(0) + p'(0)x + p''(0)\frac{x^2}{2!}$
$$+ p^{(3)}(0)\frac{x^3}{3!} + p^{(4)}\frac{x^4}{4!} + p^{(5)}(0)\frac{x^5}{5!}$$

(b) $p(x) = p(0) + p'(0)x + p''(0)\frac{x^2}{2!}$
$$+ p^{(3)}(0)\frac{x^3}{3!} + p^{(4)}\frac{x^4}{4!} + \cdots$$
$$+ p^n(0)\frac{x^n}{n!}$$

5 $f(x) = e^{2x} \Rightarrow f'(x) \quad = 2e^{2x}$
$f''(x) \quad = 2^2 e^{2x}$
$f^{(3)}(x) = 2^3 e^{2x}$
$f^{(4)}(x) = 2^4 e^{2x}$

$\Rightarrow f(0) \quad = 1$
$f'(0) \quad = 2$
$f''(0) \quad = 2^2$
$f^{(3)}(0) = 2^3$
$f^{(4)}(0) = 2^4$

The polynomial
$$1 + 2x + 2x^2 + \frac{4x^3}{3} + \frac{2x^4}{3}$$

will pass through the same point with the same gradient, and with the same second derivative, third derivative and fourth derivative, as the function e^{2x} does when $x = 0$.

Hence it is a good approximation to e^{2x} for values of x near $x = 0$ and this is confirmed by plotting the functions. The approximation gives a percentage error of within $\pm 1\%$ for $-0.45 < x < 0.64$.

7.2 C

1 (a) $f(x) = \cos x \quad \Rightarrow f(0) = 1$

$f'(x) = -\sin x \Rightarrow f'(0) = 0$

$f''(x) = -\cos x \Rightarrow f''(0) = -1$

$f^{(3)}(x) = \sin x \Rightarrow f^{(3)}(0) = 0$

$f^{(4)}(x) = \cos x \Rightarrow f^{(4)}(0) = 1$

and the cycle repeats itself.

$$\Rightarrow \cos x = 1 + 0x + \frac{(-1)x^2}{2!} + \frac{0x^3}{3!} + \frac{1x^4}{4!}$$

$$+ \frac{0x^5}{5!} + \frac{(-1)x^6}{6!} + \cdots$$

$$= 1 - \frac{x^2}{2!} + \frac{x^4}{4!} - \frac{x^6}{6!} + \cdots$$

(b) $f(x) = e^x \Rightarrow f(0) = 1$

$f'(x) = e^x \Rightarrow f'(0) = 1$

and it is clear that all derivatives will take the value 1 when $x = 0$.

$$\Rightarrow e^x = 1 + x + \frac{x^2}{2!} + \frac{x^3}{3!} + \frac{x^4}{4!} + \cdots$$

2 (a) $\ln 0$ is undefined.

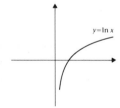

(b) Since $f(0)$ cannot be found, it is not possible to find a Maclaurin's series. Geometrically, it is not possible to approximate a function at a point that is not defined!

3 (a) $f'(x) = \dfrac{1}{1+x}$

(b) $f''(x) = -1(1+x)^{-2} = -(1+x)^{-2}$

(c) $f^{(3)}(x) = -(-2)(1+x)^{-3} = 2(1+x)^{-3}$

$f^{(4)}(x) = 2 \times -3(1+x)^{-4}$

$\qquad = -3!(1+x)^{-4}$

$f^{(5)}(x) = 4!\,(1+x)^{-5}$

(d) $f(0) = 0; \quad f'(0) = 1; \quad f''(0) = -1;$

$f^{(3)}(0) = 2; \quad f^{(4)}(0) = -3!; \quad f^{(5)}(0) = 4!$

(e) $\ln(1+x) = 0 + 1x + \dfrac{-1x^2}{2!} + \dfrac{2x^3}{3!}$

$$+ \frac{-3!\,x^4}{4!} + \frac{4!\,x^5}{5!}$$

Note that $\dfrac{2}{3!} = \dfrac{2}{3 \times 2} = \dfrac{1}{3}$,

$$\frac{3!}{4!} = \frac{3 \times 2 \times 1}{4 \times 3 \times 2 \times 1} = \frac{1}{4}$$

and $\dfrac{4!}{5!} = \dfrac{1}{5}$

gives

$$\ln(1+x) = x - \frac{x^2}{2} + \frac{x^3}{3} - \frac{x^4}{4} + \frac{x^5}{5} \cdots$$

4E (a) $n(1+x)^{n-1}$

(b) $f''(x) = n(n-1)(1+x)^{n-2}$

$f^{(3)}(x) = n(n-1)(n-2)(1+x)^{n-3}$

(c) $f(0) = 1; \quad f'(0) = n; \quad f''(0) = n(n-1);$

$f^{(3)}(0) = n(n-1)(n-2)$

$$(1+x)^n = 1 + nx + \frac{n(n-1)}{2!}x^2$$

$$+ \frac{n(n-1)(n-2)}{3!}x^3 + \cdots$$

7.2 Exercise 3

1 (a) $f(x) = e^{\frac{1}{2}x}, f'(x) = \dfrac{1}{2}e^{\frac{1}{2}x}, f''(x) = \dfrac{1}{4}e^{\frac{1}{2}x}$, etc

$f(0) = 1, f'(0) = \dfrac{1}{2}, f''(0) = \dfrac{1}{4}$, etc.

$$\Rightarrow e^{\frac{1}{2}x} = 1 + \frac{x}{2} + \frac{1}{4}\frac{x^2}{2!} + \frac{1}{8}\frac{x^3}{3!} + \cdots$$

$$= 1 + \frac{x}{2} + \frac{x^2}{8} + \frac{x^3}{48} + \cdots$$

(b) Replacing x by $\frac{1}{2}x$ in

$$e^x = 1 + x + \frac{x^2}{2!} + \cdots$$

gives $e^{\frac{1}{2}x} = 1 + \dfrac{x}{2} + \dfrac{\left(\dfrac{x}{2}\right)^2}{2!} + \dfrac{\left(\dfrac{x}{2}\right)^2}{3!} + \cdots$

$$= 1 + \frac{x}{2} + \frac{x^2}{8} + \frac{x^3}{48} + \cdots$$

2 (a) $0.877\,582\,561\,9$

(b) $1 - \dfrac{0.5^2}{2!} = 0.875$

$1 - \dfrac{0.5^2}{2!} + \dfrac{0.5^4}{4!} = 0.8776$

so three terms are needed.

(c) $\cos 1.0 = 0.540\,302\,305\,9$

$1 - \dfrac{1}{2!} + \dfrac{1}{4!} = 0.541\,67$

$1 - \dfrac{1}{2!} + \dfrac{1}{4!} - \dfrac{1}{6!} = 0.540\,28$

so four terms are needed.

3 (a) $\dfrac{x^{n-1}}{(n-1)!}$ (b) $(-1)^{n-1}\dfrac{x^{2n-2}}{(2n-2)!}$

(c) $\dfrac{x^{2n-2}}{(n-1)!}$

4 (a) Replacing x by $-x$ in the series for $\ln(1+x)$ gives

$$\ln(1-x) = -x - \frac{x^2}{2} - \frac{x^3}{3} - \frac{x^4}{4}\cdots$$

(b) $\ln(1-x^2) = \ln(1-x)(1+x)$

$= \ln(1-x) + \ln(1+x)$

$= 2\left(-\dfrac{x^2}{2} - \dfrac{x^4}{4} - \dfrac{x^6}{6}\cdots\right)$

$= -x^2 - \dfrac{x^4}{2} - \dfrac{x^6}{3}\cdots$

5 (a) $e^x = 1 + x + \dfrac{x^2}{2!} + \cdots$

$e^{-x} = 1 - x + \dfrac{x^2}{2!}\cdots$

For small values of x
$(-1 < x < 1)$, $e^{-x} \approx 1 - x$

(b) $\sqrt{(1-e^{-x})} \approx \sqrt{(1-(1-x))} = \sqrt{x}$

(c) $\sqrt{0.1} = 0.3162$
$\sqrt{(1-e^{-0.1})} = 0.3085$
$\Rightarrow$ percentage error $= 2.5\%$

7.3 Differential equations
7.3.1 Introduction

7.3 Exercise 1

1 (a) $y = e^x + c$

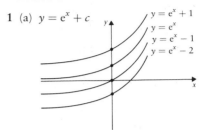

$y = e^x + 1$
$y = e^x$
$y = e^x - 1$
$y = e^x - 2$

(b) $y = \frac{1}{2}\sin 2x + c$

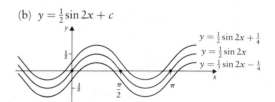

$y = \frac{1}{2}\sin 2x + \frac{1}{4}$
$y = \frac{1}{2}\sin 2x$
$y = \frac{1}{2}\sin 2x - \frac{1}{4}$

(c) $\dfrac{dy}{dx} = \dfrac{-1}{x^2} \Rightarrow y = \dfrac{1}{x} + c$

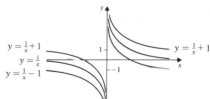

$y = \frac{1}{x} + 1$
$y = \frac{1}{x}$
$y = \frac{1}{x} - 1$

$y = \frac{1}{x} + 1$

2 (a) $y = x^4 - 1$ When $x = 3$, $y = 80$

(b) $y = x^3 - x^2 + 2x - 2$
When $x = 3$, $y = 22$

(c) $y = \frac{1}{2} - \frac{1}{2}x^{-2}$ When $x = 3$, $y = \frac{4}{9}$

(d) $y = e^{2x} - e^2$ When $x = 3$, $y \approx 396$

3 (a) $y = 8t - \dfrac{2t^2}{2} + 32$

so when $t = 4$, $y = 53\frac{1}{3}$

(b) $\dfrac{dy}{dt} = 0$ when $t = 6$. After this time, $\dfrac{dy}{dt} < 0$
and so the water is no longer being heated. The model is probably no longer valid.

4E (a) $y = -\frac{1}{3}\cos(3x+2) - 0.139$ (to 3 d.p.)
When $x = 2$, $y \approx -0.090$

(b) $y = \frac{1}{3}e^{x^3} - \frac{1}{3}$ When $x = 2$, $y \approx 993$

(c) $y = \frac{1}{2}\sin(x^2 + 1) - 0.421$ (to 3 d.p.)
When $x = 2$, $y \approx -0.900$

7.3.2 Direction diagrams

7.3 A

1 $\dfrac{dy}{dx} = x$

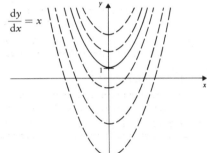

2 $\dfrac{dy}{dx} = -y$

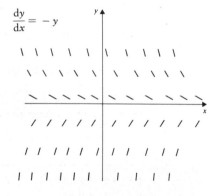

If y is initially negative, then y increases as x increases. However, y never becomes positive; it just gets closer to $y = 0$.

3 The direction diagram for $\dfrac{dy}{dx} = x - y$ is shown below.

(Note how $\dfrac{dy}{dx} = 0$ for all points with $y = x$.)

Solution curves for $\dfrac{dy}{dx} = x - y$

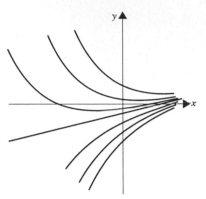

As x increases, y tends more and more to the value of x. (The line $y = x - 1$ is an asymptote to each solution curve.)

7.3 Exercise 2

1 The curves are a family of ellipses.

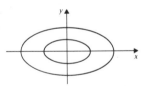

2 The curves are similar to that of the Normal distribution in statistics.

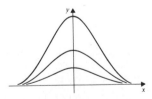

3 m represents the mass of reacting substance at time t.

$\dfrac{dm}{dt}$ represents the rate at which the mass is changing, i.e. the rate of reaction.

$\dfrac{dm}{dt} = -km$ represents the fact that the rate of loss of mass is proportional to the mass.

$$\frac{dm}{dt} = -0.5m$$

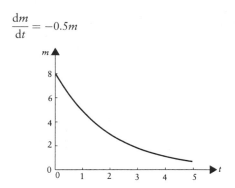

8 is the value of m at time $t = 0$, i.e. the initial mass of the substance.

7.3.3 Numerical methods

7.3 Exercise 3

1 (a) $y = \sin x$

(b)

x	0	0.5	1.0	1.5	2.0	2.5	3.0	3.5	4.0	4.5	5.0
Numerical y	0	0.5	0.9	1.0	1.0	0.7	0.2	−0.3	−0.7	−0.9	−0.9
Exact y	0	0.5	0.8	1.0	0.9	0.6	0.1	−0.4	−0.8	−1.0	−1.0

From the table you can see that the numerical and exact values appear to differ by at most 0.1.

2 (a) $y = x^4 + c \Rightarrow y = x^4 - 1$
When $x = 2$, $y = 15$

(b) To 1 decimal place, successive points are
$(1, 0)$, $(1.2, 0.8)$, $(1.4, 2.2)$, $(1.6, 4.4)$,
$(1.8, 7.7)$, $(2, 12.3)$
When $x = 2$, $y \approx 12.3$

3 (a) $y = -\frac{1}{2}\cos 2x$

(b) An exact solution is $-\frac{1}{2}\cos 2 \approx 0.208$.
The numerical solution is 0.160.

The percentage error is
$$\frac{0.048}{0.208} \times 100 \approx 23\%.$$

4 (a) $y = x^2 + 1$

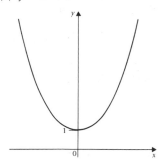

(b) With a step of $\delta x = 0.2$,

x	1	1.2	1.4	1.6	1.8	2.0	2.2	2.4	2.6	2.8	3.0
y	2	2.4	2.9	3.4	4.1	4.8	5.6	6.5	7.4	8.5	9.6

With a step of $\delta x = -0.2$,

x	1	0.8	0.6	0.4	0.2	0.0	−0.2	−0.4	−0.6	−0.8	−1.0
y	2	1.6	1.3	1.0	0.9	0.8	0.8	0.9	1.0	1.3	1.6

5E The solution to the equation is $y = e^x + k$.
The particular solution through $(0, 1)$ is
$y = e^x$.
The values for a step size of 0.1 will be
(to 3 s.f.):

x	0	0.1	0.2	0.3	0.4	...
y	1.00	1.10	1.21	1.33	1.46	... and so on.

6E

x	0	0.5	1.0	1.5	2.0	2.5	3.0	3.5	4.0
y	0	0.5	0.8	1.0	1.1	1.2	1.3	1.3	1.4

x	0	−0.5	−1.0	−1.5	−2.0	−2.5	−3.0	−3.5	−4.0
y	0	−0.5	−0.8	−1.0	−1.1	−1.2	−1.3	−1.3	−1.4

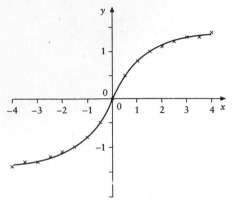

The shape of the 'turned round' graph suggests the tangent function.

The relationship is $y = \tan^{-1} x$.

7.3.4 Growth and decay

7.3 Exercise 4

1 $y = A e^{-x}$
   $y = 2$ when $x = 0$, therefore $A = 2$
   $y = 2 e^{-x}$

2 (a) $m = A e^{-0.1t} \Rightarrow m = 2 e^{-0.1t}$
   (b) $1 = 2 e^{-0.1t}$
   $\Rightarrow e^{-0.1t} = 0.5$
   $\Rightarrow -0.1t = \ln 0.5$
   $\Rightarrow -0.1t \approx -0.693$
   $\Rightarrow \quad t \approx 6.93$ hours

   It takes approximately 6 hours 56 minutes.

3 Assume Newton's law of cooling.
   y is the temperature in °C above room temperature, t is the time in minutes after boiling.
   $\dfrac{dy}{dt} = \lambda y \Rightarrow y = A e^{\lambda t}$
   $t = 0, \quad y = 80 \Rightarrow A = 80$
   $t = 5, \quad y = 70 \Rightarrow 70 = 80 e^{5\lambda}$
   $\Rightarrow \lambda = \dfrac{1}{5} \ln \left(\dfrac{70}{80} \right) = -0.0267$

   The water cools to 60 °C when $y = 40$.
   $40 = 80 e^{-0.0267t} \Rightarrow t = 26$ minutes

4 The differential equation is $\dfrac{dN}{dt} = \lambda N$.
   N is the number of insects and t is the time in days.
   When $N = 100$, $\quad \dfrac{dN}{dt} = 50 \Rightarrow \lambda = 0.5$
   $\dfrac{dN}{dt} = 0.5N \Rightarrow N = A e^{0.5t}$
   When $t = 0$, $\quad N = 100 \Rightarrow A = 100$
   Therefore $N = 100 e^{0.5t}$ and so when $t = 10$,
   $N = 14\,841$
   There will be nearly 15 000 insects after 10 days.

5 (a) $\dfrac{dm}{dt} = \lambda m$
       When $m = 0.020$,
       $\dfrac{dm}{dt} = -0.001 \Rightarrow \lambda = -0.05$
       The differential equation is $\dfrac{dm}{dt} = -0.05m$

   (b) $\dfrac{dm}{dt} = -0.05m \Rightarrow m = A e^{-0.05t}$
       A is the mass when $t = 0$, so
       $A = 0.020 \Rightarrow m = 0.020 e^{-0.05t}$
       When $m = 0.010$, $\quad 0.010 = 0.020 e^{-0.05t}$
       $\Rightarrow t = -20 \ln 0.5$
       $= 13.86$

   The substance will decay to half its mass after 13.86 days. This is called the **half-life** of the substance.

7.3.5 Formulating differential equations

7.3 Exercise 5

1 (a) For a snowball of radius r cm and time t days
       $\dfrac{dV}{dt} = -4k\pi r^2 \Rightarrow \dfrac{dr}{dt} = -k$
   (b) $r = c - kt$
       $r = 30$ when $t = 0$ and $r = 0$ when $t = 10$,
       so $r = 30 - 3t$
   (c) (i) $15 = 30 - 3t \Rightarrow t = 5$
            The radius will be halved after 5 days.

(ii) $\dfrac{30}{\sqrt[3]{2}} = 30 - 3t \Rightarrow t = 2.1$

The volume will be halved after 2.1 days.

2 (a) $0.1 = 10\%$; -0.1 is used because there is a reduction of 10%. $\alpha = 2000$.

(b) y is the number of fish and $\dfrac{dy}{dt}$ is the change in the number of fish per year.

(c) About 16 years

(d) $\dfrac{dy}{dt} = 2500 - 0.12y$

3E V is the volume of liquid in the urn in cupfuls.
t is the time in seconds.

The rate of change of volume, $\dfrac{dV}{dt}$, is proportional to the square root of V (assuming that the urn has a uniform cross-section).

So $\dfrac{dV}{dt} = -\lambda\sqrt{V}$, where λ is a constant.

Numerical method

When $V = 100$, $\dfrac{dV}{dt} \approx -\dfrac{9}{60}$ cups per second

$\Rightarrow -\dfrac{9}{60} \approx -\lambda\sqrt{100}$

$\Rightarrow \lambda \approx 0.015$

You need the solution curve through $(0, 100)$ and require t when $V = 52$ (when 48 cups have been filled).

With a step of $\delta t = 1$ (second), this occurs after 6 minutes 12 seconds.

Analytical method

$\dfrac{dV}{dt} = -\lambda\sqrt{V}$

$\Rightarrow \dfrac{dt}{dV} = -\dfrac{1}{\lambda\sqrt{V}}$

$\Rightarrow t = -\dfrac{2}{\lambda}\sqrt{V} + c$

When $t = 0$, $V = 100$ and when $t = 60$, $V = 91$

The simultaneous equations give $\lambda = 0.015\,35$, $c = 1303$.

$t \approx 1303 - 130.3\sqrt{V}$

When $V = 52$, $t \approx 363$

It takes 6 minutes 3 seconds.

7.3.6 Separating the variables

7.3 **Exercise 6**

1 (a) $\dfrac{dy}{dx} = xy$

$\displaystyle\int \dfrac{1}{y}\,dy = \int x\,dx$

$\ln|y| = \tfrac{1}{2}x^2 + k$

$y = \pm e^{(\frac{1}{2}x^2 + k)}$

$y = A e^{\frac{1}{2}x^2}$

(b) $p^2 = t^2 + k$ (c) $m = A e^{2t}$

(d) $y^2 = 2e^x + k$ (e) $y + 1 = k(x + 1)$

2 $y = \tfrac{3}{2}(1 - e^{-2x})$

3 14 800

4 (a) $0.02\,e^{-\frac{1}{20}t}$ (b) 13.9 days

(c) 27.7 days   (d) 6.07×10^{-4} g per day

5 $1.03 \times 10^7 N_0$

Miscellaneous exercise 7

1 $\dfrac{16}{3}\pi$

2 (a) $\tfrac{1}{2}\pi^2$ (b) 45.6   (c) 17.4

3 (a) 1   (b) $1 - \tfrac{1}{4}\pi$

4 (a) $-\frac{1}{4}(1-x^2)^4 + c$ (b) $-\frac{1}{2}(x^2+4)^{-1} + c$

(c) $-\frac{2}{9}(1-x^3)^{\frac{3}{2}} + c$ (d) $-\frac{1}{2}(1-x^4)^{\frac{1}{2}} + c$

(e) $\frac{1}{6}\sin^6 x + c$ (f) $\dfrac{1}{\cos x} + c$

5 (a) 17.1   (b) 6.08   (c) 33.8   (d) $\frac{16}{81} = 0.20$

6 (a) $-x^2 \cos x + 2x \sin x + 2 \cos x + c$

(b) $x^3 \sin x + 3x^2 \cos x - 6x \sin x$
$\quad -6\cos x + c$

(c) $\frac{1}{4}x^2 - \frac{1}{4}x \sin 2x - \frac{1}{8}\cos 2x + c$

7 (a) 1   (b) 4

8 (a) $A = 1, B = 2$

(b) $A = -1, B = 2, C = -1$

9 (a) $7\ln|x-3| + 2\ln|x+1| + c$

(b) $\ln\left|\dfrac{x-4}{x+4}\right| + c$

(c) $-\frac{1}{5}\ln|x+4| + \frac{1}{5}\ln|x-1| + c$

(d) $x + \ln|x-2| + \dfrac{6}{x+3} + c$

10   1.53, -1.88

11   Exact root $= 0.739$

12   1.834

13 (a) $1 - x + \frac{1}{2}x^2 - \frac{1}{6}x^3$

(b) $1 + 2x + 2x^2 + \frac{4}{3}x^3$

(c) $2x - 2x^2 + \frac{8}{3}x^3$

14 (a) $1 + \frac{1}{2}x - \frac{1}{8}x^3$ $|x| < 1$

(b) $1 - x + x^2$ $|x| < 1$

(c) $\frac{1}{2} - \frac{1}{4}x + \frac{1}{8}x^2$ $|x| < 2$

15 (a) $x + \frac{1}{3}x^3$

(b) $1 + \frac{1}{2}x^2 + \frac{5}{24}x^4$

(c) $x + x^2 + \frac{1}{3}x^3$

16 (a) $2x \cos(x^2 + 1)$ (b) $2\sin(1-2x)$

(c) $2x\,e^{x^2+1}$ (d) $(\cos x)\,e^{\sin x}$

(e) $(\cos x - \sin x)\,e^{(\sin x + \cos x)}$

17   $S = A\,e^{kt}$;   57 000

18 (a) $y = 10\,e^x$ (b) $y = 3.297\,e^{-\frac{1}{2}x^2}$

(c) $y = \dfrac{2}{2x+1}$

The equation of a straight line   Commentary

This tasksheet is intended to introduce or revise the concepts of gradient, intercept and the equation $y = mx + c$.

The tasksheet explains that the equation $y = mx + c$ represents a straight line with gradient m, passing through the point $(0, c)$, the intercept with the y-axis.

As well as noting how to calculate gradient precisely, it should be observed that:

- a numerically large gradient means a steeply sloping line;

- a numerically small gradient means a flatter line;

- a gradient of zero means that the line is flat or horizontal (parallel to the x-axis);

- a positive gradient slopes upwards to the right;

- a negative gradient slopes downwards to the right.

1 (a), (b)

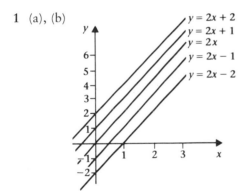

Varying c translates the line up and down. The value of c is where the line crosses the y-axis.

2 (a), (b)

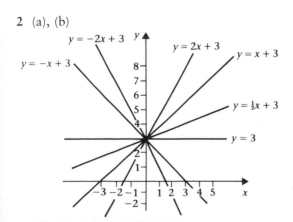

Varying m changes the gradient of the line. When m is positive, the line slopes up as x increases. When m is negative the line slopes down as x increases.

3

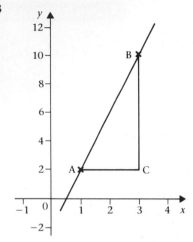

$$\text{Gradient} = \frac{BC}{AC} = \frac{8}{2} = 4$$

4 (a) $\text{Gradient} = \dfrac{11 - 2}{2 + 1} = \dfrac{9}{3} = 3$ (b) $\text{Gradient} = \dfrac{8}{-4} = -2$

(c) $\text{Gradient} = \dfrac{0}{3} = 0$

5 (a) $\text{Gradient} = \dfrac{4}{2} = 2$

(b) The line crosses the y-axis at $(0, 1)$ so the y-intercept is 1.

(c) When $x = 0$ When $x = 2$
$$y = 2 \times 0 + 1 \qquad\qquad y = 2 \times 2 + 1$$
$$y = 1 \qquad\qquad\qquad\quad y = 5$$

(d) For $y = 2x + 1$

1 represents the y-intercept.

2 represents the gradient.

6 (a) Choose any two points on the line, for example $(-1, 2)$ and $(-3, 8)$, which give the gradient -3.

(b) The line crosses the y-axis at $(0, -1)$, so the y-intercept is -1.

(c) For any point on the line, substituting the x-coordinate in the equation will give the y-coordinate; for example, take the point $(1, -4)$.

When $x = 1$
$$y = -3 \times 1 - 1$$
$$y = -4$$

(d) For $y = -3x - 1$

-1 represents the y-intercept.

-3 represents the gradient.

7 (a) The equation of the line is $y = -2x + 6$

gradient y-intercept

(b) The equation of the line is $y = 5x - 2$

gradient y-intercept

8 (a) $m = -4, \quad c = 9$

(b) $y = 3x + \frac{3}{2} \quad \Rightarrow \quad m = 3, \quad c = \frac{3}{2}$

(c) $y = 2x + \frac{5}{2} \quad \Rightarrow \quad m = 2, \quad c = \frac{5}{2}$

(d) $y = -\frac{3}{5}x - 2 \quad \Rightarrow \quad m = -\frac{3}{5}, \quad c = -2$

(e) $y = 5x - 7 \quad \Rightarrow \quad m = 5, \quad c = -7$

(f) $m = \frac{1}{3}, \quad c = -\frac{5}{4}$

(g) $y = -\frac{5x}{4} + 5 \quad \Rightarrow \quad m = -\frac{5}{4}, \quad c = 5$

9 (a) $y = 3x - 11$ (b) $y = 2x + 4$

Multiplying brackets

1 (a) $5x + 15$ (b) $2x - 8$

   (c) $16x + 40$ (d) $-2x - 12$

   (e) $-4x + 28$ (f) $6x - 12y$

2 (a) $3 + 2x + 6 = 9 + 2x$

   (b) $3x - 12$

   (c) $a + 40 - 5a = 40 - 4a$

   (d) $t - 4 + 4t = 5t - 4$

   (e) $p - 1 + 6p - 16 = 7p - 17$

   (f) $5 - 30x + 54 = 59 - 30x$

   (g) $y - 9y + 18 = 18 - 8y$

   (h) $4x - 2x + x^2 = 2x + x^2$

   (i) $2 - 3x - 6x^2$

3 (a) $x^2 + 6x + 8$ (b) $x^2 - 2x - 3$

   (c) $x^2 + 3x - 4$ (d) $x^2 - 7x + 10$

   (e) $x^2 - 2x - 35$ (f) $x^2 + 10x + 16$

   (g) $x^2 - 11x + 18$ (h) $x^2 + 3x - 28$

4 (a) (i) $x^2 + 6x + 9$

     (ii) $x^2 + 14x + 49$

     (iii) $x^2 - 18x + 81$

     (iv) $x^2 - 12x + 36$

  (b) (i) $b = 2p$

     (ii) $c = p^2$

Further factorisation

Commentary

This tasksheet provides a background from which a strategy for factorising $x^2 + bx + c$ can be developed. The relationship between the constant term c and the factorised form is examined and this relationship is used to help select appropriate pairs of factors.

1 (a)   (i) $x^2 + 5x + 6$ (ii) $x^2 - 5x + 6$

     (iii) $x^2 + 9x + 20$ (iv) $x^2 - 9x + 20$

  (b) The constant term c is obtained by multiplying together the numbers in the brackets, together with their signs ($+$ or $-$). For example,

$$(x - 2)(x + 3) = x^2 + x - 6$$
$$-2 \ \times \ 3 = -6$$

  (c) The coefficient b is obtained by adding together the numbers in the brackets. For example,

$$(x - 2)(x + 3) = x^2 + x - 6$$
$$-2 \ + \ 3 = 1$$

2 (a) $(x + 2)(x + 7)$ (b) $(x + 8)(x + 5)$ (c) $(x - 2)(x - 7)$

   (d) $(x + 6)^2$ (e) $(x - 8)(x + 1)$ (f) $(x + 7)(x - 4)$

   (g) $(x - 6)(x - 2)$ (h) $(x - 9)(x + 4)$ (i) $(x - 8)(x + 6)$

   (j) $(x + 6)(x - 4)$

3 (a) $x(x + 2)$ (b) $(x + 3)(x - 3)$ (c) $x(x - 8)$

   (d) Not possible   (e) $x(x + 25)$ (f) $(x + 5)(x - 5)$

   (g) Not possible   (h) $(x + 1)(x - 1)$ (i) $x(x - 1)$

   (j) $(2x + 1)(3x + 1)$ (k) $(2x + 3)(x + 2)$ (l) $(2x - 1)(2x + 1)$

  (m) $(3x - 2)(3x + 2)$

Review of equations

1. (a) $x = -6$

   (b) $x = -\frac{3}{2}$

   (c) $x = -\frac{9}{2}$

   (d) $x = -6$

   (e) $x = -3$

   (f) $x = -\frac{1}{3}$

2. (a) $x = 3$ or -5

   (b) $x = 0$ or 2

   (c) $x = 3$ or -6

   (d) $x = -2$ or 5

   (e) $x = 0$ or 4

   (f) $x = 3$

3. (a) $x = -7$ or 7

   (b) $x = -3$ or 3

   (c) $x = -3$ or 3

   (d) $x = -7$ or 5

   (e) $x = 0$ or 5

   (f) $x = -1$ or 1

   (g) $x = -2$ or 1

   (h) $x = -2$ or 3

   (i) $x = -1$ or 2

4. (a) $x = 7, y = 1$

   (b) $x = 4, y = 3$

   (c) $x = -2, y = 5$

Working in surd form

1 (a) $u_1 = \sqrt{2}$ $u_2 = \sqrt{3}$ $u_3 = \sqrt{4}$

2 (a) $14 + 6\sqrt{5}$ (b) $17 - 4\sqrt{13}$ (c) $29 - 12\sqrt{5}$

(d) $45 - 29\sqrt{2}$ (e) $5 - 2\sqrt{6}$ (f) $120 - 30\sqrt{15}$

4 (a) $x = \dfrac{-5 \pm \sqrt{21}}{2}$ (b) $x = \dfrac{3 \pm \sqrt{45}}{2}$ (c) $x = \dfrac{-7 \pm \sqrt{85}}{6}$

5 (a) $2\sqrt{2}$ (b) $2\sqrt{15}$ (c) $4\sqrt{2}$ (d) $\dfrac{16\sqrt{2}}{3\sqrt{7}}$

6 (b) (i) 1   (ii) -19 (iii) 1

7 (a) $\dfrac{\sqrt{3} - 1}{2}$ (b) $-\left(\dfrac{1 + \sqrt{2} + \sqrt{3} + \sqrt{6}}{2} \right)$ (c) $\dfrac{\sqrt{10} + \sqrt{15}}{5}$

(d) $\sqrt{10} + 4\sqrt{2} - \sqrt{5} - 4$ (e) $\dfrac{2\sqrt{5} - 2\sqrt{2}}{3}$

8 (a) $2 - \sqrt{2}$ (b) $2\sqrt{3} + 2\sqrt{2}$ (c) $7 + 4\sqrt{3}$ (d) $\dfrac{4 + 2\sqrt{3}}{3}$

Expanding brackets

1. (a) $x^3 - 1$

   (b) $x(x^2 + 2x + 4) - 2(x^2 + 2x + 4) = x^3 + 2x^2 + 4x - 2x^2 - 4x - 8$
   $$= x^3 - 8$$

   (c) $x^3 + 1$

   (d) $x^3 + 8$

2. (a) $(x + 1)(x^2 - 2x - 8) = x^3 - x^2 - 10x - 8$

   (b) $(x - 2)(x^2 - 7x + 12) = x^3 - 7x^2 + 12x - 2x^2 + 14x - 24$
   $$= x^3 - 9x^2 + 26x - 24$$

   (c) $(x - 1)(x^2 + 6x + 5) = x^3 + 5x^2 - x - 5$

   (d) $(x^2 - 2x + 1)(x + 3) = x^3 - 2x^2 + x + 3x^2 - 6x + 3$
   $$= x^3 + x^2 - 5x + 3$$

3. (a) $(x^2 - 1)(x^2 - 4) = x^4 - 5x^2 + 4$

   (b) $(x^2 - 4)^2 = x^4 - 8x^2 + 16$

   (c) $(x - 1)(x + 3)(x^2 + 6x + 9) = (x^2 + 2x - 3)(x^2 + 6x + 9)$
   $$= x^4 + 6x^3 + 9x^2 + 2x^3 + 12x^2 + 18x - 3x^2$$
   $$- 18x - 27$$
   $$= x^4 + 8x^3 + 18x^2 - 27$$

   (d) $(x + 1)(x - 2)(x^2 - x - 12) = (x + 1)(x^3 - 3x^2 - 10x + 24)$
   $$= x^4 - 2x^3 - 13x^2 + 14x + 24$$

Functions of functions $\qquad$ Commentary

1 (a) (i) $f(4) = 4^2 = 16$ $\qquad$ (ii) $g(16) = 3 \times 16 + 1 = 49$

(b) $g(f(4)) = g(16) = 49$

(c) (i) $g(f(2)) = g(4) = 13$ $\qquad$ (ii) $g(f(-3)) = g(9) = 28$

(iii) $f(g(-2)) = f(-5) = 25$

(d)

$x \longrightarrow \boxed{f} \longrightarrow x^2 \longrightarrow \boxed{g} \longrightarrow 3(x^2) + 1 = g(f(x))$

(e) For example, from (a) $g(f(2)) = 13$, and $3(2^2) + 1 = 13$

(f)

$x \longrightarrow \boxed{g} \longrightarrow 3x + 1 \longrightarrow \boxed{f} \longrightarrow (3x+1)^2 \quad f(g(x)) = (3x+1)^2$

2 (a) (i) $gf(x) = \dfrac{1}{x} - 3$, $\quad fg(x) = \dfrac{1}{x-3}$

(ii) $gf(x) = \sqrt{(2x)}$, $\quad fg(x) = 2\sqrt{x}$

(iii) $gf(x) = (x+5) - 9 = x - 4$, $\quad fg(x) = (x-9) + 5 = x - 4$

(iv) $gf(x) = fg(x) = 10 - (10 - x) = x$

(v) $gf(x) = fg(x) = \dfrac{1}{1/x} = x$

(b) When $fg(x) = gf(x)$, the order in which the functions are applied does not matter.

In (iii), the order in which successive addition and subtraction is carried out does not matter.

In (iv) and (v), the composite function is in both cases the identity function. Since functions f and g are the same in each example, they are both **self-inverse** functions.

3 (a) $x + 2$ $\quad$ (b) x^2 $\quad$ (c) $\dfrac{1}{x}$ $\quad$ (d) $\sqrt{x}$

4 (a) $x + 8$ $\quad$ (b) x^2 $\quad$ (c) $3x + 1$ $\quad$ (d) $\dfrac{12}{x}$ $\quad$ (e) $\sqrt[3]{x}$ $\quad$ (f) $4x - x^2$

Rearranging formulas

1 $x = \pm\sqrt{\left(\dfrac{y}{5}\right)} + 7$

2 (a) $x = \pm\sqrt{\left(\dfrac{y+7}{3}\right)}$

   (b) $x = \frac{1}{2}(\pm\sqrt{(9y)} - 1)$

   (c) $x = \frac{1}{9}(y+1)^2$

3 $x = \dfrac{3}{y+4}$

4 (a) $x = \dfrac{1}{2-y}$ (b) $x = \pm\sqrt{\left(\dfrac{3}{y}\right)}$ (c) $x = \dfrac{1}{4(y-5)^2}$

   (d) $x = \dfrac{2}{y} - 1$ (e) $x = \dfrac{1}{2}\left(\dfrac{4}{y} - 1\right)$ (f) $x = \dfrac{1}{2}\left(1 - \dfrac{7}{y}\right)$

   (g) $x = \pm\sqrt{(y)} - 1$ (h) $x = \frac{1}{2}(1 \pm \sqrt{(y)})$ (i) $x = \pm 2\sqrt{(1-y)}$

Solving equations

1 $\cos x° = \frac{3}{4} = 0.75$

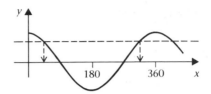

One solution is $x = 41.4$

The other solution between 0 and 360
is $x = 360 - 41.4 = 318.6$

2 (a) $\cos x° = 0.56 \Rightarrow x = 55.9, \quad 304.1$

   (b) $\sin x° = -0.23 \Rightarrow x = 193.3, \quad 346.7$

   (c) $\cos x° = -0.5 \Rightarrow x = 120, \quad 240$

3 (a) $\sin x° = 0.65 \Rightarrow x = 40.5, \quad 139.5$

   (b) $\cos x° = -0.38 \Rightarrow x = 112.3, \quad -112.3$

   (c) $\sin x° = -0.47 \Rightarrow x = -28.0, \quad -152.0$

4 (a) $3 \sin x° = 2 \Rightarrow x = 41.8, \quad 138.2$

   (b) $5 \cos x° + 2 = 0 \Rightarrow x = 113.6, \quad 246.4$

   (c) $2 \cos x° + 5 = 0 \qquad$ No solution for x

5 $5 \sin (3t + 40)° = 4$

   $\Rightarrow \sin (3t + 40)° = \frac{4}{5}$

   $\Rightarrow \sin x° = 0.8, \quad$ where $x = 3t + 40$

   From a calculator, $x = 53.1$

   $x = 53.1, \quad 126.9, \quad 413.1, \quad 486.9, \quad 773.1, \quad 846.9$

   $t = 4.37, \quad 28.97, \quad 124.37, \quad 148.97, \quad 244.37, \quad 268.97$

6 (a) $\sin 2t° = 0.7 \Rightarrow t = 22.2, \quad 67.8, \quad 202.2, \quad 247.8$

   (b) $2 \cos 3t° = 1 \Rightarrow t = 20, \quad 100, \quad 140, \quad 220, \quad 260, \quad 340$

   (c) $3 \cos (0.5t + 20)° = 2 \Rightarrow t = 56.4$

Laws of indices

1 (a) 2^{12} (b) 2^3 (c) 2^1 (d) 2^2

   (e) 2^0 (f) 2^6 (g) 2^6 (h) 2^{16}

2 (a) y^{12} (b) b^3 (c) $c^1 = c$ (d) x^2

   (e) $y^0 = 1$ (f) a^6 (g) a^6 (h) b^{16}

3 (a) $\frac{1}{32}$ (b) $\frac{1}{5}$ (c) $\frac{1}{16}$ (d) $\frac{1}{16}$

   (e) $\frac{1}{25}$ (f) $\frac{1}{64}$ (g) 2 (h) $\frac{1}{243}$

4 (a) $x^1 = x$ (b) a^{-2} (c) $b^0 = 1$ (d) d^{-6}

   (e) x^{-10} (f) y^{-3} (g) $a^0 = 1$ (h) x^2

5 (a) 2 (b) $\frac{1}{2}$ (c) 9 (d) $\frac{1}{9}$

   (e) 8 (f) $\frac{1}{10}$ (g) 1 (h) 1000

   (i) 16 (j) 1 (k) 8 (l) $10\,000$

   (m) 27 (n) $\frac{1}{25}$ (o) 100 (p) 1000

Differentiation practice

Commentary

1 By the chain rule: $\dfrac{dy}{dx} = 2\sin x \cos x$ (or $\sin 2x$)

2 By the chain rule: $\dfrac{dy}{dx} = -12\sin 4x$

3 $y = \dfrac{1}{x^2}$ or x^{-2} $\dfrac{dy}{dx} = -2x^{-3}$ or $\dfrac{-2}{x^3}$

4 By the chain rule: $y = (2x + 5)^{-1}$

$$\frac{dy}{dx} = -2(2x + 5)^{-2}\ \text{ or }\ \frac{-2}{(2x + 5)^2}$$

5 Using parametric differentiation: $\dfrac{dy}{dx} = \dfrac{6}{2t}$ or $\dfrac{3}{t}$

6 Using the product rule and the chain rule: $\dfrac{dy}{dx} = 2\,e^{2x}\sin\tfrac{1}{2}x + \tfrac{1}{2}\,e^{2x}\cos\tfrac{1}{2}x$

$$\frac{dy}{dx} = e^{2x}\big(2\sin\tfrac{1}{2}x + \tfrac{1}{2}\cos\tfrac{1}{2}x\big)$$

7 By the chain rule: $\dfrac{dy}{dx} = 12x(2x^2 - 3)^2$

8 By the chain rule: $\dfrac{dy}{dx} = 4\left(\dfrac{1}{4x}\right) = \dfrac{1}{x}$

Or: $y = \ln 4x = \ln 4 + \ln x.$ So $\dfrac{dy}{dx} = \dfrac{1}{x}$

9 By implicit differentiation: $2xy + x^2\,\dfrac{dy}{dx} = 0,$ so $\dfrac{dy}{dx} = \dfrac{-2xy}{x^2} = \dfrac{-2y}{x}$

Or: $y = \dfrac{36}{x^2} = 36x^{-2};$ $\dfrac{dy}{dx} = -72x^{-3} = \dfrac{-72}{x^3}$

10 By parametric differentiation: $\dfrac{dy}{dx} = \dfrac{3\cos\theta}{-4\sin\theta}$ or $-0.75\cot\theta$

11 Using the product rule and the chain rule: $\dfrac{dy}{dx} = (2x - 3)^4 + 8x(2x - 3)^3$

12 $y = x^4(2x - 3) = 2x^5 - 3x^4$

$\dfrac{dy}{dx} = 10x^4 - 12x^3$

13 By parametric differentiation: $\dfrac{dy}{dx} = \dfrac{-6\sin 3\theta}{2\cos 2\theta} = \dfrac{-3\sin 3\theta}{\cos 2\theta}$

14 By implicit differentiation: $2x + 2y\dfrac{dy}{dx} = 0$

$$\dfrac{dy}{dx} = \dfrac{-x}{y}$$

15 By the chain rule: $y = (5x)^{\frac{1}{2}}$

$$\dfrac{dy}{dx} = (\tfrac{1}{2} \times 5)(5x)^{-\frac{1}{2}} \quad \text{or} \quad \dfrac{2.5}{\sqrt{(5x)}}$$

16 By parametric differentiation: $\dfrac{dy}{dx} = 3t^2 \div -\dfrac{1}{t^2} \quad \text{or} \quad -3t^4$

17 By implicit differentiation: $2x + 3y + 3x\dfrac{dy}{dx} + 4y\dfrac{dy}{dx} = 0$

$$\dfrac{dy}{dx} = \dfrac{-(2x + 3y)}{(3x + 4y)}$$

18 By the quotient rule: $\dfrac{dy}{dx} = \dfrac{\cos 2x \cos x + 2\sin x \sin 2x}{\cos^2 2x}$

19 By implicit differentiation: $3\,e^{3x}y + e^{3x}\dfrac{dy}{dx} = 2x$

$$\dfrac{dy}{dx} = \dfrac{(2x - 3y\,e^{3x})}{e^{3x}}$$

Or : $y = \dfrac{x^2}{e^{3x}}$ and use the quotient rule:

$$\dfrac{dy}{dx} = \dfrac{2x\,e^{3x} - 3x^2\,e^{3x}}{(e^{3x})^2} = \dfrac{2x - 3x^2}{e^{3x}}$$

20 $y = 12 - x^2$, so $\dfrac{dy}{dx} = -2x$

Using sigma

Commentary

1 (a) $\displaystyle\sum_1^n u_i$

(b) The sum is multiplied by the constant.

(c) $\displaystyle\sum_1^n au_i = au_1 + \cdots + au_n$

$$= a(u_1 + \cdots + u_n)$$

$$= a\sum_1^n u_i$$

2 (a) The sum is increased by n times the constant.

(b) $\displaystyle\sum_1^n (u_i + b) = u_1 + b + u_2 + b + \cdots + u_n + b$

$$= u_1 + \cdots + u_n + nb$$

$$= \sum_1^n u_i + nb$$

(c) $\displaystyle\sum_1^n (au_i + b) = \sum_1^n au_i + nb$

$$= a\sum_1^n u_i + nb$$

3 (a) $\displaystyle 2\sum_1^n i - 3n = n(n+1) - 3n$

$$= n^2 - 2n$$

(b) $\displaystyle 5\sum_1^n i + n = \tfrac{5}{2}n(n+1) + n$

$$= \tfrac{5}{2}n^2 + \tfrac{7}{2}n$$

4 $\displaystyle\sum_1^n (u_i + v_i) = u_1 + v_1 + u_2 + v_2 + \cdots + u_n + v_n$

$$= (u_1 + u_2 + \cdots + u_n) + (v_1 + v_2 + \cdots + v_n)$$

$$= \sum_1^n u_i + \sum_1^n v_i$$

5 (a) $(n+1)^3 - 1^3$. The other terms cancel out in pairs.

(b) This is part (a) written in $\sum$ notation.

(c) $(i+1)^3 - i^3 = 3i^2 + 3i + 1$

$$\sum_1^n (i+1)^3 - \sum_1^n i^3 = \sum_1^n [(i+1)^3 - i^3]$$

$$= \sum_1^n (3i^2 + 3i + 1)$$

$$= 3\sum_1^n i^2 + 3\sum_1^n i + n$$

(d) $3\sum_1^n i^2 + 3\sum_1^n i + n = (n+1)^3 - 1$

$$3\sum_1^n i^2 + \frac{3n(n+1)}{2} + n = n^3 + 3n^2 + 3n$$

$$3\sum_1^n i^2 = n^3 + \frac{3n^2}{2} + \frac{n}{2}$$

$$\sum_1^n i^2 = \frac{(2n^3 + 3n^2 + n)}{6}$$

$$\sum_1^n i^2 = \frac{n(n+1)(2n+1)}{6}$$

6 $\dfrac{99 \times 100 \times 199}{6} = 328\,350$

7 (a) $2\sum_1^n i^2 - 6\sum_1^n i + 4n = \dfrac{n(n+1)(2n+1)}{3} - 3n(n+1) + 4n$

$$= \frac{n(2n^2 - 6n + 4)}{3}$$

$$= \frac{2n(n-1)(n-2)}{3}$$

(b) $\displaystyle\sum_{1}^{n}(2i-1)^2 = \sum_{1}^{n}(4i^2 - 4i + 1)$

$\displaystyle = 4\sum_{1}^{n}i^2 - 4\sum_{1}^{n}i + n$

$\displaystyle = \frac{2n(n+1)(2n+1)}{3} - 2n(n+1) + n$

$\displaystyle = \frac{n(4n^2 - 1)}{3}$

$\displaystyle = \frac{n(2n-1)(2n+1)}{3}$

Zeno's paradox

Commentary

1 (a) Since the rabbit is running at half the speed of the dog, the rabbit will have run 64 m.

   (b) By the same argument, the rabbit will have run a further 32 m.

   (c) 16 m.

The argument appears to suggest that the dog will never catch the rabbit because the dog always has to reach the spot last occupied by the rabbit. In the meantime, the rabbit will have moved on ahead again. However, you know that, in practice, the dog will catch the rabbit!

2 This is a G.P., first term 128, common ratio $\frac{1}{2}$.

   (a) $D = \dfrac{128\left(1 - \left(\frac{1}{2}\right)^n\right)}{1 - \frac{1}{2}} = 256\left(1 - \left(\frac{1}{2}\right)^n\right)$

   (b) As n approaches infinity, $\left(\frac{1}{2}\right)^n \to 0$ and so $D \to 256$.

3 This is a G.P., first term 64, common ratio $\frac{1}{2}$.

   (a) $R = 64 \times \dfrac{1 - \left(\frac{1}{2}\right)^n}{1 - \left(\frac{1}{2}\right)} = 128\left(1 - \left(\frac{1}{2}\right)^n\right)$

   (b) As n approaches infinity, $\left(\frac{1}{2}\right)^n \to 0$ and so $R \to 128$.

4 (a) $40 \times 8 = 320$ m

   (b) $40 \times 4 = 160$ m

   (c) Since the dog will have run 160 m farther than the rabbit it will have caught up with it.

5 The answer to question 2 suggests that the dog will never travel more than 256 m. You know this must be false! The paradox is resolved when you realise that *time* must be taken into account. The distances in question 2 are taken over decreasing periods of time and so give a false impression of the motion.

The dog runs 128 m in 16 seconds, the next 64 m in 8 seconds, the next 32 m in 4 seconds and so on. The total time is therefore

$$16 + 8 + 4 + 2 + \cdots = \frac{16}{1 - \frac{1}{2}} = 32 \text{ seconds}$$

In 32 seconds the dog will have run 256 m, as predicted. However, the dog does not stop moving after 32 seconds and will now overtake the rabbit, who has run $4 \times 32 = 128$ m and is level at this point.

Regular pentagons and the Fibonacci sequence

1

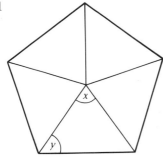

$$x = 360° \div 5 = 72°$$

$$\Rightarrow y = \frac{180° - 72°}{2} = 54° \text{ (isosceles triangle)}$$

$$\Rightarrow \text{interior angle} = 2y = 108°$$

2 $\angle ABC = 108°$ (interior angle)
Since triangle ABC is isosceles,

$$\angle BCA = \angle BAC = \frac{180° - 108°}{2} = 36°$$

3 BC = CD (triangle BCD isosceles)
$\Rightarrow CD = 1$

CA = CD + DA $\Rightarrow$ DA = $\phi - 1$
But $\phi \times DA = CD$
$\Rightarrow \phi(\phi - 1) = 1$

4

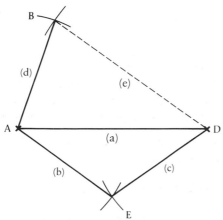

(a) Draw and measure a line segment AD= 8.1 cm. This is 5ϕ to the nearest 0.1 cm.

(b) Use compasses to draw an arc with a radius of 5 cm and centre at A.

(c) Use compasses to draw an arc with a radius of 5 cm and centre at D.

Join the point of intersection of the arcs at E to A and D, to give two sides, AE and DE, of the pentagon.

(d) Use compasses to draw an arc with a radius of 5 cm and centre at A.

(e) Use compasses to draw an arc with a radius of 8.1 cm and centre at D.

Join the point of intersection of the arcs at B to A, to give the side AB of the pentagon.

Two 5 cm arcs with their centres at B and D will give the position of C and hence the other two sides of the pentagon.

5

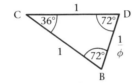

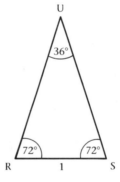

RUS is an enlargement of BCD, scale factor ϕ, hence SU $= \phi$.

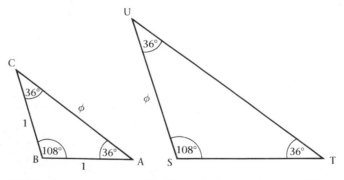

SUT is an enlargement of BCA, scale factor ϕ; hence UT $= \phi^2$

6 UT is the edge of the new pentagon.

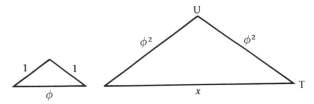

The new pentagon is an enlargement of the original pentagon, scale factor ϕ^2, hence

$$x = \phi^2 \times \phi = \phi^3$$

7 $\phi^7 = \frac{1}{2}(29 + 13\sqrt{5})$ $\qquad$ $\phi^8 = \frac{1}{2}(47 + 21\sqrt{5})$

8 $\phi^7 = \frac{1}{2}(29 + 13\sqrt{5})$ $\qquad$ $\psi^7 = \frac{1}{2}(29 - 13\sqrt{5})$

$$\phi^7 + \psi^7 = \frac{1}{2}(29 + 13\sqrt{5}) + \frac{1}{2}(29 - 13\sqrt{5})$$

$$= \frac{1}{2}(29 + 29 + 13\sqrt{5} - 13\sqrt{5}) = 29$$

$$\frac{1}{\sqrt{5}}(\phi^7 - \psi^7) = \frac{1}{\sqrt{5}}\left[\frac{1}{2}(29 + 13\sqrt{5}) - \frac{1}{2}(29 - 13\sqrt{5})\right]$$

$$= \frac{1}{\sqrt{5}}\left[\frac{1}{2}(29 + 13\sqrt{5} - 29 + 13\sqrt{5})\right] = 13$$

$$\phi^8 = \frac{1}{2}(47 + 21\sqrt{5}) \qquad \psi^8 = \frac{1}{2}(47 - 21\sqrt{5})$$

$$\phi^8 + \psi^8 = \frac{1}{2}(47 + 21\sqrt{5}) + \frac{1}{2}(47 - 21\sqrt{5})$$

$$= \frac{1}{2}(47 + 47 + 21\sqrt{5} - 21\sqrt{5})$$

$$= 47$$

$$\frac{1}{\sqrt{5}}(\phi^8 - \psi^8) = \frac{1}{\sqrt{5}}\left[\frac{1}{2}(47 + 21\sqrt{5}) - \frac{1}{2}(47 - 21\sqrt{5})\right]$$

$$= \frac{1}{\sqrt{5}}\left[\frac{1}{2}(47 - 47 + 21\sqrt{5} + 21\sqrt{5})\right]$$

$$= 21$$

9

n	ϕ^n	ψ^n	L_n	F_n
1	1.618 034	−0.618 034	1	1
2	2.618 034	0.381 966	3	1
3	4.236 068	−0.236 068	4	2
4	6.854 102	0.145 898	7	3
5	11.090 170	−0.090 170	11	5
6	17.944 272	0.055 728	18	8
7	29.034 442	−0.034 442	29	13
8	46.978 714	0.021 286	47	21

As n increases, ψ^n becomes numerically smaller and oscillates between positive and negative values.

10 $\dfrac{L_n}{L_{n-1}}$ 3,   1.333,   1.75,   1.571,   1.636,   1.611,   1.621...

$\dfrac{F_n}{F_{n-1}}$ 1,   2,   1.5,   1.667,   1.6,   1.625,   1.615...

Both ratios get closer to the golden ratio, because that is the ratio of successive terms given by the approximate formulas in both cases.

Tangents and normals

1 The normal line has gradient $-\dfrac{1}{g}$.

2 (a)

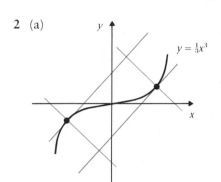

$y = \frac{1}{3}x^3$

(b) $y = x - \frac{2}{3}, \quad y = x + \frac{2}{3}$

(c) $y = -x - \frac{4}{3}, \quad y = -x + \frac{4}{3}$

(d) $\left(1, \frac{1}{3}\right), \left(\frac{1}{3}, 1\right), \left(-1, -\frac{1}{3}\right), \left(-\frac{1}{3}, -1\right)$

(e) The rectangle has edges of lengths $\frac{2}{3}\sqrt{2}$ and $\frac{4}{3}\sqrt{2}$. Its area is $\frac{16}{9}$ square units.

3 (a) The tangents and normals must have gradients of ± 1. At the corners of the square on $y = x^2$,

$$\frac{dy}{dx} = \pm 1 \Rightarrow 2x = \pm 1 \Rightarrow x = \pm \frac{1}{2}$$

The corners are $\left(\frac{1}{2}, \frac{1}{4}\right), \left(0, \frac{3}{4}\right), \left(-\frac{1}{2}, \frac{1}{4}\right), \left(0, -\frac{1}{4}\right)$.

(b) The square has edge of length $\frac{1}{2}\sqrt{2}$. Its area is therefore $\left(\frac{1}{2}\sqrt{2}\right)^2 = \frac{1}{2}$ square unit.

4 The normal has gradient $-\frac{1}{2}$ and equation $y = -\frac{1}{2}x + \frac{3}{2}$. At A,

$$-\frac{1}{2}x + \frac{3}{2} = x^2 \Rightarrow 2x^2 + x - 3 = 0 \Rightarrow x = 1 \text{ or } -\frac{3}{2}$$

A has coordinates $\left(-\frac{3}{2}, \frac{9}{4}\right)$.

Optimisation problems

Commentary

1 (a) If $x > 5$ or $x < -5$, then the base of the cone lies outside the sphere and the design constraint has been violated. x must be smaller than the radius of the sphere if the cone is to be inside it.

(b) The diagrams indicate that the volume increases to a maximum value, then gets smaller again.

(c)

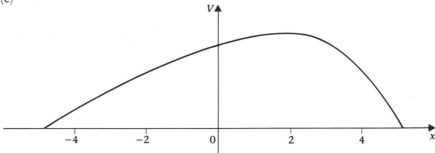

The maximum volume appears to correspond to $x = 2$.

(d) $V = \frac{1}{3}\pi r^2 h$
If $x = 2$, then
$h = 5 + 2 = 7$ and $r^2 = 5^2 - 2^2 = 21$
$V = \frac{1}{3}\pi \times 21 \times 7 = 154 \, \text{cm}^3$

(e)

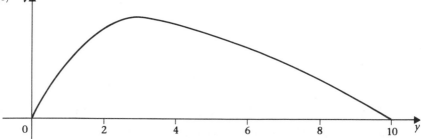

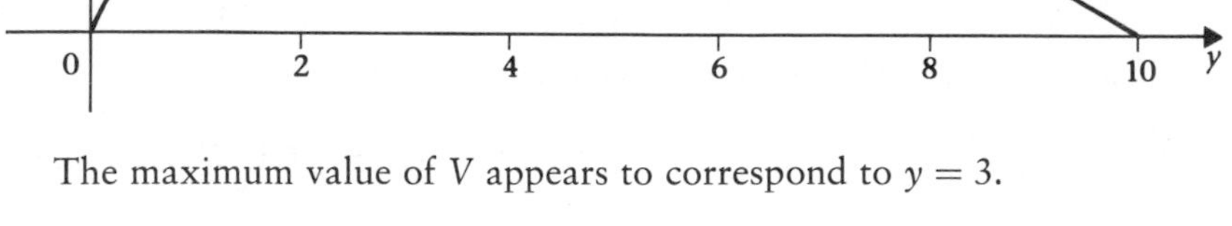

The maximum value of V appears to correspond to $y = 3$.

(f) $V = \frac{1}{3}\pi(5^2 - x^2)(5 + x) = \frac{1}{3}\pi(5 - x)(5 + x)^2$

Writing the equation in this form makes the graph easier to sketch.

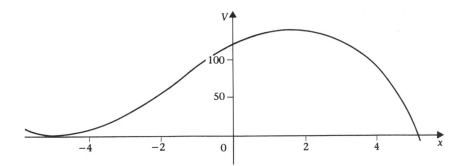

$V = \frac{1}{3}\pi(125 + 25x - 5x^2 - x^3)$

$\frac{dV}{dx} = \frac{1}{3}\pi(25 - 10x - 3x^2) = \frac{1}{3}\pi(5 + x)(5 - 3x)$

$\frac{dV}{dx} = 0 \Rightarrow x = -5 \quad \text{or} \quad x = \frac{5}{3}$

The minimum is at $(-5, 0)$. The maximum is at $(1.67, 155.1)$.

The maximum volume is 155 cm^3.

(g) Using y as the variable, the height of the cone $h = 10 - y$ and the radius is given by $r^2 = 5^2 - (5 - y)^2$.

$V = \frac{1}{3}\pi\{5^2 - (5 - y)^2\}(10 - y) = \frac{1}{3}\pi(y^3 - 20y^2 + 100y)$

$\frac{dV}{dy} = \frac{1}{3}\pi(3y^2 - 40y + 100) = \frac{1}{3}\pi(3y - 10)(y - 10)$

$\frac{dV}{dy} = 0 \Rightarrow y = \frac{10}{3} \quad \text{or} \quad y = 10$

The minimum is at $(10, 0)$. The maximum is at $(3.33, 155.1)$.

Note: $1.67 + 3.33 = 5.00$, as would be expected.

(h)

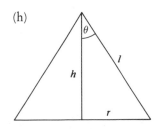

$V = \frac{1}{3}\pi r^2 h$, where $r = l \sin\theta$, $h = l\cos\theta$

Hence

$V = \frac{1}{3}\pi l^3 \sin^2\theta\cos\theta$

In finding this expression you have introduced a new variable, the slant height l. This must be eliminated from the expression for V, so that the expression for V is in terms of θ only. This can be done easily by substituting $l = 10 \cos \theta$.

This result follows directly from the well-known geometrical result that the angle subtended on a diameter is a right angle.

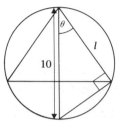

So

$$V = \tfrac{1}{3} \pi 1000 \cos^4 \theta \sin^2 \theta$$

which is a maximum when $\theta = 35.3°$, giving a volume of $155.1 \, \text{cm}^3$.

2   Let the price per bike be £P. The number sold drops by 40 for each increase of £1 in the price, and so the number sold is

$$5000 - 40(P - 100) = 9000 - 40P$$

$$\text{Total revenue} = £(9000 - 40P)P$$

$$\text{Total costs} = £50\,000 + 85(9000 - 40P)$$

$$\text{Profit} = \text{revenue} - \text{costs} = £(-815\,000 + 12\,400P - 40P^2)$$

$$\frac{\text{d(Profit)}}{\text{d}P} = 0 \text{ when } 12\,400 - 80P = 0, \quad \text{i.e. } P = 155$$

$$\text{Number sold} = 9000 - 40P = 2800$$

Approximately 2800 should be manufactured and they should be sold at a price of £155 each.

Traffic

Commentary

1   $\displaystyle\int_0^{10} \frac{t(20-t)}{5}\,dt = 133\tfrac{1}{3}$

Car A travels about 133 m during the 10 seconds in which it accelerates from rest.

2   During these 10 seconds, car B will travel $20 \times 10 = 200$ m. So car B must be at least 67 m from car A at the start if it is to avoid slowing down.

(In practice, rather more than 67 m will be required since it would be dangerous for the cars to get very close to each other. The actual length of the cars has not been considered, nor has the fact that A initially has to travel around a bend.)

3   If the traffic is moving at $20\,\mathrm{m\,s}^{-1}$, then in one hour the length of traffic passing is $20 \times 3600 = 72\,000$ m.

The average space between cars is $\dfrac{72\,000}{1200} = 60$ m.

So car A is unlikely to find a gap of sufficient length if the traffic is evenly spaced. The traffic is very unlikely to be evenly spaced and so A is likely to find a gap without having to wait too long.

Derivative of $\sin^2 x$ Commentary

1 (a)

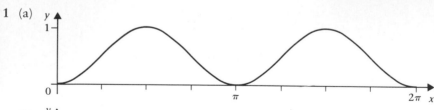

(b)

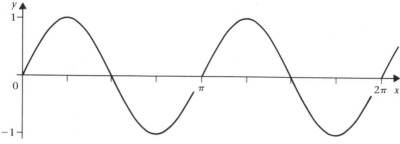

The derivative of $\sin^2 x$ is $\sin 2x$.

2 (a) $\sin^2 x = \frac{1}{2} - \frac{1}{2}\cos 2x \;\Rightarrow\; a = -\frac{1}{2}, \quad b = 2, \quad c = \frac{1}{2}$

(b) If $y = \frac{1}{2} - \frac{1}{2}\cos 2x$, $\dfrac{dy}{dx} = -\frac{1}{2}(-2\sin 2x) = \sin 2x$

3 $\dfrac{d}{dx}(\cos^2 x) = -\sin 2x$, using a method similar to that used in question 1.

$$\cos^2 x = \tfrac{1}{2} + \tfrac{1}{2}\cos 2x \Rightarrow \frac{d}{dx}(\cos^2 x) = \tfrac{1}{2}(-\tfrac{1}{2}\sin 2x) = -\sin 2x$$

4 (a) $\dfrac{d}{dx}(\sin^2 x + \cos^2 x) = \sin 2x - \sin 2x = 0$

(b)

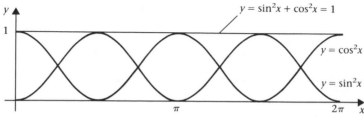

(c) $\sin^2 x + \cos^2 x = 1$, a constant whose derivative is zero.

5 $\quad \cos 2x = 1 - 2\sin^2 x \Rightarrow \sin^2 x = \dfrac{1}{2} - \dfrac{\cos 2x}{2}$

$$\frac{\mathrm{d}}{\mathrm{d}x}(\sin^2 x) = \frac{\mathrm{d}}{\mathrm{d}x}\left(-\frac{\cos 2x}{2}\right)$$

$$= -\tfrac{1}{2}(-2\sin 2x) = \sin 2x$$

6 $\quad \cos 2x = 1 - 2\sin^2 x$

$$= 1 - 2(1 - \cos^2 x)$$

$$= 2\cos^2 x - 1$$

$$\cos^2 x = \frac{\cos 2x}{2} + \frac{1}{2}$$

$$\frac{\mathrm{d}}{\mathrm{d}x}(\cos^2 x) = \frac{\mathrm{d}}{\mathrm{d}x}\left(\frac{\cos 2x}{2}\right)$$

$$= -\sin 2x$$

Prime number formulas Commentary

1 It is worth spending some time in exploring particular cases and establishing subsidiary results such as that if $an^2 + bn + c$ is always to be odd then c must be odd and a and b must have the same parity.

2 In the first attempt at a proof, the cases $c = \pm 1$ and $ac + b + 1 = \pm 1$ all invalidate the method. It is worth remembering that any one of these suffices as a counter-example.

3 When $n = 1 + 2p$,

$$an^2 + bn + c = a(1 + 2p)^2 + b(1 + 2p) + c$$
$$= 4ap^2 + (4a + 2b)p + a + b + c$$
$$= (4ap + 4a + 2b + 1)p$$

The second attempt is sound and the method may be extended to show that no polynomial form $P(n)$ of degree one or more generates only primes. If the degree of the polynomial is k it is sufficient to show that $P(n)$ takes the same value for $(k + 1)$ different values of n.

Extending the method

Commentary

1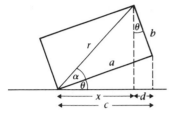

(a) (i) $x = r \cos (\theta + \alpha)$

(ii) $x = c - d = a \cos \theta - b \sin \theta$

(b) $a \cos \theta - b \sin \theta = r \cos (\theta + \alpha)$

2 $y = c - d$

$= a \sin \theta - b \cos \theta$

Also $y = r \sin (\theta - \alpha)$

$\Rightarrow a \sin \theta - b \cos \theta = r \sin (\theta - \alpha)$

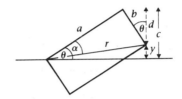

3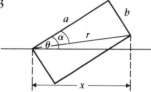

Considering the projections on the x-axis,

$$x = a \cos \theta + b \sin \theta$$

Also $x = r \cos (\theta - \alpha)$

$\Rightarrow a \cos \theta + b \sin \theta = r \cos (\theta - \alpha)$

4 (a) $r_1 = \sqrt{(49 + 16)} = \sqrt{65}$ $\alpha_1 = \tan^{-1} \frac{4}{7} = 29.7°$

(b) $r_2 = \sqrt{(16 + 49)} = \sqrt{65}$ $\alpha_2 = \tan^{-1} \frac{7}{4} = 60.3°$

(c) You can consider the function either as a sine graph with a phase shift of $-29.7°$ or as a cosine graph of phase shift $+60.3°$.

(d) $\alpha_1 + \alpha_2 = 90°$. This relationship may be seen clearly from the triangle.

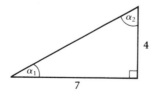

5 (a) $25 \cos (\theta - 73.7°)$ (b) $13 \sin (\theta + 22.6°)$

(c) $41 \sin (\theta - 77.3°)$ (d) $4.47 \sin (\theta + 30°)$

6 (a) $3 \sin \left(\theta + \dfrac{\pi}{6} \right)$ (b) $3 \cos \left(\theta - \dfrac{\pi}{3} \right)$

(c) $3 \sin \left(\theta + \dfrac{11\pi}{6} \right)$ (d) $3 \cos \left(\theta + \dfrac{5\pi}{3} \right)$

Intersections

1 (a) (i) $\mathbf{r} = \begin{bmatrix} 0 \\ 2 \\ 5 \end{bmatrix} + \lambda \begin{bmatrix} 2 \\ 0 \\ -3 \end{bmatrix} + \mu \begin{bmatrix} -1 \\ -1 \\ 1 \end{bmatrix}$

  (ii) $\mathbf{r} = \begin{bmatrix} 2 \\ 2 \\ 2 \end{bmatrix} + \lambda \begin{bmatrix} -3 \\ -1 \\ 4 \end{bmatrix} + \mu \begin{bmatrix} -2 \\ 0 \\ 3 \end{bmatrix}$

(b) (i) $\left. \begin{array}{ll} x = & 2\lambda - \mu \quad ① \\ y = 2 & - \mu \quad ② \\ z = 5 - 3\lambda + \mu \quad ③ \end{array} \right\} \Rightarrow 3x - y + 2z = 8$

  (ii) $\left. \begin{array}{l} x = 2 - 3\lambda - 2\mu \quad ① \\ y = 2 - \lambda \quad\quad\quad ② \\ z = 2 + 4\lambda + 3\mu \quad ③ \end{array} \right\} \Rightarrow 3x - y + 2z = 8 \quad \text{as before}$

2 $3x - y + 2z = 8 \quad ①$

   $x - 2y + z = 1 \quad ②$

  If $x = 0$, $2 \times ① - ②$, $z = 5$, $y = 2$

  If $y = 0$, $① - 3 \times ②$, $z = -5$, $x = 6$

  so two points are A $(0, 2, 5)$ and B $(6, 0, -5)$.
  (There are many others and many ways of finding just two points!)

  Hence, a vector in the direction of the line of intersection is $\overrightarrow{AB} = \begin{bmatrix} 6 \\ -2 \\ -10 \end{bmatrix}$

  and the equation of the line of intersection is $\begin{bmatrix} x \\ y \\ z \end{bmatrix} = \begin{bmatrix} 0 \\ 2 \\ 5 \end{bmatrix} + \lambda \begin{bmatrix} 6 \\ -2 \\ -10 \end{bmatrix}$.

3 At the point of intersection, the point (x, y, z) satisfies the equations of both
   the line and the plane.

  i.e. $x = 3t$

    $y = 2 - t$

    $z = 5 - 5t$

So, $2x + 3y + z = 7 \Rightarrow 2(3t) + 3(2 - t) + 5 - 5t = 7$

$$\Rightarrow \qquad\qquad t = 2$$

Thus the point of intersection is $(6, 0, -5)$.

4 The point of intersection is $(5, -1, 2)$.

5 $x - 2y + z = 1 \qquad$ ①
$3x - y + 2z = 8 \qquad$ ②
$4x - 3y + 3z = 5 \qquad$ ③
$2 \times$ ② $-$ ① $\Rightarrow 5x + 3z = 15 \qquad$ ④
$3 \times$ ② $-$ ③ $\Rightarrow 5x + 3z = 19 \qquad$ ⑤

But equations ④ and ⑤ are inconsistent – it is not possible for $5x + 3z$ to be equal to 15 and 19 simultaneously.

Using the method of question 2, the line of intersection of ① and ③ is

$$\begin{bmatrix} x \\ y \\ z \end{bmatrix} = \begin{bmatrix} 2 \\ 0 \\ -1 \end{bmatrix} + \lambda \begin{bmatrix} -\frac{3}{5} \\ \frac{1}{5} \\ 1 \end{bmatrix} \quad \text{(taking points } (2, 0, -1), (\tfrac{7}{5}, \tfrac{1}{5}, 0) \text{ on the line)}$$

and the intersection of ② and ③ is

$$\begin{bmatrix} x \\ y \\ z \end{bmatrix} = \begin{bmatrix} \frac{19}{5} \\ \frac{17}{5} \\ 0 \end{bmatrix} + \lambda \begin{bmatrix} -\frac{19}{5} \\ \frac{19}{15} \\ \frac{19}{3} \end{bmatrix} \quad \text{(taking } (\tfrac{19}{5}, \tfrac{17}{5}, 0) \text{ and } (0, \tfrac{14}{3}, \tfrac{19}{3}))$$

But the direction vector of each line is $\begin{bmatrix} 3 \\ -1 \\ 5 \end{bmatrix}$.

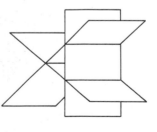

Thus, the three planes intersect in three parallel lines – a prism.

If the third equation is $4x - 3y + 3z = 9$,
$3 \times$ ② $-$ ③ $\Rightarrow 5x + 3z = 15$, which is the same as ④ above.

In this case all three planes intersect in a single straight line.

Drawing parametric curves — Commentary

1 (a)

θ	0	$\frac{1}{6}\pi$	$\frac{1}{4}\pi$	$\frac{1}{3}\pi$	$\frac{1}{2}\pi$
x	1	0.65	0.35	0.125	0
y	0	0.125	0.35	0.65	1

(b) As θ increases from $\frac{1}{2}\pi$ to π, the values of x become negative, but equal in magnitude to the values in the table. The values of y remain positive and equal to the values in the table, i.e. x decreases from 0 to -1 while y decreases from 1 to 0.

(c) For $\pi < \theta \leq \frac{3}{2}\pi$, x and y are both negative, while for $\frac{3}{2}\pi < \theta \leq 2\pi$, x is positive and y is negative.

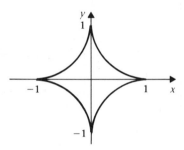

2

θ	0	$\frac{1}{6}\pi$	$\frac{1}{4}\pi$	$\frac{1}{3}\pi$	$\frac{1}{2}\pi$
x	0	0.02	0.08	0.18	0.57
y	0	0.13	0.29	0.5	1

As θ increases, x will continue to increase, though not steadily. y will oscillate between 0 and 2 (since $1 - \cos\pi = 1 - (-1) = 2$, after which $\cos\theta$ increases again).

The resulting curve is a **cycloid**, the path taken by a point on a moving circle.

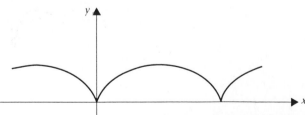

3 (a) $x = 0 \Rightarrow t = -1, \quad y = \frac{1}{5}$

$y = 0 \Rightarrow t = -2, \quad x = -\frac{1}{4}$

i.e. the curve cuts the axes at $(0, \frac{1}{5})$ and $(-\frac{1}{4}, 0)$.

(b) As $t \to 2^{-}, \quad x \to +\infty, \quad y \to 2^{-}$ ($t \to 2^{-}$ means t approaches 2 from below.) i.e. $y = 2$ is an asymptote.

(c) $t \to 4$ also yields an asymptote since it makes the denominator of y zero.

As $t \to 4^{+}, \quad x \to -\frac{5}{2}, \quad y \to -\infty$

$t \to 4^{-}, \quad x \to -\frac{5}{2}, \quad y \to +\infty$

(d) When $t = 0, \quad x = \frac{1}{2}, \quad y = \frac{1}{2}$ (It may be necessary to find a few more points to increase your confidence.)

(e)

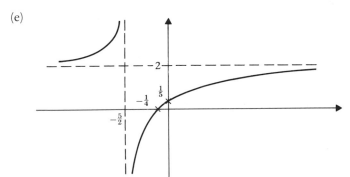

4 $x = 0 \Leftrightarrow t = 0 \Leftrightarrow y = 0$
As $t \to 1^{+}, \quad x \to -\infty, \quad y \to -\infty$
As $t \to 1^{-}, \quad x \to +\infty, \quad y \to +\infty$
As $t \to \infty, \quad x \to -2, \quad y \to -\infty$
As $t \to -\infty, \quad x \to -2, \quad y \to +\infty$

Again, plotting a few points will help.

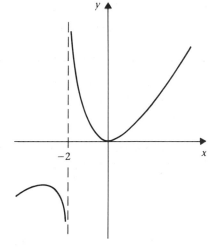

By parts

1 $I = e^x \sin x - \displaystyle\int e^x \sin x \, dx$

$I = e^x \sin x - \left[-e^x \cos x + \displaystyle\int e^x \cos x \, dx \right]$

$I = e^x \sin x + e^x \cos x - I$

$2I = e^x \sin x + e^x \cos x$

$I = \tfrac{1}{2} e^x (\sin x + \cos x)$

2 $u = \cos x \Rightarrow \dfrac{du}{dx} = -\sin x \quad$ and $\quad \dfrac{dv}{dx} = e^x \Rightarrow v = e^x$

$I = \displaystyle\int e^x \cos x \, dx = \cos x \times e^x - \int - \sin x \times e^x \, dx$

For $\displaystyle\int \sin x \times e^x \, dx$, let $u = \sin x \Rightarrow \dfrac{du}{dx} = \cos x \quad$ and $\quad \dfrac{dv}{dx} = e^x \Rightarrow v = e^x$

$\displaystyle\int \sin x \times e^x \, dx = \sin x \times e^x - \int \cos x \times e^x \, dx + c$

$\Rightarrow I = e^x \cos x + e^x \sin x - I + c$

$\Rightarrow 2I = e^x \cos x + e^x \sin x + c$

$\Rightarrow I = \tfrac{1}{2} (e^x \cos x + e^x \sin x) + K \qquad$ (where $K = \tfrac{1}{2} c$)

In this case, the choice of u and $\dfrac{dv}{dx}$ does not matter.

3 (a) $u = e^x \Rightarrow \dfrac{du}{dx} = e^x \quad$ and $\quad \dfrac{dv}{dx} = \sin x \Rightarrow v = -\cos x$

$I = \displaystyle\int e^x \sin x \, dx = -e^x \cos x + \int e^x \cos x \, dx$

For $\displaystyle\int e^x \cos x \, dx,\quad$ let $u = e^x \Rightarrow \dfrac{du}{dx} = e^x \quad$ and $\quad \dfrac{dv}{dx} = \cos x \Rightarrow v = \sin x$

$\displaystyle\int e^x \cos x \, dx = e^x \sin x - \int e^x \sin x \, dx + c$

$\Rightarrow I = -e^x \cos x + e^x \sin x - I + c$

$\Rightarrow 2I = e^x \sin x - e^x \cos x + c$

$\Rightarrow I = \tfrac{1}{2} (e^x \sin x - e^x \cos x) + K \qquad$ (where $K = \tfrac{1}{2} c$)

4 (a) Put $u = \sin x \Rightarrow \dfrac{du}{dx} = \cos x$ and $\dfrac{dv}{dx} = \cos x \Rightarrow v = \sin x$

$$I = \int \sin x \cos x \, dx = \sin^2 x - \int \cos x \sin x \, dx + c$$

$$= \sin^2 x - I + c$$

$$\Rightarrow 2I = \sin^2 x + c$$

$$\Rightarrow I = \tfrac{1}{2} \sin^2 x + K \qquad \text{(where } K = \tfrac{1}{2} c)$$

(b) $\dfrac{d}{dx} (\tfrac{1}{2} \sin^2 x) = \tfrac{1}{2} \times 2 \sin x \cos x = \sin x \cos x$

$$\Rightarrow \int \sin x \cos x \, dx = \tfrac{1}{2} \sin^2 x + c$$

Also, $\sin x \cos x = \tfrac{1}{2} \sin 2x$

Hence, $\displaystyle\int \sin x \cos x \, dx = \int \tfrac{1}{2} \sin 2x \, dx = -\tfrac{1}{4} \cos 2x + c$

$$= -\tfrac{1}{4} (1 - 2 \sin^2 x) + c = -\tfrac{1}{4} + \tfrac{1}{2} \sin^2 x + c = \tfrac{1}{2} \sin^2 x + K$$
$$\text{(where } K = c - \tfrac{1}{4})$$

5 $\displaystyle\int \ln (x \times 1) \, dx = \ln x \times x - \int x \times \dfrac{1}{x} \, dx$

$$= x \ln x - \int 1 \, dx$$

$$= x \ln x - x + c$$

$$\int_2^3 \ln x \, dx = \Big[x \ln x - x \Big]_2^3$$

$$\approx 0.910$$

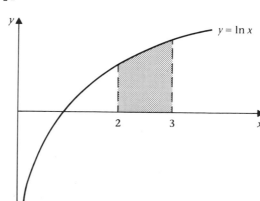

Integrating the circle

1 A circle of radius 1 unit has area π. A quarter of the circle therefore has area $\frac{1}{4}\pi$.

2 (a) $\dfrac{du}{dx} = -2$ and the integral therefore becomes:

$$\int \sqrt{u} \times \left(-\frac{1}{2x}\right) du = -\frac{1}{2}\int \frac{\sqrt{u}}{\sqrt{(1-u)}} du$$

The integral has not been simplified.

(b) $x = \sin\theta \Rightarrow \dfrac{dx}{d\theta} = \cos\theta$

$$\int \sqrt{(1-x^2)}\, dx = \int \sqrt{(1-\sin^2\theta)} \times \cos\theta\, d\theta$$

$$= \int \cos^2\theta\, d\theta$$

$$= \frac{1}{2}\int (1 + \cos 2\theta)\, d\theta$$

$$= \frac{1}{2}\left(\theta + \frac{1}{2}\sin 2\theta\right) + c$$

$$= \frac{1}{2}\theta + \frac{1}{2}\sin\theta\cos\theta + c$$

$$= \frac{1}{2}\sin^{-1} x + \frac{1}{2}x\sqrt{(1-x^2)} + c$$

(c) $\displaystyle\int_0^1 (1-x^2)\, dx = \frac{1}{2}\sin^{-1} 1 = \frac{1}{4}\pi$

$$\int_0^{\frac{1}{2}} \sqrt{(1-x^2)}\, dx = \frac{1}{2}\sin^{-1}\frac{1}{2} + \frac{1}{2} \times \frac{1}{2}\sqrt{(1-\frac{1}{4})} - \frac{1}{2}\sin^{-1} 0$$

$$= \frac{1}{12}\pi + \frac{1}{8}\sqrt{3}$$

3 $\sin 0 = 0$ and $\sin\frac{1}{6}\pi = \frac{1}{2}$

4 $\displaystyle\int_0^{\frac{1}{6}\pi} \cos^2\theta\, d\theta = \frac{1}{2}\int_0^{\frac{1}{6}\pi} (1 + \cos 2\theta)\, d\theta$

$$= \frac{1}{2}\left[\theta + \frac{1}{2}\sin 2\theta\right]_0^{\frac{1}{6}\pi}$$

$$= \frac{1}{12}\pi + \frac{1}{4}\sin\frac{1}{3}\pi$$

$$= \frac{1}{12}\pi + \frac{1}{8}\sqrt{3}$$

5 (a) For triangle OAB, $\frac{1}{2} \times$ base $\times$ height $= \frac{1}{2} \times \frac{1}{2} \times \sqrt{\frac{3}{4}} = \frac{1}{8}\sqrt{3}$

angle BOC $= \frac{1}{6}\pi$

and so sector BOC is $\frac{1}{12}$th of the unit circle. Its area is therefore $\frac{1}{12}\pi$.

(b) The shaded area is therefore $\frac{1}{12}\pi + \frac{1}{8}\sqrt{3}$, as established in questions 2(c) and 4.

6 Let $x = 3\sin\theta \Rightarrow \dfrac{dx}{d\theta} = 3\cos\theta$

$$\int_{1.5}^{3} \sqrt{(9 - x^2)}\, dx = \int_{\frac{1}{6}\pi}^{\frac{1}{2}\pi} \sqrt{(9 - 9\sin^2\theta)} \times 3\cos\theta\, d\theta$$

$$= 9 \int_{\frac{1}{6}\pi}^{\frac{1}{2}\pi} \cos^2\theta\, d\theta$$

$$= \frac{9}{2}\left[\theta + \frac{1}{2}\sin 2\theta\right]_{\frac{1}{6}\pi}^{\frac{1}{2}\pi} = \frac{3}{2}\pi - \frac{9}{8}\sqrt{3}$$

7 (a) $\displaystyle\int \frac{\sec^2 u\, du}{1 + \tan^2 u} = \int 1\, du$

$$= u + c = \tan^{-1} x + c$$

(b) Let $\tan u = 2x$

$$\int \frac{dx}{1 + 4x^2} = \frac{1}{2}\tan^{-1}(2x)$$

8 $\displaystyle\int 1\, du = u + c = \sin^{-1} x + c$

9 $\displaystyle\int -1\, dv = -v + C = -\cos^{-1} x + C$

10 (a) 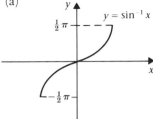 (b)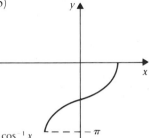

$\sin^{-1} x = \frac{1}{2}\pi - \cos^{-1} x$

The answers to questions 8 and 9 are the same if the arbitrary constants are related by $c + \frac{1}{2}\pi = C$.

Carbon dating

1   When $t = 5730$, $\quad N = 0.5N_0$ $\quad$ and $\quad N = N_0 e^{-5730k}$

$\Rightarrow \quad 0.5 = e^{-5730k}$

$\Rightarrow \ln 0.5 = -5730k$

$\Rightarrow \quad k = 1.21 \times 10^{-4} \quad$ (to 3 s.f.)

$\Rightarrow \quad k \approx \dfrac{1}{8300}$

2   $\dfrac{R(0)}{R(t)} = \dfrac{N_0 e^0}{N_0 e^{-t/8300}} \Rightarrow \quad \dfrac{R(0)}{R(t)} = e^{t/8300}$

$\Rightarrow \ln\left(\dfrac{R(0)}{R(t)}\right) = \dfrac{t}{8300}$

$\Rightarrow \quad\quad t = 8300 \ln\left(\dfrac{R(0)}{R(t)}\right)$

3   2700 BC is about 4700 years ago.

2550 BC is about 4550 years ago.

Assuming a radioactivity level of 6.68 when alive: $\quad t = 8300 \ln\left(\dfrac{6.68}{3.8}\right)$

$= 4680$ years

This agrees with historical records.

4   4500 BC is about 6500 years ago.

Assuming an original radioactivity level of 6.68: $\quad t = 8300 \ln\left(\dfrac{6.68}{2.8}\right)$

$= 7200$ years

There was strong evidence that the origins of agriculture were even earlier than at first thought.

Appendix

Core A and AS level formulas

The formulas listed here are assumed to be memorised by students taking any A or AS level examination after 1998. You would not be provided with such a list in an exam.

Quadratic equations

$ax^2 + bx + c = 0$ has roots $\dfrac{-b \pm \sqrt{b^2 - 4ac}}{2a}$

Laws of logarithms

$\log_a (xy) = \log_a x + \log_a y$

$\log_a \left(\dfrac{x}{y} \right) = \log_a x - \log_a y$

$\log_a (x^k) = k \log_a x$

Arithmetic series

$u_n = a + (n - 1)d$

$S_n = \frac{1}{2}n(a + l) = \frac{1}{2}n(2a + (n - 1)d)$

Geometric series

$u_n = ar^{n-1}$

$S_n = \dfrac{a(1 - r^n)}{1 - r}$

$S_\infty = \dfrac{a}{1 - r}$ for $|r| < 1$

Binomial series

$(1 + x)^n = 1 + nx + \dfrac{n(n - 1)}{2!}x^2 + \cdots + \dbinom{n}{r}x^r + \cdots$

A level only

Trigonometry

In the triangle ABC

$$\frac{a}{\sin A} = \frac{b}{\sin B} = \frac{c}{\sin C}$$

$$a^2 = b^2 + c^2 - 2bc \cos A$$

$$area = \tfrac{1}{2}ab \sin C$$

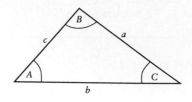

$\cos^2 A + \sin^2 A = 1$

$\sec^2 A = 1 + \tan^2 A$

$\operatorname{cosec}^2 A = 1 + \cot^2 A$

$\sin (A \pm B) = \sin A \cos B \pm \cos A \sin B$

$\cos (A \pm B) = \cos A \cos B \mp \sin A \sin B$

$\tan (A \pm B) = \dfrac{\tan A \pm \tan B}{1 \mp \tan A \tan B}$

A level only

Differentiation

Function	Derivative
x^n	nx^{n-1}
$\sin kx$	$k \cos kx$
$\cos kx$	$-k \sin kx$
$\tan kx$	$k \sec^2 kx$
e^{kx}	ke^{kx}
$\ln x$	$\dfrac{1}{x}$
$f(x) + g(x)$	$f'(x) + g'(x)$
$f(x)g(x)$	$f'(x)g(x) + f(x)g'(x)$
$\dfrac{f(x)}{g(x)}$	$\dfrac{f'(x)g(x) - f(x)g'(x)}{(g(x))^2}$
$f(g(x))$	$f'(g(x))g'(x)$

A level only

Integration

Function	Integral
x^n	$\dfrac{1}{n+1}x^{n+1} + c . n \neq -1$

$\cos kx$	$\dfrac{1}{k}\sin kx + c$	
$\sin kx$	$-\dfrac{1}{k}\cos kx + c$	A level only
$\sec^2 kx$	$\dfrac{1}{k}\tan kx + c$	

e^{kx}	$\dfrac{1}{k}e^{kx} + c$
$\dfrac{1}{x}$	$\ln |x| + c, \quad x \neq 0$

$f'(x) + g'(x)$	$f(x) + g(x) + c$	A level only
$f'(g(x))g'(x)$	$f(g(x)) + c$	

Area

$$\text{Area under a curve} = \int_a^b y\,dx \quad (y \geq 0)$$

Vectors

$$\begin{bmatrix} x \\ y \\ z \end{bmatrix} \cdot \begin{bmatrix} a \\ b \\ c \end{bmatrix} = xa + yb + zc \qquad \text{A level only}$$

Index